ROYAL AIR FORCE

by DENIS RICHARDS, *sometime Principal of Morley College, and* HILARY ST. GEORGE SAUNDERS, *sometime Librarian of the House of Commons.*

The authors of this history have been given full access to official documents. They alone are responsible for the statements made and the views expressed.

Faher

AIR CHIEF MARSHAL SIR CYRIL NEWALL,
G.C.B., O.M., G.C.M.G., C.B.E., A.M.

CHIEF OF THE AIR STAFF, 1937–1940

ROYAL AIR FORCE
1939–1945

Volume 1

The Fight at Odds

DENIS RICHARDS

LONDON
HER MAJESTY'S STATIONERY OFFICE
1974

ISBN 0 11 771592 1

Produced in England for Her Majesty's Stationery Office
by Product Support (Graphics) Limited, Derby
Dd 504476   K40   2/74

Contents

v

APPENDICES

MAPS AND DIAGRAMS

PLATES

Preface

THE history of the Royal Air Force contained in these volumes is a history of operations and the policy which governed them. In focusing attention on this aspect we are fully conscious that we have done much less than justice to the work of all those members of that Force who were concerned with maintenance and repair, signals, training, administration, and a hundred other activities without which the operations could never have taken place. Our reason, apart from the fact that one or two special subjects, such as the R.A.F. Medical Service, will be the theme of individual histories, is simply the limitation of space. To have given these subjects the consideration they deserve would have involved writing a history not in three volumes but thirty. Fortunately the authors of the full-length official military history of the war, now being prepared under the direction of Professor J. R. M. Butler, will have more space at their disposal.

In this context we must make it clear that while our work is based throughout on official documents and has been officially commissioned, it is no part of the final official history. It should be regarded, in fact, as an interim history based on such official material as we have been able to digest during the four years it has taken to write. By the same token we must make it clear that although our manuscript has been read by the staff of the Air Ministry Historical Branch, we are, in the last resort, responsible for the accuracy of the facts we have stated, and, of course, for the interpretation we have placed upon them.

We have thought it right, although our subject is the Royal Air Force in the Second World War, to include a brief introduction covering the years 1934–1939. We are sorry that—again through reasons of space—this could not be longer; for the difficulties of building up an adequate and efficient air force in peace may be even more acute than those of building up such a force in war, and are certainly equally deserving of study.

Since the operations of the Royal Air Force were but one aspect of a larger story, we have also thought it right, where necessary, to sketch in such naval, military or diplomatic background as appeared essential for the air activity to be seen in its true perspective. For this background we can naturally not claim the same degree of authority as for the air operations; it is derived from official documents, but from official documents perforce subjected to a less critical scrutiny than the air documents.

The student of history will wish to know what, in fact, were our sources. Broadly speaking, we had at our disposal everything relevant which was known to exist—including the decisions of the War Cabinet and the Chiefs of Staff, the directives, the signals between the Air Ministry and the Commands, the official and demi-official correspondence of the leading commanders, the commanders' reports, the Operations Records Books of Commands, Groups, Stations and Squadrons, the combat and sortie reports of the pilots. In the way of secondary sources we also had available for some campaigns a number of valuable 'preliminary narratives' prepared in the Air Historical Branch. In response, too, to an appeal in the Press we received a large number of personal diaries and the like, for all of which we offer our grateful thanks to the senders, and from many of which we derived information, or more usually 'atmosphere', of great value. On the German side we had the extremely useful, if incomplete, collection of *Luftwaffe* documents captured in 1945. We had very little official documentation from the Italian side, and still less from the Japanese. On occasion we have thought it legitimate to expand our enemy sources by reference to published personal documents, such as the diaries of Göbbels and Ciano.

To all this material the Air Ministry gave us free and unfettered access. In view of the general nature of this history, however, and the fact that most of the documents are in any case not available for public study, we have not felt it necessary to quote sources for our statements. We are indebted to Mr. Alan Moorehead and Messrs. Hamish Hamilton for permission to quote from *Mediterranean Front*; to Wing Commander E. Howell and Messrs. Longmans for the use of the quotations from *Escape to Live*; to Brigadier Desmond Young and Messrs. Collins for the use of the extracts from *Rommel*; and to Mr. Roderic Owen and Messrs. Hutchinson for the quotations from *Desert Air Force*.

Finally, we must express our warmest thanks to those many who have helped us in what has certainly been a long and arduous task. Our debt is especially heavy to the Air Historical Branch: to its narrators—among them Captain D. V. Peyton-Ward, C.B.E., R.N. (retd.), perhaps more than any; to Mr. E. Wilson; to its enemy documents section, under Mr. L. A. Jackets; to Miss S. I. Brown and Mr. C. Colgrave of its records section; to its draughtsmen, under Corporal S. K. Fowler; and above all to its Head, Mr. J. C. Nerney, to whose encouragement, advice, and unshakable common sense we

owe more than we can say. To the labours of our own personal staff
—among them at various times Wing Commander P. L. Donkin,
C.B.E., D.S.O., Wing Commander C. R. J. Hawkins, O.B.E., A.F.C., Wing
Commander N. H. F. Unwin, the late Squadron Leader W. T. S.
Williams, D.S.C., Squadron Leader R. G. M. Walker, D.F.C., Squadron
Leader G. Collinson, Miss J. G. Gaylor, Miss E. Baker, Miss B.
Butcher, and Miss N. Hendry—we are also deeply indebted. And to
all those, from air marshals to aircraftmen, who by letter or in person
gave us the benefit of their experiences and impressions, we again
express, what we hope we made plain at the time, our heart-felt
gratitude.

October 1950   D. R.

                                                   H. St. G. S.

The first proofs of this History were just about to flow from the
printers when the life of my friend and fellow-author was suddenly
cut short. I owe it to his memory, and to that of a happy and har-
monious partnership, to make it clear that the work thus appears
without any final amendments he might have wished to make—though
his widow, Dr. Joan Saunders, has very kindly read through the
proofs and made a number of most valuable suggestions.

I should also like to record my own indebtedness to him for his
generosity towards a younger author, and, at all times, for the en-
chantment of his conversation and company.

February 1952   D. R.

This new edition has enabled me to correct any literal or factual
slips which have come to my notice since the work first appeared.
In other respects, I have made no attempt to re-write this history;
for though many excellent studies of various aspects of Royal Air
Force activity in 1939–45 have since been published, their broad
effect has been—I venture to think—to supplement rather than to
supplant these three volumes. The full-length Official Histories of
the Second World War are indeed now available—which they were
not when this book was first printed; but apart from the four
volumes on the strategic air offensive they treat of more than one
service. Readers who wish to acquaint themselves from the Official
Histories with Royal Air Force policy and operations have, as a
result, to consult all the thirty-odd volumes devoted to strategy

and campaigns; and this is perhaps sufficient justification for the reprinting of this shorter and more specialised work, written for a wider section of the public but equally based on unfettered access to the official documents.

My warmest thanks are again due to the staff of the Air Historical Branch of the Ministry of Defence for their continued help, and in particular to its Head, Mr E B Haslam.

January 1974   **D.R.**

PROLOGUE

The Awakening

MONDAY, the twenty-third of July 1934, was a day of deep national preoccupation. At Leeds the implacable Bradman was completing a remorseless triple century, but there was always the chance of rain, and the fate of the Ashes still hung in the balance. While affairs of such moment were in issue a debate in the House of Lords—a mere incident in the game of politics—naturally attracted little attention. It was, nevertheless, an important debate; for it vitally concerned the future of the Royal Air Force, and therefore of the country.

Four days previously the Government had announced its intention of increasing the Royal Air Force by forty-one squadrons within five years. Motions of censure had at once been tabled in both Houses; and to the critics in the Lords now fell the honour of proceeding to the charge. 'What is the object of this sensational increase . . .?' demanded one of their number. 'Where is the imminent danger? . . . I do not believe that there has been a time when nations have been so intent on internal policy as they are today. You see that wherever you turn. We find that the various changes that have been going on in Germany are of such a character as to make internal questions the one interest of the moment . . .' 'What is the reason?' cried another outraged voice; 'what is the war? I will not discuss France, but if it is Germany, it is only right to point out that Germany is the one power in Europe which has unconditionally offered to abolish air warfare . . .'

Though the critics had perhaps some excuse for imagining that internal questions were the one interest of the moment in Germany, since the slaughter of Röhm and his associates three weeks earlier had left the Nazis with a wide field for domestic reconstruction, their Lordships were not impressed by this argument, and negatived the motion of censure by 54 votes to 9. Two days later Hitler's capacity for simultaneous activity in more than one direction was strikingly demonstrated by events in Vienna, where an attempted *putsch* did not fail for lack of a murdered Chancellor.

It was now the turn of the Commons. On Monday, 30th July, the Lord President of the Council rose to rebut the charge that the

Government had entered upon '. . . a policy of rearmament neither necessitated by any new commitment, nor calculated to add to the security of the nation . . .'. The barometer, the speaker complained, had never been stable. There was a restless spirit abroad, while our defences, it was rumoured in the whispering gallery of Europe, were so small as to offer but little contribution to collective security. For eight years disarmament negotiations had proceeded, for two and a half years the Disarmament Conference had been sitting, and though we had not abandoned hopes of a pact we could not afford to wait indefinitely while others reorganized and increased their air forces. France, Italy, Belgium, the United States and Russia had all recently taken steps in this direction; as for Germany, where the position was difficult to estimate, it was at least certain that 'the greatest interest' was being taken in aviation.

Thus far the Lord President had confined himself to reasons of a general nature, and had been careful to avoid naming any potential aggressor. Up to this point it was perhaps possible to agree with *The Times*, which considered that Mr. Baldwin sounded 'sincere but a little disjointed'. The Lord President, however, rarely spoke without letting fall, either by accident or design, some phrase which compelled attention. As his speech drew to a close he referred once more to the spirit increasingly evident in the world, 'a spirit which, if it became powerful enough, might mean the end of all that we in this country value and which we believe makes our life worth living'. 'Let us never forget this,' Mr. Baldwin then continued; 'since the day of the air, the old frontiers are gone. When you think of the defences of England you no longer think of the chalk cliffs of Dover; you think of the Rhine.' 'That,' he added after a loud 'Hear, Hear!' from the agreeably startled Sir Austen Chamberlain, 'is where our frontier lies.'

The Lord President's remark, which—as a later speaker prophesied —soon travelled from one end of the world to the other, was clearly significant. In fact it reflected the conclusion, reached a few days earlier, that developments in Germany warranted not only the expansion of the Royal Air Force, but the creation of a British Expeditionary Force primarily intended for service on the Continent. To critics uninformed of this chain of cause and effect so blunt a statement came as a bolt from the blue. 'We want to know what is this increased danger,' demanded the Opposition. The Government might do lip service to collective security, but at the back of their minds there was always a belief in 'the old anarchic principle of self-defence'. Besides, actual defence against the air menace was impossible, since, in the Lord President's own words on an earlier occasion, 'the bomber will always get through . . . the only defence is in offence, which means that you have to kill more women and children more quickly than the enemy if you want to save yourselves'. In sum, the projected expansion of the Royal Air Force was not only inopportune, but also likely to be ineffectual. The Opposition standpoint was therefore clear : 'We deny the proposition that an increased British Air Force will make for the peace of the world, and we reject altogether the claim to parity.'

The voice of reality was overdue. It came in those ripe and chesty tones which in later days were so often to rally and inspire the nation. The honourable Member for Epping, untrammelled by the reticences of office, plunged to the heart of things. We were a country of extra-ordinary vulnerability to air attack, 'with our enormous Metropolis here, the greatest target in the world, a kind of tremendous fat cow, a valuable fat cow tied up to attract the beasts of prey'. We were exposed to a specific danger, the danger of Germany. Since precise information on this subject was not forthcoming from official quarters, he proposed to venture upon 'some broad facts' which he would be delighted for the Government to contradict. He would therefore assert, first, that Germany, in violation of the Treaty of Versailles, already possessed a military air force nearly two-thirds as strong as our existing home defence force : secondly, that at the present rate of expansion, even if the proposals for increasing the Royal Air Force were approved, the German Air Force would nearly equal our home defence force in numbers and efficiency by the end of 1935, and would be substantially stronger in 1936 : and finally, that once the Germans had established a lead, we might never overtake them. In civil aircraft readily convertible to military uses, in trained pilots and in glider pilots, Germany already far surpassed us. 'Nothing,' Mr. Churchill concluded, 'would give me greater pleasure than to learn that I have discovered another mare's nest . . . but unless these facts can be contradicted, precisely and categorically, it seems to me that our position is a very serious one, and that not only should we brush aside a vote of censure on this small increase, but that we should urge a much greater degree of action, both in scale and speed, upon the responsible Ministers.'

During the following four hours of discussion these assertions remained entirely uncontradicted from either side of the House. But if facts were neglected, verbal portraiture was not, and Mr. Churchill was depicted by the Opposition first as a medieval baron, then, some-what more imaginatively, as holding the reins of the Apocalypse. His assertions attracted only one official reference. In winding up the debate the Foreign Secretary (Sir John Simon) declined to make 'statements which would amount to charges,' but felt himself free

4 ROYAL AIR FORCE 1939-1945

to say that Germany's interest in air development was 'very marked'.

At 11 p.m. the House divided: the Ayes 60, the Noes 404. The Royal Air Force was assured of its forty-one squadrons. England was stirring from her slumbers.

* * *

Forbidden to maintain military or naval air forces and at first closely controlled in civil aviation, the Germans had nevertheless remained obstinately air-minded. Even when Allied restrictions were at their height, gliding, soaring and flying in light aeroplanes had flourished under the name of sport, and experienced pilots had occupied army posts in the Ministry of Defence. At that period German aircraft manufacturers and designers, stifled by the oppressive atmosphere of Occupied Territory, had found the air of Sweden, Turkey, Switzerland and Italy more conducive to the exercise of their skill. But when the Paris Agreement of 1926 withdrew the limitations on the construction of civil aircraft and the Inter-Allied Control Commission departed in 1927, the way was clear; the nest was no longer under the watchful eye of strangers, and Claude Dornier, Ernst Heinkel and others came quickly home to roost.

Since Germany was still forbidden to manufacture or maintain military aeroplanes, the public products of the German aircraft firms were still for some time purely commercial. Even so, they frequently exhibited possibilities of another kind. The Junkers 52, for instance, operated as a bomber in the Spanish Civil War, while the Heinkel 111, first produced in 1932 as a ten-seater passenger aircraft, also proved well adapted to martial use. In fact the protean properties of these and other German aircraft of the time call to mind the contemporary story of the German labourer who, assembling a set of spares which his wife had induced him to steal from a perambulator factory, found that they kept coming out as a machine-gun. German civil aircraft might be built as airliners, but they kept coming out as bombers.

While the German aircraft firms revelled in their new-found liberty of design, General von Seeckt kept pace at the Ministry of Defence. The key move was the establishment of one of his nominees as head of the Civil Aviation Department in the Ministry of Transport; that done, there was no difficulty in arranging for military pilots to be trained in secret sections of the civil flying schools. By 1927 an air armament programme for the years 1927-1931 had been agreed between the Ministry of Defence and the Ministry of Transport, and in the following year a clandestine flying training centre for regular army officers was opened at Lipezk, in Russia. This school produced not only pilots—bomber, fighter and reconnaissance—but also observers and air gunners. Through its various courses in the years 1928–1931 there passed many of the officers who later held high rank in the German Air Force.

Meantime, German civil aviation had been strengthened by the formation, in 1926, of the *Lufthansa*. Enjoying a monopoly of internal German traffic and a large government subsidy, the new organization soon established an enviable position among European airlines. But its airfields, experimental establishments, signals organization and meteorological facilities were naturally susceptible of a double use, while its schools and pilots readily lent themselves from the first to military training. Significantly enough its first chairman was Erhard Milch, later to rank inferior only to Göring in command of the German Air Force. If the *Reichswehr* was one parent of the infant *Luftwaffe*, the *Lufthansa* was certainly the other.

The tempo thus far had been nothing more than *andante*, with an extended *rallentando* during the worst of the economic crisis. But now the baton was to pass to another hand—a hand which rarely called for less than *molto vivace*. From the advent to power of Hitler in January 1933, the secret development of the German Air Force was immensely accelerated. Within three months Germany boasted an Air Ministry—nominally, of course, to control civil aviation. The newly appointed Air Minister was Hermann Göring, whose qualifications included flying service with von Richthofen, experience of commercial airlines (and nursing homes) in Sweden, an early Party ticket, a superficial *bonhomie*, and a fundamental ruthlessness.

Under Göring and his deputy Milch, aided on the technical side by the famous 'ace' and stunt-flyer Udet, the basic organization of the *Lufthansa* and the secret Air Force grew apace. So, too, did the aircraft factories; existing firms were encouraged by loans and large orders, and new firms—or old ones like the locomotive company of Henschel, the shipping company of Blohm and Voss—were attracted into the industry. By 1934 military aircraft were coming off the production lines in quantity. Not all were designed for combat; since rapid development was the order of the day, a large number of training machines was required, and Milch's programme of over 4,000 aircraft for the period January 1934–September 1935 called for 1,760 elementary trainers in addition to 1,863 operational types. It is noteworthy that of this programme, which ran until January 1935 before it was superseded by something bigger and better, only 115 aircraft were earmarked for the *Lufthansa*. Over the whole of 1934 an average rate of production of 160 aircraft a month was achieved. So it continued until March 1935, when, with Hitler fortified by the Chancellorship and the Oath of Allegiance, the Saar plebiscite

B

safely over, and a convenient diversion for other Powers looming ahead in Abyssinia, the time was deemed ripe to bring into the open the units which had lain concealed in the Flying Clubs and the Army and the Storm Troops, and to declare to the world the existence of the reborn German Air Force.

How things were managed on the training side may be seen from the early career of Adolf Galland, the distinguished fighter pilot and Inspector of the German fighter forces. Galland was already well known at the age of seventeen for his gliding exploits. Determined to become a *Lufthansa* pilot when he left school in 1932, he applied for admission to the German Airline Pilot School and found that some 20,000 others had the same ambition. After various tests which reduced the 20,000 to 100, the youthful aspirant was then subjected to intensive examination—a matter of some ten days of various physical and mental ordeals—and finally gained a place among the successful twenty. Posted to a training establishment he soon found that it sheltered a secret flying course on heavy aircraft for 'discharged' army officers. Many of his companions failed to attain the necessary standards, but Galland survived the rigours of the course and was summoned with a few others to the school headquarters in Berlin. Here he was asked if he would undergo a secret training course for military aviators. Readily agreeing, he was sent to an airfield near Munich, where he applied himself to military subjects, aviation history, formation flying, air combat and air-to-ground firing. The supervisor of his studies was a product of the clandestine school in Russia.

Still on the roll of the *Lufthansa*, but already initiated into military training, Galland in May 1933 was next bidden to a meeting of some seventy young airmen, most of whom were in the Army. The speaker at the gathering was Göring, who invited those present to a 'marvellous' course of fighter training with the Italian Air Force. Nothing loth, Galland joined the party and submitted to two months of inefficient instruction in Italy, bored by the intensive security precautions and the consequent lack of feminine society, and vexed by the acquisitive nature of the Italian orderlies. Returning to Germany he put in some fifty hours of blind flying on multi-engined transport aircraft, then in October 1933 began work as second pilot on a scheduled *Lufthansa* route. Shortly afterwards he received, and accepted, an invitation to enter the Army in preparation for a career in the secret Air Force. With his basic infantry training and officer course completed by the summer of 1934, he was discharged from the Army, granted an Air Force rank and posted to a secret Air Force Training School. There, to his great pleasure, he was selected for fighters. In February 1935, in common with the rest of the school, he paraded to listen to Göring. The occasion consisted of a warning that the German Air Force would soon be brought into the open, and a preview, on the corpulent person of its Chief, of the uniform of the new Service. The following month, when the existence of the German Air Force was publicly announced, Galland started duty with a fighter squadron.

*   *   *

By July 1934, when Mr. Churchill made his assertions in the House, a secret Air Force thus undoubtedly existed in Germany. Indeed, the knowledge of its existence, and still more of its intended development, were what had stimulated the Government to undertake the expansion of the Royal Air Force. The information in the possession of the Ministerial Committee on Disarmament, on whose recommendations —ironically enough—the Cabinet were now acting, showed that the German Air Force already comprised Area Commands, a Schools Command and at least one purely operational Command, while Army Co-operation and Naval Commands were projected for the future. In regard to strength, it was calculated that Germany possessed some 400 purely military aircraft, some 250 readily convertible types and some 1,450 civil and training aircraft, with a supporting industry capable of turning out at least 100 aircraft a month. It was also believed that manufacture of bombs and aircraft guns was proceeding at a comparable pace. More alarming still was the future programme, many details of which had conveniently found their way from the new Air Ministry in Berlin to the older one in London. In this respect, it was thought that by October 1935 the Germans 'should be able to put into the air 1,000 military machines, or more'.

All this information was accurate enough for practical purposes. We now know that in December 1934 the German Air Force numbered 1,888 aircraft, of which 584 were operational types, the remainder trainers and miscellaneous. This concurs reasonably well with our contemporary estimate of 550 operational aircraft in October. On the other hand, we were not at that date aware of the full extent to which a large and efficient training organization was being built up inside the secret Air Force, as opposed to a looser form of training organization outside. We were therefore inclined to underrate the capacity of the Germans for the rapid formation of Air Force units in the future.

How far did these developments in Germany approach our own air strength? The Royal Air Force, with a first-line strength of 3,300 aircraft in 1918, had withered away in the post-war resettlement until by 1922 it stood at a tenth of its former size. The process had by then gone so far, and the pacification of Europe was so little achieved, that substantial additions to our air strength at home had been approved. The following year, alarmed at the increasing danger of a clash with the French over the Ruhr, the Government had accepted the principle that 'in addition to meeting the essential air power requirements of the Navy, Army, Indian and overseas commitments, British air power must include a Home Defence Air Force of sufficient strength adequately to protect us against air attack by the strongest air force within striking distance of this country'. This belated recognition of the obvious came at a date when we could exhibit at home a grand total of eight squadrons, of which four were allocated to co-operation with the Navy and one to co-operation with the Army, leaving three for Home Defence proper. A scheme was therefore approved to create in the next five years a Home Defence Force of fifty-two squadrons, divided roughly in the proportion of two bombers to one fighter—for counter-offensive operations were rightly regarded as an essential element of defence. The necessary additions were made regularly until 1925, but by then the doves of peace were at last airborne. More, they returned from the waters of Locarno bearing small, but perceptible, sprigs of olive, whereupon the Government promptly decided to defer completion of the 52-squadron scheme from 1928 to 1936. By March 1932, under this delayed programme, the total of Home Defence squadrons had crept up to 42 (of which 13 were non-regular), but in the next two financial years no further squadrons were formed—a gesture inspired by the existence of the Disarmament Conference, and convenient enough in the midst of the economic crisis. At forty-two squadrons, or 488 first-line aircraft, the Home Defence Force thus stood when Germany's progress in the air startled the Government into renewed action.

In addition to the forty-two squadrons of the Air Defence of Great Britain, as the Command which embraced them was called, the Royal Air Force at home included four flying-boat squadrons for co-operation with the Navy, and five reconnaissance squadrons for co-operation with the Army. Overseas, there were six squadrons in Egypt, the Sudan and Palestine, eight in India, five in Iraq, three in the Far East, one at Aden and one at Malta. Sufficient to secure our imperial position and to maintain internal security against purely tribal or local action, the overseas squadrons were obviously inadequate for the vast areas over which they would operate in a major war. Still less could they be summoned home to strengthen Air Defence of Great Britain. They could not, accordingly, be regarded as available to oppose the German Air Force, or numbered in any comparison of strengths with Germany. This applied also to the

Fleet Air Arm of twelve squadrons and six flights, which at that date was still part of the Royal Air Force, but which would serve afloat wherever the manifold duties of the Navy demanded. The Home Defence squadrons, and the Home Defence squadrons alone, were those on which we could count to oppose, offensively and defensively, a German air assault against this country. Even this calculation, however, was provisional; for Home Defence as a title described only the primary, and not the total, role of these squadrons. In various contingencies they might be sent overseas, notably to support an Expeditionary Force or to implement the Defence Plan for India.

In comparing the German Air Force with our Home Defence squadrons alone, and in omitting consideration of overseas squadrons and the Fleet Air Arm, Mr. Churchill was thus setting up an accurate standard. It is clear, too, that the purely operational aircraft in Germany numbered, in July 1934, at least two-thirds of the first line strength of our Home Defence squadrons. This, however, was a very different matter from the Germans possessing at that date, as Churchill asserted, a military air force nearly two-thirds as strong as our Home Defence Force; for few of the German military aircraft were as yet formed into complete units, and the Germans were still deficient in most of the items which constitute an Air Force as opposed to a collection of aircraft and pilots.

In July 1934 the position was thus dangerous, but not desperate. The Royal Air Force was still considerably stronger than the secret *Luftwaffe*. The Government, recognizing the menace of a rearming Germany, had begun to look to its defences. Everything now depended on the vigour with which this was done. Was the lead to be kept, and increased—or relinquished? Was the sleeper fully awake— or was the sandman's dust still in his eyes?

The next five years were to tell.

CHAPTER I

The 'Dreadful Note of Preparation'
1934–1939

THE goods ordered in July 1934 were mostly for the shop-window. Nearly everything went into the first line, and the provision for reserves—£1,200,000 over five years—was insignificant. The first great scheme of expansion was designed more to impress Germany than to equip the Royal Air Force for early action.

Unfortunately Germany refused to be impressed. 'Above all,' the Ministerial Committee on Disarmament had reported, 'the mere announcement of a substantial increase would act as a deterrent to Germany and inspire confidence at home.' But the voices of the critics at home were not silenced. On the contrary, they were soon to grow more strident. And still less were the Nazis—as the Committee apparently imagined—the sort to be deterred by 'mere announcements'. So far from slackening the pace of German rearmament after July 1934, Hitler sharply increased it.

By the autumn of 1934 the continued growth of a secret air arm in Germany was so obvious that the National Government, in answer to a motion of criticism by Mr. Churchill, felt constrained to refer to the matter. 'I think it is correct to say,' admitted Baldwin on November 28th, 'that the Germans are engaged in creating an air force. I think that most of the accounts given in this country and in the Press are very much exaggerated. I cannot give the actual number of Service aircraft, but I can give two estimates between which, probably, the correct figure is to be found.' The lower of these two estimates—600 military aircraft *altogether*—was, as we now know, substantially correct.

By way of comparison, Mr. Baldwin then stated that our own *first-line strength in regular units*, home and overseas, was 880 aircraft. But he was careful to explain that a total of military aircraft was very different from a first-line strength. '. . . The House must realize that behind our regular first-line strength of 880 aircraft there is a far larger number either held in reserve to replace the normal peace-time wastage or in current use in training and experimental work. . . . It is not the case that Germany is rapidly approaching equality with us. . . . Even if we confine the comparison to the German air strength and the strength of the Royal Air Force immediately available in Europe, her real strength is not fifty per cent of our strength in Europe today.'

Thus far the Lord President was unquestionably on firm ground. He then went on to speak of the future. 'As for the position this time next year, *if she* [*Germany*] *continues to execute her air programme without acceleration* and if we continue to carry out at the present approved rate the expansion announced to Parliament in July . . . so far from the German military air force being at least as strong and probably stronger than our own, we estimate that we shall still have in Europe a margin—in Europe alone—of nearly fifty per cent. . . . I cannot look with any certainty either into their figures or our own for more than the two years that I have given. All I would say,' he concluded, 'is this, that His Majesty's Government are determined in no conditions to accept any position of inferiority with regard to what air force may be raised in Germany in the future.'

Though Mr. Baldwin was later to declare that he had been misled in arriving at this future estimate, his speech was in fact—as the italicized parts indicate—very carefully phrased, and it contained only one sentence of which he might reasonably have felt ashamed. This was the statement that His Majesty's Government would never accept any position of inferiority. To contemplate, however unwittingly, a descent from a fifty per cent superiority in Europe alone to a mere parity was indeed to display the cloven hoof. The Lord President's peroration should have run, not that His Majesty's Government would never accept inferiority, but that they would in all circumstances maintain superiority.

Hope springs eternal, and by March 1935 Sir John Simon and Mr. Eden were in Berlin, discussing an Air Pact with Hitler. During the conversation the German *Führer* set the Nazi cat squarely among the democratic pigeons. He stated, first, that the German Air Force, which had enjoyed an official existence of only a fortnight, was already as strong as the Royal Air Force; and, secondly, that his objective was parity with France.

Unfortunately the truth of Hitler's first statement cannot be checked by any German document now in British or American possession. So far as we know, there is no *Luftwaffe* strength return in existence covering any date between December 1934 and August 1938. But as the secret German Air Force in December 1934—to our positive knowledge—numbered no more than 584 operational types all told, and as the German aircraft industry was then producing only some 200 aircraft—operational, training and civil—each month, it is inconceivable that Germany's whole total of operational aircraft in March 1935 should have been greater than a thousand. And the Royal Air Force in March 1935 certainly possessed operational aircraft (including reserves) to the number of at least three thousand.

Hitler, then, was either lying, or confusedly equating Germany's total strength with Britain's first-line strength. Since his claim was afterwards played down by Milch and others, the latter explanation is the more probable. But the former can certainly not be excluded. Hitler and Truth seldom made good bed-fellows; and to paralyse the will of opponents by magnifying his own strength was a regular trick in the *Führer's* repertoire. In any case it is clear, despite the lack of precise figures, that he was exaggerating in claiming parity with Britain, just as he was guilty of understatement in giving his ultimate objective as parity with France.

The report of the Hitler-Simon conversation caused consternation in the Cabinet. Other evidence becoming available made it plain that German aircraft production was increasing at a faster rate than we had anticipated—a new German programme had been introduced in January 1935—and the time was obviously ripe to speed up our own measures of expansion. Here, however, the politicians and the airmen to some extent parted company; for the Air Staff maintained— correctly—that the Royal Air Force was still considerably stronger than the *Luftwaffe*, while the Cabinet preferred to believe Hitler. Translated into practical terms, this meant that the Cabinet now favoured faster action than the Air Staff; for the latter, so far from grasping at the long withheld opportunity to expand on a really grand scale, believed that a very large or rapid expansion at this stage would merely destroy the quality of the Service.

The result was a fresh expansion scheme accompanied by an extraordinary admission on the part of Mr. Baldwin. In placing the new programme before the House on 22nd May 1935 the Lord President shocked his critics and delighted his supporters by—as it seemed—an almost unprecedented display of candour. 'On that subject [his statements in the House the previous November] I would say two things,' he declared. 'First of all, with regard to the figure I then gave of German aeroplanes, nothing has come to my knowledge since that makes me think that that figure was wrong. . . . *Where I was wrong was in my estimate of the future. There I was completely wrong.*[1] I tell the House so frankly, because neither I nor

---

[1] Author's italics.

any advisers from whom we could get accurate information had any idea of the exact rate at which production was being, could be, and actually was being speeded up in Germany in the six months between November and now. We were completely misled on that subject. I will not say we had not rumours. There was a great deal of hearsay, but we could get no facts, and the only facts at this moment that I could put before the House, *and the only facts that I have, are those which I have from Herr Hitler himself*[1] . . .'

So far from revealing the truth, as the House imagined, this striking confession was in fact inaccurate and unnecessary. In the first place Mr. Baldwin had not been wrong in the estimate for the future that he had given to the House in the previous November: for he had carefully qualified that estimate with the words 'if she [Germany] continues to execute her air programme without acceleration'—a condition which had not been fulfilled. And in the second place he had not been misled; for what he was now doing, as the last phrase in italics clearly indicates, was to swallow Hitler's figures and therefore to conclude that those of the Air Staff were wrong.

The essence of the matter, however, lay not in past estimates but in future plans. Since Hitler had said that the Germans were out to equal France, and since the French were reckoned to have a first-line strength of 1,500, the first line of the Royal Air Force at home was now to be built up to 123 squadrons, or 1,512 aircraft. This was to be done by March 1937, at which time the Germans, it was thought, would also attain the 1,500 level. The programme, modest enough, would have been still more modest but for the insistence of the politicians; for the Air Staff originally proposed March 1939 as the target-date, on the ground that though the Germans might have a first line of 1,500 aircraft by 1937, two further years must elapse before it could be ready for war.

The most remarkable thing about all this, apart from the Air Ministry's belief that the German Air Force would settle down to two years of consolidation after 1937, was the emphasis on parity. A year earlier the Royal Air Force at home had been immeasurably stronger than anything that Germany could have put into the air. Much of that advantage had now disappeared, but not all. Yet by March 1937 we were to have no more than parity—if we could get it; so soon had we descended from superiority into a struggle for mere equality. But at bottom the position was still worse. The new scheme aimed at parity on a basis of 1,500 first-line aircraft by March 1937. This estimate of Germany's future strength, which ignored Göring's

---

[1] Author's italics.

assertion that the Nazis would achieve parity with France on the basis of 2,000 aircraft by the end of 1935, was repeatedly attacked by Mr. Churchill as too low. It was justified by the Air Staff on the ground that the Germans would not be able to support a higher figure with the necessary reserves, maintenance organization and trained men by the date in question. The Air Staff thus visualized the German Air Force of March 1937 as a force backed by reserves in some strength. But the provision of reserves for the Royal Air Force under the new scheme was again trifling. In effect, then, we were now accepting a future German superiority in reserves.

How had it come about that a country which, in 1935, was still considerably stronger than Germany in the air, should contemplate surrendering any tittle of that advantage within two years? There were many reasons. Economy was only just beginning to loosen its stranglehold; the country was gravely divided on the need for arms; the Government felt it impolitic to speak too frankly about Germany; the Air Staff itself, while strongly in favour of expansion, was all against a hothouse or mushroom growth which, by piling up reserves of outdated aircraft and swamping skilled men with novices, would destroy the efficiency of the Service. But fundamentally all these reasons reduced themselves to one—that the Nazi threat to European peace, though apprehended in a general way, was not yet recognized in its true and terrible terms. This led to a sense of time, if limited time, in hand: a sense of urgency, but not of immediate and overpowering urgency. In consequence the Government, fairly reflecting the opinion of the country (which it made little attempt to educate), was at this stage prepared only to take measures which would not upset the peace-time basis of industry and trade—measures which would still leave freedom in the factory, goods in the home, and cash in the pocket. The Germans were able to expand their Air Force and aircraft industry so rapidly because their rulers had adopted an appropriate, and very different, formula: guns before butter. With us, until the direst hour of national danger, it was butter, butter, all the way.

The weaknesses of the expansion scheme of May 1935 were fully realized by both Cabinet and Air Staff. They were accepted because the hope of 'deterring' Germany from rearmament still persisted, and because it was thought that the number of aircraft called for was the greatest which the normal industry could produce on a peace-time footing by the stipulated date. But when, to the entirely un-deterred progress of Germany in the air, there was added the quarrel with Italy over Abyssinia and the continued pressure by Japan in the Far East, the Cabinet was forced to think again. This time the Air Staff secured agreement to a scheme which took account of strategic commitments as a whole besides recognizing the need for stronger reserves of aircraft and men. Approved in February 1936 for completion by March 1939, it set up a target of 1,736 first-line aircraft (124 squadrons) for the Metropolitan Air Force, added ten squadrons each to the Air Force overseas and the Fleet Air Arm, and provided £50,000,000 for reserves. Within the Metropolitan Air Force it increased the number of Army Co-operation Squadrons—since these would be needed for the Air Component of the Expeditionary Force now being planned—and greatly improved our striking power by replacing light bombers with medium bombers. And as the normal aircraft firms could not produce the required number of reserve aircraft—which were now to be held at 225 per cent of first-line strength —the 'shadow factory' scheme, under the strenuous impulse of Lord Swinton (who had succeeded Lord Londonderry as Secretary of State for Air in 1935), was brought into operation in advance of war. With some of the leading motor manufacturers laying down new capacity for aero-engine and airframe production, the expansion of the industry, the essential condition for the continued expansion of the Air Force, was now under way.

Reserves of aircraft were one requirement. Reserves of men were another. The professional Air Force, 30,000 strong in 1934, was already expanding with the first line, but only at the cost of a reduced flow into the regular Reserve—for many of those completing their short-service engagements now signed on for a further term on the Active List. It was therefore essential to recruit a large reserve direct from civil life—a reserve willing to sacrifice holidays and week-ends. Here the Auxiliary Air Force, which had existed since 1924, and which was now taking over an ever-greater share of the front line, might have seemed a natural nucleus. The Auxiliary Air Force, however, with only 1,500 officers and men in 1934, was a *corps d'élite*. Somewhat against its will—though it did the job magnificently when the decision was taken—the Auxiliary Air Force in 1936 found itself required to form a large number of balloon squadrons for the newly approved London barrage; and it also discharged with great success the entirely congenial task of building up more flying squadrons. But it was neither organized nor equipped to absorb and train the many thousands of young men who would now be needed both in the air and on the ground. As a result there was called into being a new organization—the Royal Air Force Volunteer Reserve. Drawing its strength not from the County Associations but from the industrial areas and 'the whole range of secondary school output', its first aim was to recruit through its town centres some 800 potential pilots a year, all initially in non-commissioned rank. When entry began in

April 1937 the desired intake was easily exceeded; and by the outbreak of war 5,000 young men of the Volunteer Reserve had undergone, or were undergoing, training as pilots. Aircrew, medical, equipment, administrative and technical branches followed, to form an invaluable reservoir of trained manpower. At the same time—or a little later—the Air Ministry also recognized the need for trained womanpower. The Auxiliary Territorial Service, formed in July 1938, included companies for work with the Royal Air Force; in June 1939 these were given a separate identity as the Women's Auxiliary Air Force. Three months later the new service numbered nearly 8,000 officers and airwomen.

The programme of February 1936 governed expansion for three years. But it was not unaccompanied by further efforts to catch the electric hare of German rearmament. In February 1937 the Cabinet rejected a fresh Air Ministry plan, but agreed that airfields should be provided, and pilots and skilled tradesmen recruited, beyond the needs of the current programme. Before the end of the year the Air Staff were back again, but their admirably balanced scheme was turned down on grounds of expense. They then put forward a cheaper variant. This was still before the Cabinet when the Nazis marched into Austria. Within a few days the original version was approved, with time-schedules advanced.

After the rape of Austria a new earnestness marked our preparations. Economy ceased to exert its malign spell, and the Cabinet withdrew the principle of 'no interference with the course of normal trade'. Aircraft production, thus far increasing but slowly, could now forge ahead. There was still, however, a limiting factor—no longer finance or reluctance to disturb peace-time conditions, but the degree to which the industry could be expanded in the absence of full war-time controls over resources and labour. It was one matter for the Cabinet or the Air Ministry or the aircraft firms to see the need for double-shifts; it was quite another to secure the labour to work them. But with orders placed to the maximum capacity of the industry under the new dispensation, and with the shadow factories making their contribution, production began to mount. Output rose steadily from the 158 aircraft of April 1938 until, at nearly 800 per month by the outbreak of war, it had equalled that of the Germans.

Big results were now assured for the future. A further expansion programme, to run on until 1942, was drawn up under the compelling influence of the September crisis—a programme in which the emphasis was on fighters and heavy bombers. No amount of progress in the last eighteen months of peace, however, could immediately wipe out the adverse balance of the preceding years. By

September 1939, five years' expansion within the successive limits laid down by the Government had increased the first-line strength of the Metropolitan Air Force from 564 aircraft to 1,476, that of the Air Force overseas from 168 aircraft to 435. It had seen the personnel strength rise from 30,000 regulars and 11,000 reservists in 1934 to 118,000 regulars and 68,000 reservists in 1939. But during those same years the Germans had expanded a semi-organized and secret collection of 400 aircraft into a fully efficient first line of 3,609, supplemented by 552 transports. From 20,000 officers and men in 1935 their Air Force had grown to over half a million in 1939—with a further million for anti-aircraft defence. Over the whole period the Royal Air Force had been multiplied by three or four, the German Air Force by at least ten. Dictatorship had been travelling at full boost; democracy at economical cruising speed.

*   *   *

The size of the Royal Air Force was primarily determined by the political authorities, and in a wider sense by the nation. Within the financial provision available, its quality rested largely in the hands of the Air Ministry. In September 1939 the Royal Air Force was out-matched in size. It was not outmatched in quality.

In the years immediately following 1918 the Royal Air Force, like the older Services, had to make do with equipment produced during the war. No new bomber could be introduced until 1923, no new fighter until 1924. Thereafter the twin principles of disarmament and economy, buttressed by the 'Ten Years Rule' until its withdrawal in 1932, continued to restrict technical progress not only in the Royal Air Force but also in the British aircraft industry. And only by carefully scraping the jam of its contracts over very large slices of industrial bread could the Air Ministry preserve the existence of many firms for the days to come, when the country would demand from them every machine they could produce.[1]

With the purse-strings held thus tight, the aircraft firms and the Royal Air Force could neither devote to research the resources they would have wished, nor embark on changes involving great capital

---

[1] The 'Ten Years Rule' was first laid down in 1919 when the War Cabinet decided that 'it should be assumed, for framing revised Estimates, that the British Empire will not be engaged in any great war during the next ten years'. In 1928, to clarify this, it was agreed that the 10-year basis should advance from day to day, but that the validity of the assumption should be reviewed annually by the Committee of Imperial Defence. Under this ruling the C.I.D. reaffirmed the 10-year assumption in 1929, 1930 and (more reservedly) in 1931. In 1932, following the aggression of Japan in Manchuria, the Chiefs of Staff recommended and the C.I.D. and the Cabinet approved, the cancellation of the rule; but no positive action under any different hypothesis was taken until 1933.

outlay. Prodigious periods therefore elapsed between 'specification' and the entry of the new aircraft into the Service—seven years was reckoned normal for a medium bomber, eight years for a 'heavy'. And as there was no financial margin for mistakes, novelties could not be ordered until they had been so thoroughly tested, outside the Service and in, that they were no longer novelties. Add to this the Air Ministry's prolonged insistence on the highest standards of safety and manœuvrability, and the result was that by 1934 the aircraft in service with the Royal Air Force had fallen behind the van of aeronautical progress. Capable of holding their own with Service aircraft elsewhere, they were outclassed in speed and load-carrying capacity by the metal monoplanes of the American and German civil airlines.

When the signal was given for expansion, the Air Staff, under Air Chief Marshal Sir Edward Ellington, therefore conceived their task as not merely to increase, but to re-equip the Royal Air Force. This was a decision which inevitably retarded the rate of expansion, for to rely on the existing aircraft types—and these had perforce to be ordered for the first two schemes, until the more advanced types under development were tested and tried—would have produced a large number of aircraft far more quickly. But it was also a decision which was vital to the future efficiency of the Service. What happened when the contrary course was taken may be seen in France, where 'panic' orders in 1933–1935 soon produced hundreds of out-of-date aircraft. By 1938 the French Air Force was stocked with machines unfit to fly against the Germans, who had kept abreast of modern developments. It had then to begin afresh the whole laborious task of re-equipment—far too late to avert disaster.

The Royal Air Force in 1934 was a force of wooden bi-planes. By 1939, with a few exceptions at home and rather more overseas, it was a force of metal monoplanes. The fastest fighter of 1934, the Fury II, carried two machine guns and had a top speed of 223 miles per hour at.15,000 feet; the Spitfire I of 1939, with eight guns, was capable of 355 miles per hour at 19,000 feet. The most up-to-date bomber in 1934, the Heyford III, with an armament of three guns and a bomb load of 1,500 pounds for a range-out-and-home of 749 miles, had a maximum speed of 137 miles per hour. A representative bomber of 1939, the Wellington IA, armed with six guns (mounted in three turrets) and capable of 235 miles per hour, enjoyed a range-out-and-home of 1,200 miles with a bomb load of 4,500 pounds, or 2,500 miles with a bomb load of 1,000 pounds. These differences, for which monoplane construction, the retractable undercarriage, the variable pitch propeller and the increased power of aero-engines were largely responsible, illustrate the general improvement in performance achieved during the pre-war expansion. By 1939 the aircraft which had been in service with the Royal Air Force five years earlier, strong, safe and admirable in many ways as they were, seemed like relics from the days of the Wrights and the Farmans.

Among the decisions of the Air Staff in the realm of re-equipment two stand out. The first was taken in 1934, when the new fast monoplanes under development at Supermarine's and Hawker's were required to carry eight machine guns in place of the four which had previously been the maximum armament of a fighter. This involved placing the guns in the wings, where they could not be attended to by the pilot; and this in turn could now be done because a reliable weapon, in the Browning '1930', was at last available. The other crucial choice was made in 1938, when the ultra-heavy bombers specified two years earlier were selected as the standard aircraft of the Metropolitan striking force. The results of the first decision were seen in 1940, when the Spitfire and the Hurricane saved Britain. The results of the second became evident later, when the Halifax and the Lancaster—the former one of the 1936 class itself, the latter a direct descendant—tore the heart out of industrial Germany.

*   *   *

New aircraft were but one part of the story. To support them a vast expansion on the ground—airfields and their associated buildings, storage and repair depots, schools of flying and technical training and the like—was called for. The sheer task of building was in itself formidable and by the summer of 1939 the annual expenditure on works had risen to more than three times the cost of the entire Air Force in 1934.

Purely constructional difficulties, however, were far from being the only obstacle. Since 'business as usual' was until 1938 the Government's motto for industry, the land-owner and farmer could fairly claim its application to agriculture. The result was that the Air Ministry's proposals for new airfields, schools and camps met with constant opposition in the countryside. Air gunnery and bombing ranges were especially unpopular, for even if some miracle of selection lighted on a spot at once suited to the purpose and void of human haunt or habitation, voices were rarely lacking to defend the rights of the local wild-fowl. In one case a colony of swans was held to be threatened, but fortunately the birds, when their supporters lost the day, rapidly adjusted themselves to their new and noisier surroundings. This did not prevent similar opposition in other cases. Indeed, as Sir Philip Sassoon pointed out when introducing the Air Estimates in 1937, the bird difficulty was apparently two-fold: either they might be driven away from sanctuaries where it was hoped to preserve them, or else they might be driven away from shooting coverts where it was the intention to destroy them.

Difficulties of this kind, and others more serious, existed to be overcome. The schools and the depots and the dumps were built; and by the end of 1939 there were 138 airfields available for use at home—excluding civil airfields taken over at the outbreak of war—as against a total of 52 five years earlier. Further, the new stations enjoyed a high standard of operational and domestic equipment—even if concrete runways were still a rarity, and the only hard surface was usually an apron of tarmac in front of the hangars.

The operational airfields of 1939 were not only more numerous and more elaborate than those of 1934; they were also disposed in a very different pattern. In 1934 the Metropolitan bomber squadrons, organized in the 'Western Area' and the 'Central Area' of the Air Defence of Great Britain were, apart from those at Bircham Newton in Norfolk, based in the counties of Wiltshire, Hampshire, Berkshire and Oxfordshire. The fighters of the 'Fighting Area', with the key task of defending London, were grouped on airfields in Essex, Kent, Surrey, Sussex and Middlesex with but one station—Duxford—further north. It was a disposition based on the assumption that any attack on us in a European war could only be made by France—a hypothesis which had little reality after the Ruhr crisis of 1923, which had continued to exist for want of a better, and which disappeared like a puff of smoke on the advent of Hitler. A contrary, and by no means unreal, hypothesis, that of war in alliance with France against Germany, governed the expansion of the Royal Air Force from 1934 onwards, and the new airfield locations soon gave evidence of a *Drang nach Osten*. By 1939 the surviving short-range bombers, earmarked for transference to Continental bases, still occupied the central airfields, but the new long-range striking force was based in the Eastern half of the country—in Yorkshire, Lincolnshire, and East Anglia, where five years before there had been only a single operational station. Still more strikingly, a continuous system of fighter defence already stretched from Southampton east and north to Newcastle, while beyond these limits fighters also guarded the Clyde-Forth area and Bristol. Good progress had been made in what official circles were pleased to term the 're-orientation' of our air defence.

* * *

No subject during the expansion of the Royal Air Force received, or repaid, closer study than this problem of air defence. It was a

c

problem easy to pose, infinitely difficult to answer. The hostile bomber, holding the initiative, had the choice of time, target and approach; and no place in England was more than twenty minutes' flight from the nearest coast. In such circumstances how could the fighter, which might spend ten minutes merely in climbing to its operational height, intercept before the bombs dropped—even in good visibility—unless it were already airborne on standing patrol? And how could standing patrols, extravagant beyond measure in flying hours, and therefore in aircraft, men and everything else, be maintained at the requisite strength for the requisite length of time round every area to be protected? Only with a truly gigantic fighter force could this be done—a force so enormous that it would leave us with few resources for guns, tanks or ships, and none at all for bombers.

From this central dilemma of air defence, already clearly evident in 1917, had arisen the conviction of the Air Staff that the whole defensive apparatus of fighters, guns, searchlights, balloons, acoustical mirrors and observer posts could be only a part—and not the major part—of our protection against the enemy. The real solution, the Air Staff held, must lie in offence, in reducing the scale of the enemy's attack by crippling his air force on and over his own soil. This in its turn would bring other dividends; for when the freedom of the enemy's skies was won, all the immense potentialities of air superiority could be exploited, and the destruction of enemy war potential and morale could proceed to the full. The essence of well-directed air warfare clearly lay in attack, not defence. On the doctrine of the offensive, tirelessly preached by Lord Trenchard—a great man whose vision saw first things steadily and saw them whole—the Royal Air Force was thus built; and until the last declining year of peace at least two new bomber squadrons were formed for every new squadron of fighters.

A belief in the virtues of the offensive, however, did not imply that defence could be neglected. While the fruits of Milch's husbandry were emerging from the German aircraft factories, the Air Ministry was casting about for means of nullifying the tactical advantages of the bomber. These, powerful enough before, had now become positively overwhelming, for acoustical detection had broken down in face of the increased speed of aircraft. Desperate cases, the proverb has it, produce desperate remedies. Popular imagination was already attracted by the idea of disabling cars—or their drivers—by some form of energy ray, and the same principle might well be applied to aircraft. Towards the end of 1934 the Air Ministry Director of Scientific Research, Mr. H. E. Wimperis, therefore urged that research into this, and other defensive possibilities, should be carried out in association with two or three distinguished scientists. To this end he suggested that Mr. H. T. Tizard, Chairman of the Aeronautical Research Committee and a former pilot in the Royal Flying Corps, should be invited to preside over a small committee consisting of Professor A. V. Hill, Professor P. M. S. Blackett and himself, with Mr. A. P. Rowe, a scientist of his Directorate, as secretary. The proposal was approved, the scientists were agreeable, and the Committee was duly instituted.

No body of men bearing the name of Committee was ever less dilatory. It needed only one meeting for Tizard and his colleagues to reach three conclusions of the greatest importance. The first of these was negative: that there was little possibility of using electromagnetic radiation to cripple aircraft or their crews. The second was positive: that the *detection*, as opposed to the destruction, of-distant aircraft by radio was a field of some promise. The third, that on both matters they should seek the advice of Mr. R. A. Watson Watt, Superintendent of the Radio Department of the National Physical Laboratory, proved decisive. For with the advent of Watson Watt there occurred, in an incredibly brief period, nothing less than a revolution in the science of air defence.

The sequence of events in early 1935 would be accounted rapid anywhere. For work in which Government circles were involved it was almost miraculous. The Committee held its first meeting on 28th January. Within less than a week, in response to its invitation, Watson Watt had submitted a detailed paper showing the impracticability of radio-destruction. At the same time he offered to supply a study of the possibilities of radio-detection. The offer was at once accepted, and this second memorandum was in the hands of the Committee by 12th February. Using as a basis his experiments in calculating the height of the ionosphere by the reflection from it of radio pulses, Watson Watt explained how pulses would be similarly reflected from the metal components of an aircraft, and how this reflection could be recorded. The method propounded made so great an impression on Tizard and Wimperis that they proposed an immediate approach to the Treasury for £10,000 for experimental purposes. But the natural caution of Wimperis's chief, Air Marshal Sir Hugh Dowding, Air Member for Research and Development, first insisted on a practical demonstration.

So it came about that on 26th February a Heyford aircraft from the Royal Aircraft Establishment at Farnborough might have been seen flying backwards and forwards between Daventry and Wolverton as though the crew were in doubt of their position. The pilot, however, had everything under control, for a well-defined section of the L.M.S. main line to Rugby was enabling him to navigate by the best Bradshaw methods. Under the impression that he was participating in 'some B.B.C. job', his aim was to fly on a course corresponding to the lateral centre of the Daventry 50-metre beam; and he had naturally no idea that at Weedon, over which he passed three times, his progress was being observed by novel means. For at Weedon, Watson Watt, A. P. Rowe and others were gathered round a wireless receiving set to which was attached a cathode-ray oscillograph. The small group of men, gazing into the oscillograph, saw the radiation from Daventry depicted as a straight line. But as the Heyford entered the path of the beam, they saw the line oscillate until when the aircraft was most nearly overhead a deviation of over an inch was observed. Without specially designed equipment, without control of wave-length, and without any great transmission power, it had been demonstrated beyond doubt that electro-magnetic energy was reflected from an aircraft, and that these reflections could be depicted visually by the cathode-ray apparatus.

Though this was far from being a demonstration of Watson Watt's proposed method of aircraft detection, since continuous wave radiation, and not pulse, had been used, it was sufficiently striking to convince everyone present that a new hope had dawned for air defence. By 4th March Wimperis was minuting Dowding in these terms:

> We now have, in embryo, a new and potent means of detecting the approach of hostile aircraft, one which will be independent of mist, cloud, fog or night-fall, and at the same time be vastly more accurate than present methods in the information provided and in the distances covered. I picture the existence of a small number of transmitting stations which will between them radiate the entire sky over the Eastern and Southern parts of this country, using a wave-length of probably 50 metres. This radiation will cause every aircraft then in the sky to act as a secondary oscillator (whether it wishes to or not) and these secondary oscillations will be received by a number of local receiving stations (equipped with cathode-ray oscillographs) dotted around the coast much as acoustical mirrors might have been under the older scheme. These receiving stations would thus obtain continuous records of bearing and altitude of any aeroplanes flying in the neighbourhood (including those still 50 miles out at sea) and deduce course and ground speed.

A few days later, arrangements were made for the services of Watson Watt and other staff of the National Physical Laboratory to be available to the Air Minstry, and for research to be carried out at the Orfordness establishment of the Radio Research Board. By the end of March, only two months after the Committee's first meeting, sites for laboratories and towers had been selected at Orfordness, and work had begun on the design of suitable transmitting and receiving apparatus.

The developments that followed, first at Orfordness and then at Bawdsey Manor, quickly made it clear that R.D.F.—or radar, as it was later called—was capable of many applications.[1] The use of the new technique was soon visualized not only for detecting aircraft (both at long range to help the fighters and at short range to help the guns and searchlights), but also for detecting shipping. Its possibilities, too, were not confined to ground stations, for sets might be developed for use both in naval vessels and in aircraft. For the time being, however, the detection and continuous location of aircraft at long range was accounted the most important task; and by September 1935 the Air Council was sufficiently impressed with progress to recommend the construction of a chain of ground stations from Southampton to the Tyne. As an intermediate step the Treasury agreed to the erection of five stations between Dover and Bawdsey. The building of these, however, was beset with all kinds of difficulty and delay, and approval for the main chain of twenty stations did not follow until August 1937.

By the outbreak of war progress had reached the point where there were twenty stations in Great Britain and three overseas; aircraft flying at medium heights could be detected at a range of a hundred miles from our shores; special sets had been ordered for the detection of low-flying aircraft; and a device (I.F.F.—identification friend or foe) had been developed for distinguishing friendly aircraft from 'hostiles'. Equally important, the radar stations had been incorporated into the general air defence system. A network of new communications had been laid down; the information from the radar stations could be 'told' to the filter and operations rooms, and represented visually at these points; large numbers of radar operators were under training; and the system had been tried out successfully in air defence exercises. The result, quite simply, was that with early warning of this kind our fighters could now dispense with standing patrols, remain on the ground until the enemy was known to be approaching, and still take off in time to intercept. And this, which was equivalent to multiplying our fighter force many times over, was only one, if the most developed, of the uses already foreseen for radar. All told, it may be doubted whether any project of equal

---

[1] R.D.F. = Radio Direction-Finding. Its existence was not publicly acknowledged until 1941, when it was referred to as Radiolocation. Radar, an American term (=Radio Direction and Ranging), was adopted in 1943 as part of the effort to establish a joint Anglo-American nomenclature.

complexity was ever evolved from untried theory to practical application on so large a scale within so short a time.

* * *

With expansion and technical development came the need for reorganization. After the 1935 scheme, which aimed at doubling the existing strength of the Metropolitan Air Force, it was clear that the old arrangements for command would no longer serve. If Air Defence of Great Britain continued to direct all the home-based fighters and bombers its commander would be hopelessly overburdened. Moreover—an important point when bigger and better bombers were soon to be available—air attack on Britain might subject him to pressure to retaliate against the enemy population instead of carrying out a scientific policy of bombardment. In 1936 the old structure of A.D.G.B. and the Areas was therefore abolished, and in its place appeared a division by function—the now familiar Bomber, Fighter and Coastal Commands, supported by Training Command and a Maintenance Group (later Maintenance Command). Balloon Command followed in 1938, when the barrage was extended beyond London. Only one other Command was set up before the war—Reserve Command, to control the Volunteer Reserve aerodrome centres and the civil elementary flying training schools; but in 1940 this merged with Training Command to produce Flying Training Command and Technical Training Command. In this shape, apart from the addition of Army Co-operation Command in December 1940, Transport Command in 1943, and a special variation for the invasion of the Continent, the Royal Air Force at home was to remain until victory was won. Overseas, where forces were smaller, the Commands at the outbreak of war—Middle East, Palestine and Transjordan, Iraq, India, Mediterranean (Malta), Aden, and Far East—embraced all operational functions and many of the non-operational.

The new functional basis of the home organization, besides limiting Commands to manageable proportions, was intended to develop specialized efficiency and ensure that no arm was neglected. It also helped the Air Ministry to shed the load of detailed administration—a task which could be undertaken centrally only when the Service was small. While broad administrative policy continued to be formulated at the Air Ministry, the actual work of administration was for the most part therefore delegated to the Commands. The Air Officer Commanding-in-Chief at the Command Headquarters, whose principal subordinate in operational matters was the Senior Air Staff Officer, had the main weight of administrative matters taken from his shoulders by an Air Officer in charge of Administration; and the pattern of staff organization stemmed from these two heads. After the September crisis had revealed that even at Command level administration was still too centralized to be effective, the operational Groups within the Commands were also empowered to deal with a wide range of administrative detail, and the Group Headquarters became organized on the same dual pattern. This organization, with few modifications, was to be called upon to sustain the enormous burden of war. It withstood the strain with complete success.

The reorganization of 1936 thus produced the chain of command which governed operations throughout the war. The Cabinet, of which the Secretary of State for Air was a member, decided general strategic policy and the appropriate allocation of national resources, with the advice of the Chiefs of Staff. Responsibility for the execution of such Cabinet policy, in so far as it concerned the growth and development of the Royal Air Force, rested with the Air Council. Translation of the higher strategy into practical terms was a matter for the Chief of Air Staff (as a member of the Air Council) who issued directives for the guidance of commanders and preserved broad control over operational policy. The Air Officer Commanding-in-Chief at the Command acted within the role and system of priorities laid down at the Air Ministry, using his forces in accordance with his own judgement to secure the desired results. Below the Commands were the operational Groups; within the Groups were the Stations; and on the operational Stations and their associated airfields were the Squadrons, the fighting formations. So the chain ran—from Cabinet to Air Ministry, from Air Ministry to Command, from Command to Group, from Group to Squadron, with the Station between for administration. Different Commands had their distinctive variations, such as the 'Sector' organization in Fighter Command, but the broad pattern was the same. At each stage the orders, narrowing in application, were translated into greater detail. No stage could be dispensed with at home; none, with the communications provided, was to occasion any material delay.

* * *

The expansion of the Royal Air Force between 1934 and the outbreak of war is not a story without imperfections. It is not even a story without gross and palpable faults. But it is a story in which the merits far outweigh the defects.

Some of the deficiencies, such as those relating to quantity, are obvious enough. The nucleus for expansion was very small; the start was at least a year later than the situation demanded; the Government—and by no means only the Government—was slow to realize the fuli menace of Hitler, and hence failed to think from the outset on really big lines. In the result the Royal Air Force, which had been far stronger than the *Luftwaffe* in 1934, was numerically much inferior in 1939. The responsibility for this, the primary fault, was very widespread; though it can at least be urged in the general extenuation that whereas the Nazis knew what they were heading for, we could only guess.

Beyond this primary fault there were others less obvious in September 1939, but obvious enough soon afterwards. The organizations for repair and operational training were inadequate. Except in the coastal reconnaissance squadrons and the few squadrons with the primary role of night bombing, there had been too little attention to long distance navigation and blind-flying. More strangely, there had been too little attention to the distinctive weapon of the Service —the bomb. In the task of building up a high-quality force quickly on a limited amount of money, all these things had received less than their due. They provide the main instances—there are not many—in which the Air Ministry may be charged with lack of foresight.

That all these deficiencies could be, and were, overcome is not solely the measure of the work accomplished during the war. It is also a measure of the work put in before the war; for the expansion, whatever its limitations in quantity, had fostered a strength which was not to be expressed in numbers. In September 1939 our aircraft were fewer than those of our opponent, and far too few to discharge all their commitments equally well. But they were, on balance and with some exceptions such as the obsolescent Battle, rather better and more up to date than their opposite numbers across the North Sea; and the projects already commissioned for the future, such as the four-engined heavy bomber, held out good hope that this slight but vital lead would be kept. Above all, in the all-important matter of radar, on which the whole air war in Europe was to depend, we were several stages ahead of the enemy. Whatever else the Germans could boast, they could not boast a general technical advantage.

Strong in its technical excellence—especially on the defensive side —the Royal Air Force of 1939 was also strong in its structure. To begin with, it was still itself. 'Peace hath her victories', and during the 1920's Trenchard's fierce devotion had brought the youngest Service unscathed through the cross-fire of its seniors. Renewed assaults had marked the expansion period; but though the recurrent struggle of twenty years ended in 1937 with the loss of the Fleet Air Arm to the Admiralty, the shore-based aircraft for work over the sea still remained part of the Royal Air Force, and the claims of the Army to a virtually separate force—claims so large that they would have swallowed up our entire production of aircraft—were success-fully withstood. A single and unified control of our air forces, apart from those carrier-borne, had thus been preserved: a control which avoided the fatal error of dividing our slender resources into self-contained compartments. Only by such a control could the problems of the air be viewed as a whole; only thus could deployment and reinforcement be handled in a spirit above sectional interest; only thus could the striking force be directed now at the enemy's air force, now at his warships, now at his armies, now at his industrial centres, in accordance with over-all strategy and the needs of the moment. The principle of a unified Air Force—the First Article of the Air Staff Creed—had triumphed over all opposition; thanks to that, the new organization of the Home Commands remained undisturbed, and it was possible to fight the air war with efficiency and economy.

If the conception—and the fact—of a unified Air Force was a prime source of strength, there were other Air Staff tenets scarcely less valuable. The principle of first gaining and then exploiting air superiority: the importance of preserving both the technical and the tactical initiative: the concept of air warfare, not only in association with the land and sea forces, but also in its own right, particularly in an offensive against the enemy's war industry—these were the central positions of a doctrine far more cogent and coherent than any which impelled the enemy. For the *Luftwaffe*, independent though it was in organization, was in effect the hand-maid of the German Army; its solitary venture into the realm of the strategic offensive was to earn few dividends and no laurels.

Up-to-date equipment, sound organization, correct principles—these were all very vital. But in the last analysis they were either derived from, or secondary to, the main strength of the Royal Air Force—the men. The Service was well staffed and well led. In the Air Ministry alone at the outbreak of war there was an enormous array of talent. The Air Staff, under Air Chief Marshal Sir Cyril Newall, included such names as Peirse, Sholto Douglas, Slessor and Saundby; Portal was Air Member for Personnel; Supply and Organization, under Welsh—soon to be succeeded by Courtney—could show Donald, Hollinghurst, Musgrave Whitham, Garrod; and in Develop-ment and Production, a vastly expanded department built up and ruled by Wilfrid Freeman, there was the civilian Director General of Production, Lemon, a whole range of civilian scientists—Watson Watt, Buchanan, Pye, Farren—and scientifically minded airmen like Tedder and Roderic Hill. Nor were the planets of the system lost in the brilliance at the centre. Ludlow-Hewitt at Bomber Command, Dowding at Fighter Command, Bowhill at Coastal Command—these were sufficient guarantee that operations would be conducted by men rich in ability, experience and character. Out at the Groups there were commanders of the calibre of Harris, Gossage, Leigh Mallory, Coningham. And the talent went deep, reaching far beyond the Headquarters staffs through the blithe spirits of the air to the sturdy, self-reliant technicians of the ground.

With the ability there was also the will. Only the picked volunteer had any place in the Royal Air Force of 1939; and to the end of the war those who served and flew were but a fraction of those who so desired. Sometimes the will was a little disguised. The buoyancy of youth, or an elaborate pretence of the casual, may have cloaked it to the onlooker. But the protective shell merely fortified an intense inward resolution. Our air crews were immensely imbued with the temper of the offensive. Men of the modern age, they sought the element kindred to their spirit, determined to do well by their comrades, their country, and their professional standards. And though the parties that interested them most were not political, they had a clear conviction of the justice of their cause. They were certainly no sober company of Puritans; but, like Cromwell's troopers, they knew what they fought for, and loved what they knew.

The architects of the pre-war expansion, from Ellington and Newall downwards, set themselves two objectives. They were determined not only to increase the technical competence of the Royal Air Force, but also to preserve its distinctive quality in flesh and blood and spirit. It was this combination of aims which enabled their structure to endure. For battle in the air is beyond all else a supreme test of the individual; and no degree of mechanical efficiency can atone for human failure. 'The heart of an aeroplane', wrote the first historian of the Service a generation ago, 'is the engine; but the pilot is its soul.'

*   *   *

The dismal days of Munich, when Britannia's shield was suddenly a gas-mask and her trident a peripatetic umbrella, cost much in self-respect. Only the ducks in the parks, sailing unperturbed along the newly dug trenches, seemed to lose nothing in dignity. But whatever the moral, political and military deficiencies of Franco-British policy at that juncture, so far as the French and British air forces were concerned there was much to be said for buying a little time. For after the wild surge of relief, the waved scrap of paper and the faltering echo of Disraeli, the realities undoubtedly proceeded at a quickened pace. The French Air Force, for instance, set about acquiring some modern planes. As for the Royal Air Force, the value of a year's grace—not Chamberlain's intention in concluding the Munich agreement, but its only possible justification—may perhaps be seen from this: that in September 1938, to oppose the German long-range striking force of some 1,200 modern bombers, Fighter Command could muster, including all reserves, only 93 of the new eight-gun fighters. All the remainder of its 666 aircraft were the outdated biplanes. No Spitfires were yet in the line; and the Hurricanes, being without heating for their guns, could not fight above 15,000 feet, even in summer. A year later, when war came, over five hundred of these modern fighters were immediately available for operations.

We had gained a breathing-space. The accent must now be on readiness. While the great armaments machine gathered momentum, strenuous efforts were made to complete our operational plans. Fortunately, though the start in this direction had been slow, much had been done already. In 1934, when the Cabinet decided that we must be ready to face the possibility of war with Germany by 1939, only two major war plans had existed. One of these was for the defence of India, the other for the defence of our possessions in the Far East. During the next two years, when the Abyssinian crisis was adding Italy to our possible foes and exposing our utter weakness at home when reinforcements were required abroad, plans had ripened for the defence of Egypt and the Middle East. Meanwhile the Committee of Imperial Defence, through its sub-committees, the Chiefs of Staff and the Joint Planners, was examining the probable form of a defensive war in alliance with France against Germany. Not until February 1937, however, were the roles of the Services in such a war sufficiently clear for the Chiefs of Staff to recommend the preparation of detailed operational plans. By that date the Air Ministry was already well ahead with administrative plans for mobilization and war organization.

The operational plans for preparation in the Air Ministry had been classed under three heads—those to help the Navy, those to help the Army, and those for independent air action. The last included plans for attacking Germany's main airfields, depots of war-like stores and industrial resources. In the subsequent detailed development, priority went to action against the airfields and maintenance organization of the German Air Force, since this would directly reduce the scale of German air attack on this country. The degree of importance attached to this plan (for nothing was more feared than a 'knock-out blow' from the air), its independence of the other Services, and its reliance on normal Air Ministry intelligence material, all speeded its preparation. Alone of the air plans for war against Germany, it was complete by September 1938.

After Munich, plans for co-operation with the Navy and for independent air assault against German industry were quickly brought to

a state where they could be carried out. Plans for co-operation with
the Army, however, presented more difficulty. For no one, in September 1938, quite knew where the Army was going to fight. By that
date military arrangements were more or less complete for the impressive total of two divisions to be transferred to France, if a
decision were taken that way; but there was no plan for their
employment, nor had any promises been made to the French. On
the air side, in the same way, a scheme was reasonably complete for
the despatch to France, if necessary, of an Advanced Air Striking
Force; but though arrangements for the reception, maintenance and
defence of the Force had been discussed with the French, no agreement had been sought on its use. The Advanced Air Striking Force,
in fact, was to be what its name implied; it was to go to France, if it
did go, not to help the French Army, or even the British Army, but
to get the shorter-ranged bombers within striking distance of German
industry. As befitted their degree of importance, arrangements of this
nature had been concerted largely through the Attachés. But if it was
a question of framing a joint system of command and a joint strategy,
full Staff Conversations on a higher level would clearly be required.
And now, after Munich, the Chiefs of Staff at length agreed with the
Foreign Office that the advantages of these would outweigh their
dangers.

The time was indeed ripe. Not only was the German threat mounting in Europe; it was opening up fearful vistas of simultaneous
conflict all over the world. At some stage it would almost inevitably
encourage Japan to attack us in the Far East. Still more certainly
would it lead to trouble in the Mediterranean and Middle East. For
Mussolini, smarting from 'sanctions', convinced of French deca-
dence, lusting for easy loot, and lost in a mixture of fear and
admiration of his Nordic imitator, already seemed determined to
range Italy alongside Germany. In February 1939 the Cabinet
accordingly endorsed the view of the Chiefs of Staff that we should
now concert detailed arrangements with France, and if possible with
Belgium and Holland, for the event of war against Germany, Italy
and Japan. The die was cast; but the casting was done with due
discretion. Anxious to avoid either general alarm or 'precipitate
action on the part of Herr Hitler', the Chiefs of Staff delegated the
duty of conducting the Conversations to the less conspicuous Joint
Planning Committee.

Two weeks before the British and French delegations were due to
meet, Germany added further point to their deliberations by occupying Prague and dismembering Czechoslovakia. Even those who had
given Hitler the benefit of the doubt the previous September were

now convinced: behind the fervour of the fanatic they at last perceived, what indeed had been there all too obviously from the start,
the morals of the gangster. To tolerate further aggression from such a
source would be merely to invite our own ultimate downfall. Anglo-
French guarantees were therefore hastily extended to the next potential victims; and the Cabinet, having by now concluded that more
than two divisions must be earmarked for the Continent after all,
decided to double the Territorial Army and introduce conscription.

The Anglo-French Staff Conversations which opened in London
on 29th March 1939, continued at various places, stages and levels,
until they were caught up in the closer collaboration of war. They
revealed from the start a broad identity of view. Germany and
Italy, initially the stronger both on land and in the air, but unable to
increase their potential during the conflict to the same degree as their
opponents, would stake their chances on a short war. It was thus the
interest of the democracies to buy time and gather strength—to
secure their industry from air attack and their communications from
interruption, to build up armaments, to ensure 'the benevolent
neutrality or active assistance of other powers, particularly the
U.S.A.', to apply economic pressure and harass Axis trade—but not
to launch a major offensive, either by land or air. Rather must the
Allies await the German offensive and, if it took the form of a land
movement through Holland, Belgium or Switzerland, hold it as far
forward as possible. The German assault once contained, the Allies
could then proceed to capture the Italian colonies, eliminate Italy,
and, in the fullness of time, defeat Germany—though 'no date and
no possible line of action' could yet be fixed for this final task. As for
the broad chances of success, we should probably be able to win only
with the help of further allies if Japan intervened; but if Japan
remained neutral, 'once we had been able to develop the full fighting
strength of the British and French Empires we should regard the
outcome of the war with confidence'.

This appreciation was arrived at before the Anglo-French guarantee to Poland. When that guarantee was accepted, it became necessary
to consider in detail the implications of the Polish alliance. The small
Polish Air Force, it was concluded, might compel Germany to keep
one-fifth of her fighters and anti-aircraft guns in the East. This would
reduce Germany's power to resist British and French air attack in the
West. The Polish contribution on land would be still more important;
for though Germany could certainly knock out Poland by concentrating against her in force, the divisions required to hold down a
captive Poland and guard against a possible Russian attack might be
scarcely fewer than those required for the initial conquest. All the

same, the Poles could not survive for any length of time unless they were supplied by a friendly Russia. Against a German invasion Britain and France could give them no direct help, either by land, sea or air.

The real power behind an enduring Eastern front was thus acknowledged to be Russia. This was a fact on which the French placed greater stress than the British. The British view was that the Russian army, for all its 200 divisions, could not overcome the effects of purges, political commissars, and poor communications, and would be incapable of operating outside its own country. The Russian Air Force, too, in spite of its numbers, was thought to show many weaknesses. The Eastern force could probably not reinforce the Western, there was no great store of reserves, most of the bombers were slow and obsolescent, and the fighters were not up to British or German standards. Although the vital importance in the East of a neutral and friendly Russia was clearly recognized, we thus placed equal, or even greater, emphasis on the benefits of an alliance with Turkey.

This, then, was the shape of things to come as it appeared to the Allies. Poland would be a useful, but far from decisive, helpmate; she could be restored to the map of Europe after our victory, but not saved from conquest meanwhile. Our basic strategy of gathering strength and friends, holding the German offensive, knocking out the Italian colonies and then Italy, and finally attacking Germany, remained unaffected. And indeed the course of the war, in its broadest outline, was to conform remarkably to this general conception; though no one foretold that the German onslaught in the West would sweep unchecked through Denmark, Norway, the Low Countries and France before it faltered and failed in the skies of Britain.

As the spring and summer of 1939 wore on, and all the sickeningly familiar preliminaries to a fresh German aggression were set in train over Danzig, Anglo-French plans crystallized. The reception of the Advanced Air Striking Force, the protection of British bases and airfields in France, the collaboration of British bombers with the Allied Armies in resisting a German attack through the Low Countries, the arrangements for liaison and command, the division of labour in an air counter-offensive against the *Luftwaffe*—all these matters were arranged in some detail. In this spirit of preparation, bombs for the Advanced Air Striking Force were laid down in the Rheims area under the guise of a sale to the French Air Force; and a link between Jersey and the Cherbourg Peninsula, forged largely by the energy of the British Post Office, brought into being a new cross-Channel cable at a respectful distance from the Belgian frontier. Many other subjects of mutual concern, however, received less attention. Discussion of a joint air offensive against German war industry, for instance, was still in its infancy. This was not because British plans were insufficiently advanced. It was partly because we did not contemplate operations of this character for the opening phase of the war, partly because the French had no bombers capable of penetrating German territory.

As the arrangements between Great Britain and France proceeded, and as the international situation grew steadily worse, the two countries quickened their efforts to gain allies. But a request for staff conversations with Belgium was rebuffed on the orders of a King wedded to the hope of neutrality, and there seemed little point in seeking contacts with the Dutch if the Belgians refused to co-operate. With the Turks a more realistic attitude prevailed, and by June a political agreement had been concluded and military discussions initiated. Meanwhile, in the direction which mattered most, a blank greeted all efforts. For reasons best known in Moscow, but which certainly included the understandable reluctance of the Poles to allow a Russian army on their soil, the democratic advances were met with an early but choice example of negotiation *à la Molotov*. An Anglo-French Military Mission at length arrived in the Russian capital, only to cool its heels while the Russians concluded their agreement with the Germans. With the Kremlin thus deliberately showing Hitler the green light, the world waited for war.

There was not long to wait. The Russo-German Pact was announced on 21st August. On 22nd August the German Commanders-in-Chief foregathered at Obersalzberg; many of them, having already heard from their *Führer*'s lips on 23rd May that he would attack Poland at the first suitable opportunity, had spent the summer months perfecting the necessary plans. Now they were informed by Hitler that, after a 'special step' on his part, an agreement with Russia had been reached the previous day: that Poland at last was where he wanted her: and that living space in the East must be acquired while Germany was still guided by his own unique self, Italy by Mussolini, Spain by Franco, and England and France by no one more significant than the 'miserable worms' he had seen at Munich. France, Hitler assured his commanders, lacked men, arms and stomach for the venture; as for Britain, her vaunted rearmament was largely a sham, with the naval programme in arrears, the Expeditionary Force limited to three divisions, and only 150 anti-aircraft guns available for home defence. 'We need not be afraid of a blockade,' the *Führer* continued, 'the East will supply us with grain, cattle, coal, lead and zinc . . . I am only afraid that at the last minute some *Schweinehund* will make a proposal for mediation.' All was ready; frontier incidents would be created; and the attack would begin the following Saturday, 26th August.

The day after this meeting, on 23rd August, the British Cabinet decided to initiate various confidential measures scheduled for an emergency, and in the evening Royal Air Force Units received orders to mobilize unobtrusively to war establishment. On the morning of 24th August green envelopes bearing the word 'MOBILIZATION' in large letters—a curious divulgence, hastily rectified by over-stamping—began to descend on the homes of the Auxiliary Air Force, the main body of the Reserve, and 3,000 of the Volunteer Reserve; while visitors to the Royal Air Force Club in Piccadilly noted with surprise the floods of telegrams which threatened to engulf the entrance. The Reservists made their brief farewells and hastened off to the mobilization centres—some, indeed, who were caught up on their annual training, had no need to travel. But Hitler, as it turned out, was smitten by a momentary doubt—a doubt which arose, not from the appeals of Chamberlain or Daladier or Roosevelt or the Pope, but from the fact that on 25th August the British guarantee to Poland was confirmed by a hard and fast alliance between the two countries. It was thus now abundantly clear, even to Ribbentrop, that an attack on Poland would mean a general European war; and at the same time Hitler also learned that in such a war he would not at the outset receive the help of his ill-prepared Italian ally. The opera-tion against Poland was therefore postponed for a few days while the *Führer* made a cursory effort to secure the fruits of conquest without resort to arms. The attempt failed; and on 31st August the order was given to march against Poland the following morning.

The last week of peace saw British and French Staff delegations—this time led by the military advisers designate to the Supreme War Council—again conferring in a series of formal meetings in London. Since the Italians seemed as yet to have little zest for a conflict—Hitler had forced the pace before they were quite ready—and since Italian neutrality was preferable to Italian hostility, British com-manders overseas had already been ordered to avoid any action which would bring in Italy against us. The French were now invited to issue similar instructions. British commanders had also been instructed to limit bombardment to purely military objectives in the narrowest sense of the term; and it was agreed to issue a joint declara-tion of this policy and of our determination to observe the rules con-cerning gas, submarines and air attack on shipping. This was the logical outcome not only of a sincere desire to limit the horrors of war, but also of our decision to stand on the defensive until we had gathered strength—a decision which naturally entailed avoiding all provocative action.

While bombardment was so restricted, we should, of course, be unable to carry out our most far-reaching plans, including those for attack on German industrial resources. But this aspect of the matter did not unduly disturb the Air Staff, who had long before perceived the solution . . . 'this delicate and difficult problem may well be solved for us by the Germans, who are perhaps unlikely to refrain, for more than a limited period at most, from actions that would force the Allies from all legal restrictions'.

With the invasion of Poland on 1st September, full mobilization was publicly proclaimed in Great Britain. By that time the process was already virtually complete in the Royal Air Force. Units, both at home and overseas, had moved to war stations; the air defence system was manned, and 'look-out' begun; civil aircraft and air-fields were about to be requisitioned; Coastal Command's North Sea patrols were on the watch for German commerce-raiders. In the afternoon of 2nd September the ten Battle Squadrons of the Advanced Air Striking Force winged their way across to the heart of the champagne country, landed, refuelled and bombed up. When, shortly after eleven o'clock the following morning, the embittered accents of a disillusioned Prime Minister announced that we were at war with Germany, the Royal Air Force, if not complete down to the last button on the last Mae West, was ready—and more than willing.

D

CHAPTER II

La Drôle de Guerre:
Bomber Command

'THE war was only 24 hours' old', writes Flight Lieutenant K. C. Doran, 'but already the bomb-load had been changed four times. Lunch-time on 4th September found us standing by at an hour's readiness, the Blenheims bombed up with 500-pound S.A.P.' [Semi Armour-Piercing].

Suddenly we got some more 'gen'. Units of the German Fleet had been sighted, but the weather in the Heligoland Bight, it appeared, was bloody, and the only attack possible would be a low-level one.

We could not carry torpedoes, so off came the 500-pound S.A.P. and on went 500-pound G.P. [General Purpose] with 11 seconds delay fuse. At last everything was ready, and the final briefing had been given by the Station Commander, who finished up with these words to the rear gunners: 'Don't shoot till you see the whites of their eyes.' Owing to the weather over the target, only ten aircraft from Wattisham were to take part, five from No. 110 Squadron and five from No. 107 Squadron. Each squadron was to proceed independently.[1]

Soon after crossing out over the North Sea we ran into the bad weather. The Met. forecast was only too accurate, a solid wall of cloud seemed to extend from sea-level to about 17,000 feet. We obviously had to keep below it to stand any chance of finding our target. So we went down to sea-level and flew in and out of cloud between 50 and 100 feet. We turned on E.T.A. [Estimated Time of Arrival] by what should have been Heligoland and flew on towards Wilhelmshaven. Suddenly a couple of barges appeared out of the murk and vanished. At the same time we got our first sight of the German coast.

After a bit of feverish map-reading, we decided we were in the approach to the Schillig Roads. By an incredible combination of luck and judgment we were bang on our track.

---

[1] Five Blenheims of No. 139 Squadron (Wyton) also took part, but failed to locate the enemy.

Within a few minutes, cloud base lifted to 500 feet and we saw a large merchant ship; just beyond it was the *Admiral Scheer*.

No. 110 Squadron had planned to attack in two sections of three and two, hoping to get all the aircraft from each section attacking from different directions and over the target within the 11 seconds delay before the bombs exploded. Nos. 4 and 5 of the formation were therefore ordered to break away, and Nos. 1, 2 and 3 opened out to make their attack.

The *Scheer* was anchored in shallow water, near the bank and protected from the landward side by a 'pin-cushion' balloon barrage. So we decided to make our attack slightly across the fore and aft line of the ship, and make our getaway by a sharp turn to port to avoid the balloon barrage.

We climbed as high as we could, which was about 500 feet, and made our attack in a shallow dive. As we approached, we saw the matelots' washing hanging out around the stern and the crew idly standing about on deck. It seemed as though we had caught them, literally, with their pants down.

However, when they realized that our intention was hostile they started running like mad, and as aircraft No. 1 came over at mast-head height and dropped its bombs bang amidships, their A.A. got into action, and this together with shore-based A.A. kept us pretty busy carrying out evasive measures. The bombs from the second air-craft undershot by about ten yards and exploded in shallow water directly under the ship. No. 3 found he could not get over within the 11 seconds and dropped his bombs on another target.

The leader of the second section, who attacked another target, did not return, and only one of the other five aircraft (from No. 107 Squadron), who attacked other units of the German Fleet, returned to base.

For leading this, the first Royal Air Force attack of the war, Doran was awarded the Distinguished Flying Cross. The intention behind the attack, of course, was to bomb the German fleet in its North Sea bases at the very outset of hostilities, before the enemy's defences grew too strong.

In accordance with this plan, a Blenheim aircraft of No. 139 Squadron had been standing by at Wyton since 1st September. Its function was to reconnoitre and photograph the German bases. From 2nd September a striking force was also waiting. Forty-eight minutes after war was declared on 3rd September the Blenheim, piloted by Flying Officer A. McPherson and carrying a naval observer, had departed on its mission. The two men saw several enemy warships emerging into the Schillig Roads from Wilhelmshaven; but the aircraft was flying at 24,000 feet and the intense cold had frozen the wireless. Not until the Blenheim landed could the crew report their vital information. With afternoon already turned to evening the striking force had then taken off, only to be baulked by thunder-storms and the oncoming darkness.

Shortly after half-past eight the following morning McPherson, whose daring and persistence were also rewarded with the Distinguished Flying Cross, had again left Wyton. Thick low clouds forced him down almost to the surface, but he persisted with his task; and from 300 feet he and his observer saw and photographed warships in Brunsbüttel, Wilhelmshaven and the Schillig Roads. Once more there was an attempt to radio an advance report, and once more it failed—the message was received, but in corrupt form. Nothing could be done until the aircraft landed. Two hours of intense activity followed while the ground crews worked frantically to change the bombs of the striking force; then Doran and his companions took off for the attack. Of what occurred from this point Doran's account gives an accurate description, which it is necessary to supplement only from German sources. From these we now know that the bombs which hit the *von Scheer* failed to explode—being fused for 11 seconds delay they probably bounced overboard from the armoured decks— and that one of the missing Blenheims crashed on the fo'c'sle of the *Emden*, killing and injuring many of the cruiser's crew.

The Blenheims were not the only British bombers to be active that afternoon. While Doran was attacking near Wilhelmshaven, fourteen Wellingtons of Nos. 9 and 149 Squadrons were making their way towards Brunsbüttel. Here McPherson had reported two battleships. But bad weather and fierce anti-aircraft fire shielded the targets, and only one crew claimed a possible hit. Two of the Wellingtons which penetrated the harbour failed to return.

These operations of 4th September, which cost seven of the twenty-nine aircraft taking part, may be regarded as characteristic of our first attempts to damage the enemy from the air. The over-optimistic view of what might be achieved: the care taken to avoid harming the German civil population: the large proportion of aircraft failing to locate the objective: the ineffective bombs and inconsiderable results: the expectation that crews would be skilful enough to find and bomb in atrocious weather a precise and hotly defended target on the other side of the North Sea: and the unflinching courage with which the attacks were pressed home—all these were typical, not merely of September 1939, but of many months to come.

*   *   *

The Blenheims and Wellingtons which thus early carried the war into German waters were aircraft of Bomber Command, the largest command of the Royal Air Force. In attacking enemy warships on the scale of 4th September, the Command was clearly not striking the most dramatic blow of which it was capable at the outbreak of war. It was, however, doing its best within the limits laid down by the War Cabinet; for Bomber Command, though big by existing Royal Air Force standards, was by no means big enough, and for some time to come its actions were to be carefully circumscribed.

Fifty-five squadrons strong in the last month of peace, Bomber Command slimmed down by the end of September to a front-line force of thirty-three squadrons, or 480 aircraft. The balance, except two squadrons, was 'non-mobilizable'—reserved, that is to say to cover initial war wastage or the needs of operational training. Of the thirty-three effective squadrons no less than ten were now in France as the Advanced Air Striking Force. These were armed with the obsolescent Battle—a single-engined aircraft advanced in its day, but now slow, short-ranged, poorly defended, and completely incapable of bombing Germany from England. Fortunately the twenty-three squadrons which remained in this country were all equipped with something better. Six of them, in No. 2 Group, based in East Anglia, had the twin-engined Blenheim IV, our fastest bomber, the virtues of which were qualified by short range and a small bomb load. The rest flew Wellingtons, Whitleys and Hampdens, twin-engined aircraft slower than the Blenheim, but of considerably longer range and greater bomb-carrying capacity. The six squadrons of No. 3 Group, also in East Anglia, operated with the Wellington I and I A, whose six guns, mounted in three turrets, were reckoned to confer outstanding defensive power; the five squadrons of No. 4 Group, in Yorkshire, had the Whitley III or IV, with the longest endurance and slowest speed of the heavier bombers, and therefore restricted to bombing by night; and the remaining six squadrons, of No. 5 Group, in Lincolnshire, were equipped with Hampdens, slightly faster than the Wellingtons but with no turrets and fewer guns. These were the forces which the Air Officer Commanding-in-Chief, Air Chief Marshal Sir E. R. Ludlow-Hewitt, had at his disposal to implement our offensive air plans.

As against our thirty-three effective squadrons in Bomber Command and the Advanced Air Striking Force, the Germans could show a long-range offensive force some 1,500 machines strong. The French having no bombers worth mentioning, 'all-out' air action was obviously against our interests until a more satisfactory balance of forces could be achieved. With expediency reinforcing the dictates of humanitarianism, the Allies had therefore determined to avoid not merely unrestricted bombing but anything remotely resembling it. In the spirit of this fundamental decision the Cabinet, on 1st September, had approved the initial programme for the employment of our main striking force. If Germany began unrestricted air action,

Bomber Command would attack those objectives, such as oil plants, which were most vital to the enemy effort, even if civilians suffered in the process. But if Germany confined her air offensive to purely military targets, our bombers would attack the German fleet at Wilhelmshaven and at sea, and enlighten the German people by the delivery of leaflets.

The first days of war had now passed, and no German air action worth the name had taken place in the West. London's sirens, it is true, had wailed their first lament a few minutes after the Prime Minister's broadcast on 3rd September, but only because someone had been doubtful about the silhouette of a friendly civil aircraft. No hordes of Nazi bombers had blackened the British sky; no knock-out blow, or indeed any other kind of blow, had been attempted from the air, and the whole weight of the German offensive had been hurled eastwards. The measures open to Bomber Command were accordingly those which could be carried out under the policy of conserving and expanding the bomber force until we were at liberty, in one of the favourite phrases then current in the Air Ministry, to 'take the gloves off'. Since a raid on the enemy fleet in Wilhelmshaven had already been tried, and found too costly, attention was now devoted to the remaining projects under the 'conservation' policy—the attack on warships at sea and the delivery of propaganda.

By 19th September single aircraft of Bomber and Coastal Commands had carried out seven reconnaissances into the Heligoland Bight. Six of these had reported German warships at sea. But the vessels, which were exercising, were all too near their bases to warrant the despatch of a striking force; for even if a wireless report got through from our reconnaissance—a rarer event than might be imagined—our bombers could not reach the spot under four hours, by which time the ships would be safely back in port. It was accordingly decided to resort to the reconnaissance in force, in which nine aircraft or more, carrying bombs, would sweep the Bight under orders to attack any warships or U-boats they might discover. The crews, however, were strictly enjoined not to seek out the German fleet in its bases: not to infringe Danish or Dutch territorial waters: and not to attack warships escorting merchant vessels if there was any danger of damaging the latter.

The first reconnaissance in force was flown uneventfully by Bomber Command on 26th September. Three days later the next operation met disaster. Eleven Hampdens found and attacked two destroyers near Heligoland, but lost five of their number to fighters from the North Frisian Islands. Thenceforward the reconnaissance in force was less popular, but twenty-four Bomber Command aircraft stood by each day at the call of Coastal Command. Opportunities to strike, however, were severely limited by the weather, the lack of information, and the unenterprising nature of the German fleet movements. In October there were two attempts, both ineffective, to find units reported at sea, but in November all that occurred was a series of armed sweeps by half a dozen aircraft. These were sent off in the afternoon, after the chance of bringing the main striking force into action had virtually disappeared. Patrols of this kind served, if nothing else, to sustain the morale of the impatient crews.

Offensive action of so limited a character, however well it conformed to our general strategy, was clearly doing little to help the conduct of the war at sea. So it was not surprising that the First Lord of the Admiralty, with his partiality for vigorous measures, should have shown signs of restiveness after an incident on 17th November. On that day an aircraft reconnoitring the Wilhelmshaven area reported back by wireless the position of several enemy warships, only for these to return to port without any attempt on our part to send off a striking force.

The reasons which decided the Air Officer Commanding-in-Chief, Coastal Command, to take no action on the reconnaissance report were entirely adequate: the ships were heading back for the defended base of Wilhelmshaven, to which he was forbidden to despatch his force, and in any case the bombers could not have made contact before dusk. The implications of the matter were nevertheless debated at some length in the War Cabinet, and it was decided that the situation at sea, with the mounting success of the enemy's mines and U-boats, warranted a more aggressive policy. The Air Ministry was accordingly authorized to carry out attacks on the German fleet of a nature 'not likely to result in losses to our own air forces disproportionate to those inflicted on the enemy'. This meant that, although the policy of generally conserving the bomber force was to be maintained, it was no longer to be interpreted as prohibiting attack on a target within the shelter of strong anti-aircraft defences. For the first time since the opening days of the war an operation could thus be launched, if the occasion seemed propitious, against ships in the immediate vicinity of the German naval bases.

All was now in order for more vigorous action, or, in the words of the instruction to Bomber Command, 'a major operation with the object of destroying an enemy battle-cruiser or pocket battleship'. For this purpose the technique of the reconnaissance in force was to be employed; as soon as weather conditions permitted high-altitude attack, at least twenty-four aircraft were to seek out a major unit in the Wilhelmshaven or Heligoland area. As usual, the 'greatest care' was to be taken to avoid injuring the civil population. For this reason no bombs were to be aimed against warships in dock or berthed alongside the quays.

On 3rd December the weather at last promised well, and shortly before ten o'clock in the morning the inhabitants of Yarmouth observed with interest a formation of twenty-four Wellingtons heading out to sea. The aircraft, which came from Nos. 38, 115 and 149 Squadrons at Mildenhall and Marham, flew in a north-easterly direction; then, some 250 miles from our shores, they turned south-east and set course for Heligoland. Half an hour's flying brought the leading aircraft within sight of the narrow roads between the islands, where two cruisers lay at their moorings. Fortunately for the health of the British airmen, if not for the accuracy of their bombing, they had been strictly enjoined to attack from a high level; and at 7,000 feet there was now 5/10ths cumulus. The waiting anti-aircraft gunners on Heligoland—radar had given them eight minutes warning of the impending attack—thus found their aim confused by large masses of cloud. Enemy fighters also appeared during the attack, but were no more effective; one of the few to close to lethal range was promptly shot down by Leading Aircraftman J. Copley, a rear gunner of No. 38 Squadron, who first learnt of a hostile presence when an armour-piercing bullet lodged in the quick-release box of his parachute harness. Under cover of cloud, and by judicious use of tail-guns and the retractable under-turrets known as 'dust-bins', the Wellingtons then made good their escape. The results of their exploit were one minesweeper sunk by a bomb which passed through the bottom of the vessel without exploding, and some accidental damage on land to an anti-aircraft gun and an ammunition store. Not a single German, service or civilian, was killed in the attack, which an enemy report describes as 'cleverly delivered from the sun and executed with great certainty in avoiding the residential area of the island'.

While the operation of 3rd December achieved no great results, it was nevertheless encouraging in that our bombers had penetrated a vital and highly defended area by day, and had fought their way back without loss. This was attributed in part to the virtues of the Wellington, with its turrets and strong geodetic construction, in part to the protective merits of flying in formation. High hopes were therefore entertained of success on the next attempt, which was to take place as soon as the weather permitted.

For some days conditions remained unsuitable for high-level attack. Then, late on 13th December, one of our submarines reported German warships in the middle of the North Sea, and a large force of Wellingtons and Hampdens was brought to 'stand-by'. Despite bad visibility and low cloud, the Hampdens took off at dawn the following day, but saw nothing. Some hours later, twelve Wellingtons of No. 99 Squadron penetrated the Schillig Roads on armed reconnaissance. There they sighted a number of the warships, only to find the cloud base, at 800 feet, too low for attack with S.A.P. bombs. Under heavy fire from the warships and from nearby trawlers or '*flak*-ships', the Wellingtons maintained formation and shot it out with the fighters who soon came up to join battle; but five of the twelve failed to return, and another crashed when almost home, as against the enemy's loss of one fighter. The immunity enjoyed on 3rd December had not been repeated.

From subsequent investigation of the losses on 14th December it appeared that none of the missing bombers had succumbed to fighters. It was therefore still possible to preserve the official belief in the defensive power of Wellingtons in formation. The contemporary tactical analysis of the operation began by expressing this in eloquent terms.... 'The maintenance of tight, unshaken formations in the face of the most powerful enemy action is the test of bomber force fighting efficiency and morale. In our Service it is the equivalent of the old 'Thin Red Line' or the 'Shoulder to Shoulder' of Cromwell's Ironsides. . . .' Nevertheless, a somewhat different note was sounded in later paragraphs, which stressed the paramount importance of concealment, rather than self-defence. 'It cannot be emphasized too strongly', concluded the report, 'that the success of the bombers in future must depend largely on their ability to fly with the utmost confidence for long periods in clouds.'

If 14th December had been disappointing, 18th December proved disastrous. 'Met' promised clear conditions over North Germany, and at 1000 hours twenty-four Wellingtons of Nos. 9, 37 and 149 Squadrons joined up over King's Lynn for an armed reconnaissance of the Schillig Roads and Wilhelmshaven. Two aircraft soon returned to base; the remainder, flying in four formations, kept well north of the direct line of approach to avoid '*flak*-ships', then turned south on a course which took them to the east of Heligoland. Barely had they passed the islands when the German fighters, already airborne as a result of radar warning and now directed by R/T, pounced upon them. From this point until some eighty miles out to sea on the way home the Wellingtons suffered continuous fighter attack, interrupted only when the anti-aircraft guns of the naval bases came into play. Despite the fury of the opposition the Wellingtons covered the whole area; but though the crews saw many warships they made no attack. Every vessel was in dock or harbour, where the fall of bombs would endanger the lives of German civilians.

Once more the skill and determination of our airmen had left no mark on the German fleet; and this time the cost of failure was even higher than before. Having studied the operations of 3rd December and 14th December to good effect the Germans had ordered their fighters to attack, not from the stern, but on the beam from above. The result was that many of the Me.109's and 110's caught our bombers in an utterly defenceless position; for the front and rear turrets of the Wellington lacked the traverse to oppose attack from the side, while the 'dust-bin' could not fire above the level of the fuselage. So it came about that ten of our aircraft were last seen plunging into the sea or struggling in flames towards the Dutch coast, two more 'ditched' on the way home, and three of the ten which regained our shores were so badly damaged that they forced-landed away from base. The heaviest price was paid by No. 37 Squadron, which lost five of its six aircraft.

The lessons of 18th December were sufficiently clear to be summed up in similar terms on both sides of the North Sea. The contemporary report by *Jagdgeschwader 1*, the German fighter group involved, gave credit to our pilots for flying 'rigidly to their course' and to our gunners for their 'excellent shooting ability'; but it also commented on the ease with which the Wellingtons were set ablaze, and on their lack of defence against the beam attack from above. The corresponding British analysis, by No. 3 Group, was no less explicit. 'Many of our aircraft were observed during and after the combat to have petrol pouring out of their tanks', wrote the Air Officer Commanding, Air Vice-Marshal J. E. A. Baldwin, '. . . . the vital necessity of fitting self-sealing tanks to all bombers cannot be overemphasized.' And the report continued by acknowledging the helplessness of the individual Wellington against the new German tactics. 'Wellingtons cannot defend themselves from a beam attack from above . . . since it has never previously been thought that a beam attack would be developed, in view of modern speeds and the consequent deflection-shooting involved.'

There was, however, one finding in No. 3 Group's post-mortem with which the enemy disagreed. Most of our losses had occurred in the third and fourth formations, which had been set too hot a pace to maintain their correct positions and had loosened up still further under anti-aircraft fire. No. 3 Group accordingly drew the standard moral about the need to keep a tight formation. 'A very close formation of six Wellingtons', ran the British report, 'will emerge from a long and heavy attack by enemy fighters with very few, if any, casualties to its own aircraft.' J.G.1 viewed the matter differently. 'The British seemed to regard a tightly closed formation as the best method of defence, but the greater speed of the Me.109 and Me.110 enabled them to select their position of attack. Rigid retention of course and formation considerably facilitated the attack. . . .' A trifle over-elated by its estimate of thirty-six Wellingtons shot down— fourteen more than the entire force present—for the loss of four fighters, J.G.1 went on to conclude. . . . 'It was criminal folly on the part of the enemy to fly at 4,000 to 5,000 metres in a cloudless sky with perfect visibility. . . . After such losses it is assumed that the enemy will not give the *Geschwader* any more opportunities of practice-shooting at Wellingtons.'

The British divergence from this conclusion was more prominent in the theory of the moment than in subsequent practice. From 18th December onwards we tacitly abandoned the belief that our Wellingtons and Hampdens could operate by day in the face of German fighter opposition. Detachments of the striking force con- tinued to stand by for action against fleeting naval targets; bombers were still sent off on frequent sweeps over the North Sea; an ineffec- tive attack was made, in atrocious weather, on German ships fast in the ice near Heligoland; the Blenheims, whose losses had been lower, went singly or in pairs to reconnoitre the naval bases; unsuccessful attempts were made to bomb the more outlying '*flak*-ships'; but Wellingtons and Hampdens were no longer required to approach the shores of Germany by day. At first this decision was linked with the supply of protective armour and self-sealing petrol tanks; yet though the first days of spring saw most of our bombers equipped with a French self-sealing covering for their tanks, they witnessed no tight formations fighting their way through to Wilhelmshaven. Nor, when Hitler struck out against Norway in April, or against the Low Countries and France in May, was there any attempt to reverse the unspoken verdict. The Wellingtons and Hampdens were then flung unsparingly into the struggle; but, like the Whitleys, they operated by night, when there was little or no fighter opposition. Only the lighter bombers, the Battles and Blenheims assigned to tactical work with the armies, carried out their tasks by day.

The offensive (if such it may be called) against enemy warships during the long months of inactivity on land was singularly unim- pressive in its immediate results. In the course of 861 sorties Bomber Command dropped only 61 tons of bombs; and the material achieve- ment—some slight damage to the *Emden* and the *Scheer*, the sinking of a U-boat and a minesweeper, and the destruction of ten fighters— was not worth the loss of forty-one bombers. But the lessons learned in the process—learned, that is to say, not in some disastrous major campaign, but in the course of a few minor operations—were of the highest value to our cause. The improvement of operational technique; the fitting of self-sealing petrol tanks; the policy of using the 'heavies' of the time only·by night—these were the real consequences of our failure. And, as lessons, they were learnt not only at little cost but in full time for the days of stress that were to come. Had this not been so, had the Air Staff been less sensitive to the early promptings of experience, the bomber force might well have been exposed, in the catastrophic days of May 1940, to losses that would have blunted its power at the moment of our greatest need.

                         *   *   *

While the Blenheims, Wellingtons and Hampdens were discovering the difficulties of locating and attacking German warships, the Whitleys of No. 4 Group were engaged on Bomber Command's second main task in the opening phase of the war—the 'propaganda' raids. These had begun on the first night of hostilities, when ten aircraft of Nos. 51 and 58 Squadrons dropped leaflets over Hamburg, Bremen and the Ruhr. The message delivered on that occasion contained truths which the Germans were to recognize only when the Third *Reich* had gone down in utter ruin. The German people, the leaflet stated, had their minds imprisoned, so to speak, in a concentration camp: they had been led into an unnecessary war: they would be worn down inexorably by the Allies: and they could have peace as soon as they established a peace-loving government. The Whitleys completed the job of distributing these elementary facts without interference by the enemy, but electric storms and severe icing provided sufficient hazards of their own, and one aircraft crashed in France. This was a fair sample of the operations to follow.

The dropping of leaflets from the air was not, of course, a novelty. It had achieved notable results in 1918, when the niceties of Lord Northcliffe's propaganda, arriving at the psychological moment of imminent defeat, had speeded the disintegration of the Austro-Hungarian armies. Later, pamphlet-dropping had become a regular element in the Royal Air Force technique of dealing with recalcitrant tribes in the Middle East and along the North-West Frontier; for adequate warning always preceded, and often obviated, punitive action. What was good for recalcitrant tribes in these areas was also, it seemed, good for recalcitrant tribes nearer home, and when the September crisis of 1938 threw the shadows of war once more upon the European scene arrangements were promptly made for our aircraft to distribute leaflets over Germany. In the months that followed, a ministerial committee on the planning of propaganda was set up, and a scheme was developed for releasing small leaflet-carrying balloons over the Franco-German frontier. Suitable balloons were quickly perfected at the Balloon Development Establishment, Cardington; operators were trained in the closing weeks of August 1939; and on 1st October 'M' Balloon Unit, established near Toul, sent off its first balloons into Germany.[1]

The main burden of the pamphlet work, however, rested on the Whitleys, joined after 8th September by a few Wellingtons. According to the met. forecast and the area of Germany to be covered, these aircraft operated either direct from home bases or else refuelled in France. But delivery had been in progress for only a week when the War Cabinet, sensitive to criticism, changed its mind and suspended operations. For it was everywhere remarked that while Poland bled and burned, we were bombarding the Germans with nothing more lethal than copies of Mr. Chamberlain's latest broadcast.

In the official view there were, however, many advantages to be derived from leaflet operations by aircraft apart from any effect produced by the leaflets themselves. Enforced evacuation, diversion of resources to air defence, dispersal of industry, interruption of night shifts, loss of production, decline of morale—all these, if the precedent of the enemy's raids on England in 1917 meant anything, might come about from our aircraft ranging the German skies by night. Later it became clear that such results could hardly be expected from bombers that never dropped bombs. But if the merits of the work from this aspect were at first overrated, at least the flights had an undoubted value from the intelligence and preparatory point of view; for the crews were under orders to observe the enemy territory beneath them, and to report on such interesting items as the effectiveness of the black-out, the whereabouts of dummy towns, the degree of activity at various airfields, the position and accuracy of searchlights and anti-aircraft guns, and the trend of movements by road, rail and water. The leaflet operations, in short, served the needs of reconnaissance and training as well as propaganda, and before the end of September the Cabinet withdrew its ban. But the dropping of leaflets, or 'Nickels'—since even leaflet-dropping had its code name —was in future to be less of a primary task, and more of an incidental to night reconnaissance; it was to be done no more than two or three times a week; and it was to be referred to in public only as 'special reconnaissance'.

---

[1] The balloons were at first called 'P' Balloons—an abbreviation for Propaganda. Later it was thought that this revealed too much, and the letter 'M'—for Meteorological—was substituted. Those clever enough to guess the meaning of the initial were thus misled as to the purpose of the balloon.

With the resumption of operations on the night of 24/25th September 1939, the Whitleys carried their bundles further afield, and on 1st/2nd October three aircraft of No. 10 Squadron shed their load over Berlin. But a few of the aircraft, whose navigators were less skilled than others, had by now infringed the neutral air of Holland and Belgium, and another temporary halt was soon called. When operations were once more permitted, the Ruhr was for some time *verboten*.

The Whitleys were not, as a rule, harassed by the guns or fighters of the enemy. The opposition they were liable to suffer from weather —a hazard trebly formidable in the absence of reliable cockpit heating, electrically heated clothing, and oxygen apparatus usable in all positions—may be seen from the operations of 27th October. At 1700 that evening five Whitleys of No. 51 Squadron, which had been standing by for the past three days at Villeneuve awaiting suitable weather, were ordered to take off before dark. The task was to reconnoitre southern Germany, and to drop leaflets over some of the principal towns. It can only be concluded that those responsible for these orders were impatient of the delay which had already occurred, for the afternoon weather forecast included the promise of 'rain, hail and sleet showers, risk of thunder: cloud 7 to 9/10ths, low base 1,000 feet, but 500 feet in showers: freezing level 1,500 feet: heavy icing anticipated in shower clouds up to 12,000 feet'. Better conditions, however, were expected over base for the return; and with this consolation the crews took off as dusk fell. They had eaten nothing since midday, and had had no time, on the large and unfamiliar airfield, to pick up the usual sandwiches and hot drinks before departure.

The weather was soon too much for one crew, who turned back. The remaining four carried on, and it says everything for their endurance and skill that all dropped their leaflets over the prescribed areas. But what this cost in human endeavour and material loss may be seen from their reports. The ceiling of the Whitleys, even in the best of conditions, was only some 17,000 feet—and over much of the route the snow clouds rose a thousand feet higher. Trouble began for the first aircraft near its objective, Stuttgart; for it was impossible to use oxygen during the unloading of the leaflets, and the two unloaders—the navigator and wireless-operator—became very sick. The real difficulties, however, occurred on the homeward journey. Inches of ice on the control surfaces, making handling desperately difficult: the air speed indicator frozen: the temperature at −38 degrees Centigrade: huge lumps of ice breaking from the airscrews and crashing with alarming thuds against the fuselage: the observer at the front covered with snow and ice, unable to see ahead, and numbed to the bone, but repeatedly operating the turret to prevent its freezing; these were some of the features of the return. Yet despite them all the wireless-operator got his fixes, and after six hours' blind flying the pilot put down safely at base.

Another of the Whitleys also regained Villeneuve. In this case the front gun and the trimming tabs froze on the outward journey, and the 'dustbin' jammed when it was lowered for the release of the leaflets. In the ensuing struggle with the reluctant turret the crew reached for their oxygen, to discover that only one of the bottles was charged—a legacy of the hasty departure. To drop the leaflets with the turret jammed it was necessary to transfer the bundles from one side of the aircraft to the other and then push them down the launching tube. This was eventually accomplished, but only with frequent rests and pauses. Meantime the front gunner lay slumped in a semi-frozen heap, while the second pilot and the navigator, seeking the relief of some other pain than the intense cold, butted their heads against the floor and the navigation table. Finally compelled by the lack of oxygen to descend into the thick of the cloud, the crew then ran into anti-aircraft fire. This was not the last of their troubles. During the return flight the captain suffered from sickness, the ice on the surfaces became still thicker, the rear gun and the air speed indicator froze; but again the wireless-operator got his bearings from base and again the pilot brought the aircraft to a safe landing.

The third Whitley was not so fortunate. Apart from the extreme cold and the unserviceability of the vacuum pump on the port engine, the outward journey to Frankfurt was uneventful. The leaflets, too, were successfully released. After that the trouble began. First the mid-turret, lowered for the dropping of the leaflets, stuck fast in the down position. Eventually the combined strength of the crew got it up again, but the navigator fainted from the effort. Then, after five and a half hours' flying, the exhausted captain handed over the controls to the second pilot and collapsed. When he recovered, flames were pouring from the starboard engine. This was at once switched off; but the second vacuum pump had now gone, the blind-flying panel was no longer functioning, and with six inches of ice on the wings the aircraft soon went into a steep dive. From this it was pulled out by a united effort on the part of both pilots. Then the captain gave the order to jump, only to cancel it when he got no response from the front and rear gunners, knocked unconscious during the dive. By this time the Whitley was heading down at a shallow angle towards a forest. By desperate coaxing the second pilot held it up over the first belt of trees, brushing the topmost branches, then 'pancaked' in a clearing. The half-stunned crew crawled out as quickiy as they could, extinguished the fire in the starboard engine, and sought help. The first call at a neighbouring farm was discouraging—an elderly Frenchwoman took one look at them, slammed the door, and shot the bolts home. She made ample amends later in the light of fuller knowledge, but meanwhile the crew spent the night in their damaged aircraft, mounting guard in turn. The next morning they were still able to bring a sense of humour to their aid when a local inhabitant asked at what hour they would be taking off.

Even greater hardships were experienced by the crew of the remaining Whitley, whose objective was Munich. Ice blanketed the windows and snow lay on the floor of the front gunner's cockpit, but the men kept up their spirits on the outward journey by well-established methods: strains of 'Roll out the Barrel', 'Hang out the Washing on the Siegfried Line' and 'East of the Border'—a slight geographical adaptation for operations over the Franco-German frontier—echoed over the inter-com., and some of the more meritorious solo performances earned vigorous applause. But when the 'Nickel' dropping was done the 'dust-bin' remained frozen in the down position, and the effort to move it manually soon reduced the crew to complete exhaustion. Then the starboard engine gave trouble, and near the frontier a cylinder head blew off. As the Whitley lost height, it descended into thicker and thicker snow clouds, and the port engine began to fail. Finally, at 2,000 feet, and with hills ahead, the captain ordered the crew to abandon aircraft. The front gunner jumped first. Fouling the inter-communication leads, he hung by the neck until pushed out by the navigator. Knocked out by the opening of his parachute, he eventually came to in a field, surrounded by a herd of cows. Next the navigator left; loosening his boots during the descent in the mistaken belief that he was over water, he sprained his ankle on landing. Then came the turn of the wireless-operator, who jumped with one hand on his rip-cord and the other clasping an oxygen bottle which had frozen to his fingers. Alighting gently in a field, he instantly discovered the exception to the rule about the female of the species, but a smart hundred yards in full flying kit beat the bull to the nearest hedge. Meanwhile, the captain, after trimming the aircraft to a slight descending angle, had baled out without difficulty. When all this was done the Whitley glided down, bumped heavily, and burst into flames; and from the rear turret stepped Sergeant A. Griffin, air-gunner. Blissfully ignorant of the parachute descents—his inter-communication point had failed at the last moment—he dashed to the front of the burning aircraft to save his comrades. The cockpit was empty. Dazed, cut, burned, and more than a trifle puzzled, the sergeant limped his way to the nearest village, where the sight of familiar figures taking refreshment in a café rapidly restored his full powers of movement and expression.

The pamphlets which our crews were delivering at such hazards were not, of course, compiled by the Air Ministry. But the Royal Air Force, though its role in connection with the leaflets was purely that of carrier, had in fact a very real interest in their contents. The reputation and morale of the Service would certainly suffer if our aircraft distributed unworthy or ineffective material; while a pamphlet which offended against international law might stimulate the Germans into reprisals against the crews who delivered it, should they be unfortunate enough to fall into enemy hands. By the end of October the interest of the Royal Air Force in the contents of the pamphlets was fully conceded, at any rate from the negative point of view, and all stocks of leaflets of which the Air Ministry disapproved were reduced to pulp. After this the standard of material was higher. Interesting innovations soon occurred, and on 25th November our aircraft dropped the first issue of a miniature two-page newspaper. Out of compliment to the notorious *Völkischer Beobachter* ('People's Observer') this was known as the *Wolkiger Beobachter* ('Cloud Observer').

Early in 1940 Bomber Command began to carry pamphlets still farther afield, and releases were made over Prague and Vienna. By then the Hampdens of No. 5 Group were also bearing a share in the work. But they had hardly begun when operations again came to a standstill. The halt, which lasted from 20th January to 17th February, was not on this occasion due to any change of policy. It arose from weather which for weeks on end locked Europe in a grip of snow and ice.

When operations were again resumed, the Advanced Air Striking Force and the Air Component of the British Expeditionary Force were brought into the scheme. But leaflet delivery in itself was no longer the main consideration. The primary task was now for each Bomber Group to reconnoitre a different area of Germany in preparation for a large-scale mining campaign against the enemy's estuaries and inland waterways. Leaflets would be dropped during the reconnaissance, partly for the sake of the propaganda, but still more to avoid arousing the suspicions of the enemy.

The new plan was introduced in March 1940, a month which also saw the first damaging encounter with a German night fighter. Another landmark of the month was the delivery of leaflets to Poland. During the second operation to this new territory, on the night of 15/16th March, one of our crews performed a feat which probably remained without parallel for the rest of the war. Having sent their

E

cargo drifting towards the undimmed lights of Warsaw they returned safely across Germany, only to run short of petrol. They accordingly put down as soon as possible after crossing—as they thought—the Franco-German frontier. Half a dozen words with the local peasantry rapidly disillusioned them, but by that time German troops were approaching on cycles. The quick-witted crew promptly dashed back into the aircraft, took off under rifle-fire, and landed safely over the border with a few gallons to spare.

After 6th April leaflet operations were suspended, except by the Advanced Air Striking Force, for the minelaying was now imminent. But the enemy, too, had plans, and far more drastic ones; and on 9th April the invasion of Norway confronted the Royal Air Force with a sterner task than delivering propaganda. It was not until Norway was overrun and France, too, lay beneath the Nazi jackboot that pamphlet-dropping was revived. The basis, however, was then very different. From that time onwards the leaflets carried information and hope to the forces of resistance across the Channel; while across the North Sea they made a useful little addition to the bomb-load.

The first phase of the 'Nickel' operations was thus at an end. On the whole, Berlin had not taken our efforts lightly. No less than twenty-five accounts of the excellence of the Me.109, for instance, appeared in one week's German radio programmes after our pamphlets had referred to that originally somewhat unstable aircraft as a 'Flutterschmitt'. Mere words, however, could not compete with the brute fact of German victory; and our aircraft losses over the whole period from 3rd September 1939 to 6th April 1940—six per cent of sorties engaged primarily on pamphlet-dropping—were certainly far too expensive for any immediate effect achieved on the enemy. But beyond this, and far more important, the leaflet operations had built up a fund of information about the enemy, and had subjected our own aircraft and operational technique to the sharp proof of experience. From this experience emerged improvements of the highest value. New devices for ensuring the well-being of aircrews at high altitudes: better arrangements for landing and ditching in emergency, and for escaping from the aircraft: the development of navigational aids; these were but part of the legacy from the pioneers who bombed Germany with paper.

CHAPTER III

La Drôle de Guerre: Coastal and Fighter Commands. Training

W<small>HILE</small> the bomber crews dropped their 'Nickels' or fretted for the sight of a German warship, their comrades in Coastal Command were busy on the unspectacular but arduous work of maritime reconnaissance and convoy protection. For our strategy, it will be remembered, was a mixture of defence and economic pressure, in which—so long as the German Army and Air Force remained quiet —the main burden must fall on the Royal Navy. And the function of Coastal Command, in the new element of air, was to help the Navy in the old, traditional tasks at sea—the maintenance of our own communications, the severance of the enemy's.

The Command was well organized for the purpose. Contrary to popular legend, liaison with the naval authorities was from the very beginning close and effective. At Command Headquarters, for instance, there was a small naval staff, while the Groups—Nos. 15 (H.Q. Plymouth), 16 (H.Q. Chatham) and 18 (H.Q. Rosyth)—carried out their day-to-day conduct of operations in Area Combined Head-quarters where naval and air staffs shared the same operations room.

Organization, however, is a very different matter from equipment; and if the Command was well organized for its duties, it was certainly not yet well equipped for them. There was, of course, good reason for this: the task of producing a fighter force capable of protecting our cities and a bomber force able to strike back at Germany had absorbed most of our energies and output, leaving very little over for purely maritime aircraft. To accept such a situation did not, as some critics would have us believe, argue any lack of foresight on the part of the Air Staff or the politicians. With the Allies' great superiority in naval resources, anything higher than third place for Coastal Command in the pre-war expansion would have been utterly unwarranted.

The Coastal force at the outbreak of war was accordingly small compared with that disposed by Bomber or Fighter Command. It was equipped, in the main, with obsolescent aircraft, though new maritime types were on order. All but one of the eleven general reconnaissance squadrons were still operating with Ansons—excellent and highly reliable machines, but limited to a speed of 178 miles per hour and a radius of action, under normal operational conditions, of some 250 miles; the remaining squadron was flying the first of the Hudsons ordered from the Lockheed firm in America—aircraft of twice the range, as well as greater speed and bomb load. Of the six flying-boat squadrons, intended for long-range work, only two had Sunderlands, with their seven machine guns, 2,000-pounds bomb load and normal operational radius of 850 miles; the rest were on Londons and Stranraers, greatly inferior in all respects. Worst of all, the two squadrons of 'strike' aircraft were both armed with the completely out-of-date Vildebeest torpedo-bomber, of top speed 153 miles per hour and normal radius 185 miles. This entailed calling on Bomber Command for every attack against a major warship.

First and foremost of the routine duties assigned to Coastal Command was reconnaissance over the North Sea. The greatest danger to our sea-borne trade, in the official opinion of the Admiralty before the war, was likely to be the surface raider, not the submarine; and the North Sea patrols were designed with this appreciation in mind. As a surface raider trying to break out into the Atlantic from North Germany was virtually bound to pass between Scotland and Norway, the main Coastal Command patrol took the form of an 'endless chain' in daylight from Montrose up to the Ansons' operational limit, which was some fifty miles from the south-west tip of Norway. Reconnaissance over the remaining fifty miles depended for a few weeks entirely upon our submarines, until there were sufficient Hudsons to take on the job. North of this continuous patrol, dawn patrols were flown by flying-boats based at Sullom Voe (Shetlands) and Invergordon; while to the south dusk patrols were carried out by Hudsons from Leuchars. These routine sorties—which were constantly readjusted in the light of circumstances—were supplemented by special searches whenever necessary. So the watch for the surface-raider was planned; the detection of contraband traffic and U-boats on passage were useful, but subsidiary, functions.

The North Sea patrols began on 24th August, just too late to detect the *Graf Spee*, which had sailed from Wilhelmshaven three days earlier. The *Deutschland* also slipped by before the outbreak of war, passing through the patrol area at a time when our aircraft were grounded by fog—a feat she was to repeat on her homeward voyage in November. Coastal Command, however, had at least one crumb of consolation. On 2nd November, after an intensive hue and cry, a London of No. 201 Squadron spotted the *Deutschland's* returning prize, the *City of Flint*, in Norwegian territorial waters.

Unfortunately the first cruise of the *Deutschland* was by no means the only example of the Germans' skill in picking suitable conditions for their rare naval ventures. On 8th October, for instance, a Hudson of No. 224 Squadron on patrol from Leuchars reported a battleship, a cruiser and four destroyers off the south-west coast of Norway; but heavy rain and low clouds made it impossible for the bomber force to gain contact. Again, in the following month vile weather hampered the search for the *Scharnhorst* and *Gneisenau* after their clash with the gallant *Rawalpindi*. On this occasion there were two days when the crews at Pembroke Dock could not even get into their flying-boats; and on the last day of the search a Sunderland, after alighting safely at Sullom Voe in a 60-knot gale, tossed helplessly at her moorings for over ten hours before her crew could be taken off. Better conditions, however, attended the hunt in February 1940 for the *Altmark*, auxiliary and prison ship of the *Graf Spee*. After agents' reports had indicated her presence off Norway, a Hudson of No. 220 Squadron was able to pick her up and direct our naval forces to the scene.

Meanwhile the watch between Scotland and Norway, if the most important part of Coastal Command's work in the North Sea, had become increasingly complicated by other tasks. The Skagerrak, the Heligoland Bight, the Dutch and the Belgian coasts—all these had also to be kept under observation, besides many other areas where sea-borne raids or invading forces could be detected early in their passage. Such work, of course, called for far better-armed aircraft than the Command possessed at the beginning of the war. So, too, did the duty, carried out in conjunction with Fighter Command, of protecting our East Coast convoys. Aircraft with a sting in them were what was needed; and for the time being all that could be done was to produce a fighter version of the long-ranged, long-nose Blenheim (the Mark IV), and to modify a few of the Hudsons to take a mid-upper turret.

Well armed or poorly armed, the Coastal aircraft were certainly now being called upon for a bewildering variety of tasks. Apart from those before mentioned, there were our mine-layers to be guarded as they laid the great barrage from Dover to the north of Scotland. There were crippled ships and submarines to escort safely back to port. There was the enemy's mine-laying campaign to defeat. And, since the *Luftwaffe's* determination to dominate the North Sea

stopped short neither of triviality nor terrorism, there were even the
herring fleet and the lightships to look after. All this had to be done
with the few aircraft which could be spared from the major commitment. How seriously the force was pressed may be seen from the
history of the four 'trade protection' squadrons of Blenheim
fighters. Formed in October 1939 specifically for the protection of
East Coast convoys, they were soon required not only to carry out
long-range reconnaissance, but also to act as escort to purely naval
forces. Thus early did the hard test of experience shatter the doctrine,
long entertained by the Admiralty, that a fleet at sea had nothing to
fear from the air.

The threat of the German surface raiders came to little; and the
harrying of our East Coast trade and our vessels in the North Sea by
German aircraft, though vexatious, could not be decisive. But when,
in November 1939, Secret Weapon No. 1 arrived, in the form of
magnetic mines laid close inshore by aircraft and U-boats, the
enemy at first registered a real success. Over a quarter of a million
tons of shipping were sunk by this method alone within three months.
Fortunately, however, the menace was defeated with remarkable
speed. 'Degaussing' and the LL sweep proved the ultimate answer,
but before these could be fully applied the Royal Air Force did much
to reduce our losses. On the offensive side, Bomber Command
carried out nightly patrols over the seaplane bases in the North and
East Frisians to discourage mine-laying aircraft from taking off; and
on the night of 19/20th March 1940, after we had suffered our first
civilian air raid casualties during a raid on Scapa, the War Cabinet
went so far as to permit the Command to bomb the hangars and
slipway at Hornum. On the defensive side, Balloon Command put
up a barrage from barges and lighters in the Thames Estuary; Fighter
Command carried out night patrols, somewhat expensive in crashes;
and Coastal Command, besides patrolling the east-coast estuaries
by moonlight, formed special flights of Tiger and Hornet Moths in
the north and west. This last action was done in the conviction, not
ill-founded, that the sight and sound of any aircraft would scare the
mine-laying U-boats into remaining beneath the surface.

Another task of Coastal Command in the campaign against the
magnetic mine was to operate the D.W.I. Wellingtons.[1] As the
mines could not be swept by normal means, the object of these aircraft, which were evolved by a joint effort on the part of the Admiralty
and the Royal Aircraft Establishment, was to explode them. Fitted
underneath with a great hoop containing a magnetic coil activated

---

[1] D.W.I.=Directional Wireless Installation: more misleading initials

by an auxiliary and extremely smelly engine inside the fuselage, the D.W.I.s carried out sweeps at 25–40 feet over suspected waters; anything from a slight tremor to a heavy bump with bits-and-pieces flying off the aircraft informed the crews of an addition to their score. Beginning operations in January 1940, the half a dozen or so aircraft engaged on this task exploded one-eighth of all the magnetic mines swept or detonated in the period from November 1939 to May 1940. Typically enough, the crews obtained most of these successes by disregarding the safety regulations laid down for their benefit.

The magnetic mines were a menace speedily mastered. Very different were the U-boats, whose potentialities as a weapon, though decisively curbed between 1943 and 1945, were still as great at the end of the war as at the beginning. Seven or eight of these pests were already stationed westward of the British Isles on 3rd September; and the sinking of the *Athenia* that evening, though, as we now know, carried out against orders, was a grim warning of what was to come. The disaster was certainly no false alarm. Before the month was out nearly 150,000 tons of British shipping had gone to the bottom.

During this difficult initial period, when convoy was being established (it had not been ordered during the precautionary stage), when isolated homecoming ships and stragglers abounded, and when destroyer escort went out no farther than 13° W., Coastal Command did its best to provide close and continuous cover in coastal waters. Escort beyond a hundred miles out from the Scillies, however, was extremely intermittent, for most of the long-range aircraft were needed on the primary task of North Sea reconnaissance. Nor could aircraft well be spared for distant work when a stream of S.O.S. signals and reports of U-boats was pouring in from the South Western Approaches. The gaps in our air cover at sea, it was already painfully apparent, were all too great. And when the Admiralty tried to fill in some of the nearer ones by using aircraft-carriers the narrow escape of the *Ark Royal* and the loss of the *Courageous* soon brought the attempt to an end.

It was during this opening phase of the U-boat offensive that Coastal Command accomplished a rescue which was much written of at the time, and which still remains outstanding. The *Kensington Court*, a tramp bringing in 8,000 tons of grain, had been torpedoed without warning some seventy miles off the Scillies. Two Sunderlands, one from No. 204 and the other from No. 228 Squadron, on separate patrols, picked up the distress signals. The first flying-boat reached the reported position in forty minutes, to find the ship down by the bows. Some way off from the wreck was a drenched and overcrowded lifeboat. To this a number of men were clinging with their bodies in the sea—for the ship's other boat had been swamped as soon as lowered. After a brief look-round for the U-boat, the crew of the Sunderland, disregarding a heavy swell, put their aircraft down on the surface and made ready to bring the survivors aboard by means of the rubber dinghy. Then the second Sunderland appeared, carried out a quick search, and also alighted. Between them the rescuers got all thirty-four of the seamen safely aboard, though many were utterly exhausted and helpless. Then, having jettisoned their bombs, the aircraft took off; and a little over an hour after their ship was hit the crew of the *Kensington Court*—not a man missing—were back on dry land. Meanwhile a third Sunderland had appeared on the scene of the disaster, and, after keeping watch till the rescue was completed, had sighted the U-boat breaking surface. The flying-boat at once attacked. Unfortunately for the artistic unity of the story, the first bomb hung up, and the enemy escaped by a smart dive.

By October convoy routine was settling down, and the sinkings, though heavy, showed a perceptible decline. The following month the losses from U-boat attack decreased still further, partly on account of the casualties thus far inflicted by the Navy, partly because the enemy was now concentrating on the magnetic mine. By then Coastal Command was flying 'police' patrols throughout daylight along the east coast route, while the Atlantic convoys could rely on regular air escort up to 200 miles from our shores—a figure on which it would doubtless have been possible to improve, had we possessed bases in Southern Ireland. At the same time the North Sea patrols, designed primarily against surface raiders, were proving so successful in their secondary task of spotting U-boats that an excellent picture of enemy movements round the north of Scotland was being built up. Special air patrols to harry these craft on passage were accordingly 'laid on'; and by mid-November the location and attack of the enemy's submarines was officially rated as of equal importance to the location of his surface warships. Henceforward, Coastal Command's routine patrols were to be flown at the height which afforded the best chance of success against the under-water menace. The Command was becoming increasingly 'U-boat minded'.

These new measures in the air proved their worth from the start. Reduced to travelling submerged for much of their passage, the U-boats perforce spent less time in their operational areas; and on more than one occasion the Coastal patrols brought our asdic-fitted vessels into position for the kill. But no directly lethal effect was yet achieved by the aircraft themselves. This was largely because the 100-pound A/S. (Anti-Submarine) bomb carried by the Ansons

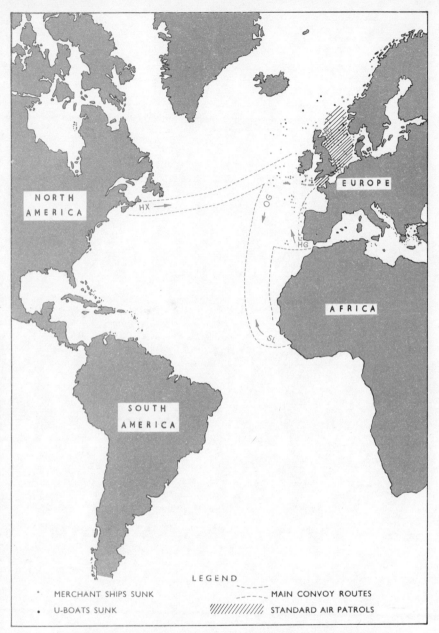

THE BATTLE OF THE ATLANTIC (I), 3 SEPTEMBER 1939—MAY 1940

Note (i) No consistent air cover over convoy routes.

       (ii) Most Coastal Command aircraft engaged on standard
North Sea reconnaissance.   [*facing page* 60]

proved to be almost harmless even when it scored a direct hit; while the 250-pound A/S. bomb carried by the flying-boats needed to explode within six feet of the pressure hull to inflict serious damage. Accuracy of aim, too, was at this stage almost a matter of luck. Up till the end of 1939 only the Hudsons of the coastal aircraft had a distributor capable of ensuring a properly spaced stick of bombs; and the Mark IX bomb-sight, which required a steady run up at a height above 3,000 feet, was useless against such small and elusive targets as submarines.

The worthlessness of our anti-submarine bombs was not entirely a surprise. Various critics had had their suspicions before the war; but in peace-time it is never an easy matter to test bombs against the actual objects they are intended to destroy. The war was not many days old, however, before misgivings deepened. On 5th September 1939, two of our own submarines were attacked in mistake by Ansons; both escaped with nothing more than a slight shaking. This was disquieting enough, if fortunate for the submarines; but a similar incident on 3rd December left no room for doubt. On that day the *Snapper* received a 100-pound anti-submarine bomb directly at the base of her conning-tower. The only damage to her pressure hull occurred in the control room, where four electric light bulbs were broken.

A week after this episode arrangements were made for the Admiralty to develop depth charges for use from the air. Until these became available, Coastal Command might harass the U-boats, but it was impotent to destroy them. Of the twenty-three successes scored between the outbreak of war and the fall of France, Coastal Command was credited with a direct share in only one, and even this was partly thanks to the enemy. On 30th January 1940, a U-boat, after being damaged by our surface forces, found itself unable to escape the attentions of a Sunderland of No. 228 Squadron. Losing his nerve, the German captain scuttled his vessel.

Fortunately this lack of ability to kill made little difference to the broad picture of success. For by April 1940, in spite of a renewed spell of U-boat activity in the first two months of the year, the war at sea was definitely going well for the Allies. The long-range blockade was operating to good effect, the surface raiders were well under control, the magnetic mine was being mastered, and the U-boats, if much more of a menace than had been anticipated before the war, were inflicting nothing like the losses of 1917. The credit for all these achievements belonged primarily, of course, to the Navy. But to each of them Coastal Command had made a useful, and indeed a vital, contribution. It had done this at a time when it was beset with

difficulties—when new and unexpected commitments were arising
every month, when aircraft were scarce and obsolescent, and when the
re-equipment programme had collapsed through the entire failure of
the two scheduled replacements, the Lerwick flying-boat and the ill-
starred Botha. Perhaps more significant than any positive achievement, however, was the fact that the Command, designed almost
entirely for reconnaissance on behalf of the Navy, was now developing an anti-U-boat offensive in its own right. The day of its triumph
in that direction was not yet; but the signs and portents were there
for the future.

*   *   *

To the intense dismay of the Air Officer Commanding-in-Chief,
Fighter Command also found itself involved in the struggle for
control of the North Sea. Upon Sir Hugh Dowding rested what was
undoubtedly the most important operational duty of the Royal Air
Force at the time—the air defence of Great Britain; and with forces
already insufficient, as he deemed, for this vital task, Sir Hugh was
naturally reluctant to extend his commitments.

To discharge his duties effectively against an estimated force of
2,000 long-range bombers operating from Germany, it had been
calculated that Dowding should dispose forty-six squadrons for the
general defence of the country, four for the protection of the East
Coast convoys, two for Scapa Flow and one for Northern Ireland.
But the last three of these requirements had been put forward only
in the closing months of peace, and in September 1939 none of the
seven squadrons to meet them existed. Still more serious, ten of the
forty-six squadrons for the general defence of the country were not
due to form until the financial year 1940–1941. Of the fifty-three
squadrons reckoned as essential, Dowding in fact had no more than
thirty-five at the outbreak of war. Allied to his inherent singleness of
purpose, this inevitably prompted him to a rigid regard for priorities.

Given the full number of squadrons, Dowding felt confident of
breaking the assaults of the *Luftwaffe*. But at anything less—and
certainly at only two-thirds—he was not so sure. He accordingly
threw his whole strength and prestige into achieving his due complement. This involved not only demanding the approved additions
ahead of schedule, but also ensuring that, in the temporary absence of
German attack against this country, his existing squadrons were not
diverted to purposes beyond their main role. In the course of this
struggle—as he conceived it—to preserve and build up his Command
for the great battle to come, Dowding looked neither to left nor right:
he scouted difficulties and opposed all competing claims, whether of
Allies, sister Services, or other Royal Air Force Commands. At

every suggestion to lay hands on one of his precious squadrons or to extend his already great commitments, he directed to the Air Ministry a stream of forceful, cogent and entirely outspoken protests. Others might plan attractive schemes for fighter flexibility, by which our Hurricanes might be defending the British Expeditionary Force in France one moment and southern England the next. But Sir Hugh Dowding knew better. A squadron lent might be—almost certainly would be—a squadron lost; and every distraction from the main task was playing the game of the enemy. Before his eyes there was the spectre of an overstretched fighter force vainly trying to plug the gaps and slowly wilting under the inexorable pressure of overwhelming numbers; and after that, of ports choked with sunken shipping, of aircraft and arms factories pulverized into rubble, of London undefended and burning, of the whole Allied cause collapsing from the paralysis of the British nerve-centres. However many calls there might be on our resources, Dowding was convinced that one call—the safety of the base—was primary and absolute; and till that was met, he proposed neither to understand other arguments, nor to compromise, nor even to accept with good grace the decisions that went against him.

The war was not many days old when Dowding began to press the Air Ministry for the immediate formation of twelve more fighter squadrons. But the Air Staff, fully alive to the problem, were already enquiring into possibilities of this sort. The result was not encouraging. Current production of Hurricanes and Spitfires totalled less than a hundred a month—not enough to cover the estimated wastage in existing units, let alone create a large block of new squadrons. Two new fighter squadrons at most might be formed, reported the Air Member for Supply and Organization—two squadrons, not of Spitfires or Hurricanes, but of Blenheims. Confronted with this verdict, Dowding merely reduced his demand to eight squadrons; and at the same time he complained bitterly that the four fighter squadrons intended for the Expeditionary Force had been sent to France before the *Luftwaffe* had engaged, and failed, in its grand assault on England. This decision, he foretold, had 'opened a tap through which will run the total Hurricane output'. For he had already been ordered just before the war to put six more Hurricane squadrons on a mobile basis; and though he had been promised that these would never be withdrawn from Fighter Command unless they could be spared with safety, he knew 'how much reliance to place on such assurances'. As for the claims of other Commands, he felt he must 'put on record' his view 'that the home defence organization must not be regarded as co-equal with other Commands, but that it should receive priority to all other claims until it is firmly secured, since the continued existence of the nation, and of its services, depends on the Royal Navy and Fighter Command'.

The Air Staff, for all their anxiety to ensure the defence of Great Britain, could not regard the matter in the same uncomplicated light as Sir Hugh Dowding. Their responsibilities were far wider, and they could hardly admit an absolute priority on the part of Fighter Command. The Army, the Royal Air Force in France, and the French were all clamouring for more fighters to be sent across the Channel; and the Air Ministry was committed, as its main contribution to victory, to building up a powerful force not of fighters but of bombers. Clearly it was impossible to satisfy everyone; but clearly it was also essential to create more fighter squadrons. And this emerged all the more plainly because the Germans had selected for their opening air action in the West precisely those objectives for which special fighter forces had been approved but not yet formed—our East Coast convoys and the new naval base at Scapa Flow.

In the end, thanks partly to his own pertinacity and partly to Sir Cyril Newall, Chief of Air Staff, Dowding got what he wanted. Supply and Organization had acknowledged that it was possible to form two Blenheim squadrons. Dowding, who had a use for Blenheims as night fighters, asked that these might take the form of four half-squadrons, to be built up to full strength as occasion permitted; and he further requested that an extra squadron previously approved for training and reserve should be allocated to the first-line, also in the form of two half-squadrons. To both these suggestions Newall gave his consent; and he also agreed that two more squadrons should be formed as an insurance against two of the mobile squadrons going to France. This gave Dowding the eight squadrons—or potential squadrons—to which he had reduced his original demand.

Here the matter might have rested for the time being, had not Newall become convinced that the demand for fighters would soon grow still more insistent. From all aspects of logistical possibility no more fighter squadrons could be formed at that moment; for the entire output, not only of single-engined machines but of Blenheims, was already fully earmarked—the latter largely to cover wastage among the bombers. And yet, if only more fighter squadrons could be formed, even on the wrong aircraft types, they might be ready for action—on the right types—precious weeks earlier than if their formation were delayed until the production position improved. So, since he had no good argument except the sheer desirability of more squadrons, Newall decided not to argue. Calling a meeting of the Air Members and some of the Air Staff on 17th October 1939, he briefly announced not only that the eight extra squadrons recently approved must be completed by the end of the month, but that an additional ten squadrons must be formed in the following fortnight. He then invited those present to suggest how this could be done.

The act of faith more than justified itself. By December all eighteen squadrons had been formed. Most were armed with Blenheims, but some had Battles—machines as well adapted for air fighting as hackneys for winning the Derby. The struggle of these squadrons towards full operational status was slow and painful. But in the spring of 1940 production of single-engined fighters rose sharply, and by May nine of the eighteen squadrons had changed their Battles and Blenheims for Hurricanes or Spitfires. Since four of the Blenheim squadrons were finally handed over to Coastal Command for shipping protection, and two more of the mobile squadrons were despatched to France during one of the periodic 'flaps', Fighter Command finished up with a net increase of twelve squadrons. In other words, the forces available for the air defence of this country rose from 35 squadrons (of which 22 were armed with Hurricanes or Spitfires) in September 1939, to 47 squadrons (of which 38 had Hurricanes or Spitfires) in May 1940. Had Newall not settled the pattern of this so early by forming squadrons before the supply of aircraft warranted, it is almost certain that our fighter array when the German offensive opened in the West would have been neither so extensive nor so modern. On the other hand, the expansion of Fighter Command inevitably retarded the already slow development of Bomber Command; indeed it upset all previous notions of the correct balance between offensive and defensive forces, for by May 1940 our fighter squadrons in Britain and France outnumbered our bomber squadrons. But Newall and Dowding did not over-insure; and the narrow margin of victory in the Battle of Britain was the proof of their wisdom.

The decisions of October 1939 kept Dowding quiet (if the phrase may be used without offence) for nearly six months. During this time his main operational problem was the German attack against our east coast shipping and naval bases. The protection of shipping, it has already been made clear, was not a task that he accepted willingly. The existing radar stations were little use against low-flying aircraft; the fighter squadrons were unaccustomed to working over the sea; and fighter airfields near the coast were a rarity. After making it plain that his other responsibilities—of which the protection of the aircraft industry ranked highest—would correspondingly suffer, Dowding at length agreed to defend a coastal belt stretching five miles out to sea. At first his squadrons had little success in this, but once they could operate from Coastal Command's airfields they were soon able to bring about a reduction in sinkings. All told, from the outbreak of war until the opening of the Norwegian campaign, some forty German aircraft were destroyed out of the 400 odd which were reported over or near our shores—no mean feat for fighters operating at the fringe of their interception system against bombers attacking widely dispersed targets.

To protect our main naval base on the east coast in the autumn of 1939 was scarcely less of a problem than to safeguard our shipping. There was no great difficulty about Rosyth, which could be covered from Drem and Turnhouse by the two Scottish auxiliary squadrons —Nos. 602 (City of Glasgow) and 603 (City of Edinburgh). But Scapa Flow, in the Orkneys, was a very different proposition, for it was far outside the general Fighter Command system. Not until March 1939 had the Air Ministry learnt of the intention to use Scapa as a main base, and though a scheme of defence had been settled in the following July the squadrons for this were not due to form until 1941. Scapa was thus without fighter protection when war broke out; and by no possibility did it seem, even then, that fighters could be provided before the summer of 1940. By that date, according to new decisions taken in September 1939, two squadrons and a Sector Operations Room capable of handling up to five more were to be available at Wick, an incomplete Coastal Command station on the mainland. A full balloon barrage was also to be in position. Meanwhile, as emergency measures, some of the London balloons were rushed north, and the Admiralty agreed to operate two Fleet Air Arm fighter squadrons from the small civil airfield at Hatston.

On the other side of the North Sea, one person at least was anxious to take advantage of this situation. Göring—if his own tale may be believed—longed to open hostilities by flinging his bombers in full force against the Home Fleet. It is certainly interesting to speculate what would have happened had he done so. But political considerations and the demands of the German Army prevailed, and for the time being the entire German air effort was concentrated against the Poles. Only with Poland vanquished and the *Führer's* magnanimous peace offer rejected by the Allies could the *Luftwaffe* get down to business in the West.

It was on 14th October 1939, some forty-eight hours after Hitler's proposals had met their inevitable answer, that Lieutenant Prien nosed the *U.47* into Scapa Flow and directed two well-placed salvoes of torpedoes into the *Royal Oak*. The defences of the base were immediately declared inadequate, and arrangements were made for the Commander-in-Chief, Home Fleet, to move to Rosyth within a week. Two days later, on the morning of 16th October, reconnais-sance aircraft appeared over the Forth and the wireless interception service reported signs of a forthcoming operation against Rosyth. With this warning No. 607 (County of Durham) Squadron was promptly ordered up to Drem; and during the afternoon the threatened raids developed. Unfortunately the local radar ceased to function at the critical moment through a failure of the power appara-tus, with the result that the enemy bombers, who numbered about a dozen, got their first blows in unmolested. Being at this stage of the war under orders as stringent as our own, they made no attempt to damage targets on land, but concentrated entirely on our ships. One bomb went through three decks of the *Southampton* and out of the side before exploding and sinking the Admiral's barge; another damaged the *Edinburgh:* and a third caused several casualties on board the *Mohawk*. But despite the lack of early warning or coherent direction, Nos. 602 and 603 Squadrons got in amongst the bombers and shot down two He.111's—the first German aircraft to be destroyed over British soil since 1918.[1]

Apparently well satisfied with the venture against Rosyth, the next day the *Luftwaffe* turned its attention to Scapa Flow. Shortly before 1100 hours a small force of bombers swept into the anchorage, only to find that most of the fleet was at sea. In the ensuing attack our light guns disposed of two of the enemy, but the raiders scored a near miss against the depot ship *Iron Duke*, which was so badly damaged that she had to be beached.

Coming on top of the loss of the *Royal Oak* and the raid on Rosyth, this was too much for the Admiralty, who now decided to move the Home Fleet to the west coast until the two north-eastern bases offered greater security. While work on the approved schemes was hastened forward at Scapa, with a new target date of February 1940, and while some of the Glasgow balloons were redeployed for the benefit of Rosyth, the Home Fleet accordingly retired to the Clyde. Thence it would be difficult, to say the least, for our ships to intercept with due speed a surface-raider breaking into the Atlantic or a force descending on our east coast. By two or three boldly directed strokes, and at a total cost of four aircraft, the German Air Force and the U-boat Service had between them scored a resounding strategic success—of which, very fortunately, the German Navy was to take little advantage.

---

[1] Some of the combats, including a chase at roof-top height, were witnessed by the boys of Fettes, one of whom wrote an entertaining description of the fighting to the Secretary of State for Air. 'The College', he concluded, 'remains quite unconvinced of the horror of war on the doorstep.'

The winter months saw the development of a fighter sector for the Orkneys pressed on apace. In spite of the remoteness of the locality and the extraordinary severity of the weather the work was accomplished up to schedule. By the end of February 1940 a new airfield was under construction on the mainland at Castletown, more radar stations were being built, a Sector Operations Room had been opened up at Wick (in an elementary school), and three Hurricane squadrons—Nos. 43, 111 and 605—were deployed on Wick airfield. Possibly the hardest task was that of No. 950 Squadron, whose duty was to install and operate a balloon barrage. Suitable sites on the islands were few and far between; the naval authorities at first rejected the idea of water-borne sites; and the rough seas repeatedly held up supplies. Then in February, when the first balloons were installed and 'bedded down' on screw pickets, violent winds tore them adrift. After this the airmen, who had already gained a nodding acquaintance with the art of building from having to erect their own huts, turned their hands to laying concrete beds. In the face of such obstacles it was no small achievement that by the end of March there were twelve balloons flying, and that arrangements were well advanced for a total barrage of fifty-six. In the end all difficulties were triumphantly overcome; but the job of flying the barrage remained a tough one, and balloon-operators continued to display a touch of pallor in their weather-beaten countenances at the mention of a posting to the Orkneys.

With the defences of Scapa Flow strengthened in the air, on the ground, and under water, early in March 1940 the Home Fleet returned. Within a few days No. 111 Squadron shot down a German raider. A more determined assault followed on 16th March, just before dark, when the *Norfolk* and the *Iron Duke* were damaged, Hatston airfield was attacked, and some bombs on the island of Hoy caused the first fatal casualties among British civilians. On this occasion our fighters failed to intercept; but, as recorded above, the fall of bombs on British soil stung the War Cabinet into retaliation against the sea-plane base at Hornum. Doubtless with the intention of damaging as many of our vessels as possible before the invasion of Norway, the enemy then made three more raids on Scapa in the following month. All were broken up and defeated by the Hurricanes.

By March 1940 the general system of air defence embracing Nos. 11, 12 and 13 Fighter Groups and running from Portsmouth round the south and east of the country to the Forth had thus been supplemented by an isolated sector for the protection of Scapa Flow. But the enemy, finding his efforts against our shipping off these sections of the coast too expensive, was already now beginning to concentrate his attacks on shipping in the virtually undefended reaches between the Forth and the Orkneys. For the time being the only answer to this—and a very imperfect one—was to operate detached squadrons of fighters from Coastal Command airfields like Dyce (Aberdeen) and Montrose, even though these places were not linked with the main Fighter Command System. Worse still, however, was the danger at the other extremity of the system; for the enemy was now thought to be developing aircraft with the range to outflank our defences in the south, so that he could attack not only our shipping in the South-Western Approaches but also the whole country west of Portsmouth. Against this threat there was as yet only the isolated sector at Filton for the protection of Bristol and the Bristol Aeroplane Company. It was with these problems in mind, sharpened by his ever-present dread of being ordered to send further fighters to France, that Dowding now approached the Air Ministry once more to augment his forces. What he asked for, in effect, was the extension of the air defence system to the largely uncovered north-east and south-west of Great Britain.

In point of fact, a new Fighter Group, No. 10, had already been projected to cover the gap between Portsmouth and Filton. What Dowding wanted—and got—was a further extension of this embryonic Group to Cornwall, Devonshire and South Wales; while in the north he visualized an entirely new Group, No. 14, with responsibility for all fighter operations between the Firth of Tay and the Shetlands. For these extensions Newall agreed that Dowding must have seven new squadrons within the next six months; and in a general review of the whole problem of fighter expansion, the Air Staff came to the conclusion that beyond these seven squadrons, a further twenty, bringing the Metropolitan Fighter Force to a total of eighty squadrons, would be needed by April 1941. It was, in the words of the Air Staff appreciation, 'a staggering requirement'.

Neither the seven new squadrons nor the two new groups had been formed by the time the German offensive broke in the West. But that they had been envisaged and approved and were in the process of creation, was the measure of the foresight of both Dowding and the Air Staff; for whereas in March 1940 these additions were certainly desirable, a few months later, with German aircraft based in Norway and France, they were not merely desirable but essential.

* * *

So the war continued—a war of alarums and excursions, but singularly little major action. Americans, watching from comfortable seats outside the arena the cautious sparring and pulled punches of

F

the opposing heavyweights, dismissed the contest as 'phoney'. The epithet was hardly justified. One of the contestants was nursing his strength for the later stages of the fight; the other was about to launch an all-out effort in the next round. Certainly there was nothing 'phoney' about the war for our aircrews, despite the strange restrictions on bombing observed by both sides. For restrictions or no restrictions, our airmen had still to drone their way over Germany through night and the enemy defences, or ceaselessly scan the wastes of ocean, or speed to combat with the molester of our shipping, or—and this to most was the true hardship—sit long, bitter hours at dispersal, waiting for the call that did not come.

The French, too, had a word for it—'*la drôle de guerre*'. And up to a point the Royal Air Force in France was inclined to agree with them. It was odd to be in the first party to leave England, travelling in an aircraft on the nose of which was chalked the prophetic words '*Où sommes nous?*' It was odd to arrive and to find few of the promised arrangements for one's reception in existence. It was odd to be—if only for a brief time—without blankets, shelter or sufficient food. It was odd to be sent off on daylight reconnaissance of enemy territory in a Battle, and to be shot down almost before crossing the border; it was almost equally odd to be sent off in a Blenheim I, and to run out of petrol short of home. It was still more odd to carry out night training over Germany because of the French restrictions on flying after dark. It was odd, when the soldiers below were not yet at grips, to be fighting hard with the enemy in a corner of sky near Luxembourg; and odd to be a hero of the fighting, like young 'Cobber' Kain of New Zealand and No. 73 Squadron, and find oneself the hapless subject of a clash between Service and Press on the merits of publicity for individuals. On a humbler plane, it was odd, when all starting devices from batteries to hot bricks and blow lamps had failed in forty degrees of frost, to hear the flight sergeant's optimistic injunction to 'whip out them plugs'—with frozen fingers and one plug-spanner per six aircraft. But it was also a great deal more than odd: how much more, the Royal Air Force, whose adjectival vocabulary is strictly limited, would have found it difficult to express in polite society.

However phoney or odd or anything else the comparative calm of these early months might appear, it was what the Allies had hoped for. But it was also far more than they had expected. For though it was clearly in the interests of the Allies to postpone the decisive clash until they had amassed their full strength, it was less clear why Germany should apparently be playing the same game. The answer, as we now know, lay in a combination of factors. Until his peace offer was turned down in mid-October, Hitler still hoped to do a deal with Britain and France. Then there was some delay while the apprehensions of his General Staff about attacking France were overcome; but by November the decision to violate the neutrality of Belgium, Holland and Luxembourg had been taken. After that it was a question of waiting for the right weather to make the best use of German superiority in tanks and aircraft. But there were also additional complications. In January 1940—incredible as it sounds—a German aircraft carrying certain details of the plan crashed in Belgium, and a fresh variant had to be devised. By this time Admiral Raeder and the German Naval Staff had persuaded the *Führer* that Norway would make a most palatable addition to the ensuing banquet. For a while there was discussion on the correct sequence of the courses, but in the opening days of March the chef (and principal diner) made up his mind: Denmark and Norway the *hors d'œuvre*, France and the Low Countries the *entrée*. The repast was to begin in April; and by the time the *entrée* was demolished, the roast—England—would undoubtedly be done to a turn.

Meanwhile the Allies were presented with a heaven-sent gift: eight months of that most precious of all commodities for ill-armed but wealthy democracies—Time. The Air Ministry and the Royal Air Force well understood that the value of the gift was strictly conditioned by the use that was made of it. Lessons of the highest value were extracted from the operations carried out, limited in scale and restricted in scope though these were. Plans were perfected for the inevitable battle in the Low Countries, and for much else. Technical development and production were speeded on; the fruits of earlier research were gathered and the seed of fresh invention sown. The first use of the specially stripped and unarmed Spitfire, camouflaged light blue—a momentous innovation due largely to the prescience of Flying Officer M. V. Longbottom—gave birth to the revolutionary technique of high-altitude photographic reconnaissance. In the all-important matter of radar, ground stations for the detection of low-flying aircraft and airborne sets for the detection of shipping began to come into service. The control of fighter aircraft from the ground was improved out of all recognition by the introduction of V.H.F. (Very High Frequency) radio telephony. New and better aircraft were specified; and in December 1939, thanks in great part to the individual insistence of Air Marshal Sir Wilfrid Freeman, the first order was placed for that most remarkable of 'private ventures', the de Havilland Mosquito. Equally important, the powerful pressure from the British aircraft industry to close down on the development and production of the four-engined heavy bomber in favour of a greater output of existing aircraft was firmly resisted. A mass of useful, vital work was done in nearly every field; for the expansion of the Royal Air Force, started in 1934, and jerked into successively greater speeds many times since, was now set firmly in top gear.

No feature of this activity was more important than the extension of training facilities. The requirement was immense. The ground training alone was a formidable commitment, for its purpose was to produce not well-drilled automata but highly skilled technicians— men whose training in peace-time had taken as much as seven years. Excellent progress was made, and by April 1940 the number of technical schools had more than doubled compared with September 1939. But the ground training was the least part of the difficulty. The flying training, with its tremendous demands on airfields, aircraft and skilled instructors, and its vital, complex relation to first-line strength and efficiency, was the heart of the problem. And here, in September 1939, there were two tasks beyond all others which called for attention. The first was to ensure that aircrew posted to squadrons were not merely accustomed to an intermediate type of Service aircraft, but were operationally efficient on the particular aircraft of that squadron with a particular crew for the particular tasks they would have to perform; the crews, in other words, must come to the squadron with much of the knowledge and experience which in peace-time—since squadrons must have something to do in peace-time—they usually picked up when they got there. The second and even greater task was to provide facilities for elementary and Service flying training on a vast scale in some less crowded and vulnerable place than the British Isles.

Both these problems were well on the way to solution by the spring of 1940. The danger of having the squadrons either cluttered up with half-trained aircrew or else waiting for replacements who were queuing for the final stages of their training in the few existing 'Reserve' squadrons, was averted by the creation of operational training units (O.T.U.s). These large organizations, holding as many as seventy aircraft and maintained economically on a station basis, were highly developed in Bomber Command, where the problem was greatest—and where Ludlow-Hewitt was fully prepared to risk unpopularity in high places by insisting on the need to divert first-line aircraft and skilled crews to the duty of instruction. The system, however, was applied generally throughout the operational Commands, and rapidly proved the key to efficiency in the air.

The other danger, that the earlier stages of flying training would be cramped by enemy action and lack of space, was overcome by Canning's classical remedy of calling in the New World to redress the balance of the Old. The Air Ministry had seen the need for this well before the war; indeed, one of the oldest Service Flying Training Schools was at Abu Sueir, in Egypt. From 1936 onwards Canada, which enjoyed an ideal strategic position and a convenient proximity to the vast industrial resources of the United States, was repeatedly approached; but the Canadians, largely for domestic reasons, felt unable to accept our proposals, and until the outbreak of war undertook no commitments for the Royal Air Force beyond training fifty Canadian recruits a year. During these years Australia and New Zealand were considered too remote for Royal Air Force training, but both provided trained cadets for service with the Royal Air Force, and shortly before the war New Zealand promised a substantial contribution in trained men. For the rest, Southern Rhodesia had both formed and trained an air unit for work with the Royal Air Force, and was prepared to give hospitality to Royal Air Force training; but only in Kenya, of the Commonwealth territories, was there a school actually planned and in prospect when war broke out.

This picture was transformed in the first weeks of hostilities. Canada, Australia and New Zealand, having taken up their stand at our side, at once set out to develop large Air Forces for service with the Royal Air Force. Very early the decision was taken to make the training of the Dominion aircrews to some extent a common enterprise, and on 17th December 1939 there was signed in Ottawa the agreement which brought into being the great Empire Air Training Scheme. By the terms of this, the United Kingdom was to supply nearly all the aircraft and a nucleus of skilled men, the Dominions all other requirements. Canada, training Canadians, Australians, New Zealanders and a small number of pupils from Britain or Newfoundland, would build up thirteen Elementary Flying Training Schools, sixteen Service Flying Training Schools, ten Air Observer Schools, ten Bombing and Gunnery Schools and two Air Navigation Schools. Australia, training her own citizens, would create nine Elementary Flying Training Schools, seven Service Flying Training Schools, four Air Observer Schools and four Bombing and Gunnery Schools. New Zealand, also training her own citizens, would form three Elementary Flying Training Schools and two Service Flying Training Schools. By mid-1942, when the organization would reach full size, it was to be capable of producing no less than 11,000 pilots and 17,000 other aircrew each year.

This assured us of a magnificent flow of trained aircrew who, though members of their own Dominion Air Force, would mostly work in or alongside the Royal Air Force. But it was also necessary to find training space and hospitality overseas for large numbers of our own men. Here Southern Rhodesia led the way by agreeing to accommodate, administer and partially pay for three Service Flying Training Schools, all of which were to be, in the main, staffed by and run for the Royal Air Force. Then, hard on top of the Ottawa Agreement in December, South Africa offered a share of her expanding training organization to Royal Air Force pupils. At about the same time it was also arranged—with less fruitful results—that five Royal Air Force schools should be built in France.

The opening courses in the first of the new schools in Canada, Australia and New Zealand began on 29th April 1940. As the months went by, it was to become apparent that the early plans, richly conceived as they had been, had far from exhausted the genius of the architects. All the Dominions were to undertake, and to fulfil, much more than they had originally promised—Canada in particular, with mounting pride in the splendid edifice rising before her eyes, was to become an ever more lavish deviser and donor of improvements and additions. Meantime, in April 1940, it was much that the plans had been made and the work begun: that the ardent British boy might learn to handle his Moth and Anson in the space and security of veldt or prairie, and that the stalwart sons of the Dominions, hastening to our aid, would soon need no more than the final experience of the Operational Training Unit before they entered the lists of battle. For in Europe, Time had at last run out. Hitler's armies were once more on the march.

CHAPTER IV

Scandinavian Misadventure

THE advantages of a controlling position in Norway, so strongly urged on the *Führer* by Admiral Raeder, were not unappreciated in Whitehall. From the end of November 1939, when the Russians attacked Finland, the possibilities of fishing profitably in Scandinavian waters were seriously considered by the British Government. Of the voices that were raised in favour of active measures of this sort, one in particular was clear and insistent—the voice of Mr. Churchill, then First Lord of the Admiralty; for Norway—or some of it—was within easy reach of the Navy.

Clearly the Allies had every justification for supporting Finland. The wanton aggression committed against a weak and unoffending neighbour by a vast dictatorial power on terms of intimacy with the Nazis cried for redress in the name of morality and the democratic cause. Cries for redress, however, are apt to pass unheard unless they fall on willing ears. In this case the ears were already well down to the ground.

For some time past the Allies had been studying the possibilities of depriving Germany of the high-grade iron-ore which is found so abundantly in Sweden, and which is so important in the manufacture of armaments. When the Russians attacked the Finns it was at once seen that Allied intervention, by establishing a military force in Scandinavia, might achieve this desired end. The prize was not one to be despised. All our economic surveys pointed to the peculiar significance of Swedish iron-ore in the German war economy; the least optimistic estimate of its worth was that without it the German war effort would collapse within a year; and a confidential memorandum to the French government from Fritz Thyssen, Frankenstein fearful of his own creation, only confirmed the verdict. Nor has post-war research done anything to upset these conclusions. According to recent German admissions, during the opening months of the war iron-ore from Sweden and Norway in fact supplied two-thirds of Germany's total consumption of the product.

The iron-ore of Sweden is found in two widely separated areas—the fields around Grangesberg, within easy access of Stockholm, and those around Kiruna and Gallivare, in the extreme north. It is the latter which produce in such great quantities the high grade phosphoric ores. The export of the ore from the fields in the south presents no difficulty, for these are served by the network of railways covering southern Sweden; but the export of ore from Kiruna and Gallivare is another matter. From both these towns there is railway communication to the port of Luleå, at the head of the Gulf of Bothnia; but from mid-December to mid-May Luleå is ice-bound. Much of the ore in consequence travels by a single-track railway, overhung by great rocks and mountains, to the Norwegian port of Narvik, which remains open to traffic all the year round. Thence it proceeds by sea to its destination. And in the early months of the war its destination was largely Germany—by way of Norway's territorial waters.

The approach of the War Cabinet to what could now be considered the combined problems of Finland and the Swedish iron-ore was hesitant. Sabotage, though it might help, could not interfere seriously with the trade with Germany; only the occupation of the ore-fields and the communications on which they depend would suffice. But a naked seizure of the ore-fields would set all Scandinavia by the ears, alienate neutral opinion generally, and violate the principles for which we were fighting. Moreover, since the fact of German control over the Baltic meant that we should have to approach the ore-fields by way of the scanty communications and mountain barriers of northern and central Norway, a mere descent in force would be militarily unsound. The expedition must thus be undertaken unobtrusively, in the course of carrying aid to the Finns, and only if both Norway and Sweden agreed to co-operate—or at least, not to oppose. And even this would be risking war with Russia.

It was with these difficulties in mind that the War Cabinet in December 1939, after agreeing as a first step to send some aircraft to the Finns, considered the proposal of the First Lord of the Admiralty that we should interrupt the traffic from Narvik to Germany inside Norwegian territorial waters by a combination of mine-laying and naval action. In accordance with the Cabinet's determination not to offend Scandinavian opinion, Mr. Churchill's proposal was accepted only to the extent of inquiring how the Norwegian and Swedish governments would regard such measures. The reply was entirely unfavourable. There, for a few weeks, the matter rested.

By February 1940, however, it was clear that without substantial

BOMBER AIRFIELD AT DUSK
The crews go out to their Wellingtons

HURRICANES ON PATROL

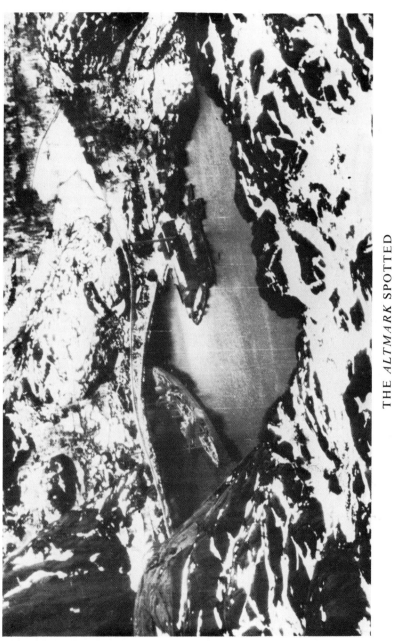

THE *ALTMARK* SPOTTED

Coastal Command reconnaissance discovers the prison-ship in Josing Fjord on 24th February 1940

SEVEN YEARS AFTERWARDS
The wreckage of one of No. 263 Squadron's Gladiators, still visible on the shores of Lake Lesjaskog in 1947

reinforcements the Finns could not hold out against Russia for more than a matter of weeks. The prospect of having 'the great barbarians' within easy reach of the Swedish iron-ore and the North Sea being more than a little distasteful, it was decided to ask Norway and Sweden to allow the transit of Allied units across their territory into Finland—units formed on the model of the Italian 'Volunteer' brigades in the Spanish Civil War. The necessary military and air forces were detailed, and in early March the request was duly made. Once again the only result was a blank refusal. Faced with this, and with the continued insistence of the Norwegians and Swedes on maintaining their exports to Germany, the First Lord of the Admiralty then reverted to the lesser project of mining the route from Narvik. Since this was at best only a partial solution of the problem—the Narvik route accounting, as we now know, for one third of Germany's total imports of iron-ore from Scandinavia—it was once more rejected by the Cabinet.

The Allies had not reached this point without arousing German suspicions; indeed our intention at least to carry help to Finland had been proclaimed to the world. On 12th December 1939, when Hitler formally decided to secure control of Norway, he was not yet sure how far he could achieve his object by fostering the influence of the traitor Quisling. During the ensuing months he had accordingly catered for both contingencies, at once encouraging the Norwegian Nazis and at the same time preparing a military expedition. The news that the British were actually contemplating intervention in Scandinavia, coupled with our violation of Norwegian territorial rights during the *Altmark* incident, now convinced Hitler and his Naval Staff that they must act swiftly if they were to safeguard their supplies of iron-ore and obtain their desired vantage-points for the air and sea war against England. As Quisling, by his own admission, could not produce the goods in time, on 4th March Hitler ordered the German armed forces to make ready with all speed.

Hostilities between the Russians and the Finns ended on 13th March 1940. The following day the British War Cabinet considered Mr. Churchill's view that we should still proceed with our Scandinavian expedition, partly to secure the ore-fields, partly to forestall an eventual Russian advance to the Atlantic. But once more the Cabinet, in default of Norwegian and Swedish consent, rejected extreme courses. Indeed, it now decided to disperse the forces thus far collected—forces which included, among the Royal Air Force units, an air component headquarters, two bomber squadrons, three fighter squadrons, one and a half army co-operation squadrons, a balloon squadron and an observer screen.

After the signature of the Russo-Finnish Peace Treaty the Germans sensed some relaxation in the British preparations, and at the end of March Admiral Raeder gave his opinion that a British descent on Norway was no longer imminent. But at the same time he urged that the Germans must ultimately take over Norway, and that they should do so sooner rather than later. The *Führer* was entirely of the same mind. On 26th March the German 'D-day' for operation *Weserübung* —the 'Weser exercise', or occupation of Norway and Denmark— was fixed for the period of the next new moon.

Meanwhile the Allies, almost equally reluctant to abandon the chance of a cheap strategic success, were haggling. The French, sensitive to the loss of 'face' over Finland, urged that some positive action to control Norwegian territorial waters, either by naval measures or by seizing Norwegian ports, would have a tonic effect on neutral opinion. The British countered that Scandinavian co-operation was essential, even for the most limited project; but at a meeting of the Supreme War Council on 28th March, some ground was yielded on both sides, and agreement was reached. Fresh notes were to be addressed to Norway and Sweden informing them that their interpretation of neutrality had worked against our interests: that they must not oppose us if we decided to carry aid to Finland in a future struggle: and that we reserved the right to take such measures as we thought necessary to prevent vital resources flowing to Germany This message delivered, mines were to be laid in Norwegian territorial waters along the route from Narvik, and operations were to be undertaken against German shipping thus forced out to sea. Should these measures provoke a German invasion of southern Norway, or should there be clear evidence that such an invasion was intended, and should the Norwegians then welcome our support, a few units retained from the original expeditionary force would be rushed across to occupy Narvik, Trondheim and Bergen, and to effect demolitions at Stavanger. With the Germans forestalled at the key points on the west coast, further forces could then be despatched to Norway as necessary—or as available. In all this the Royal Air Force was expected to bear no great part. 'No air forces', wrote the Chiefs of Staff, 'need accompany the . . . army forces in the first instance. We may, however, have to despatch the air contingent which was included in the original Narvik plan, if the opportunity to move to Gallivare should subsequently arise. A decision on this can be deferred.'

The warning notes were presented to the Norwegian and Swedish governments on 5th April 1940—two days after the first supply ships of the German expedition had quietly set sail. The Swedes immediately complained that the British note 'brought our countries very close to war'. The reply of the Norwegians was still awaited when the progress of events made it superfluous.

* * *

A few hours after the Allied notes were delivered in Oslo and Stockholm, most of the forces intended to cover the mine-laying left Scapa. The operation, scheduled for the early hours of 8th April, was to take place in two areas; one field was to be sown in the Vest Fjord, on the direct approach to Narvik, the other farther south. While the vessels for these tasks proceeded towards Norway, the troops who were to forestall the Germans at the west coast ports embarked in transports and cruisers, ready to sail, if need be, as soon as the mines were laid.

By 8th April, however, the situation had lost its pristine clarity. By that time reports of unaccustomed movements by German naval units had been coming in for many hours. On 6th April a sizable German force, including the *Scharnhorst* and the *Gneisenau*, had been photographed at anchor in the Wilhelmshaven roads; but in the course of the evening it sailed, and the leading ship, the cruiser *Hipper*, was reported during the night by Bomber Command aircraft as proceeding on a northerly course twenty miles north of Heligoland. The following morning—the 7th—Coastal Command Hudsons were ordered to search for this vessel. They spotted a cruiser and attendant destroyers on a northerly course, but were driven off by German aircraft. Their information, however, was good enough to warrant an attack, and at 1325 hours twelve Bomber Command Blenheims of No. 107 Squadron came up with the target. Unfortunately their bombs missed; but their sighting report was of the highest value, for it now gave the composition of the force as a battleship, a pocket battleship, two or three cruisers, and a large destroyer escort. This estimate was not entirely accurate, for the force in fact consisted of two battle-cruisers (*Scharnhorst* and *Gneisenau*), a cruiser (*Hipper*) and destroyer escort; but at least it was clear that a very substantial number of German warships was proceeding north. A further attempt to impede its progress was accordingly made later in the afternoon by two squadrons of Wellingtons. Bad visibility robbed them of success.

While the Blenheims were attacking what in fact was the German expedition for the seizure of Trondheim and Narvik, a signal was on its way from the Admiralty to the Commander-in-Chief, Home Fleet. It ran thus: 'Recent reports suggest German expedition is being prepared. Hitler is reported from Copenhagen to have ordered unostentatious movements of one division in ten ships by night to land at Narvik with simultaneous occupation of Jutland. Sweden to

be left alone. . . . Date given for arrival at Narvik was 8th April.'
This was a very significant warning; so significant, that the information was also passed to the Norwegian government. It was, perhaps,
a little unfortunate that the signal went on to say: 'All these reports
are of doubtful value and may well be only a further move in the war
of nerves.' Nevertheless its general purport, coupled with the news
of the large German force proceeding north and the failure of our
bombing attacks, determined the Commander-in-Chief to put to sea
that evening in an effort to intercept the enemy. At the same time, for
fear of a clash with powerful forces, the Admiralty recalled the more
southerly mine-laying group. The following day—the 8th—anxious
to free as many ships as possible for the forthcoming battle in the
North Sea, the Admiralty turned the waiting expeditionary battalions
and their stores out of the cruisers in the Forth, so that these vessels
might join the fray.

When 8th April dawned, one British mine-laying expedition was
thus completing its work off Narvik; another was on its way home
with its mission unfulfilled; a powerful German naval force was
heading north; and the Commander-in-Chief, Home Fleet, as yet
with scanty resources, was hastening east to intercept. Throughout
the day, the Royal Air Force continued its efforts to throw further
light on the situation. Patrols by Hudsons and Sunderlands covered
as many areas and contingencies as possible, but in a day of mist and
rain only one contact was made with the enemy. A Sunderland of
No. 204 Squadron, detailed to escort the Home Fleet in its progress
east, had been diverted by the Commander-in-Chief to search for the
German force. The aircraft reached the Norwegian coast, flew
coast-wise to Ulla, near Kristiansund, and thence proceeded due
north. Visibility at this time was no more than one to two miles in
constant rain, with 10/10ths cloud at 800 feet. Suddenly the captain,
who was sitting in the second pilot's seat, saw warships about one
mile ahead. Seizing the controls, he turned steeply to starboard, then
ordered the second pilot to fly round the force at visibility distance.
It was instantly recognized to be German and was judged to consist
of a battle-cruiser, two cruisers and two destroyers. Within a few
minutes the flying-boat had paid for its discovery by receiving a
stream of bullets in the hull and petrol tanks; but despite this damage
it succeeded in drawing clear of the vessels and reporting to base
their composition, course and speed. Unfortunately the course was
reported without qualification as 270 degrees (due west), though the
crew of the aircraft, under fire and manœuvring rapidly, were hardly
in a position to make sure, and the second pilot disagreed with the
estimate.

This report misled the Commander-in-Chief, Home Fleet, in two important respects. The vessels in fact were the cruiser *Hipper* and four destroyers, which had broken off from the larger force reported earlier; and they were heading north-east for Trondheim, not west for the Atlantic. But in view of the Sunderland's report of a powerful force steering west, and the failure of later reconnaissance that day to regain contact on account of the persistent bad weather, the Commander-in-Chief placed himself in the path of a break-out into the Atlantic. He thus remained far to the west of his quarry. Meanwhile Admiral Whitworth, who had been covering the mine-layers further north, was warned to guard the approaches to Narvik; but though he had a brush with the *Scharnhorst* and *Gneisenau*, the two battle cruisers had already parted company with the destroyers bound for Narvik, and so the Narvik expedition itself eluded him.

This preoccupation with the German units in the North Sea, coupled with the extremely bad weather, resulted in the remaining German forces escaping detection from the air. These, as it proved, were destined for Bergen, Egersund, Kristiansand, Arendal and Oslo. But in conditions of very low visibility aircraft of Bomber Command failed to notice any unusual activity in the Heligoland Bight; while those of Coastal Command, finding visibility nil in the Skagerrak, had to return home with their task unaccomplished. Strong enemy forces were reported by the Naval Attaché in Copenhagen passing up towards the Kattegat in the afternoon of 8th April, and during the evening British submarines reported enemy vessels steering west past the tip of Jutland; but these were thought to be shaping to follow the other enemy units into the North Sea. The Norwegian government, indeed, took warning at the last moment from the fact that a German vessel bound for Bergen, and sunk by submarine, turned out to be carrying large numbers of soldiers; by the time, however, that the Cabinet had met and decided upon partial mobilization it was past 9 p.m. So it came about that, in spite of the many signs and portents, and in spite of our glimpses of the various task forces, the German warships achieved a large measure of surprise when, less than three hours later, they began to appear off the Norwegian ports.

The German vessels entered Norwegian territorial waters under cover of darkness. Only in Oslo Fjord, where the minelayer *Olaf Trygvesson* damaged the *Emden*, and a stiff fight off the island fortress of Oskarsborg disposed of the *Blücher*, were the enemy's plans disrupted. Elsewhere the German Navy, despite gallant opposition by Norwegian ships, had matters all its own way. Arendal and Egersund, almost undefended, were there for the taking; at Kristiansand the first attack was beaten off, but enemy destroyers later gained an unopposed entry by flying the French flag; at Bergen merchant vessels lying peacefully in harbour suddenly ran up the Swastika and revealed themselves as supply ships for the expedition; at Trondheim the batteries at the entrance to the fjord were undermanned, short of ammunition, and baffled by a snow-storm; at Narvik the bravery of the Norwegian naval units was stultified by the treachery of the local military commander—a supporter of Quisling—who handed over the town without resistance. Everywhere brutal force and base cunning swiftly attained their ends.

By daybreak on 9th April, despite the failure of the attack upon Oslo Fjord, the German Minister had presented himself at the Norwegian Foreign Office to demand the country's instant capitulation. Meanwhile an impressive bonfire of documents in the gardens of the British Legation was being extinguished with great promptitude by the Oslo Fire Brigade. Three hours later the *Luftwaffe*, somewhat delayed by fog, appeared on the scene. For *Weserübung* nearly six hundred operational and over six hundred transport aircraft had been made available, and powerful forces of twin-engined fighters now swept in and overwhelmed the small Norwegian Air Force at Stavanger/Sola and Oslo/Fornebu airfields. Next came clouds of parachutists, to be followed almost immediately by airborne infantry; indeed, at Fornebu some of the aircraft bearing the latter actually landed before the paratroops—the one mishap in an otherwise perfectly timed programme. By midday Oslo/Kjeller airfield was also in enemy hands, and both at Oslo and Stavanger/Sola—which was captured entirely from the air—transport aircraft were streaming in with men and supplies, while bombers, fighters and reconnaissance machines were already taking off in support of the German troops. During the afternoon enemy forces moved into Oslo itself and by nightfall the German stranglehold was complete. Within a few hours King Haakon and his Cabinet, having appealed to the Allies and rejected the German demand to surrender power to Quisling, were vainly seeking some stable seat of government north of Oslo. From successive refuges they now strove to mobilize their army—a desperately difficult task with the capital, the main railway terminals and the chief ports all in German hands. Meanwhile the almost bloodless occupation of Denmark had assured Germany of easy access by air and sea to the new theatre of war.

*　　*　　*

The full implications of the enemy's initial success were not at first generally appreciated in England. Instead, there was some tendency to believe that, since Hitler had committed his forces across the water, and since Britannia ruled the waves, German communications would be rapidly severed and the whole expedition brought to disaster. Unfortunately such agreeable anticipations were to be quickly dashed to the ground. For the regrettable truth of the matter was that the sea routes from Germany and Denmark to southern Norway were controlled, not by the Royal Navy, but by the German Navy and the German Air Force: that the Germans had seized control of every airfield and port of consequence in the whole of Norway: and that the *Luftwaffe* was now either based in Norway or could refuel there, or could operate from Danish bases no more than 200 miles away. The Allies, on the other hand, were faced with the problem of operating over sea lines of communication anything from 600 to 1,000 miles long; and they would be compelled to rely—unless they could recapture a major port—on tiny harbours and exiguous railways. Without airfields in a country in which there are few natural landing grounds, Britain and France could not possibly bring to bear anything like the weight of air effort which the Germans were capable of applying. Once, then, the enemy had succeeded in his first swift blows, the situation was in fact highly unpromising.

While the Allies concerted their military plans, the Royal Air Force and the Royal Navy took what immediate measures were possible. The first concern was to hunt down the German warships which had been engaged in the expedition, and which were under orders to return to their home ports as soon as they had discharged their troops and stores. From 9th April to 12th April Coastal Command accordingly strained every nerve to spot the enemy vessels. On 9th April, though tasks in other areas were not neglected, coastal aircraft flew extensive patrols over a large part of the North Sea and the Norwegian coast and repeatedly reconnoitred the occupied ports. Five sorties were over Bergen during the day, confirming the presence of two cruisers—the *Köln* and the *Königsberg*[1]; two sorties reported a light cruiser—the *Karlsruhe*—in Kristiansand; and a Sunderland of No. 204 Squadron confirmed the presence of another cruiser—the *Hipper*—in Trondheim. Urgent naval requests also led to the despatch of a Sunderland—the only coastal aircraft with the necessary range—on a task which was particularly unsuitable for a flying boat; for the crew were instructed to make landfall at German-occupied Stavanger, cross the 150-odd miles of mountains to Oslo, and search for naval vessels in the neighbouring fjords. Not unexpectedly, the aircraft 'failed to return'.

---

[1] The identifications of these ships are as established from German records. The aircraft at the time reported the class of the vessel, not the identity.

Acting on the information thus gathered, Bomber Command rapidly despatched twelve Wellingtons of Nos. 9 and 115 Squadrons against the two cruisers at Bergen. Their attack, according to the enemy, was 'vigorously pressed home', but it resulted in nothing better than some near misses and a few wounded German sailors. The *Köln* made good her escape that evening, but the *Königsberg* had been damaged by the Norwegian shore batteries during her approach; and after a dawn reconnaissance by an aircraft of Coastal Command had established that she was still there the following morning—April 10th—Fleet Air Arm Skuas from Hatston caught her with two well and truly aimed bombs, and so earned the distinction of being the first aircraft to sink a major warship in battle. Apart from this, the *Karlsruhe*, sailing from Kristiansand in the evening of 9th April, was sunk by a British submarine; and the destroyers which had carried the landing parties to Narvik were disposed of by the naval actions of 10th and 13th April. Almost all the remaining German naval forces regained their home ports in safety. Early in the morning of the 12th the *Scharnhorst* and *Gneisenau*—now joined by the *Hipper*, which had left Trondheim on the night of the 10/11th—were picked up by Hudsons of Coastal Command off the south-west coast of Norway; but the striking forces despatched the same day, amounting in all to ninety-two aircraft, were once more frustrated by the weather. As a last resort twelve of these machines—Hampdens of Nos. 44 and 50 Squadrons—tried to attack a warship in Kristiansand. They were caught by German fighters, and having no defence against a beam attack were 'hacked down from the wing man inwards' until half their number had perished.

Thus ended the first phase of the invasion of Norway. The German Navy had got there in safety; had landed enough troops and supplies to capture all the key points; and had subsequently suffered losses which were severe in relation to German naval strength, but insignificant when weighed against the hazards, and the success, of the venture. The Allies could take consolation, however, from the fact that the most daring part of the stroke could not be repeated. Though the German troops in southern Norway could be supplied both by sea and air, the *Luftwaffe* alone must revictual and reinforce the isolated units at Trondheim and Narvik. And supply on this scale purely by air, if it was to be accomplished, would mark a new achievement in the history of warfare.

* * *

The attempt to bomb the German Navy on its return voyage having failed, our air attacks were now concentrated against the German-held airfields. Of these, the most immediately important to the enemy was Oslo/Fornebu, since the main German advance northwards would be directed from that area. As far as our own needs were concerned, however, the most important was the ill-developed but commodious landing ground at Vaernes, near Trondheim; for whereas Allied forces could not possibly sail through the Skagerrak and land near Oslo, they had every prospect of securing a lodgment in the neighbourhood of Trondheim. Moreover, Trondheim was perhaps the best centre of communication for the country as a whole; it was the third largest port in Norway; and the German force in occupation was both small and isolated. To put the *Luftwaffe* out of business at Vaernes would therefore be of the utmost benefit to our plans. Unfortunately, however, neither Fornebu nor Vaernes was within the effective striking distance of our daylight bombers; the former was 580 miles away from our nearest bomber bases, the latter 760 miles. Only the Whitleys could strike at this range without undue risk, and these had to operate by night, when the chances of identifying an airfield in Norway were slender. The result was that our main air effort came to be directed against the airfield which was the easiest to reach, to locate, and to attack—that of Stavanger/Sola, where for once the mountains of Norway sweep down, not to the sea, but to an open coastal flat.

Stavanger/Sola, 450 miles from our bomber bases on the east coast, was raided for the first time on the night of 11/12th April, and more heavily on 14th April. Thereafter it was bombed regularly; for by 14th April British forces were landing on Norwegian soil, and the bombing of Stavanger was one of the few available means of reducing the weight of German air attack against them.

The key to recovery in Norway was of course Trondheim. If we could recapture this large and flourishing port, with Vaernes airfield no great distance away, the northern half of Norway could almost certainly be held—for near Trondheim the country narrows sharply, and the distance across to Sweden is only sixty miles. Forces could then be built up for a subsequent advance to the south. With this in mind, and with the knowledge that the German troops in possession numbered as yet no more than two thousand, the Norwegians therefore urged the Allies to undertake an immediate and direct assault. But an operation of this kind could not be carried out without heavy losses among our ships, and though the plan was adopted in principle it was not applied. Instead a beginning was made with a subsidiary movement—an overland advance on Trondheim from two directions. One wing of this was to land at the small harbour of Namsos, 125 miles by road to the north of Trondheim, the other at the equally small harbour of Aandalsnes, 200 miles by road to the south.

G

Meanwhile, a third and entirely independent force was to recapture the remote and isolated port of Narvik.

The first naval party put ashore at Namsos on 14th April. The same day British forces began to land near Harstad in Vaags Fjord, the base selected for operations against Narvik; and on 17th April an advanced party disembarked at Aandalsnes. All these landings were unopposed, and since some initial progress was quickly made from Namsos and Aandalsnes the plan of a direct assault on Trondheim up the fjords was abandoned with relief, and all efforts were concentrated on the advance over land.

The troops at Namsos were under the command of Major General Carton de Wiart, v.c., a soldier whose gallantry from the days of the Boer War onwards had become almost a legend. De Wiart, who arrived by Sunderland flying-boat on 15th April to the accompaniment of German bombs, lost no time in pushing forces south through the vital defile of Steinkjer. A halt then ensued while further troops —a French demi-brigade—were brought into Namsos on 19th April. But the Frenchmen were no sooner landed and the ships withdrawn than the *Luftwaffe*, whose activities over this area had thus far been sporadic, appeared on the scene in strength. In the absence of anti-aircraft defences their task was not difficult, and by nightfall on 20th April Namsos was virtually destroyed. 'The whole place', wrote a naval eye-witness, 'was a mass of flames from end to end, and the glare on the snows of the surrounding mountains produced an unforgettable spectacle'. The railway station, the rolling stock and the storehouses on the jetties all suffered in the general devastation, and the road transport disappeared with the evacuating Norwegian population.

The lesson of this was not lost on de Wiart. The following morning he signalled the War Office : 'I see little chance of carrying out decisive, or indeed, any operations, unless enemy air activity is considerably restricted'. Two days later, after German forces shipped along the fjords from Trondheim had landed on the flank of his advanced troops, and after the *Luftwaffe* had twice subjected the forward units and the town of Steinkjer to the same treatment as the base at Namsos, de Wiart put it more strongly—that there was 'no alternative to evacuation' unless he could have superiority in the air. From this point onwards the General could act only on the defensive, and his best hope, when the order to withdraw was given, was that he would succeed in getting his forces back to Namsos. The advance on Trondheim from the north had failed.

Meanwhile, the other jaw of the would-be pincers was trying in vain to operate from Aandalsnes. The first formation to land

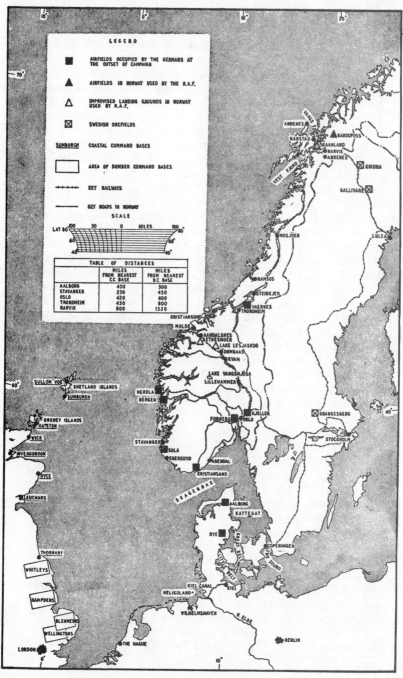

THE NORWEGIAN CAMPAIGN, 1940

consisted of some sixteen hundred men, containing a very high proportion of raw troops and a very low proportion of transport and guns. Before advancing north the brigade was ordered to secure the vital junction of Dombaas, where the railway from Oslo divides for Aandalsnes and Trondheim. The bulk of the Norwegian army was at this time well south of the junction, fighting a stout delaying action against the main German drive from Oslo; and if this advance could be halted before it reached Dombaas our own movement towards Trondheim could be conducted without interference. But the hard-pressed Norwegians were naturally reluctant to see our troops merely consolidating a position in their rear, and it was to meet their requests that Brigadier Morgan pushed his men well down the valley past Dombaas to the advanced positions around Lillehammer. Before our men were properly established in the line, however, the forward Norwegian troops had been driven back. At the limit of endurance, they succumbed to the combined assault of German land and air forces; for the pilots of the *Luftwaffe*, taking advantage of a settled spell of fine weather most unusual in Norway at this time of the year, were flying up and down the snow-bound valleys at will, selecting their targets with the greatest deliberation. The full shock therefore fell on Morgan's brigade, who at first fared little or no better than the Norwegians. While they strove to restore the situation, a second brigade which had been landed at Aandalsnes was rushed down to give them support. The Aandalsnes expedition, so far from driving north against Trondheim, was thus desperately engaged in trying to hold off the Germans to the south.

While our troops were struggling to establish themselves in central Norway the Royal Air Force had not been idle. It had repeatedly bombed Stavanger/Sola airfield; it had attempted the more difficult tasks of bombing the two vital airfields at extreme range—Trondheim/Vaernes and Oslo/Fornebu; and it had made its first attacks on the Danish airfield at Aalborg, of which the enemy was making great use. It had not, however, attacked airfields in Germany, of which the enemy was making even greater use—for the policy of not provoking German air action against this country was still maintained. Nearly two hundred sorties were flown against the airfields in Norway and Denmark between 14th April and 21st April; but the distance was considerable, the weather over the North Sea often unfavourable, and the enemy defences too strong to allow our aircraft to operate except by night or under cover of cloud. The net effect on German air activity over Norway was therefore small.

The Royal Air Force had also joined battle against the enemy's sea communications. Beginning on the night of 13/14th April our aircraft had laid magnetic mines in the Great and Little Belts, The Sound, the Kiel Canal, the Elbe estuary, and many other areas which our ships could not approach. Though undoubtedly less dangerous than operating over Germany, this was by no means easy work. The flights were long, and might take the aircraft to such hotly defended places as the Kiel Canal or Oslo Fjord; the mines, weighing fifteen hundred pounds each and attached to a parachute, had to be dropped from only five hundred feet or so above the water; and in thick weather there was every likelihood of having to turn back and land with the mines still on. By the end of April Bomber Command's Hampdens had sown 110 mines at a cost of seven aircraft, while others had been laid by Coastal Command, the Fleet Air Arm and the submarines. All this was to prove very profitable in the long run, but it was certainly not decisive for the campaign in Norway. In fact, the enemy took across everything he wanted. Between mid-April and mid-June the Germans lost on the Norwegian route only eight or nine per cent of their shipping and only 1,000 of the 100,000 officers and men transported.

The mining and the attacks on airfields had their value, but it was not apparent to troops who were spending their time dodging German bombs. Our men in Norway, ludicrously short of anti-aircraft guns, were also desperately in need of fighter protection. The problem was easier stated than solved. No Royal Air Force units had been detailed for central Norway; all the known airfields had been seized by the enemy; and emergency landing grounds could hardly be constructed with any great speed in mountainous country several feet under snow. To achieve what was possible in the circumstances, the aircraft carriers *Glorious* and *Ark Royal* were recalled from the Mediterranean and despatched on 23rd April to give support off Namsos and Aandalsnes; and on board the *Glorious* went one fighter squadron of the Royal Air Force. It was No. 263, from Filton; it was chosen because its obsolescent Gladiator biplanes could operate from small landing grounds.

The selection of an operational site for the Gladiators had been no easy task. In that wild and mountainous country, where a forced landing is an impossibility and the parachute is the pilot's sole hope in emergency, only a frozen lake offered any chance of a flat surface. At Lake Vangsmjösa, where there was very little snow, some remnants of the Norwegian Air Force were operating off skis. To Squadron Leader Whitney Straight, who had been sent to explore the district, the best solution seemed for the Gladiators to join the Norwegians there; but the Chiefs of Staff rejected this recommendation on the ground that the site was exposed to a German advance and could be supplied only along a separate and dangerous route. Instead, they approved Straight's second choice, Lake Lesjaskog, which lies in the valley connecting Aandalsnes and Dombaas, and was therefore along our existing lines—or line—of communication. This decision taken, Straight at once got down to business. Within two hours of his arrival at Lesjaskog he had 200 civilians—an almost incredible number in a place so sparsely populated—hard at work on the task of clearing a runway through the two feet of snow that covered the ice.[1]

Shortly before midnight on 22nd April a Royal Air Force advanced party under Wing Commander Keens arrived at Aandalsnes. Its function, until a full Royal Air Force Headquarters could be set up, was to establish a base at the port and servicing facilities at Lake Lesjaskog. The night was spent in clearing stores from the jetty, and the following morning some of the servicing party proceeded up the valley to the lake. There they arranged fuel dumps around the newly cleared runway and in the woods which go down to the water's edge. Twenty-four hours later, at midnight on the 23rd, the servicing equipment arrived at Aandalsnes. It was rapidly unloaded, but only two lorries—impressed from the local population, for the British authorities had none—were available to transport it up the valley to the lake. Only the most vital items could go forward; and this meant opening every box to examine its contents, since no schedule of equipment had been provided. But by midday on the 24th the essential gear and the remainder of the servicing flight had left for the lake, and during the afternoon Wing Commander Keens signalled the waiting carrier—by way of the Air Ministry—that the Gladiators could land at 1800 hours.

When the time came for Squadron Leader Donaldson, the Commanding Officer of No. 263 Squadron, to fly his aircraft off, the *Glorious* was 180 miles from the shore in the thick of a heavy snowstorm. Donaldson was a brave man, but he had little relish for the task that lay before him; for his squadron, with four maps between them and no more navigational facilities than those usually to be

---

[1] This was done by sheer manual labour. Straight did not enjoy the good fortune of a small remnant of the Norwegian Air Force from Vaernes, which was faced with the problem of clearing even deeper snow from a lake in a still less populated district. While the dispirited Norwegians wondered how to begin, three thousand reindeer happened to pass nearby on their annual spring journey from the valleys to the mountains. Their keeper, a Lapp with a weakness for strong drink, responded to the bribe of 100 per cent alcohol offered by the medical officer—no weaker form being available—and consented to direct his herd across the lake. Following their leader, a highly-trained white reindeer, the beasts dutifully pounded the snow into a hard, compressed mass six inches thick. From this the aircraft could have taken off admirably, had there been any petrol.

found in fighters, had to make their first take-off from the deck of a carrier, locate in poor visibility an unknown spot set among mountains, and land on ice. He asked the captain if a Fleet Air Arm Skua might lead the squadron to the lake. The request was readily granted; the eighteen Gladiators flew off without mishap; and without mishap they landed on Lake Lesjaskog.

What they found at Lesjaskog might have dismayed less cheerful hearts. The valley being wide at this point, there was no difficulty about the approach, and the single road and railway from Aandalsnes ran close to the lake. But the prepared runway was some distance from the shore, for the ice at the edges was already beginning to melt; the only transport available to take stores from the road to the runway was an occasional horse-drawn sledge; the servicing party, designed and equipped simply to operate until the squadron ground staff arrived, had no petrol-bowser and only two refuelling troughs; the starter trolley batteries were uncharged and had no acid; and there was no warning system to report the approach of hostile aircraft. It was to conditions of this sort that the Gladiators arrived, in a district over which German aircraft swarmed at will; indeed, the preparations on the lake had already been systematically observed by the enemy. But, though their Commanding Officer had noted with apprehension the bomb damage along the railway, the pilots of No. 263 Squadron were far from downcast. They were young, they were amid the glittering beauty of the snow and the ice and the stars, they were comfortably housed in the little summer hotel nearby, they were at last on the threshold of action, they were superbly cheerful. They would have been still more cheerful that evening but for the bore of having to disperse their aircraft. Their outlook was that of the British soldier in Aandalsnes who, seeing them fly over on their way to the lake, remarked to a local inhabitant, 'Here come our fighters—no more German bombers now'.

The dawn brought swift disillusion. The Gladiators were to put up a patrol over the Dombaas area at 0300 hours. But the sharp frost of the spring night had frozen the carburettors and the controls, and ice locked the wheels to the runway. Only after two hours' struggle did the first pair of aircraft get off the lake and proceed to Dombaas, where their appearance over our lines put fresh heart into the troops. Meanwhile, the desperate efforts of the squadron to start up the rest of the Gladiators were surveyed by two German aircraft, which dropped a few ineffectual bombs. Two hours later the serious business began. In relays of threes, unescorted Ju.88's and He.111's returned again and again, while the engines of the Gladiators still defied attempts to wake them to life. At length some accumulators were commandeered from passing lorries, and under attack from bombs and machine-guns two more Gladiators managed to start up and take off. While they circled the lake others succeeded in joining them, and from then on the squadron was able to give a good account of itself. Starting up, however, was merely the first of its difficulties; for the party included only one armourer, and with the limited equipment available and the enemy constantly overhead, refuelling and re-arming was a painful, lengthy and dangerous process. Such conditions could have only one end. Despite the pilots' best efforts in the air and despite the heroic work of a small naval party manning two Oerlikon guns near the lake, by midday ten of the eighteen Gladiators had been put out of action on the ground.

It says everything for the pilots of the squadron that in conditions such as these they were able to make upwards of thirty sorties during the day, to fight many combats, and to shoot down several of the enemy. But one day was enough. Towards evening, when the runway as well as the squadron was virtually destroyed, the Squadron Commander flew down to Setnesmoen, near Aandalsnes, and landed on a small plateau which was being hastily cleared as an emergency landing ground. Finding it reasonably satisfactory, and well placed to protect the base, if far removed from the front line, he ordered the four remaining Gladiators to join him. During the night the few available lorries brought down to the coast such fuel, stores and ammunition as remained; and when the morning sun rose on Lesjaskog, it revealed only a scene of smashed and splintered ice, broken trees and burnt-out aircraft.[1]

From Setnesmoen on 26th April the surviving Gladiators made their last effort. Between them the five carried out a useful reconnaissance and a patrol over the forward lines; then there were three. These three attempted to engage the German aircraft which attacked Aandalsnes at leisure throughout the day, but with no oxygen the pilots were completely unable to operate at the 20,000 feet from which the enemy, respecting their presence, chose to bomb. Finally, one Gladiator alone remained doubtfully serviceable; and for this there was no petrol. Nothing remained but to withdraw the pilots in a cargo vessel. Surviving several attacks from German bombers they reached Scapa Flow safely on 1st May—exactly ten days after they had sailed to Norway from the same place. Their adventure had been

---

[1] The skeletons of some of these aircraft could still be seen on the shores of the lake, and protruding above its surface, as late as 1947. They are probably still visible to this day. One machine, recovered from the lake, has been polished up by a pious Norwegian and preserved as a museum-piece in a neighbouring boathouse.

brief, and expensive in aircraft, but at least well rewarded in experience. For the story of No. 263 Squadron at Lesjaskog will for ever stand witness to the futility of exposing a handful of machines, with hastily contrived and inadequate arrangements on the ground, to the full blast of operations by a powerful enemy.

The destruction of No. 263 Squadron meant that there was now little hope of keeping Aandalsnes in use; for the gallant and skilful work of the Fleet Air Arm pilots of the *Glorious* between 24th April and 27th April could not avail to save the base from the frightful effects of German air superiority. In the words of the naval officer in charge, '. . . the wooden quays destroyed, the area surrounding the single concrete quay devastated by fire, the roads pitted by bomb craters and disintegrated by the combined effect of heavy traffic and melting snow, the recurrent damage to the railway, the machine-gunning of road traffic—all made it patent to those on the spot that it was only a question of time for the port activities to diminish to such an extent that the line of communication could not be maintained.' With the neighbouring port of Molde in no better case, our ships in harbour in constant danger, and Namsos—despite fine work by the aircraft of the *Ark Royal*—as badly hit as Aandalsnes, the end was indeed certain. Though everywhere hard-pressed and withdrawing, our troops in contact with the enemy ground forces could have held on longer; it was the air bombardment of their bases which threatened disaster complete and irreparable. Recognizing this, Lieutenant-General Massy, the Commander-in-Chief of the Expeditionary Force—whose headquarters were still in London—regarded the destruction of No. 263 Squadron as decisive; almost as soon as he heard of it, on 27th April, he advised the Chiefs of Staff to abandon the entire Central Norwegian project. The following day the local commanders received the order to withdraw their forces.

The function of the Royal Air Force during the evacuation was to reduce the enemy's air activity by bombing his airfields, and to give what cover it could to the withdrawal from Aandalsnes. The second part of this task demanded what we so conspicuously lacked at the time—a good long-range fighter. The makeshift Blenheim fighter was all that we could boast in this category; and of these only one squadron was available for the operation. The intention was that these aircraft should land and refuel at Setnesmoen, but before they could do so the *Luftwaffe* had put the landing ground out of action. All operations were accordingly carried out from this country, with the result that each sortie could spend no more than an hour near Aandalsnes. As for Namsos, this was quite beyond the range of any Royal Air Force fighters; but protection was to be given by the

Ark Royal and the *Glorious*, which had returned home to refuel and were due back off Norway on 1st May.

In accordance with this plan Bomber Command attacked Stavanger/ Sola and Oslo/Fornebu airfields by day and night throughout the entire period of the evacuation, besides directing a lesser number of sorties against the Danish airfields of Aalborg and Rye. The heaviest raid was on the night of 30th April/1st May, when twenty-eight Wellingtons and Whitleys bombed Stavanger at a cost of five aircraft. This effort, coming on top of those already undertaken, had its effect, for by 1st May the Germans were confining the use of the surface to emergency landings. During the critical days the weight of enemy air attack on Aandalsnes and Namsos was therefore materially less. All the same, there was plenty of activity against our ships at sea—so much, in fact, that when the two aircraft carriers duly reappeared off Norway on 1st May, and were promptly selected for special attention by the *Luftwaffe*, they were soon ordered home. This meant that our forces had to make good their escape from Namsos with no air cover whatsoever.

In spite of the scanty measure of protection that could be supplied by the Blenheims the evacuation from Aandalsnes went well. The enemy air force made no attempt to interfere with the embarkation during the hours of darkness, the final parties were cleared on the night of 1st/2nd May, and all vessels reached British ports safely. Up to this point the Germans, strangely enough, seem to have been unaware of our intentions; having captured the plan for building up our forces through Aandalsnes, they perhaps imagined that we were still coming, not going. But on 2nd May, before de Wiart's men at Namsos had even begun to embark, Chamberlain announced in the House that we had withdrawn from Aandalsnes. The inference that we might also be withdrawing from Namsos was not difficult to make, and perhaps because of this the *Luftwaffe* was able to subject the Allied convoys to repeated assaults on their homeward passage. Two destroyers were sunk. Only when our ships came within the orbit of Coastal Command did the attacks cease.

*   *   *
•

While Central Norway was witnessing the first of those evacuations which were to feature so prominently in our military efforts during 1940 and 1941, the expedition in the North was in a fair way to success. For whereas Namsos and Aandalsnes were within easy reach of airfields held by the enemy, Narvik was not.

The port of Narvik is some 600 miles north of Oslo as the aeroplane flies, and 400 miles north of Trondheim. Within the Arctic circle and set amidst mountains wild to the last degree, it gives the impression of some desperate triumph of man over nature. The port remains open throughout the year, but between September and the beginning of May the country is entirely covered with snow and ice, and in mid-winter the only light of day consists of two hours of murk and gloom. Remote and inhospitable, Narvik has few communications with southern Norway: the single track railway runs directly east to the Swedish orefields, and the traveller who attempts the journey south by road—if road it may be called—faces the prospect of shipping his car across several fjords. Even the all-conquering aeroplane, which bids fair to 'put a girdle round about the earth in forty minutes', is at a disadvantage. A flight between North and South Norway is usually marked by swift and treacherous changes of weather which may spell death to the airman who ventures on; great down-draughts snatch at the aircraft as it tops the mountain peaks or noses its way through the defiles; and there are few places within fifty miles of Narvik where anything other than a float-plane or flying-boat could possibly alight. Of such landing grounds as there were in 1940, though one or two of them were normally occupied by small detachments of the Norwegian Air Force, none could be dignified with the name of airfield.

The British element of the Narvik expedition sailed on 12th April, a few hours before Admiral Whitworth disposed of the German destroyers by his action in the fjords. The military commander was Major General Mackesy, whose instructions were to establish a base at Harstad, a small fishing port on an island in Vaags Fjord, fifty-five miles by sea from Narvik. When the news of Whitworth's victory reached the commander of the naval forces, Admiral of the Fleet the Earl of Cork and Orrery, he at once proposed that the Harstad project should be cancelled in favour of an immediate and direct assault on Narvik; but the suggestion made no appeal to Mackesy, whose brigade had embarked for an unopposed landing, had been neither trained nor equipped for movement over snow, and would have had to advance unsupported through snow waist deep in the face of enemy gunfire. Although the German forces in Narvik were small, our troops therefore landed, as originally intended, at Harstad. A plan was then made to capture the ground north and south of the peninsula on which Narvik stands so that the port itself might be taken from the rear. This involved waiting for reinforcements—and the thaw.

The reinforcements, consisting of French Alpine troops under General Béthouart, Foreign Legionaries and Poles, began to arrive on 27th April. Thus far, enemy aircraft had not been unduly troublesome

—many of those that appeared were float-planes carrying stores. With the *Luftwaffe* rapidly establishing itself at Trondheim/Vaernes airfield, however, we could soon expect attack of a far heavier order —attack which could be countered only by land-based fighters. While the Allied troops improved their positions, two Royal Air Force officers, of whom the senior was Wing Commander R. L. R. Atcherley, were accordingly sent out from England to examine the landing grounds—or sites for landing grounds—in the neighbourhood of Narvik.

The arrival of Atcherley's Sunderland at Harstad coincided with an enemy air raid, which it inadvertently scared away. After reporting to General Mackesy, whom he found in a half-dressed state retrieving possessions from the headquarters building, which had just been hit, Atcherley went on to explain his mission to the local Norwegian Army Commander. His reception was not encouraging. The news of the evacuation of Aandalsnes had just reached the Norwegian forces in the north, and Atcherley was asked to sign a formal undertaking not only that large quantities of British supplies would be available for the Norwegians but also that the Royal Air Force did not intend (in Atcherley's phrase) 'to cut and run'. Eventually the General was pacified—the Staff Officer bearing his representations apparently succumbed to a judicious mixture of eloquence and whisky from Lord Cork—and the reconnaissance proceeded. Deep snow made the task one of the utmost difficulty, but fortunately the Norwegians placed a ship, and Lord Cork a Walrus Amphibian, at Atcherley's disposal. Even so, the searchers were compelled to confine their investigation to places of good local report. In the end the most promising sites were found to be the existing Norwegian landing grounds at Bardufoss and Banak, and some undeveloped ground at Skaanland. The last of these was the best placed geographically, being only fifteen miles by air from Harstad and twenty-five from Narvik. Bardufoss, at fifty-five and fifty miles respectively, was also within fighter range of both base and objective; but Banak, over two hundred miles north-east of Narvik, would be useful only for bombers.

What was achieved at Bardufoss gives some idea of the appalling obstacles that were overcome. The local authorities having gathered together an impressive, if predominantly amateur, labour force (first of Norwegian territorials and later of civilians) on 4th May work began. Atcherley was in charge, and he was assisted by technical officers of the Royal Air Force, the Royal Engineers and the Norwegian Army. With daylight almost continuous, and a thousand men to call on—after a broadcast appeal, volunteers, according to Atcherley, 'rolled up in their hundreds'—work proceeded for twenty hours out of twenty-four. First, the two existing landing strips, 715 by 95 yards, were cleared of snow five feet deep. This meant not merely moving the snow aside, but taking it some distance away—otherwise the advent of the thaw would have spelled disaster. Then the six-inch layer of ice beneath the snow was attacked with pick and gelignite. The soil being at last exposed to view, more drains were dug, soft spots of clay were cut out and filled with gravel, and the whole surface was flattened by means of a roller made from two forty-gallon drums welded together and filled with concrete. After this the better of the two runways was extended to 1,000 yards—a task which involved clearing bush and felling trees. It was scarcely completed when the thaw arrived. Only mass digging of the most feverish kind prevented torrents of water engulfing the newly cleared surface.

All this was but part of the undertaking, for Atcherley, warned by the Air Ministry of the vital necessity of protective measures, was determined to avoid another fiasco on the lines of that at Lesjaskog. Four taxying lanes, each eight yards wide, were cut from the runway to the heart of the woods surrounding the landing ground; snow, ice, trees, bushes, moss and top surface were all cleared, and the whole laid with gravel. Blast-proof pens made from double lines of tree trunks filled with gravel were built for the aircraft, camouflaged, and connected by satellite lanes to the taxi tracks. Shelters of a still stronger kind, dug down to a depth of five feet, were constructed for the men, both in the woods and at convenient points near the runway. Twenty miles of road leading to the nearest fjord was cleared and repaired. Two hundred hastily recruited mules speeded the painful progress of supplies.

The crises which arose in the course of these Herculean labours were frequent and acute. Food gave out, there were too few tools, the weekly Walrus failed to arrive from Harstad to drop the labourers' wages. But every set-back was triumphantly overcome by the combined efforts of the three Services and the Norwegians, and within the incredibly short space of three weeks Bardufoss was fit for use. Skaanland, too, was declared ready; while at Banak all difficulties yielded before the cheerful onslaught of a thousand Lapps under the inspired direction of one British able seaman.

All this time the headquarters of the somewhat grandiloquently styled Royal Air Force Component of the North-Western Expeditionary Force was waiting to sail. Formed at Uxbridge on 22nd April under the command of Group Captain M. Moore, it was originally designed to control air operations both in central and northern Norway. With their field of activity now confined to the Narvik area, the headquarters staff sailed on 7th May. The same vessel carried Lieutenant-General Auchinleck, whose instructions were to assume command (if he thought fit) of the Allied troops, and to report on the forces needed for the tasks of holding northern Norway as the seat of King Haakon's government, stopping German supplies of iron-ore through Narvik, and interfering with shipments from Luleå. The General landed at Harstad on 11th May, just twenty-four hours after the German invasion of France and the Low Countries had knocked the bottom out of his mission.

The threat of a German offensive in the West had throughout gravely handicapped Allied efforts in Scandinavia. Now the act proved decisive. The forces which Auchinleck considered necessary to hold northern Norway—he dismissed as impracticable any idea of interfering with the ore shipments from Luleå—included seventeen infantry battalions, one hundred and four heavy and ninety-six light anti-aircraft guns, and four squadrons of aircraft. These could not possibly be spared at a time when the Allied armies were reeling under the impact of the German blows in Belgium and France. Even the small but steady effort of Bomber Command against the enemy-occupied airfields in Norway and Denmark had now to be abandoned in favour of sterner tasks elsewhere. So, when the Chiefs of Staff made their final survey on 21st May—it was the day on which the enemy first gazed across the English Channel at his next objective—their summary of the position was very clear: 'The security of France and the United Kingdom is essential; the retention of northern Norway is not.' They accordingly recommended to the War Cabinet that the Allied force should proceed to capture Narvik, that the harbour and its installations should be demolished, and that the expedition should then be withdrawn.

It was while these matters were approaching decision in London that No. 263 Squadron, with a fresh supply of Gladiators, once more appeared on the Norwegian scene. The pilots had sailed in the *Furious* on 14th May, and had spent some days waiting offshore while the final preparations were made at Bardufoss. In the early morning of 21st May the first flight took off. But visibility was no more than three hundred yards, the savage outlines of the coastal peaks were obscured by low cloud, and the navigating Swordfish, slightly off course, led the first section straight into a mountain side. Two of the Gladiators crashed, and the pilot of a third saved himself only by turning violently as the white and black mass suddenly loomed up before him; the remainder turned back to face the further peril of their first deck landing—assuming they could find the carrier. Fortunately all landed safely. The next day, in better weather, the Squadron established itself successfully at Bardufoss and flew nearly fifty sorties before the brief Arctic twilight called a halt to operations.

By this time the Allied ground forces were well enough placed— numerically, administratively and geographically—to make their attempt on Narvik. The enemy's frequent air attacks, mounted from Trondheim/Vaernes (and its neighbouring fjords) 400 miles to the south, had made matters unpleasant for our ships, but had not prevented our forces gathering strength. Before long, however, these attacks might be many times heavier; for German troops were forcing their way up the coast from Trondheim towards Bodö, where there was flat ground suitable for an airfield within thirty minutes' flight of Narvik. Tactical as well as strategic considerations therefore dictated an immediate move by the Allied forces. Advanced detachments accordingly attempted to hold the enemy south of Bodö while the assault on Narvik was prepared. The thaw had arrived, and the attack was to begin as soon as the rest of the fighters assigned to the expedition—the Hurricanes of No. 46 Squadron— were established at Skaanland.

The Hurricanes had already made the passage to northern Norway with No. 263 Squadron, and had been sent back because Skaanland was not then ready. They returned to Norway in the *Glorious* on 26th May. When they came in to land at Skaanland they found the runway soft and patchy, and after three aircraft had gone up on their noses the remainder of the squadron was ordered to join No. 263 at Bardufoss. This meant that both squadrons had to face some fifty miles of mountain mist and cloud before they could appear over Harstad, Narvik or the fleet anchorage at Skaanland. But distance and climate were by no means the only obstacles to efficient operation. A fighter depends not merely on its own powers of performance but on information of the enemy's movements; and in Norway arrangements for reporting enemy aircraft were primitive in the extreme. The nature of the coast was such that radar could not be installed without the most prolonged trials; the Royal Air Force and Norwegian observer posts, valuable as they were, possessed in such country an extremely restricted field of view; and the W/T and the R/T sets then in use were ineffective among high iron-bound mountains. Reports over the ordinary telephone system from the observer posts provided useful warning at Harstad and Bardufoss; but the information they gave was neither quick nor continuous enough for fighters to be controlled from the ground, even had the R/T worked properly. For the most part our aircraft were thus forced to rely on the wasteful method of standing patrols.

Despite all these handicaps, No. 263 Squadron had already enjoyed considerable success by the time it was joined by No. 46. For several days the Gladiators had kept up a daily average of over forty sorties to the benefit of Harstad, Skaanland and their own base. What spirit animated their pilots may be seen from one brief episode. At midday on 26th May three Gladiators took off from Bardufoss for Bodö, where a hastily prepared landing ground was now available for the support of our troops resisting the German advance north. The leader of the section was Flight Lieutenant Caesar Hull, an extraordinarily skilful pilot and a lively character for whom, in the words of a fellow-pilot, 'every night was guest night'; the other two aircraft were flown by Pilot Officer Jack Falkson and Lieutenant Anthony Lydekker, a Fleet Air Arm armament officer with flying experience, who had volunteered to take the place of a sick pilot during the voyage out to Norway. After surviving a few shots from two passing He.111's *en route*, the three Gladiators came in to land on the newly constructed runway. They were immediately caught fast in the mud. Frantic taxying brought them to somewhat drier soil, the aircraft were eventually refuelled from four-gallon tins, and the softest patches in the runway were laboriously covered with wooden snow-boards. While this was going on a He.111 appeared on the scene. Disregarding the state of the runway, Lydekker, whose tanks were less full than the others, promptly got his aircraft off the ground and engaged. Then Hull and Falkson, who had meanwhile been briefed by Wing Commander Maxton, the officer in charge of the landing ground, prepared to follow. Hull's diary records the events of the next few hours:

> The Wing Commander explained that the Army were retreating up a valley east of Bodö, and were being strafed by the Huns all day. Sounded too easy, so I took off just as another Heinkel 111 circled the aerodrome. God! What a take-off! Came unstuck about fifty yards from the end and just staggered over the trees. Jack followed and crashed. I thought the expedition was doomed to failure and that I had better do as much damage as I could before landing again, so told Tony to land over the blower, and set off towards the valley.
>
> Saw some smoke rising, so investigated, and found a Heinkel 111 at about 600 feet. Attacked it three times, and it turned south with smoke pouring from fuselage and engines. Broke off attack to engage a Junkers 52, which crashed in flames. Saw Heinkel 111 flying south, tried to intercept, and failed. Returned and attacked two Junkers 52's in formation. Number one went into clouds, number two crashed in flames after six people had baled out.

Attacked Heinkel 111 and drove it south with smoke pouring from it. Ammunition finished, so returned to base. The troops were very cheered by the report, and I thought another patrol might produce more fun. The Wing Commander didn't like the idea of risking another take-off, but after a lot of persuasion he agreed to it. It was quite shattering, in spite of some wooden planks laid across the bad patches.

This time the valley was deserted, and the only thing I could do was amuse the troops by doing some aerobatics. They all cheered and waved madly every time I went down low—I think they imagined that at last we had air control and their worries were over. Vain hope!

The state of the runway made further operations distinctly inadvisable. But some of the troops were being withdrawn by sea during the night, and the tiny Royal Air Force contingent at Bodö was determined to give what help it could. All hands fell to the task of laying down more snow-boards, until these covered almost the entire runway, and an hour before midnight Lydekker took off again. At midnight Hull followed, and in the absence of enemy aircraft amused himself by 'beating up' the retiring vessels—much to the delight of the troops. Two hours later he was relieved by Falkson, after which, convinced that further attempts to use the runway would end only in the loss of valuable aircraft, he asked Maxton to call off the patrols. The Wing Commander agreed; and Hull and Lydekker, having despatched a well-earned breakfast, were enjoying—at readiness—the cheering warmth of the morning sunshine, when they experienced something all too familiar to those members of the squadron who had been at Lesjaskog. Hull's diary again tells the story:

Suddenly at 0800 hours the balloon went up. There were 110's and 87's all round us and the 87's started dive-bombing a jetty about 800 yards from the aerodrome. Tony's aircraft started at once and I waved him off, then after trying mine a bit longer got yellow and together with the fitter made a dive into a nearby barn. From there we watched the dive-bombing in terror until it seemed that they were not actually concentrating on the aerodrome. Got the Gladiator going and shot off without helmet or waiting to do anything up. Circled the 'drome climbing and pinned an 87 at the bottom of a dive. It made off slowly over the sea and just as I was turning away another 87 shot up past me and his shots went through my windscreen knocking me out for a while. Came to, and was thanking my lucky stars when I heard rat-tat behind me and felt my Gladiator hit. Went into right-hand turn and dive but could not get it out. Had given up hope at 200 feet when she centralized and I gave her a burst of engine to clear some large rocks. Further rat-tats from behind, so gave up hope and decided to get her down. Held off, and then crashed.

With Hull out of the combat—and on his way to hospital—Lydekker received the full attention of the enemy. Wounded, and with his

H

aircraft badly shot up, he managed by skilful evasive action to get back to Bardufoss, where his machine was promptly classed as a complete 'write-off'. All three Gladiators had now been put out of action; but the *Luftwaffe* was taking no risks. That evening they returned to Bodö in force. He.111's laid waste the town, and twelve Ju.87's and four Me.110's made a systematic job of wrecking the runway. So ended the brief history of Bodö landing ground. The attempt to use it had brought about its destruction; but the Gladiators had shot down at least three enemy aircraft, and, at a highly critical moment, had diverted many more from attacks on the Allied troops.

While the *Luftwaffe* was concentrating on Bodö the Allies were beginning the final moves against Narvik. French and Norwegian forces were now firmly established along the farther side of Rombaks Fjord, north of the Narvik peninsula; and the plan was to cross the Fjord, gain a footing on the peninsula—where the enemy was in no great strength—and approach the town from the rear. At the same time the Poles would launch an attack in the Ankenes peninsula, to the south. The task of the two fighter squadrons, beginning some hours before the initial assault, was to maintain continuous patrols at a strength of three aircraft over the area of operations.

The patrols during the evening and night of 27th May, when the Allied troops made their landing, were agreeably uneventful. Early the following morning fog descended on Bardufoss, and for a brief spell our aircraft were grounded. During this time the *Luftwaffe*—which was now reported to have Ju.87 dive-bombers operating from an emergency ground at Mosjöen, only 200 miles to the south—appeared on the scene. The Admiral's flag-ship was damaged; then one of our patrols came up and drove away the attacking aircraft. After that the Hurricanes and Gladiators combined with the misty weather to hold off the enemy, and before the day closed Narvik was in Allied hands. Nothing remained but to destroy the facilities of the port—and withdraw.

The destruction was well and truly accomplished. No cargo of iron-ore left Narvik for Germany until January 1941. The evacuation presented problems of greater complexity. In the first place our intention to withdraw had to be kept secret from all except the principal commanders; the remainder—including the Norwegians— were to be encouraged to believe, until the last moment, that we were preparing to move to other bases in Norway. Secondly, to allow time for the arrangements, and to reduce the difficulties in which the Norwegian ground forces would find themselves by a sudden with- drawal of the British, French and Poles, the evacuation was not to begin until 3rd June, and was then to be spread over five days.

The work of the two Royal Air Force squadrons was thus by no means finished. From 29th May to 1st June they were busy, but mainly with single enemy aircraft. Then, on 2nd June, the *Luftwaffe* arrived in force. Throughout the day wave after wave of a dozen bombers or dive bombers, escorted by Me. 110's, sought to destroy our shipping and the base at Harstad; but the Gladiators and Hurricanes so harassed every attempt that the German crews either jettisoned their bombs or aimed them wide. By the end of the day the two squadrons had flown seventy-five sorties, fought twenty-four engagements, and brought down at least nine enemy aircraft, all for no loss to themselves. Many of the actions took place in full view of the troops; and General Auchinleck was moved to send a handsome message of thanks.

That evening the Norwegians were informed of our intention to withdraw, and the following morning the evacuation began. The movement presented a most tempting series of targets, for many of the troops had to be picked up by the local 'puffers', taken out to destroyers in the fjords, and then transferred to liners standing off the coast. But a kindly cloak of mist and low cloud concealed the vessels for many hours, and until the last day the enemy's effort in the air was very small. Such as it was, it was well contained by Nos. 46 and 263 squadrons, and by the aircraft of the *Glorious* and the *Ark Royal*, which had returned to take part in the evacuation.

The orders under which the Royal Air Force operated during the final phase were clear and precise. Patrols were to be flown over the vital areas until evacuation was virtually complete; the Gladiators were then to fly on to the *Glorious*; the Hurricanes, which could not, it was then thought, land on a carrier's deck, were to be destroyed; and Bardufoss airfield, with the exception of a small strip for the use of the few surviving Norwegian Fokkers, was to be thoroughly demolished. This programme was duly completed, but with one significant exception. The Commanding Officer of No. 46 Squadron, Squadron Leader K. B. Cross, begged that his ten remaining Hurricanes should be allowed to attempt a landing on the *Glorious*. The risk appeared considerable; for unsuccessful tests had been made with Hurricanes when the squadron was being shipped to Norway, with the result that the aircraft had finally been hoisted aboard from lighters. In Norway, at the tail end of the evacuation, and with their airfield far distant from the waters where the carrier lay, the squadron could clearly not re-embark in the same fashion. The only alternative to destruction was thus to hazard the aircraft and their pilots in a deck-landing. Mindful that Britain stood in need of every Hurricane she could muster, Group Captain Moore agreed to Cross's request, and a call was made for volunteers. Every one of the eighteen pilots responded. So, in the clear Arctic midnight of 7th June, the Hurricanes took off from Bardufoss for their last flight. By then the Gladiators had left, led by Swordfish, and were already stowed away in the *Glorious*. An hour's flight and the Hurricanes too came on, each to an admirable landing.

Fate was to mock this last achievement. The *Scharnhorst* and the *Gneisenau*, moving up the Norwegian coast under orders to penetrate the fjords around Narvik, had learnt from air reconnaissance and intercepted wireless messages that traffic was heavy between Northern Norway and Scotland. They had learnt too, that the *Glorious* and the *Ark Royal* were at sea. No hunter could neglect so splendid a quarry. The two battle cruisers headed up for the convoy routes, and in the afternoon of 8th June they sighted the *Glorious* and her attendant pair of destroyers. The German crews, noting with alarm that a number of aircraft were already visible on the flying decks of the carrier, hastened to open fire. Their first salvoes found the mark, and all the valiant efforts of the destroyers could only postpone the end. After two hours the *Glorious*, blazing furiously, rolled over beneath the waves; and with her went the pilots who had crowned their triumph over the *Luftwaffe* by their determination to bring their aircraft home. Only Squadron Leader Cross and one other, gaining a Carley float, and defying the Arctic cold, the promptings of despair, and the sight of twenty-five of their fellow survivors on the raft dying before their eyes, were picked up later by a passing fishing vessel.

* * *

The expeditions to Central and to Northern Norway had one fundamental point of difference. The former was conducted from poor bases and along exiguous lines of communication within easy reach of strong forces of the *Luftwaffe*, and beyond the effective range of the Royal Air Force; it therefore came to swift disaster. The latter was conducted, for most of the time, within effective range of only a single enemy air base, while in its later and more critical stages it enjoyed the protection of Royal Air Force fighters; it had therefore achieved a fair degree of success when the situation on the western front demanded its recall.

This lesson was certainly not ignored by the Commanders concerned, who spoke up with remarkable unanimity of voice. Major General Paget, whose forces could have held on longer had their base at Aandalsnes not been destroyed by the *Luftwaffe*, wrote thus:

> My considered view in the light of experience remains that which I expressed to the D.Q.M.G. before I embarked. It is that the possibility of maintaining any force through the single port of Aandalsnes

depended primarily upon whether or not local air superiority could be established and maintained. To that view I would add that, since the necessary degree of air superiority could scarcely be expected to exist throughout the whole length of the line of communication, and since that line was peculiarly vulnerable to both air action and to seasonal changes, the Aandalsnes project was not administratively practicable. Operationally, therefore, it was doomed to failure.

Very similar views were expressed by Major General Carton de Wiart about the fighting at Namsos:

> Then came the air situation, which was the dominating factor. We had no A.A. defence at all and were completely at the mercy of enemy planes. Only twice in the course of operations did we have any British planes over us, and then the enemy planes cleared off at once.

Lieutenant General Auchinleck, too, though he bore witness to the difference at Harstad when the two Royal Air Force squadrons arrived, was powerfully impressed with the performance of the *Luftwaffe* in supplying Narvik by air, in landing small detachments at strategic positions along the coast, and in blasting our troops out of the Bodö area:

> The predominant factor in the recent operations has been the effect of air power . . . the first general lesson to be drawn is that to commit troops to a campaign in which they cannot be provided with adequate air support is to court disaster.

In all of this General Jodl, in his official report to the *Führer*, wholeheartedly concurred. 'The Air Force,' wrote Jodl, 'proved to be the decisive factor in the success of the operation.'

The campaign in Norway witnessed the first completely conclusive employment of air power. Around Narvik two squadrons of Royal Air Force fighters held at bay an enemy operating from long range; elsewhere it was the enemy, swiftly and strongly established on all the available airfields, who dictated events. The Royal Air Force at home, too far away, too small, and too much handicapped by the need to conserve its effort for the western front, was unable to intervene effectively. And though there were many purely military factors in our defeat in Central Norway, nearly all of them applied the more sharply because of the presence of an enemy air force which, at the peak-point, employed in *Weserübung* no less than 615 bombers, fighters and reconnaissance machines, and 650 air transports.

The primary and over-riding importance of air power was not new as a conception. The Air Ministry, of course, had harped on it for years; and had always given the clearest warnings, whenever intervention in Scandinavia was discussed, that the *Luftwaffe* by virtue of its size and proximity to the theatre of operations must enjoy a powerful advantage. If not new as a theory, however, it was new as a fact—new as a fact so abundantly plain, for instance, to the military. And though the Navy had escaped with comparatively light losses for the outstanding work it had accomplished and the many perils it had run, even the saltiest of sea-dogs could, if he chose, now read the writing on the wall.

CHAPTER V

Collapse in the West

At first light on 10th May 1940, while the German columns were streaming westwards across the frontiers of the unfortunate neutrals, the *Luftwaffe* went into action against some seventy French, Belgian and Dutch airfields. At the same time German airborne forces seized four vital points in the Belgian defences and struck deep into the heart of Holland. The third and most impressive demonstration of the *Blitzkrieg* had begun.

The event was one for which the Allies had had ample time to prepare. The general direction of the enemy's attack, through Holland, Belgium and Luxembourg, as opposed to a frontal assault on the Maginot Line, accorded completely with Allied anticipations. Neatly formulated plans for dealing with the situation were duly available. The necessary orders were at once—or almost at once—given.

The predetermined *riposte* of the Allied Armies, if the circumstances appeared favourable, was Plan 'D' (Dyle). While the troops in Lorraine and Alsace stood ready to repulse any attempt on the Maginot Line, the forces further north, drawn up along the Franco-Belgian frontier, would advance to the line Meuse–Namur–Antwerp. The movement would be smallest on the right, most extensive on the left. The French Second Army, the pivot on the right, would hold the southern exits of the Ardennes; the Ninth Army would move forward to the line of the Meuse from Mézières to Namur; the First Army would hasten into the natural gap between the Meuse at Namur and the Dyle at Wavre; the British Expeditionary Force would travel still faster to gain the Dyle from Wavre to Louvain; and the Seventh Army, on the extreme left, would execute a veritable *pas de galop* to reach Antwerp and the Dutch islands at the mouth of the Scheldt. Between the British Expeditionary Force and the Seventh Army a gap would thus be left, stretching from Louvain to Antwerp. It would be filled by the retiring Belgians, whose resistance along the Albert Canal, their main defence line further forward, was expected to last no more than three or four days.

Compared with standing still on the Franco-Belgian frontier this manœuvre seemed to offer many advantages. Belgian resistance would be stimulated; the line to be held would be shorter; cover would be given to the French industrial regions of the north-east; and, equally important to both Allies, the enemy would be unable to operate aircraft and submarines from bases in Belgium. These advantages would have been still more convincing had the Belgians and Dutch been prepared to co-operate effectively beforehand, and had there not been that stretch of unbroken, poorly fortified country around Gembloux, between the Meuse and the Dyle. For the First Army, which was to defend this sector, had to be specially strengthened for the task, just as the Seventh Army, which was to travel farthest, had to be given special treatment in the matter of mechanical transport; and this could be done only by starving the Second and Ninth Armies of such desirable items as guns, tanks, aircraft and lorries, to say nothing of able-bodied young men. Above all it was the Ninth Army which went short; for the Ninth was to hold by far the most easily defended section of the line, the great ravine of the Meuse from Montmédy to Namur—a position of enormous natural strength shielded by the dense woods and narrow tracks of the Ardennes. Through such country, Pétain had once declared, the enemy could never move enough armour and artillery for a major attack. And through such country, the French General Staff reaffirmed in 1940, the enemy could build up a dangerous concentration of force only by fifteen days of intense movement—movement which would certainly be observed in good time to make the necessary counter-movement of the French reserves.

The tasks of the Royal Air Force in the Dyle manœuvre, and in the campaign which was expected to follow, had been closely worked out with our ally. Though the home commands would play their part, the main burden would fall on the British Air Forces in France, commanded by Air Marshal A. S. Barratt. One of Barratt's two subordinate formations, the Royal Air Force Component of the British Expeditionary Force, commanded by Air Vice-Marshal C. H. B. Blount, would cater for the requirements of the British troops. Its five squadrons of Lysanders would be responsible for tactical reconnaissance and photographic survey on the B.E.F. front, its four Blenheim squadrons for strategical reconnaissance beyond the British and Belgian lines as far as the Rhine, its four Hurricane squadrons—or six, under the reinforcement plan—for protecting the British troops, bases and reconnaissance aircraft. The other subordinate formation, the Advanced Air Striking Force under the command of Air Vice-Marshal P. H. L. Playfair, had much wider responsibilities. As the French could muster less than one hundred bombers, of which only twenty-five were really modern, the A.A.S.F. was to serve the needs of the whole Allied front. Its ten squadrons of Battle and Blenheim bombers were to attack the advancing German columns, preferably at such natural bottle-necks as bridges and road-junctions, while its two squadrons of Hurricanes—which would be increased to four when the German attack was launched— were to support the bombers and help to defend the area around Rheims, where the A.A.S.F. was based. The original purpose behind the despatch of the A.A.S.F. to France, to bring the short-range bombers within effective striking distance of German industry, was thus in abeyance. The reason for this was partly the urgent need to support the Allied armies, partly the utter helplessness of the Battles before fighter attack of the strength experienced over Germany.[1]

Though the A.A.S.F. would be able to reach all points of the front, it was expected in the main to support the southern sector. The enemy columns approaching the more northerly sectors would be attacked by the home-based medium bombers—the seven Blenheim squadrons of Bomber Command. In addition, two squadrons of home-based 'heavy' bombers—Whitleys—were to operate by night against the German road and rail communications immediately west of the Rhine. These were the bombing forces assigned to the campaign. But though Barratt, working alongside General d'Astier de la Vigerie of the *Armée de l'Air* at Chauny, could issue direct orders to the A.A.S.F., to Bomber Command he could only address 'requests'.

The decision to commit the medium bombers to collaboration in the land battle was not taken without certain misgivings on the part of the Air Staff. Still stronger were these feelings at Bomber Command. Two days before the German attack, Air Marshal Portal, who had succeeded Ludlow-Hewitt in April, expressed his fears to the Chief of Air Staff in the most striking terms. 'I am convinced,' he wrote, 'that the proposed employment of these units (the Blenheims of No. 2 Group) is fundamentally unsound, and that if it is persisted in it is likely to have disastrous consequences on the future of the war in the air . . .' At the enemy's chosen moment for the advance, Portal went

---

[1] Battles had been sent on reconnaissance ten to twenty miles over the Franco-German border in the opening weeks of the war. The missions were abandoned after an incident on 30th September 1939, when, of five Battles of No. 150 Squadron, four were shot down by Me.109's and the fifth damaged beyond repair.

on to urge, the area concerned would be literally swarming with enemy fighters and we should be lucky to avoid crippling losses. Really accurate bombing under such conditions was not to be expected, and he felt serious doubt whether the attacks of fifty Blenheims, based on information necessarily some hours out of date, were likely to make as much difference to the ultimate course of the war as to justify the losses that he expected them to sustain.

This objection by a Commander on the very eve of a battle to the use proposed for his force may be judged sufficiently remarkable. It was, however, less remarkable than the corresponding fears evinced in the actual operational instructions issued by B.A.F.F. and Bomber Command. These stated that 'Bomber aircraft have proved extremely useful *in support* of an advancing army, especially against weak anti-air-craft resistance, but it is not clear that a bomber force used *against* an advancing army, well supported by all forms of anti-aircraft defence and a large force of fighter aircraft, will be economically effective'. It was thus to a virtually untried course of action, in which those responsible for its execution had far from complete confidence, that something over one half of the British bomber force was committed. Clearly, however, these bombers could not stand idle; and as they could not attack Germany itself with any prospect of success, and as the Allied armies would certainly need their help, the Air Staff had virtually no alternative but to commit them to collaboration in the land battle.

If there was some misgiving about the proposed employment of the medium bombers there was open controversy about the role of the 'heavies'. The Wellingtons, Hampdens and remaining Whitleys of Bomber Command—sixteen squadrons in all—were our sole strategic striking force. On these Barratt had no official right of call, though he might request their help in emergency. By May 1940 experience had shown that daylight operations by these aircraft in the face of fighter opposition would be impossible. Their ability to inflict damage by night, however, was still considered great, and it was with them that the Air Staff hoped to carry out its most cherished project—the great strategic offensive against the industrial capacity, and in particular the oil resources, of Germany. Soaring beyond the bloody, prodigal clash of the armies, the 'heavies' would strike at the very root of the enemy's capacity to wage war. The French, how-ever, had other ideas, with the result that the winter of 1939/1940 witnessed a sustained and a lively debate between the Allies.

During these months the Air Staff consistently urged that a German invasion of the Low Countries should be the signal for the heavy bombers to attack the Ruhr. Most of the arguments remained constant. The heavy bombers had not been designed for work near the battlefield. The Ruhr, the heart of which was no bigger than Greater London, contained an unequalled concentration of industrial objectives, amounting to some sixty per cent of Germany's vital war plant. The ideal moment to begin the assault on this unique area was when the Germans violated the neutrality of the Low Countries; for our aircraft could then fly directly across Holland and Belgium, and might reap full advantage of the brief interval before the Germans set up forward air defences. Moreover, attacks on carefully selected objectives in the Ruhr, in addition to their long-term economic effects, would greatly impede the progress of the German armies into the Low Countries. Not only would the enemy suffer incidental damage to his rear communications: he would also be constrained to hold back fighters and anti-aircraft guns for the protection of the *Reich*, thereby exposing his advancing armies to the attacks of our medium bombers. These arguments held good whether the favourite project at the moment was to attack general industry and communications in the Ruhr, or, as it finally became, to single out the oil industry in the Ruhr for particular attention.

The French had no effective and reasoned body of air doctrine to oppose to these arguments. Nevertheless, they remained obstinately unconvinced on one point. Whatever the merits of bombing German industry, they entirely doubted whether the correct time to begin this was at the opening of a great land battle. The heavies, they maintained, should drop their bombs somewhere less remote from the front line. And as for the idea that an attack on the Ruhr would impose any immediate or material delay on the advancing enemy (which after all was the vital consideration)—that was fantastic. Our own air leaders, however, could hardly take these opinions at their face value, for they were painfully aware that the views of the French were coloured by an apprehension which was sometimes expressed, sometimes concealed, but never absent. Not to put too fine a point upon it, our Allies were desperately afraid of the *Luftwaffe*; and in truth the state of their air defences gave them every reason to be. They accordingly opposed any course which could possibly provoke German air action against French cities. Despite certain merits in their general case, the French were thus led into absurdities; for in trying to extend the initial policy of avoiding provocation into the period when the armies came to grips, they were merely shutting their eyes to the general extension of air action that would then automatically occur.

There is nothing remarkable in controversies between Allies, but in this particular controversy one feature at least deserves that adjective. This was that the French, holding such opinions, should ever have agreed—as they finally did in the Supreme War Council on 22nd and 23rd April 1940—that 'in the event of a German aggression against Holland, or against Belgium, or against both these countries, the British Air Force should be authorized, without further consultation between the Allied governments or the Allied High Commands, immediately to attack marshalling yards and oil refineries in the Ruhr'. Less strange, considering the comparatively untried nature of strategic air bombardment, but also very noteworthy was the fact that neither French nor British based their objections on technical grounds. Both parties considered the British 'heavy' bombers—for all that they were only two hundred strong and were compelled to operate by night and navigate largely by dead reckoning—to be capable of accomplishing either of the tasks proposed. For the objection of the Air Staff to the view of the French was not that our heavy bombers would be unable to locate and attack a particular bridge or crossroads near the battlefield, but that they might be doing something much more useful. And the objection of the French to the view of the Air Staff was not that the 'heavies' would be unable to locate and attack the oil factories and marshalling yards of the Ruhr, but that such operations would have no immediate effect on the German advance.

Though the objections of the French were overcome—momentarily, as it proved—the way was still far from clear for the Air Staff to apply their plans. The views from which General Gamelin had been so reluctantly weaned were immediately embraced by the Chief of the Imperial General Staff, who had hitherto favoured the Ruhr project; and the discussion continued with all that ardour which characterizes a debate between two British government departments. Moreover, the War Cabinet was still anxious to restrict air attack to purely military targets, at least until the enemy had himself acted otherwise in the West—even though the sufferings of Warsaw and the Polish villages were held to justify a wider choice of objectives. Not until 8th May was the Air Ministry given definite authority, if the Germans invaded Holland or Belgium, to attempt, by harassing operations at night, to extinguish the lights necessary for the efficient working of the German marshalling yards. As for the main assault against oil or power plants in the Ruhr, this was still not to be launched without express permission from the War Cabinet. Such permission would be given, or withheld, in accordance with the circumstances of the moment, including the extent to which the bombs of the enemy were slaughtering Allied civilians.

*   *   *

From the *Luftwaffe's* opening assault on 10th May the A.A.S.F. and the R.A.F. Component escaped lightly. Nine of the airfields occupied by the British were attacked, but few of our aircraft were destroyed. The Hurricane pilots were at full stretch from first light onwards. 'A day too crammed with incident to do anything like justice to it', reported No. 73 Squadron, which, like No. 1, had spent the spring sharpening its claws against enemy fighters along the Franco-German border, and now withdrew to a pre-arranged airfield in the A.A.S.F. area. The verdict was endorsed by No. 501 Squadron, which flew out from England to join the A.A.S.F. in accordance with the reinforcement plan, and was in combat with forty He.111's within an hour of arriving in France. The fighter squadrons with the Component—Nos. 85, 87, 607 and 615—were kept equally busy, some of the pilots putting in as many as six, or even seven, sorties before nightfall; and in the evening Group Captain P. F. Fullard, commanding the Component Fighter Group, was able to report 'I have never seen squadrons so confident of success, so insensible to fatigue and so appreciative of their own aircraft'. During this and the following day these four squadrons were joined by three more Hurricane squadrons (Nos. 3, 79 and 504) from England, so bringing the Royal Air Force fighter squadrons in France up to the promised total of ten.

While the Hurricanes were taking a tremendous toll of the enemy and protecting the forward movement of the B.E.F., long-range fighters from England were guarding the seaward flank of the Seventh Army and reconnaissance Blenheims were spying out the main lines of the German advance. Meantime Barratt was impatiently awaiting Gamelin's permission to unleash his bombers against the invading columns. The small hours gave place to mid-morning, but still no word came—for the Generalissimo clung with supreme obstinacy to the hope that a 'bombing war' would somehow be avoided. Tiring of this unseemly delay, at midday Barratt took matters into his own hands and ordered Playfair to send off the first wave of Battles. Their target was a German column reported by a French reconnaissance aircraft some hours earlier as advancing through Luxembourg.

This first attack was a fair sample of what was in store for the Battles. Since the defensive armament of these aircraft was limited to one gun firing forward and one gun firing aft, it was clear that they might fall easy prey to enemy fighters. After the unfortunate reconnaissance missions over the German border in September 1939, efforts had indeed been made to add a 'free' gun underneath, but though various mountings had been tried none had proved entirely satisfactory. When the Battles went into action on 10th May, they were thus known to be still extremely vulnerable to fighter attack from below. Unfortunately this weakness could not be countered by close fighter escort, for there were not enough Hurricanes to provide more than a brief offensive patrol over the target area. The pilots were accordingly ordered to make a very low approach to the target, and to attack at 250 feet, using bombs fused for eleven seconds' delay.

The orders were carried out. But a storm of machine gun and small arms fire rose from the German columns, and three of the first eight crews were at once shot down. No better fate attended their comrades who attacked during the afternoon. Of the thirty-two Battles despatched that day, thirteen were lost and all the rest damaged—a severe price for operations whose effect on the enemy advance was negligible.

Though there were already clear indications that important enemy thrusts were developing through Luxembourg and Belgium, the black spot of this first day seemed to be the position in Holland. The Dutch had not been caught unawares, and their vigorous action had frustrated the airborne attempt against The Hague. The Germans, however, retained a grip on a number of important airfields, including those at Waalhaven, near Rotterdam, and Ypenburg, near The Hague. Requests for Royal Air Force action accordingly soon flowed in. In response to these the War Cabinet, fearing that some of our bombs might miss their mark and kill friendly civilians, would at first permit attack by fighters only; and at mid-day six Blenheims of No. 600 Squadron, Fighter Command, duly swept down on Waalhaven. They had barely delivered their attack when they were pounced on by a dozen Me. 110's, and one pilot alone returned to Manston to give an account of the operation. Blenheim bombers were then employed against the same target, with better success.

The attempt to shake the German hold on Waalhaven was continued during the night by thirty-six Wellingtons of Bomber Command. Portal would certainly have preferred to send them against the oil plants and marshalling yards of the Ruhr, but the *Luftwaffe* seemed to be operating against military targets in the narrowest sense, and the War Cabinet would not yet sanction attacks which were bound to result in the death of German civilians. Action by the two squadrons of Whitleys under Barratt's control against communications in Germany west of the Rhine was not, however, ruled out; for though the Germans were expected to react violently against damage to their towns east of the Rhine, they would doubtless appreciate the military necessity of attacks west of the river. After the French High

Command had once more made clear its reluctance to bombard urban targets, nine Whitleys accordingly departed to attack roads, railways and bridges in and near four German towns on the enemy's route to southern Holland. Doubtless the occasional crash of a five hundred-pounder was very alarming that night to the inhabitants of Geldern, Goch, Cleve and Wesel. The only regret at Barratt's head-quarters was that the alarm could not be greater.

By 11th May the pattern of the enemy's advance was becoming clearer. Apart from the situation in Holland, which grew more critical every hour, two main thrusts were developing. One was aimed through the Ardennes; the other further north, through Maastricht towards Brussels. The first was fully reported by French reconnais-sance aircraft, but the second accorded more with the preconceived ideas of the French High Command. It was therefore on the second that attention was mainly focused. And certainly the threat in this direction appeared serious enough; for the Germans, thanks to the glider-borne troops who had captured intact the bridges immediately west of Maastricht, were already over the Albert Canal, and there was grave doubt whether the Belgians could hold on long enough to cover the Allied advance to the Dyle.

Throughout the morning of 11th May Blenheims of the R.A.F. Component flew repeated sorties to establish the strength of the enemy drive through Maastricht. By midday three aircraft had been lost and two damaged out of eight despatched. As German fighters were over the area in such force it was then decided to risk no further reconnaissance; but later in the day urgent French requests led to another Blenheim being sent off to reconnoitre the Albert Canal. Not unexpectedly it failed to return. In spite of this two Bomber Command Blenheim squadrons (Nos. 21 and 110) attacked enemy troops and communications along this line of advance during the afternoon; most of the aircraft returned safely to their bases, but in No. 21 Squadron eight out of twelve were severely damaged by fire from the ground. During the night thirty-six 'heavies' of Bomber Command carried on the work by attacking the exits of the West German town of München-Gladbach—for the War Cabinet still refused to sanction operations against the Ruhr.

Against the more southerly thrust only one operation was under-taken on 11th May. Eight Battles of Nos. 88 and 218 Squadrons were ordered to deliver a low-level attack on a column in German territory moving up towards the Luxembourg border. Whether they managed to reach their target area is doubtful. The only pilot to return saw three of his companions succumb to ground fire in the Ardennes.

By 12th May the bulk of the Franco-British forces had gained their chosen line. To General Georges, the commander of the entire north-east front, the enemy movement through Maastricht still appeared the greatest threat and it was in accordance with his wishes that Barratt now concentrated against this axis of advance. At dawn the British air commander sent off nine A.A.S.F. Blenheims of No. 139 Squadron to attack a column on the road from Maastricht to Tongres. Running into the swarms of fighters previously reported over the area, they lost all but two of their number—a disaster which ended the life of the A.A.S.F. Blenheims as a useful force before it had begun, for the other squadron (No. 114) had been virtually destroyed on its airfield the previous day.

A grim task now faced the Battles. Ever since the early hours of 10th May the Belgians had been striving to remedy the initial disaster of the bridges over the Albert Canal. Counter-attacks had made no headway; shell-fire had produced no result; and aircraft had succeeded only in inflicting some slight damage on one bridge at prohibitive cost. The Belgians then appealed to the Allies, and, after French aircraft had fared no better, the Royal Air Force took its turn. Since the ever-increasing strength of the German defences made any further attempt against the bridges almost suicidal, Barratt took an exceptional step. He instructed Playfair to despatch six Battles manned by volunteer crews. Protective patrols were to be flown over the area by Hurricanes of both A.A.S.F. and Component, but again there was no attempt to supply close escort.

When No. 12 Squadron—the 'Dirty Dozen', in the playful language of the Service—learned that they had been chosen for the task all the pilots present at once volunteered. The briefing officer then asked the six pilots next on the duty roster if they were prepared to go. They were; and their normal crews went with them. Three were detailed to attack the concrete bridge at Vroenhoven, on the Maastricht–Tongres road, the other three the metal bridge a mile or two farther north at Veldwezelt, on the Maastricht–Hasselt road. The bridges were alike in size—370 feet long, 30 feet wide—but the concrete structure was less likely to be affected by the Battles' 250-pound bombs.

When the six aircraft came to take off, the wireless in one refused to function. The crew promptly transferred to another aircraft, only to find its hydraulics unserviceable. Five machines eventually left Amifontaine. Before they departed the leaders of the two sections, Flying Officer N. M. Thomas and Flying Officer D. E. Garland, had what Thomas has described as 'a rather heated discussion'. 'Garland was determined', wrote Thomas, 'to carry out a low-level attack

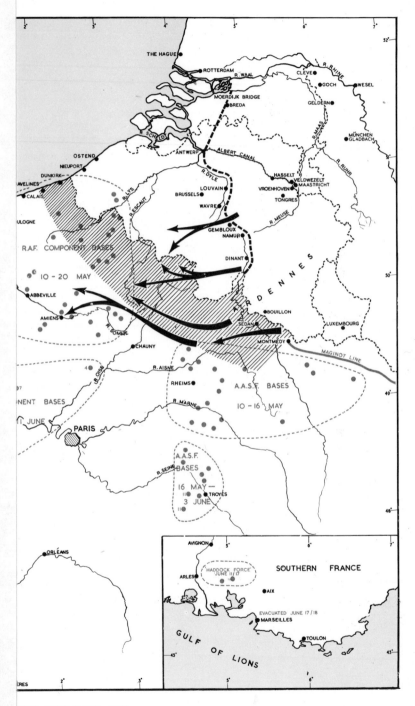

thinking it not only the best form, but the safest. I was set on high dive and tried to persuade him to do likewise. My parting words to him were "it will be interesting to see the result, and may we both be lucky enough to return".'

The results were indeed interesting, for they were invested with all that poignancy which surrounds the death of the young and the brave. Thomas and the other pilot of his section, Pilot Officer T. D. H. Davy, approached the Vroenhoeven bridge above 7/10ths cloud, ran into enemy fighters, dived from 6,000 feet through a storm of *flak*, and nearly blew themselves up with the last of their bombs. For a few minutes Thomas managed to keep his battered aircraft going; then, as the engine failed, he touched down to a fairly smooth landing. Unfortunately it was within 150 yards of a German convoy. Under a hail of fire he emerged and negotiated a surrender, while the wireless-operator stood imperturbably by his gun awaiting orders to open up on the enemy. Davy's machine, also riddled, travelled farther. Ordering his crew to bale out, he succeeded in coaxing the aircraft almost back to base before it crashed. Between them these two pilots slightly damaged the bridge and cratered the approaches.

Meanwhile Garland's section had headed for the metal bridge at Veldwezelt. Garland, a coldly determined youngster of twenty-one, was resolved to let nothing interfere with his aim. But cloud base was at 1,000 feet. As he approached the target he accordingly radioed back to his No. 2 and 3, Pilot Officer I. A. McIntosh and Sergeant Marland, to set the fuse setting control at '11 seconds delay'; he was going in 'low level'. Through the growing volume of *flak* the three swept towards their objective. Then, with flames pouring from his machine, McIntosh aimed his bombs and crashed. Pulled from the burning wreck by his crew, he was soon listening to a lecture delivered with full Teutonic solemnity: 'You British are mad. We capture the bridge early Friday morning. You give us all Friday and Saturday to get our *flak* guns up in circles all round the bridge, and then on Sunday, when all is ready, you come along with three aircraft and try and blow the thing up.' His captor refused to reveal whether the bridge was damaged, but McIntosh noted with satisfaction that the lorry which bore him to five years' captivity made a detour and crossed the canal by another route.

McIntosh's bombs had been dropped in desperation from a burning aircraft. It is unlikely that they hit the target. But either Garland or his No. 3—and all the available scraps of evidence indicate that it was Garland—found the mark; for though the Battles lay broken and burning on the ground, the western truss of the bridge hung shattered in the air. From the ditch in which he was hiding, McIntosh saw one

I

of these two aircraft trying to fight its way back. 'Then it suddenly stood on its tail, climbed vertically for about 100 feet, stalled, and nose-dived to earth.' At a cost of five machines out of five, and four crews killed or captured, No. 12 Squadron had achieved half its allotted task.

For their valour in ensuring success even at the sacrifice of their lives, Garland and his observer, Sergeant T. Gray, an ex-aircraft apprentice from Halton, were posthumously awarded the Victoria Cross. This was the first occasion during the war on which a member of the Royal Air Force won the supreme recognition. Since Victoria Crosses are distributed sparingly, and there was no other appropriate honour which might be conferred on a dead man, the third member of the crew, Leading Aircraftman L. R. Reynolds, the wireless-operator/air-gunner, received no award. Let his name then at least stand recorded with those of his companions, in tribute not only to himself but to all the 'part-time' air crew of the early days of the war—the men who forsook the safety of the ground for the love of flying, and whose efforts were rewarded by the princely addition of a daily eighteen pence to their pay.

While the Battles were attacking the bridges over the Albert Canal immediately west of Maastricht, Bomber Command was concentrating against the bridges over the Maas in the old town itself. Officially, these had already been 'demolished' by the Dutch; but an Allied demolition in 1940, carried out with the utmost respect for neighbouring property and the future possibilities of reconstruction, was a very different matter from a German demolition in 1944, and the bridges were already under repair. No serious damage was done by our aircraft, and ten out of the twenty-four Blenheims failed to return. But an evening operation against the road exits at Hasselt and Tongres was more successful; and the day's work, costly as it was, evoked a signal from Georges thanking Barratt for delaying the German advance and relieving the situation. The Germans, too, were impressed. 'Great destruction by enemy bombing at Maastricht,' confided General Halder, the Chief of Staff at German Army Supreme Headquarters, to his diary that evening.

The pressure through Maastricht may have appeared to slacken. That through the Ardennes was obviously increasing. Before the end of the day the A.A.S.F., called on to operate once more in this region, had lost six out of fifteen Battles in attacks near Bouillon. Again the French High Command signalled its appreciation, reporting that the British bombers had saved the position. But it was not to be saved for long, for the effect of bombing bridges and troop columns is inevitably brief unless the ground forces can follow up the air attacks, or the bombing can be repeated as often as necessary. Determined action on the part of the ground forces there was not to be. As for the Battles, these could obviously not continue to suffer a rate of loss which, taking no account of aircraft merely damaged, was forty per cent of sorties on 10th May, one hundred per cent on 11th May and sixty-two per cent on 12th May.

On 10th May there had been 135 bombers serviceable in the A.A.S.F. By the close of 12th May this number had dwindled to 72. So it was not surprising that during the evening Barratt received a less welcome message than those from Georges. 'I am concerned', signalled the Chief of the Air Staff, 'at the heavy losses incurred by the medium bombers . . . I must impress on you that we cannot continue indefinitely at this rate of intensity . . . If we expend all our efforts in the early stages of the battle we shall not be able to operate effectively when the really critical phase comes . . . ' The following day—13th May—Barratt accordingly made no call on the Blenheims. The Battles he despatched on only one small operation, during which No. 226 Squadron brought a factory down over a cross-roads near Breda. According to the French this helped the Seventh Army, which was now retreating even faster than it had advanced, to take up new positions in safety.

It was while the medium bombers were being rested that von Kleist broke through the French line of defence along the Meuse. In theory this should have been impossible; in practice it was accomplished with the utmost ease. For the enemy, well aware of the difficulties of bringing any great force of artillery through the Ardennes with the necessary speed, set about the task of forcing a crossing of the Meuse by other means. If German guns could not dominate the river, German aircraft could, and two hundred Ju. 87's screeched down on the dismayed defenders with that fury of personal hostility which distinguishes the dive-bomber. It was all too simple. The Ninth Army, barely established on its line, and with only a handful of fighters, very few anti-aircraft guns, indifferent troops, and artillery drawn by horses, was the ideal target. The troops went to ground, the horses were killed, the guns stuck fast, and in a few hours the Germans were across. The Second Army, attacked at its junction with the Ninth, was at first also overwhelmed, but rallied later. So began the legend of the *Stuka*. And so began the severance of the Allied armies and the German drive towards the Channel.

The text-book remedy, apart from a counter-attack by what little was immediately available, was now for the French to throw their reserves into the battle. But these reserves consisted of only one Army Headquarters without troops, and a few poorly equipped divisions;

everything else had been put into the front line. It was therefore essential to pull units out of the Maginot Line, where the pressure was slight, and rush them north. The Maginot troops, however, were not 'mobile': their speed would be that of the French railways. This fact was fully appreciated by the Germans, who now directed most of their 2,000 long-range bombers against communications, and in particular the railways leading from eastern to northern France. When the French strove to hasten towards the fatal gap, they found their power of movement destroyed by the *Luftwaffe*.

The enemy had forced the Meuse in strength at two points. One was at Houx, a few miles north of Dinant; the other, farther south, was at Sedan—a name which for the third time in seventy years struck chill into French hearts. The news in all its full gravity was reported to Barratt during the late evening of 13th May. Before midnight he had warned Playfair not only that the A.A.S.F. would be required to operate at full strength the following day, but that he should also prepare plans for retirement.

The events of 14th May determined the future both of the A.A.S.F. and of the campaign. In the early morning ten Battles of Nos. 103 and 150 Squadrons pin-pointed the German pontoon bridges in the neighbourhood of Sedan and attacked them without loss—for no enemy fighters were encountered, and the tactical low approach had now been abandoned. It was then in Barratt's mind to attack the bridgehead near Dinant; but before he could do this he was called on by the French High Command for a supreme effort at Sedan, where the ground forces massing for a counter-attack had been rudely scattered. Arrangements were accordingly made for the whole strength of the Allied bombers in France to be hurled against the Sedan bridgehead in a series of waves, and soon after noon the few French aircraft available went into action. Attacking bridges and columns of troops, they suffered losses so severe that their remaining operations for the day were cancelled. Then came the turn of the A.A.S.F. Between 1500 and 1600 hours the entire force of available Battles and Blenheims was flung in against the same objectives. But the Me.109's, absent in the morning, were now on guard. No. 12 Squadron lost four aircraft out of five; No. 105 Squadron, six out of eleven; No. 150 Squadron, four out of four; No. 139 Squadron, four out of six; No. 218 Squadron, ten out of eleven. In all, from the seventy-one bombers which took off, forty did not return. No higher rate of loss in an operation of comparable size has ever been experienced by the Royal Air Force.

The day's work was not yet done. In the evening twenty-eight Bomber Command Blenheims continued the attack. They encountered fewer Me.109's than the Battles, and their own fighter protection was stronger. Their losses were accordingly less severe, though at twenty-five per cent of sorties they were bad enough.

These suicidal efforts were not without effect. The evidence of captured prisoners testified to the alarm and fatigue produced by the bombing, and the French High Command entertained a momentary belief that the air assault, coupled with a counter-attack by the Second Army, had saved the situation. During the evening Georges informed Barratt that the air action had slowed down reinforcement of the foremost German troops, and had enabled the French counter-attack to contain the bridgehead. By the following day, Georges thought, the 'centre of interest' would have shifted to the Dinant area. He was sadly wrong, though the interest at Dinant was to be real enough. At Sedan the Germans merely paused for a few hours. Then they brushed aside whatever was still in their path and began their joy-ride across France.

* * *

While the wrecks of the Battles lay strewn about the valleys of the Ardennes, events were moving to their climax in Holland. The Dutch had always refused to concert plans in advance with the Allies; their country, apart from the islands at the mouth of the Scheldt, was beyond our chosen line of defence; and we had never expected that their resistance could last more than four or five days. Gallantly though they had fought, and heavy as were the losses they had inflicted on the invaders, they had failed to dislodge the German airborne forces from Waalhaven airfield and the great Moerdijk bridge —the key to 'Fortress Holland'. Simultaneously punched in the face and stabbed in the back, the Dutch put up a brave but inevitably brief struggle. By the evening of 13th May their Air Force was virtually destroyed, Queen Wilhelmina was aboard a British destroyer, and the position was everywhere desperate.

It was to speed the inevitable admission of defeat that during the following afternoon some forty Ju.87's delivered a systematic bombardment of Rotterdam, while negotiations for the surrender of the town were still in progress. There was opposition neither in the air nor from the ground, and the bombing, conducted in a leisurely fashion from 100–200 feet, was a bitter lesson in the potentialities of air supremacy. With the water low in the canals from the dry weather and the main supply pipe quickly severed, the old town was soon a raging inferno. The most densely built-up square mile of the city was devastated, 20,000 buildings destroyed, 78,000 people rendered homeless and nearly 1,000 of the inhabitants killed. The following morning, except in the Zeeland province, the Dutch forces were ordered to lay down their arms.

The destruction of Rotterdam settled not only the question of further resistance in Holland, but also the question of how far the German Air Force was respecting civilian life and property. When on 15th May the War Cabinet once more considered the propriety of attacking the Ruhr, its remaining doubts had vanished, and the Air Staff was at last given the signal to go ahead. Of the many benefits that this decision was expected to bring, the greatest would be the anticipated effect on the German Air Force; for German air superiority had so paralysed the French ground forces that some diversion of the enemy's bombers from their present objectives was imperative. If the Royal Air Force raided the Ruhr, destroying oil plants with its more accurately placed bombs and urban property with those that went astray, the outcry for retaliation against Britain might prove too strong for the German generals to resist. Indeed, Hitler himself would probably head the clamour. The attack on the Ruhr, in other words, was an informal invitation to the *Luftwaffe* to bomb London.

The decision to bombard objectives in the Ruhr brought in its train a further ruling of great importance. This concerned the des-patch of British fighter squadrons to France—a matter on which so many inaccurate statements have since been made, on both sides of the Channel, that it is as well to set out the facts in detail. Before the war we had agreed to base four of our fighter squadrons in France. These had duly flown out in September 1939. Then, in the quiet months before the German attack, we had sent two more; and at the same time, in response to pressure from the French, we had under-taken to bring the total up to ten when the enemy offensive was launched—for until the Germans were inextricably committed against France their opening move might well have been the dreaded 'knock-out blow' against England. This promise had been fulfilled on 10th and 11th May, and ten squadrons of Hurricanes were now fighting desperately in France against great odds. Their performance was magnificent, and the enemy was suffering heavy losses, but they were obviously far too few. The campaign was not many hours old when Barratt, Blount and Gort accordingly with one voice besought more fighters, and on 13th May thirty-two Hurricanes and pilots— the equivalent of two squadrons—flew out to join the Component. The next day the full extent of the disaster on the Meuse became clear, and French demands took on a new note of urgency. 'You were kind enough,' telephoned M. Reynaud, 'to send four squadrons [i.e. the four reinforcing squadrons sent on the 10th and 11th], which is more than you promised; but if we are to win this battle, which might be decisive for the whole war, it is necessary to send at once, if possible today, ten more squadrons.' Immediate reinforcement on this scale was of course impracticable, and for the moment no promises were made. Pending a final decision, however, the Chief of Air Staff was instructed to make all necessary preparations for despatching the squadrons.

This at once brought Dowding up from Fighter Command to plead against any further weakening of our air defences. However great the need on the Continent, and however tempting the opportunity to send our fighters where there were certainly large numbers of German bombers to be shot down, Hurricanes abroad could not fight as effectively as Hurricanes at home. For though we had built a few radar stations in the North of France, the apparatus as yet worked poorly overland, and the basis of the warning system was still the French observer posts, supplemented by our own 'wireless intelligence screen'.[1] If the drain of fighters to France continued, Dowding could only visualize his forces 'bled white and in no condition to withstand the bombing attack which will inevitably be made on this country as soon as our powers of resistance fall below a level to which we are already perilously close'. Everything for which he had fought, all that he had striven so painfully to build up, was in jeopardy. The military leaders might see in France the decisive struggle which would determine the war, but Dowding's eyes were fixed nearer home. For while Britain survived unconquered the Allied cause was not lost; and while Fighter Command retained its strength, Britain might still survive.

In response to his own request Dowding appeared before the War Cabinet on 15th May. His arguments prevailed. A meeting, as he saw it, originally hostile to his opinions, was converted to his viewpoint, and to his 'inexpressible relief', it was decided for the moment to send no more fighter squadrons to France. And this was the necessary counterpart of the decision to attack the Ruhr; for we could not with good sense at once invite Germany to attack London and at the same time divest ourselves of our means of defence. Indeed, this close relation between the two subjects had already prompted Dowding to recommend to the Air Staff 'an immediate assumption of the air offensive against Germany, and particularly her oil supplies'. For he was determined to fight his battle—in his opinion the one decisive battle—over England, not France; and this he could do only if the

---

[1] Forward Observer posts reporting back by W/T.

Germans attacked England before Fighter Command had been offered up on the altar of Anglo-French solidarity.

After the intensity of the struggle to persuade the War Cabinet, the Army and the French that the heavy bombers would be best employed against the Ruhr, the result of their operations came as something of an anti-climax. On the night of 15/16th May, ninety-six Wellingtons, Whitleys and Hampdens, took off for objectives east of the Rhine. Seventy-eight were directed against oil plants. Only twenty-four of the crews even claimed to have found them.

The following day our bombing policy was again in the melting pot. The Prime Minister hastened across to France to protest against withdrawals executed, as it seemed to the War Cabinet, 'on account of the penetration of the French line by a force of some 120 German Armoured Fighting Vehicles'. Finding out the real situation, he accepted the French view that our night bombing should be concentrated against the crossings of the Meuse. From then onwards the effort of the heavies was either divided, or else pursued an uneasy alternation, between the objectives east of the Rhine favoured by the Air Staff and the objectives nearer the battle proposed by the French. At Hamburg and Bremen, where the lines of the coast and the relatively clear atmosphere made identification easier, our bombers did some damage, but they were repeatedly baffled by the industrial haze of the Ruhr. No better results were achieved against the crossings of the Meuse, where the general unsuitability of the targets for night attack was increased by the mist which invariably shrouded the river valley. In sum, during the next few nights the heavy bombers achieved none of their objects. Industrial damage was negligible; whatever delay was inflicted on the German Army was insignificant; not a single German fighter or anti-aircraft gun was withdrawn from the Western front to protect the Reich; and not a single German bomber was diverted from attacking the French armies and their communications to reply to the provocation from England. The assault on the Ruhr, most cherished of all Air Staff projects, was a failure. The conception had been admirable; the timing doubtful; the available means utterly inadequate.

A fresh bombing programme for the 'heavies' was not the only consequence of the Prime Minister's visit to France. Early on 16th May the War Cabinet had decided, in spite of the impression made by Dowding the previous day, to send four of the extra ten fighter squadrons requested by Reynaud. This reinforcement, in the form of eight half squadrons with only a few key ground staff, left to join the Component within a few hours. Meanwhile from Paris Mr. Churchill now telegraphed to urge that six more squadrons, to make up Reynaud's requirement of ten, should be at once despatched across the Channel. Late that night the War Cabinet met to consider the demand. By that time, however, Sir Cyril Newall had been in communication with B.A.F.F. The Chief of Air Staff was thus able to point out to the political leaders that our bases in northern France could accommodate only three more squadrons, and to make this point decisive. As a compromise he suggested that three squadrons should be sent over to operate from France in the mornings, and that another three should relieve them in the afternoons—a proposal which brought six squadrons into action yet committed none of them so fully that they would be lost in a French *débâcle*. This scheme was applied during the next three days. After that the approach of the Germans to the Channel coast at once prevented the use of bases in northern France and at the same time enabled fighter patrols to be flown over the battle area from southern England.

By 16th May the A.A.S.F. bases astride the Aisne were threatened by the German break-through. Fortunately the force had somewhere to go. An extensive scheme of airfield construction had been under-taken by the Royal Air Force and the Army during the quiet months before the German attack, and a number of grass landing grounds were almost ready in the south Champagne, around Troyes. A with-drawal south to this district would place not only the Aisne but the Marne between the Germans and the British units. Such an order, however, would be easier given than obeyed; for the A.A.S.F., until Barratt's urgent representations during the winter months, had been regarded as a static body well protected by the Maginot Line, and its transport resources were still hopelessly insufficient for a simul-taneous move of the kind now required. Six hundred vehicles short even of its official complement, the Force would have been crippled but for two pieces of good fortune. In the first place the Germans made no serious attempt to cross the Aisne, but held the river as their left flank while they pressed across France to the Channel coast. This meant that once the few units north of the Aisne had been with-drawn, the A.A.S.F. had ample time to complete its move and salvage the equipment that would otherwise have been left behind. In the second place three hundred new American lorries were borrowed from the French, and, in spite of protestations, retained until the final evacuation. How the Air Attaché and his colleagues in Paris were able to persuade our Allies, who could not move their own reserves for lack of transport, to part up with so valuable a prize is something of a mystery—but there was always much more war material in France than ever found its way into the front line. Be that as it may, the lorries proved a godsend. They would, however, have been still more useful had the drivers hastily flown out from England known anything of their workings, or of France, or of the A.A.S.F. locations, and had someone not loaded all the starting handles, jacks and tools into one of the lorries and sent them down to the west coast under the impression that they were unwanted spares.

The French lorries were one part of the answer to the problem of making the A.A.S.F. mobile. The other part was the drastic expedient of 'rolling up' four of the ten bomber squadrons. The selection was easy. Two of the Battle squadrons—Nos. 105 and 218—had only four aircraft left between them; these and the surviving crews were transferred to the other Battle squadrons. The two Blenheim squadrons (Nos. 114 and 139) had between them nine aircraft; these joined the reconnaissance Blenheims of the Component. Thus reduced, the A.A.S.F. continued the fight at a strength of six Battle and three Hurricane squadrons. It was this combination of contraction and extra transport which enabled the force to carry out three further withdrawals during the remaining weeks of the campaign and finally to escape from the west coast.

The A.A.S.F. had barely reached safety when danger loomed before the Component. With the Ninth Army shattered on the Meuse, the First Army on its left could only retreat towards the Escaut, and the B.E.F. was forced to conform. By 17th May the most advanced Component units were being withdrawn westwards, and land-line communications with Barratt's headquarters—south of the enemy penetration, like the A.A.S.F.—had already gone. Still the Panzers rolled on unchecked, and by 19th May, Gort, Blount and the Air Ministry were in agreement that the Component could operate as effectively, and with a great deal more security, from the south of England. First the reconnaissance aircraft left, then the fighters. By the evening of 21st May a few Lysanders of No. 4 Squadron assigned to G.H.Q. were the only Component aircraft left in France.

The evacuation of the Component was carried out in such haste that most of its equipment and stores fell intact into the hands of the enemy. One loss was especially grievous. The equivalent of thirteen Hurricane squadrons, plus replacements, amounting in all to 261 aircraft, had operated with the Component; 75 had been destroyed and 'written-off'; but only 66 returned to England. The balance of 120 consisted of damaged machines which could not be repaired in time for them to be flown back to this country. The cost of ten days' operations in northern France was thus 195 Hurricanes. This loss of something like a quarter of Britain's entire strength in modern fighters was bad enough. It would have been far worse but for the good sense of Newall and the obduracy of Dowding in resisting the demands of the French.

While a new 'Back Component' Headquarters was forming at Hawkinge, near Folkestone, the Battles of the A.A.S.F. continued the attack against enemy communications. But they now operated mainly by night, and with few losses. That so radical a change was possible reflected the greatest credit on those who had earlier persisted, in spite of many accidents, in an ambitious programme of night training. Flying and landing a Battle by night was no easy task —there was a brilliant glare from the exhaust which dazzled the pilot, and the view from the observer's seat was poor—but those difficulties which were not overcome were ignored, and there was an immediate and dramatic decline in the casualty rate. During the intense daylight operations of 10th–14th May, one aircraft had been lost in every two sorties; during the night operations of 20th May–4th June the loss was just over one in every two hundred. In this the Battles confirmed what the experience of the 'heavies', whose average loss was about two per cent, had already demonstrated—that as our bombers could not survive in daylight against enemy fighters, and as we had no good long-range fighters to provide escort, our long-range bombing must be done under cover of darkness, or not at all. Such a policy, however, was by no means all gain, for safety could only be achieved at the expense of accuracy. In fact, so many Battle crews now dropped their bombs with no more precise identifications of their target than that provided by their watches, that Barratt was compelled to forbid bombing on 'estimated time of arrival'. After that the phrase ceased to appear in the pilots' reports. The practice, however, continued.

By 21st May the enemy panzers, keeping the Aisne and the Somme on their left flank, had reached Abbeville and were wheeling north along the Channel coast. The Allied armies in the north, completely isolated and already hard-pressed on front and flank, were thus also being hemmed in from the rear. Clearly the situation demanded some action to close the gap between the two groups of armies, either by those in the north fighting their way south, or by those in the south fighting their way north, or by each advancing to meet the other. That this was the correct course in theory there could be no doubt; but only those furthest from the battle believed that it was possible in practice. Weygand, recalled from the Middle East to assume the mantle of Gamelin, was at the moment strong for the plan. So, too, was the boldest and stoutest heart of all. Others may not have known their own minds, but unquestionably the Prime Minister did. When the War Cabinet met on 19th May it agreed that the B.E.F. should be directed to move southwards upon Amiens, attacking all enemy forces encountered, and to take stand on the left of the French Army.

When this order reached G.H.Q. it was received aghast. Commanded to thrust his forces into the very jaws of the German armoured divisions, Gort promised to do his best to mount a counter-attack in due course, but made it clear that a general fighting withdrawal to the south-west was (in the language of his printed despatch) 'entirely impossible until the situation had been retrieved on the front of the French First Army'. Disappointed in Gort, the Prime Minister tried Reynaud. 'Salvation (of the northern armies)', he telegraphed, 'can only be obtained by immediate execution of Weygand's plan. I demand that French commanders in North and South and Belgian G.Q.G. be given most stringent orders to carry this out and turn defeat into victory'. But a lion-like resolution in Downing Street could not now alter the facts of the battlefield. On 24th May the Belgians, between the B.E.F. and the sea, were heavily attacked by infantry and aircraft; forced away from the B.E.F., they obliged Gort to extend his left with the two divisions earmarked for an attack to the south. Meanwhile the enemy forces which had turned north from Abbeville were eating their way along the coast. Boulogne fell, Calais was surrounded. The French First Army, so far from striking south, began to retire north. The armies along the Somme and Aisne, thin and poorly equipped, made no move to strike across the gap to the rescue of their comrades. The game was up. On 26th May Gort was given permission 'to operate towards the coast forthwith in conjunction with the French and Belgian armies'. Thenceforth the hopes of 200,000 men, and a nation, centred on Dunkirk.

During these desperate days, when fantastic and incredible disasters shook established habits of thought to their foundations, the Air Staff were compelled to modify a principle of more than twenty years' standing. From the war of 1914–1918 they had deduced that the correct employment for the fighter in offence was not to furnish escort to the bomber but to sweep the air clear of the enemy. Only thus, it seemed, could the basic canon of successful air warfare—the relentless concentration on the offensive—be observed; for systematic escort would demand vast numbers of fighters beyond those needed for territorial defence, and if these were provided there would be little chance of building up the great bomber force without which victory would be unattainable. Ideally, the bomber should be able to look after itself; and if it obviously could not, like the Battle and Blenheim, it should have the air swept clear over the target area, but not expect to travel under a heavy protective guard the whole way. This system, in which undoubtedly was enshrined much truth—the offensive fighter patrol over the battle area is still one of the keys to tactical air superiority—was now, in the special circumstances of a great numerical inferiority, proving an unqualified failure. Half a dozen Hurricanes might perform prodigies of valour over the target area, but they could hardly be expected to sweep the air clear when they always encountered twenty or thirty Me.109's. Indeed, as often as not they simply advertised the forthcoming arrival of our bombers. This was already becoming plain when on 17th May No. 82 Squadron, Bomber Command, was ordered to attack German columns near Gembloux. Hurricanes were over the target area, but the bombers were caught *en route* by fifteen Me.109's. Eleven of the twelve Blenheims were shot down, and only the exceptional determination of the squadron commander, Wing Commander the Earl of Bandon, prevented the temporary disbandment of the squadron. Within forty-eight hours, in fact, Bandon had scraped together enough crews and new machines to lead six aircraft on a night operation.

Clearly a repetition of this sort of disaster could not be risked. Newall's first reaction was accordingly to confine the medium bombers, like the 'heavies', to operations by night. Then the full extent of the threat to the B.E.F. became clear, and the decision was at once reversed. Daylight attacks from England were to continue; but unless good cloud cover could be relied upon, the bombers were to have strong and close protection. However extravagant, however defensively-minded it might appear, escort was henceforth the rule. And since the battle was now moving within the range of Fighter Command, the rule could be applied—even if it jeopardized still more of Dowding's precious squadrons.

The development of fighter escort, so vital to the success of the operations that were now to ensue, supplemented, not superseded, offensive patrols. While escorted Blenheims, aided on occasion by Lysanders and even a few ancient Hectors, hammered away by day at the immediate threat to the B.E.F., fighter patrols were scouring the air over the Channel ports. And by night, while the A.A.S.F. and the 'heavies' attacked the enemy's supply lines further afield, Blenheim fighters of No. 604 Squadron continued the patrol over the Pas de Calais. From 22nd May onwards something like two hundred fighter sorties a day were flown from England over northern France. As the main force of German armour reached this area it perceived a sharp difference. 'For the first time now,' noted General Halder in his diary on 24th May, 'enemy air superiority has been reported by Kleist.' 'Enemy fighter resistance,' recorded the War Diary of the German XIX Corps on the same day, 'was so strong that our own air reconnaissance was practically impossible.' But still the pressure grew; and soon Dowding was forced to draw upon his most treasured possessions of all, the carefully husbanded Spitfires. The whole resources of Fighter Command were being sucked inexorably into the battle. The life-blood of Britain's air defence was ebbing away in the skies of France.

* * *

While hope was entertained for the best, preparations were wisely made for the worst. On 19th May, that fateful Sunday which saw the order to Gort to fight his way south, the War Office and Admiralty had begun to discuss the 'possible but unlikely evacuation of a very large force in hazardous circumstances'. It was decided that such an operation, to which the code name 'Dynamo' was given, should be prepared, and if necessary, executed, by Vice Admiral Ramsay at Dover. As a result of the measures which followed, Boulogne was successfully evacuated on May 23rd/24th; the heroic garrison of Calais, too, could have been saved had the British Government not decided, in the greater interest of the Allied armies south of Dunkirk, that it must fight on to the death. There was thus an organization in being, though as yet without anything like adequate forces at its disposal, when at 1857 hours on 26th May, Ramsay was ordered to start up 'Dynamo'.

Obviously the devotion and skill of the Royal Navy, coupled with that of the merchant seamen and amateur yachtsmen, was the prime factor in ensuring the success of the Dunkirk evacuation. But there were others of great importance which are apt to be overlooked. Even Rundstedt (backed by Hitler) played a part; for as a result of his pre-occupation with the forthcoming offensive against the French armies south of the Somme, coupled with his fear of risking tank formations in an area protected by canals and inundations, the main force of German armour was for three days held back. 'The left wing,' recorded the infuriated Halder on 24th May, 'consisting of armoured and motorized forces, which has no enemy before it, will thus be stopped dead in its tracks upon direct orders from the *Führer*. Finishing off the encircled enemy army has to be left to the air force.' We must not, however, give too much credit to a German mistake which was soon rectified. The evacuation owed more to the elements of the French First Army who acted as covering troops, to say nothing of the B.E.F.'s own valour and skill in holding off the enemy. And certainly no list of the prime authors of the achievement can exclude the Royal Air Force.

Dunkirk, like the operations which preceded it, was for the Royal Air Force a battle of all arms—not, as is sometimes imagined, an affair of fighters alone. The fighters indeed bore the main share by covering the bridgehead and the sea lanes, but we must remember, too, the reconnaissance aircraft which brought back details of the military position and kept watch against U-boats and E-boats, and the bombers which harassed and held up enemy troops and silenced vital batteries.

This combined action was co-ordinated by Blount from the Back Component Headquarters at Hawkinge. His task was one of the utmost difficulty. The military basis on which he had to work was distinctly sketchy—a broad requirement was received from the small Component staff still with Gort, or from the War Office, but little positive information of the positions of our own or the enemy's forces was provided. Only by piecing together the results of reconnaissance, the reports of returning bombers, intelligence material from the Air Ministry, and the messages intercepted by the wireless station at Hawkinge, could Blount get much idea of what was happening on the other side of the Channel. Indeed, in his subsequent report, he complained that he received no information whatever of the enemy land forces from any Army source except the combined R.A.F./Army Reconnaissance Mission—which ceased to operate on 27th May.[1] He also stated that information of greater value about our own forces was provided by intercepted German messages than by the War Office. To add to these handicaps there were the defects of his own hastily improvised Headquarters, including an extremely small staff. Moreover, he was dependent, for all tasks other than reconnaissance, upon 'requests' to the chiefs of the operational commands. Fortunately Portal, Dowding and Bowhill were all men who recognized a crisis when they met one, and the organization, though cumbrous, somehow worked.

Indeed, it worked to great effect, though the results were not apparent to everyone. Subjected to an utterly exhausting and terrifying experience, our soldiers and sailors returned home with a single question on their lips—'Where was the R.A.F.?' So general and so bitter was the criticism that the newly appointed Chief of the Imperial General Staff, Sir John Dill, felt impelled to point out to his commanders that the Royal Air Force had gone 'all out', and

---

[1] The work of this organization was outstanding, and later inspired the formation of the Reconnaissance Corps. It consisted of No. 3 Air Mission, under Wing Commander J. M. Fairweather, and an attached military section under Lieut. Col. G. F. Hopkinson. The Mission was lavishly equipped with armoured cars, mobile high-powered wireless, and motor-cycles. Fairweather and the Air Mission proper acted in a liaison capacity at Belgian G.Q.G., while the military staff visited lower formations and carried out direct ground reconnaissance of the Belgian Front. Reports were transmitted by wireless to Fairweather at G.Q.G., sifted there, and thence relayed to Barratt and Gort. Unfortunately most of the Mission staff perished at sea on the voyage home.

that they should discourage contrary opinions in their units. If mistaken, however, the outcry was fully understandable. The B.E.F. was under the severe emotional and physical shock of being bundled out of France within three weeks of the opening of the campaign, and its members were not for the most part disposed to view matters in a wide context. Conscious of having fought well, and of being fully equal to the enemy troops 'man for man', they could only blame their misfortunes on French faint-heartedness and Royal Air Force wrong-headedness. Their reasoning took little account of the fact that the *Luftwaffe* was far stronger than the Royal Air Force, and therefore that they must expect to be bombed; rather it told them that they could have held the enemy on the ground if only the Royal Air Force had played its part in the air. We must also remember that the British soldier—and for that matter any soldier—customarily expects as his right not merely a greater freedom from air attack than his enemies are enjoying, but nothing less than complete immunity. The Royal Air Force may be blasting his opponents from their strong points, strangling their communications and reducing their cities to smoking rubble, but if it permits a single enemy bomb to fall near Private Atkins then for Private Atkins it has failed in its duty. And at Dunkirk it was not a question of single bombs.

The anonymous critic in the ranks, though his viewpoint is necessarily limited, has direct experience and is not to be ignored. Still more difficult is it to dismiss the strictures of the responsible Commander. Admiral Ramsay, after complaining in his subsequent report to the Admiralty that our air action was often brought to bear either at the wrong place, or at the wrong time, or with inadequate force to meet a particular situation, put matters in no uncertain terms. 'Rightly or wrongly,' wrote the Admiral, 'full air protection was expected, but instead, for hours on end the ships off-shore were subjected to a murderous hail of bombs and machine-gun bullets. Required by their duty to remain off-shore waiting for the troops, who themselves were unable to move down to the water for the same reason, it required the greatest determination and sense of duty, amounting in fact to heroism, on the part of the ships' and boats' crews, to enable them to complete their mission. In their reports, the C.O.s of many ships, while giving credit to the R.A.F. personnel for gallantry in such combats as were observed from the ships, at the same time express their sense of disappointment and surprise at the seemingly puny efforts made to provide air protection during the height of this operation . . .'

Yet while matters appeared in this light to Ramsay, Air Vice-Marshal K. R. Park, who as Air Officer Commanding No. 11 Group was responsible for by far the greater part of the protective patrols, was reporting in a completely opposite sense to Dowding at Fighter Command. 'Our fighter pilots', Park asserted, 'obtained such ascendency over the German bombers that during the last phase of the operation the German bombers jettisoned their bombs in the sea on sighting even small formations of our fighters. On one occasion, a fighter pilot who had used up all his ammunition made a feint attack at a sub-formation of German bombers who immediately fled east, one of them losing control and crashing in the sea.' Park was not an impartial witness—though he was certainly a witness, for he flew over Dunkirk more than once in his own Hurricane. It was a weightier voice than his which, again partly to silence criticism, pointed out to the nation that 'there was a victory inside this deliverance which should be noted. It was gained by the Royal Air Force.'

Ramsay and the men on the beaches and in the ships—or Park and Churchill? The difference is striking, but not impossible to resolve. The air action undertaken on behalf of the evacuating forces was, it has been mentioned, of many kinds. Reconnaissance alone occupied some thirty sorties a day, apart from any fighter escort. The bomber effort, too, was certainly as great as the Royal Air Force was capable of at the time. Every day some fifty Blenheims, escorted or under cloud cover, attacked enemy troops closing in on the B.E.F. Every night an equal number of Bomber Command 'heavies' concentrated against the road approaches to the Dunkirk area, while as many more, aided by the A.A.S.F., attacked enemy communications further back. Very little of this work could possibly be seen by our ground forces. Occasionally, however, an operation was carried out within sight of the troops, and then it earned its full meed of praise. 'On the afternoon of 31st May', reported the Commander of the 12th Infantry Brigade to Divisional Headquarters, 'this brigade was holding a sector from opposite Nieuport to the sea. Between 1500 and 1700 hours a determined attack was launched upon our front—the third within a period of twelve hours. The leading German waves were stopped by our light machine-gun and mortar fire, but strong enemy reserves were observed moving through Nieuport and on the roads to the canal north-west of Nieuport. At this moment some R.A.F. bombers arrived and bombed Nieuport and the roads north-west of it. The effect was instantaneous and decisive—all movement of enemy reserves stopped: many of the forward German troops turned and fled, suffering severely from the fire of our machine-guns . . .'

The attack at Nieuport was exceptional in that it was close enough to our troops to be witnessed and appreciated. A similar exception

K

may be found in the operations against the enemy batteries which increasingly harassed Dunkirk, the beaches and the shipping approaches. Almost every day during the evacuation fresh gun-sites were spotted and attacked either by Royal Air Force Blenheims, Lysanders and Hectors, or else by Fleet Air Arm squadrons operating under Coastal Command control; and to this type of work Ramsay paid full tribute. These were the exceptions. In general, our soldiers and sailors at Dunkirk were in no position to appreciate the bombing and reconnaissance operations undertaken on their behalf. Their expressed grievance, however, was not lack of bomber support but lack of fighter cover. There was no 'air umbrella' over their heads. There was not even a continuous battle fought out between opposing hordes of aircraft. They were just bombed.

There were many reasons why the troops had so poor an opinion of the protective effort. Even the briefest air combat may take place over a vast area of sky, and the fatal bullets or shells may finish their work many minutes after they hit the aircraft. Moreover, our soldiers and sailors in 1940 were mostly unable to distinguish British from enemy aircraft. Since Spitfires more than once attacked Hurricanes over Dunkirk this lack of skill in aircraft recognition need cause no surprise, but it had some very curious results. On 1st June, for instance, two typical episodes were noted by the same officer. 'As the mists and clouds dispersed', recorded Rear Admiral Wake-Walker, 'many aircraft appeared on the scene and fighters constantly came low over us. More often than not they were Spitfires, but our ships were not taking chances and nearly always opened fire indiscriminately on them. As this kept happening, I hoisted 6 flag—"cease fire"—and blew the siren to draw attention and try and stop the firing. In spite of this I can remember our own machine-gun aft in *Keith* firing away regardless of the "cease fire" gong. Once started firing, they could hear nothing.' A few hours later the Admiral was on shore, but the situation there was little different. 'Back on the pier again I waited for Tennant, who presently walked down. His tin hat had been decorated with the letters S.N.O. cut out of silver paper and stuck on with sardine oil—it looked very distinguished all the same. As we stood talking there a Lysander Army Co-op. plane came over very low and flew down the pier. It was fired at by several Bofors guns and Tennant said "I am sure that damn fellow is a Hun—he has been flying over here all day". I then realized it was the plane flying over at my request to see if the pier was being shelled, and felt rather sorry for the poor chap; though he seemed none the worse.'

Incidents like these were by no means uncommon. Exposed to heavy and repeated attacks, our ships and ground forces automatically, assumed that all aircraft were hostile. It was, of course, the safe thing to do. Ships' crews in particular can afford to take no chances, and are notoriously light on the trigger. In this connection it is worth noting that even four years later, when the *Luftwaffe* scarcely dared to raise its head, and Allied aircraft painted in huge black and white stripes swarmed in their hundreds over the Normandy beachheads. many naval vessels still went on shooting with the same gay abandon.

If much of the air fighting took place out of sight of Dunkirk, and if many of the aircraft our troops thought were German were in fact British, it remains true that for the greater part of the operation our fighters were heavily outnumbered. Indeed, they were perhaps more heavily outnumbered than they need have been. The average force at Park's disposal was limited to some two hundred serviceable aircraft. This was the number which Dowding was prepared not merely to operate, but to keep operating; and to do so he had, in fact, to call on almost every one of his single-engined squadrons. He could, however, have achieved a larger initial concentration of force over Dunkirk if he had been willing to strip the entire North and Midlands of their defence against the enemy. This risk Dowding was not prepared to take; nor, with one eye on the greater struggle that lay ahead, was he anxious to expose his entire force, including many squadrons incompletely trained or recuperating, to the heavy wastage entailed in fighting over the Continent. It is however possible—if not profitable—to contend that a bigger initial concentration over Dunkirk might have resulted not, as Dowding feared, in higher losses, but in lower.

It was thus with two hundred aircraft—and the rest of Fighter Command in immediate reserve—that Park had to frustrate the assembled might of the *Luftwaffe*; for it was to the German Air Force, not the German Army, that Hitler had entrusted the task of thwarting the evacuation. Weakness in numbers, however, was by no means Park's only difficulty. The area to be protected was fifty or sixty miles away from his nearest bases; operating beyond their normal defensive system, our fighters would have no information from radar and would be compelled to rely on the wasteful method of standing patrols; and the endurance limits of the Hurricane and Spitfire allowed not more than forty minutes on the actual patrol lines. It is with these handicaps in mind that the course of the air operations at Dunkirk must now be traced, and the achievement of our fighters assessed.

The evening of 26th May, when full evacuation began, went well. 'Enemy fighter activity very strong,' recorded German XIX Corps: 'our own fighter protection completely lacking. Use of *Luftwaffe* against sea transport ineffective.' The following day, however, cumulative disasters threatened to overwhelm the whole project. Early in the morning the French on the western side of the perimeter were forced back to within five miles of Dunkirk. With the enemy's guns dominating the town and the normal approach from Dover, our ships were thereupon forced to approach the port by a roundabout route from the East until a more central channel could be swept clear of mines. As this eastern route was over twice the length of the direct passage the number of journeys made by the ships was correspondingly reduced. Then the *Luftwaffe*, concentrating its attacks against the town and harbour, wrought such havoc that all British troops were ordered outside the town; and the newly arrived Senior Naval Officer, Captain Tennant, informed Admiral Ramsay that evacuation would have to take place solely from the beaches. On top of all these calamities the Belgians capitulated with only the briefest notice, leaving a twenty-mile gap on the left of the B.E.F. Fortunately this had been anticipated, and appropriate movements had been planned for our troops.

It was, of course, impossible for the Royal Air Force with its available resources to prevent the destruction of Dunkirk; for the initiative throughout lay with the *Luftwaffe*, which could strike when it pleased. At first the task of the British fighters was complicated by War Office requests for protection and supply-dropping over Calais, as it was not known that the heroic garrison had surrendered the previous evening. Meanwhile, the Admiralty naturally expected continuous cover over Dunkirk throughout the hours of daylight. With a total of sixteen squadrons, however, Park could achieve continuity only at the expense of strength. Even when he learned that the fight in Calais was over, he could still not provide continuous cover for the Dunkirk evacuation at more than single squadron strength, for the perimeter stretched back some distance inland, the beaches alone extended for ten miles, and the shipping was liable to be attacked almost anywhere on passage. In consequence our fighters on 27th May, though present the entire day on one or other of the different patrol lines, were usually greatly outnumbered. Eleven Spitfires of No. 74 Squadron, for instance, gave battle to thirty Do.17's and Me.109's; five Hurricanes of No. 145 Squadron attacked the rear section of a Do.17 formation only to find themselves set upon by twenty or thirty Me.110's; twenty Hurricanes and Spitfires of Nos. 56 and 610 Squadrons, trying to pick off a single He.111, at once ran into thirty or forty Me.110's. But though our fighters could not prevent the enemy reducing the town and port of Dunkirk to rubble, they certainly spoiled his aim against the targets that mattered most—the harbour moles and the ships. For the damage did not, in spite of first impressions, make evacuation from the port impossible; and though there were a dozen concerted assaults against our vessels, as well as many individual attacks, not more than two ships were sunk.

After the disasters of 27th May, the following day brought renewed hope. This was thanks in part to the worsening weather and the pall of black smoke that hung over the town from the burning oil-tanks. Indeed, the greatest danger on 28th May came not from the *Luftwaffe*, but from the confusion on the beaches, to which evacuation had now been confined. For embarkation was not yet under naval control, and the small craft at work were far too few for the tremendous task of ferrying the troops to the ships off shore. Confidential reports of the time tell of wild scrambles to get aboard the boats, which, launched by inexpert hands, were all too often swamped in the surf. Worst of all, many thoughtless or selfish groups cut their boat adrift after reaching the waiting vessel, instead of arranging for its return to shore. Mercifully it became apparent towards evening that use could still be made of the harbour. Meanwhile on this side of the Channel steps were taken to organize naval beach parties and muster large numbers of small craft.

From an early hour, the Royal Air Force was in no doubt of its responsibilities. 'To-day,' signalled Newall to the Chiefs of Bomber, Fighter and Coastal Command, 'is likely to be the most critical day ever experienced by the British Army. The extreme gravity of the situation should be explained to all units. I am confident that all ranks will appreciate that it is the duty of the R.A.F. to make their greatest effort today to assist their comrades of both the Army and the Navy.' In this spirit, Fighter Command was instructed to 'ensure the protection of Dunkirk beaches (three miles on either side) from first light until darkness by continuous fighter patrols in strength' and to have 'due regard to the protection of bomber sorties and the provision of support in the B.E.F. area'. Meanwhile Coastal Command, which was already scouring the Channel for enemy surface craft and submarines, was ordered to maintain a continuous daylight patrol from the North Goodwins to Gravelines and thence along the coast to Ostend. It was asking much for formations of no more than three Blenheims, Hudsons, Skuas or Rocs to fly over waters where the very thick of the enemy's single-engined fighters would be found, but the duty was faithfully and profitably discharged until the end of the evacuation.

Once again, then, the demand was for continuity. Though the area to be covered had now somewhat shrunk, Park was still unable to put up patrols at any greater average strength than two squadrons. And the 321 sorties flown by No. 11 Group in the course of the day still left short intervals when there was no cover at all. During the morning the *Luftwaffe* was up in force, and our fighters intercepted many powerful formations, one of which was thought to consist of no less than 150 aircraft; then the weather closed in, and in the afternoon our patrols sought in vain for the enemy. Though six ships were sunk and others damaged during the day, 28th May thus saw the evacuation once more making headway. By nightfall, Tennant was informing Ramsay 'Fighter protection has been invaluable, and . . . bombing only sporadic'.

By 29th May the greater part of the B.E.F. was inside the organized defences of the perimeter, our mine-sweepers had cleared a new middle route from Dover to Dunkirk, and destroyers and personnel vessels were again being directed to the port by day. Park, who had protested strenuously against the policy of continuous weak patrols, was now authorized by the Air Ministry to operate less often and at greater strength.

From this day onwards he accordingly arranged the No. 11 Group patrols so that up to four squadrons—sometimes in two separate formations—were over the Dunkirk area at the same time. The result on 29th May was stronger protection for eleven of the seventeen daylight hours, though during the other six there was no cover except by the small Coastal Command patrols. In the morning, when the enemy's attacks were light, these intermissions had no serious results; but we were not so fortunate during the afternoon and evening, when the German airmen began a new and devastating series of attacks against our shipping. At least five times they developed a concerted assault in strength; and though our fighters engaged the enemy on three of these occasions on the other two we had none present. The effect of the bombing on the evacuation is difficult to assess. From some accounts it appears to have been very great: eight vessels were lost from air attack, the harbour was again reported blocked, and the Admiralty withdrew our most modern destroyers. On the other hand many of our shipping losses occurred not from German bombs but from torpedo-boats and the ramming and firing of our own vessels. The harbour, too, was not in fact blocked, and had our vessels closed during the night they could doubtless have lifted large numbers of men. More definite pointers to the success of our air action were a report from the B.E.F. that it had suffered little bombing during the day, and an appreciative signal from Admiral Ramsay to Fighter Command—'I am most grateful for your splendid co-operation. It alone has given us a chance of success . . .'

The governing factor on 30th May was undoubtedly the weather. It was known from intercepted wireless messages that three hundred bombers, with fighter escort, were waiting to take off against our ships, but in the morning they were baulked by 10/10ths cloud between 300 and 3,000 feet. After the clouds had lifted a little during the afternoon, another intercept informed us that the attacks were about to begin. Small, spasmodic raids then followed, without much profit to the enemy. Once again No. 11 Group provided fighter protection at four-squadron strength for the greater part of the day, but this time there were no major battles. The small Coastal Command patrols more than once drove off single bombers.

The weather was not the only reason for the quickening of the evacuation on 30th May. The immortal flotillas of the 'little boats' had by now arrived; powered craft were rounding up the boats which had been cut adrift; the troops had built a pier of lorries at Bray; and the Admiralty allowed the modern destroyers to return. By the end of the day hopes ran high that the night of 31st May/1st June would see the last of the B.E.F. brought to safety. All this, of course, was gall and wormwood to Halder, who recorded: 'The consequence of the blunders forced upon us by Supreme War Headquarters (OKW) is beginning to be felt now. . . . The pocket would have been closed at the Coast if only our armour had not been held back. As it is, the bad weather has grounded our air force and now we must stand by and watch how countless thousands of the enemy are getting away to England under our noses.'

After early morning haze, 31st May cleared into a fine day. From intercepted signals it was known that the enemy's objective would be our shipping, not the town or the harbour installations. Sporadic attacks only, however, developed during the morning. Very different was the afternoon, when fierce assaults were aimed at our ships every thirty minutes or so. But nearly all were engaged, at some time or other, by our patrols. The three biggest raids in particular, while not entirely beaten back by our fighters, were sufficiently harassed for much of the bombing to go astray. As a result only one vessel was sunk by direct air attack, though no less than six destroyers were damaged in collisions. Things were thus still going well, even if artillery fire against the town at one end and the eastern beaches at the other was an ever-increasing menace. Still more strenuous efforts, however, would be needed; for the French had now decided to share in the withdrawal and the War Cabinet gave orders that they should be taken off in equal numbers with our own troops. The end of the evacuation, in sight the previous day, receded into the distance.

As 1st June broke, mist and low cloud again hung over Dunkirk, only to disperse with the rising sun. Never was the cool splendour of an early summer morning less appreciated by the men on the beaches. There had already been some fitful and ineffective raiding during the night. Now the real thing began, and No. 11 Group's first patrol was at once among the bombers. Then came a respite, while our second patrol was on the line. But as soon as this had turned for home, and before the third patrol could come up, a series of vicious attacks again developed. Thirty or forty Ju.87's made free with the shipping off shore and in the absence of our fighters descended, in more than one sense, to attacking struggling figures in the water. Only with the arrival of our third patrol did the raiders make off back to their bases. Furious fighting marked the rest of the morning—on one occasion twenty-eight Hurricanes were in combat with fifty or sixty Me.109's and 110's—but for a second time the enemy managed to deliver a major assault in an interval between our patrols. Then the clouds mercifully rolled over again, and the German effort dwindled and died away. Meantime ten vessels had been sunk, including three destroyers, and several others had suffered serious damage. Worse still, the enemy's guns were by this time covering the newly swept central route to Dunkirk as well as the direct and the eastern approaches. Confronted with this prospect of heavy losses from both aircraft and artillery, Ramsay felt himself bound to call a halt to evacuation in daylight. From now on the work could be done only by night. The operation would drag on even longer. Still more extreme demands would be made on the endurance of the devoted rescuers.

These events, disastrous as they seemed, nevertheless proved something of a blessing in disguise. For if the troops were to be lifted only during the night, the demand for continuous air cover would be relaxed and our fighters could be concentrated over the evacuation area in great strength at the two critical periods. These would be at dusk and dawn, when our ships were approaching and leaving Dunkirk.

The advantages of the new arrangements were soon seen. Although the beaches were shelled and a trawler was sunk in the harbour during the night of 1st/2nd June, loading went on according to plan and the early morning haze helped to cover the departure of our ships. In fact our first patrols found the skies clear of the enemy. Not until 0800 hours did the *Luftwaffe* appear on the scene; and it then encountered five full squadrons on patrol. A series of heavy engagements developed, in which the five squadrons took on something like 120 enemy aircraft. In spite of the odds against them the British squadrons inflicted severe losses on their opponents; but what was more important, the Germans were kept far too busy fighting for their lives to molest our ships. For the rest of the morning the enemy was largely content to send over single bombers, some of which were driven off by a Coastal Command patrol. No further incident occurred until the evening. By then our shipping was again approaching Dunkirk, and the four squadrons on patrol proved quite capable of thwarting a determined attack by escorted Ju.87's. The new plan had thus proved an unqualified success. Over the whole day no ships had been sunk and only two damaged—apart from the hospital carriers which had bravely but rashly presumed on German sentiments of humanity by approaching the harbour in daylight. And though the embarkation of our allies was going slowly—not through air attack or lack of ships, but through the French failure to organize a continuous flow of men—before midnight Tennant was able to send the signal for which Ramsay was waiting. It was brief, and infinitely welcome: 'B.E.F. evacuated'.

But the French were still waiting in their thousands, and for two nights more the heroic work of rescue continued. On 3rd June, as on 2nd June, embarkation ceased at first light and began again during the evening. Once more our fighter patrols were concentrated at the dawn period, but the mist was mercifully heavy, and the *Luftwaffe* remained on the ground. At about 0730 hours there was an inconclusive encounter with some Ju.87's, then the weather closed in entirely. No further patrols were flown for the remainder of the day, but the fighters remained on call to answer any appeal for help. None came.

Under an extremely effective combination of fog and fighter cover, more men were lifted on the morning of 4th June, but by then the time had come to call a halt. Twenty or thirty thousand French troops still remained in and around Dunkirk, but all ammunition was expended, the Germans were in a position to reach the sea along the whole front, and the end could not be long delayed. After the early morning embarkation had been completed the French accordingly acknowledged that further resistance was useless, and during the afternoon the machinery of 'Dynamo' was brought to a stop.

If the sequence of events during the evacuation is examined, it will be seen that the *Luftwaffe* enjoyed outstanding success only on 27th May and 1st June. On all other days it was in effect frustrated either by our fighter patrols or by bad visibility. Large numbers of attacks were still delivered on these lesser days, and for the men in the ships or on the beaches the ordeal was long and terrible. It would, however, have been far worse but for our fighters, whose interventions over and over again prevented prohibitive losses to our ships. Judged by the acid test of results the evacuation, carried out under the nose of superior forces both on land and in the air, was not merely a success but a triumph. In that triumph our airmen, as well as our sailors and soldiers, certainly bore their share.

In spite of any contemporary opinion to the contrary, then, the Royal Air Force was present, and effectively present, at Dunkirk. It was so much present that during the nine days its bombers flew 651 sorties, its reconnaissance aircraft 171 sorties and its fighters 2,739 sorties directly connected with the evacuation, apart from other work further afield. To assess its presence only in terms of numbers, however, would be very wrong. For its strength lay much less in its numbers than in its superb fighting spirit.

The quality of that spirit may perhaps be judged from two examples of the many that could be quoted. On the evening of 31st May, when our patrols were still endeavouring to cover the evacuation area throughout the whole day, Flight Lieutenant R. D. G. Wight of No. 213 Squadron wrote thus to his mother:

> Well, another day is gone, and with it a lot of grand blokes. Got another brace of 109's today, but the whole *Luftwaffe* seems to leap on us—we were hopelessly outnumbered. I was caught napping by a 109 in the middle of a dog fight, and got a couple of holes in the aircraft, one of them filled the office with smoke, but the Jerry overshot and *he's* dead. If anyone says anything to you in the future about the inefficiency of the R.A.F.—I believe the B.E.F. troops were booing the R.A.F. in Dover the other day—tell them from me we only wish we could do more. But without aircraft we can do no more than we have done—that is, our best, and that's fifty times better than the German best, though they are fighting under the most advantageous conditions. I know of no R.A.F. pilot who has refused combat yet—and that sometimes means combat with odds of more than fifty to one. Three of us the other day had been having a fight, and were practically out of ammunition and juice when we saw more than eighty 109's with twelve Ju.87's, all the same we gave them combat, so much so that they left us alone in the end—on their side of the Channel, too. This is not a tale of stirring heroism. It is just the work that we all do. One of my sergeants shot down three fighters and a bomber before they got him—and then he got back in a paddle steamer. So don't worry, we are going to win this war even if we have only one aeroplane and one pilot left—the Boche could produce the whole *Luftwaffe* and you would see the one pilot and the one aeroplane go into combat. All that sounds very involved, but I am trying to convey to you something of the spirit of 'Per ardua ad astra' today. The spirit of the average pilot has to be seen to be believed.

It may be added that Flight Lieutenant Wight continued to live up to the spirit of which he wrote. Ten weeks later, during the Battle of

Britain, he was killed leading three Hurricanes into a formation of sixty Me.110's.

Our bomber pilots were cast in no different mould. The story of Wing Commander B. E. Embry, Commanding Officer of No. 107 Squadron, is unusual in its details, but typical in its substance.

Embry was shot down on 27th May while leading an attack on a German column approaching Dunkirk. Though wounded in the leg, he baled out successfully, but on landing was at once captured. His morale never for one moment faltered. Ordered to salute a Prussian captain, he maintained that the captain should salute him. Subjected to the usual 'grilling', he resolutely refused to divulge the slightest information; indeed, he later reversed the process by systematically collecting intelligence of the enemy's anti-aircraft defences. For when he had been set to march towards Germany, he quickly detached himself from the long column of half-starved men, and (after two days of attempting to move without being seen), discarded his uniform, fitted himself up with a civilian coat from a scarecrow, and was soon making for the Allied lines south of the Somme.

His subsequent adventures had all the elements of good schoolboy fiction. Trapped raiding an empty farmhouse for food, he spent 36 hours in a loft, hiding in straw, with German troops billeted below. Seized by a German patrol and lodged in a farmhouse under armed guard—with a warning that he would be shot if he turned out to be English—he knocked out his gaoler with a well-timed blow to the jaw, snatched the German's rifle, brought it down on the head of the guard outside the door, delivered a passing blow against a third German encountered in the hall, and dived into a huge pile of manure in the farmyard, where he remained undetected until nightfall. Later, after operating on his own leg to remove shrapnel, he was once more 'picked up'; his pose as a Belgian breaking down before the fluent French of his German interrogator, he stated that he was really a Southern Irishman 'wanted' for bomb outrages in London—and satisfied his captor's request to talk Gaelic by rattling off a few sentences in Urdu. Then, failing to find either the Allied armies or a boat on the coast, he broke into a garage, built himself a bicycle from spare parts, and—though he knew that Paris had by then fallen— made for the capital with the intention of seeking help as an American. A German soldier commandeered his bicycle, but he got to Paris all the same; and though he failed to hoodwink the American Embassy, he at length acquired another bicycle and set off for the south of France. Over and over again he was challenged; always he put up some convincing story. At last he reached a district still held by the French, and after many difficulties left Perpignan for Gibraltar.

Thence he was brought back to England by the Royal Navy, to arrive at Plymouth ten weeks after being shot down.

The story of Wing Commander Embry is, in a sense, the story of Dunkirk. According to the laws of probability his chances of surviving all these incidents were negligible—but he did. In the same way, on 26th May 1940, some 340,000 Englishmen and Frenchmen had, in theory, little or no chance of escaping from Dunkirk—but they did. Granted a measure of good fortune, Embry owed his freedom to his resourcefulness, his skill, his toughness, his optimism and his courage. It was because these qualities were so widely shared by his fellow airmen that the Royal Air Force, for all its slender numbers, was able to play so worthy a part in the 'miracle of deliverance'.

*   *   *

After the Battle of the North, the Battle of France. It was hardly worthy of the name. If 134 Allied divisions at the opening of the campaign had been unable to hold the enemy, the 63 divisions now remaining were not likely to fare much better. During the brief respite of Dunkirk, while the Germans regrouped for their drive southwards, the French hastily pulled what units they could out of the Maginot fortifications. Their intention was not only to contain the enemy along the Aisne and the Somme, but also to form, somewhat belatedly, a *masse de manœuvre*. But the troops along the Aisne–Somme line remained ridiculously thin on the ground—each division held, on the average, twelve kilometres in place of the prescribed six—while whatever was scraped together as a reserve was neither massive nor manœuvrable.

When the Germans opened their new offensive on 5th June they accordingly broke through wherever they pleased. By the evening of the 5th their right was across the Somme; by the 7th, their left was over the Aisne. By the 10th they were beyond the Seine at one end of the front and the Marne at the other, while the French government was in flight to Tours. Where the lion led the way the jackal was ready to follow, and by the 11th France faced Mussolini's Italians in the Alps. By the 14th the forces which had crossed the Marne were wheeling east to take the Maginot Line in the rear, the French government was seeking safety at Bordeaux, and German boots were once more ringing down the Champs Elysées. By the 15th the Maginot had been pierced from the front, the French armies were in isolated groups scattered across the breadth of France, and coherent defence was at an end.

The opening of the battle found the Bomber Command 'heavies' in the course of a renewed attack against German oil targets, to which they had at once been redirected by the Air Staff as soon as the B.E.F. was saved. By 8th June their main objective was once more the enemy's communications in northern France, and against these they now maintained a steady effort until the end of the campaign. The Blenheims continued to operate by daylight against German columns, and in particular those pressing towards the Seine, while the Battles of the A.A.S.F. attacked troop movements by day and communications by night. In addition Fighter Command for some days flew intensive patrols over the remaining British troops in the coastal sector, including the 51st Division in its march to captivity and glory at St. Valéry. The evacuation from Le Havre was also covered. But from then on fighters from England could no longer reach the main battle zones by direct flight, and the overrunning of our newly opened bases near the lower Seine prevented them refuelling in France.

During these desperate days the Royal Air Force spared no effort to stem the flood of disaster. An air force very much larger, however, would have battled in vain where the ground forces were so unequally matched. Only in one matter were French requests or expectations rebuffed. To all the fervent pleas for the transfer of Fighter Command's resources to French soil—General Vuillemin, the French Chief of Air Staff, demanded at least twenty more of our squadrons—a firm front was presented. In the three and half weeks between 10th May and the end of the Dunkirk evacuation we had expended no less than 432 Hurricanes and Spitfires. To continue at the same rate was impossible. While their range permitted, our fighters would accordingly operate from England or refuel at French bases, but on no account must further squadrons be sent across the Channel. Only on 7th June, when Nos. 17 and 242 Squadrons were ordered to join the A.A.S.F., was this decision in any way modified; and by then the War Cabinet and the Air Staff were looking ahead to the problem of fighter protection over the final withdrawal.

Another, though lesser, source of disagreement between the Allies was the policy to be adopted towards Italy. This had already been thrashed out during the previous months, when both countries were taking all possible steps to placate Mussolini; and on 31st May, when the *Duce*'s decision to intervene became clear, the Supreme War Council had finally agreed that an Italian declaration of war should be the signal for British aircraft to bomb the industries of northern Italy. To this end, No. 71 Wing Headquarters, which had operated Battles during the opening days of the campaign, had been sent down to the Marseilles area on 3rd June with the task of making the necessary preparations on two French airfields. The intention was that this organization, which laboured under the uninspiring code-name of 'Haddock', would act as a refuelling and operational base for Wellingtons from England, while the longer range Whitleys refuelled in the Channel Islands. In the circumstances of the moment, when the survival of France depended on her ability to beat back the new German offensive, the venture naturally appeared somewhat super-fluous to those on the spot. Despite this, 'Haddock' force was ready to receive its Wellingtons when Italy declared war as from midnight on 10th June.

By then, however, France was dissolving into chaos. Further, the French fighters normally concerned with defence against Italy had long since been thrown into the battle in the north. At such a time it seemed to the French the worst of policies for the Royal Air Force to open an offensive against an enemy whose retaliation might well fall, not on London, but on Marseilles, Lyons and Paris. And on the evening of 11th June this conviction led to remarkable happenings.

The sequence of events that night amply bears out the truth of the old military proverb: 'Order—Counter-order—Disorder'. Group Captain R. M. Field, the commander of 'Haddock' force at Salon airfield, must surely have thought that he was in the grip of some fiendish nightmare. At 1530 hours a squadron of Wellingtons— No. 99—arrived from England. They had barely touched down when the nearest French Bomber Group telephoned to say that in no cir-cumstances were Italian targets to be attacked. Field was still think-ing this over when he received the executive order from Air Ministry to despatch the aircraft. Then the telephone rang again. From one French authority after another the same message arrived: operations against Italy were forbidden.

Meanwhile the same scene was reproducing itself on a higher level. At 2145 hours General Vuillemin phoned B.A.F.F. Headquarters— would Barratt cancel operations against Italy? Confronted with this demand, Barratt felt obliged to consult the Air Ministry: he got through to Whitehall only to be told to ask the Prime Minister, who had left for France. A call to Weygand's Headquarters then elicited from General Ismay the Prime Minister's opinion that the operations should proceed. But Barratt had scarcely hung up the receiver when Field came through to explain what was happening at Salon. Again Barratt appealed to Ismay, who this time returned a more forcible reply: the French had officially agreed to the operation, the Whitleys were already on their way from the Channel Islands, the Wellingtons must take off as arranged.

These proceedings were duly made known to the perplexed com-mander of 'Haddock' force, who thereupon prepared to send off his aircraft. Then once more his telephone began to ring. For the next two and a half hours it scarcely stopped. Successively higher tiers of French officials informed Field, not once but many times, that on no account must his bombers take off against Italy. All this Field ignored, and at last, a few minutes after midnight, the first Wellington began to taxi into position. As it lumbered along, several French lorries appeared from beside the hangars and drove rapidly across the airfield. They then stopped in a pre-arranged pattern admirably designed to block take-off and landing.

This move could have been countered only by force; for the orders of the local French commander, it appeared, were to keep the Wellingtons on the ground at all costs. But since it was now very late, and the weather was growing worse over the mountains, there was little point in pressing matters to the exchange of blows, or still worse, shots. Bowing to the inevitable, Field called off the night's operations.

Meanwhile the Whitleys of Nos. 10, 51, 58, 77 and 102 Squadrons, which had refuelled in the Channel Islands, were having little better fortune. Thirty-six aircraft had taken off, but only thirteen reached Turin and Genoa; the rest found the heavy storms and severe icing conditions over the Alps too great a strain on their engines. Indeed there were so many cases of engine failure that it was widely, though wrongly, suspected that saboteurs had 'sugared' the petrol.

Four nights later, after the episode of the lorries had been sorted out in high places and strong terms, eight Wellingtons of Nos. 99 and 149 Squadrons took off from Salon to bomb industrial objectives in Genoa. They ran into violent thunder-storms and had great difficulty in finding their targets. Only one aircraft attacked; the remainder returned with their bombs. The next night, 16th/17th June, a further attempt was made by nine Wellingtons, four of which failed to find their objectives. The following day the French negotiations for an armistice ended a singularly unprofitable venture.

The 'Haddock' organization in the South of France, whatever its other difficulties, was at least fairly safe from the immediate attentions of the German Army. Not so the main body of the A.A.S.F. With great foresight Barratt had withdrawn this force from the South Champagne to the region around Orléans and Le Mans in the brief lull before the enemy's second offensive. From this central position and from the refuelling bases retained in the South Champagne it was well placed to intervene along the whole line of battle. But when on 11th June the enemy broke through the French positions on the Marne, Oise and Seine—the last line on which any hope of successful resistance could be built—every unit was endangered. By 12th June Air Vice-Marshal Sholto Douglas, the Deputy Chief of Air Staff, was writing to warn Barratt to prepare for a quick withdrawal from

France. His letter crossed with one from Barratt requesting direction on the same subject. Thoughts of this kind came none too soon. The next day Mr. Churchill learned in Tours that Weygand was pressing for an immediate armistice, and that even Reynaud was begging to be released from the obligation not to treat separately with the enemy.

There was nothing for it now but to take the last step towards the west coast. Fresh bases were secured near Angers, Saumur, Rennes and Nantes, but only with great difficulty; for as the enemy covered the breadth of France, so the few airfields left to our allies became more and more congested. No. 1 Squadron, for instance, arrived at Nantes to find 'so many aircraft on the airfield that it looked like several Empire Air Days all at once'. To retain the whole force in such a position would have been to invite its destruction on the ground. Bearing in mind that his bombers could operate from home, Barratt took a generous interpretation of his instructions and on 15th June ordered the Battles back to England. The surviving aircraft reached Abingdon that afternoon.

It remained for the A.A.S.F. fighters to cover the evacuation of the ground staff and of the three remaining British divisions under Lt. General Alan Brooke. But evacuation, other than that of 'surplus stores and personnel' had not yet been officially ordered from home. For though there was now no conceivable military justification for retaining our forces in France, there was some natural fear that our withdrawal would prejudice the French against continuing the fight from North Africa. By midnight on 16th June, however, that question, though not yet decided, was heavily compromised. Spurning the hastily considered and quixotic offer of union with Great Britain, the French Ministers entrusted the fate of their country to Pétain. The aged victor of Verdun had been agitating since 5th June for the premiership and peace. He now had the one; and he at once set out to get the other. His approach to the Germans on 17th June was the signal for the complete evacuation of the British forces.

Barratt's task was now to cover seven ports with five squadrons. It was merely another variant of a problem with which the Royal Air Force was already thoroughly familiar—how to make a pint go as far as a gallon. To La Pallice and La Rochelle, the ports of which the least use would be made, Barratt sent the anti-aircraft batteries which had defended the A.A.S.F. airfields. For Nantes and St. Nazaire, whence the flow of troops would be heaviest, he grouped three squadrons—Nos. 1, 73 and 242. For Brest he arranged a small detachment from the squadrons at Nantes. And for St. Malo and Cherbourg he ordered protection by two squadrons—Nos. 17 and 501—at first from Dinard, then from the Channel Islands. Fighter

Command aircraft from Tangmere would also give help over Cherbourg, while Coastal Command would protect returning vessels. With these arrangements made, Barratt then took off for England. The final operations came under the control of his Senior Air Staff Officer, Air Vice-Marshal D. C. S. Evill, who had been throughout the campaign, in Barratt's words, 'a tower of strength'.

In spite of the inevitably sparse nature of the cover provided, and in spite of 'scenes of indescribable confusion' at Nantes, the evacuation was entirely successful. The *Luftwaffe* dropped bombs by day and mines by night, but achieved remarkably little. Only off St. Nazaire, where on the afternoon of 17th June German bombers making their third attempt within two hours sank the *Lancastria* with five thousand troops aboard, was there a major disaster. In this case the enemy made clever use of cloud cover to elude our patrolling Hurricanes.

By the afternoon of 18th June the ground forces had made good their escape, and the fighters, most of whom had flown six sorties on the previous day, were free to depart. After No. 73 Squadron had flown the final patrol, the last Hurricanes left Nantes for Tangmere and the mechanics set fire to the unserviceable machines. A little time was lost while a thoughtful sergeant gave one of the staff cars to a well-disposed café proprietor nearby, and while a more commercially-minded airman endeavoured to sell an Austin Seven. Then the rear parties of the ground and operations staff took off in transport aircraft. A few hours later German tanks came rumbling into Nantes.

* * *

Except at Dunkirk, where decisive results were achieved by a concentration in space impossible at any other time in the campaign, the effect of the Royal Air Force on the course of the German advance was very limited. Some delay was imposed on the enemy ground forces by the Battles and Blenheims in the opening days, though only at prohibitive cost; while the Wellingtons, Hampdens and Whitleys, operating by night and handicapped by cross-currents in policy, proved a harassing, not a deterrent, force. Valuable information was obtained by the reconnaissance aircraft, among which the high-flying Spitfires were a triumph, the Blenheims useful but expensive, the Lysanders altogether too slow and defenceless to survive in the face of the German fighter patrols. But even when the enemy's columns were spotted and his intentions realized, his attacks still proved irresistible.

The work of our fighters, however, was truly rewarding. For whatever else it did, the *Luftwaffe* scored no cheap or easy success. How many of the 1,284 aircraft lost by the enemy can be credited to the Royal Air Force, and how many to the air forces and ground

L

defences of our allies, is entirely uncertain, but there is no doubt that a very substantial proportion fell to the Royal Air Force, and particularly the Component. This, it is true, made no difference to the result of the campaign. But it was not without importance for the campaign that was to follow.

The British air forces involved in this first great clash were very small compared with those which later assailed the enemy in Africa, in Italy, in France, in his homeland, on the seas, and wherever else he reared his unattractive head. But they were very much the heart, soul and body of the Royal Air Force at the time; for the whole strength of the A.A.S.F., the Component and Bomber Command was continuously engaged in the struggle, together with a great part of the resources of Fighter and Coastal Commands. Any extensive misuse or mishandling of our squadrons would thus have destroyed virtually our entire Air Force, at once shattering our only offensive weapon and throwing open the British Isles to invasion.

Fortunately the Air Force was not misused. Or rather, such misuse as became apparent was at once corrected. After the first few days the low-flying attacks by Battles were stopped, the Blenheims were given stronger and closer fighter protection. Defects in organization were also remedied: by desperate means the A.A.S.F., originally designed as a static formation, was given the mobility essential for an air force in the field. Above all, two temptations were firmly resisted. The main strategic striking force of Wellingtons, Whitleys and Hampdens was used only by night, where its losses, at two per cent of sorties, were low enough to ensure its continued existence and expansion. And the main strength of Fighter Command, deeply committed though it was to the conflict, was safeguarded by the refusal to continue the flow across the Channel.

In May and June 1940, 959 of our aircraft, of which 477 were fighters, were lost to little apparent avail. Every operational command at home and in France suffered heavily: the A.A.S.F. lost 229, the Component 279, Fighter Command 219, Bomber Command 166, Coastal Command 66. All this sacrifice, and all the abiding heroism of the crews that came back, could not compensate for the weakness of the French Army. Yet the work of the Royal Air Force was far from wasted. Our squadrons had exacted a high toll of the enemy, had contributed notably to the salvation of the B.E.F., and had learned many lessons in the bitter school of experience. And though nothing within the bounds of sense had been withheld from the struggle, the Service had still emerged strong enough to fight, and win, the crucial battle of the war—not after long years of painful reconstruction, but within a few brief weeks.

CHAPTER VI
The Battle of Britain

'What General Weygand called the Battle of France is over. I expect that the Battle of Britain is about to begin... The whole fury and might of the enemy must very soon be turned on us. Hitler knows that he will have to break us in this island or lose the war. If we can stand up to him, all Europe may be free and the life of the world may move forward into broad sunlit uplands. But if we fail, then the whole world, including the United States, including all that we have known and cared for, will sink into the abyss of a new Dark Age made more sinister, and perhaps more protracted, by the lights of perverted science. Let us therefore brace ourselves to our duties, and so bear ourselves that, if the British Empire and its Commonwealth last for a thousand years, men will still say, "This was their finest hour".'

The Prime Minister's call evoked its due response. A fierce determination inspired the armament industry. Tired workers emerged from long hours in office and workshop to march with the Local Defence Volunteers. Dawn and dusk found men on church towers and hilltops, scanning the skies for the white flutter of parachutes. Barbed wire and concrete sprouted surrealistically from south coast beaches; trenches scarred the immemorial green of the downs. Crazy obstructions blocked the roads, sign-posts disappeared overnight, bewildered motorists were 'picked up' for members of the fifth column. Recruits on the front at Blackpool drilled with dummy rifles roughly shaped from pieces of wood. Airmen in maintenance units armed themselves with two-foot lengths of gas-piping.

The German occupation of France and Belgium, which had prompted this activity, confronted the Royal Air Force with new and immense problems. Apart from the greatly heightened menace to our sea-borne trade and the imminent prospect of invasion, there was the brute fact that the world's largest air force was now within an hour's flight of the world's largest target. Our defences, too, could be easily outflanked. The radar cover round our shores had been built up against an enemy based in Germany and perhaps occupying some portion of the Low Countries; it could certainly not yet cope with an enemy established all round the coast of Europe from the Arctic to the Pyrenees.

Two needs were paramount: the extension of the air defence system to the relatively unprotected north and west, and the greatest possible increase in the strength of Fighter Command. By good fortune, or rather, good management, schemes for the defence of the unprotected areas were already approved and under way. They were at once speeded up. At the beginning of June there was only one fighter squadron based further west than Middle Wallop, in Hampshire; two months later there were seven. With the fighter squadrons went the radar chain and the observer posts. At the time of Dunkirk there were still only three fighter groups—Nos. 11, 12 and 13. By the opening of the Battle of Britain a new group in the south-west (No. 10) was fully operational, and two other groups for the defence of north-west England and northern Scotland (Nos. 9 and 14) were nearing completion.

This extension of the reporting and control organization supplied the basis on the ground for efficient operation in the air; it did not, of course, provide the necessary aircraft and crews. Of these two needs, that for more aircraft was at the moment the greater. Indeed, the urgency of this demand had already, on 14th May, caused the Air Ministry's research and production departments to be detached from their parent body and formed into a separate Ministry of Aircraft Production under Lord Beaverbrook.

It is in the history of our war production rather than in the history of the Royal Air Force that the work of that dynamic and controversial figure must be fully assessed. Here it is enough to mention the details of the planned and the actual production in the three months before and after the creation of M.A.P., and to indicate some of the governing conditions at the time. The figures are so important that they should be set out in full:

Month	Planned production of all types by the Harrogate[1] programme of January 1940	Actual production of all types	Planned production of fighters by the Harrogate programme	Actual fighter production
February 1940 .	1,001	719	171	141
March 1940 .	1,137	860	203	177
April 1940 . .	1,256	1,081	231	256
May 1940 . .	1,244	1,279	261	325
June 1940 . .	1,320	1,591	292	446
July 1940 . .	1,481	1,665	329	496
August 1940 .	1,310	1,601	282	476

[1] The production departments of the Air Ministry were evacuated to Harrogate in September 1939.

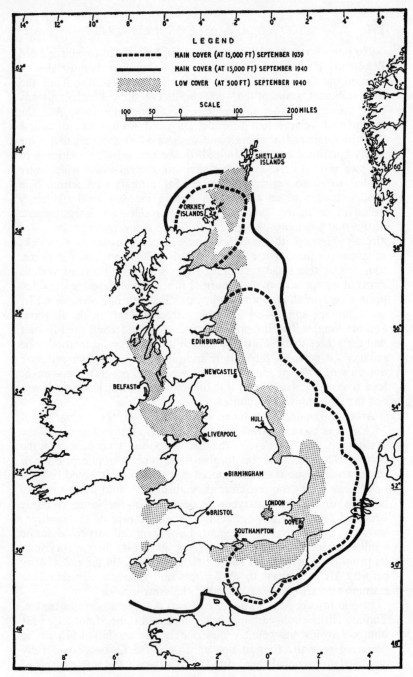

RADAR COVER, SEPTEMBER 1939 AND SEPTEMBER 1940

No one who studies these statistics will be inclined to belittle Lord Beaverbrook's work. In justice to others, however, it must also be pointed out that, as the substantial rise in output during April and May indicates, some of the worst production difficulties had already been overcome before the creation of the new ministry. And the magnificent achievement of June, July and August was of course the achievement of the aircraft industry as a whole, not only that of the newly appointed Minister. Indeed, Beaverbrook had, in addition to his own unique drive and determination, several assets which were denied to those earlier responsible for aircraft production. The deadly danger which confronted Britain in May 1940 obviously called for an 'all out' policy of immediate results; and it was because of this that Beaverbrook was able to secure an overriding priority for aircraft above all other munitions, as well as permission to use stocks of spares for the construction of new aircraft. The Royal Air Force, too, was at this stage prepared to accept aircraft short of various items of equipment which in normal times would have been insisted upon as essential. And above all, Lord Beaverbrook was helped by the 'Dunkirk spirit'—by the great surge of effort in the factories and the long, willing hours of overtime. All these assets the Minister had the genius to exploit to the full. In the long run his method—the reliance on personal inspiration and 'hunches', the utter rejection not only of red tape but of all closely planned programmes—might lead to confusion and even loss of production. But just now it was not the long run which counted.

Among the decisions taken immediately on the formation of M.A.P. was to concentrate on producing five types of aircraft—the Wellington, the Whitley V, the Blenheim, the Hurricane and the Spitfire. The intention was to give these types absolute priority of materials and labour for some months; other aircraft would be built only in so far as the resources they absorbed could not be readily diverted to the selected types. Production of the latter certainly benefited from this arrangement. The importance of the decision, however, has been vastly exaggerated. A rule of this sort could not be applied for long without creating chaos; in fact it failed to survive in its primitive simplicity for more than a fortnight. By the end of May priority 1A was given to all fighters and bombers. By mid-June training aircraft had to be placed in the same category.

In one respect M.A.P. and the Royal Air Force were fortunate. Though Hitler could certainly have unleashed some, if not all, of his bombers against this country immediately after the fall of France, he preferred to wait: to wait not only until the *Luftwaffe* was fully deployed on French, Belgian and Dutch airfields, and thus capable of a much bigger effort, but also to wait until the British had enjoyed a few weeks' grace in which to consider surrender. The days passed, and no British 'feeler' emerged—could the obstinate islanders be banking on the intervention of America, or even Russia? The *Führer* was not to know that the matter had been virtually decided at the very depth of our misfortunes, when to the defeat of France it appeared that there would be added the loss of the entire British Expeditionary Force. For on 25th May the British Chiefs of Staff, reviewing the course of action to be adopted if France fell, had reported, on the strength of information supplied by the Ministry of Economic Warfare, that—always provided we had full Pan-American economic and financial co-operation—we might well produce a critical economic situation in Germany by the middle of 1941.

Reasonably unmindful of this invincible optimism, Hitler did not seriously consider the necessity for invading England until mid-July—though as a precautionary measure he had instructed the German Services to begin planning a little earlier. The German Navy, though not the German Army, had in fact already anticipated this order. The rejection of his public peace offer of 19th July then confirmed what had by now become clear even to Hitler—that the British had no intention of giving up without a struggle. Three days before this he had issued his personal directive for invasion—an invasion which in the given state of German preparations could not possibly take place before mid-September.

It was to this project—Operation 'Sealion', as it was called—that Hitler harnessed German air action. Six weeks before the date when all was to be ready, the *Luftwaffe* would launch a major offensive against the Royal Air Force; and in the light of the degree of air superiority attained in the following fortnight, Hitler could then decide if the German Army's journey across the Channel would be either practicable or really necessary. Meanwhile, until the end of the first week in August, Göring's aircraft would reconnoitre and probe our defences, molest our shipping, and husband their strength for the great day. As for what would then happen, the Germans were supremely confident. 'It will take', reported General Stapf to Halder on 11th July, 'between a fortnight and a month to smash the enemy air force.'

The German decision to postpone major air action was of the utmost service to Beaverbrook and to all those who were so feverishly working to repair our deficiencies. From Dunkirk to the opening of the Battle of Britain there were two whole and entirely precious months in which our fighters, though busily engaged, were not exposed to unduly heavy wastage. The grievous losses incurred in the fighting over France could thus be made good, and a respectable reserve built up for the days of intensive action which lay ahead. Indeed, some of this reserve was actually incorporated in the front line, for an extra flight of four aircraft, without pilots, was added to most of the single-engined fighter squadrons. They were to be flown in emergency by those pilots who at less critical moments would have been resting or on leave.

In certain circumstances the production of aircraft may be rapidly accelerated. It is more difficult to speed up the production of trained crews. The severe winter of 1939-1940 had been bad for flying training; the front line had already been enlarged at the expense of the training organization; and nearly 300 fighter pilots had been lost over France and the Low Countries. In spite of the timely and altogether invaluable loan of fifty-eight pilots from the Fleet Air Arm, it was thus quite impossible at one and the same time to bring the existing fighter squadrons up to full strength and to form new squadrons which would be capable of fighting in the immediate future. The existing squadrons were duly built up and several new ones were formed; but from the end of July to the end of September only five of the new squadrons could be added to the operational strength of Fighter Command. One of these was No. 1. Squadron of the Royal Canadian Air Force, which reached this country on 20th June; the other four—Nos. 302, 303, 310 and 312—were flown by the heroic remnants of the air forces of Poland and Czechoslovakia.

In mid-August, when the Battle of Britain opened, Dowding's squadrons were not very different in number from those available at the close of the Dunkirk evacuation. But they were in altogether better fettle. For whereas on 4th June he had 446 operationally serviceable aircraft, of which 331 were Hurricanes and Spitfires, on 11th August he disposed 704 operationally serviceable aircraft. among which the Hurricanes and Spitfires totalled no less than 620, Even in the front line, then, his effective fighting force had almost doubled. And behind this there was now a far stronger backing of reserves. On 4th June there had been 36 Hurricanes and Spitfires immediately available for issue to the squadrons from the Aircraft Storage Units. On August 11th there were 289.

The fighter defences were thus restored, strengthened and extended; but they were still, of course, far short of what was considered necessary. When the Air Staff reviewed the strategical consequences of the fall of France they concluded that Fighter Command needed at least double its existing strength of sixty squadrons. Since there was not the slightest chance that this number, or anything like it, could be produced in the near future, the review was to that extent

DUNKIRK

A Hudson of Coastal Command patrolling during the evacuation

FEW

his pilots, photographed during a reunion

and Bar, Wg. Cdr. I. R. Gleed, D.S.O., D.F.C., Wg. Cdr. M. Aitken, D.S.O., D.F.C.,
Hugh C. T. Dowding (now Lord Dowding), G.C.B., G.C.V.O., C.M.G., Flt. Off. E. C.
g. Cdr. C. B. F. Kingcome, D.F.C., Sqn. Ldr. D. H. Watkins, D.F.C. and Wt. Off.

AIRCRAFT CEMETERY

German aircraft shot down during the Battle of Britain being dismantled for raw material

academic. All the same, it showed how far Dowding was from having a fully adequate force for the situation in which he now found himself. Still more alarming, however, was the shortage of anti-aircraft guns, both heavy and light. Even before the war the Chiefs of Staff had recommended the provision of just over 4,000 guns; a fresh survey of requirements now placed the figure at something over 8,000; but the total number actually possessed by Anti-Aircraft Command at the beginning of August was less than 2,000. And with our small output of these weapons—the average number of heavy guns added to the home defences throughout the latter half of 1940 was only forty a month—there could be no quick improvement. Searchlights and balloons were more nearly up to the approved totals, though far below what was desirable.

Since the immediate additions to the gun defences could be so few, Dowding had to find some other answer to the problem of close protection. His solution, effected in concert with General Pile of Anti-Aircraft Command—who was operationally responsible to Dowding as head of the entire air defence system, but in practice a colleague rather than a subordinate—was to redeploy the existing resources. He accordingly lessened the gun density in many areas, including London, and concentrated no less than a quarter of our entire strength in heavy guns for the defence of the aircraft industry—on which our capacity to resist now more than ever depended. At the same time, so far as his means allowed, he strengthened the defence of many of the aircraft factories by balloon barrages. These, like the balloons protecting our towns, were installed, administered and operated by Air Vice-Marshal O. T. Boyd's Balloon Command under the operational control of Fighter Command. Finally, Dowding was able in some cases to protect the aircraft factories with the installation known as P.A.C. (Parachute and Cable). By this device a system of rockets arranged in line and attached to light steel cables carrying parachutes was electrically discharged on the approach of a hostile aircraft. The rockets ascended to some 600 feet, the parachutes opened, and the dangling cables formed a brief but deadly obstacle in the path of the raider.

* * *

Meanwhile the *Luftwaffe* was preparing for its task. Three *Luft-flotten*, or Air Fleets, were to take part in the operations against the British Isles. *Luftflotte* 2, under Kesselring, was based in Holland, Belgium and north-east France: *Luftflotte* 3, under Sperrle, in north and north-west France: *Luftflotte* 5, under Stumpff, in Norway and Denmark. Together their resources amounted to some 3,500 aircraft; and with 75 per cent of these serviceable they could be sure of having at least 250 dive-bombers, 1,000 long-range bombers and 1,000 fighters ready for the opening of the offensive. Throughout the last week of July the operations staff at *Luftwaffe* Headquarters and the staffs of the three *Luftflotten* laboured on their plans for the great *Adlerangriff*, or Eagle-attack, which in a few swift strokes would shatter the Royal Air Force as it had earlier shattered the air forces of Poland and France. On 2nd August the final directive was issued to the *Luftflotten*; all was decided save the exact date. A few days later and that too was settled. Given the right weather, the grand assault would begin on 10th August.

While these plans were being perfected, and while all was being made ready on the newly occupied airfields, the *Luftwaffe* used no more than five to ten per cent of its strength on active operations. Its main tasks during this preliminary period were reconnaissance of our airfields, 'experience' flights over the English coast, night training, and attacks on our Channel shipping. All these duties except the last were combined with the further function of harassing the British population and testing its morale.

The first operations over England in any strength were flown on the night of 5/6th June, when some thirty aircraft attacked airfields and other objectives near the east coast. Similar attacks were made on the following night; then there was a lull until the French request for an armistice on 17th June. But from the moment France was disposed of, and until the daylight offensive was well under way, German aircraft ranged over England almost every night. The force employed was never more than sixty or seventy bombers; its losses rarely amounted to more than one or two aircraft. Apart from their reconnaissance and training value, the operations were thus a cheap means of maintaining pressure until the full weight of the German air arm descended upon us. At first they caused great inconvenience and some loss of production—not from the actual damage inflicted, but from the perpetual and protracted air raid alarms; on 24/25th June, for instance, the whole of the country south of a line from Hull to Liverpool was under the 'red' warning, though only Bristol was threatened by more than one or two aircraft. But as soon as we accepted the chance of the odd bomb falling unannounced and sounded the siren more sparingly (a remedy also adopted in Germany at this time against the activity of Bomber Command) the *Luftwaffe's* night operations were seen to be singularly ineffective—almost as ineffective as the efforts of our guns, searchlights and night-fighters to prevent them.

German operations over the Channel were not much more fruitful, though these confronted Fighter Command with difficulties beyond its immediate capacity to resolve. The *Luftwaffe* had no lack of targets, for though most of our ocean-going convoys were by now taking a route west of Ireland a few still used the Channel, and there was an almost continuous procession of coastal convoys. In terms of vessels sunk, the enemy's daylight attacks were but moderately rewarded—in the month preceding the Battle of Britain they sank some 40,000 tons—and the Germans obtained an almost equal return, at far less expense, from their mine-laying by night. But the flying-effort forced on Fighter Command by the daylight attacks was very large, amounting to some 600 sorties a day; and since the fighter escorts with our ships were of necessity small, and the warning usually too short for further squadrons to reach the convoys before the attack developed, most of the combats found our pilots at a grave disadvantage. Over and over again a mere handful of Spitfires and Hurricanes found themselves fighting desperately with formations of a hundred or more German aircraft. It says everything for the skill and valour of our airmen that in these circumstances 227 enemy air-craft were shot down between 10th July and 10th August, while we ourselves lost only 96.

These days of chase and combat over the Channel soon revealed the need for some better means of rescuing 'ditched' aircrew. The existing system depended on search by ships in the vicinity, Royal Air Force high-speed launches, and whatever aircraft could be spared by Coastal Command or the station of the lost aircraft. What was needed was on the one hand the certainty that specially-equipped aeroplanes would be instantly available, on the other hand the development of all possible devices by which crashed airmen could indicate their position and remain alive until help arrived. In both respects the Germans were well ahead. They already had some thirty He.59 float-planes equipped for rescue work over the sea; and their single-engined fighters, like the bomber and reconnaissance aircraft on both sides, carried an inflatable dinghy at a time when our Hurricane and Spitfire pilots had to rely entirely on their Mae Wests. The German aircrews were also provided with fluorescine, a chemical which stained the sea around their dinghy bright green. For our part we refused to recognize the right of the He.59's to bear the Red Cross —they would certainly have used their immunity to report our convoys—and from 14th July our fighters were under orders to shoot them down. As a more constructive measure we imitated the device of fluorescine. By the end of July, Air Vice-Marshal Park at No. 11 Group, acting in co-operation with the Vice-Admiral at Dover, had also succeeded in borrowing some Lysander aircraft to work syste-matically with the launches and other craft—an event which marked a start towards a truly comprehensive organization for Air-Sea Rescue. Few investments of aircraft were to yield more precious dividends.

How badly we needed special aircraft for this purpose may be seen from the almost fortuitous fashion in which our airmen were being picked up from the sea. The case of Pilot Officer Stevenson of No. 74 Squadron is not unrepresentative. Early on 11th August his squadron was ordered to intercept enemy aircraft over Dover. Stevenson sighted a single Me.109. His combat report tells the rest of the story:

> I climbed up to him. He must have thought I was a Me.109 but when he suddenly dived away I followed him and gave a two-seconds deflection burst. The E/A [enemy aircraft] lurched slightly and went into a vertical dive. I kept my height at 15,000 feet and watched. I saw the E/A dive straight into the sea fifteen miles South East of Dover and disappear in a big splash of water. I then climbed to 23,000 feet up sun and saw a formation of twelve Me.109's 2,000 feet beneath me, proceeding North of Dover. It was my intention to attach myself to the back of this formation from out of the sun, and spray the whole formation. As I was diving for them, a really large volume of cannon and machine-gun fire came from behind. There were about twelve Me. 109's diving at me from the sun and at least half of them must have been firing deflection shots at me. There was a popping noise and my control column became useless. I found myself doing a vertical dive, getting faster and faster. I pulled the hood back. I got my head out of the cockpit and the slipstream tore the rest of me clean out of the machine. My trouser leg and both shoes were torn off. I saw my machine crash into the sea a mile off Deal. It took me twenty minutes to come down. I had been drifted eleven miles out to sea. One string of my parachute did not come undone, and I was dragged along by my left leg at ten miles an hour with my head underneath the water. After three minutes I was almost unconscious, when the string came undone. I got my breath back and started swimming. There was a heavy sea running. After one and a half hours a M.T.B. came to look for me. I fired my revolver at it. It went out of sight, but came back. I changed magazines and fired all my shots over it. It heard my shots and I kicked up a foam in the water, and it saw me. It then picked me up and took me to Dover.

The fighting over the Channel waxed fiercer, and floating balloon barrages began to form part of the convoys. Dover, too, acquired a barrage, and the *Luftwaffe* took with such relish to the sport of shooting down the balloons, and lost so many aircraft and crews in the process, that Göring hastily ordered a close season. And everywhere the preparations went forward—on the one side for ensuring an easy and agreeable trip across the Channel, on the other side for giving the visitors a warm, not to say hot, welcome.

Defence at its most effective is very seldom purely defensive. Fortunately the Royal Air Force was also able to disturb the enemy by offensive action. But before either defensive or offensive action could be applied with much profit, the nature of the German plans had to be laid bare. This task, too, our aircraft discharged to the full.

Thanks to the brilliant work of a few individuals, among whom due credit must be given to the adventurous and unorthodox F. S. Cotton, there now existed a means of extensive, efficient and economical air reconnaissance. The high-altitude Spitfires, no longer merely a promising innovation, had already become one of our most important weapons. The time was therefore ripe to bring them into line with normal Royal Air Force organization; and in preparation for the tasks that lay ahead the Photographic Development Unit in which most of them worked was renamed the Photographic Reconnaissance Unit, placed under the command of a regular officer (Wing Commander G. W. Tuttle), and embodied in Coastal Command. At the same time steps were taken to improve and expand the facilities for photographic interpretation.

From Norway to the Spanish frontier these Spitfires and the lower-flying Hudsons now ranged, photographing the ports held by the enemy. Of the danger points where an expedition might be in preparation only the Baltic was still beyond their reach. At first they brought back little evidence of anything unusual; but during the second week of August their prints began to reveal small concentrations of barges which might be explicable in terms of invasion. The German plan was maturing. So Coastal Command kept watch, building up a picture remarkable not only for its accuracy but also for its low cost.[1]

Meanwhile Bomber Command was hitting out. At first the main intention was to reduce the potential weight of German air attack against this country. To this end the night bombers operated for the most part against the German aircraft industry, the day bombers against airfields in occupied territory. During July enemy ports and shipping were officially rated 'top priority', but until the shipping concentrations became very marked in August aircraft plants and airfields remained our prime objectives. Throughout the period, however, attacks were delivered on other target systems, such as oil plants and communications; and, as in the crisis of May and June, our bombing policy displayed a variety which was perhaps too great for the circumstances.

Whether much good was done by our attacks on the enemy's airfields is an open question. The Air Staff at the time had no love for work of this kind. There were over 400 airfields from which the Germans could, and did, operate against this country; well dispersed

---

[1] Between July and October 1940 only 7 P.R.U. Spitfires were lost in 650 sorties.

aircraft offered a very unprofitable subject for attack; the small fragmentation bomb which later gave such good results in this type of operation was not yet in existence; and 'shooting up' by fighters, which was known to be effective, was at the moment a luxury we could not afford. Nevertheless, the situation demanded attacks on airfields, and the bombers did their best to provide them. On occasions that best was very good indeed; but all too often our attempts resulted only in a depressing waste of effort.

The bulk of these operations against airfields were carried out in daylight by the Blenheims of No. 2 Group; the 'heavies', operating by night, usually attacked airfields only when they had failed to identify their prime objectives in Germany. As they had little chance of surviving against German fighters, the Blenheim pilots were soon under orders to abandon the task if there was less than 7/10ths cloud near the target area. This was certainly a wise precaution, but in the latter part of July it resulted in no less than 90 per cent of the sorties proving abortive. It was to avoid this waste of effort that from then onwards the Blenheims, aided by some of the Battles which had returned from France, began to operate by moonlight.

What was liable to happen during the daylight operations before the pilots were bound down by hard and fast instructions about cloud cover may be seen from the experience of Nos. 21 and 57 Squadrons on 9th July. Their target was the airfield at Stavanger, where a large concentration of enemy aircraft was reported. After standing by at 0500 hours for some days, waiting for a suitable report from 'Met', six aircraft from each squadron at last took off in good weather—too good, as it proved. A hundred miles from the Norwegian coast not a cloud was in sight, but the pilots kept on. At least one of the navigators was doubtful of the wisdom of this. 'I suggested we should turn back,' writes Sergeant T. Hudspeth, 'but the pilot would not hear of it; the others were going on and we were simply obliged to follow the leader. We were under strict W/T and R/T silence, so therefore unable to exchange opinions. I quite saw his point, for if we turned back as I suggested our two outside aircraft would have followed us, and the strength of the formation would have been weakened considerably. Also, of course, we should no doubt have received a good raspberry from the powers that be, so on we stooged.'

The Blenheims made their landfall without incident, then turned for their run up to the target. The enemy had been caught unawares: his fighters were still on the ground. But up came the *flak*, and down went the bombs, and then the crews 'had only one ambition in life, and that was to get to Hell out of it'. Three aircraft had now broken formation; the other nine, still in company, made off west at full throttle. They were not many miles out from shore when the enemy fighters came up with them—three Me.110's and thirty Me.109's.

Most of the nine were by now already badly damaged. Of what followed, Hudspeth had an excellent view, since the Blenheims were not more than ten yards apart. 'I could see through my mirror', he records, 'the enemy fighters manœuvring to attack. On one occasion I saw six fighters queuing up getting ready for the kill. It was not long before casualties started to pile up. First I saw our port machine and its valiant crew smashed to smithereens when it was shot down and hit the sea. Then came the starboard machine's turn. He got a packet in the petrol tank and was burning like a torch. The pilot screamed out over his R/T that he was on fire but there was little we could do about it. The Jerry fighter on his tail, with the usual Teutonic thoroughness, would not ease up in the slightest, and continued to pour a stream of lead into the doomed machine till I saw him, too, disintegrate into the sea, legs and arms and parts of the machine being scattered far and wide. Both of our wing aircraft had now been shot down, and according to the law of averages we were next on the list. My pilot therefore did his best to catch up with the rest of the formation, but this was easier said than done, for they were taking absolutely wizard evasive action and we simply could not get in, no matter how we tried. Nor could we get below them, for they were at deck level, about 10 feet off the water; we had no alternative but to keep above them and slightly behind.'

By this time the nine had been reduced to four, but still the attacks continued. One of the pursuers was shot down, then another of the Blenheims. Then came what Hudspeth describes as his climax. 'We stopped a packet in the starboard engine. I was kneeling up at the time, watching the fighters off our starboard, when to my great amazement our starboard propeller flew off—literally flew off. There was the prop. calmly sailing on ahead, leaving us stooging along behind. I felt like putting my hand out and dragging it back . . . By now my ammunition had almost run out and it seemed just a matter of time before we joined the others, so I took what was, to me, a coward's way out. I sat back on my heels and offered up a prayer. I prayed for a cloud, for something that would ease this one-sided battle; and then, fantastic as it may sound, when I opened my eyes, there, about a mile away and about 1,000 feet above us was a cloud—a big, beautiful cloud. "Look, look," I screamed to the pilot, "Clouds." He did not want any second telling.'

Shaking off the enemy in the cloud-bank, the Blenheim eventually reached Wick and made a successful belly-landing. Of the twelve aircraft which had set off, four others, all damaged, also regained our shores.

*   *   *

As the day for the launching of the great *Adlerangriff* drew nearer, the Germans intensified their attacks against Channel targets. For the operations against our south coast ports and shipping had the treble purpose of weakening the Royal Navy, damaging our trade and wearing down our fighter forces. Indeed, the German activity on 8th August (when repeated assaults were made on our convoys off Dover and the Isle of Wight, and we lost twenty aircraft and the enemy twenty-eight) was so great that it afterwards appeared to us to mark the beginning of the Battle of Britain. But in truth Göring had not yet opened his main offensive, nor did the weather permit him to do so on his appointed date of 10th August. The 11th, with attacks on Dover and Portland and two convoys, and thirty-two of our air-craft destroyed as against thirty-five of the enemy's, was another big day; but it was not until 12th August that the Germans, doubtless unaware of the significance of the date in the sporting calendar, went all-out against the Royal Air Force. By that date Raeder, forced by the German Army to agree to landings on a far wider front than he felt himself able to protect, had already lost confidence in the whole plan of invasion. 'Paradoxical situation,' noted Halder on 6th August, 'where the Navy is full of misgivings, and the Air Force very reluctant to undertake a mission which at the outset is exclusively its own. And O.K.W. [Supreme Headquarters], which for once has a real combined forces operation to direct, just plays dead. The only driving force in the whole situation comes from us . . . '

The Germans themselves reckon that they began the Battle of Britain on the afternoon of 13th August. They admit, however, that two formations misunderstood orders and took off in the morning. But the attacks of 13th August did not differ materially from those of the previous day, and it is from 12th August that the beginning of the battle proper must be dated. For it was on that day that the enemy, while not yet ignoring our shipping and Channel ports, began a systematic assault on our airfields and radar stations.

The operations of 12th August displayed a number of features characteristic of the days to follow. The German bombers, which included Ju.87's, were heavily escorted; five or six major operations, involving many hundreds of aircraft, were undertaken; and attacks on one area were timed either to coincide with, or to follow closely upon, attacks or threats against some other area many miles away. As the targets were on or near the coast our fighters were hard put to it to intercept, and the German bombing was not unsuccessful. All

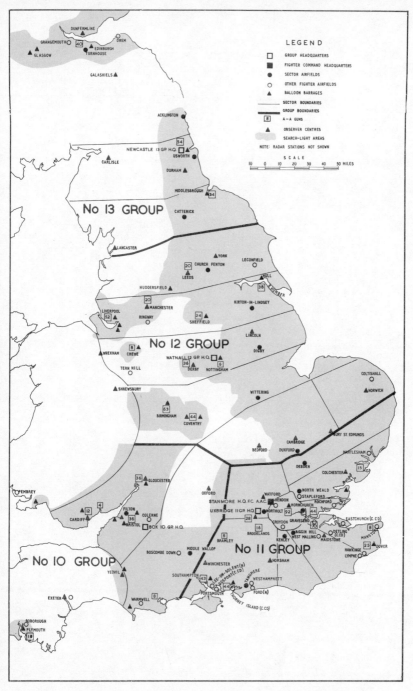

THE AIR DEFENCES OF ENGLAND AND WALES, AUGUST 1940

[facing page 164]

the five radar stations attacked were damaged, Manston airfield was put out of action, and at Lympne and Hawkinge take-off and landing had to be confined to very narrow strips. But though many structures were destroyed, the general effect on our air activity was small. At one radar station on the south coast, for instance, every building was smashed except the three that really mattered—the transmitting and receiving blocks and the watch office. By dint of hard work all the attacked units except the radar station on the Isle of Wight (which was not replaced until 23rd August) were in operation again by the following morning. Moreover, though a few small formations had penetrated unchallenged, none of the major raids had escaped detection and combat, and some—including one aimed at Manston—had been entirely frustrated. No. 11 Group had managed to put its fighters into the air, if not in time to meet the raiders in force, at least in time to interfere with their bombing and harass their departure; and though our fighters were consistently outnumbered they had lost only twenty-two of their number in shooting down thirty-six of the enemy.

The following day the Germans left the radar stations alone. Three times they came over in strength, with one prong of their attack directed at airfields in the south and the other at airfields in the south east. Their intention was to find a loophole in our defence: to see if we could fight over Kent and Essex only at the expense of our resistance over Sussex and Hampshire. Much of the day was cloudy, favouring attack rather than defence; but the enemy was sadly disappointed if he expected, after the previous day's damage to our warning system, to cross our shores undetected and unchallenged. Our radar continued to plot the enemy's approach towards our shores; the Observer Corps continued to track his progress inland. The result was that serious damage was confined to the Coastal Command stations at Eastchurch and Detling and the 'fringe' target of Southampton. Split up and harried by our fighters, the enemy pilots dropped a few bombs on seven Royal Air Force stations, including Middle Wallop, Benson and Thorney Island, but nowhere achieved an effective concentration. Three of their main objectives—the airfields at Odiham, Farnborough and Rochford—remained entirely untouched. And this time the balance of losses was still more in our favour—thirteen against forty-seven. The Germans, however, thought otherwise. Reporting on the results of the attacks since 8th August, Stapf informed Halder that eight of our major air bases had been virtually destroyed, and that the ratio of German to British aircraft losses was one to three for all types, one to five for fighters.

On the night of 13th August the enemy embarked on a fresh departure. Not content with the minor operations and mine-laying

M

thus far reserved for the hours of darkness, and closely pursuing their main plan of reducing British air power, the Germans began nightly attacks on our aircraft plants. On this first evening eleven high-explosive bombs hit the Nuffield factory at Castle Bromwich—a factory producing Spitfires. The bombers were from *KG. 100*, one of the few bomber *Gruppen* in the German Air Force which specialized in night operations, and one which was to lead many of the heavy raids of the autumn and winter. The success of this initial attack, however, did not truly represent German ability to find specific factories by night. Between 14th and 23rd August, the Bristol Aeroplane Company's Works at Filton were selected for attack on at least eight occasions, but bombs fell on them only twice. And during the same period, in nine attempts to bomb the Westland, Rolls-Royce and Gloster works, the Germans only twice got their bombs within five miles of their objective. Indeed, they were so far astray that in this whole series of attacks only one German pilot so much as claimed to have hit his target—the Rolls-Royce works at Crewe, on the night of 20th August. Fortunately he was mistaken.

After the intense fighting of 13th August the following day was quieter. In the morning Manston was attacked by nine Me.110's carrying bombs—a clear indication that Göring already doubted the ability of his Ju. 87's to survive against our Hurricanes and Spitfires. Some rather pointless attacks were also made on the Dover balloon barrage and the Varne lightship. In the afternoon and evening single enemy aircraft, or aircraft in very small formations, made scattered raids over the west and north west, and bombs fell on eight Royal Air Force stations as far apart as Middle Wallop, Cardiff, Andover and Sealand, near Chester. But our capacity to put our fighters into the air was almost unaffected; and the enemy had lost nineteen aircraft to eight of ours.

During the hours of darkness that followed, the enemy's usual nightly activity—a matter of between sixty and a hundred sorties, ranging far and wide over the country—was strangely absent. Apart from a few individual reconnaissances the quiet continued well into the next morning. It was the calm before the storm. August 15th saw the heaviest fighting of the whole battle.

For some time now the Germans had been waiting for this moment—the moment when the weather would be right for a concerted onslaught by all three *Luftflotten*. This, it will be remembered, was how they had planned to open the intensive phase of their campaign. While *Luftflotte* 2 attacked the south-east, and *Luftflotte* 3 the south, *Luftflotte* 5, in Norway and Denmark, would operate against the north-east. The British fighters would thus be engaged all along the line. If Dowding had stripped the north to thicken up his defences in the south, Tyneside and the bomber airfields of Yorkshire would suffer in full measure.

The first blow was struck at the south-east. At 1129, two German formations, amounting to about sixty Ju.87's escorted by fifty Me.109's, crossed the coast between Dover and Dungeness; a third formation, of fighters only, was driven back before it reached our shores. Two of the four British squadrons ordered up—Nos. 54 and 501—made skilful interceptions; and of the several airfields that were attacked, only the little-used Lympne suffered much damage.

Then, while the Channel remained the scene of repeated alarums and excursions, so that No. 11 Group was continually forced to put up patrols, the attacks began against the north-east. At 1208, nearly an hour before the enemy eventually crossed the coast between Blyth and Acklington, the Operations Room table at No. 13 Group showed its first plot of German aircraft. They were opposite the Firth of Forth, nearly a hundred miles out to sea; and they were heading south-west. With such good warning five British squadrons were soon on patrol. No. 72 Squadron intercepted thirty miles out beyond the Farne Islands; it reported that the enemy, so far from numbering some thirty, as indicated by our radar, consisted of about a hundred He.111's and seventy Me.110's. This sort of mistake was not infrequent in 1940, for though our radar stations at this time gave very accurate information about the enemy's bearing, they were much less reliable in their estimates of height and number. Nothing daunted, the squadron sailed in, caught the Germans by surprise, inflicted heavy losses, and split the broad mass of the raiders in twain. One of the resulting formations was savagely mauled by No. 79 Squadron before it reached the coast; and as soon as our shores were gained the Me.110's, short of petrol and very unhappy in the presence of Hurricanes and Spitfires, turned and fled. Despite our attacks most of the He.111's managed to cross the coast, but they were then so harassed by Nos. 41, 605 and 607 Squadrons, with the Tees and Tyneside guns joining in, that their bombing went entirely astray. Not a single factory or airfield was hit. All that the enemy pilots could show for their efforts was the destruction of twenty-four houses at Sunderland.

Meanwhile another German formation from the Scandinavian bases was heading for Scarborough, a hundred miles to the south. Against this threat, four British squadrons were already on guard. No. 616 Squadron was the first to engage, ten miles out beyond Flamborough Head. No. 73 Squadron followed. Together their attacks resulted in the destruction of several of the enemy; but the bulk of the formation, consisting of fifty Ju.88's, pressed on and crossed the coast. Some then turned north to join in the attacks on Tees and Tyneside, while others turned south. They were pursued, completely in vain, by the makeshift Blenheim fighters of No. 219 Squadron, one of which chased a Ju.88 for 160 miles over land and sea without getting closer than 600 yards. Nevertheless, the enemy bombers managed to hit only two military objectives. One of these, presumably struck by accident, was an ammunition dump near Bridlington. The other was the aerodrome at Driffield, where ten aircraft were destroyed and much damage was done to buildings and hangars.

The bombing of Driffield was the one item on the credit side that the Germans could display for their operations from Norway and Denmark. Indeed, their losses were so severe that throughout the remaining weeks of the Battle of Britain they never again attempted a daylight raid against the north-east. Yet on the British side not a single fighter had been lost. The whole episode was a remarkable demonstration of the German bombers' complete impotence in the face of our defences when forced to operate by day without the company of Me.109's.

By 1420 the last German aircraft had disappeared from the scene of the attacks in the north. At the same time the third great operation of the day was just beginning in the south-east. After a number of feints, the enemy flew beyond the Thames estuary and crossed the coast in some force near Felixstowe, Harwich and Orfordness. But the six British squadrons which had been sent up were less skilfully controlled than usual, and few interceptions were made—part of No. 17 Squadron from Martlesham Heath, for instance, was sent off on search, and had then to be ordered back to its own airfield, which the enemy was bombing at leisure. Meanwhile at precisely the same moment another raid consisting of nearly a hundred aircraft was plotted in over Deal. Twenty minutes later, at 1530, yet another formation, nearly 150 strong, came in near Folkestone. Both of these formations were challenged and harried all over Kent and Essex by our pilots, who though consistently and heavily outnumbered prevented any serious damage to our airfields. The Germans were much more successful, however, against their other main object of attack—the aircraft industry at Rochester. Pobjoy's and Short's were both heavily hit, with resulting loss of output for several weeks.

Two hours later the enemy struck at yet another point. Between 1700 and 1720 the south-coast radar stations detected no less than seven strong formations, containing in all between 200 and 300 aircraft, approaching the shores of Hampshire and Dorset. Before

THE MAIN GERMAN ATTACKS, 15 AUGUST 1940

the Germans could cross the Channel eight British squadrons were in the air; and altogether about 150 Spitfires and Hurricanes left the ground in the course of the raid—the largest force which Fighter Command had as yet put up to meet one attack. Fierce battles developed near Portsmouth and Portland, where many of the Germans were beaten back before they could cross the coast, and long straggling encounters took place all over the southern counties. Yet such was the ascendancy of our pilots, and so small was the proportion of the enemy's bombers to his fighters, that once again the damage on the ground was insignificant. Only at Middle Wallop airfield, where two hangars and a few aircraft were affected, did the German crews reap the slightest reward for their efforts; and even then they spoilt the effect by reporting on their return that they had bombed Andover.

Scarcely were these attacks over when large forces were again plotted in the region of Calais. By 1815 sixty or seventy enemy aircraft were heading for the coast between Dover and Dungeness, and within the next ten minutes four British squadrons were ordered up. Six others followed later, as the enemy penetrated inland. Some of the Germans were intercepted over Folkestone and others were turned back near Maidstone; but one formation of Me.110's, carrying bombs and escorted by Me.109's, got through to Croydon. Here they were sharply engaged by No. 32 Squadron from Biggin Hill and by No. 111 Squadron from Croydon itself. Several of the enemy were shot down; but the Germans managed to bomb not only Croydon and West Malling airfields, but also the Rollason and Redwing aircraft factories. Damage in both cases was severe—though Redwing's started up on a new site within twenty-four hours—and another factory engaged in making switches for aircraft radio sets was completely destroyed. That evening Londoners became uncomfortably aware that the great battle in the air was moving their way. Its significance, however, they as yet barely apprehended.

So 15th August closed. Five major assaults, some of them almost simultaneous, had been launched by the enemy against areas as far apart as Portland and the Tyne. The attacks had had their profitable moments, as at Driffield, Rochester and Croydon; but considering that no less than 1,790 aircraft—520 bombers and 1,270 fighters—had been hurled against our shores, the damage was infinitesimal. Everywhere the Germans had been checked and harried by our Hurricanes and Spitfires; nowhere had they discovered a serious gap in our defences. And if the emphasis of their operations was on wearing down our fighters rather than destroying objectives on the ground, they had achieved any success in that direction only at a great price; for though we lost thirty-four aircraft the enemy lost seventy-six.

This figure of seventy-six enemy aircraft destroyed, though impressive enough in all conscience—especially as many were bombers carrying a crew of three or four—came as a great disappointment when it was discovered from secret German archives after the war. Our estimate of the day's successes given to the public at the time was that we had certainly destroyed 182 enemy aircraft and probably destroyed another fifty-three. The circumstances, however, were unusual. Raids came in so thick and fast that there was often barely time to interrogate pilots before they were again leaping into their cockpits; aircraft were landing away from base; communications were affected; No. 11 Group and Fighter Command, besieged by the Press for the day's results, could give only the roughest check to the claims pouring in from the stations; and with the size of the formations involved it was inevitable that two pilots, or a pilot and a gun crew on the ground, should sometimes claim the same aircraft. The enemy, too, had a trick of breaking away in a steep dive, emitting black smoke, and pulling out near the ground to escape at deck-level. As our pilots were rightly forbidden to follow suspected victims down for the satisfaction of witnessing the crash, this also swelled the score. This unwitting exaggeration was to be repeated on all the big days of the battle, though whenever the fighting was less intense the pilots' claims were extremely accurate. That the figures were inflated, then, is not to be taken as a criticism of anyone at the time—least of all the pilots. The only charge that may justly be made is that in the years to follow, until the discovery of the true figures, the Air Ministry did not sufficiently insist on the provisional character of those given to the public at the time. Statistics which of their nature could only be estimates were allowed to take on the guise of hard facts. Yet it must also be admitted that the figure of 182, like that of 185 for 15th September, though subsequently shown to be wrong, had an important psychological effect during the battle. For it undoubtedly inspired not only the fighter pilots but the whole nation to still greater miracles of effort.

While the three *Luftflotten* were engaged in the massive onslaught of 15th August, their commanders were enjoying the hospitality of their corpulent chief at his Prussian country-seat. On this occasion the guests had more important business than to study the activity of their host's prize stallions, and a general conference took place on the progress of the operations against England. After some discussion Göring issued directions on a number of points. Among other matters, he found it necessary to remind his subordinates that the object of the battle was to crush the Royal Air Force. 'Until further orders', ran his instructions, 'operations are to be directed exclusively against the enemy air force, including the targets of the enemy aircraft industry allocated to the different *Luftflotten*. Shipping targets, and particularly large naval vessels, are only to be attacked where circumstances are especially propitious. For the moment other targets should be ignored. We must concentrate our efforts on the destruction of the enemy air forces. Our night attacks are essentially dislocation raids, made so that the enemy defences and population shall be allowed no respite; even these, however, should wherever possible be directed against air force targets.' Moreover, insisted Göring, there had been too many attacks on alternative targets which had 'absolutely no connection with our strategic aim'. Henceforth even the alternative targets must be chosen for the degree to which their destruction would speed the victory over the Royal Air Force.

On this point Göring's guidance was certainly sound. But on another matter his judgement, doubtless corresponding with the general sense of the meeting, was crucially at fault. For the ninth item in his summary of conclusions ran thus: 'It is doubtful whether there is any point in continuing the attacks on radar sites, in view of the fact that not one of those attacked has so far been put out of operation.' In fact, these attacks had done more harm than the enemy thought, for on 12th August the station on the Isle of Wight had been virtually destroyed. But Göring's decision, tentative in form, was acted upon as if it were absolute, and only two more attacks were made on these objectives.

The 15th of August thus witnessed not only the enemy's plan of operations at its most extensive, but also a fateful, and fatal, turn of policy. The decision to stop attacking radar stations was not, however, the only remarkable order issued by Göring that day. For it was on 15th August, only two or three days after the battle had begun, that he gave instructions that no aircrew operating over England should contain more than one officer. Thus early did the fear of heavy losses weigh on the German commander's mind.

After the great battles of the day came the usual minelaying and other minor activity during the hours of darkness. Forty-two of our night fighters were sent up. Only one claimed an interception.

Then, with the morning of 16th August, the *Luftwaffe* returned in force. The day was marked by three great assaults. At midday the Germans operated over Kent and the Thames Estuary; a little later they attacked objectives in Sussex and Hampshire; and in the early evening they crossed the coast almost simultaneously at four points between Harwich and the Isle of Wight. Once more the forces employed were very large, amounting in all to some 1,720 aircraft; and it was no small tribute to the defenders that of this number all but

400 were fighters. Despite this the balance of losses in the air fighting—forty-five of the enemy, twenty-one of ours—was in much the same proportion as before. The day was cloudy, and for that reason the evening attack was able to penetrate well inland. For precisely the same reason it petered out in much scattered and ill-directed bombing, though the two Ju. 88's which attacked the Maintenance Unit and Flying Training School at Brize Norton, in Oxfordshire, scored the biggest single success of the whole battle by destroying no less than forty-six aircraft in the hangars. Other air-fields bombed during the day were Manston, West Malling, Tangmere, Gosport, Lee-on-Solent, Farnborough and Harwell, while the radar station on the Isle of Wight, already out of action, suffered another pounding. It was typical, however, of the weaknesses of the German plan, or German intelligence, that only three of the eight airfields attacked were used by Fighter Command.

It was during the second of the day's great operations, when the Germans were attacking Gosport, that one of our pilots performed an action typical of the spirit of the hour. Flight Lieutenant J. B. Nicolson, of No. 249 Squadron, was hotly engaged with the enemy when his Hurricane was hit by four cannon-shells. Two struck him, a third set fire to the reserve petrol tank behind the instrument-panel. Flames at once poured into the cockpit, and Nicolson was about to jump when he saw a Me.110 in a vulnerable position. Disregarding his intense pain and danger, he stayed in the blazing aircraft and delivered an attack which sent the German diving down out of control. Only then, badly wounded and severely burned about his face, neck, hands and legs, did he take to his parachute—to be promptly shot in the buttocks by an over-zealous Local Defence Volunteer. Nicolson's great gallantry was later recognized by the award of the Victoria Cross, the first to be won by a pilot of Fighter Command.

The huge efforts on 15th and 16th August evidently imposed some strain on the Germans, for on 17th August they paused to recover. Though the weather was not unfavourable, only seventy-seven raiders crossed our shores. But by 18th August the enemy was back again in force, with 750 sorties. Soon after midday part of a formation which had crossed the coast at Beachy Head got through to Kenley, one of the vital sector stations in No. 11 Group. Despite spirited intervention by Nos. 64 and 111 Squadrons, and despite the success of the local P.A.C. rockets in bringing down a Do.17—the first victim to fall to this device—the enemy attack was delivered with skill and success. Every hangar except one was destroyed; six Hurri-canes were put out of action on the ground; the runways, though they could still be used, were heavily cratered; and signals communications were so badly affected that the Sector Operations Room had to be closed down and the organization transferred to an emergency room in a disused butcher's shop in the main thoroughfare of Caterham. From then on the station controlled only two squadrons instead of its normal three.

Ten minutes after the bombing of Kenley a small detachment from the main body of the enemy again attacked Croydon airfield and the Rollason aircraft factory. West Malling was also hit once more, but a large force which headed for another of the all-important sector stations—Biggin Hill—was largely beaten off by Nos. 32 and 610 Squadrons. Later in the afternoon the airfields at Gosport, Ford and Thorney Island were all heavily attacked, and another radar station —the last of these objectives to suffer during the battle—was put out of action. But the enemy was less successful in the evening, when an onset by strong forces against our airfields in the Thames Estuary was entirely frustrated. On the whole, though the damage was in some places serious, we had done well to prevent the raiders knocking out Kenley and Biggin Hill. As for the tally of losses, this was still more in our favour. We lost twenty-seven; the enemy seventy-one.

For all the German advantage in numbers, the exchanges up to this point had been well in our favour. This was the more remarkable since the enemy's numerical superiority was even greater in actual combat than in total resources. For since the *Luftwaffe* was operating for the most part against targets near our coasts, the warning we received was usually much too short to mass our squadrons into larger formations before challenging the enemy; only by allowing the Germans to bomb their objectives unhindered for the sake of concentrating a large force against them on their way home could Park have overcome this difficulty. So it was squadron by squadron that our Hurricanes and Spitfires were coming into action against the enemy; and in any given combat they might be, and usually were, outnumbered by as many as twenty to one. Yet it was in conditions of this kind that our pilots were shooting down two of the enemy for every loss they themselves suffered.

The enemy's advantage in numbers was to be expected. For that reason it was less galling to our pilots than his all too frequent advantage in height. Over and over again our squadrons, ordered to intercept the enemy at 10,000–15,000 feet, found themselves 'jumped' from above. This occurred partly because the radar height readings were unreliable, partly because the controllers had to keep some of our fighters below cloud-level to protect our airfields, and partly because Spitfires and Hurricanes in 1940 were unable to climb to 25,000 feet in less than about twenty minutes. All the same the orders were not entirely to our pilots' disadvantage, for above 18,000 feet the relative performances of the Hurricane and the Me. 109 turned in favour of the latter.

Despite all adverse factors, then, our pilots had so far more than held their own. The first German formations had come over with the bombers low, the fighters high above them; and on Park's orders our squadrons had met them by splitting up, one flight engaging and holding off the fighters, the other flight dealing with the bombers beneath. These tactics had proved so successful that from 16th August onwards the Germans resorted to much tighter formations, with their fighters not only close on top of the bombers, but also ahead and on the flanks at the same level. To that extent our pilots' manœuvre was soon countered. There was nothing, however, that the enemy could do to disguise the now obvious vulnerability of the Ju.87. For though the Stukas had bombed some of the coastal airfields with great accuracy, they had suffered the heaviest losses of all; so heavy that after the raid on Gosport on 18th August they were withdrawn from the battle. From that date they were condemned to wait on airfields behind Calais until the great day of invasion, when in the absence of the defeated Royal Air Force they could demonstrate their powers against the Royal Navy.

But though our pilots were proving more than a match for their opponents, and though the German attacks on our airfields had resulted in only West Malling being out of action for more than twenty-four hours, there was every prospect that the enemy's superior resources might tell in the end. From 8th to 18th August the Germans had lost 367 aircraft, Fighter Command 183 in combat and 30 on the ground. This number of Hurricanes and Spitfires, however, could not be made good from production when the combined weekly output of these types was little over a hundred. To replace our losses we were thus having to eat into our scanty reserves. If this went on for many weeks there could be only one end—defeat for the Royal Air Force.

In this situation the work of those engaged in making, repairing and servicing our fighters took on a degree of urgency greater than ever before or since. All responded overwhelmingly to the demands of the hour. Typical of the efforts was that of No. 24 Maintenance Unit at Tern Hill, in Shropshire. This unit, a Service-manned Aircraft Storage Unit in No. 41 Group, Maintenance Command, was primarily engaged in preparing Spitfires flown to it from the manufacturers. 'We worked', wrote the Commanding Officer, 'two twelve-hour shifts daily, and the Spitfires were received, checked, modified, and had their guns removed, cleaned, re-fitted, tested and harmonized; the aircraft were fitted out with radio, filled with ammunition, and were ready for collection within 48 hours. They were frequently collected by the Fighter Squadron pilots and were in action against the enemy on the same day . . .'

Alarming as was the shortage of aircraft, it was not the worst danger. Long before our fighters gave out we should have reached crisis-point in the supply of trained fighter pilots. Between 8th August and 18th August we had lost 154 pilots killed, missing and severely wounded; and the number of new fighter pilots produced during the same period was only 63. Moreover these newcomers, though of equal spirit, as yet possessed only a tithe of the fighting skill of their predecessors. To meet the need of the hour volunteers from among the Lysander and Battle squadrons, the air forces of our allies, and those about to embark on the final stages of Bomber and Coastal training were rushed through specially shortened fighter courses. Emergency measures, however, could only reduce the gap, not close it. Throughout the battle the supply of pilots remained Dowding's gravest anxiety.

The replacement of casualties was the most serious aspect of the pilot problem, but it was not the only one. There was also the growing strain on those who survived. Incidents such as befell Flying Officer E. S. Marrs of No. 152 Squadron, and recorded below in his own words, were happening every day. They could not be suffered very often without some effect on the nervous system.

> I got in a burst of about three seconds when—Crash! and the whole world seemed to be tumbling in on me. I pushed the stick forward hard, went into a vertical dive and held it until I was below cloud. I had a look round. The chief trouble was that petrol was gushing into the cockpit at the rate of gallons all over my feet, and there was a sort of lake of petrol in the bottom of the cockpit. My knee and leg were tingling all over as if I had pushed them into a bed of nettles. There was a bullet-hole in my windscreen where a bullet had come in and entered the dashboard, knocking away the starter button. Another bullet, I think an explosive one, had knocked away one of my petrol taps in front of the joystick, spattering my leg with little splinters and sending a chunk of something through the backside of my petrol tank near the bottom. I had obviously run into some pretty good cross-fire from the Heinkels. I made for home at top speed to get there before all my petrol ran out. I was about fifteen miles from the aerodrome and it was a heart-rending business with all the petrol gushing over my legs and the constant danger of fire. About five miles from the 'drome smoke began to come from under the dashboard. I thought the whole thing might blow up at any minute, so I switched off my engine. The smoke stopped. I glided towards the 'drome and tried putting my wheels down. One came down and the other remained stuck up. I tried to get the one that was down up again. It was stuck down. There was nothing for it but to make a one-wheel landing. I switched on my engine again to make the aerodrome. It took me some way and then

began to smoke again, so I hastily switched off. I was now near enough and made a normal approach, and held off. I made a good landing, touching down lightly. The unsupported wing slowly began to drop. I was able to hold it up for some time and then down came the wing-tip on the ground. I began to slew round and counteracted as much as possible with the brake on the wheel which was down. I ended up going sideways on one wheel, a tail wheel and a wing-tip. Luckily the good tyre held out and the only damage to the aeroplane, apart from that done by the bullets, is a wing-tip which is easily replaceable. I hopped out and went off to the M.O. to get a lot of metal splinters picked out of my leg and wrist. I felt jolly glad to be down on the ground without having caught fire . . .

The long hours at dispersal, the constant flying at high altitudes (two or three sorties a day was normal, six or seven not uncommon), the repeated combats, the parachute descents, the forced landings—all took their toll, even where the harm was not at once apparent. The growing tiredness of those who had been most actively engaged was a factor which Dowding could neglect no more than his casualties. Fighter Command was still successfully resisting the enemy. Its own strength was being steadily sapped in the process.

*　　*　　*

From 19th August to 23rd August there was much heavy cloud, and the Germans were unable to operate in strength. Nevertheless they carried out many scattered raids; Manston was heavily attacked, and on the afternoon of 19th August a single aircraft bombed the oil storage depot at Llanreath, starting a fire which burned for a week and destroyed ten out of the fifteen oil tanks. By night the enemy again damaged the Bristol works at Filton and some industrial targets at Castle Bromwich, but otherwise his efforts resulted in little beyond the now customary catalogue of rural incidents. Satisfaction at the ineffectiveness of the night attacks, however, was marred by the sobering thought of how little this was due to our defences. During these five nights none of the three enemy aircraft claimed by the guns was found on the ground, and 160 sorties by night fighters resulted in only one pilot so much as gaining contact with the enemy.

On 24th August the Germans were able to resume mass attack by daylight. From then until 6th September there was only one day—27th August—on which they despatched less than·600 sorties. Over the whole period they put an average of almost a thousand aircraft a day into the air; and on two days—August 30th and 31st—they operated more than 1,600 machines against us. Yet the number of bombers included in these vast formations never rose above 400, and was usually not much over 250.

The governing object of the enemy was still the destruction of the Royal Air Force, and especially of Fighter Command. At another conference at Karinhall on 19th August Göring was again explicit on this point. 'We have reached', he said, 'the decisive period of the air war against England. The vital task is to turn all means at our disposal to the defeat of the enemy air force. Our first aim is the destruction of the enemy's fighters. If they no longer take the air, we shall attack them on the ground, or force them into battle by directing bomber attacks against targets within range of our fighters. At the same time, and on a growing scale, we must continue our activities against the ground organization of the enemy bomber units. Surprise attacks on the enemy aircraft industry must be made by day and by night. Once the enemy air force has been annihilated, our attacks will be directed as ordered against other vital targets.'

The enemy's basic strategy might remain the same, but he took care to alter his tactics. Clearly the attacks on coastal airfields and other 'fringe' targets had not decisively weakened the British fighter force, while the simultaneous assaults at widely separated points had only proved that our defences were intact all along the line. A new approach to the task was badly needed; and the Germans accordingly determined to concentrate the whole weight of their onslaught by day against Royal Air Force objectives in the south east. The full fury of their attack was thus turned on No. 11 Group, and more particularly on its inner airfields. For only by penetrating well inland could the enemy reach the vital sector stations from which our squadrons were controlled; and only in this way could he be sure of bringing the largest possible number of British fighters to battle. If still more Hurricanes and Spitfires could be shot down—the German pilots were far more lavish in their estimates of success than ours—and if the control system could be paralysed, London and the invasion coast would soon lie at the attackers' mercy.

Command and Group were the brain of our defensive system; the sectors were the nerve-centres. Once Group had ordered aircraft into the air, the control of those aircraft and their direction by R/T towards the enemy was in the hands of sector. In No. 11 Group there were seven of these master stations, each normally controlling three squadrons. Tangmere, on the South Downs behind Bognor, and Debden, near Saffron Walden, were rather apart from the rest; the others formed a close guard round London. Kenley, an unexpected plateau above the wooded slopes of the North Downs near Caterham, and Biggin Hill, farther along the ridge into Kent, protected the southern approaches to the capital; Hornchurch, a sudden expanse of grass beyond the factories of Romford and Dagenham, and North

Weald, on the outer fringe of Epping Forest, guarded the east; Northolt, on one of the great arterial exits, stood sentinel against attack from the west. It was against this inner ring of airfields that the enemy now struck.

The attack on 18th August had already restricted our use of Kenley. Now, on the 24th, North Weald was heavily hit; but the enemy's second main objective, Hornchurch, was well protected by the local guns and suffered less severely. Two days later a new series of attacks against Hornchurch and North Weald was beaten off, though bombs fell on Debden. But on the 30th the enemy twice got through to Biggin Hill, wrecking the workshops, the M.T. yard, the equipment and barracks stores, the armoury, the Met. Office and—a grave blow at the morale of the airmen—the N.A.A.F.I. The attacks also severed the gas and water mains and all telephone communications on the northern side of the station. A direct hit on a shelter trench killed several officers and men.

The next day the enemy was equally successful. After Debden had been bombed in the morning, and Croydon and Hornchurch at midday, Hornchurch and Biggin Hill were again attacked in the evening. At Hornchurch three aircraft of No. 54 Squadron were destroyed as they were taking off. 'The Squadron', recorded the Station diary, 'was ordered off just as the first bombs were beginning to fall. Eight of our machines safely cleared the ground; the remaining section, however, just became airborne as the bombs exploded. All three machines were wholly wrecked in the air, and the survival of the pilots is a complete miracle. Sgt. Davies, taking off towards the hangars, was thrown back across the River Ingrebourne two fields away, scrambling out of his machine unharmed. Flight Lieutenant Deere (in yet another role) had one wing and his prop. torn off; climbing to about 100 feet he turned over and, coming down, slid along the aerodrome for 100 yards upside down. He was rescued from his unenviable position by Pilot Officer Edsell, the third member of the Section, who had suffered a similar fate except that he landed the right way up. Dashing across the aerodrome with bombs still dropping, he extricated Flight Lieutenant Deere from his machine. "The first and last time I hope" was the verdict of these truly amazing pilots, all of whom were ready for battle again by the next morning.'

But once again it was at Biggin Hill that the damage was worst. More telephone lines were severed; many buildings and hangars were destroyed; the operations room block was set on fire, and an emergency room outside the station—in an estate office in the neighbouring village—had to be brought into use. The station still continued in action; but as the emergency equipment could not deal with the normal number of aircraft, two of the three squadrons had now to operate under the control of adjoining sectors.

All this was not accomplished cheaply, for the enemy lost thirty-seven aircraft on the 30th and thirty-nine on the 31st. Moreover the Germans, beaten off over and over again from their main targets, had been reduced to bombing a number of airfields, like Eastchurch, which were of little significance in their immediate plan. All the same their attacks were now beginning to strike home and make a real impression. Manston was no longer in use, Kenley and Biggin Hill were working at greatly diminished efficiency.

On 1st September Biggin Hill had its sixth raid in three days. Most of the buildings left standing were by now unsafe, and the equipment had to be moved into the open. Yet the station still functioned. It did so not only because of the adaptability and determination of its airmen, but also because of the bravery of its airwomen. This quality came as a surprise to many, though not to officers like Wing Commander Carnegie, who had already been given some inkling of how the W.A.A.F. would behave under fire. In the early months of the war Carnegie, having received a draft of W.A.A.F. at Wittering 'only because the C.O. at a nearby bomber station refused to take them', ordered them away from the airfield when an approaching raider was plotted. The next day the W.A.A.F. officer in charge demanded an interview and informed him that if he ever gave a similar order she could not be responsible for the discipline of the girls or for their obedience to his instructions. This admirable spirit was now being maintained at Biggin Hill under actual bombardment. During the big attack of 18th August Sergeant Joan Mortimer, a telephone operator who was also in charge of the despatch of ammunition to the gun positions, remained at her very dangerous post throughout the raid, then, as soon as the bombs stopped falling—and long before the 'all clear'—began planting red flags round the craters in which there were unexploded bombs. Again, on 1st September, two telephone operators, Sergeant Helen Turner and Corporal Elspeth Henderson, continued to maintain communications even after the operations block in which they were working received a direct hit. Such calm behaviour, to which the superb example of the W.A.A.F. officer in charge—Assistant Section Officer Felicity Hanbury—greatly contributed, was an inspiration not only to airwomen on other stations but also to their male comrades.

Continuing the plan of attacking the sector stations, on 2nd September the enemy concentrated against Hornchurch. All assaults were repelled except one, and that was so harried that of the hundred or so bombs dropped only six fell on the airfield. Then on 3rd September raiders again got through to North Weald, setting two hangars on fire and severing nearly all the telephone lines to the Observer Corps. Fortunately a bomb which hit the roof of the new operations room did no damage, and the landing area could still be used by day. The following day, 4th September, the sector stations escaped further harm, but the enemy succeeded in bombing four other airfields in No. 11 Group and the Vickers aircraft factory at Weybridge—a plant responsible for two-thirds of our entire output of Wellingtons. So many raids were being plotted at the time of this incident that the operations room table at Fighter Command was 'saturated' and Weybridge received no air raid warning. As a result there were heavy casualties, though the twenty Me.110's which carried out the bombing were intercepted at the moment of attack by No. 253 Squadron, and only six bombs hit the works.

On 5th September Biggin Hill was again attacked, but under pressure from No. 79 Squadron the German crews aimed wide. Later in the day others made amends by hitting the oil farm at Thameshaven. This may have been an alternative target for the Estuary airfields, but the enemy's success encouraged him to a repetition of the attack on the 6th. Stoked by further enemy bombs, huge fires burned all through the night. They were still burning when the heavy attack of 7th September was launched. Another industrial target to be bombed on 6th September was Hawker Aircraft Ltd. at Weybridge, a factory producing more than half of our total supply of Hurricanes. Fortunately the intervention of our fighters prevented serious damage.

It was at this stage, when the German efforts were straining our defences to the utmost, that Hitler, as at Dunkirk, once more came to our aid. The credit for the change in the enemy's tactics which now occurred cannot, however, be assigned exclusively to the German leader. The *Führer*'s mental processes were powerfully assisted by Bomber Command.

Up to the end of August our daylight bombing had been directed almost entirely against the enemy's airfields in occupied territory; but by night we had never ceased to attack targets in Germany. These were all precise objectives—aircraft factories, airfields, oil plants, ports, shipping and communications (among which the marshalling yards at Hamm held a place of honour). Doubtless it was somewhat optimistic to expect any great result from the fifty or so aircraft which carried out these tasks every night. Doubtless, too, much of the bombing went astray. The operations, however, had moments of outstanding success, among which special mention must be made of a

N

raid on the night of 12/13th August. On that night five Hampdens of Nos. 49 and 83 Squadrons, operating under the cover of diversionary bombing, attacked an aqueduct forming part of the Dortmund–Ems canal. Two of the first four aircraft were shot down, the other two badly hit; but the fifth, piloted by Flight Lieutenant R. A. B. Learoyd, dived to 150 feet through the storm of *flak* and the blinding glare of the searchlights to drop his bomb within a few yards of the target. He then struggled home in his badly damaged aircraft, waited for dawn, and landed without injury to his crew, so completing an exploit which brought him a richly deserved Victoria Cross. Ten days afterwards the canal was still blocked, with the result that the movement of barges and motor-boats from the Rhineland to the invasion ports fell seriously behind schedule. In concert with many other difficulties, this proved too much for the enemy. At a time of the year when the deteriorating weather made every hour precious to the enemy, the German D-day was postponed from 15th September to 21st September.

Incidents of this nature were naturally galling to the *Führer*. It was also galling, however small the damage to industry, to have bombs falling on German cities. And it was still more galling to learn that even Berlin, 600 miles from the British bases, was not immune; for on 25/26th August, in retaliation for some bombs which had fallen on the City of London the previous night—the first since 1918 —eighty-one British aircraft raided targets in the German capital. The same medicine was administered several times during the next few nights. It was not a prescription in which the Air Staff had any great confidence, as there were plenty of more important objectives much nearer; but there were political advantages to consider, which the Prime Minister was not slow to point out.

It would, of course, be too much to see in these raids on Berlin the whole cause of Hitler's next move; but they unquestionably added to his anger at the activities of Bomber Command. It would not be long now before D-day. What better policy, then, for this final phase, than to enjoy a swift and sweet revenge by hurling the *Luftwaffe* in force against London? For if the British capital could be reduced to chaos, the task of the invading armies would be enormously simplified; indeed, if Göring's pilots did their work well enough the need for a military expedition might entirely disappear. And nothing could be more agreeable than to be freed from the necessity of crossing the Channel while the Royal Navy and the Royal Air Force were still in being.

While the German ships were moving secretly towards their appointed stations, Hitler accordingly informed the world that his patience was once more exhausted. 'The British', he screeched, 'drop their bombs indiscriminately and without plan on civilian residential quarters and farms and villages. For three months I did not reply because I believed that they would stop, but in this Mr. Churchill saw a sign of our weakness. The British will know that we are now giving our answer night after night. We shall stop the handiwork of these night pilots.' Three days later, on 7th September, the *Luftwaffe* abandoned its offensive against the sector stations and began the assault on London. From the point of view of winning the battle, Dowding himself could not have made a more satisfactory decision.

* * *

Each day now, for many weeks past, the Spitfires and Hudsons of the Photographic Reconnaissance Unit had scoured the Channel coast from Cherbourg to the Texel. On 1st September their prints showed barges moving in great and unaccustomed numbers towards the sea along the South Beveland and Terneuzen–Ghent canals. During the next few days the growing concentrations at Ostend and Flushing were steadily watched and photographed. On 31st August 18 barges lay in the port of Ostend; on 2nd September the photographs revealed 70; on 4th September, 115; on 6th September, 205. During the same week the number of barges at Flushing increased by 120. And every day processions of barges and motor-boats could be seen moving westwards along the Channel coast in the company of merchant shipping. Between 4th September and 6th September 34 extra barges appeared at Dunkirk, 53 at Calais. By the close of 6th September, there could no longer be much doubt: the Germans would not be massing their craft in ports so exposed to our bombing unless the hour of trial were at hand. That evening, after the Combined Intelligence Committee had studied the interpretation reports of the day, the authorities ordered Invasion Alert No. 2—'attack probable within the next three days'.

Saturday, 7th September, opened quietly. But in the late afternoon, from the usual maze of activity over the Channel and northern France, the radar stations picked up a number of German formations shaping for Kent and Sussex. The reaction of No. 11 Group—helped by No. 12 Group, which sent down three squadrons from Duxford to guard North Weald—was to concentrate on protecting the vital airfields. This time, however, the enemy's objective was different. One formation forced its way up the estuary, bombed the Arsenal and other industrial targets at Woolwich, and took a fierce drubbing from the Duxford and Northolt pilots (including the Polish Squadron, No. 303) on its way out. Another group bombed Thameshaven, a third the docks at West Ham. Then, while the raiders were fighting their way back, three fresh formations headed in towards Dover. All were engaged soon after they crossed the coast, but the enemy escorts were very strong, and our own squadrons came into action only one by one. Weight of numbers told. Beyond the inferno of Thameshaven the roar of burning warehouses mingled all along the river with the grey dust of humble homes.

As the enemy had steadily converged in one direction for an hour and a half, no less than twenty-one of the twenty-three squadrons we had sent up succeeded in engaging. The German losses were therefore severe—forty aircraft as against twenty-eight of ours. The powerful escorts, however, had safeguarded the German bombers, and nearly all the machines shot down by our pilots were fighters. Weighed against the enormous damage the attackers had inflicted, the price doubtless appeared cheap enough to Göring. All the same it was not one which he could afford to pay very often.

Indeed, there was an instructive contrast in the enemy's immunity during the next few hours, when the *Luftwaffe* returned under cover of darkness to improve on the havoc it had wrought. For the previous fortnight *Luftflotte* 3 had been practising concentrated bombing at night, though its efforts against Birmingham and Merseyside had been marked by no great success. Now, with a target near at hand, vast in extent, and lit by the lurid glare of a hundred dockside fires, the task was somewhat easier. From 8 o'clock that night to 4 o'clock the next morning 250 bombers kept up a slow, agonizing procession over the capital. Between them they dropped some 300 tons of high explosive and 13,000 incendiaries, or rather more than their comrades had dropped during the day. Barrage shooting by the anti-aircraft batteries being forbidden, and many of the guns having been moved to protect the aircraft factories, Londoners heard only a few brief and pitiful bursts of shell-fire to relieve the drone of the planes and the steady crash of the bombs. The next morning, weary from lack of sleep, they learned that their defenders had claimed between them one enemy aircraft.

It was a battle now not only against the British air force but against the British people. But the people could 'take it', and none better than the long-suffering sons and daughters of the East End, upon whom the first cruel blow had fallen. For as on each succeeding night the German bombers returned to their task and the toll of broken bodies and buildings mounted, there was still no sign that nerve would crack or falter, no hint that London would prove unequal to its ordeal. Instead, a cheerful and unwavering fortitude, an immense patience, possessed the population; and in the flame and fury of 'The Blitz' were forged the links of a wider friendship and a deeper humanity.

Clearly the Londoners were not to be frightened easily, and the invasion plans must be pressed forward. Yet if to the virtually indiscriminate damage at night there could be added the destruction of key-targets by day, the task before the German armies might not prove so difficult after all. Besides, London was still farther inland than most of the 11 Group sector stations; it was certain to be defended in the greatest possible strength by the British fighters; and no other objective could offer the same chances of a vast and decisive air battle—a battle which would end, once and for all, the obdurate resistance of Fighter Command. So the German tactics were settled. The main weight of attack would fall on London by night, when losses would be agreeably small; and huge fighter formations, covering a small number of bombers, would force their way through to the capital by day, destroying in their path the final relics of Dowding's force.

For the leaders of the *Luftwaffe*, misled by the exaggerated claims of their own pilots, were now convinced that Fighter Command was down to its last hundred aircraft. A few more daylight operations against London might thus complete the ruin of our defences. The German hopes were sadly and speedily disappointed. On 8th September an attempt by 100 aircraft to repeat their success of the previous day against the Thames docks was entirely frustrated; on 9th September an attack by somewhat larger forces was also beaten off; on 11th September, after the weather had interfered with operations on the 10th, a number of bombers got through to the capital, but achieved no concentration; and on the 12th and 13th heavy cloud prevented attacks, though it enabled single aircraft to score hits on the Admiralty, the War Office and Buckingham Palace.[1] Not until the 15th, a day of heavy and sustained fighting during which the Germans flew over a thousand sorties and lost fifty-six aircraft for our loss of twenty-six, did an enemy formation of any size again force its way through to London; and even then it was so harried by the British fighters and guns that the damage to the capital was insignificant compared with that of 7th September. After this, cloud was again prevalent until 23rd September, and the enemy was restricted to harassing activity and attacks on fringe targets.

During the whole of the vital fortnight from 7th September to 21st September, when the *Luftwaffe* was supposed to be delivering the

---

[1] One of the enemy bombers crashed just outside Victoria Station. It was rammed, in the heat of combat, by Sergeant R. Holmes of No. 504 Squadron. Holmes had already shot down two Dorniers, and his ammunition was exhausted. He himself made a successful parachute descent to land on a roof in Chelsea, from which he rolled into a dustbin.

knock-out-blow, it thus failed completely in every one of its immediate aims. The night raids, whatever their results against bricks and
mortar, had no effect on morale; while the day raids inflicted neither
systematic damage on the London key-points nor decisive losses on
Fighter Command. Indeed, as soon as the enemy turned against
London, the Command, which was perceptibly weakening, at once
began to recover strength. Not only was the pressure of bombardment taken off the sector stations and the greater part of the enemy
bombing carried out by night; the enemy's concentration on an
objective farther inland also gave time for the British squadrons to
join up in pairs and yet intercept before the German bombs fell.
Wherever possible a Hurricane and a Spitfire squadron now operated
together, the Hurricanes attacking the bombers, the Spitfires with
their greater effectiveness at big heights holding off the fighters. These
tactics completed the enemy's undoing. Göring's harassed bombers
called for ever-closer escort, and his fighters were finally so tied down
that they lost all power of initiative, and with it much of their ability
to defend either themselves or their charges. The result may be seen
from the casualties on either side. In the fortnight before 7th September, when the sector stations were under attack, Fighter Command
lost 277 aircraft as against 378 by the *Luftwaffe*—five British machines
for every seven of the enemy. In the fortnight from 7th to 21st September, when the main German objective was London, Fighter
Command lost 144 aircraft as against 262 by the *Luftwaffe*—five
British machines for every nine of the enemy.

Meanwhile the continued existence of the Royal Air Force was
being demonstrated with equal emphasis by Bomber Command. On
7th September the ever-increasing numbers of barges, coupled with
the attack on London, caused the country's defences to be brought to
their highest pitch of readiness; and a few hours after the issue of
Alert No. 1—'Invasion imminent, and probable within twelve hours'
—our heavy bombers delivered their first attack on the waiting craft
on the other side of the Channel. The Blenheims had already been
dealing with the same objectives since 5th September, and by 13th
September the whole of the bomber force was attacking invasion
targets—the ships in harbour, the communications behind the ports,
the gun emplacements on the coast.

As the month entered its third week German preparations reached
their peak. On the 15th there were 102 barges in Boulogne, on the
17th, 150. By the same date the 136 barges at Calais on 13th September
had been increased to 266. By 18th September the Channel ports held
more than a thousand of these craft and a further 600 waited up river
at Antwerp. But night after night the Battles and the Blenheims, the

Wellingtons, the Whitleys and the Hampdens went forth. There was no trouble now in finding the targets, and the short distance allowed the aircraft to carry their maximum bomb-load. In a fortnight of extremely profitable work our bombers crippled 12 per cent of the invasion fleet and greatly hampered the Germans in their task of organization, minesweeping and assembly.

It was on one of these raids, on the night of 15/16th September, that Sergeant John Hannah, a wireless operator/air gunner of No. 83 Squadron, won the Victoria Cross. While over Antwerp his Hampden was hit by an incendiary shell, which burst in the bomb compartment. Both petrol tanks were also pierced. Fire quickly enveloped the navigator's and rear-gunner's cockpits, and the rear-gunner baled out. Forcing his way aft, Hannah seized two extinguishers and fought the fire, though ammunition was bursting all round him and the heat was so great that it melted the aluminium floor. When the extinguishers were spent he finished the job by beating at the dying flames with his logbook. Badly burned, he then crawled forward, found that the navigator had also taken to his parachute, and passed the maps and log to the pilot, who brought the aircraft safely back to base.

An excellent description of a successful attack at this time was written soon afterwards by the pilot of a Blenheim, Flying Officer R. S. Gilmour. 'The whole of "Blackpool Front" [wrote Gilmour], as we call the invasion coastline stretching west from Dunkirk, was now in near view. It was an amazing spectacle. Calais docks were on fire. So was the waterfront of Boulogne, and glares extended for miles. The whole French coast seemed to be a barrier of flame broken only by intense white flashes of exploding bombs and vari-coloured incendiary tracers soaring and circling skywards.' Gilmour's target was Ostend. He approached and dived, dead on line:

Then came the great surging kick on the stick as the bombs left the plane. A second later the bomb-aimer was through to me on the 'phones . . . 'Bombs gone'. My waiting hand threw open the throttle levers in a flash. The motors thundered out. Hauling back on the stick, kicking at the rudder, we went up in a great banking climb. As we went I stared down and out through the windows. There they were! One, two, three, four vast flashes as my bombs struck. In the light of the last one, just as lightning will suddenly paint a whole landscape, I saw the outline of the jetties in vivid relief. Between them the water boiled with thin black shapes. They were barges flung up-end and fragments turning slowly over and over in the air.

Then came a most gigantic crash. We were nearly 2,000 feet up now and well away from the jetties but the whole aircraft pitched over as if a giant blow had struck us underneath. A vivid flash enveloped us and lingered as the sound burst round our ears. It was a blinding white flash like a great sheet of daylight stuck in between the dark. While all hell broke loose round us, I fought like mad to get control of the bomber. But all the time my mind was blankly wondering—half-stunned as I was—what the devil we had hit. Afterwards I learned that the last bomb had struck a group of mines stacked on a jetty waiting to be loaded aboard the mine-layers. Photographs taken the next morning showed two stone jetties blown away to the water's edge; all barges vanished from the inner basins; and devastation over a mile radius!

These anti-invasion operations of Bomber Command had a direct effect on the German programme, and on 11th September the enemy's prospective D-day was once more postponed—from 21st September to 24th September. The German naval authorities had always stipulated that Hitler must take the final decision—the yea or nay—ten days before D-day. On 14th September Hitler accordingly gathered again in conference with his commanders. The omens were scarcely inspiring. The previous night the Royal Navy had bombarded four of the Channel ports and at Ostend the Royal Air Force had sunk eighty barges. It was not surprising, then, that Admiral Raeder, never an optimist about the subject, should come armed with a memorandum which began: 'The present air situation does not provide the conditions for carrying out the operation, as the risk is still too great.' Hitler, however, was not yet prepared to abandon hope. 'The accomplishments of the *Luftwaffe*', he declared, 'are beyond praise. Four or five more days of good weather, and a decisive result will be achieved.' In this spirit he refused to accept the Admiral's wily suggestion that a decision should be left over until October, and insisted on reviewing the position yet again on 17th September.

As Raeder expected, the next three days made little difference, except to witness the consignment of further quantities of German shipping to the bottom of the English Channel and to demonstrate on 15th September that even the *Luftwaffe*'s greatest efforts availed little against Fighter Command. When 17th September came, the compiler of the War Diary at German War Headquarters was thus left to record: 'The enemy air force is still by no means defeated; on the contrary it shows increasing activity. The weather situation as a whole does not permit us to expect a period of calm. . . . The *Führer* therefore decides to postpone "Sealion" indefinitely.' To avoid the attentions of the British bombers the invasion vessels were to be widely dispersed; but some hope was still entertained for the unlikely combination of fine weather and German air supremacy, and the expedition was not yet to be disbanded.

This relaxation of tension was soon sensed by our reconnaissance aircraft. Between 19th and 22nd September photographic cover of the Channel ports was incomplete, but by the 23rd there were signs that the immediate crisis was past. By then several destroyers were seen to have moved round to Brest, and the number of barges in the ports between Flushing and Boulogne had decreased by nearly one-third.

For another month the German threat was still maintained, though in a less immediate form. By day there were dangerous blows against the aircraft factories of the south and south-west, as well as renewed attempts to penetrate in force to the capital. But however much the enemy varied his tactics by strengthening escorts, or using fighter-bombers, or sending over great diversionary sweeps of fighters, Dowding's forces remained equal to their task. On 27th September, one of the last of the great days, there were three major raids against London, as well as one against the Bristol aeroplane factory at Filton. Bristol's escaped damage; only a few bombers got through to the capital; and in the attempt the Germans lost forty-five aircraft. We lost twenty-eight. Even more discouraging for the enemy were his last full-scale daylight operations against London on 30th September. Again there were three distinct raids, as well as attacks and diversions elsewhere; but in every direction the German pilots were baulked, and the balance of losses—forty-seven against twenty—was still more in our favour.

After treatment of this kind the *Luftwaffe* could be forgiven for not wishing to continue the daylight onslaught in that precise form. The invasion, though not yet cancelled, was most unlikely to be mounted that year, once September was over; and if it was simply a question of conducting a long-term campaign against British morale and economic life the whole thing could be done by night without such distressing losses. It would still, of course, be necessary to keep up pressure against Fighter Command by day; but that could be done by the Me.109's and Me.110's, which would doubtless be able to look after themselves so much better when not escorting Do.17's, He.111's and Ju.88's.

From the beginning of October the Germans accordingly reserved their bombers for the hours of darkness, and almost the whole burden of the daylight offensive passed to their fighters and fighter-bombers. Flying at a great height and taking every advantage of the cloudy weather, these aircraft set Fighter Command new and difficult problems and imposed many fruitless hours of climb and chase upon the British pilots. But they did little else; and Dowding's forces continued along that path of recovery which had opened up on 7th September.

As October wore on, it became only too clear to the German commanders—even to those who had some appetite for the venture—

that the situation in the air was unchanged. The Royal Air Force was as far from defeat as ever. On 12th October Hitler therefore postponed operation 'Sealion' until the spring of 1941. In the meantime a winter of night-bombing, coupled with the activities of the U-boats, would no doubt help to soften up British resistance. But the plans of a dictator are liable to strange and sudden metamorphoses. Long before the spring of 1941, Hitler's eyes were fixed on what appeared to be bigger and better game.

* * *

The Battle of Britain has been the subject of much misconception and not a little controversy. There was the British misconception about the German losses; there was the far greater German misconception about the British losses[1]; and there have been any number of misconceptions about the extent to which Dowding's forces became depleted. Until the post-war publication of the *Führer*'s conferences on Operation 'Sealion', there was even a growing misconception that the battle had had no relation to a German invasion. This, however, was only a tribute to the very completeness of our victory. The controversies, as opposed to the misconceptions, were fortunately limited to fairly narrow circles within the Royal Air Force; but they were concerned with matters so important as Park's tactics and Dowding's strategy.

After the battle there was much exaggerated talk about our shortage of fighters. It is therefore worth emphasizing that Fighter Command was at no time reduced to a reserve of half-a-dozen aircraft, or any similar number. The critical period of the battle was the fortnight from 24th August to 6th September, when the enemy's main objective was the airfields of the south-east, and in particular the sector stations of No. 11 Group. Not only was there very considerable damage to the ground organization during this period, but the British losses in fighters so greatly exceeded the output from production that in three more weeks of activity on the same scale— if the Germans could have stood three more weeks—the fighter reserves would have been completely exhausted. But on 7th September the enemy not only turned against London, but also—so heavy were his own losses—began to drop his main weight of bombs by night. From then on Dowding's forces once more grew numerically stronger. For in the week from 7th September to 14th September the gross wastage of Hurricanes and Spitfires from all causes fell below the gross output, and continued so until the end of the battle. The

---

[1] Between 10th July and 31st October we claimed the destruction of 2,698 enemy aircraft and actually destroyed 1,733. The Germans claimed 3,058 and actually destroyed 915.

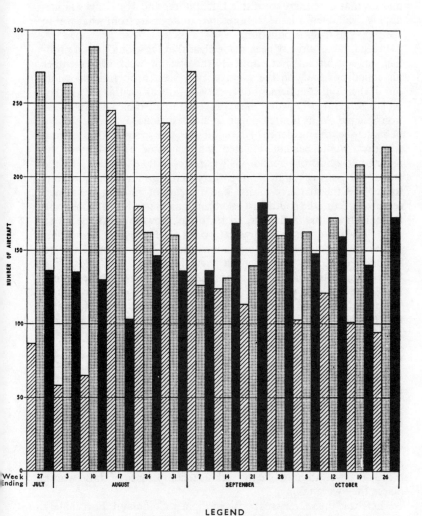

LEGEND

▆ Gross weekly output of Spitfires and Hurricanes

▨ Gross weekly wastage of Spitfires and Hurricanes

▦ Spitfires and Hurricanes immediately available for issue
from aircraft storage units on last day of week

**PRODUCTION AND WASTAGE OF SPITFIRES AND HURRICANES,
JULY—OCTOBER 1940**

position in reserve aircraft was thus at its worst about 7th September; and on that date there were still 125 Spitfires and Hurricanes immediately available for issue from reserve, quite apart from what was in the pipe-line from production.

Indeed, it has already been made clear that Dowding's main problem was not aircraft but pilots. By the opening week of September his squadrons had, on the average, only sixteen operational pilots out of their full complement of twenty-six. It was for this reason that on 8th September Dowding was compelled to introduce his Stabilization Scheme. As he himself puts it in his Despatch: 'By the beginning of September the incidence of casualties became so serious that a fresh squadron would become depleted and exhausted before any of the resting and reforming squadrons was ready to take its place.' By the end of the first week in September there were thus no fresh squadrons to replace the battered units, and instead of moving exhausted squadrons from the south-east and bringing in rested squadrons from the quieter sectors, as he had so far done, Dowding was forced to divide his squadrons into three categories. The 'A' class squadrons, for No. 11 Group and the adjoining Middle Wallop and Duxford sectors, were to be kept up to strength in fully-trained pilots; the 'B' class squadrons, for Nos. 10 and 12 Groups, were also be to kept up to strength—only five in number, they were intended to relieve 'A' squadrons when the latter needed replacement as whole units; the 'C' class squadrons, for all groups except No. 11, were allowed only five or six experienced pilots, and existed largely to 'bring on' the new pilots so that they could eventually take their place in the 'A' and 'B' squadrons. Dowding would never have introduced a scheme of this sort, with its depressing effect on the 'C' squadrons, unless the position was desperate; and the very nature of the scheme exhibits clearly where our main weakness lay. For though the number of pilots in Fighter Command was distressingly less at the beginning of September than at the beginning of August, it was not so much the smaller quantity as the lower quality that gave Dowding so much anxiety. The new pilots were, of course, magnificent material; but they had as yet nothing like the technical competence of those whose places they were taking.

There was thus a very real crisis in Fighter Command. Fortunately there was an equally real crisis in the *Luftwaffe*. Though the Germans' first-line strength greatly exceeded ours, they had now lost their lead in aircraft production. They could therefore not easily replace their heavy and repeated losses. Further, they had not been able to solve the problems of large-scale escort; yet without such escort their bombers were powerless. That the Germans began to attack London by day was a mistake of tactics. That they then virtually abandoned daylight bombing in favour of night operations was the measure of Fighter Command's triumph.

That triumph, for all its completeness, was achieved by a narrow margin. The margin was narrower, in fact, than some of those in high positions thought necessary. Dowding's initial policy of concentrating only one-half of his force in the most threatened area, and relieving tired squadrons as necessary, was not one which commanded unqualified approval. One school of thought maintained— mostly after the battle—that a larger number of squadrons should have been packed into No. 11 Group and the adjoining sectors at the outset of the offensive, so that the enemy could have been met on more equal terms; for with the given position of London and the limited range of the Me. 109, the struggle was virtually bound to be fought out in the south-east. Dowding, however, had good reason to believe that the congestion on the south-eastern airfields and the technical difficulties would be too great, and that the Germans would be quick to take advantage of any drastic weakening elsewhere. And indeed, that the enemy intended to deliver subsidiary attacks against the north and east, but was deterred by the strength of his reception, was amply proved by the events of 15th August. It must be remembered, too, that Dowding throughout remained responsible for protecting our coastal shipping, and that unlike subsequent critics he had no means of knowing how long the battle would last.

The tremendous odds which our pilots had so constantly to face gave rise to criticisms not only of Dowding's deployment but of Park's tactics. During the final stages of the battle, when victory was assured, Park found that his handling of operations had suddenly become the subject of an informal inquiry. The impetus for this came not from his own outnumbered units, but from No. 12 Group, where the Air Officer Commanding, the bluff, forceful Air Vice-Marshal Trafford Leigh-Mallory, was strongly critical of Park's direction. When called upon to provide support in the No. 11 Group area, Leigh-Mallory had operated a number of squadrons together— usually three, four or five, but once as many as seven—as a mass formation, or 'wing'. This wing, normally operated from Duxford, had obtained some striking successes at very little cost, under the inspiring leadership of Squadron Leader Douglas Bader.[1] In the

---

[1] Bader had lost both his legs in a flying accident in 1931. Having demonstrated his continued ability to fly, he refused to accept a job on the ground, but was informed that there was 'nothing in King's Regulations' to cover his case, and was invalided from the Service. At the outbreak of war he by-passed the medical authorities through a little influence in the right places, and was accepted back for flying duties.

result, growing differences between the two Group Commanders eventually reached the point where the Air Staff felt obliged to consider the main tactical issue between them—the respective merits of the wing and squadron formations.

This involved several very debatable factors. Should the successes of the Duxford wing be ascribed rather to the fact that the enemy formations had already been broken up by No. 11 Group? Had the wing neglected its appointed role of guarding No. 11 Group's northern airfields to chase the enemy all over the southern counties? Had No. 12 Group's keenness for battle resulted in perplexed controllers in No. 11 Group ordering up Spitfires and Hurricanes to investigate what was presumably a large hostile formation? But whatever the merits of these matters, it was difficult to disagree with the general principle that the wing formation was stronger than the squadron formation. It was, in fact, so elementary a precept that Park himself would surely have acted upon it—as he did over Dunkirk—could he have done so without harm to the objectives he was supposed to defend. For the unhappy truth was that the two commanders were largely at cross-purposes. Since there was nearly always good warning of the enemy's approach before No. 12 Group was required to come into action, Leigh-Mallory had time to mass his squadrons into a wing; No. 11 Group, on the other hand, usually had much shorter warning, and Park did well if he could get his squadrons into pairs, let alone wings, before the bombing began. And neither then, nor subsequently in Malta, was he prepared to allow bombs to fall on an important target for the sake of securing better results in the air fighting.

Be this as it may, Leigh-Mallory's tactical conceptions won a warm measure of approval from the authorities at Whitehall. So it came about that when the Air Ministry decided in November to give Dowding and Park some comparative rest after the enormous strain to which they had been subjected, Leigh-Mallory was appointed to succeed Park in command of the all-important No. 11 Group. At about the same time the Deputy Chief of Air Staff, Air Marshal W. Sholto Douglas, took over from Dowding at Stanmore. These changes reflected the end of one phase of the air war, and the beginning of another; for, besides the fact that the Germans had been forced into attacking mainly by night, the British Air Staff was now resolved to pass from the defensive to the offensive and to carry the daylight fighter battle to the other side of the Channel. For this new phase, Douglas and Leigh-Mallory were admirable choices. Equally, there was no lack of careful thought behind the selection of Dowding to serve on a mission to the United States, and of Park to command a flying training group, where he could give the new generation of pilots all the fruits of his hard-won experience. Both Dowding and Park, however, were naturally reluctant to leave the forefront of the struggle; and their translation to quieter spheres, though doubtless wise in itself, was not perhaps the most impressive immediate reward that might have been devised for the victors of one of the world's decisive battles.

* * *

The Battle of Britain has often been compared with the Battle of the Marne. Its general relation to the Second World War was indeed the same as that of the Marne to the earlier conflict; but there the resemblance ends. For the Marne was a miracle of good fortune born of the enemy's mistakes, an incredible victory snatched from the jaws of defeat. The Battle of Britain, on the other hand, was the result of years of careful thought and scientific preparation. It was the testing time of the whole British system of air defence—the radar stations and the observer posts, the pip-squeak and the R/T, the balloons and the guns, the Spitfires and the Hurricanes. That system had been built up to defeat unescorted bombers operating from Germany; it proved good enough to defeat escorted bombers operating from France. Fighter Command's victory in 1940 thus followed logically—though not, of course, inevitably—from the decisions of the Air Ministry in 1934 and thereabouts. It would be difficult to maintain that Joffre's—or Galliéni's—victory in 1914 followed logically from any decision of the *Ministère de la Guerre* or the War Office in 1908.

There is another difference no less striking. The Marne was fought by vast masses who were not unequally matched in numbers. In the Battle of Britain the enemy's numerical superiority was at least two to one in terms of general strength, and often twenty or thirty to one in terms of particular combats. And though large numbers of our men and women on the ground carried out their duties under fire, from the unwearying maintenance crews to the W.A.A.F. tellers whose quiet voices never faltered amid the droning crescendo of the approaching 'hostiles', the numbers engaged in the actual fighting were very small. Our bomber and reconnaissance crews amounted to some six thousand men. The fighter pilots who bore the brunt of the battle numbered, all told, not much more than a thousand.

This element had already been stressed by Winston Churchill in an eloquent prophecy before the battle opened: 'The great French Army was very largely, for the time being, cast aside and destroyed by the onrush of a few thousands of armoured vehicles. May it not also be that the cause of civilization itself will be defended by the skill and devotion of a few thousand airmen?' And it was again what he crystallized for posterity at the height of the battle, on 20th August, in his famous tribute that 'Never in the field of human conflict was so much owed by so many to so few'. Indeed, it was this very slenderness of the fighting force, allied to the greatness of the issue, that has given to the Battle of Britain the quality of an epic.

But 'epic' is a word which would certainly have drawn disrespectful comments from Dowding's pilots. For one of the supreme qualities of those young men—few of them were older than 25—was their light-hearted refusal to take either their dangers or their achievements seriously. They had that natural buoyancy of spirit which comes from robust youth, perfect health, and an adventurous disposition; they demanded of existence not that it should be long or leisured, but that it should be lively. Hence they applied to celebrations and 'parties' the sentiments of Voltaire about the Deity: if a 'party' did not already exist, it would be necessary to invent one. But usually it did exist; and if it was a party with the enemy, so much the better. In the main gloriously extrovert—the self-analysis of a Richard Hillary was quite untypical—they drank cheerfully of life with few questions as to the quality of the beverage; and if death struck the cup from their hands long before the dregs were reached, there were worse ends than one which was sudden, swift, and encountered in the service of what they held dear.

The Battle of Britain was fought by the gayest company who ever fired their guns in anger. Indeed, their gaiety was such that it penetrated even the official records. Into the tedious catalogue of moves and visits, postings and sorties, casualties inflicted and casualties suffered, there intrudes the alien note of youthful laughter. No. 73 Squadron debags a sergeant for identifying an Anson as a Blenheim; No. 54 Squadron hears with delight that one of its flight leaders has shot a cow during combat; Tangmere, heavily raided, watches with approval while the station commander sets one of the captured German crews to sweep up the remains of three hangars; an officer of No. 43 Squadron complains, not of his wounds, but of the M.O.'s description of them as 'multiple foreign bodies in both legs'. No. 609 Squadron rags the pilot who spins down from 15,000 feet and admits to feeling 'rather unwell'; No. 87 Squadron rejoices to see a Pilot Officer who has landed 'in the drink' return to base 'dressed in a tunic and blue underpants—a somewhat fearsome spectacle'.

This lightness of heart, a lightness which defied even tired limbs and jangled nerves, only adds to the quality of the epic. It would not, however, have carried our pilots very far had their equipment or their skill been inferior to that of the enemy. But of that there was no danger.

The eight-gun Spitfire or Hurricane, powered by the Rolls-Royce Merlin engine, was a magnificent weapon. The training our pilots had undergone was second to none.

The combination of gay hearts, admirable equipment, good leadership, first-class training, and devoted service on the ground, proved too much for the *Luftwaffe*. For though high and even supreme courage was also necessary, that could be taken for granted. The pilot who delayed his jump until his burning aircraft was clear of a town, or chased the enemy from a convoy when his ammunition was exhausted, or took the air again within a few hours of baling out, or waded alone and undismayed into a sea of enemy aircraft—was the rule, not the exception. The German aircrews, too, were brave men; but Dowding's pilots had something more than courage. They had that restless spirit of aggression, that passion to be at grips with the enemy, which is the hall-mark of the very finest troops. Some—like 'Tin-legs' Bader, 'Sailor' Malan and Stanford Tuck—were so fiercely possessed of this demon, and of the skill to survive the dangers into which it drew them, that their names were quickly added to the immortal company of Ball, Bishop, Mannock and McCudden. But all possessed it to a high degree; and it was this which gave them a strength not to be measured in terms of numbers.

The Battle of Britain was not won in the air alone. It was won, too, in the factories, the repair shops, the maintenance units, the flying training schools, the radar stations, the operations rooms—and a host of other places, including the Air Ministry. And even in the air it was the achievement of bombers and reconnaissance aircraft as well as fighters. But all the devoted labour on the ground existed only that more men might operate the better in the air; and the work of Bomber and Coastal Commands, important as it was, was secondary to that of Fighter Command. The public verdict, though it has done much less than justice to others, has thus rightly acclaimed Dowding's pilots as the foremost artisans of victory; and when the details of the fighting grow dim, and the names of its heroes are forgotten, men will still remember that in the summer of 1940 civilization was saved by a thousand British boys.

CHAPTER VII

'The Blitz'

SHORTLY after 10 o'clock on the evening of 21st June 1940, an Anson of the Blind Approach Training and Development Unit took off from Wyton, in Huntingdonshire. In the fuselage was a wireless set of a type used by the American police. It was specially designed to receive frequencies in the neighbourhood of 30 megacycles per second.

The pilot, who had rejoined the unit the previous day, was a little vague about the object of the exercise. He was clear enough, however, about his immediate orders, which were to attempt to find a beam signal on frequencies 30, 31.5 or 33 mcs. Though the weather was murky below, the aircraft was soon clear of the clouds, and at 10,000 feet, under the starry canopy of the midsummer night sky, the search began. It was not long before the wireless operator—a peace-time radio enthusiast who continued to twiddle his knobs with the chevrons of a Royal Air Force corporal on his sleeve—picked up very loud and clear signals on 30 mcs. They consisted of dashes repeated sixty times a minute—as in the British standard beam-approach and the German Lorenz system for blind landing.

This was promising, and the pilot headed north with high hopes. About twenty miles beyond Wyton the dashes changed into a continuous note. The aircraft was in the beam. It proved to be less than half a mile wide, with very clearly defined dot and dash edges; and by keeping towards one edge the pilot found that he could fly along it with an accuracy of 100-200 yards. Having confirmed his position from a 'fix' the navigator then plotted the path of the beam. In one direction it extended towards Western Germany, whence in fact it was originating; and in the other, doubtless for reasons not unconnected with the presence of the Rolls-Royce aero-engine works, it passed across the town of Derby.

When the pilot landed he telephoned the news of his success to Fighter Command. Thence it was passed to the Air Ministry, where it was received with great satisfaction by Dr. R. V. Jones, a youthful and extremely versatile physicist who was in charge of Scientific Intelligence. Working on the evidence of agents, captured German aircrews and other sources, Jones had concluded that the Germans possessed a radio beam system capable of being used for 'blind' bombing over England, and that the receiving apparatus in the aircraft was the blind-approach landing set common to every German bomber. His opinion was challenged, however, by another scientist, outside the Intelligence organization, who was an acknowledged authority on the propagation of radio waves; for according to this expert it was impossible to make a short wave beam which would bend sufficiently round the curve of the earth from Germany for it to be heard in a bomber over England. Coming from so authoritative a quarter this pronouncement had threatened to place Jones's hypothesis out of court, and even to cancel the search which he had just arranged. But the Prime Minister, who had a firm belief in the value of positive experiment, had directly concerned himself in the matter; and it was by his personal order that Jones was allowed to have his way, and that the Anson took off. Its subsequent success was, of course, no more than Jones expected; for the intelligence already at his disposal had enabled him to put the aircraft in the right locality, and on the right frequency, for bringing back confirmation of his theory.

The beam which the Anson had picked up was in fact part of a system known to the enemy as *Knickebein* ('crooked leg'). The pilot using it travelled along the beam until it was intersected by another beam, at which point a different note sounded in his ear-phones and he released his bombs. Alternatively, for tactical reasons such as avoiding heavy anti-aircraft defences at a particular place, the beams might be made to intersect a little distance from the target, and the pilot would then drop his bombs after a short timed run along a given course from the point of intersection. The system was accurate to within roughly a square mile, and was thus an admirable device for the mass bombardment of urban areas by night.

The fact that one of these beams was picked up as early as 21st June, several weeks before German night bombing began on a large scale, is good evidence that the Air Ministry was fully alert in the matter of night defence. This is the more worth emphasizing since our failure to inflict any appreciable loss on the enemy raiders was soon to be all too obvious. Indeed, the main problem of the night bomber at this juncture, as long as it kept reasonably high, was not the opposition it would encounter, but the difficulty of locating and identifying its objective in bad weather or absence of moon.

It was this problem which the Germans hoped to solve by the use of radio beams. The early discovery of *Knickebein* was thus a distinct score for the defence. As soon as the nature of the system was confirmed, a series of listening posts was set up, and jamming apparatus of a crude type, made up from hospital diathermy sets, was fitted to a number of vehicles, ready for despatch to target areas. Jammers were also installed in police stations along the East and South coasts, where they could be operated on receipt of a message from Fighter Command. The object of this somewhat rudimentary jamming was simply to blot out the *Knickebein* signal in the pilot's ears. Far more subtle forms of interference, however, were also devised. These depended on adapting some of our own beam approach beacons to receive the enemy signals, and to retransmit them. The beam along which the pilot was flying could thus be broadened until it lost its original accuracy—an effect which was popularly known as 'bending the beam'—or a cross-beam could be inserted just short of the enemy's planned point of intersection. In either case the bombs were likely to fall wide of the target. By the time the Germans turned to night operations on a grand scale, we were accordingly ready with a number of well thought-out counter-measures. They went, appropriately enough, under the code name of 'Headache'.

But *Knickebein* was not the enemy's only radio aid to navigation at this time. The raiding aircrews also made great use of their medium frequency direction-finding beacons, which had been extended from Germany up to the Channel. By tuning in to the signals from any two of these beacons, whose locations were well known to them, the raiders could periodically fix their position and ensure that they were steering an accurate course. Fortunately the Post Office radio engineers had already devised in advance a counter-measure to this practice. The enemy signals were picked up and retransmitted in sufficient strength to swamp the original sound in the ears of the German crews, who, ignorant of the true source of the signal, thus made a false calculation of their bearing. Since the process consisted of 'masking' the enemy beacons it was known as 'Meaconing'. Its success depended not only on the skill of the operators but also on up-to-date information of enemy transmissions derived from the ever-alert wireless interception service.

There were other means of misleading the German raiders besides interfering with their radio aids. The experience of 1914–18 had amply demonstrated the value of camouflage in all its many forms, and shortly after the outbreak of war the retired Director of Works and Buildings in the Air Ministry, Colonel J. Turner, had been charged with the development of devices intended to deceive and decoy the enemy. The Colonel, already an expert in such matters, gave his name to a special branch devoted to this praiseworthy pursuit—

'Col. Turner's Department' stands unique in the history of Air Ministry nomenclature—and rapidly succeeded in his object of making the true appear the false, and the false the true. By the time the Germans had finished with France his bogus creations included some seventy dummy airfields, the majority of which had flare paths and appropriate lights to be illuminated on the approach of a raider. The enemy was attracted to these from the very beginning of his night operations over this country, and in June 1940 alone, before the major offensive opened, they drew no less than thirty-six attacks.

It was just as well that there existed these various devices for confusing the German night bombers, since by night neither fighters nor guns possessed a tithe of their daytime efficiency. The basic reason for this was our inability to track enemy aircraft accurately in the dark once they had crossed our shores. Winston Churchill, lamenting the fact that when a raid crossed the coast it left radar to come within the province of the Observer Corps, had once described this as 'a transition from the middle of the twentieth century to the early Stone Age'. By day, in anything like clear weather, the skill of the observers—whose visual plots were extremely accurate, and whose estimates of height and number were a great deal better than those afforded at the time by radar—fully justified reliance on the human eye (and a pair of binoculars). But by night, or in heavy cloud, the absence of effective inland radar told heavily. For the Observer Corps then became dependent on sound; and though their tracking was invaluable for the issue of air raid warnings, it was not sufficiently exact for systematic interception or engagement of the enemy.

The guns and the searchlights in fact depended on their own sound-locators for more detailed information of the enemy's approach. But sound-location apparatus varies greatly in accuracy in different kinds of weather, and with the increased speed of modern aircraft it was becoming entirely out of date. An aircraft flying at 20,000 feet and 300 miles per hour would be one and a half miles further on before its sound reached the listening apparatus on the ground, and five or six miles further on before the burst of the shells; and during this time it would not—if its pilot was sensible—maintain a constant course.

In mid-1940 neither the gun nor the searchlight could thus open up against the night raider with any reasonable prospect of success. Moreover, even if the enemy were accurately located, guns and searchlights alike were still subject to other limitations. The searchlights, of which there were some 4,000 in Great Britain in July 1940, could neither hold an aircraft for a satisfactory length of time, nor penetrate cloud, nor illuminate effectively above 12,000 feet. After the first few raids in June, when searchlight-aided fighters scored several successes, the Germans accordingly took care to operate well above that height. The guns were also far from adequate both in numbers and performance. In July 1940 only 1,200 heavy and 549 light guns were deployed in the whole of the United Kingdom. Of the 'heavies' some 200 were of the obsolescent 3-in. type; the remainder were the effective 4.5-in. and 3.7-in.weapons, with a theoretical 'ceiling' of over 30,000 feet, but a practical limitation to 25,000 feet because the predictor in use could not accept greater heights. The light guns, about half of which were of the admirable Bofors model, dealt with aircraft only up to 6,000 feet.

From all the disadvantages of inaccurate tracking and location the fighters suffered fully as much as the guns. It had also proved difficult, with the deadly menace of daylight attack still undefeated, to concentrate on the development and production of a specialized night fighter. When the Germans opened their main night offensive in September, we had, in fact, only eight squadrons of fighters primarily allocated to a night role. None of these was equipped with aircraft specially designed for the purpose. Two squadrons of Defiants had recently been turned over to night fighting because they had proved incapable of holding their own against enemy fighters by day; the other six squadrons—Blenheims—were night fighters for much the same reason. The Blenheims, however, in spite of their lack of speed —they were slower than some of the bombers they were supposed to pursue—had certain advantages. They were a twin-engined type, with a reasonable endurance; and many of them were already fitted with the airborne radar system known as A.I. (Air Interception).

From very early days in the study of radar, Watson Watt and others had foreseen the possibility of developing suitable apparatus for use in aircraft, both against other aircraft and against vessels at sea. The technical difficulties were very great, however, and priority of research and development was inevitably accorded to the coastal chain of ground stations, which promised immediate results of revolutionary importance. Though intensive work on airborne radar was begun at the Bawdsey Research Station under Dr. E. G. Bowen in 1936, it was thus perforce slower to achieve fruition.

A ground radar station, with its static position, huge aerials on 60-foot masts, and transmitting and receiving apparatus weighing many tons, is naturally capable of detection at a far greater distance than a set carried in an aircraft. In the summer of 1940, a ground radar station could 'see' over water for as much as a hundred miles; an A.I. set could 'see' at distances only between two miles and eight hundred feet. It was therefore not surprising that the first three marks of A.I., though full of promise, and though used operationally by a few aircraft of the Fighter Interception Unit from November 1939 onwards, had not achieved any great success in practice. On 22nd July 1940, an enemy aircraft was at last shot down by an A.I. Blenheim, but in general interceptions were disappointingly few. This was primarily because the limited range of the set demanded more accurate tracking on the ground than was yet available. But there were also other handicaps, including the slowness of the Blenheims and the fact that the A.I. apparatus was not yet mechanically reliable. On the night of 13/14th August, however, the first tests were made with a new mark of A.I., the Mark IV, which had a maximum range of nearly four miles and a minimum of only six hundred feet. Its worth was soon proved; and about the same time the first Beaufighters—strong, fast machines developed from the Beaufort bomber—began to trickle into service. An effective A.I. in an effective aircraft—the conjunction seemed, and was, highly promising. But in September 1940, such aircraft were too few in number to have much operational significance. In any case they still lacked the information which could put them within A.I. range of the enemy.

Since the number of specialized night fighters was so small, the ordinary Hurricane and Spitfire squadrons, or rather their more experienced members, were thus expected to do duty by night as well as day. They were neither properly trained nor equipped for this, nor had they good night-flying facilities at their airfields. In bright moon the pilots had no great difficulty in taking off, navigating and landing, but dark or cloudy nights brought fearful hazards. Indeed, it often proved impossible to send our fighters into the air in conditions which presented no obstacle at all to the beam-assisted German bombers.

In sum, our defence against night attack in September 1940, was entirely inadequate. Radar promised well in several directions; but until it had developed to the point of replacing sound-location over land, neither inland tracking, nor gun-laying, nor searchlight exposure could be done effectively. And though an excellent night-fighter with an efficient A.I. had just come into service, the main burden of night fighting still rested with the day squadrons.

What chance of success the Hurricanes and Spitfires had may be seen from an incident in July. It is told in the words of the pilot, Flying Officer T. S. Wade, of No. 92 Squadron:

Although a day-fighter squadron, circumstances demanded that we should make some attempt at continuing our activities into the night, and attempt it was. Of the many night patrols we made between June and August only one, so far as I can remember, achieved success.

Alan Wright not only saw something, but effectively shot at it. For most of us it was a case of showing the flag to the locals, who no doubt got some satisfaction out of hearing a couple of Spitfires screaming overhead, even if the screams were brought about by our endeavours to get out of our own searchlights and subsequent A.A. fire.

One of the quieter nights, at least as far as A.A. Command and the German Air Force were concerned, was that of July 27/28th. A local dance had prematurely accelerated my promotion to the then thin ranks of night-fighter pilots, with the result that after some four nights of practice I found myself defending South Wales against the German invader.

Needless to say, it was an entirely uneventful one-and-a-half hours stooge—uneventful, that is, from an operational point of view.

Almost before I had finished congratulating myself on getting down in one piece, I was being persuaded into a further venture. The fact that the weather was rapidly becoming typical of this country did not apparently outweigh the need for further flag-showing.

I therefore climbed into my Spitfire, climbed up to 10,000 feet, and three-and-a-quarter hours later climbed over the side of my Spitfire at 4,000 feet. In that time all sorts of nasty things had happened.

Soon after getting settled down on the patrol line over the Swansea area—marked, incidentally, by an invariably invisible triangle of lights at each end—10/10ths cloud at about 8,000 feet and a thick ground haze up to 1,000 feet effectively cancelled out any idea of maintaining position.

Having already warned Control that conditions were deteriorating, I felt fully justified in calling the whole thing off and repeating my request to be allowed to return to base, the first occasion in which I had done so having been turned down by higher authority. I might just as well have not wasted my time. My radio had decided to go on strike. It was a doubly aggravating strike, because whilst I could hear with ever-decreasing clarity the Controller's ever-increasing concern for my well-being, he could hear nothing. For me, very lost and very lonely, it was a very unsatisfactory state of affairs. After flying around for something like an hour on highly inaccurate reciprocal courses, I heard a faint and frantic voice suggest that I steer South as there was some suggestion of a plot North of base. It soon became obvious that it must have been some other sucker.

By this time, I had quite naturally lost faith in relying on communication with the ground, and resigned myself to putting in further night-flying practice in the optimistic hope of benefiting therefrom at a later date.

Careful engine-handling enabled me to prolong the agony for a total of three-and-a-quarter hours. Not wanting to hasten my extinction by trying to crash land, left me with only one alternative—which I took. Before doing so, however, I ineffectively tried to get my own back with a final crack at the Controller.

So far as I know, nobody heard my 'Baling out: listening out'. Perhaps it was just as well.

*   *   *

When the Germans opened their main night offensive, they thus had little to fear from our fighters, and the bulk of the opposition was

Wing Commander J. Cunningham, D.S.O., D.F.C.

Flight Lieutenant C. F. Rawnsley, D.S.O., D.F.C., D.F.M.

NIGHT FIGHTERS — THE TOP-SCORING TEAM

ST. CLEMENT DANES, 10th May, 1941

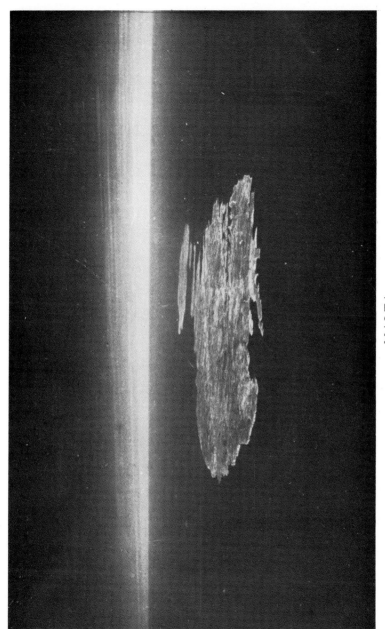

MALTA

supplied by the guns. It was not very effective, as Londoners soon discovered. The first great attack, on 7/8th September, found only 92 'heavies' deployed for the defence of the capital. Most of the raiders came in between Dungeness and the Isle of Wight; and the sound-locators, which were largely concentrated along the Estuary approach, were either out-flanked or swamped by the large numbers of aircraft. In addition communications failed between many of the vital points. In fact the system broke down completely, and many of the guns did not go into action at all.

Within forty-eight hours of this opening blow London's heavy-gun defences were more than doubled. But numbers in themselves were no guarantee of efficiency, and since existing methods of fire control showed no signs of being able to deal with the attacks, on 11th September many of the crews were given a free hand. The result was an orgy of what General Pile describes in his despatch as 'largely wild and uncontrolled shooting'. Expenditure of ammunition was prodigious, but no enemy aircraft were shot down. Nevertheless the German pilots showed a healthy respect for the increased volume of fire; all of them operated from a greater height, and some of them turned back short of their objective. The damage to the centre of the capital was correspondingly less than on the previous night, while the sound of the 'barrage', after the spasmodic firing to which they had thus far been treated, came as music to the ears of the inhabitants.

The nightly assault on London continued without respite from 7/8th September to 12/13th November. Over the whole of this period there were only ten nights in which the Germans' effort did not, according to their own method of reckoning, amount to a 'major raid'—one, that is to say, in which they dropped at least 100 metric tons of high explosive. Occasionally the enemy's activity was reduced because of bad weather, but normally the attack, extending over many hours, was carried out by between 150 and 300 bombers. It was an ordeal which for sheer continuity was not to be exceeded on either side during the war. But London is a large place, with a spirited population; and few of the enemy aircraft carried much more than a ton of bombs. Unless the raiders could destroy key points like power-stations and gasworks—and fortunately they showed very little ability in this direction—they would be in for a long job.

The point was not at once appreciated by the enemy. 'German airmen, comrades!' wrote Göring in an Order of the Day to the *Luftwaffe* crews on 18th October, 'you have, above all in the last few days and nights, caused the British world-enemy disastrous losses by uninterrupted, destructive blows. Your indefatigable, courageous attacks on the heart of the British Empire, the city of London with its

8½ million inhabitants, have reduced British plutocracy to fear and terror. The losses which you have inflicted on the much vaunted Royal Air Force in determined fighter engagements are irreplaceable. . . .' Later this confidence was to evaporate.

By mid-November, when the Germans adopted a change of plan, over 13,000 tons of high explosive and nearly 1,000,000 incendiaries had fallen on London. Outside the capital there had been widespread harassing activity by single aircraft, as well as fairly strong diversionary attacks on Birmingham, Coventry and Liverpool, but no 'major raids'. The London docks and railway communications—the enemy's favourite aiming points—had taken a heavy pounding, and much damage had been done to the railway system outside. In September there had been no less than 667 hits on railways in Great Britain, and at one period between five and six thousand wagons were standing idle from the effect of delayed action bombs. But the great bulk of the traffic went on; and Londoners, though they glanced apprehensively each morning at the list of closed stretches of line displayed at their local station, or made strange detours round back streets in the buses, still got to work. For all the destruction of life and property, the observers sent out by the Ministry of Home Security failed to discover the slightest sign of a break in morale. Over 13,000 civilians had been killed, and nearly 20,000 injured, in September and October alone; but London had adjusted itself to its new existence with astonishing calm. Wardens, firemen, rescue and salvage teams, repair gangs, bomb disposal squads, ambulance drivers, nurses—and plain workers and housewives—all were cheating the *Luftwaffe* of its triumph.

More than 12,000 night sorties were flown by the Germans over Great Britain during this phase of concentrated offensive against the capital. But in the whole period from 7th September to 13th November our night defences were able to claim the destruction of only 81 enemy aircraft—54 by the guns, 8 by the fighters, 4 by the balloons, and the remainder by other causes. Assuming that these claims were under-estimated by about a third—it is impossible to distinguish on all occasions the night losses from the daylight losses in the German records, but after the daylight attacks died down the one-third margin of error becomes apparent—the German casualty rate, at less than one per cent of sorties, was extremely light. With a first-line strength of over 1,400 long-range bombers, and some 300 emerging each month from the factories, the enemy would have no difficulty in sustaining his attacks indefinitely.

The defences might be having little immediate success, but at least every effort was being made to improve them. During these autumn months many projects, most of which had already been under consideration or development before the attacks opened, were pressed forward with the utmost speed. In the First World War the Services had been widely accused of resistance on principle to all new ideas, but no such charge could be laid against them in 1940. Indeed, they proved willing to try almost anything. The P.A.C. apparatus had already shown what fantastic feats of ingenuity the Air Ministry was prepared to incorporate in our defensive system, but even this was overshadowed by the 'long aerial mine'. Under pressure from the Prime Minister and the Admiralty, much time and energy was expended on this weapon, which was nevertheless given the somewhat discouraging code-name of 'Mutton'. It consisted of 2,000 feet of piano wire with a parachute at the top end and a small bomb at the bottom. The intention was to unspool a number of these contraptions from patrolling aircraft, so that they formed an apron in the predicted path of the enemy bombers. When a raider struck one of the wires the pull of the parachute would bring the bomb up against his wing, where it would explode.

Many tedious hours, with occasional interludes of unpleasant excitement, were spent by the test pilots of the Royal Aircraft Establishment flying into practice weapons of this character.[1] By October No. 420 Flight (later No. 93 Squadron), Middle Wallop, was detailed to employ 'Mutton' operationally. In spite of great efforts on the part of scientists and aircrew alike the project enjoyed singularly little success, and after the main enemy assault was over it was officially abandoned. A similar lack of success met the attempt to operate a free-balloon barrage—a curtain of bombs suspended by wire from balloons released in the path of the enemy. Both ideas failed, not from technical imperfections, but from the sheer immensity of space open to the attackers.

It was also during this period that Wing Commander W. Helmore's proposal for an airborne searchlight came to the fore. The scheme involved fitting a suitable light in an A.I. aircraft, and then operating this for the benefit of an accompanying fighter, which would carry out the actual attack. The technical problems involved were formidable, and though the device was developed with exceptional speed, it was not until the enemy's main offensive against this country had ended that 'Turbinlite' aircraft were ready for use. Ten flights were then rapidly fitted, but the difficulty of co-operating with the

---

[1] 'Impact trials' were also carried out by these pilots to develop, amongst other things, cable-cutters, de-icing equipment, rocket-projected mines, and the 'double-parachute-link' (steel cable joining two parachutes, either for incorporation in a balloon-barrage cable or for firing by rocket).

attendant fighter and the inherent imperfections of searchlights in thick weather prevented any great success.

Though the Air Ministry rightly neglected no field of experiment, the real hope for the future depended, as Dowding and Pile constantly stressed, on perfecting and producing certain radar apparatus. A few radar sets for gun-laying (G.L.) were already in existence, but they were unable to give readings of height until an elevation-finding attachment was developed. This was introduced into the London defences at the beginning of October, after which 'unseen' barrages could at last be fired with a reasonable chance of success. The set, however, still had many defects at angles of sight above 45°, and these had to be overcome, and the new equipment produced in quantity, before the guns could inflict any great losses on the raiders. Meanwhile radar was also adapted for the special requirements of searchlight control (S.L.C.).

A most promising prospect had in addition opened up for the fighters. By the summer of 1940, the scientists at the Air Ministry Research Establishment (later the Telecommunications Research Establishment), aided by a powerful contribution from the radio industry, had evolved radar apparatus for long-distance inland tracking. As soon as its worth was established a 'crash' programme of twelve sets was put in hand, and in mid-October the first operational station opened at Shoreham. Its range was some 45 miles; and by a novel scheme known as the Plan Position Indicator the controller was able to witness a simultaneous presentation of the attacking bomber and the intercepting fighter in relation to the surrounding countryside. By passing directions over the R/T the controller could place the fighter within a thousand yards of the bomber; once the fighter pilot was within that distance, his A.I. would bring him into visual contact with the enemy. The new apparatus, which became known as a ground-controlled interception set (G.C.I.) was, in conjunction with A.I., to revolutionize the science of night defence. It had, however, the serious limitation that it could not control more than one, or at the most two, interceptions at a time.

In essence, our chances of success now rested on the speed with which the new radar apparatus and the Beaufighters could be brought into service. But many subsidiary improvements in the night fighting system were also required. The investigations of a specially constituted Night Defence Committee under Marshal of the Royal Air Force Sir John Salmond, and including such agile brains as those of Air Marshals Freeman, Joubert, Tedder and Sholto Douglas, showed the way. The Committee recommended special optical tests in the selection of night fighter pilots, specialized night training at a night fighter O.T.U., a special night operations staff at Fighter Command, and navigational aids for night fighters. All these suggestions were carried out in the ensuing months.

At last, then, there was hope of better things for the future. Meanwhile, if we were not shooting down any great number of enemy aircraft, we were certainly—though the public did not know it— diverting many of them from their objectives. Colonel Turner's dummy airfields, decoy fires and the like were drawing some five per cent of the enemy effort, and a great deal more was going astray through our interference with *Knickebein*. Indeed, by November the German pilots had become thoroughly distrustful of this radio aid. Experienced crews, according to the evidence of captured prisoners, were able to disregard our counter-measures, but there was a general, and natural, reluctance to steer a course which was apparently well-known to the defences. A number of our fighters equipped with 'Lorenz' apparatus had, in fact, been instructed to 'hunt up and down the beam'. They had not secured any victims, but their presence —or their suspected presence—was thus proving a powerful deterrent.

One of the early German advantages had now been largely nullified. But war in the ether is a relentless battle of wits between experts who are adept at seeing more than one step ahead at a time. The Germans were not without an alternative radio navigational system for the fresh phase of their offensive which was about to begin; and Air Vice-Marshal Addison's No. 80 Wing, our newly formed radio counter-measures headquarters at Radlett, was not without a shrewd idea both of what it was, and of how to deal with it.

*   *   *

'During the night air offensive I finally secured the *Führer*'s permission to attack other objectives besides London, because it was always my contention that attacks on the British war industries would be much more valuable. I argued that it was no use to us to have another hundred houses go up in flames. I wished for attacks on the aircraft plants in the South of England and around Coventry, the shipping yards, Glasgow, Birmingham and the ports . . . I told the *Führer* again and again that in as much as I knew the British people as well as I did my own, we should never force them to their knees by bombing London.'

Thus Göring to the author of the latter part of this history in April 1946. At such a date the ex-Commander-in-Chief of the *Luftwaffe* was naturally inclined to minimize his own responsibility for the assault on London; but there is little doubt that as the attacks on London progressed, his own enthusiasm for them diminished. Indeed, after 12th October, when the projected invasion was postponed until the following spring, it was clear that their primary purpose had failed. Henceforth correct strategy would aim, not at the demoralization of the capital, but at the emasculation of British trade and war industry.

The forthcoming change in German objectives was sensed by our Intelligence, and by 12th November we knew that three great attacks, called by the Germans with unwonted humour 'Moonlight Sonata', 'Umbrella' and 'All-One-Price', were soon to be delivered against Coventry, Birmingham and Wolverhampton. Indeed, there was just time to plan a counter-operation—'Cold Water'—by which Bomber Command would simultaneously harass the enemy's bomber airfields and retaliate against a selected German town. It is a striking illustration of the advantage then held by the Germans that though this information was in our hands, and though attacks against their airfields were duly carried out, Coventry and Birmingham were both heavily smitten within the next few nights. Wolverhampton, more fortunate, escaped. The sudden increase in its anti-aircraft defences was possibly observed by the enemy.

The new phase of the German offensive began on the night of 14/15th November, as the inhabitants of Coventry will long remember. The weather—full moon and good visibility—favoured the attack, and the German operation went more or less according to plan.

The first raiders crossed our coast at 1817 hours, when about a dozen enemy aircraft made landfall at Lyme Bay. They were the He.111's of *Kampfgruppe* (*K.Gr.*) *100*, the unit which specialized in blind-bombing against precision targets. Using a highly complicated radio-aid system known to the Germans as the '*X*' *Gerät*,[1] the unit had already enjoyed some success in individual attacks against bridges in Warsaw and aircraft factories in the British Midlands. Now, however, its role was different. Since our interference with *Knickebein* had proved so successful, and since there was no other radio-aid with which the whole of the German bomber force was fitted, K.Gr.100 were to employ their special technique in a path-finding capacity. Their task was to find the target, shower it with incendiaries, and leave it well ablaze. The rest of the bomber force would follow up and bomb the fires.

K.Gr.100 arrived over Coventry at 2015 hours. Meanwhile the main force was already approaching from a number of different

---

[1] The aircraft flew along a fine beam in the centre of a coarse beam. This was intersected by three beams near the target—the first as a general warning, the second as the 'preliminary signal', the third as the main signal. From this third point of intersection it was then a short predetermined distance to the target. A device set in motion by the observer on arriving at these cross-beams released the bombs automatically.

directions. One stream led in across the Lincolnshire and Norfolk coasts: another between Selsey Bill and Portland: a third between Selsey Bill and Dungeness. All told, 437 enemy aircraft operated, keeping up the attack until shortly before 6 o'clock the following morning. Between them they dropped 56 tons of incendiaries, 394 tons of H.E. bombs and 127 parachute mines.

In view of our popular conception of this raid as a virtually indiscriminate assault on a city centre—and certainly the parachute mines were not a precise weapon—it is not without interest to discover that many of the German aircraft were given specific targets. I/L.G.I. was to attack the works of the Standard Motor Company and the Coventry Radiator and Press Company; II/K.G.27 the Alvis aero-engine works; I/K.G.51 the British Piston Ring Company; II/K.G.55 the Daimler works; and K.Gr.606 the gas-holders in Hill Street. Most of these objectives were in fact fairly heavily hit.

Twelve important aircraft plants and nine other major industrial works suffered directly from the attack, but output was also affected by general damage to utilities. Only one power plant was actually hit, but many cables, pipes and lines were severed—there were nearly 200 fractures of gas mains—and the shortage of gas and water was felt for some time. Indeed several factories were compelled to suspend production solely for this reason. The disorganization of transport was another great handicap—all railway lines were blocked, and all road traffic except the most essential had to be diverted round the city—and the loss of some 500 retail shops greatly hampered the distribution of food.

Recovery from the general disorganization, however, was surprisingly quick. Help was rapidly forthcoming both from the regional authority and the ministries in London. All railway lines except one were re-opened by the 18th. The large numbers of unexploded bombs were speedily dealt with, and within three or four days there was an excellent service of transport to take workers to the factories, evacuate the homeless, and disperse key tools from the damaged works. And despite the fact that 380 people had been killed and 800 seriously injured, morale remained unshaken. On the evening of the 16th arrangements were made to transport 10,000 people out of the centre of the city. Only 300 used them.

The results of the raid would, of course, have been much worse but for the fine work of the local civil defences and the voluntary helpers. The guns, too, had maintained a fierce barrage which kept the enemy high. Among the many who carried out their duties unflinchingly throughout the grim ordeal were the men of the Observer Corps, whose operations room was uncomfortably close to the blazing

Cathedral. Mr. Gilbert Dalton, a Chief Observer, has described how for twelve hours members of the Corps sat around the table and plotted the tracks of the raiders. 'The building', he writes, 'was frequently shaken by bombs—more than twenty detonated within a short distance—and surrounding buildings were on fire, but the work went on. Lights failed; candles were lit. Smoke drifted in through the ventilating system. Water from firemen's hoses swilled into the room. Telephones went dead; plots were still received and told to the R.A.F. on the lines that remained. Men whose homes and families were in the city went on stolidly with their work; one member that night lost his house, his business and his car, but he reported for duty next day. A number of members got through as reliefs during the height of the blitz; one man took three hours to come two miles because of the fires and obstructions.'

The next two nights the enemy, anxious not to let the capital benefit unduly from his change of plan, reverted to attacks on London. On the 17/18th November he struck at Southampton; then followed three nights of heavy raiding against Birmingham. In the last week of the month Southampton, London, Liverpool, Bristol and Plymouth all received 'major raids'. Further ordeals followed in December, and Manchester and Sheffield were added to the list of stricken cities. The year went out with the City of London still smouldering from the fire-raising attack led by K.Gr.100 on 29th December.[1]

Göring pursued his policy of ringing the changes between three main target groups until the latter part of February, 1941. Of the thirty-one 'major raids' carried out between mid-November and that date, fourteen were on ports, nine on inland industrial towns and eight on London. Apart from minor nuisance activity, the enemy's effort was usually concentrated each night against a single centre; and he developed the unpleasant habit of bombing the same city twice or three times at brief intervals in the hope of impeding recovery. In January, though three fresh centres—Cardiff, Portsmouth and Avonmouth—had their first heavy night attack, the German attacks were much reduced by the weather. February saw a still further decline, with only 1,200 sorties as against over 6,000 in November and 4,000 in December.

During this time the defences were certainly not idle, though they were still destroying very few enemy aircraft. In the four months

---

[1] The damage caused purely by fire in this raid, and in those on Manchester, showed the vital need for teams of fire-watchers in office premises, public buildings, streets, etc. A general obligation to fire-watch was introduced on 18th January 1941. The creation of the National Fire Service followed in August.

from the beginning of November to the end of February the enemy put at least twelve thousand sorties over this country, but the total number of aircraft claimed as destroyed by the defences was not more than seventy-five. Of these approximately two-thirds were claimed by the guns, one third by the fighters.

Fortunately our success in diverting, as opposed to destroying, enemy aircraft was much greater. Although at first we had nothing available with the correct frequency range for interfering with K.Gr.100's '*X*'-*Gerät*, suitable jamming apparatus was soon developed. Indeed, during the early months of 1941 the Germans became so impressed with our radio counter-measures that they no longer set up their beams the afternoon before the attack—except sometimes to mislead us by directing them against a false target. Instead they waited until their aircraft were crossing the British coast. Our customary foreknowledge of the enemy's objective—a surprising feature which would have caused some disquiet had it been commonly appreciated—was to that extent reduced; but there was also a corresponding reduction in the efficiency of the German system. Moreover, by January we were using one of Colonel Turner's devices —the decoy fire, or 'Starfish'—in very effective conjunction with our information of German intentions; for a decoy will naturally deceive the enemy more completely and attract a much greater number of his bombs if it is ignited along his predetermined line of approach.

All told, though we were still far from having the measure of the night bomber, we were on the verge of better things. Above all, the active defences were being developed along the right lines. Pupils from the new night fighter O.T.U. were beginning to enter the squadrons; night-flying facilities were improving; the first G.C.I. programme was being completed with astonishing speed. The guns, too, were growing steadily more efficient. The 20,000 rounds per aircraft destroyed in September had dropped to less than 3,000 in February, and the first of the new batteries of rockets, or unrotating projectiles (U.P.), was at last in action. The results were to be seen in the next, and final, phase of 'The Blitz'.

* * *

By February 1941 the German High Command was becoming critical of what had thus far been achieved. The doubts of Keitel and Jodl were powerfully reinforced by those of Raeder, who took the opportunity of a conference with Hitler on 4th February to point out that the *Luftwaffe*'s attacks had neither crippled British production nor shaken British morale. Britain's vulnerable points, the German admiral urged, were her dependence on imports and her shortage of

P

shipping space. German air strategy should concentrate on exploiting these weaknesses.

This, of course, was already part of the German plan of campaign. But from now on it was given 'top priority'. Since the German Army, according to the plan now current, would be fully occupied with Russia by the following May, Britain must be brought to her knees through a blockade exercised jointly by the German Navy and the German Air Force. While the U-boats dealt with our ships at sea, Göring's bombers must shatter our ship-yards and lay waste our ports. At the same time they must still keep the Royal Air Force in check by occasional attacks against the air armament industry. On 6th February this policy was incorporated in a formal directive from Hitler.

When better weather again made intensive operations possible, the *Luftwaffe* thus turned in strength against the ports, and in particular against those most used in the vital traffic across the Atlantic. Between 19/20th February and 12th May the enemy carried out sixty-one attacks involving more than fifty aircraft. Seven of these— most of them very heavy—fell on London, five on Birmingham, two on Coventry and one on Nottingham. The remaining forty-six were all directed against the ports. Portsmouth, Plymouth, Bristol and Avonmouth, Swansea, Merseyside, Belfast, Clydeside, were all heavily and repeatedly bombed. On the east coast Hull became an increasingly favoured target, while Sunderland had one big raid and Newcastle—thanks to a suggestion made by a former French Consul —two. In addition there were many minor raids, as well as individual attacks on ships and constant mine laying.

In each of the places attacked the enemy certainly left his mark. But his triumph was no longer cheap or easy. By March the A.I. squadrons in Fighter Command were all equipped with the new Mark IV apparatus, and five of the six had changed their Blenheims for Beaufighters. The following month the number of G.C.I. stations handling these aircraft rose to eleven. Moreover, the eight squadrons of ordinary Hurricanes and Defiants allocated exclusively to night operations were gaining rapidly in skill and experience. There was also the 'Intruder' Squadron—No. 23—which since December had harassed the German airfields and generally interfered with their night activities at source. As soon as the enemy's new plan of campaign became apparent, all these resources were skilfully disposed by Sholto Douglas to give the greatest possible protection to the ports.

In January the night fighters had been able to claim only three enemy aircraft destroyed, the guns twelve. In February the figures were much the same—four by the fighters, eight by the guns. But from then on the totals showed a welcome and encouraging rise—a rise, moreover, in which the fighters began to outstrip the guns. During March the fighters claimed twenty-two of the night raiders, the guns seventeen. In April the figures were better still—forty-eight and thirty-nine. In May, though the enemy's effort had already slackened before the end of the month, a peak was reached with a claim of 96 by the fighters, 31½ by the guns, 10½ by other causes.

This, though still no more than 3.5 per cent of the German sorties over the month, was a far cry from the complete failure of the previous autumn. Numerically the fighter successes were divided fairly equally between the ordinary 'cat's eye' fighters and the A.I. aircraft operating under G.C.I. control. But it was noticeable that since January the latter had obtained nearly twice as many 'contacts' as the former, though they had flown less than half the number of sorties. It was thus with A.I./G.C.I. that the future lay; for the normal fighter, even when flown by a fully trained night-pilot, was really effective only against a highly concentrated attack delivered on a very bright night—a 'fighter night', when gun-fire could be kept down (much to the chagrin of the gunners and the perturbation of the local population) and the skies above the target given over to close patrols of Defiants and Hurricanes or even, on occasion, Hampden bombers. The A.I./G.C.I. combination, on the other hand, did not depend for its success on a dense concentration of raiders; and though it was many times more efficient in moonlight than otherwise it was capable of securing results in conditions which completely baffled the 'cat's eyes'.

How the pilot and his A.I. operator in the air worked with the G.C.I. controller below may be seen from a typical combat report. The date is the night of 11/12th April 1941, the aircraft a Beaufighter of No. 604 Squadron, the A.I. operator Sergeant C. F. Rawnsley, the reporting pilot Squadron Leader John Cunningham. The necessary explanations have been added.

> Put on to north-bound raid 13,000 feet. Final vector 360° and buster [full speed].
> Told to flash [to operate A.I.] but no contact received. [G.C.I. station] then told me to alter course to 350° and height 11,000 feet. While going from 13,000 to 11,000 feet a blip [flash of light in A.I. set] was picked up at max. range ahead. On operator's instructions I closed in and obtained a visual at 2,500 feet range (checked on A.I. set) and about 30° up.
> Identified E/A [Enemy aircraft] as He.111 which was flying just beneath cloud layer and occasionally going through wisps which allowed me to get within 80 yards of E/A and about 20–30 ft. beneath before opening fire.
> Immediately there was a big white flash in the fuselage centre section and black pieces flew off the fuselage. E/A went into a vertical dive to

the right and about half a minute later the sky all around me was lit
up by an enormous orange flash and glow. Bits of E/A were seen to be
burning on the ground.

I estimated my position to be about Shaftesbury but called Harle-
quin and asked for a fix so that my exact position could be checked.

One He.111 destroyed.

Rounds fired 64.

Cunningham and Rawnsley, it may be remarked, were to continue
on these lines for a long time to come. They soon became the outstanding night-fighter crew of the war, and won between them no less
than nine British decorations.

The diversionary defences, like the night fighters, proved very
successful during the final phase of the German attack. On the night
of 17/18th April, for instance, when a heavy raid was taking place on
Portsmouth, a 'Starfish' site was lit on Hayling Island. It attracted
170 high explosive bombs, 32 parachute mines and 5,000 incendiaries.

Radio counter-measures were no less effective. As a result the
'X'-Gerät, subjected to continued interference, rapidly declined in
favour. Instead the enemy tried to employ a fresh beam system known
as the 'Y'-Gerät.[1] The essential features of this had been deduced in
advance by R. V. Jones of Scientific Intelligence, and it was jammed
at the enemy's very first attempt to bring it into use. By the end of
April, III/K.G.26, the pathfinding unit trained to operate with this
device, had as little confidence in it as K.Gr.100 had in the 'X'-
Geraet.

How the decoy fires and the radio counter-measures worked
together was shown very strikingly in the closing weeks of the enemy's
offensive. On the night of 8/9th May German bombers were ordered
to attack Derby and Nottingham. The attack on Derby was to be led
by K.Gr.100, and 'X'-Gerät beams were set up to cover the
Rolls-Royce works. They were detected, and radio counter-measures
applied, with the result that Derby escaped entirely and the German
effort spent itself on the moors to the north-east of the town. Apparently in the course of this diversion, some of the bombers attacked
Nottingham, the target for the other force. To distract them, a decoy
fire was lit outside the city. Seeing this ahead, many of the pilots
scheduled to attack Nottingham imagined the fire to be Derby
burning from the attack of their comrades, and concluded that they
were slightly off course. They accordingly 'corrected' by steering
further to the east. The result was that the Vale of Belvoir, which is

---

[1] This depended on the combination of a single beam with a system of ranging—
i.e. determining the position of the aircraft along the beam at any given time, so
that a signal for the release of the bombs could be sent at the right moment.

roughly the same distance east of Nottingham as Nottingham is of Derby, received 230 high explosive bombs, one oil bomb, and several groups of incendiaries, with a total casualty roll of two cows and two chickens. The following morning the German communiqués claimed great success at both Nottingham and Derby, including heavy damage to the Rolls-Royce works. The whole episode was the more surprising in that it occurred on a night of bright moon, when the difference between town and country—and real and decoy fires—should have been perfectly apparent to the enemy.

As the German Army began to mass in the East and to secure its right flank in Greece and Yugoslavia, the German Air Force struck with redoubled fury in the West. If the intention was to cover up the forthcoming offensive against Russia, it was singularly unsuccessful. But doubtless the main motive was to do as much damage as possible in the short time remaining. In the second half of April London was twice raided with a greater weight of high explosive than ever before —876 tons on the memorable 'Wednesday' (16/17th), 1,010 tons on the 'Saturday' (19/20th). Between came Portsmouth's heaviest attack; then followed four grim nights for Plymouth. The next month was ushered in by the sustained assault on Merseyside and by savage raids against Clydeside and Belfast; and in a final fling on 10/11th May, London was treated to another 700 tons.

But by then Göring's units were on the move, and in the next two months only four attacks of over a hundred tons were delivered against British targets. By the end of June two-thirds of the *Luftwaffe*'s strength had been withdrawn east and south. Like a prisoner slow to comprehend the news of his release, England saw 'The Blitz' degenerate into 'seaside tip-and-run' and was scarcely aware that the long ordeal was over.

In terms of strict economics, the German offensive had certainly been a profitable venture for the enemy. British aircraft production had been seriously impaired, both by direct damage and enforced dispersal of plant: not until February 1941 did output again approach the level of the previous August. The steel and ship-building industries, communications, power supplies, stocks of food and oil, all had suffered. Over 600,000 men had been kept tied down to ground and civil defence. Some 40,000 British civilians had been killed, another 46,000 injured, and more than a million houses damaged. All this had been accomplished for the loss on night operations of some 600 German aircraft—nearly a third as many again as we claimed at the time, but still only 1·5 per cent of sorties. The great Coventry raid, which for a short time caused a decline of 20 per cent of our aircraft output and cost us many hundreds of machines before production was fully restored, had been carried out for the loss of one German bomber.

Yet 'The Blitz' was very far from being a great strategic victory for the enemy. Widespread though the damage was, its effect on general industrial production was not of vital importance. In five months of intensive raiding on docks and ports in 1941, only some 70,000 tons of our food stocks were completely destroyed, and only one half of one per cent of our oil stocks. Damage to communications was quickly repaired. Everywhere except in the aircraft industry the loss was too small a fraction of total output to matter seriously.

This was partly because the German night offensive, like the day-light attacks in the Battle of Britain, suffered from confused direction. Our great power installations provided one good target system; the aircraft industry was another—though dispersal complicated the German task; the ports and dockyards were a third. But the Germans vacillated between these different systems, and mingled attacks on all three with mere terrorism. And since most of the bombs in any case fell wide of their target—an effect which must be ascribed in great part to our defences—much of the German activity was wasted, although it certainly made matters uncomfortable for the civil population. The campaign was conducted cheaply enough, and the Germans had good value for their expenditure in aircraft and crews. But except in so far as it forced us to retain at home guns and fighters which were badly needed by our hard-pressed forces in the Middle East, it got them nowhere.

CHAPTER VIII

German Blockade, British Bombing

THE Battle of Britain and 'The Blitz' were the most dramatic aspects of Hitler's effort to subdue us while we stood alone. But throughout the long months of the German assault on our homeland the enemy was also at work with a weapon which was quieter, more insidious, slower in its effects, but equally dangerous—the long-range blockade.

Until the spring of 1940 the war at sea had gone steadily in our favour. We had brought Germany's overseas commerce to a standstill, held her surface-raiders in check, cut short the success of her U-boats, mastered her magnetic mines. Even from the disastrous Norwegian episode we had emerged with at least one consolation— the campaign cost the German Navy one-third of its cruisers and nearly one-half of its destroyers.

The German occupation of Norway, however, was the beginning of a profound transformation which was all too rapidly completed by the overrunning of France and the Low Countries and the entry of Italy into the war. By virtue of these events, the enemy U-boats, E-boats and aircraft at once assumed new and deadly powers of destruction. From bases on the French Atlantic coast U-boats and aircraft such as the Focke-Wulf 200, an adapted civil machine of 2,000 miles range, began to haunt our Western Approaches or reach far out into waters previously free from their predatory attentions. From Norway the Germans harassed our east coast shipping and challenged our reconnaissance over the North Sea. From Sardinia and Sicily, southern Italy and the Dodecanese, Mussolini's ships and planes threatened the short route to Egypt and forced us into the 'long haul' round the Cape. Everywhere in a few swift strokes the prospect became charged with gloom and menace.

In common with the Royal Navy, which found itself desperately short of escort vessels for the new situation, Coastal Command was faced with a bewildering variety of fresh tasks. Anti-invasion patrols had to be flown over the North Sea and the English Channel, long-range fighter protection supplied over our Atlantic approaches, watch and ward maintained over thousands of miles of hostile coast. Escort patrols for convoys, offensive patrols against U-boats—all must be extended to distances unthought-of in earlier months. Yet for these and all his other duties Air Chief Marshal Bowhill in June 1940 had only some 500 aircraft. And a mere thirty-four of these— the Sunderlands—could operate beyond 500 miles from our shores.

At first the German U-boats and aircraft found their happy hunting ground in our South-West Approaches. The simplest answer to this was to route our convoys so that they approached British ports by the north-west. This was quickly done. The new traffic lane, however, was at once discovered, and the battle promptly shifted to the waters north and west of Ireland. In the absence of suitably placed airfields and flying-boat bases, the result was a still greater strain on Coastal Command. Hard on top of this, in August 1940, the U-boats made matters worse by adopting new tactics. Following up on the surface during the day at a respectful distance from the convoy and its attendant aircraft, they delayed closing in till nightfall. Still on the surface to escape detection by the Asdics of the escort vessels, they then attacked under cover of darkness.

To these tactics Coastal Command had as yet no reply. Facilities for night flying were still in a very rudimentary stage in the north-west, and except in bright moon an ordinary aircraft stood no chance of spotting a U-boat. On darker nights, the only hope thus lay in A.S.V. (Air to Surface Vessel) radar, with which about a sixth of the Coastal aircraft were already equipped. Unfortunately this was still subject to serious limitations. As the radiations might guide the U-boat to its prey, the apparatus could not be switched on until a convoy was already threatened; even if a 'contact' was obtained, the aircraft had no means of lighting up the target; and in any case pilots would run grave risks in descending to 'depth-charge' height in bad visibility without a reliable low-reading altimeter—which did not yet exist. The A.S.V. sets at this time also showed little response unless the U-boat was fully surfaced and within a distance of three miles. All told, the immediate outlook was unpromising.

In this situation, and with air and surface escorts alike so weak, our convoys were forced to depend for their safety mainly on evasive routing. This was planned in the light of intercepted wireless signals. The same means also enabled us to concentrate our air patrols over areas where the U-boats intended to operate. But information of this

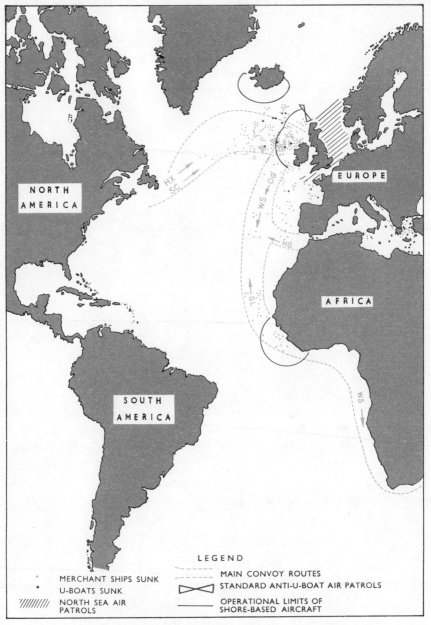

LEGEND

· · · MERCHANT SHIPS SUNK   ‑ ‑ ‑ MAIN CONVOY ROUTES
· U-BOATS SUNK   ▷◁ STANDARD ANTI-U-BOAT AIR PATROLS
////// NORTH SEA AIR PATROLS   ── OPERATIONAL LIMITS OF SHORE-BASED AIRCRAFT

THE BATTLE OF THE ATLANTIC (II), JUNE 1940—MID-MARCH 1941

Note (i) Standard anti-U-boat patrols in N.W. approaches from Oban and Aldergrove.

   (ii) Limited air escort supplied during this period. Sunderlands 300 miles, Hudsons 150 miles.

   (iii) U-boat attacks mainly at night.

   (iv) Intermittent local air escort from Gibraltar.

[facing page 220]

kind was not always available or reliable, and when it failed, losses were apt to prove disastrous. Between the beginning of June and the end of 1940 over 3,000,000 tons of British, Allied and neutral merchant shipping were sunk by the enemy—an average of some 450,000 tons each month. Fifty-nine per cent of this tonnage fell to the U-boats and twelve per cent to the Focke-Wulf Condors and other aircraft. The remainder was accounted for by mines and surface-raiders. Over the whole period British losses exceeded replacements by more than 2,500,000 tons, and our volume of imports shrank by one-fifth.

At this stage, then, we were in desperate need of more and better weapons: more aircraft, more destroyers, more A.S.V., more depth-charges, more R/T sets for communication between air and surface escorts—but aircraft of longer range, A.S.V. of higher performance, depth-charges specially designed for dropping from the air. Means of illumination by aircraft, such as searchlights and slow-dropping flares, were also urgently required. Of all this Bowhill at Coastal Command was entirely aware. Yet a mounting volume of criticism now began to threaten his Command—criticism which, instead of fastening on the need to provide all these things with the utmost speed, called in question the whole system of naval and air co-operation. Once more there appeared the demand that the Admiralty should be responsible for all maritime aircraft. At the height of the U-boat crisis Coastal Command was confronted with the danger of being severed from the Royal Air Force and handed over *en bloc* to the Navy.

In an earlier form this demand had resulted in the compromise of 1937, when all carrier-borne aircraft were transferred to the Admiralty. The main advocate of completing the job by handing over the shore-based maritime aircraft as well was now, curiously enough, the Minister of Aircraft Production. Yet it was far from clear how the proposal would result in any increase of aircraft, which after all was the main consideration; and it was completely certain that the morale of the Command would suffer a grievous, if not irreparable, blow. Lord Beaverbrook's proposal, too, took no account of the fact that Bomber and Fighter Commands also played a great part in the war at sea. Fortunately it was a case of being more Catholic than the Pope. The Admiralty, while terming Coastal Command the 'Cinderella' of the Royal Air Force and criticizing its training and equipment, were not prepared to go as far as the Minister. In peace-time My Lords Commissioners might have felt otherwise; in the middle of a war they were rightly chary of assuming at one stroke so vast and unfamiliar a responsibility.

The great sailor and the great airman who headed their respective Services had therefore little difficulty in arriving at an agreement which went some way towards meeting naval criticisms without shattering the hard-won unity of British land-based air power. Coastal Command, whose rate of expansion since the outbreak of war already exceeded that of Bomber Command and would have been greater still but for the lamentable failure of the Lerwick flying-boat and the Botha, was to be increased by three squadrons at once and fifteen squadrons by June 1941. It would remain an integral part of the Royal Air Force, alike for administration, technical development and training; but its squadrons could not be diverted to non-maritime work without the consent of the Admiralty. As from April 1941 the Command would also come under the Admiralty's operational control, which would be exercised through the Air Officer Commanding-in-Chief. Apart from some improvement in the means of liaison between the Admiralty and the Command, this made no great alteration to the position, which remained in fact, if not in theory, much what it had always been. The Admiralty specified the broad requirement: the Command decided how, and with what, it should be met.

A more important innovation was the decision to operate Coastal Command aircraft from Iceland. The strategic value of Iceland had been long recognized, and on 26th September 1939 our only Catalina flying-boat had been sent off to reconnoitre its south and south-western coasts. Forced down by fog, the pilot had been technically interned, but within two days had taken off again for Scotland. On official orders he had then returned to Iceland, where the conditions of his internment enabled him to fill in the time to good purpose. When British forces forestalled the Germans by landing at Reykjavik on 10th May 1940, a valuable report on the possibilities of the island as an air base was available, and in August a squadron of Battles—No. 98—was sent out to strengthen the local defences against a German invasion. Its first flight over Reykjavik, according to the squadron diary, 'stirred one-half of the townspeople to enthusiasm'—the other half apparently being convinced that the dreaded Hun had at last arrived. But the enemy made no effort to challenge our position, and in the absence of any such attempt No. 98 Squadron came to be occupied more and more with purely naval reconnaissance. For this task its aircraft were unsuited and its crews largely untrained. In January 1941, the decision was accordingly taken to send out a squadron of Hudsons and a squadron of Sunderlands, and by April No. 30 Wing Headquarters had been set up to control the three squadrons. It worked under No. 15 Group, which had been transferred from Plymouth to Liverpool on the formation of the new Western Naval Command.[1] A few weeks later the Battles were withdrawn in favour of Northrop float-planes flown by the gallant young Norwegians of No. 330 Squadron, and by mid-summer Iceland was the base of a small but highly specialized and skilful maritime air force.

The year 1941 opened with tempestuous weather which hampered the U-boats and brought about some decline in the Allied losses. Then the enemy's successes again began to mount. By 24th February Hitler felt sufficiently sure of himself to prophesy that the struggle would be over within sixty days. The next two months saw the German effort reach a climax. New ocean-going U-boats, powerful reinforcements of aircraft—He.111's as well as F.W.200's—surface raiders like the *Hipper, Scharnhorst, Gneisenau* and *Scheer*, all played their part. In March the sinkings reached 532,000 tons, in April 644,000 tons. In the latter month no less than 296,000 tons were sent to the bottom by aircraft alone.

This intensified campaign was met by Winston Churchill's Battle of the Atlantic directive on 6th March, by the creation of the Battle of Atlantic Committee, and by a host of practical measures on a lower plane. Blenheims withdrawn from Bomber Command took over some of the reconnaissance duties in the North Sea, so enabling Coastal squadrons to be moved to the vital north-west. The inestimable boon of bases in Eire remained unhappily denied to us, but new airfields quickly appeared in Northern Ireland, the Hebrides and Iceland. Convoys were strengthened by the arming of merchant vessels and the development of the fighter-catapult ship. A mounting weight of attack fell on the German naval bases; bombs and air-laid mines hemmed in the *Scharnhorst* and *Gneisenau* at Brest. At last strong enough to act offensively as well as defensively, Coastal Command began to scour the seas for U-boats far beyond the immediate vicinity of our convoys. All this, and more, was done. To one suggestion, however, the Air Staff remained resolutely deaf; the new long-range Halifaxes were preserved, as they were intended, for Bomber Command. Otherwise there was some danger, as Air Marshal A. T. Harris, then Deputy Chief of Air Staff, put it in his own characteristic fashion, that 'twenty U-boats and a few Focke-Wulf in the Atlantic would have provided the efficient anti-aircraft defence of all Germany'.

It was not long before more ample resources, improved equipment and revised tactics brought their reward. The U-boats, vulnerable to

---

[1] A new Group—No. 19—was formed at Plymouth to work with the re-organized Plymouth Naval Command.

attack on the surface for several hours each day while they recharged their batteries and emitted foul air, soon showed their sensitiveness to our increased air activity by retiring farther and farther from our shores. By May 1941, when air escort and offensive sweeps stretched out to 400 miles from the coasts of Great Britain and Iceland, the U-boats were largely reduced to operating off West Africa or in the central Atlantic. The West African threat—the lesser of the two— was met by basing Sunderlands and Hudsons near Freetown. The central Atlantic was as yet beyond the range of Coastal Command; but it was also beyond the range of the F.W.200's, and without their co-operation the U-boats were nothing like so formidable. At the same time the improved anti-aircraft defences of the convoys and the advent of the first Coastal Command Beaufighter squadron (No. 252) helped to master the 'Big Bad Wulf'. The difference was soon clear enough. In May 1941 Allied and neutral shipping losses fell below 500,000 tons. In June they declined still further. In July and August they averaged no more than 125,000 tons. The immediate crisis was over.

The turning-point in this struggle was undoubtedly the sinking of five U-boats in March. When our destroyers put paid to the activities of Commanders Prien, Schepke and Kretschmer, they profoundly influenced the course of the whole battle. But the death-blow to Hitler's hopes of a quick victory at sea came with the crippling of the *Gneisenau* and the pursuit and destruction of the *Bismarck*.

The enemy's original plan was for the *Bismarck*, a newly completed battleship of immense power, to co-operate in the North Atlantic with the *Scharnhorst* and *Gneisenau*. The two battle-cruisers had destroyed 115,622 tons during the cruise which finished at Brest on 22nd March, but they had been handicapped by their inability to face the battleship escort of our convoys. The presence of the *Bismarck*, which was reputed to be more than a match for anything else afloat, would remedy this weakness, and in company the three German ships would wreak unprecedented havoc on the British trade routes. Such was the broad German conception in April 1941.

This intention was frustrated by the Royal Air Force. After the Prime Minister's directive of 6th March our air striking force was ordered to concentrate on objectives connected with the Battle of the Atlantic. When photographic reconnaissance on 28th March confirmed the presence of the two battle-cruisers at Brest, they thus at once became a target of great importance not only for Coastal but also for Bomber Command. During the next few nights weather conditions were unfavourable, and though some 200 bombers attacked they scored no hits. But the effort was not wasted, for an unexploded

250-pound bomb caused the *Gneisenau* to be removed on 5th April from dry dock to the outer harbour. There it was at once detected by a photographic Spitfire, and a strike by Coastal Command torpedo-bombers was arranged for first light the following morning.

As 6th April dawned, a Beaufort of No. 22 Squadron—the only one of four aircraft to locate the target in the haze—penetrated the outer harbour. The *Gneisenau* was lying in the inner harbour alongside one of the shore quays. To her seaward was a long stone mole; behind her was sharply rising ground; in dominating positions all round were anti-aircraft guns—some 270 of them. Three *flak*-ships moored in the outer harbour and the battle-cruiser's own formidable armament added to the strength of the defences. Even if the Beaufort survived the fury of its reception, its crew could scarcely hope, after delivering a low-level attack, to avoid crashing into the rising ground beyond. The pilot—Flying Officer Kenneth Campbell—was nothing daunted. Sweeping between the *flak*-ships at less than mast height, he skimmed over the mole and launched his torpedo at a range of 500 yards. Greeted by a searing hail of fire, his aircraft was instantly shot down, with the loss of all its gallant crew; but the torpedo ran true and pierced the *Gneisenau*'s stern beneath the water-line. Eight months later the starboard propeller shaft was still under repair.[1]

With great difficulty the crippled battle-cruiser was redocked on 7th April. During the next few days unfavourable weather again frustrated our attacks on both ships, but on the night of 10/11th April Bomber Command inflicted further injury on the *Gneisenau* by four direct hits and two near-misses. Many of the vessel's crew were killed or wounded, and extensive damage was done to one of the turrets, to the gunnery and damage-control rooms, and to the living quarters. The *Scharnhorst*, more fortunate, escaped direct hurt, but her refitting was delayed by the damage to dock facilities.

The enemy's grand design of a combined break-out into the Atlantic trade routes was thus thwarted, and the *Bismarck* and an accompanying cruiser, the *Prinz Eugen*, were left to carry out the mission alone. How they in turn were harried and frustrated, and the *Bismarck* destroyed, is a striking example of the inter-dependence of modern sea and air forces.

The two German vessels were first sighted, though not identified, by a Swedish warship on 20th May, while passing through the Kattegat. Within a few hours a report reached the Admiralty from our Naval Attaché in Stockholm. The next day both ships were

---

[1] Flying Officer Campbell was posthumously awarded the Victoria Cross. The other members of the crew were Sergeants J. P. Scott, W. Mullis and R. W. Hillman.

spotted near Bergen by a Spitfire of the Photographic Reconnaissance Unit, and from the photographs then taken correct identifications were made. Bad weather hampered air action, but on 22nd May, in 10/10ths cloud down to 200 feet, a Fleet Air Arm Maryland forced its way up the Bergen fjords at very low level and established that the German vessels had departed. In continued bad weather our aircraft remained unable to pick up the enemy, and it was a surface vessel in the Denmark Strait, between Iceland and Greenland, which detected the two ships as they attempted to break through into the Atlantic. This was done by radar—a possibility for which the Germans had not bargained. Coastal Command and the Fleet Air Arm as well as our surface vessels then set about shadowing the enemy. The credit for putting our forces firmly on the trail was thus shared by ships and aircraft alike.

The chase then took a fresh turn with the naval action of 24th May, when the ill-fated *Hood* blew up and the *Prince of Wales* scored hits which pierced the *Bismarck*'s oil tanks and reduced her speed. It was this which forced the German commander to make for a French port. But the agonizing uncertainties of the next stage, when the German battleship had covered up the departure of the *Prinz Eugen* and shaken off her pursuers, were ended mainly by brilliant work at Coastal Command. On 26th May, after many hours had passed with no sign of the enemy, Bowhill on his own initiative laid a patrol farther south than the Admiralty appreciation required, and in so doing put Catalina 'Z' for Zebra of No. 209 Squadron, piloted by Pilot Officer D. A. Briggs, right on to the missing vessel. Circling to confirm her identity, but unluckily breaking cloud only a quarter of a mile away, the flying boat was at once hit. It lost touch, but another Catalina, of No. 240 Squadron, was soon there to regain contact. By then it was too late for our heavy forces to come up before the quarry reached Brest, and every mile would bring the pursuers into greater danger from German bombers based in Britanny. So once more all depended on aircraft—on aircraft directed from the sea. 'Homed' on to the target by a shadowing cruiser, which they at first attacked in error, Swordfish from the *Ark Royal* settled the matter when a well-aimed torpedo crippled the *Bismarck*'s steering gear. Defiant still, the pride of the German Navy was left a dangerous but certain victim for our oncoming surface forces. The whole pursuit had been a drama in which the two elements, air and sea, in turn dominated successive scenes.

A few days later, on 14th June 1941, Bowhill was posted from Northwood to form Ferry Command. The day before, the pilots of No. 42 Squadron gave him a parting present of his favourite kind by torpedoing the *Lützow* off Norway. By that time, the worth and importance of Coastal Command were established beyond dispute. From being concerned almost entirely with reconnaissance, the Command had developed into an offensive weapon capable of inflicting serious damage on enemy warships, merchant shipping, aircraft and shore targets. Its equipment had improved out of all recognition. The nineteen squadrons of 1939 had grown to forty. The average range of its aircraft had doubled. Efficient torpedo-bombers and long-range fighters—though still all too few—had taken their place in the line of battle. More than half the aircraft of the Command had been fitted with A.S.V.—an improved A.S.V., effective at twice the range of the initial model. Experiments in the camouflage of Coastal aircraft and the development of an airborne searchlight were about to be crowned with success. It was with the knowledge that many, though by no means all, of the basic problems and difficulties had been overcome that Bowhill handed over to his successor, Air Marshal Sir Philip Joubert.

Joubert, an extraordinarily keen-witted and versatile officer, was no newcomer to Coastal Command. He had already presided over its infant destinies in 1936–1937, when his ever-active intelligence had stimulated the development of airborne radar for locating ships at sea. After a spell in India just before the war, he had taken up the new position of Assistant Chief of the Air Staff (Radio) at the Air Ministry, in which capacity he had held a watching brief on all the manifold aspects of radar—no hint of which was as yet allowed to appear in his deservedly popular broadcast commentaries. It was because the air war at sea, like the bombing offensive, was becoming increasingly dependent on radar that Joubert was now re-appointed to his old command. His first task was accordingly clear: to develop the most effective operational technique for A.S.V. aircraft, and in so doing to make the aeroplane at last a 'U-boat killer'.

There were other subjects, too, in which there would be ample scope for Joubert's talents. But in one respect he would be well content to leave matters as he found them. Under Bowhill, for all the shortages and difficulties of the period, the spirit of the Coastal crews had remained superb. Every demand, whether for the steely determination and cold courage of a daylight attack on Brest, or the patient, alert endurance of a U-boat hunt, had been met with equal fortitude. Only rarely had the crews been rewarded by the sight of some really satisfactory piece of destruction—'The chimney', reported one pilot lyrically after attacking an oil refinery in Brittany, 'was tossed from its base like a caber'. Promising-looking enemy vessels, too, had a disappointing habit of turning out, on closer inspection, to be wrecks, or shoals of porpoises, or even basking whales. Yet the keenness and skill of Bowhill's airmen had never become blunted. Cheerful and unwearying, they had faced long, monotonous hours of flying in which danger, if not ever present, had never been far distant. The newly made landing ground, with its toll of fatal crashes: the faulty engine or compass 400 miles out to sea: the fierce Atlantic 'front': the all-too-frequent attack from friendly *flak* or fighters: the landing with base blanketed in mist or cloud and the aircraft too short of fuel to fly elsewhere—these, no less than the sharp, unforgiving clash with the enemy, were among the hazards they had accepted undeterred.

To turn the pages of the Operations Record Books of the Coastal squadrons is to recapture, despite the stereotype entries, something of these slow, uneventful hours so sharply broken by moments of deadly danger. Sometimes—it is the exception—a recording officer with a gift for putting pen to paper gives us not merely fact, but atmosphere. Such a record is that of No. 217 Squadron at St. Eval, where the mist rolling in from the Atlantic, the absence of convenient alternative landing grounds, and the frequent attentions of the enemy, provided no lack of incident:

> St. Eval. 29.1.41.
> Beaufort A, which returned because of a faulty airspeed indicator, crashed on landing. When the remainder returned, conditions were very awkward at St. Eval. A mist had formed over the aerodrome, about 200 feet thick, and prevented the returning pilots from seeing the ground. The goose-neck flares were lighted, but the Chance Light was almost useless because of reflection from the mist . . . P/O. W— circled for some time without being able to see anything, then saw a break in the mist and recognized Mawgan Porth. He made several darts at the flare-path, but, as he said later, 'every time it came into view it was in a different place!' Eventually he landed anyhow, but ran into a patch of mist just as he was holding off. The machine must have touched and ballooned, because next time it hit, one wheel was pushed up through the wing. None of the crew was hurt.
> Another machine landed across the flare-path and swung. It was sliding sideways in the mud when the undercarriage hit the runway and collapsed sideways. No one was injured.
> Sergeant S— had rather a shaky do. He was circling just above the mist when he felt his wheels hit something, probably the hills to the south east. He hastily climbed.
> Flight Lieutenant O— landed rather roughly, overshot and finished up in the Hurricane Dispersal Point. He taxied out, rather shaken, between two picketed machines.

A few months later, the diarist presents another angle:

> St. Eval. 8.5.41.
> About midnight, Group decided they wanted three machines for a moonlight convoy, though they had already released the squadron.

Flying Officer K—, who was duty officer, nearly howled himself hoarse over the phone trying to find crews who had been released, and finally he got a large transport and drove around the countryside pulling out every aircrew he could find from bed, billet or hotel. Eventually he got two complete crews into camp, and the Station Commander washed out the job. Were the crews pleased!!!

But 'higher authority', that convenient repository of all the sins, is not the only enemy:

St. Eval. 10.5.41.

Pilot Officer K— and Squadron Leader R— were just taxying out to take off, when they were stopped by the 'Alert'. They taxied back to the perimeter track and switched off. After sitting in their cockpits for a while, it suddenly struck them that sitting on top of 2,000 pounds of bombs during a raid was rather a silly business. So they got out. Then the stuff began to fall, and R—'s aircraft was written off by a direct hit. R— himself went into a ditch, and his observer head first into a bed of nettles. Altogether seven aircraft of the squadron were damaged—mostly written off. A/C.s Collier and Ball put up a very good show by towing a bowser which was on fire away so that it could burn out in safety. One of them actually had to climb under the bowser to attach a cable to it. Their prompt and courageous action undoubtedly saved another aircraft from destruction.

And when Group and the Germans fail to come up to expectations, there is always the weather:

St. Eval. 22.5.41.

One of the 'St. Eval' speciality days—that is, fog and rain, consequently no flying. Four Beaufighters were expected to come in from Gibraltar. Flying Officer M— (late of this squadron and therefore knowing the local weather) took one look at the south coast and went down in the sea in Mount's Bay. His aircraft floated for $1\frac{1}{4}$ hours, but the fishing boat beside which he landed left them bobbing about in the water for half an hour before deciding that they were not Huns! Another Beaufighter got in at Perranporth. The third went down in Ireland, and the fourth at Weston Zoyland.

*   *   *

'The Navy can lose us the war, but only the Air Force can win it. Therefore our supreme effort must be to gain overwhelming mastery in the air. The Fighters are our salvation but the Bombers alone provide the means of victory. We must therefore develop the power to carry an ever-increasing volume of explosives to Germany, so as to pulverize the entire industry and scientific structure on which the war effort and economic life of the enemy depend, while holding him at arm's length from our Island. In no other way at present visible can we hope to overcome the immense military power of Germany . . . '

Thus the Prime Minister to the War Cabinet on the first anniversary of the outbreak of war. It was a policy with which the Air Staff

R

was in entire agreement. Indeed, their only regret was that a more powerful bombing offensive against German industry was not already under way.

Since the fall of France much of Bomber Command's work had been defensive––first in reducing the threat from the enemy's air force, then in disrupting the preparations for invasion. Targets in the directly offensive category, such as oil plants, had received less attention than they were normally reckoned to deserve. This arose from no fault of the Air Staff, whose belief in the value of a strategic offensive never wavered. Still less did it represent the ideals of Portal, who in the brief interval before the Battle of Britain protested against the use of Bomber Command to 'bolster up Fighter Command, the A.A. defences and the A.R.P. before these had been really tried and found wanting'. Nor could it rightly be blamed on the Admiralty, whose incessant desire for the bombing of German naval objectives was entirely natural in the circumstances. The concentration on defensive bombing was, of course, simply a reflection of the general military situation. For nearly a year after the fall of France, the Germans, being free to devote their whole military effort to our destruction, could dictate the sequence of operations. The Battle of Britain, 'The Blitz', the blockade, were the changing facets of their offensive. With a huge numerical superiority on land and in the air, and a powerful fleet of surface-raiders and U-boats to challenge our superiority at sea, they held the initiative firmly in their hands. It would remain there until we had defeated their onslaught by the use of every weapon in our armoury.

By the end of September 1940, when the Germans had been forced to abandon massed bombing by day and disperse their invasion flotillas, the first and greatest crisis was over. It is a remarkable indication of the Air Staff's faith in the conception of a strategic offensive that even in these grimmest hours Bomber Command was never entirely confined to defensive activity. In July and August 1940 twenty-four per cent of our bombing effort had been aimed at German oil plants; only in September, when fifty-four per cent of the effort was devoted to barge concentrations alone, were operations against oil reduced to a mere four per cent. This decline was not allowed to persist a moment longer than the situation required. On the first clear signs of a break-down in the German invasion plans, the Air Staff at once seized the opportunity to reshape the pattern of our bombing policy nearer to their hearts' desire.

In this determination to resume the strategic offensive our air leaders were powerfully supported by the Prime Minister. But the military and the political conceptions of the forthcoming operations were by no means identical. With London under heavy bombardment, the politicians desired above all things retaliation on Berlin. The Air Staff, however, being more keenly aware that to reach Berlin British aircraft had to fly five times as far as German aircraft attacking London, favoured raids on objectives within easier range. The difference of opinion, however, went deeper than a choice between bombing the German capital and bombing the Ruhr. The political authorities, exasperated by the German 'Blitz' and gauging the feeling in London, wanted—in the popular phrase—to 'give it 'em back!' They desired, in other words, not merely attacks on Berlin, but indiscriminate attacks—to which end the War Cabinet on 19th September recommended the use of parachute mines. Nothing could have accorded less with the ideas of the Air Staff, who drew an instructive contrast between the results of four German bombs which fell on the Fulham Power Station and several thousand German bombs which fell elsewhere.

The dispute ended in a compromise. The Air Staff agreed to give a high place to Berlin in their forthcoming bombing directive. But they insisted that the attack should be aimed, not against the population at large, but against precise objectives—power stations, gasworks, the electrical industry. In this, of course, they were moved by professional rather than humanitarian considerations. They wanted to do their job as quickly and efficiently as possible; and indiscriminate bombing against a well-disciplined population is—or was, before the atom-bomb—of all means of attack the most extravagant. They were fully as anxious as the political authorities to lower German morale, but they thought that this would best be achieved by, and in the course of, destroying vital industrial plant. Of actual physical injury the civilians would receive quite enough from the bombs that failed to find their mark on the factories.

The bombing directive of 21st September 1940, an interim measure which contemplated as yet only the release of the Whitley Group from anti-invasion work, accordingly gave a high place to power plants in Berlin. Other selected target systems elsewhere in Germany were oil plants, aircraft component and aluminium factories, railways, canals, and U-boat construction yards. The directive was not many hours old when Berlin was selected for a special retaliatory effort. On 23rd/24th September the Whitleys were joined by all available Wellingtons and Hampdens and 119 aircraft took off for the German capital. Their main objectives were the city's gas-works and electric power stations, with the local marshalling yards and the Tempelhof airfield as subsidiary targets. Weather and icing conditions proved unexpectedly severe, but eighty-four of the bombers managed to reach Berlin. The only significant success was at Charlottenburg, where incendiaries set fire to a gasometer. Many of the bombs failed to explode, including one which dropped in the garden of Hitler's Chancellery. Several houses were damaged in the Tiergarten district —the Berlin West End—and 781 persons lost their homes. Twenty-two Germans were killed—ten more than our own losses in aircrew.

Unsatisfactory as operations of this kind were, they were not without some effect on the enemy. Berlin looked forward to a visit from the Royal Air Force no more enthusiastically than London looked forward to a visit from the *Luftwaffe*. Apart from direct damage to industrial targets and town property, the raids interfered with transport, caused loss of production, and showed the German people that war was not one unvarying succession of German victories. A minor but not unpleasing by-product was Hitler's discomfiture when the arrival of our bombers coincided with that of distinguished foreign visitors. On 26th September, Ciano, travelling to Berlin, was turned out of the train at Munich: 'Attacks by the Royal Air Force endanger the zone, and the *Führer* does not wish to expose me to the risk of a long stop in the open country. I sleep in Munich and will continue by air.'

Attacks on the scale of 23rd/24th September against the German capital were not yet the rule, and until the end of the month the invasion ports continued to attract the attention of the bulk of our bombers. An incident which occurred on the night of 9/10th September provided a good example of the dangers of adverse weather even on one of these short-range trips. Near its objective, the port of Boulogne, a Wellington of No. 149 Squadron ran into a severe electric storm. Climbing to avoid this, the aircraft was caught in even more turbulent conditions which for a few seconds left it uncontrollable. Badly iced up, it began to lose height, while the pilot, his vision obscured by the ice on the windscreen, and his compass hopelessly defective, turned for home. Within a few minutes the port engine failed and burst into flames. Ahead the crew could catch glimpses of searchlights on the English coast, but as the aircraft drew nearer the lights went out. Then the starboard engine fell silent. For a few minutes the Wellington glided down, while the crew peered anxiously into the murk beneath. By now, it seemed, they should be over land, and in any case they could not delay their jump much longer. But the aircraft, unknown to its occupants, had turned on a course parallel with the coast, with the result that the crew took to their parachutes some miles out to sea. Only one of the six men survived. Aided by his 'Mae West', Pilot Officer C. W. Parish, the second pilot, and a comparative newcomer to operational work, floated and swam for several hours towards land, to which he guided himself at times by glimpses of searchlights, at times simply by the North Star. Despite cramp and sickness he kept going till dawn, when a final effort brought him to the shore. In full flying kit, save for his discarded boots, he had swum something like seven miles in the dark —an ordeal which apparently left him little the worse, for he was back to duty and bombing Berlin within a fortnight. Two and a half years later, his brief career—long only for a bomber pilot—was to end on his fifty-fourth operation.

At the close of September more bombers were released from anti-invasion work, and on 6th October renewed attacks against Italy were authorized. Less than a hundred sorties in all had thus far been directed against Italian targets, and many of these had gone astray. Indeed, the most satisfactory feature had been, not the bombing, but the understanding attitude of the Swiss towards our use of their air. This may be gauged from the two wishes good-humouredly expressed by a Swiss representative—that if we had to pass over Switzerland, we would use the Geneva route, and that when the weather made it impossible for us to fly over his country we would draw attention to the correctness of our attitude. But the hope of attacking Italian industry in much greater force, like that of attacking Germany, was soon disappointed. The needs of defence again came to the fore, the Admiralty pressed for action against the *Scharnhorst* and *Gneisenau* in Kiel, and in October over a third of our bomber sorties were directed against naval and coastal objectives.

Before October was out Sir Cyril Newall, whose services in building up the Royal Air Force and guiding it through its greatest hour of trial had been second to none, reached the age of retirement. He was succeeded by Portal from Bomber Command. The new Chief of Air Staff, a man of quiet but powerful resolution whose polite address, discretion and immense ability made an immediate impression on all who met him, came to Whitehall imbued not only with enthusiasm for the bombing offensive against Germany, but also with a first-hand appreciation of its difficulties. His place at Bomber Command was taken by Air Marshal R. E. C. Peirse, who as Vice-Chief of Air Staff had already been closely concerned with our bombing policy.

The effect of Portal's appointment was seen in the new 'winter' directive issued on 30th October 1940. Oil plants remained 'top priority', but they were to be attacked only in bright moonlight, when there was some chance of hitting them. 'Fringe' coastal targets, mining (by the inexperienced crews), Italian targets, marshalling yards, Berlin, all figured in the directive. But the essence of the new policy was that the precise objective selected for attack—the power station, or oil refinery, or aircraft plant—should be situated in a well-populated centre. In the words of the directive, 'regular concentrated attacks should be made on objectives in large towns and centres of industry, with the primary aim of causing very heavy material destruction which would demonstrate to the enemy the power and severity of air bombardment'. While still intent on damaging individual factories, the Air Staff thus recognized that these were being hit less frequently than might appear from the crews' reports, and that at the same time some retaliation for the sufferings of British towns would not be amiss. Accordingly, they were now choosing, not merely profitable targets, but profitable targets in profitable surroundings.

From this to 'area bombing' was a short and natural progression. In November a small force of bombers attacked Berlin, Essen, Munich and Cologne; in each case a target in the middle of an industrial area was chosen as the general aiming point. Then, on 16/17th December, as the result of a War Cabinet decision four days earlier, came an experiment in heavy concentration in the 'Coventry' manner. Two hundred and thirty-five aircraft were ordered, under the not inappropriate code-name 'Abigail', to bring about the 'maximum possible destruction in a selected German town'. Fourteen of the most experienced Wellington crews were to bomb first with incendiaries; the rest, navigating individually but helped by the fires, and carrying incendiaries, land-mines and the biggest available bombs, were to arrive in succession over the target area throughout the night. The choice of objective was to be made at the last moment, in accordance with the weather forecast, from three towns in different areas of Germany—Bremen ('Jezebel'), Düsseldorf ('Delilah') and Mannheim ('Rachel').

At 1015 on 16th December the waiting squadrons obediently booked a date with 'Delilah', only to have it changed three hours later for a rendezvous with 'Rachel'. Good weather was reasonably certain for the first part of the night, but not for the early hours of the following morning, and the number of aircraft was accordingly cut down to 134. The moon was bright, with excellent visibility, and 103 aircraft claimed to have made their way successfully to Mannheim. All the later sorties had no difficulty in recognizing the town from the *flak* and the fires. The aiming point was officially 1,500 yards south of the Motorenwerke-Mannheim—a works engaged in the production of Diesel engines for submarines—and 89 tons of H.E. and nearly 14,000 incendiaries (including a number of special 250-pounders) were dropped in the six hours of attack. Total casualties, including crashes on return, were ten aircraft. Among the more noteworthy incidents, Pilot Officer Brant of No. 10 Squadron brought his Whitley back from south-west Germany to Bircham Newton on one engine, jettisoning guns, ammunition and all loose objects to maintain a height of 2,000 feet over the sea.

The contemporary German record of the raid makes somewhat disappointing reading. The scale of attack was estimated at 40–50 aircraft, and the number of bombs dropped at 100 H.E. and 1,000 incendiaries. Most of the damage occurred in the residential area of Mannheim, but several bombs fell across the river at Ludwigshafen. Many aircraft were reported to have bombed from a great height without aiming, owing to the strength of the anti-aircraft defences. Sixteen large and seventy-five medium and small fires were caused, fire-fighting being made difficult by bomb damage to the main water system and by the freezing of water brought from the Rhine. A sugar and a refrigerator factory were put out of action, the Mannheim-Rheinau power station was damaged, and output of armoured fighting vehicles and tank components from the Lanz works was cut by a quarter. Four other industrial plants were also hit. Twenty-three Germans were killed and eighty injured.

No further attacks of this sort were made during the rest of December. The Admiralty was now clamouring for action against the U-boat bases at Lorient and Bordeaux as well as the construction yards in Germany, and by the end of the year as big a weight of bombs was being aimed against naval targets as against all other types of objectives put together. A run of bad weather also helped the German towns to escape further serious damage for the time being, and enabled both sides to make a virtue of necessity at Christmas.

The next experiment in area bombing was an attack on Bremen early in January 1941. Then, following the latest report of the Lloyd Committee on German oil production, came a sharp revulsion of opinion. The new report emphasized once more that the Axis powers would be dangerously short of oil until Germany had increased her domestic production and overcome the difficulty of transporting supplies from Rumania. The critical period would be the first six months of 1941, during which time any further significant reduction in German output of the synthetic product—the Committee considered that a cut of 15 per cent had already been achieved by our bombing—would have consequences of the highest value. If the nine largest synthetic plants could be destroyed, out of the total of seventeen, output would be reduced by eighty per cent, and a devastating blow struck at the entire German war effort. On 15th January Peirse was accordingly instructed that the whole primary aim of the bombing offensive, until further orders, should be the destruction of the

German synthetic oil plants. The secondary aim, when the weather was unfavourable for the major plan, would be to harass industrial towns and communications. The only diversions contemplated from this strict programme were such operations as might be necessary against invasion ports and enemy naval forces.

This renewed attempt to concentrate against oil broke down before the threat to our shipping, just as the first attempt broke down before the threat to the French armies. The directive was not many days old when an extra task was reimposed in the form of mine-laying. Then came requests for the bombing of the *Hipper* at Brest and of the Focke-Wulf bases at Bordeaux and Stavanger. Next it was considered essential to delay the completion of the *Tirpitz* at Wilhelmshaven; over 400 sorties were despatched against this target within two months. Finally there was the decision to divert Bomber Command Blenheims to coastal duties in the North Sea, so that Coastal Command could be reinforced in the North-West Approaches. The result, taken in conjunction with a good deal of unfavourable weather, was that during January and February 1941 the bomber force operated exclusively against its priority objective, oil, on only three nights. Against naval targets it operated exclusively on thirteen nights and partially on six. Only one attempt was made during these two months at a crash concentration against a German city by over two hundred aircraft. On 10th February 221 bombers—the largest force thus far detailed against a single town—took off to attack an industrial area in Hanover. It was chosen for its importance in the manufacture of U-boat components.

All this was before the Prime Minister's directive of 6th March 1941 gave absolute priority to the Battle of the Atlantic. During the seven weeks that followed, more than half the total bombing effort was directed against naval targets. At Brest, as already described, 1,655 tons of bombs were aimed at the German battle-cruisers in two months. From Norway to Brittany the Blenheims of No. 2 Group, reverting entirely to daylight operations, sought out and struck at enemy shipping. Mines were laid off the Biscay ports and the Frisian islands. In Germany the weight of attack fell, not upon the Ruhr or Berlin or the oil plants, but on the ports and dockyard towns of the north—Hamburg, Bremen, Kiel, Wilhelmshaven.

From the 1,161 Bomber Command sorties against the *Scharnhorst* and *Gneisenau* in the eight weeks following their arrival at Brest, only four bombs found their mark. Peirse soon grew restive at this kind of work. On 15th April, after conclusive reports of damage to the *Gneisenau* and the sowing-in of both ships by mines, he demanded impatiently whether he was 'to continue *ad nauseam* to cast hundreds

FLENSBURG

KIEL-CANAL

KIEL

WARNEMÜNDE
ROSTOCK

LÜBECK WISMAR

...HAVEN

...ILHELMSHAVEN

HAMBURG

BREMERHAVEN

STETTIN

R. ELBE

VEGESACK
BREMEN

...BURG

R. ODER

R. WARTA

R. WESER

HANOVER

BERLIN

...EN
OSNABRÜCK

BRUNSWICK

MAGDEBURG

R. ODER

BIELEFELD

PADERBORN

...MM
...SOEST
...EN

KASSEL

MERSEBURG

G E R M A N Y

...NZ

FRANKFURT

R. MAIN

C Z E C H O S L O V A K I A

MANNHEIM LUDWIGSHAFEN

NUREMBERG

KARLSRUHE

STUTTGART

R. DANUBE

MUNICH

...RLAND

...ITALY

...PO

GENOA

L I G U R I A N
S E A

EMMERICH

SCALE
10   5   0   10   20 MILES

R. RHINE

WESEL

LÜNEN

OSTERKRADE   BOTTROP

GELSENKIRCHEN

WANNE · EICKEL
DORTMUND

HOMBERG

DUISBURG   ESSEN

SCHWERTE

HÜLS

KREFELD

DÜSSELDORF

MÜNCHEN
GLADBACH

REISHOLZ

of tons more on to the quays and into the water of Brest harbour'. His complaint met a ready response at the Air Ministry, where targets in the enemy's homeland were naturally regarded with greater favour than targets in the occupied territories. By return signal he was permitted, subject to agreement by the War Cabinet, to transfer his primary effort to objectives in Germany until any fresh movement of the battle-cruisers was suspected. Unofficial approval from the Prime Minister was at once obtained, and by the time formal approval from the War Cabinet followed three weeks later the new policy was well under way.

Operations against the north German ports proved a much more profitable affair than repeated assaults against the *Scharnhorst* and *Gneisenau*. Hamburg, second largest city in the Reich, was attacked in force eight times in early 1941—twice in March, once in April, five times in May.[1] During the May raids the Blohm and Voss shipyards were hit three times in five nights, and much damage was done to the docks. Bremen, too, suffered severely. Excellent results were obtained in January, when the buildings and the river stood out vividly from the snow-covered countryside. An important machine-factory sub-contracting to the U-boat building yards of Bremer Vulkan, a searchlight and dynamo factory, a power station, the Focke-Wulf works, and large stocks of metal components and rare woods were among the industrial objectives completely destroyed or heavily damaged, and the whole city was left, according to one of our pilots, 'like a gigantic illuminated Christmas-tree'. In March, the Focke-Wulf works—which made not only the Condor but the new F.W.190 fighter and the Me.110—received further damage. In May the main objectives to suffer included the docks, the railways, the Atlas shipbuilding and naval component works, and the Weser aircraft factory, where Ju.88's and Dornier flying-boats were produced. Focke-Wulfs, too, were again hit.

Still better results were obtained at Kiel. As the main German naval base and one of the greatest centres for building ships and U-boats, Kiel had a standing claim on the attention of our bombers. In the first two months of 1941 it was attacked only lightly, since the Admiralty gave priority to Wilhelmshaven, where the *Tirpitz* was nearing completion. Between mid-March and the end of May, however, Bomber Command flew no less than 900 sorties against Kiel— the largest number against any town in Germany. The climax came in mid-April, when 288 and 159 bombers attacked on successive nights. After this there was something approaching devastation at the

---

[1] A major raid at this period would normally be carried out by a force of 50–150 bombers.

main objectives, with the three great naval shipbuilding yards—the Deutsche Werke, the Krupp Germania Werft and the Kriegsmarine-werft—reporting temporary losses of production of 60, 25 and 100 per cent respectively. Among other damage at the Deutsche Werke was the complete destruction of the U-boat welding sheds and many of the welding plants.

Oil plants, warships, merchant shipping, airfields, industrial centres, the north German and Channel ports, Berlin, mine-laying —these were the main, but by no means the exclusive pre-occupations of Bomber Command in the year following the fall of France. Among minor activity deserving of record, if only for a certain picturesqueness, was the attempt in the autumn of 1940 to fire German crops and forests by means of a new incendiary weapon invented in America. This consisted of two strips of celluloid about three inches in length, between which was a small piece of phosphorus wrapped in wet wadding. The leaves—code-name 'Razzle', or, in a larger version, 'Decker'—were packed in liquid, some 450 to a tin, and dropped through a special chute. After several hours on the ground the phosphorus dried out and ignited the celluloid, which burned for thirty seconds. A few fields and woods suffered from our attacks, but the advocates of the weapon seem to have taken too favourable a view of northern European weather, and results on the whole were insignificant. According to the *Neue Frankfurter Zeitung*, however, many souvenir-hunting Germans received an unpleasant shock after placing the leaves in their trousers pockets.

Another subsidiary task was propaganda. Leaflet-dropping, suspended during the campaign in France, was resumed in July 1940. Usually it was carried out in the course of bombing operations, but it was also undertaken as a final exercise over France for the pupils at Operational Training Units (O.T.U.s). An agreeable variation from the usual forms of propaganda occurred in March and April 1941. About 4,000 pounds of tea, a gift from the Dutch of Batavia, was dropped over Holland in small cotton bags, each weighing two-thirds of an ounce, and bearing the message 'Holland will rise again. Greetings from the Free Netherlands Indies. Keep a good heart.' The reaction of the Dutch people to the gift, as reported by their Naval Attaché in London, was—'Why not bombs?' The Free French, however, were more impressed, and asked for coffee to be dropped over France. Ten crates, suitably sub-divided, were accordingly distributed by O.T.U. crews.

By July 1941, when the immediate crisis in the Battle of the Atlantic was over, Bomber Command was free to adopt an offensive policy. The trials through which it had passed, and was still passing, had left its crews and its Commander quite undaunted. Forced into a policy of night bombing by the strength of the German defences, it had found orthodox navigation inadequate for the appalling difficulties of operating over blacked-out territory in thick weather or absence of moon. Against objectives fairly near at hand or easily identifiable by the presence of water, such as the north German or Channel ports, it had achieved excellent results, but elsewhere, and particularly in the smoke-laden maze of the Ruhr, much of its effort had gone astray. We now know, for instance, that no less than forty-nine per cent of the bombs dropped on south-west Germany between May 1940 and May 1941 fell in open country. Evidence of this waste was beginning to accumulate in mid-1941, as night photography improved and more bombers were fitted with cameras. With it would come the danger, unless the subject were carefully handled —and unless there was some prospect of a remedy—of demoralization among the crews and the abandonment of the whole strategic offensive on which so many hopes had been built; for clearly no one could justify devoting so large a share of the national resources to the bomber force unless it held a real promise of consistently impressive results. Fortunately the Command was to hold firm through its gravest hours, while the skill of the scientists at the Telecommunications Research Establishment had already evolved, even before the imperative need for it was put before them, the first of the great radio navigational aids for bombers. By August 1941 the merits of this new system, which was to be known first as 'G' and then as 'Gee', were clearly established, but many months were yet to pass before sets could be produced in sufficient quantity for effective use. Meantime the Command would have to battle not only against its two constant adversaries, the weather and the Germans, but also against the more insidious foes of domestic doubt and criticism.

Inaccurate navigation and bombing, though in fact the biggest obstacle to the progress of our offensive, had not thus far been the Air Staff's main worry, for the seriousness of that particular problem was only gradually becoming realized. What was more obvious was that the total bombing effort had been disappointingly small. Bombers had been diverted—quite inevitably—to O.T.U.s, to the Middle East, to Coastal Command. Bomber crews had been called upon to ferry Blenheims and Wellingtons out to Egypt, and for one reason and another throughout the winter little more than half the full establishment of crews had been operationally fit. On top of this, naval targets had absorbed most of the available effort. All told, it was little wonder that German industry had escaped lightly.

Yet if the phase now passing had proved a time of trial and not infrequent error, Bomber Command had done much valuable work. It had played a notable part in upsetting the German invasion plans, had made a useful contribution to the defeat of the blockade, and had tied down more than a million Germans to civil and anti-aircraft defence. Even in its weakness, alone of the British forces it had carried war to the heart of Germany. Now it was building up into a more formidable force. In May 1941, with better weather, and a new group (No. 1) operational, it had managed to put down an impressive weight of bombs on the German ports. Nineteen raids of over fifty bombers had been despatched during the month, and on one night— 8th May—over 300 bombers had operated. The size of the bombs, too, was increasing—the first 4,000 pound bomb had been used against Emden at the end of May—and the new heavy bombers, the Manchesters, Stirlings and Halifaxes, were coming into service. Problems and difficulties of the utmost complexity still lay ahead, even with the aircraft—the Manchester was to prove a failure, the Stirling a disappointment—but the tactical and technical requirements for an efficient night offensive were becoming clear, and fuller understanding would assuredly breed greater success.

So, as the spring of 1941 gave place to summer, the Air Staff looked forward to better things. 'The Blitz' had died away, the shipping losses were falling well below the danger line, the strategic initiative was passing into our hands. No longer compelled to concentrate on defence, our fighters were winning air superiority on the other side of the Channel. In the Balkans a hastily constituted and ill-provided front had broken down in swift and utter collapse, but the back door of Egypt in Iraq had been held as firmly as the front door in the Western Desert. Everywhere the future seemed to hold greater promise. On 22nd June, as the Nazi hordes drove east against Russia, it became certain that Hitler's folly and our own exertions had indeed earned us a respite. The German onslaught against Britain, so long and so valiantly defied, had faltered to an uneasy pause. The British onslaught against Germany, for many months to come the exclusive privilege of Bomber Command of the Royal Air Force, could at last gather momentum.

CHAPTER IX

'Middle East': The Opening Rounds

THOUGH it turned out to be with something less than the traditional Italian genius for picking the winning side that Mussolini launched his country into war, the prospects in June 1940 appeared rosy enough. On all sides the fruits of victory—Savoy, Nice, Corsica, Tunisia, Egypt, the Sudan, Kenya—glistened in alluring profusion. Better still, all seemed within easy reach. No longer would Italian aggression be rewarded only with deserts and mountains. By the green banks of the Nile even a new Caesar might rest content.

Only one doubt troubled the *Duce*. In common with the *Führer* he had planned for war against Britain and France in 1942, and in the summer of 1940 the Italian armed forces were not all he might have wished. But with the Germans pouring across the Meuse only quick action could secure a share in the spoils. From 14th May, Mussolini's intentions were plain, and the final ultimatum on 10th June surprised nobody.

Up to the last, Britain and France strove to avoid provocation, and not until the day of 10th June did No. 202 Group—the Royal Air Force units in the Western Desert of Egypt—complete its forward concentration. Nine minutes after midnight the Group Commander, Air Commodore R. Collishaw, who was waiting in his underground operations room near Maaten Bagush, received the signal he was expecting from Air Chief Marshal Sir Arthur Longmore, the Air Officer Commanding-in-Chief at Cairo. We were at war with Italy; reconnaissance aircraft were to be despatched in accordance with the pre-arranged plan; in the north, where concentrations of enemy aircraft had been observed, the search was to be accompanied by bombers. By dawn on the 11th, twenty-four hours before their curiously unready opponents proved able to reply, Collishaw's squadrons were in action. Their target was El Adem, the main air base in Cyrenaica.

The outbreak of hostilities in the Middle East—an elastic term in its war-time usage, covering any territory which was absorbed into the Middle East Command—found us with forces exiguous even by our own standards of military preparation. On 11th June Longmore received an official definition of his sphere of action. He was to command 'all Royal Air Force units stationed or operating in . . . Egypt, Sudan, Palestine and Trans-Jordan, East Africa, Aden and Somaliland, Iraq and adjacent territories, Cyprus, Turkey, Balkans (Yugoslavia, Rumania, Bulgaria, Greece), Mediterranean Sea, Red Sea, Persian Gulf'—an area of some four and a half million square miles. Unfortunately his resources were not on the same generous scale as his responsibilities. Twenty-nine squadrons, or some three hundred first-line aircraft, comprised the total. For the main types there was a hundred per cent reserve available, but in the circumstances of June 1940, replacements and reinforcements from home would not be forthcoming very easily. Nor was there a local aircraft industry to help in the work of repair.

Almost half of these three hundred aircraft were based in Egypt, with the remainder in Palestine, the Sudan, Kenya, Aden and Gibraltar—a deployment corresponding with their primary role, which was defined as 'the defence of Egypt and the Suez Canal and the maintenance of communication through the Red Sea'.[1] The squadrons in Egypt, where the heaviest fighting was expected, were mainly those with the more up-to-date aircraft; the older types were relegated to the subordinate theatres. Few of the machines, however, were really modern. Nine of the fourteen bomber squadrons were armed with the reasonably efficient but very short-range Blenheim I, and two of the four naval co-operation squadrons had Sunderlands; but even the best equipped of the tactical reconnaissance squadrons flew the virtually defenceless Lysander. None of the five fighter squadrons had anything better than the obsolescent Gladiator biplane. Together, the Blenheims, Sunderlands, Lysanders and Gladiators made up eighteen of the twenty-nine squadrons. The remaining eleven were mounted on a remarkable assortment of miscellaneous and out-dated oddments, including Bombays, Valentias, Wellesleys, Vincents, Battles, Ju.86's (of the South African Air Force), Hardys, Audaxes, Harts, Hartebeestes, and Londons. This did not prevent their rendering effective, and indeed noble, service.

---

[1] The exact disposition on 10th June was 13½ squadrons (and a few D.W.I. Wellingtons for minesweeping) in Egypt, 1 in Palestine, 3¼ in the Sudan, 5½ (South African, Rhodesian and local auxiliary units) in Kenya, 3½ in Aden, 1¼ in Iraq, 1 in Gibraltar. On 12th August the R.A.F. Group at Gibraltar was transferred to Coastal Command.

Against these slender British resources the Italians could pit 282 aircraft in Libya, 150 in Italian East Africa, 47 in the Dodecanese, and as many more of their home strength of 1,200 machines as they were able, or cared, to concentrate in southern Italy and Sicily, or send over to Africa. Of the aircraft already in Africa in June 1940, the best fighter, the Cr.42, was about evenly matched with the Gladiator, while the main bomber, the S.79, though rather slower than the Blenheim I, had a longer endurance and carried a greater bomb-load. In terms of performance, the aircraft of the two sides were on the whole not unequal. It was in numbers, and in ease of reinforcement, that the Italian advantage lay.

No great success could be registered by the Italians in the first few days of the conflict, for the French and British navies jointly dominated the Mediterranean and there were military forces of some strength in Tunisia and Syria. But with the signature of the Franco-Italian armistice on 24th June the balance of naval power in the Mediterranean swung down heavily on the enemy side, and the Italians in Libya were soon free from any concern with their western boundary. By July the melancholy naval actions at Oran and Mers-el-Kebir, the fiasco of Dakar, and the acceptance of the Vichy writ almost everywhere in the French Colonial Empire made it clear that French resistance overseas was a broken reed. The whole strategic picture in the Mediterranean had changed as quickly, and as decisively, as that in Europe.

Outpaced by the swift onrush of the German armies and restrained by Hitler's policy of keeping on terms with Vichy, Mussolini saw the disappearance not only of an opponent but of his hopes of French booty. From Britain, however, he was still, in German eyes, welcome to all he could get; though whatever he got he would certainly have to fight for. Even so, Egypt, 'at the cross-roads of east and west', lying athwart the routes both to the ancient riches of India and to the more modern mineral wealth of Iraq and Iran, was well worth fighting for; and as July wore on, and the danger of a French attack from Tunisia vanished, the Italian armies under Marshal Graziani began to concentrate in eastern Cyrenaica. By that time they had already, it may be remarked, lost one Commander. On 28th June Balbo was shot down over Tobruk by his own anti-aircraft guns. His funeral was graced by a wreath from Collishaw, dropped by air.

The process of concentrating the Italian forces took some time. The Egyptian boundary is 935 miles by road—*the* road—east of Tripoli, 316 miles east of Benghazi, and 82 miles east of Tobruk, and it was not until mid-September that Graziani was ready for the great advance. Meanwhile, to the accompaniment of frontier clashes and

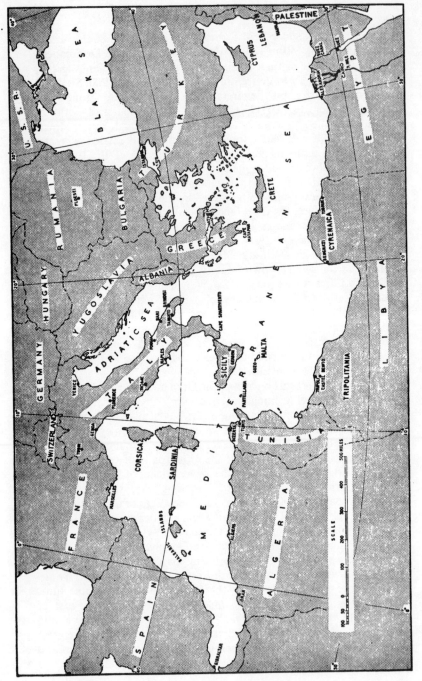

THE MEDITERRANEAN

naval activity below, Collishaw's crews got busy. The Blenheims struck by day at the Italian airfields and ports, the lines of communication between Derna and the frontier, and any troop concentrations which threatened serious trouble. The great 'bomber-transport' Bombays of No. 216 Squadron lumbered along by night, when the moon was favourable, to drop their loads on Tobruk. While the Blenheims of No. 113 Squadron reconnoitred farther afield, the Lysanders of No. 208 Squadron, assigned to tactical work with Western Desert Force, logged up details of the enemy's forward positions. And when the Gladiators were not covering the Blenheims and the Lysanders, they were fully occupied guarding our forward posts and airfields against the frequent, if ineffectual, attacks of the enemy.

Among the high-lights of this preliminary period must be reckoned the raid on Tobruk on the night of 12th June, when the old cruiser *San Giorgio* was crippled. Burned out and beached, she remained in use as a *flak*-ship, in spite of much subsequent attention from our aircraft. Some of the early instances of co-operation with the Mediterranean Fleet are also deserving of record. Full-scale support was given during two naval bombardments of Bardia, the second, on 17th August, witnessing an air battle above Admiral Cunningham's ships in which the Gladiators shot down eight S.79's for no loss to themselves. All possible help—fighter protection, reconnaissance, and 'fumigation' of enemy airfields—was again given at the beginning of September, when the naval Commander-in-Chief was escorting precious reinforcements between Malta and Alexandria. Other typical examples, on a smaller scale, were the protection given to Fleet Air Arm Swordfish during their brilliant raid against Tobruk harbour on 6th July, when a destroyer and three merchant vessels were sunk, and the attack on the flying-boat base at Bomba on 15th August, which crippled twelve Italian seaplanes.

Of the operations undertaken at this time for the benefit of Lieutenant-General O'Connor's ground forces, perhaps the most spectacular was the destruction on 1st August of a large ammunition depot near Bardia. The entire dump went up with a series of explosions which satisfied even the raiding pilots, while almost equally impressive, if more accidental, results were obtained from a near miss which burst among a huge pile of four-gallon tins. These proved to contain soup, which burst forth in reckless profusion to waste its fragrance on the desert air.

The greatest achievement of No. 202 Group in these early days was that by its aggressive tactics it established a defensive mentality in the opposing air force. In this valuable work it was aided by No. 252

s

Wing, the small fighter organization for the protection of Cairo, the Delta and the Canal. At the front the *Regia Aeronautica*, though it showed no particular keenness to join issue with the Gladiators, made things uncomfortable at our forward positions and airfields, but in strategical operations farther afield it showed a quite extra-ordinary lack of enterprise. A few sorties were directed against Alexandria from the Dodecanese, but these were promptly deterred by our fighters and naval guns. Throughout the whole of July the enemy's only real success was a raid on Haifa which set fire to three oil tanks. Strangest of all, the Italian bombers almost entirely neg-lected our great repair depot at Aboukir and its subsidiary units at Abu Sueir and Fuka, the destruction of which might well have crippled the entire Middle East Air Force.

The enemy's timidity was astonishing enough in view of his superior forces. It was still more astonishing in view of the further fact that Collishaw's squadrons were kept on a very close rein. Their Commander, a Canadian who had emerged in 1918 from the slaughter on the Western Front with the second highest total of 'kills' credited to any fighter pilot in the British Empire, had enjoyed much sub-sequent experience, including the command of Royal Air Force units in such diverse localities as South Russia, North Persia, the Sudan, East Anglia and the aircraft-carrier *Courageous*. Nothing had robbed him of the gay aggressiveness which was his by nature, and nothing would have pleased him better than to attack the enemy night and day with all the means at his disposal. He was left in no doubt, how-ever, that such a policy would not be countenanced by higher authority. After an incident on 5th July, when a pilot was wounded and an observer killed during a low-flying attack on a concentration of enemy vehicles, Collishaw received a rebuke from Longmore: 'I consider such operations unjustified having regard to our limited resources, of which you are well aware.' A fortnight later the Air Officer Commanding-in-Chief again intervened: 'We are rapidly consuming available resources of all types of aircraft in the Com-mand, and must in consequence exercise still greater economy in their employment.' Reconnaissance flights were to be confined to the barest essential minimum, and no bombing attacks were to be made on troop concentrations by forces greater than one squadron unless military operations of major importance were in progress.

These restrictions reached a climax on 13th August, when the Army was asked not to call for attacks unless an enemy offensive was imminent. The request was faithfully observed, and from then until the end of the month only two sorties were made against field targets.

Collishaw was thus reduced to keeping the enemy on the defensive by a combination of offensive fighter patrols, attacks on airfields and lines of communication, and bluff. Perhaps the outstanding example of his talent in this latter respect was 'Collie's battleship'—his one and only Hurricane, which he switched rapidly about from landing-ground to landing-ground to impress the enemy with our strength in modern fighters.

Longmore's concern to limit losses arose, of course, from his difficulty in securing not merely reinforcements but even essential replacements. For it became painfully borne in on him that very little would be sent out from home until the threat of invasion had receded, and that whatever was spared would be a long time reaching Egypt. Before June 1940, aircraft travelled to the Middle East either by sea, along the short Mediterranean route, or by flying in easy stages by way of southern France, French North Africa, Malta and the Western Desert. But now to pass a convoy along the Mediterranean meant a major naval operation, and with France unfriendly only the longer-range types like the Blenheim and Wellington could make the trip by air. Even these—and their newly trained crews—would face hazards enough, with the night-flight across the Bay of Biscay, the unpleasantly short runway at Gibraltar, and the night-landing and take-off at Malta. Aircraft of shorter range, however, could travel only by sea; and this might mean the long, time-consuming journey round the Cape.

There was, however, an alternative which the Air Ministry was quick to explore. Valuable time and shipping space would be saved if the short-range aircraft could make at least a part of the journey under their own power. Fortunately this was possible, for the pioneer flights undertaken by Squadron Leaders Coningham and Howard Williams before the war had forged a link between Egypt and the west coast of Africa. By 1936 Imperial Airways and an associate firm were running a weekly service between Lagos and Khartoum, at which point it connected with the regular route from England to the Cape. Already then, a set of primitive landing-grounds spanned the Continent—at horrifying distances apart.

As soon as Italy entered the war the Air Ministry decided to use this route for reinforcing the Middle East. It was at once seen, however, that the Gold Coast port of Takoradi, which had been developed in the previous ten years for the cocoa and manganese trade, offered better airfield and harbour facilities than Lagos. Its drier climate, too, would have less disastrous effects on aircraft left in the open. So, while the drama in France was nearing the final scene in a railway coach at Compiègne, Takoradi became the sea-terminus of the new route—the point at which the aircraft would be unshipped and erected for their 4,000-mile flight across Africa.

A Royal Air Force advanced party of twenty-four officers and men arrived at Takoradi on 14th July 1940. It was led by Group Captain H. K. Thorold, who, after his recent experiences as Maintenance Officer-in-Chief to the British Air Force in France, was unlikely to be dismayed by any difficulties in Africa. Thorold rapidly confirmed the selection of Takoradi, then set his little band to work on organizing such necessary facilities as roads, gantries, hangars, workshops, storehouses, offices and living accommodation. This activity was not confined to the port. Thorold was also charged with turning the primitive landing-grounds into efficient staging posts and perfecting wireless communication along the whole route.

It was certainly a route over which wireless would come in useful. The first stage, 378 miles of humid heat diversified by sudden squalls, followed the palm-fringed coast to Lagos, with a possible halt at Accra. Next came 525 miles over hill and jungle to an airfield of red dust outside Kano, after which 325 miles of scrub, broken by occasional groups of mud houses, would bring the aircraft to Maiduguri. A stretch of hostile French territory some 650 miles wide, consisting largely of sand, marsh, scrub and rocks, would then beguile the pilot's interest until he reached El Geneina, in the Anglo-Egyptian Sudan. Here, refreshed with the knowledge that he had covered nearly half of his journey, he would contemplate with more equanimity the 200 miles of mountain and burning sky which lay between him and El Fasher. A brief refuelling halt, with giant cacti providing a pleasing variety in the vegetation, and in another 560 miles the wearied airman might brave the disapproving glances of immaculate figures in khaki and luxuriate for a few hours in the comforts of Khartoum. Thence, with a halt at Wadi Halfa, where orange trees and green gardens contrast strangely with the desert, and a house built by Gordon and used by Kitchener shelters the passing traveller, he had only to fly down the Nile a thousand miles to Abu Sueir. When he got there his airmanship would doubtless be all the better for the flight. Not so, however, his aircraft.

The main Royal Air Force party of some 350 officers and men, including 25 ferry-pilots, joined Group Captain Thorold at Takoradi on 24th August. Small maintenance parties were sent out to the staging posts, B.O.A.C. navigators were enrolled for the initial flights, and B.O.A.C. aircraft were chartered to return the ferry-pilots from Abu Sueir. It was also laid down as a general principle that single-seat fighters should be led by a multi-engined aircraft with a full crew. With these preliminaries arranged, the first consignment

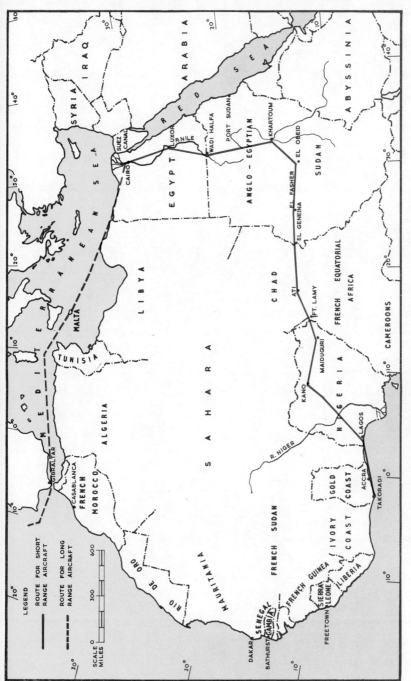

AIRCRAFT REINFORCEMENT ROUTES TO THE MIDDLE EAST, 1941

of crated aircraft—six Blenheim IV's and six Hurricanes—docked at Takoradi on 5th September. It was followed the next day by thirty Hurricanes in the carrier *Argus*. These were complete except for their main-planes and long-range tanks.

No time was lost. The Port Detachment of Thorold's unit quickly unloaded the aircraft and transported them to the airfield. There the Aircraft Assembly Unit took over, exercising much ingenuity to make up for the unexpected absence of various items, including the humble but essential split-pin. Last-minute difficulties like the collapse of the main runway on 18th September were rapidly overcome by hard work, and on 19th September the first convoy—one Blenheim and six Hurricanes—stood ready on the tarmac for the flight to Egypt. By now French Equatorial Africa had joined de Gaulle, and the pilots had the consolation of knowing that they would be flying all the way over territory which was diplomatically well disposed, if unfriendly in other respects. The Blenheim roared down the runway, climbed, and circled, to be joined in a few moments by its six charges. Seven days later, on 26th September, one Blenheim and five Hurricanes reached Abu Sueir.

* * *

The Gibraltar-Malta and Takoradi-Khartoum routes might between them serve for aircraft, but other essentials for the Royal Air Force and nearly all military reinforcements and supplies would have to travel round the Cape. Even so, their arrival in Egypt would be problematical. Apart from the menace of the German U-boats on the early part of the journey, there was the critical period when the convoys came within range of Italian aircraft and submarines operating from Somaliland and Eritrea. To make certain that our reinforcements reached Egypt we had thus to assert strict control of the Gulf of Aden and the Red Sea; and this, if it could be done, would doubtless lead in the long run to the expulsion of the Italians from the whole of their East African Empire. The prospect was certainly inviting, and not merely for reasons of prestige. An early liquidation of Italian East Africa would release our small but extremely valuable forces in Kenya, the Sudan and Aden for the decisive struggle in the Western Desert.

For the moment, however, the boot was on the other foot. The Italians in East Africa seemed more likely to liquidate us. At the end of June, the enemy forces in Eritrea, Italian Somaliland and Abyssinia amounted to over 200,000 troops and 150 aircraft, against which Wavell and Longmore could oppose slightly more aircraft but only some 19,000 men. Nevertheless, the British forces hemmed in the enemy—in so far as 19,000 men can hem in 200,000—on all sides.

To the north and west, in the Sudan, we had 9,000 troops and 50 aircraft; to the south, in Kenya, 8,500 troops and 80 aircraft, not counting Kenya's Auxiliary Air Units; and to the east, in British Somaliland, 1,500 troops and no aircraft. Across the Red Sea we had also 50 aircraft operating from the comparative security of Aden; and on the water the enemy had to reckon with the Royal Navy, Though the Italians had an overwhelming numerical advantage on the ground, they were thus well matched in the air, and at the same time cut off from reinforcement either by land or sea.

However heroic their efforts, the tiny band in British Somaliland would have been hard pressed to defend Berbera, let alone the whole Protectorate. After the collapse of French resistance at Jibuti their task was plainly impossible. When the Italians advanced on the British colony in August, the defenders accordingly soon found themselves forced to retreat. This they did with the utmost skill. Fighting all the way, and supported by the Aden squadrons—at first from two landing-grounds in Somaliland, and then, when enemy bombing made these untenable, from permanent bases across the Gulf—our troops made good their withdrawal to Berbera. Thence, under the guardian eye of a few long-range Blenheim fighters, and helped by naval and air bombardment of enemy forces advancing along the coast, they were successfully taken off to Aden.

With this evacuation, carried out on 18th August, the Italian Air Force made only one serious attempt to interfere. For it was reluctant to attack as long as there was even a single British fighter in the offing, and it was more than a little upset by an incident which had occurred that morning. Starting from Perim Island to add a few miles to their range, five Wellesleys of No. 223 Squadron—which Longmore had switched to Aden from the Sudan at the beginning of the offensive—had set off for Addis Ababa. The enemy capital had thus far been neither reconnoitred nor attacked. By a brilliant feat of navigation four of the aircraft now forced their way over wickedly mountainous country and through heavy cloud and ice to bomb the airfields outside the town. Despite severe damage from anti-aircraft fire and the opposition of one tenacious Cr.32 all four Wellesleys returned safely to base; so, too, did the fifth, which became lost, landed to find itself in French Somaliland, and took off again while the French authorities were looking up the regulations. The four pilots who reached their objective brought back with them excellent photographs and the satisfaction of having destroyed four S.79's, three hangars and the Duke of Aosta's private aircraft.

British Somaliland was poor fare for a dictator allergic to deserts, and the *Duce* looked forward with more lively interest to triumphs in

Kenya and the Sudan. In face of the ludicrous insufficiency of our forces—spaced out along the enemy frontiers they would have numbered about eight men to the mile—Wavell resolved to fight delaying actions at the main posts, and hope for the best. The delaying actions, varied by aggressive raids into Italian territory, were fought with skill and spirit; from July onwards reinforcements began to appear; and by the end of October the Italians had nothing to show for their efforts except the Sudanese outposts of Kassala and Gallabat, and a few square miles in Kenya around Moyale.

This remarkable state of affairs was the achievement of a few heroic battalions and a hotch-potch collection of aircraft. In the Sudan, where a new group (No. 203) was formed in August under Air Commodore L. H. Slatter, the three and a half Royal Air Force squadrons did work of enormous value. They defended the vital strategic points of Khartoum, Atbara and Port Sudan, protected our shipping in the Red Sea, carried out incessant raids against Italian airfields, dumps, ports and railways. Not content with giving close support to our own troops they also helped the Abyssinian 'patriots', who were almost equally inspired by the bombing of enemy strongholds and the landing of a Vincent laden with Maria Theresa dollars. All this, and much besides, including constant reconnaissances, was achieved between June and the end of October at a cost of thirty-three aircraft.

Yet the opposition was far from negligible. Though Slatter's squadrons in general had the measure of the enemy, the Italians were quite capable of bringing off an unpleasant surprise. On 16th October eight Wellesleys of No. 47 Squadron and two Vincents were drawn up on a forward landing-ground at Gedaref, to which they had flown to help the patriot forces operating near Lake Tana. With no warning—there being no local observer screen—an S.79 and seven Cr.32's and 42's swept out of the sky. Before our pilots had time to rush to their aircraft a well-placed stick of bombs from the S.79 and a spate of incendiary bullets from the fighters had reduced all ten British machines to burning wrecks.

Normally, however, it was the Italians who came off worse—much worse; and they failed just as badly in the south as in the north and west. From Kenya the Dominion squadrons under Air Commodore Sowrey and his South African Senior Air Staff Officer, Brigadier Daniel, operated with wasp-like persistence against enemy airfields, dumps, M.T. concentrations, and wireless stations. Most of their effort was at first taken up with reconnaissance, but to all their duties —whether in close support, or protecting Mombasa, or scouring the coastal waters of Italian Somaliland—the Dominion pilots brought a spirit so offensive that it almost inspires pity for the Italians. For how could such opponents cope with men like the Valentia pilot who grew tired of communication-flying, filled a forty-gallon oil drum with gelignite and scrap iron, wedged it on the sill of his cabin door, and heaved it overboard to effect impressive slaughter among the defenders of a fort?

Small in numbers as they were, the Sudan, Kenya and Aden squadrons gave astonishingly effective support to our hard-pressed ground forces. Nevertheless, the main achievement of these squadrons lay in a different sphere. For it was to them, in conjunction with our unfailing Navy, that we owed our domination of the Red Sea and its approaches. This they had achieved in part by hours of patient search and escort—between June and December the Aden and Sudan squadrons escorted fifty-four Red Sea convoys, from which only one ship was sunk by bombs and one damaged. But they achieved it much more by their unceasing attacks on the Italian air and naval forces. The offensive against the enemy air force was widespread in its application; that against the enemy navy found two focal-points in Assab and Massawa, the main ports of Eritrea. In particular, from the first day of the Italian war, when No. 14 Squadron bombed the harbour tanks and sent up 780 tons of fuel in flames, the Sudan squadrons never took their eye off Massawa. Oil stores, administrative buildings, barracks, airfield, port installations, destroyers, submarines—Massawa could always provide something worthy of their attention.

What these vital operations against the Red Sea ports and airfields meant in human terms has been recorded by a skilled pen. On 16th July, Alan Moorehead, together with one or two others of that remarkable body of men, the war correspondents, visited Port Sudan, where No. 14 Squadron was based. The target that day was a concentration of warships in Massawa.

> The town [wrote Moorehead [1]] festered in a humid shade temperature of 110 degrees and sometimes more. In the cockpits of the aircraft patrolling down the Red Sea the temperature rose sometimes to 130 degrees. Many in the town were suffering from prickly heat, the rash which blotches your face and arms and back with red scabs. The water in the pool at the front of the Red Sea Hotel was so warm that it was a slight relief in the evening to emerge from it into the less warm air. In the hotel it was wise to fill your bath in the evening so that by the morning the standing water would have dropped a degree or two below the temperature of the flat hot fluid that steamed out of the tap. One wondered how the crews of submarines in the Red Sea got along.
>
> We watched the Wellesleys take off, great ungainly machines with a single engine and a vast wing spread, but with a record of security

---

[1] Alan Moorehead: *Mediterranean Front* (Hamish Hamilton)

that was astonishing. For weeks now they had been pushing their solitary engines across some of the most dangerous flying country in the world—country where for hours you could not make a landing and where the natives were unfriendly to the point of murder—and they had been coming back. Often their great wings were slashed and torn with flying shrapnel. Sometimes they just managed to struggle back with controls shot away and the undercarriage would collapse, bringing the machine lurching down on the sand on one wing like some great stricken bird. But always they seemed to get back somehow. Now again on this second day of the attack on Massawa the control room at Port Sudan got signals that some of our aircraft had been sorely hit. We knew how many aircraft had gone out. It was a strain counting them as they came in, knowing always from hour to hour that there were still due three or two or perhaps just one machine and the chances of the lost airmen ever getting back were diminishing from minute to minute. In the late afternoon we first heard, then saw, the last flight over the sea. They cast their recognition flares, then two of the three aircraft fell behind. The progress of the leading machine was very slow. It was obvious that since this was the one most badly hit it had been sent on ahead to make its landing as quickly and as best it could. It circled twice, then settled for the landing. Crack went one wheel, down in the sand went the engine, over on one wing went the whole machine. The ambulance, fire brigade wagons, doctors and ground staff raced across the aerodrome. Out of the machine almost unharmed came the crew.

There were many incidents like that in the days that followed. The old Wellesleys were cracking up and we had no newer aircraft to replace them. They were too slow. Always the Italian fighters would wait over Massawa until one machine more badly hit than the others would lag behind. Then the enemy fighters would come and give it hell. That happened to a young squadron leader who after months of staff work on the ground had asked to take part in this all-important raid. He was given the job of rear gunner and his guns were blown away. The pilot was hit. The airman manning the two makeshift guns that sprouted out of the belly of the machine was mortally wounded. The squadron leader fixed a tourniquet, tightened it with his revolver, and got the dying man to hold it in place. Then he manned the two side guns until the pilot, lacking blood, was failing. Then the squadron leader took over the controls. That machine, too, came back though they lifted out of it a dead man still holding the revolver that tightened his tourniquet.

Such was the spirit that was bringing the convoys through the Red Sea and cheating the enemy of victory.

* * *

The British plan for the defence of Egypt was of long standing. We should take the main shock of Graziani's painfully accumulated divisions at prepared positions 120 miles back from the frontier, near the little watering place of Mersa Matruh. There, some two thousand years earlier, Cleopatra had dallied with her Anthony, and there, up to June 1940, wealthy Egyptians from Cairo and Alexandria had passed pleasant summers in well-appointed villas. Our choice of the Matruh position, however, was dictated less by these agreeable associations than by the fact that the single railway from the Delta ran no farther west. The instructions of the forward troops on the frontier—the Support Group under Brigadier Gott—were thus that they should harass the enemy's advance while withdrawing towards the main line of defence. In this delaying action they would, of course, have the aid of Collishaw's squadrons.

As the pitiless blaze of August declined into the milder flame of September, No. 202 Group carefully husbanded its resources for the approaching crisis. On 9th September reconnaissance reports made it clear that the blow would not be long in falling, and the Blenheims were at once sent out against Tobruk harbour, the vehicle concentrations on Tobruk airfield, and the landing-grounds at Tmimi, El Gazala, Derna and El Gubbi. The next evening a Lysander reported 700 lorries moving eastwards towards the frontier. The long-awaited hour was at hand.

The advancing Italian columns displayed a pattern of remarkable uniformity. A screen of motor-cyclists preceded the main bodies; behind the motor-cyclists lumbered the tanks and armoured vehicles; and in the rear of them, supported by mobile field, machine and anti-aircraft guns, came clusters of lorries bearing the infantry. At night the columns went into leaguer, protected by guns, lights, and—a significant tribute to Gott's patrols—barbed wire. It was in panoplied procession of this order, lacking only coloured costume to complete the resemblance to a military tattoo, that Graziani bore down on Egypt. He found No. 202 Group more than eager to disturb the symmetry of his dispositions. Within two days large numbers of Cr.42 fighters were to be seen patrolling closely above the enemy troops.

The original intention of the Italians was to develop two parallel lines of advance, one along the coast and the other further inland. But they found the approach inland well guarded; and in any case they preferred not to put too great an area of desert between themselves and the Mediterranean. In the event, Graziani thus concentrated on the coastal thrust, and from 13th September the enemy lorries were crossing the frontier and winding down the huge escarpment that frowns above the emerald-and-white beauty of Sollum. Constantly harassed by our ground and air forces, they pressed on through a nothing called Buq Buq, and in the evening of 16th September arrived at the small collection of houses and huts unduly dignified by the name of Sidi Barrani. Another sixty miles still lay between them and our main defences at Matruh; but at the moment Graziani had no desire to advance farther along lengthening lines of communication against increasing opposition. A few miles past Sidi Barrani, and the Italian columns ground down to a halt.

*   *   *

Six weeks passed, and Graziani was still building up supplies when his impatient master embarked on a new venture. Anxious to assert Italy's position in the Balkans and impelled by his unfailing desire to collect military laurels on the cheap, on 28th October Mussolini struck against Greece. Within a few days the harassed Air Officer Commanding-in-Chief at Cairo had yet another campaign on his hands.

As long as it was only the Italians they were fighting, the Greeks, who had a shrewd suspicion that Mussolini's move was not entirely welcome in Berlin, showed no great wish for the help of the British Army. They reasoned, not incorrectly, that their own troops were capable of withstanding an Italian attack from Albania, and that the landing of British ground forces on the Greek mainland would at once draw upon them the hostility of Germany. Unless British divisions could arrive in overwhelming strength—and of that there was little hope—it was therefore better for them to keep away. For the time being it was accordingly agreed that our troops should merely occupy an area in Crete around Suda Bay, to assure the Royal Navy of a secure base for the control of the Aegean. About help from the Royal Air Force, however, the Greeks felt differently; for they themselves had no more than seventy first-line machines, and unless some outside aid was forthcoming the Italians would soon enjoy unchallenged command of the air. What the consequences of this would be on the ground the experiences of Poland, Norway and France already amply indicated.

Until the actual launching of the Italian attack, Longmore had strongly opposed any suggestion of dispersing his few precious squadrons still more widely. The Air Officer Commanding-in-Chief—and he was backed by the Secretary of State for War (Mr. Eden), then visiting the Middle East theatre—doubted his ability, with his existing resources, to provide fully effective support for Wavell's growing forces even in the Western Desert; and he was certainly clear that he had nothing to spare for Greece. It was also self-evident that in general strategic importance the security of Greece must rank lower than that of Egypt. Nevertheless the political, and indeed military, arguments for sending at least a token air force to support the Greeks were so strong that when the Italian blow fell Longmore at once despatched a mixed squadron (No. 30) of Blenheim fighters and bombers to defend Athens—an action for which he was warmly commended by the Prime Minister.

Longmore's decision was soon improved upon in London. Four days later he received the following message from the Chiefs of Staff: 'It has been decided to give Greece the greatest possible material and moral support at the earliest moment. Impossible for anything from the United Kingdom to arrive in time. Consequently, the only course is to draw upon the resources in Egypt and to replace them from the United Kingdom . . . It is fully appreciated that this plan will leave Egypt thin for a period. Every endeavour is being made to make this period as short as possible.' Detailed orders followed; and before the end of the month two more Blenheim squadrons (Nos. 84 and 211) and a squadron of Gladiators (No. 80) had followed No. 30 Squadron. A few units of the British Army accompanied the force to provide supply services and airfield defences. A little later, at the beginning of December, a further squadron (No. 112), which was due for re-equipment, handed over its Gladiators to the Royal Hellenic Air Force.

The airfields selected for the Blenheim squadrons were the permanent bases of Eleusis and Tatoi (later renamed Menidi), near Athens. Both were of considerable size, and could be readily supplied through the Piraeus. Beyond this, however, they had few advantages. At Eleusis the imposingly planned station buildings were still under construction, and rubbish and filth of every description lay strewn about the camp, which was infested by flies. Menidi, set in a valley near the King's summer palace, and flanked by mountains 4,000 feet high covered with pines, olives and eucalyptus trees, was more attractive only from the scenic aspect. 'The cheerless, ugly two-storeyed building on the south east corner of the landing-ground', reported one of the Medical Officers, 'was, apart from a few forms and trestle-tables, completely unfurnished. Its floor-boards were rotting, and it was cold, damp and evil-smelling. Food was supplied and prepared by a rascally contractor and only served to heighten the general atmosphere of monastic gloom. . . . There were ten semi-serviceable wash-basins, with cold water, and a couple of showers which regularly flooded the corridor. There were two baths but these were filthy, and use was therefore made of the public baths in Athens. . . . The outlet pipes were small and frequently became blocked, "back-fires" flooding the corridors and bedrooms.'

Such conditions were good neither for health nor morale, but they were by no means the greatest obstacle to operational efficiency. At a time when winter was coming on, and when every aircraft would be precious, neither of the airfields had hard runways or good repair facilities. Worse still, both could be easily spied upon by officers of the German Legation in Athens, who were unlikely to neglect to inform the Italians by wireless whenever the Blenheims took off. But perhaps the gravest disadvantage was that to reach any of their targets our bombers would have to fly at least 300 miles over wildly mountainous country through weather liable to change with bewildering rapidity. Air Vice-Marshal J. H. D'Albiac, the Air Officer Commanding, could thus have no illusion about the amount of effort that was likely to be wasted by operating from these bases. Yet he had little other choice; for the airfields in the Larissa plain, south of Mount Olympus, would soon be flooded by the autumn rains, and the Greeks refused to let us occupy, or even reconnoitre, sites in Salonika for fear of offending the Germans by our proximity to Bulgaria.

At all costs, however, some place nearer to the front had to be found for the fighters. While the Blenheim fighters of No. 30 Squadron remained at Eleusis to protect Athens, the Gladiators of No. 80 Squadron were accordingly moved up to Trikkala, in the Larissa plain, in spite of its known defects at this time of the year. Within a few days they were forced to move to the bigger and better drained station at Larissa, although this was already fully occupied by the Greeks. Most of the Gladiator patrols, however, were carried out by detachments operating from a forward landing-ground at Yannina, only forty miles from the Albanian frontier. This was set amidst superb scenery which in spring, with the sun lighting the snow on the mountains, streams gurgling down the hill-sides, and sportive lambs gambolling in lush pastures, might have wrung the description 'idyllic' from the lips of a warrant officer of twenty years' service. But other times of the year might well have produced other epithets, for summer was dusty and malarial, autumn unpleasantly wet, and winter bitterly cold. Moreover the antique Turkish sanitation of the place made little appeal to airmen fresh from the effective simplicities of the desert.

While the enemy could make the most of his great numerical superiority by operating from hard runways only a few miles behind the front, our tiny force was thus handicapped by every consideration of weather, site and maintenance. From mid-November until the end of December the two and a half squadrons of Blenheim bombers, aided by a few Wellingtons sent over for the moonlight periods, in fact carried out no more than 235 sorties—an average of about one sortie a week for each aircraft. Even then, nearly a third of this total proved abortive because of unfavourable weather. More than once the Greeks expressed disappointment at so small a scale of effort; but until they could construct two all-weather airfields on the western side of the country—which they rapidly undertook to do—D'Albiac was powerless to improve matters. It was little wonder that Longmore, who naturally preferred to have his aircraft where he could make good use of them, was unenthusiastic about sending a force of any size to Greece, and angry when our Minister in Athens appealed to London for reinforcements without his knowledge.

What was achieved by this limited scale of attack is hard to assess in precise terms. Broadly speaking, two-thirds of our bombing effort was directed against the enemy's airfields, supply ports and rear communications in Albania, and one-third against 'battlefield' targets or communications close to the front. This proportion by no means satisfied the Greeks, who applied their own air effort to the front-line, and wore out their air force in doing so. But a consistent policy of 'close support' to the troops advancing into Albania, such as the Greeks desired, accorded neither with D'Albiac's ideas on the correct use of air power nor with the imperative need to keep casualties low, and the British commander preferred to concentrate on the two main ports of Durazzo and Valona. The first, at the extreme range of the Blenheims, received less attention than the second, which was attacked seventeen times before the end of the year. On the whole, captured enemy soldiers showed a healthy respect for our raids, and one group, taken in January within twenty miles of Valona, confessed that the supply situation had become so bad that they had received food only once in every three or four days. Doubtless this was due more to the Italian military system than to our bombing, but the latter undoubtedly helped.

The achievement of our handful of fighters in these early weeks was more clear-cut. The fighter-Blenheims of No. 30 Squadron were a valuable addition to the local Greek defences of Athens, and after their arrival the Italian attacks grew markedly fewer. Still more impressive was the work of the Gladiators in the forward area. Operating over the front on offensive patrols or in support of our bombers, by the end of the year No. 80 Squadron had claimed the destruction of forty-two enemy aircraft for its own loss in combat of only six. Even allowing for some overstatement, it is clear that the Gladiator pilots destroyed many more aircraft than they themselves lost, and that they established a degree of moral, if not material, superiority in the skies above the Pindus Mountains.

That our airmen greatly impressed the Greeks is evident from the many acts of generosity, kindness and devotion which rewarded their efforts. How eagerly the Greeks strove to pay these honours to those whom they considered brave allies may be seen from the experience of Squadron Leader Gordon-Finlayson, Commanding Officer of No. 211 Squadron. On 24th November, Finlayson's Blenheim was heavily hit while bombing Valona, and his port airscrew and reduction gear were shot away. With great skill he nevertheless shook off the enemy fighters in the clouds and made a belly-landing on Corfu, where he and his crew were soon succoured by the local peasants. After being treated to large quantities of cognac, coffee, sardines, cheese, bread, hard-boiled eggs and beer—in that order—they were escorted into Corfu town. Fifteen alerts and eight raids cast a damper on the festivities during the following day, but by nightfall a boat was ready and they set off for Patras. They had not gone far when bad weather forced them into the little port of Astakos. What followed from that point may be told in the words of Finlayson's own report at the time:

> We were mobbed, given flowers, kissed by old men and women, given coffee, cognac, cigarettes, cake and Greek and British flags. We were nearly brained with bouquets and complimented by the ladies, who had learnt sufficient English from our Navy to say 'Beautiful men'.
>
> An old Ford . . . drove us up mountain, down dale, across fords, through mud and finally to Aitolikon.
>
> At Aitolikon we were expected and our car was lifted off its wheels. We were carried shoulder high to the Town Hall where we were doped with cognac and introduced to the mayor.
>
> The people howled 'Zito Anglia' and clamoured to see us on the balcony.
>
> Feeling rather like Dictators we arrived on the balcony to the frantic cheers of 5,000 townsmen. Silence was called and I delivered a tub-thumping harangue, expressing the pride which we felt in fighting for Greece, congratulating them on the Albanian successes—and by mentioning the magic word 'Mussolini', and passing the hand across the throat, possessed the crowd with wild enthusiasm.
>
> The ladies of the town presented us with flowers, cigarettes and cognac. Little girls gave us more flowers and received fatherly kisses on their brows for their troubles. An old man gave me a pair of Evzone shoes, of excellent workmanship . . .

Finlayson's experience was confirmed by almost every British airman who passed through Greek hands. Another typical case was that of Flying Officer A. A. N. Nicholson, of No. 84 Squadron, who was forced down into the sea on 6th February 1941 by a storm of extraordinary violence. The Blenheim struck the water about a quarter of a mile from a small island, and sank within five minutes. The rear gunner was killed by the impact, but Nicholson and the observer clung to the dinghy, which they tried to propel towards the shore by lying across it and swimming with their legs. The observer, however, was very weak, and Nicholson's best efforts, maintained for over an hour, could not prevent him drowning. For the next two hours Nicholson was virtually in a state of coma, but he revived to find that a change of wind was driving him towards the shore. Sighting a shepherd, he shouted to attract his attention, and a boat quickly put out. The demeanour of the occupants was menacing, for the shepherd had reported the swimming figure as Italian; but Nicholson's frantic cries that he was English saved him 'from being finished off, like Agrippina's maid, with oars and boat-hooks'. He was swiftly lifted on board, taken to a house in the island, and warmed before a roaring fire. His report to his Commanding Officer tells the rest of the story:

> I cannot speak too highly of the kindness and solicitude of the little community on this island. Although these people were, I imagine, miserably poor and ill-provided with clothes and food, the best of all they had was produced for me. I was waited on constantly, and it was considered insulting if I moved from my chair . . . to do anything for myself . . . At night I was given the bed of honour by the fire . . .
>
> The second day it was too rough to leave the island. I climbed with great difficulty and much agony in bare feet up the jagged rocks to the thorn bushes on the top of the hill, where I wrote my name with stones in letters three feet high, in the hope that some searching aircraft would see it.
>
> I remained with these delightful people from the time I was picked up until the morning of 8th February, when a glorious calm prevailed. After an extremely pleasant trip we arrived at Loutraki at midday, and from then on I assumed the role of some conquering general or visiting potentate. The news of my arrival spread through the town in a moment. First I had to be photographed with my saviours, much to their delight; then on the assumption that I was hurt, shocked or otherwise ailing, I was hustled off to the hospital headquarters, where I was most courteously received by Field Marshal Belias, the Commandant, and practically bundled into bed on the spot . . . Then I committed, I believe, an atrocious *gaffe* by asking if I might have a hot bath with disinfectant in it; baths were known, it seemed, even baths with disinfectant, but a hot bath—I might almost have asked for the moon. However, if I had asked for the moon they would certainly have tried to get it for me; and orders were given that a hot bath should be prepared in an adjoining hotel, also part of the great hospital. Meanwhile the mayor had arrived, and in a speech of welcome told me of the great pride of the citizens of Loutraki in receiving for the first time a British officer, of their felicitations on my escape, and of their great sorrow at the death of my crew. I replied, I hope in suitable language, and gratefully accepted his invitation to lunch. While we waited for a telephone connection, the mayor produced a bottle of brandy and the first cork was pulled in what turned out to be a day of organized toping. In the meantime I heard that my friends the fishermen were being feted round the town, and receiving no small kudos, which gratified me. After I had telephoned Menidi, we all removed to the

neighbouring hotel for the ceremony of the bath. It was considered beneath my dignity to walk the fifty yards down the street in slippers, and I was driven through cheering crowds by the Marshal himself. In attendance on my bath were: one Field Marshal, his wife and daughter, one senior doctor, his wife and daughter, one junior doctor, one priest, the mayor, and a major and two junior officers of the Evzones, to say nothing of the matron and sundry nurses. After we had chatted for the best part of an hour, waiting for the water to heat, I decided that something was expected of me, and entered the bathroom for a noisy pretence of ablution in stone-cold water, to the great satisfaction of all concerned.

After the bath I lunched with the mayor, a party to which all his friends kept coming with contributions of Retsina; so our outlook was benevolent in the extreme as we strolled through the town to a café, surrounded by admiring crowds. Another photograph had to be taken, this time the nucleus being two Greek girls and myself; around us were grouped the mayor and most of the corporation, and innumerable wounded soldiers. The girls were a little coy, but I linked arms with them, thereby apparently giving a tremendous fillip to Anglo-Hellenic relations.

In the course of the afternoon I met innumerable people, soldiers and civilians, and of course we expressed a thousand times our mutual pride in each other's fighting forces and our united belief in our common cause. Finally we took refuge in the mayor's office, until a tremendous burst of cheering greeted the arrival of your car.

Before I left I received a most touching present of fish from the man who picked me up: I was moved by this, as I realized that he had given me as a memento his entire food supply for about a week. His name and that of his companion is Katsaneas—Anastasios and Demetrius respectively—and by way of reward they desire nothing so fervently as to see their names and the story of their exploit in print in the Greek papers.

It is to be hoped that their simple wish was gratified. If not, it may be some slight consolation that their story stands here in tribute to all whose generous actions bound the Royal Air Force, alike in victory and defeat, to the cause of Greece.

* * *

The efforts of the four British squadrons in Greece were not unsupported from outside. On the night of 28th October, within a few hours of the Italian invasion, the War Cabinet approved a plan to operate Wellingtons from Malta against supply ports in southern Italy. This decision was possible because Malta already sheltered Wellingtons on passage to Egypt, and because measures were in hand to strengthen the defences of the island. For if Malta struck out against the enemy, it must be prepared for what the enemy would do in return. The more it brandished the sword—in the metaphor of a later air commander—the more it would stand in need of a shield.

T

The island of Malta, sixty miles off Sicily and athwart the routes from Gibraltar to Alexandria and Naples to Tripoli, was clearly of great strategic importance. There were obvious limits, however, to what could be expected from a mere speck of land within a few minutes' flight of enemy territory, with no possibility of air defence in depth or proper dispersal, and dependent for food and everything else on what could be brought over several hundred miles of sea. With the growth of Italian hostility and air power in the 1930's, the need for an alternative naval base had accordingly become plain. The outbreak of war found the Mediterranean Fleet at Alexandria.

Yet even if Malta could no longer serve its old purpose, we might still perhaps make use of it in some less provocative role. It might, for instance, be employed as an air staging post and reconnaissance base, a naval refuge and emergency repair depot, or a base for light naval forces. It was therefore well worth defending, reasons of prestige apart; and in the summer of 1939 the Committee of Imperial Defence approved a long-term air defence programme amounting to four fighter squadrons and 172 anti-aircraft guns. The Air Ministry, how-ever, not unnaturally doubted whether Malta could survive under the very nose of the Italian Air Force; and fighters were badly needed elsewhere. When the Italians entered the war Malta was thus still awaiting its four squadrons, though the necessary airfields had been built, and a radar station had been in existence since March 1939.[1] And though the island was wonderfully placed for reconnaissance, and plans had been prepared for work on behalf of the Mediter-ranean Fleet, Malta was still without a proper unit even for this purpose. There were airfields at Hal Far, Takali and Luqa, a flying-boat base at Kalafrana, and a headquarters at Valletta, but the only aircraft on the island were five Swordfish, four sea-Gladiators, and a Queen-Bee.

The Swordfish, which officially existed to tow targets for the benefit of the gunners, had been employed on reconnaissance since the out-break of war. The Gladiators were a more recent development. In May 1940 Air Commodore F. H. M. Maynard, the Air Officer Commanding, had been ordered to take precautions against sudden attack by Italy. He had cast about for some means of defence. At Kalafrana there were four Fleet Air Arm Gladiators—spares for a carrier—in packing cases. Permission to use them was obtained from Admiral Cunningham; volunteers were at once forthcoming from Maynard's staff and the anti-aircraft co-operation unit; and the improvised flight was ready for action by the time of the first Italian

---

[1] Only two other radar sets had been sent overseas by the outbreak of war—one for Aden, the other for Alexandria.

raid on 11th June. One of the Gladiators was quickly damaged beyond repair. The remaining three—Faith, Hope and Charity, as they were soon dubbed—continued to defy the Italian Air Force for some weeks to come. It is sufficient indication of their success that contemporary Italian estimates placed Malta's fighter strength at twenty-five aircraft.

At the end of June, Faith, Hope and Charity were joined by four Hurricanes. These had been destined for the Middle East but were detained on Malta by permission of Longmore. Three fighters in June and seven in July, together with the anti-aircraft guns, thus made up Malta's entire defence against over two hundred Italian aircraft in Sicily. Almost every day during these two months Italian bombers attacked the island, but they were driven first into bombing from a great height, then into operating under escort, and finally, for a while, into attacking by night. Only two of our fighters were lost in combat, and no serious damage was suffered on the ground.

In such encouraging circumstances the risk of basing reconnaissance forces on the island appeared less formidable. More Swordfish (No. 830 Squadron) of the Fleet Air Arm arrived towards the end of June, together with a few oddments—a Hudson, a Skua, a French seaplane—for the longer-range tasks. About the same time one or two Sunderlands of Nos. 228 and 230 Squadrons from Alexandria began to use Kalafrana as an advanced operational base. Their *début* was all that could be desired, and more than could possibly have been expected: Flight Lieutenant W. W. Campbell of No. 230 Squadron sank two Italian submarines in the first three days. On the second occasion he returned with convincing proof of his exploit in the form of four prisoners.

Observation by such limited forces, however, could not possibly meet in full the needs of Admiral Cunningham; yet it would be rash to risk bringing in more reconnaissance aircraft until the island's defences were stronger. The Air Ministry accordingly decided to press on with the approved programme of four fighter squadrons. A beginning was made on 2nd August, when twelve Hurricanes were successfully flown off the carrier *Argus*. Ground staff and stores were carried to the island in submarines, and the new arrivals soon formed No. 261 Squadron. With the defences doubled, three Marylands were sent out from home in September, to become No. 431 Flight, and within a few days of the Italian attack on Greece No. 228 Squadron arrived *en bloc* from Alexandria.

The next instalment of fighters was now due, and on 17th November twelve Hurricanes, led by two Skuas, took off from the *Argus*. Owing to movements by the Italian fleet the Hurricanes were ordered off at extreme range, some 450 miles west of Malta. Unfortunately the operation had not been so carefully planned as the previous one. Many of the pilots had no experience of long-range flying, and in default of instructions set their engine revolutions too high for the great distance to be covered; and the observer in one of the guiding Skuas was on his first flight out of training school. The result was tragedy. Only one Skua and four Hurricanes reached Malta. What happened to the rest may be inferred from the fuel-tanks of the four fighters to arrive. They contained, respectively, twelve, four, three and two gallons of petrol.

Meanwhile, in anticipation of the arrival of the Hurricanes, the Wellingtons had already begun to attack the southern Italian ports. Naples was raided on the night of 31st October, and throughout November bombers on passage from England put in a quota of operations before leaving for Egypt. Such an arrangement was good neither for efficiency nor morale, and in December Maynard secured permission to form sixteen of the Wellingtons into a Squadron (No. 148). At first the bombing effort was applied for its original purpose—the support of the Greeks—and several attacks were made on Bari and Brindisi. But the Wellingtons could obviously be used with equal effect against the Italian supply lines to Libya, and it was on these, rather than on communications with Albania, that our bombers were soon to concentrate. At all events, Malta—shield in one hand, sword in the other—now stood forth to challenge the enemy.

The beginning of a bombing offensive from Malta meant still greater demands for reconnaissance. How much depended on this patient and daring work of search was soon seen in connection with the Fleet Air Arm's exploit at Taranto. For several days before the attack Marylands of No. 431 Flight and Sunderlands of No. 228 Squadron kept watch over the enemy naval base and its approaches, defying anti-aircraft fire and the attentions of Italian fighters. On 10th November a Maryland returned, after twenty minutes' running combat with a Cr.42, with the information that five battleships, fourteen cruisers and twenty-seven destroyers lay in the harbours. An aircraft of the *Illustrious* working from Malta then picked up full details of the enemy's dispositions, together with photographs showing the anti-torpedo nets and barrage balloons, and it was in the light of these that the Swordfish crews planned their attack. On 11th November two more Royal Air Force reconnaissance sorties established that the only alteration in the enemy positions was the arrival of another battleship, and the *Illustrious* was notified accordingly. That night her gallant pilots steered their leisurely but well-loved 'String-bags' through a storm of fire to deliver an attack which was surpassed in effectiveness only by the unexpected and treacherous blow at Pearl Harbour.[1]

The following morning one of Maynard's precious Marylands again ran the gauntlet of *flak* and fighters at Taranto. The crew brought back proof, in the form of photographs, that three of Italy's six battleships would not be troubling us for some time to come. Eleven air-launched torpedoes had transformed the naval situation in the Central Mediterranean, with benefit to the Greeks no less than to ourselves.

*　　*　　*

In Egypt, Graziani and Wavell were meanwhile competing for the honour of striking the next blow. For Graziani the problem was largely one of building up supplies in the forward area; for Wavell the immediate task was to distribute to the best advantage the reinforcements now reaching his Command. With the arrival, towards the end of September, of the armoured brigade which had been so boldly despatched from our shores at the very height of the invasion threat, offensive action on a limited scale at last came within the British commander's grasp. He responded by promptly setting a tentative date of mid-November for attack in the Western Desert. This proved too optimistic, especially when Greece called for aid; but the delay was very brief. For O'Connor pronounced himself prepared to strike in the next moonlight period, at the end of the first week in December—as long as he could count on full support in the air.

Longmore, and those behind him in London, did not fail in the assignment. Three squadrons arrived from England to offset the five squadrons sent from Egypt to Greece. Two of the new units, the Wellingtons of Nos. 37 and 38 Squadrons, flew out by way of Malta; the third, the Hurricane fighters of No. 73 Squadron, came by sea to Takoradi and thence by air to Egypt. In addition there was the regular, if somewhat thin, trickle of aircraft over both routes. Reinforcement, however, was only part of the answer. Longmore also needed to juggle with his existing resources. A practised hand at this, he promptly switched two Blenheim squadrons (Nos. 11 and 39) over to Egypt from Aden, brought a third Blenheim squadron (No. 45) up from the Sudan, and by moving a newly formed Hurricane squadron (No. 274) from Amriya to the Western Desert, left the air defence of Alexandria and the Suez Canal—'with a mental apology to the Italians for the insult'—to the care of two Fleet Air Arm

---

[1] Some of the pilots flew right through the balloon defences. According to the Admiralty pamphlet *Fleet Air Arm*, one pilot sang out to his observer, 'Where's that bloody balloon barrage?' and received the answer, 'We've been through it once, and we're just going through it again.'

Gladiators. By 8th December he had sixteen squadrons based in Egypt—only two more than in June, but now including fighters of far better performance than any boasted by the Italians.

All this was not accomplished without friction. General Wavell, Admiral Cunningham and the visiting Secretary of State for War had all joined in the cry for more aircraft, with the result that the Air Ministry was beset with appeals not merely from their Commander on the spot but from the other Service ministries. This concerted pressure did nothing to strengthen Longmore's case either in the Air Ministry or at No. 10 Downing Street, where strenuous efforts on behalf of the Middle East were already being made, and where there was naturally a more vivid appreciation of the urgent needs of the home Commands. Misunderstanding also flourished in the fertile field of aircraft statistics. The authorities at home tended to stress the number of aircraft despatched to the Middle East and the number already there. Longmore tended to stress the number of these which were fully serviceable with crews and ground staff and which he could actually deploy at the moment in the line of battle. The two figures were of course very different. 'I was astonished to find', wrote the Prime Minister in mid-November, 'that you have nearly a thousand aircraft and a thousand pilots and sixteen thousand air personnel in the Middle East, excluding Kenya. . . . Surely out of all this establishment you ought to be able, if the machines are forthcoming, to produce a substantially larger number of modern aircraft operationally fit? Pray report through the Air Ministry any steps you may be able to take to obtain more fighting value from the immense mass of material and men under your command.'

These statistics did less than justice to the Air Commander, for the total of 'nearly a thousand aircraft' included some 250 machines used for communication, training and other non-operational tasks. The general tone of the Prime Minister's message was also inspired by an assumption that was natural, but somewhat mistaken—that aircraft sent to the Middle East would take their place in the line of battle within a brief space of time. There was, however, ample opportunity for an aircraft to become unserviceable or be lost in transit; and it was perhaps not surprising that between the starting-point in England and the finishing point in the front line there existed a formidable number of machines undergoing inspection or repair, together with others awaiting anything from complete erection to missing equipment or a formal 'write-off'. There was also the fact that the aircraft usually arrived several weeks ahead of the ground staffs, who normally travelled round the Cape. By taking different categories of serviceability, or disregarding the number of crews or ground staff available, or leaving out the minor theatres, or not counting the obsolescent aircraft, it was easy to arrive at very diverse estimates of Middle East strength.

How these differences could arise may be seen very clearly from the case of No. 73 Squadron. The squadron, one of the earliest to be equipped with Hurricanes, had fought with great distinction in France, and had added to its laurels during the Battle of Britain. On 6th November it was ordered out to Egypt to replace No. 80 Squadron, which Longmore had moved across to Greece. In order that the squadron should arrive in time for Wavell's forthcoming offensive, arrangements were made for the thirty-four aircraft to be shipped with their pilots on the *Furious* to Takoradi, and for the ground staff to be run through the Mediterranean in a cruiser. After a few days of preparation and forty-eight hours' embarkation leave, the ground and aircrews sailed in their respective vessels; and in due course, having survived a brush with the Italian Fleet off Cape Spartivento, the ground party arrived safely at Alexandria on 30th November.[1] Meanwhile the *Furious* had reached Takoradi on the 27th, and had begun to fly off her charges. One of the aircraft crashed into the sea, but the other thirty-three took off successfully, and were soon *en route* for Heliopolis. On 1st December, while the first six were on the Geneina–El Fasher lap of the four thousand mile flight, the wireless of the guiding Blenheim failed, the crew lost their bearings, and in gathering darkness all seven machines were forced to land in the desert. Two Hurricanes crashed beyond repair, one of the pilots was killed, and the other four Hurricanes were all badly damaged. Of the thirty-four fighters despatched only twenty-seven thus reached Egypt at the appointed time.

But though the ground crews had arrived some days beforehand the squadron was still far from ready for operations. At this date the Royal Air Force had much to learn about the technique of moving units in a hurry, and all the stores and equipment intended for the squadron had been packed in cases which bore no distinctive mark. As the stores and equipment of the two fresh Wellington squadrons arrived in the same consignment with a similar absence of markings the resulting confusion took some time to clear up. Having flown across Africa, the Hurricanes also had to be stripped of their long-range tanks, fitted with guns, and overhauled. By intense effort eight were ready to help in the defence of Alexandria by 12th December, and three days later four more joined No. 274 Squadron in the Western

---

[1] 'To carry a ship-load of passengers into battle,' wrote Vice-Admiral Holland, 'is an unenviable lot, but their presence had perforce to be dismissed from my mind. They themselves were exhilarated at having been in a sea battle.'

Desert. But it was not until the end of December, three weeks after the opening of the offensive, that the squadron took its place as a complete whole in the line of battle.

Episodes of this nature undoubtedly explain much of the discrepancy between the statistics produced in Cairo and in London. Nevertheless for various reasons, most of them excellent ones, there were in fact too many unserviceable aircraft in the Middle East; and the heart of the matter—a point as yet not fully perceived—lay in the maintenance organization, which was still too weak to sustain the enormous burden so suddenly thrust upon it.

At the moment, however, differences of opinion about the exact strength of his forces were perhaps less important to Longmore than the fresh tasks now looming before him in the Balkans. For with the Germans occupying Rumania, the Italians at grips with the Greeks, and Graziani merely marking time in front of Sidi Barrani, the authorities at home were now convinced that the centre of interest would soon shift from Africa. Above all, there was the danger that the Germans would descend on Turkey or Greece by way of Bulgaria —a danger which might be prevented only if the Turks took their courage in both hands and joined the Greeks before they were overwhelmed. The Turks, however, were realists. They declined to challenge Germany, or even Italy, without lavish supplies of men and materials. But help on this scale could be given only at the expense of existing commitments in the Middle East. What, asked the Chiefs of Staff, could Wavell and Longmore spare? The reply of the two commanders, received in London on 4th December, failed to fulfil expectations. The Prime Minister, in fact, referred to it as 'unsatisfactory and unresponsive'.

The following day Longmore received a signal from the Chief of Air Staff. It repeated the view that by the spring of 1941 the Balkans, and not Africa, might well be the main sphere of operations. Reinforcements amounting 'very tentatively' to twelve squadrons might be sent to the Middle East, but should not be relied upon. Would Longmore's present administrative and depot organization stand the strain? In any case the Turks and Greeks should be encouraged to speed up the construction of airfields from which we could operate 'a high proportion' of both the existing Middle East forces and the future reinforcements.

'On receipt of this message,' writes Longmore in his autobiography, 'I took a deep breath, told my A.O.A. (Air Vice-Marshal Maund) to figure out the additional load on his administrative services, then turned my attention to the realities of the moment, for it was only four days before the whistle was due to blow and Wavell's offensive was to start.'

*   *   *

GLADIATORS OVER THE WESTERN DESERT

WELLESLEY OVER ITALIAN EAST AFRICA

TOBRUK. JANUARY 1941

In the background are the *San Giorgio* and signs of R.A.F. action

WRECKED ITALIAN AIRCRAFT AT EL ADEM

discovered during our first advance

Land warfare alternates between phases of fairly quiet preparation and bursts of violent and bloody action; air warfare, though it varies in intensity, pursues a more level course. While Western Desert Force was making ready for the opening of the offensive on 9th December, No. 202 Group, helped by long-range bombers from the Suez Canal airfields and Malta, was already striking at the enemy. Supply ports, lines of communication, landing-grounds, military camps—all were coming under attack. Without the Blenheims sent to Greece, Collishaw had a hard task to muster an adequate striking force, and many of his raids were carried out by single bombers. Despite all handicaps, however, his squadrons continued to keep their opponents on the defensive. And when the *Regia Aeronautica* did attempt to retaliate, it enjoyed singularly little success. On 31st October fifteen S.79's, escorted by eighteen Cr.42's, made a determined effort to bomb our forward positions. They were intercepted by twelve Hurricanes and ten Gladiators, and returned at least eight short.

Preliminary reconnaissance, both visual and photographic, was of course vital for the success of the offensive. But, as in France, the Lysanders with which the Army Co-operation squadrons (No. 208 and No. 3 (R.A.A.F.)) were equipped had proved all too vulnerable. Longmore accordingly strengthened these squadrons with a few Gladiators and Hurricanes, after which the Lysanders were normally used for close or artillery reconnaissance, the fighters for missions requiring deeper penetration. On special occasions, however, Lysanders continued to be sent off on long trips over the enemy lines—though now with the addition of heavy escort. On 20th November, for instance, a Lysander and a Blenheim, escorted by nine Hurricanes and six Gladiators, set off to photograph the entire Italian positions south of Sidi Barrani. At once a swarm of Cr. 42's rose to give combat, and for over half an hour the British formation fought a desperate engagement with some sixty opponents. It returned intact, with seven enemy aircraft to its credit and all the required photographs. The latter included excellent pictures of the Italian anti-tank defences.

The Royal Air Force also bore some share in that relentless patrolling activity on the ground which so unsettled the enemy troops. In September Longmore had brought No. 2 Armoured Car Company over from Palestine to the Western Desert. There it joined the formation furthest forward—the 11th Hussars—and fought with distinction throughout the whole of the campaign.

In the operations that now followed, Collishaw was to enjoy the help of a trained and subtle intellect. A few weeks before, it had been decided to ease the tremendous burden falling on Longmore by appointing a Deputy Air Officer Commanding-in-Chief. For this position Air Vice-Marshal Boyd was selected; but errors of navigation on his flight from England resulted in his aircraft running short of petrol and landing on Sicily instead of Malta. The choice of the authorities at home then lighted on Air Vice-Marshal A. W. Tedder, who at that time was Director General of Research and Development in the Ministry of Aircraft Production. Tedder was wiser than Boyd: he came out by way of the Takoradi route, thus avoiding the enemy and at the same time finding out for himself how the development of this vital link was progressing. Once at Cairo his main function quickly became to 'look after' the Western Desert. A scholar of Pepys's college, the author of a research thesis on the Restoration Navy, and a member of the colonial service before the war of 1914 called him to the Western Front and a pilot's wings, Tedder had a far broader outlook than many of his fellow commanders. In all the work that lay ahead his keen intelligence, quietly sardonic humour, and gift of attracting the willing service and devotion of officers and airmen from the highest to the lowest, were to be of untold value to the British cause.

As 9th December approached, Collishaw continued to attack over a very wide area. His plan—and it met with every success—was to make the Italians disperse their fighters and retain them on the defensive. Then, as the general preparations gave way to the immediate tactical preliminaries, Longmore ordered a vigorous assault against the enemy air force. On 4th December No. 202 Group Blenheims successfully bombed El Adem, the main air base in Cyrenaica. Three nights later Wellingtons from Malta did even better against the main Tripolitanian base of Castel Benito. They achieved complete surprise, hit five hangars, and in low attacks with incendiary bullets shot up large numbers of aircraft on the ground. At the same time Collishaw's Blenheims struck at Benina, a big airfield outside Benghazi.

By that time O'Connor's men were on the move. As the Italian lines were some seventy miles west of our own, our troops had to approach by dark. They set off during the night of 7/8th December, covered the first stage without mishap, while the Blenheims were raiding Benina, and at sunrise settled down to wait. All day long they lay in the desert, taking shelter among such patches of scrub and thorn as they could find. All day long the Gladiators and Hurricanes swept the forward area, alert for enemy bombers and reconnaissance. Slowly the hours passed: our men were not attacked or even observed. Then, by the bright moon of a clear, crisp night, they again moved forward. Overhead flew a Bombay, to drown the rumble and rattle of the tanks. In front, to the right, the flash of high explosive lit the sky as our ships and aircraft attacked Sidi Barrani and Maktila, the enemy's foremost camp on the coast. Far beyond in the distance, the airfield at Benina again reverberated to the crash of bombs. By the end of the long night our troops had reached the positions from which they would strike. And the Italians, disturbed and deceived by the coastal bombardment, were already fleeing from Maktila.

The enemy camps, each well defended by barbed wire and obstructions against tanks, lay in a line from Maktila in the north to Sofafi in the south. O'Connor's plan was to filter through the twenty-mile gap between Rabia and Nibeiwa, two camps north of Sofafi; to assault Nibeiwa from the west; to take the two camps further north around Tummer in a similar fashion; and to strike north-west to the coastal road, so taking Sidi Barrani and Maktila in the rear. After that we could exploit the situation as opportunity offered. We were unlikely, however, to be able to sustain the momentum of the offensive for more than five days.

All this befell exactly as planned, except that the opportunities for exploitation, and the vigour with which they were seized, surpassed all expectations. In the early morning of 9th December troops of the Royal Tank Regiment and the 4th Indian Divison attacked Nibeiwa. Surprise was so complete that many of the defenders were interrupted at their breakfast. Fortunately the heavy armour of our infantry tanks resisted the fire of the defenders, and within an hour and a half the camp was in our hands. Tummer East, assaulted at a weak spot revealed by air reconnaissance, fell during the afternoon. At Tummer West resistance lasted a little longer, but was almost broken by nightfall. Meantime part of the 7th Armoured Division 'held the ring' to the south, and other elements drove north-west to the coast and established themselves astride the road behind Sidi Barrani.

The Royal Air Force part in the first day's operations was to master the opposing air force by offensive patrols and raids on airfields, to carry out reconnaissance, and to attack enemy columns. Bad visibility failed to prevent success in all three tasks. Before the battle Longmore had ordered the Hurricanes to be used in low-flying attacks on the Italian fighter airfields and lines of communication, and the policy soon paid handsome dividends. Flying as many as four sorties each a day, our fighter pilots streamed through the Italian defences; No. 33 Squadron in particular distinguished itself by playing havoc with transport for fifty miles behind Bardia and returning with vital information about movements in the enemy rear.

Harried in this fashion, the Italians reacted in the worst way possible. Instead of striking at the root of the trouble, they tried to put up an 'umbrella' over their troops. The result was that before long the Italian fighters were completely worn out by the ceaseless demands of the Italian generals.

After a further bombardment during the night of 9/10th December, Sidi Barrani succumbed to converging attacks the next afternoon. A heavy dust storm blew throughout much of the day, cutting down air support and enabling the enemy to withdraw from around Sofafi. But on the 11th the sky cleared and the retreating enemy columns came under heavy attack from our fighters. In the days that followed the remaining forward camps were occupied, the 4th Indian Division —by one of Wavell's masterly switches—was ordered to the Sudan, and the 7th Armoured Division, supported by the Royal Air Force, kept up the pursuit. By 16th December the last of the enemy had been driven over the frontier, Bardia was invested and under repeated bombardment from sea and air, and 38,000 prisoners were in our hands. On our side the total casualties in all arms were less than six hundred killed, wounded and missing. It was little wonder that on Christmas Eve the *Duce*, gazing gloomily into the street as disgrace in Albania followed disaster in Africa, spoke bitterly to Ciano: 'This snow and cold are very good. In this way our good-for-nothing Italians will be improved. One of the principal reasons I have desired the reforestation of the Apennines has been to make Italy colder and snowier . . . '

The weather might be chilly in Rome, but in Cairo and London all was now genial warmth, and the Prime Minister paid glowing tribute to the Middle East commanders. After thanking Wavell and stating the next objective in characteristic terms ('to maul the Italian Army and rip them off the African shore to the utmost possible extent') he added 'Pray convey my compliments and congratulations to Longmore on his magnificent handling of the R.A.F. and fine co-operation with the Army. . . . Tell him we are filling up *Furious* again with another even larger packet of flyables from Takoradi.'

Thus encouraged, our commanders prepared for the reduction of Bardia. While the infantry was coming up and the 6th Australian Division was replacing the 4th Indian, the Royal Air Force operated on a reduced scale. Many machines had been damaged during the intensive work of the last few days, and towards the end of the month two of the Blenheim squadrons could muster only seven serviceable aircraft between them. With this decline the Italian Air Force at once became more active, attacking our troops and interfering with our efforts to use the little harbour of Sollum. This in turn meant that Collishaw had to direct an increasing number of sorties against enemy landing grounds; he continued, however, to make his main effort against Bardia and its neighbouring troop concentrations and supply dumps. Meanwhile the Wellingtons from the Canal attacked the ports and airfields of Tobruk and Benghazi, and Wellingtons and Swordfish from Malta struck heavy blows at Tripoli and Castel Benito.

By the beginning of January the Army was almost ready, and in the opening days of the month our ships and aircraft duly 'softened up' Bardia. On 3rd January, following night raids by Wellingtons and Bombays, the attack opened with the heaviest artillery barrage yet heard in Africa. Throughout the day our fighters were ceaselessly active, carrying out offensive patrols, protecting our naval vessels while they bombarded troop concentrations north of the Bardia-Tobruk road, and diving over Bardia every ten minutes on close reconnaissance. Meanwhile the Blenheims, having weakened the perimeter defences, resumed the pressure against the enemy air force. By nightfall two-thirds of the defended area was in our hands, and the remainder fell within the next two days.

Some of the 45,000 prisoners which the operation produced were questioned about the results of our bombing. Their answers showed that it had caused great disorganization, mainly through its moral effect. One captured general, apparently dyed deep in the khaki, asserted that 'bombing and aerial combats were only for news bulletins and did not affect the military issue,' but paid handsome tribute to the work of our Lysanders. They had directed our mechanized units so well, he considered, that the two 'appeared to be connected to each other by a string'. Another general was more impressed by our offensive activity. He explained that the garrison was so harassed by our preliminary air attacks that when the final assault came, with shelling from all sides, including the sea, and continuous bombing and machine-gunning from the air, the defenders were reduced to utter helplessness. He himself escaped the attentions of one of our fighters only by hiding beneath some desert scrub. Of the two captains with him, one was killed outright and the other died of heart failure.

The capture of Bardia brought renewed congratulations from London. This time, however, the messages contained a note of warning. 'Greatly admire your brilliant support of army operations,' wrote the Prime Minister on 7th January, ' . . . . We shall soon be as usual torn between conflicting needs. . . . Probably four or five squadrons will be required for Greece and yet you will have to carry the army forward in Libya. . . . ' Four days later the Chiefs of Staff informed the Middle East commanders that a German movement through Bulgaria appeared imminent. Once Tobruk was taken, help to Greece must come before all other considerations in the Middle East. It need not, however, prevent an advance to Benghazi if the going was good.

Reluctantly making a gesture in the required direction, Longmore now ordered Nos. 11 and 112 Squadrons over to Greece. Both of these were at half strength. He strenuously resisted, however, the proposal of the Chief of Air Staff that two or three Hurricane squadrons should go as well. This attitude brought a sharp message from the Prime Minister. 'Nothing must hamper capture of Tobruk, but thereafter all operations in Libya are subordinate to aiding Greece. . . . We expect and require prompt and active compliance with our decisions, for which we bear full responsibility.'

Bowing to the inevitable, Longmore placed No. 33 Squadron under orders to move. It was one of the only two Hurricane Squadrons in the Western Desert. Then followed difficulties from an unexpected quarter. Visiting Athens in mid-January 1941, Wavell and Longmore found the Greek General Staff convinced that the British appreciation of the situation was mistaken. The Germans, if they attacked, would not attack until well on in March. At the same time the British commanders found our immediate offer of two regiments politely refused. Unless we could send at least nine divisions, speedily and secretly, the Greeks preferred our military help to be confined to supplies of equipment. Only when the Germans cast the die by entering Bulgaria would inadequate British forces be better than none. From the Royal Air Force, on the other hand, the Greeks would accept all the help that could be given. Even that, however, would be limited by the lack of serviceable airfields.

*   *   *

While the War Cabinet's offer was being rebuffed in Athens, important developments were occurring elsewhere. Distrusting the Italians' ability either to close the Mediterranean to British shipping or to keep open their own supply routes to Africa, Hitler had pressed upon Mussolini the services of *Fliegerkorps X*. In the latter part of December 1940 the German air units began to arrive in Sicily, where their dispositions were studied by our aircraft from Malta. The war in the Mediterranean was entering a new, and very different, phase.

On 9th January, nine Ju.87's from Sicily attacked shipping in Marsa Scirocco Bay, Malta. The attacks were not pressed home, from which it was correctly concluded that the pilots belonged to the *Regia Aeronautica*. But the events of the following day dispelled any hope that the Germans were merely handing over their aircraft to the Italians. Soon after midday a British convoy from Gibraltar, bound for Malta and Greece, was attacked while running the Narrows between Tunisia and Sicily. With fanatical determination some sixty Ju.87's and He.111's delivered repeated assaults on the *Illustrious*, which suffered six hits and three near misses. Two further attacks were made during the afternoon, but under cover of darkness the aircraft-carrier managed to limp into harbour. The next day the *Southampton* and the *Gloucester*, two cruisers which had accompanied the convoy, were heavily hit while east of Malta, and the *Southampton* had to be abandoned.

With the crippled *Illustrious* in her care, Malta now awaited the full fury of *Fliegerkorps X*. By way of prevention, Wellingtons struck at the Sicilian airfields on the nights of 12/13th and 15/16th January. During most of the intervening time the weather was fortunately too bad for the Germans to operate, and repair work on the *Illustrious* made good progress. Then on 16th January the skies cleared, and seventy Ju.87's and Ju.88's escorted by Cr.42's delivered a concentrated attack on the Grand Harbour. The *Illustrious* was hit once more, the merchant vessel *Essex* was damaged, one of the docks was put out of action and much civilian property was destroyed. The next day the weather was again bad, but on the 18th the *Luftwaffe* struck in force at Luqa and Hal Far airfields—a tribute to the work of our bombers and fighters. On the 19th the dockyard and harbour came in for another pounding, and again the *Illustrious* was hit. This time, however, the attacks were noticeably less determined. Four days later, by a miracle of effort on the part of the repairers, the *Illustrious* slipped out of harbour under her own steam. Surviving further air attacks *en route*, on 25th January she anchored safely at Alexandria.

That the *Luftwaffe* was cheated of its prey was the more remarkable in view of the odds at which the battle was fought. The forces of *Fliegerkorps X* in Sicily on 9th January 1941 numbered 61 dive-bombers, 77 long-range bombers, 12 long-range reconnaissance aircraft, and 22 twin-engined fighters. There were also about 75 Italian machines available for operations against Malta, making in all a total of some 250 enemy aircraft. Against this, Malta could muster only two squadrons of bombers, one and a half squadrons of reconnaissance aircraft, and one squadron of fighters—a total of about sixty machines. Yet our heavily outnumbered forces gave much better than they got. During the period of what came to be called 'the *Illustrious* blitz'—to distinguish it from all the other 'blitzes' Malta suffered later—our fighters and guns between them accounted for eleven German aircraft and an unspecified number of Italian, while the Wellingtons in their raids on Sicily destroyed at least nine more. As against this we lost twelve aircraft in all—two on bombing operations, four in combat, six on the ground.

As some compensation for these losses, Longmore now decided to send Malta six Hurricanes. Landing-grounds having been captured in Cyrenaica the flight presented no undue difficulty, and on 30th January the aircraft took off from Gazala. The atmosphere of the occasion is preserved in the diary of the formation leader, Flight Lieutenant C. D. Whittingham. 'We joined up our escorting Wimpies', wrote Whittingham, 'the moment we saw them approach the aerodrome. We landed at Hal Far, Malta, after four hours over the sea—intact and without incident. We were met by the A.O.C. (Maynard) and Wing Commander Michie. They joined us for tea. We enjoyed two lovely eggs and bacon and the nicest cup of tea. It did not taste of salt. The two senior officers painted the life in Malta as very good, and explained that we were there only for six months. This, and the tea, and the contrast to the desert, made us all feel very happy to be in such a place. At that moment, the sirens went. Our hosts returned to Headquarters and we to the best view-point to watch the Hurricanes take the air in twos from Takali, and to climb into sun. We envied them and thought of the sport that would be ours in the near future.'

* * *

The arrival of the German Air Force in Sicily and the Greek refusal to accept military aid combined to throw the emphasis once more on Cyrenaica. On 16th January Longmore was told that he need not send No. 33 Squadron over to Greece, and on 21st January the Middle East commanders were informed that their prime objective was Benghazi. They were not, however, spared fresh commitments. The capture of the Dodecanese was of the first importance, a strategic reserve was to be created for possible use in Greece, and detailed plans were to be prepared for invading Sicily. Meanwhile there was also the Sudan, where Gallabat had now been recovered, Kassala—the gateway into Eritrea—was being forced, and the Emperor Haile Selassie was leaving Khartoum in a Valentia for the Abyssinian border. Whatever else the Middle East commanders might suffer from, they could not complain of lack of variety in their tasks.

It was in this somewhat uncertain atmosphere that our troops proceeded to reduce Tobruk. Bad weather with heavy dust storms restricted the preliminary air operations, but several raids were made on the ports and airfields of Derna and Benghazi. From 16th January the main air effort was applied within the defended perimeter around

Tobruk—a line nearly thirty miles long—and the reconnaissance planes secured valuable photographs of enemy positions and minefields just in time for the attack. Combined bombardment from air and sea during the two nights immediately before the assault softened up the defences, as at Bardia, and in the final hours protracted bombing by Wellingtons covered the assembly of our tanks.

At dawn on 21st January, the ground forces—British tanks and Australian infantry—moved forward under fighter cover and a creeping barrage. At the same time Blenheims, Lysanders and Hurricanes operated ahead of the troops to keep the threatened area clear of reinforcements. Quickly piercing the outer defences, our men poured through, and with the help of incessant attacks by our aircraft the bulk of the artillery was soon established inside the perimeter. The intensity of the effort in the air may be judged from the fact that No. 45 Squadron, with only eight serviceable Blenheims, put in thirty-two sorties during the day. Evening fell with the Australians holding a line along the top of the escarpment which dominates the harbour, where the wreckage of nineteen ships gave silent witness to the work of our bombs and shells. The next morning the Australians entered the town and quenched the last flickers of resistance, so completing an operation which brought in another thirty thousand prisoners for under five hundred casualties on our side. Throughout the whole two days only one air combat was recorded. Disorganized and demoralized, the Italian Air Force hardly put in an appearance, and Collishaw's squadrons enjoyed undisputed command of the skies.

From Tobruk the pursuit now rolled rapidly past the flat wastes of Gazala towards the green hills and red earth of the Jebel Akdar. Two big enemy formations remained to be overcome. On the coast at Derna, where trim white houses and purple bougainvillaea delight the eye wearied with too much desert *peau de lion*, was the greater part of the Italian 60th Infantry Division; inland, near the Beau Geste fort of Mechili, on the southern side of the Jebel Akdar, lay the remainder of the Italian infantry and the main body of armour. Clearly the British forces must now follow divided paths. While Collishaw's fighter and army co-operation squadrons moved up to landing-grounds at Gazala and Tmimi abandoned by the enemy, the Australians swept north round the Gulf of Bomba towards Derna, and the 7th Armoured Division struck straight ahead towards Mechili. But the enemy preferred not to wait for the encounter. On 30th January, after three days' pressure, the Australians entered Derna; and when the Armoured Division arrived at Mechili the Italian armour was already retiring on Benghazi. So hot a pace could
U

not continue. The Armoured Division settled down to a fortnight's halt for repair and replenishment. Meanwhile the Royal Air Force kept up the pressure against the retreating columns.

To Longmore this triumphal progress spelled a firm hold on Cyrenaica, the liquidation of resistance in Italian East Africa, and, in due course, the capture of the Dodecanese. Egypt would then be safe, and the enemy would have no air bases within range of Alexandria, Haifa and the Canal. To the authorities at home, with their wider responsibilities, our successes meant something very different— the chance to forestall the Germans in the Balkans. On the day the Australians entered Derna, Longmore received another signal from the Chief of Air Staff. It told him of a proposal to counter German penetration of Bulgaria by 'infiltrating' ten to fifteen Royal Air Force squadrons into Turkey. The squadrons would, of course, come mainly or wholly from the Middle East. Their transfer, which was not to take place until the situation in Cyrenaica had stabilized, would be at the expense of operations against Italian East Africa and any further help to Greece.

Longmore, who thus found he had escaped sending more squadrons to Greece only to be expected to send three times as many to Turkey, did not mince his words in reply. 'Your [message] received,' he answered forthwith. 'Quite frankly contents astounds me. . . . I cannot believe you fully appreciate present situation Middle East, in which Libya drive in full career and Sudan offensive into Eritrea progressing satisfactorily. Neither shows signs of immediate stabilization. Arrival of aircraft in Middle East all routes now hardly keeping pace witʰ casualties. . . . However strong political advantages may be of impressing the Turks, can you afford to lock up squadrons you propose in Turkey where they may well remain for some time inoperative? Would it not be forsaking the substance for the shadow?' To these doubts the Chief of Air Staff replied the following day: 'It is not a question of impressing the Turks. It is a question of trying to deter Germany by fear of bombing of Rumania from absorbing Bulgaria, Greece and Turkey without firing a shot and then dominating the Eastern Mediterranean and Aegean as she now dominates the Narrows. If we can prevent or even delay this, the squadrons in Turkey will have pulled far more weight than in helping to beat Italians in Africa.' Faced with this, Longmore reluctantly came into line.

On 1st February the Prime Minister put his proposal to President Ineunu. The advantages he held out were manifold. British air support would help to maintain the 'famous military qualities' of the Turkish army; we could 'threaten to bombard the Rumanian oilfields if any German advance is made into Bulgaria'; and we could even hope to influence the policy of the men in the Kremlin. 'Nothing,' wrote Mr. Churchill, 'will more restrain Russia from aiding Germany, even indirectly, than the presence of powerful British bombing forces which could attack the oilfields of Baku. Russia is dependent upon the supply from these oilfields for a very large part of her agriculture, and far-reaching famine would follow their destruction. We are assured that the whole soil around the oil-wells is impregnated with petroleum, making it possible to start a conflagration on a scale not hitherto witnessed in the world.'

President Ineunu, however, took a less optimistic view of what could be accomplished by a handful of squadrons than the Prime Minister and his advisers. He considered the proposal likely to call down an immediate German or Russian attack on his country, and on 7th February he rejected it outright. The Defence Committee in London then turned towards another plan—'the only way to make sure the Turks do fight is to give sufficient support to the Greeks'; and in due course further squadrons were sent to Greece, though mercifully not as many as would have gone to Turkey.

With the seeds of future tribulation thus being sown, our forces in Cyrenaica moved forward to complete their task. On 3rd February air reconnaissance revealed that the Italians were bent on abandoning the whole province. The opportunity was too good to be missed. O'Connor promptly proposed to cut short his halt and unleash his armour with a bare two days' supplies. Collishaw enthusiastically seconded. While the Australian infantry pressed on through Apollonia and Cyrene, past relics of the days when the 'grandeur that was Rome' rested on more solid foundations than a dictator's eloquence, the 7th Armoured Division accordingly struck south-west across the desert. The going would be difficult—perhaps impossible; but it was worth taking risks to slice off the Cyrenaican 'bulge' and reach the coastal road ahead of the enemy pulling out from Benghazi.

Unlike many 'left hooks' in the later desert campaigns this 'straight left' landed home with decisive effect. On 5th February, after an appalling journey across the desert, our leading armour reached and cut the road at two points beyond Benghazi. Within a few hours the enemy ran into the main body at Beda Fomm. All the next day his columns strove to force their way through. But the trap held. In the early morning of 7th February the last of the Italian troops surrendered amid a wild confusion of abandoned equipment and mutilated vehicles. Meantime the Australians, continuing their advance along the coast, entered an unresisting Benghazi.

Months of disappointment and disaster were now to follow, and all that had been won in Cyrenaica was to be cast away in the vain effort to sustain Greece. No later events, however, could or can obscure the brilliance of this early achievement. A force never exceeding two divisions, helped by an average of two hundred aircraft, had within two months utterly routed nine Italian divisions and four hundred aircraft. It had captured 130,000 prisoners, 1,290 guns and 400 tanks at a cost to itself of less than 3,000 casualties. It had advanced 600 miles over territory aptly described as the 'tactician's paradise and quarter-master's hell'. In this almost unprecedented feat of arms the Royal Air Force had borne a full share, the measure of which may perhaps be gauged from the fact that on no single occasion were our troops seriously held up by enemy aircraft.

After his forces had reached the frontier post of El Agheila, O'Connor addressed a special order of the day to Collishaw. 'I wish', he wrote, 'to record my very great appreciation of the wonderful work of the R.A.F. units under your command, whose determination and fine fighting qualities have made this campaign possible. Since the war began you have consistently attacked the enemy air force . . . dealing him blow after blow, until finally he was driven out of the sky, and out of Libya [Cyrenaica], leaving hundreds of derelict aircraft on his aerodromes. In his recent retreat from Tobruk you gave his ground troops no rest . . . '

Coming from one whose own skill and vigour had been so powerful an agent for victory, this tribute was doubly appreciated by all ranks of No. 202 Group. Nor was it undeserved praise for those who had serviced and flown and fought their aircraft alongside the General's men; had endured, like them, the dust and the heat, the flies and the sores, the hail, mud, and biting wind, the miserable ration of water and the interminable corned beef and chlorinated tea; and had found their reward in the dark outline of a Wellington on its lonely way to Tobruk, the wild swerve of a truck under the bullets of a Hurricane, the swift, triumphant roll of a victorious Gladiator, the vanquished enemy plunging in flames to meet the desert sand.

CHAPTER X

'Middle East':
The Loss of Cyrenaica and Greece

THE British offer of military formations to Greece had been, in the words of General Wavell, 'politely but quite definitely refused'. This absolute negative was soon qualified. The appearance on Greek soil of a couple of British regiments, to be built up to two or three divisions, might indeed bring down the German Army on Greece without providing the means of resistance; but once a German attack was certain any degree of help would be better than none. On 18th January 1941, only a few days after Wavell's departure from Athens, the Greeks accordingly modified their attitude. While still declining what was offered at that moment they made it clear that in one situation they would welcome a British expedition of whatever size we could muster. This was if Hitler made his intentions plain beyond doubt by moving troops into Bulgaria.

In point of fact the German dictator had set preparations in train for a southward move as far back as 12th November 1940. On 13th December had followed his first firm directive for operation 'Marita'—the occupation in the following spring of the Aegean coast and possibly the whole mainland of Greece. His main reason, strangely enough, was fear that the Royal Air Force would take over bases in Salonika and bomb the Rumanian oilfields; other factors such as the desirability of rescuing the Italians in Albania or clearing his right flank for the great venture against Russia apparently concerned him less. Of the details of all this the British Government was not aware; it had, however, impeccable grounds for believing that Germany was bent on attacking Greece. We were, therefore, not at first disposed to co-operate with the Greeks along the lines they now suggested. Already conscious that our proferred help—the most within our power—could scarcely offset the presence of some twenty

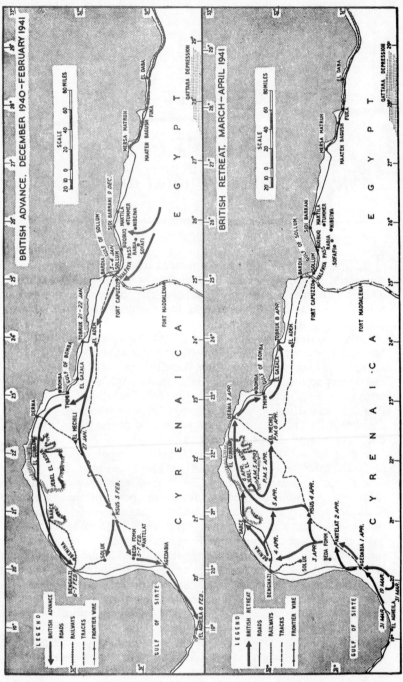

CYRENAICA AND THE WESTERN DESERT, DECEMBER 1940—APRIL 1941

German divisions in Rumania, the Defence Committee considered that delay of the kind proposed by the Greeks would sacrifice the most attractive element in the whole scheme—the chance, for once, of forestalling Hitler. But the Turks, to whom, as already related, the Prime Minister then addressed himself, proved even less willing than the Greeks to accept the questionable benefit of British help on a small scale. Understandably reluctant to allow the Germans into the eastern Mediterranean without a struggle, the Government was thus thrown back on the Greeks. Moreover it remained acutely aware both of its obligations to a singularly gallant ally and of the deplorable effect on public opinion—and not least on American public opinion —which would result from a failure to honour them. On 10th February the Defence Committee accordingly reaffirmed the policy of halting the African advance at Benghazi, and the following day the Foreign Secretary and the Chief of the Imperial General Staff were ordered to Athens to concert measures with the Greeks. At the same time General Wavell was instructed to prepare all possible forces for a move across the Mediterranean.

On 22nd February, Eden, Dill, Wavell, Longmore and D'Albiac met the Greek political and military leaders at Tatoi. The total of forces likely to be available to resist a German attack through Bulgaria and Yugoslavia was six Greek and four British divisions, excluding the Greek forces already engaged in Albania. With these it was certainly not possible to hold the long, shallow provinces of the north-east—Eastern Macedonia and Western Thrace. Indeed, British plans had always recognized that twenty divisions would be needed for Eastern Macedonia alone. On the other hand it was vitally important to stimulate the resistance of the Yugoslavs; and the Yugoslavs could hardly be expected to oppose a German move through their country if Salonika, the only port through which British supplies could reach them, was not to be defended. But as Yugoslavia at the moment appeared likely to submit to the German dictates without a fight, it was agreed that no serious opposition should be offered on the north-eastern frontiers, and that the Greek forces in the outlying territories should be withdrawn to a short, and apparently very strong, position in Central Macedonia. In its right-hand sector this followed the River Aliakmon, which gave its name to the line; the left-hand stretched towards the Yugoslav frontier. The mountainous terrain promised well for defence, while the right flank, behind which stood Mount Olympus, rested on the sea. The proposed line was not, however, to be occupied until the British Foreign Secretary had made a further effort to persuade the Yugoslavs to play their part.

The discussions at Tatoi proceeded favourably, and on 24th February the War Cabinet, after receiving Eden's report, decided that 'on balance . . . the enterprise should go forward'. Subject to the consent of Australia and New Zealand, whose troops were to make up three of the four British divisions, the Prime Minister then instructed Eden to clinch the matter. 'While being under no illusions, we all send you the order "Full steam ahead".'

On 1st March the German army began to enter Bulgaria. Within a few hours Eden, Dill and Wavell were again in Athens. The Greek Commander-in-Chief, General Papagos, had apparently not been informed of the result of the fresh British approaches to Yugoslavia, and he had therefore left his forces in their forward positions. Beseeched by the British representatives to withdraw them at once to the Aliakmon Line, he answered that it was now too late, since they might be attacked during the move; and he suggested instead that we should 'dribble our forces piecemeal' (in Eden's phrase) to join the Greeks in Eastern Macedonia. This proposal we firmly resisted. The attitude of Yugoslavia, however, was still undecided, and as a compromise between the views of the British and Greek leaders it was agreed that the Greeks should maintain their main forward position in Eastern Macedonia, but should withdraw from Western Thrace the province in the extreme north-east. This would free one division, which together with two reserve divisions would hold the Aliakmon Line until the British took over. If Yugoslavia came in, the Aliakmon forces could then move forward to Eastern Macedonia; while if Yugoslavia remained neutral the Eastern Macedonian forces would fight a delaying action and retire to the Aliakmon. On top of all the other risks of the enterprise, it was thus with General Papagos's troops committed to dispositions unsatisfactory from the purely military point of view, if unavoidable politically, that, on 7th March 1941, the British expeditionary force began to land in Greece.

By this date, in accordance with earlier orders from London, Longmore had already moved three more squadrons across from Africa—Nos. 11 (Blenheims), 112 (Gladiators and Hurricanes) and 33 (Hurricanes). Another Blenheim squadron (No. 113) arrived in Greece during March, and No. 208 Squadron (Lysanders and Hurricanes) was on the way when the Germans launched their attack. D'Albiac was accordingly confronted with the problem of finding suitable bases for five extra squadrons, in addition to his original four, in a country desperately short not only of airfields but of general communications. This he had to do in the intervals of protecting the arrival of the expeditionary force, covering its movement up to

central Greece and its assembly on the Aliakmon Line, and supporting the Greek offensive in Albania.

The programme was certainly a full one. On the Albanian front
D'Albiac's difficulties may be glimpsed from one of Longmore's
messages to the Chief of the Air Staff at the end of February: 'Have
just returned from visiting western aerodromes. All water-logged
except Paramythia, where in spite of appalling operational conditions
Blenheims and Hurricanes have kept Greeks almost clear of air interference since 13th February. . . . Line of communication for petrol
and bombs in this area unbelievable. . . . One hour's flight takes two
to three days by road.' In central Greece conditions were little better.
Most of the grass airfields were still too soft for use, and those with
firm surfaces were often in wildly inconvenient places. One of the
Blenheim squadrons, for instance, had to be based at Almyros, which
had no direct communication with the combined headquarters of the
Army and the new Royal Air Force 'Eastern Wing' at Ellason. All
messages between these points had to be relayed through the airfield
at Larissa; and since the local air raid warning centre more or less
monopolized one stretch of the only available line, the passing of a
priority telephone call during the campaign often took as much as
five or six hours. Larissa itself was a good airfield, but congested, and
the neighbourhood suffered severely in an earthquake on 1st March.
Around Athens conditions and communications were naturally
better, but the distance to the fronts was too great for effective
operation. Matters were also not improved by the presence of the
German Minister, who mingled with our arriving troops and on one
occasion actually secured an invitation to an officers' mess.

The reinforcing squadrons arrived to find their comrades taking
part in a major offensive. Conscious of the impending German move,
the Greeks had determined on an all-out attempt to capture Valona
and finish off the struggle in Albania. Their continual entreaties had
moved D'Albiac to use two of his squadrons for close support; a dry
patch for a few Blenheims had been found near the front; and a
'Western Wing' headquarters had been set up to control operations.
For two or three weeks the weather was kind, and a great effort on
13th and 14th February, when fifty sorties were flown, helped to
carry the Greeks almost into Tepeleni. With the arrival of the
Hurricanes of No. 112 Squadron, morale mounted still higher; and
it reached a peak on 28th February when twenty-eight Gladiators and
Hurricanes intercepted an enemy formation of fifty aircraft and shot
down twenty-seven for only one loss to themselves. The engagement
was fought over the Greek lines in full view of both armies, and each
success was confirmed from the ground. This remarkable feat so

impressed the local Greeks that Wing Commander P. B. Coote, in charge of the Western Wing, was able to report: 'civilians and soldiers passing us in the streets make the sign of the Cross, saying "Long life to you. Thank the Almighty who sent you to us". '

But very soon the Italian airmen, freed from any preoccupation with their own bases and spurred on by the presence of Mussolini in Albania, began to show a most unwelcome activity. In the teeth of protests from the Greeks, D'Albiac adjudged it necessary to revert to attacks on airfields and supply ports. 'In vain we tried to explain the proper employment of an air force and the disparity between our strength and that of the enemy,' wrote Wing Commander Coote; 'at the end we gained our point, but the same discussion started all over again on the morrow. Nevertheless, jokingly, we again pressed our point of view and always parted at the Greek Headquarters in a most friendly and cordial atmosphere.' But though relations between the allies remained untroubled, the Greek advance, handicapped by a renewed spell of bad weather and continued Italian reinforcement, slowed down and came to a halt a few miles north of Tepeleni. Soon the enemy struck back, only to be held. A decision in Albania was still as far off as ever. And on the southern and western borders of Bulgaria now lay Hitler's legions, poised for action.

* * *

The assignment of four divisions and five additional squadrons to Greece left the British in Cyrenaica remarkably thin on the ground. The reduced military units, under Major-General Neame, consisted of only one armoured brigade and one incompletely trained division of Australian infantry; the reduced air forces, under Group Captain L. O. Brown, amounted to no more than four squadrons—two fighter (Nos. 3 (R.A.A.F.) and 73), one bomber reconnaissance (No. 55) and one tactical reconnaissance (No. 6). Two of these were at less than half-strength. On the air side, Longmore and Brown were deeply conscious of the risk that was being run, for well before the decision to commit a British expedition to Greece German aircraft were harassing our front-line troops, frustrating our first efforts to use Benghazi, and laying mines in the Suez Canal. But on the military side General Wavell as yet saw no reason to be perturbed.

Having finally, like Longmore, come down on the side of the Greek venture, the Commander-in-Chief loyally set about obeying the Government's injunction to strip North Africa to the lowest level consistent with safety. Since on balance it appeared that the many good reasons for going into Greece out-weighed the many good reasons to the contrary, it was only logical to give the British expeditionary force at least some chance of success by making it as strong as possible. Very little would then be left in Cyrenaica; but the remaining Italian forces in Libya were so shattered as to be obviously incapable of any immediate counter-stroke. So far the reasoning was good. But unfortunately General Wavell reckoned without the Germans.

Hitler's first directive ordering German troops to Africa was issued on 11th January 1941. The unit selected was the 5th Light Division, which included one *panzer* regiment; command was in the hands of Erwin Rommel. The intention at this date was nothing more ambitious than to save Tripolitania from the fate then rapidly overtaking Cyrenaica. On 6th February a further step followed; the *Führer* decreed that German air forces, besides operating from Sicily and the Dodecanese, could also be transferred to North Africa, 'if necessary withdrawing them from warfare against the British Isles'. About the same time the first German troops landed at Tripoli. On 12th February Rommel arrived to take up his command, after a conference with the commander of *Fliegerkorps X* in Sicily the previous day, and by the middle of the month the Germans were establishing themselves in the forward area around Sirte. On 18th February Hitler named Rommel's forces the 'German Africa Corps' and decided to reinforce them with a full *panzer* division.

All these moves and decisions were of course not known to us on 24th February, when the Cabinet formally agreed to send a force to Greece. By 28th February, however—before the first British troops had sailed from Egypt—it was known in London that the Africa Corps and the 5th Light Division were at Tripoli. Moreover the handful of reconnaissance aircraft with our forward troops were already observing signs and portents of the arrival of German units at the front. On balance, however, G.H.Q. at Cairo discounted the probability of any German appearance in strength, and on 2nd March—when it was admitted that one German armoured brigade group was already in Africa, and reinforcement proceeding—General Wavell advised London that in view of the great distance from Tripoli to Benghazi, the enemy's shortage of transport, and the coming hot weather, no large-scale enemy attack was likely before the end of the summer.

During March, General Neame and the Australian divisional commander, worried by repeated reports of the appearance of German units on their front, made representations to Cairo. As the month wore on, General Wavell himself became increasingly anxious; but his considered appreciation remained that no attack was likely before May, by which time our victories in East Africa might free one of the two Indian divisions for service in Cyrenaica.

Fortunately Group Captain Brown was more impressed with the evidence of his own aircraft, including the many signs that the enemy were occupying fresh landing-grounds and making more use of the small harbours along the coast. So far as his diminutive resources allowed, Brown accordingly carried out attacks against the main air-fields and Tripoli. The four Wellington squadrons—Nos. 37, 38, 70 and 148—from the Canal and Malta, also operated against the same targets. Much damage was done, but the available effort was of course far short of what was required to stop the Germans building up the force they had planned.

Apart from the German 5th Light Division, Italian reinforcements amounting to two divisions, including one armoured, reached Tripolitania in January and February. During the same period there arrived about 110 German aircraft, of which all but a few were Ju.87's or Me.110's. Their commander, known as the *Fliegerführer Afrika*, came under the higher control of *Fliegerkorps X* in Sicily. On 10th March our aircraft, which had reported increased movement by enemy M.T. since 2nd March, observed large concentrations in the area immediately west of El Agheila. From the 19th onwards, enemy patrols became very aggressive, and on the 24th, German and Italian forces approached El Agheila and compelled us to withdraw our out-posts. Yet only the Royal Air Force took these indications at their true value. On 22nd March, Brown instructed his units to prepare for a move backwards at short notice; but Neame, his early apprehen-sions apparently dispelled by the attitude of his superiors at Cairo, maintained in a conference on 27–29th March that there were no German troops in Tripolitania except a few technical experts. On 30th March his headquarters issued an operational order stating that though enemy forces had occupied El Agheila, they had 'so far shown no signs of contemplating a further advance'. 'There is no conclu-sive evidence', the order continued, 'to show that the enemy intends to take the offensive on a large scale, or even that he is likely to be in a position to do so in the near future.' The very next day—pre-sumably while this appreciation was being distributed—the enemy counter-offensive began.

The British military commanders, it must be made clear, had this justification: that when the attack began, the enemy intended a very limited advance. It was only when the Axis forces found the going so easy that, under the spur of Rommel's aggressive genius, they went so fast and so far. As late as 3rd April, when the vital tank battle had already been decided in the enemy's favour, and Rommel was pushing hard across the base of the Cyrenaican 'bulge', Keitel was issuing orders that 'attacks . . . must not be extended . . . before the 15th

Panzer Division arrives. . . . Under no circumstances should the open right flank be endangered, which would necessarily be the case in an advance to the north on Benghazi. . . . Even after the arrival of the 15th Panzer Division, a large-scale offensive, aimed perhaps at Tobruk, should not be launched.' Such plans, Keitel concluded, could be changed only if the bulk of the British armoured forces were withdrawn from Cyrenaica. Which indeed, though he was unaware of it, was already the case.

Exposed to an attack by three armoured or motorized divisions and an air force greatly superior in numbers, within a few hours our forward units were falling back through Agedabia. The intention was to maintain our armour inland of the coastal road and so guard against both an advance along the coast and a direct outflanking thrust across the desert. Yet Neame was also under orders to fight a retiring action, if necessary, as far as the high ground east of Benghazi—a point certainly much too far north for effective control of the desert route through Msus and Mechili. Worse still, the 2nd Armoured Division, new to the forward area, short of transport and thus tied to a vulnerable series of petrol dumps, and struggling along with worn-out or Italian tanks, was in no fit shape to halt the enemy along either path they might take.

Until our armour reached Antelat, on 2nd April, the retirement went according to plan. From then on the whole British movement became disjointed. Once the commander of the 2nd Armoured Division heard that his tank losses could not be made good, and so refrained from seeking a decision south of Benghazi, there was really nothing to do—if we wished to avoid being trapped in the Jebel Akdar by the outflanking move across the desert—but pull out of Western Cyrenaica as fast as possible. Unfortunately it is not always practicable to adopt the most expedient course from the purely military point of view. By the evening of 2nd April it was clear, as foreseen in the retirement plan, that Benina and Benghazi were untenable; but Wavell still hoped to make the main stand on the high ground to the east. Coming up to examine the situation for himself, the Commander-in-Chief nevertheless found matters more critical than he had expected. Alarmed, he at once summoned the experienced O'Connor to the forward area from his new command in Egypt—in the capacity, however, of an adviser, not a commander.

During this time No. 3 (R.A.A.F.) Squadron at Benina, helped by a flight of No. 73 on detachment from Tobruk, gave valuable protection to Benghazi and the forward troops. Great efforts were also made by our bombers. Brown's single remaining squadron of Blenheims was reinforced by a flight of No. 45 Squadron from Greece, and

together these aircraft repeatedly bombed landing-grounds and concentrations of vehicles. From Egypt the three Wellington squadrons,
now joined by the Wellington squadron from Malta—German air
raids on the island having compelled its withdrawal—attacked
similar targets. By refuelling near Tobruk they were also able to
strike at Tripoli, so hampering enemy reinforcement. But though our
squadrons were not outfought they were heavily outnumbered and
far too few for the work to be done. Their most strenuous exertions—
and these they gave in full measure—could not possibly redress the
situation on the ground.

From 3rd April the situation in the forward area was chaotic. On
the night of 2nd April, No. 6 Squadron, one of the Army Co-operation units under direct military control, was with the Headquarters
of the Second Armoured Division at Antelat. When morning came
the Headquarters had disappeared, leaving the squadron completely
ignorant of its intentions. Mystified, the squadron put up search
patrols, and when these proved in vain retired north-east across the
desert to the Division's main supply dump at Msus. Here the airmen
found a Free French detachment which denied knowledge of any
other troops in the area; and it was not until noon that the missing
Headquarters was located thirty miles to the west. It had retired, not
north-east, but due north towards Benghazi with the rest of the
Division. Two hours afterwards one of the squadron pilots, taking a
'quick look' along the Msus–Antelat track, reported a small enemy
force only five miles off Msus. At this the 3rd Armoured Brigade was
directed east to investigate, leaving the Divisional Headquarters
troops and the Support Group to continue the retirement north. But
when the Brigade arrived at Msus the following morning, it found
neither the enemy—though he may well have been there overnight—
nor the petrol with which it hoped to refuel; for this had been
destroyed when the Free French left. Instead of continuing ahead
across the desert to Mechili in accordance with its orders, the Brigade
therefore—unknown to Divisional Headquarters—turned north towards petrol, the coast, and disaster.

Covered by No. 3 Squadron (R.A.A.F.) and 73 Squadron, who on
5th April claimed fourteen enemy aircraft for only two losses on their
own side, the rest of the Division had by then reached the high ground
towards which it had been steadily retiring. But there was now wide
scope for manœuvre by the enemy to the south; and there seemed no
hope of success in a pitched encounter. Sizing up the situation on his
arrival, O'Connor had already advised a general withdrawal to the
line Derna-Mechili. So back on Derna moved the Australian infantry on the right; and back on Derna, through the heart of the

Jebel Akdar, moved the Support Group, followed in the latter part
of its course by the 3rd Armoured Brigade; and back on Mechili,
under the impression that the Armoured Brigade was heading there
too, moved the troops of Divisional Headquarters. Meanwhile,
against the mounting threat to Egypt, Indian troops were ordered
post haste from the Sudan; the South African Government agreed
that their forces could be employed as far north as the Mediterranean; the 7th Australian Division, destined for Greece, was held
back; and reinforcements of Hurricanes and Wellingtons were rushed
out from home.

By 7th April, Brown's squadrons were partly at Sidi Mahmoud,
outside Tobruk, partly at Gambut, an elevated expanse of brown
dust between Tobruk and the Egyptian frontier. No. 6 Squadron,
sent forward again in response to a military request after it reached
Derna, lost a number of men in getting back; and misfortune also
befell O'Connor and Neame, who made a detour to avoid the endless
stream of vehicles and by bad luck ran into an enemy patrol. To
Tedder the gods were kinder. Forced down in the desert by engine
failure he was picked up next day by a passing Blenheim.

By 8th April all hope of holding the Derna-Mechili line had
vanished. In the north the Australians, having withdrawn without
difficulty to Derna, had been ordered farther back to defend Tobruk;
the Support Group, after a fierce encounter outside Derna, was retiring in the same direction; and the 3rd Armoured Brigade, following
a little later, had been cut off in Derna and in large part overwhelmed. Inland, at Mechili, the Divisional Headquarters, strengthened by Indian motorized troops from Tobruk, had for two nights
waited in vain for the Armoured Brigade. Surrounded on 8th April,
it then strove to break out to the east. A few elements got through but
the bulk of the force was destroyed or taken prisoner.

By that time Wavell had decided to stake a good part of his fast-
dwindling resources on holding Tobruk. The water supplies, the
ample stores, and the excellent harbour of this port were a valuable
prize, and in Rommel's hands would undoubtedly give a fresh
impetus to the enemy advance. A brigade of the Australian 7th
Division was accordingly shipped in from Egypt; the remnants of
the Support Group were concentrated a few miles to the south; and
while No. 3 Squadron (R.A.A.F.) and 45/55 Squadron retired over the
Egyptian frontier, Nos. 6 and 73 stayed behind to operate from
within the defended perimeter. With these moves the Royal Air Force
completed its withdrawal through Cyrenaica. In contrast to the hundreds of unserviceable aircraft abandoned by the Italians during their
retreat in the opposite direction, Brown's squadrons—admittedly

a much smaller force—left behind only ten. And these, of course, they destroyed.

Within three days of the disaster at Mechili the enemy was threatening El Adem and the neighbourhood south of Tobruk. Deprived of the refuelling-grounds in this district the Wellingtons from the Canal could no longer reach Tripoli. The whole burden of air operations against enemy traffic to Africa thus fell on Malta; and Malta, under the pressure of the German assault from Sicily, had just been relieved of its only bomber squadron. For the moment, however, the Germans and Italians were more interested in developments at the front. On 12th April their armour attempted to concentrate for an attack on Tobruk. It was at once spotted by our reconnaissance and broken up by our bombers, which flew up from Egypt and refuelled at landing-grounds within the perimeter. Unable to take the port in their stride, the Axis forces promptly consoled themselves by moving to Bardia and the Sollum escarpment. This they occupied on 13th April. But by then the ever-increasing difficulties of supply, the ceaseless toll of the desert and the menace of an unsubdued Tobruk had robbed the advance of its momentum. On the borders of Egypt the German and Italian columns came to rest.

Meantime events had not stood still elsewhere. On 6th April, while our hard-won position in Cyrenaica was thus crumbling into ruin, the German avalanche had descended on Greece.

* * *

On 25th March 1941 the Yugoslav Prime Minister and Foreign Secretary, summoned to Vienna to declare their attitude to the Axis Tripartite Pact, duly signed on the dotted line. Their countrymen, however, were made of sterner stuff than the acquiescent Rumanians and Bulgarians. Belgrade was at once aflame with protests; and on 27th March a military *coup* overthrew the Regent Paul and the collaborationists and installed the young King Peter in the exercise of full regal powers. From this point it was clear not only that Yugoslavia would fight to keep the Germans out, but also that she would have to do so in the very near future. It was also clear, though the point seems to have been appreciated more in theory than in practice, that everything now depended on effective co-operation between the Greeks, the Yugoslavs, and the British.

On 28th March, Admiral Cunningham, placed on the scent the previous day by a Sunderland of No. 230 Squadron, brought strong Italian naval forces to action off Cape Matapan. Blenheims from Greece joined in without success—contrary to our belief at the time—but intensive reconnaissance by Sunderlands helped to keep track of the enemy's movements, and the final result was entirely satisfactory. On the Italian side three cruisers and two destroyers were sunk and a battleship damaged, while on our side the only loss was that of one naval aircraft. Heartened by this notable contribution towards control of the Mediterranean and still more by the dramatic change in the attitude of Yugoslavia, the Greeks now shook off the pessimism which had lately fallen upon them, and addressed themselves to the future with confidence.

Unfortunately time was short, and everything still remained to be arranged with Yugoslavia. Labouring under the misfortune of common frontiers with Italy, Germany, Hungary, Rumania and Bulgaria, the Yugoslavs were exposed to attack on five sides; but with their traditional spirit, and against the advice of their allies, they were firmly resolved to defend their territory at all points. This made it impossible for them to concentrate strong forces in the vital sectors. To a British and Greek request of more doubtful wisdom, they did, however, agree; in the hope of capturing badly needed equipment they undertook to launch four divisions against the Italians in Albania. Here co-operation stopped. Sir John Dill, so heavily incognito that the Yugoslavs with whom he conferred remained unaware that he was anything more than a representative of General Wilson, paid one fleeting visit to Belgrade; a Yugoslav general paid one fleeting visit to Greece. These were the only military contacts of any significance before the German attack. Afterwards there were still less.

By the beginning of April the German army had mustered twenty-seven divisions, of which seven were armoured, on the borders of Yugoslavia and Greece. Other divisions were contributed by the Italians, the Hungarians, and the Bulgarians. German aircraft available for the occasion, under *Luftflotte 4*, amounted to some 1,200 first-line machines, to which—since they could be used to attack many targets besides those on the Albanian front—must be added the 150 Italian aircraft in Albania and as many more in Italy. Against this formidable force the Greeks could muster six divisions— the remainder of their army being already engaged with the Italians; the British under General Wilson between two and three divisions[1]; and the Yugoslavs twenty-four divisions. But the Yugoslav army, being nearly all infantry and like the Greeks dependent on horse, mule and ox-drawn transport, was hardly yet in the field; and it was not likely to give of its best against tanks and bombers if caught in

---

[1] The 1st Armoured Brigade and the New Zealand Division were fully deployed by the time of the German attack; the 6th Australian Division was still arriving.

x

the process of concentration. In the air, combined Greek and Yugoslav strength totalled no more than a hundred machines for all fronts; while D'Albiac's force amounted to nine squadrons and two visiting detachments of Wellingtons—in all something under two hundred aircraft, of which only eighty were serviceable at the beginning of April. Moreover the two squadrons of the 'Western Wing' were committed to the Italian front. To complete the catalogue of inequality, the Greeks had already borne the strain of six months' struggle against a far more powerful opponent; while the Germans, with every advantage in numbers, equipment, and communications, would also choose the place and time at which the blow would fall.

The time proved to be 0515 on 6th April; the place, or rather places, Eastern Macedonia and seven separate areas along the Yugoslav frontiers. Infuriated by Yugoslav's unexpected defiance, which had forced him to call back several divisions already under orders to proceed farther east, Hitler led off with Operation *Strafgericht* (Retribution). This enabled the *Luftwaffe* to inscribe the name of Belgrade alongside those of Warsaw and Rotterdam among its battle-honours. According to an official German report the effect of the various high explosive calibres proved in all cases 'up to expectation'. With bombers thus pounding their capital to ruins, fighters shooting up their slow-moving helpless columns, and tanks striking deep into their territory at a host of different points, the Yugoslav armies were beaten almost before they could take the field.

All this, of course, was to determine the progress of events in Greece. As there was a large gap between the Greek forces on the Albanian front and the Anglo-Greek forces in the east, the defence of Greece essentially depended on what happened in southern Yugoslavia. Unfortunately the Yugoslav Army in this area collapsed at the first thrust, and within two days the enemy was astride the Vardar. By 9th April one German force had followed the river south-east towards Salonika, cutting off the forward Greek divisions in Eastern Macedonia and compelling their surrender; another, striking south at a point farther across Yugoslavia, was heading through the Monastir gap into virtually undefended territory. Thenceforward the result was scarcely in doubt; for the Allied Army in Central Macedonia and the Greek Army in the Epirus could not be stretched to meet in the middle. Either the two armies must retire on both sides of the peninsula, or they must stand and be outflanked by a thrust down the centre. And the Greeks, having no mechanical transport worth mentioning, could not retire.

During these first critical days, when the issue of the campaign was being decided, D'Albiac strove to establish the enemy's intentions and delay the advancing forces. He also provided fighter protection for the Greeks in Eastern Macedonia, a task which produced a notable victory when twelve Hurricanes took on twenty Me. 109's and claimed five victims without loss. The bombers he at first directed against previously selected communications targets in Bulgaria, including the marshalling yards at Sofia; then, as the enemy's plan unfolded, against the columns pouring into south-east Yugoslavia; and finally, as the main danger became clear, against concentrations and bottle-necks on the roads leading to the Monastir gap. Losses were light—it was not until the hundredth sortie, on 11th April, that a Blenheim failed to return—and some of the German columns suffered severely, but bad weather baulked many of our efforts. The morning of 7th April, for instance, was a complete blank, and only heroic deter-mination in the afternoon took ten Blenheims and Wellingtons through to bomb the streams of vehicles winding their way towards the Vardar. April 8th was as bad, and again it required the utmost resolution and skill even to reach the target area. Still more dis-appointing was the 9th, when the Blenheims could attack only the enemy's route to Salonika, though the growing movement through the narrow defiles towards the Monastir gap offered a far more attractive target. On the 10th, nineteen Blenheims got through to the Monastir approaches by day, and four Wellingtons by night. On the 11th and 12th, when the German movement was at its strongest, only twelve bombers took off in the whole forty-eight hours. D'Albiac, who had been through the Staff College mill, was certainly not un-mindful of what might be achieved against an enemy caught in a narrow defile. Perhaps, indeed, his thoughts turned to the classic occasion of 21st September 1918, when seven squadrons of Bristols, D.H.9's, S.E.5a's, and R.E.8's trapped a Turkish force in the Wadi el Fara and reduced it at leisure to a shambles of shattered guns, wag-gons, beasts and men. If so, he was certainly unable to follow this desirable precedent. All his efforts were frustrated by mist, rain and unbroken low cloud.

The bad weather in the north had one advantage. Though it hampered our aircraft, it protected our airfields and ground forces from the *Luftwaffe*. For a few days the British troops therefore escaped serious attack. Moreover, it was not until 14th April, after he had attained his main objectives in Yugoslavia and Salonika, that Hitler finally decided to occupy the rest of Greece. It was thus the approach of the German Army on his left flank, not the activity of the German Air Force, which forced General Wilson to retire. Once that retirement had started, disaster succeeded disaster. The tanks of the 1st Armoured Brigade, like those of their fellow-brigade in

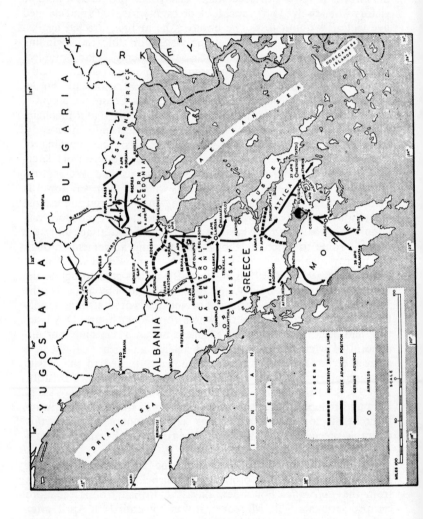

Cyrenaica, broke down by the score; the Greek divisions disintegrated when they found their mules and horses unable to keep pace
with the British lorries; the skies cleared and the *Luftwaffe* began to
appear in strength. Already on 16th April it was clear to the Greeks
that resistance was hopeless. For when Wilson proposed to move
right back to Thermopylae, Papagos not only agreed, but went one
better by suggesting complete evacuation.

To abandon the Olympus positions and retire on Thermopylae
meant surrendering Larissa and the other airfields in the Thessalian
plain. This was a grave step to take, for there was only one landing-
ground between the Athens area and the new line on which the
troops would fight. The decision, inevitable in the circumstances, was
taken for purely military reasons; but to these additional urgency
was soon lent by the increasing pressure of the German Air Force.
With the better weather on 13th April, D'Albiac's Blenheims had had
a profitable day, despite the fact that one entire formation of six was
shot down north of Monastir.[1] At night Wellingtons had also bombed
successfully. These attacks were repeated on the 14th, and that night
Wellingtons of No. 38 Squadron broke the bridge over the Vardar at
Veles. Such activity was unlikely to be tolerated by the Germans for
long. On the 14th the enemy, operating fighters and dive-bombers
from forward strips, bombed the Anzac Corps heavily in its new
positions. Our Hurricanes offered valiant resistance; and the *Luftwaffe* soon fell back on its old and well-tried principle of mastering
the opposing air force before attempting too much elsewhere. Four
times during the morning of 15th April, Me.109's appeared over the
Larissa plain without warning—for the Greek observer system had
broken down in the withdrawal. Four times they ground-strafed
No. 113 Squadron at Niamata. Not a single Blenheim escaped
damage or destruction. At Larissa itself, twenty Me.109's swept in
just as three of No. 33 Squadron's Hurricanes were taking off. Two
of the British fighters were at once shot down; the third put up a
skilful defence and claimed one of the enemy. D'Albiac, who had

---

[1] 14th April: Two survivors—Flight Lieutenant Godfrey and Sergeant
Simpson—of the six Blenheims came in, having first buried twelve of their friends
and walked back between the forces on East and West—not knowing that they
were for the most part actually between the enemy. Both very done up but
amazingly brave and eager to get back to their squadron at Larissa for more
fighting. Sergeant Simpson had only one boot and had walked through his
sock . . .
15th April: Both pilots returned to their squadron. Heard a few days later that
Simpson had been killed by being shot up on taking off from Larissa, and Godfrey
had had two fingers shot off at the same time in another machine—the sole
survivor from six Blenheims.
(Extract from diary kept by Flight Lieutenant F. S. Symondson.)

witnessed the attack, ordered the squadron back to the Athens area forthwith, but in any case it must have retired during the next few hours. The remaining squadrons of the Eastern Wing followed on 16th April.

By this time the British air commander was fully aware that the end could not be long delayed. On 15th April he reported to Longmore that he had only forty-six aircraft serviceable, apart from the Wellingtons of No. 37 Squadron. 'Even if the army establish themselves on the rear line,' he pointed out, 'I see no possibility of providing them with adequate air support in view of the scarcity of aerodromes.' The dilemma was indeed acute. If our fighters stayed on the single airfield immediately behind the Thermopylae line they would undoubtedly be wiped out by the enemy; if they retired to Athens they would be too far from the front to protect effectively either our ground forces or our bombers. Further, as all our aircraft became concentrated on the two or three grounds near Athens, they would present—in the absence of any adequate ground defence by anti-aircraft guns—a more and more tempting target to the *Luftwaffe*. Faced with so harsh a choice of evils, D'Albiac recommended immediate evacuation.

By 17th April the signs of collapse were general. D'Albiac, warned by the King that the internal situation was fast deteriorating, ordered the Wellingtons to Egypt (whence they could still operate) and recalled to Athens the two squadrons of the Western Wing. The latter's task was complicated by the remnants of the Royal Yugoslav Air Force arriving at Paramythia on 15th April, and by a vicious enemy air attack which swept down upon the airfield shortly afterwards. All forty-four of the Yugoslav aircraft were put out of action, though six bombers, three civil aircraft and ten sea-planes were later passed on successfully to Egypt. Despite this episode the Western Wing made good its retreat just in time. The following day No. 208 Squadron, the only remaining unit in the forward area, had too close an escape to be pleasant—it was in the air when a Greek Gladiator squadron sharing the airfield was annihilated on the ground. By 19th April No. 208 Squadron, too, was withdrawn, and all D'Albiac's aircraft were concentrated around Athens.

Three times that day our fighters intercepted formations of over fifty aircraft. Our pilots claimed eight of the enemy as against damage to three Hurricanes. On 20th April the fighting waxed still hotter. At 0430 hours that morning a formation of Me.110's got through undetected and destroyed or damaged a dozen Blenheims at Menidi; but on three other occasions our fighters either harassed the enemy or beat them off entirely. The climax came during the afternoon, when

Ju.88's, Me.109's and Me.110's to the number of almost a hundred attempted to bomb the Piraeus. Fifteen Hurricanes of Nos. 33 and 80 Squadrons remained serviceable, and all immediately took the air. In the combats that ensued the enemy's losses were estimated as at least fourteen, against five of our own; but five from so slender a force—and among them, Squadron Leader 'Pat' Pattle, the brilliant and much-loved leader of No. 33 Squadron—was a loss we could ill afford. Yet still the dwindling handful of Hurricanes continued to challenge the enemy, many of our pilots taking off in riddled aircraft that would normally have been considered quite unfit for flight. Against the Italians, during the earlier phase of the campaign, they had cheerfully accepted odds of five to one, and asked for nothing better. Now it was odds of ten, fifteen, twenty to one; and the men in the opposing cockpits were Germans. With the best will in the world—and it was theirs in full measure—our out-numbered airmen could not prolong the agony indefinitely.

Meantime a small inter-Service staff, on which the Royal Air Force representative was Group Captain C. B. R. Pelly, had since 17th April been preparing plans for complete evacuation. The Piraeus was too good a target for the *Luftwaffe* (and too heavily damaged already), so that obviously the men would have to be lifted from whatever suitable beaches or small harbours could be found in Attica and the Morea. The overwhelming German superiority in the air also made it essential that the operation should be carried out by night—preferably during a moonless period. Preparations were accordingly made along these lines. Fortunately a number of infantry assault ships and tank-landing craft were available for the task of going in to the beaches, but three or four days' notice would be needed for the vessels to be brought the six hundred miles from Egypt. If evacuation were decided upon, 28th April was the first practicable date on which it could begin.

On 21st April, General Wilson heard that the Greek Army of the Epirus had laid down its arms. Attempting too late to yield the territory it had so gallantly wrested from the Italians, it had found itself outflanked by the Germans. With the Adolf Hitler S.S. Motorized Division at Yannina, there was now real danger that the enemy would reach Athens from the west before the British could get back to the beaches. Nothing less than immediate evacuation could save Wilson's forces. Although preparations were far from complete, it was accordingly decided to try to pick up the first parties on the night of 24/25th April.

Until 19th April the Blenheims had continued their attempts to delay the enemy advance. From 20th April the surviving aircraft concentrated on the work of flying key airmen to Crete—first air-crew, then ground staff. On 22nd and 23rd April the squadrons took off from Menidi and Eleusis for the last time, together with the four remaining Lysanders. Only the Hurricanes of Nos. 33, 80 and 208 Squadrons—eighteen aircraft in all—then remained for the last duty of giving what protection they could to the evacuation. For this task they were ordered to Argos, a Greek training airfield in the Morea, where they would be well placed to protect our shipping approaches and the final movements of some of the parties towards the beaches.

The command of this rear force and the supervision of the Royal Air Force evacuation from this area were entrusted to Air Commodore J. W. B. Grigson. When Grigson arrived at Argos he found the main airfield so lacking in any form of cover, either for aircraft or men, that he decided to base the Hurricanes on a small satellite three miles away where the landing area was adjoined by an olive grove. Unfortunately the troops detailed for anti-aircraft protection had proceeded to the wrong airfield, and the only defences immediately available were those of the local Greeks. These consisted of two Bofors and two Hotchkiss machine-guns.

The Hurricanes arrived over Argos during the afternoon of 22nd April. The Greek Bofors at once opened up, and one machine was badly damaged. This incident over, the pilots landed, pushed their aircraft into the edge of the olive grove, and settled in for the night. The following morning they put up a reconnaissance and an offensive patrol. Then the *Luftwaffe* appeared—just when five fresh Hurricanes had landed from Crete. Four of the five got into the air and challenged the enemy; the other was destroyed on the ground. This did not satisfy the Germans, who returned in force during the afternoon. Some of our aircraft were on patrol at the time, but apparently made no interceptions. The others, at dispersal in the edge of the olive grove, were completely unable to get off the ground in time. In utter impotence their pilots watched thirty to forty Me.110's first silence the Bofors guns, then pour their bullets into the dispersed aircraft, then turn their attention to the airmen and troops in the grove. It was a leisurely performance, occupying some forty minutes; but at the end of it thirteen Hurricanes had been destroyed on the ground and one in the air, besides nearly all the Greek trainers. This was enough for Grigson, who now wisely decided to transfer his seven surviving machines to Crete, whence they could at least cover the return of our ships. At daylight on 24th April, eighteen hours before the first troops were due to embark. what remained of our fighters took off for the last time from the soil of Greece.

Meanwhile the Royal Air Force ground-crews were making their way to the evacuation points. Lack of food and sleep, frequent misdirection, and inability to use lights for fear of air attack gave a nightmare quality to most of the journeys. No. 112 Squadron, which had just reached Athens from the Epirus, had much less trouble than most of the other contingents and was among the first to be taken off. The Squadron diary tells their story:

> (22nd April.) In pitch darkness we moved off, after throwing all equipment, etc., into the sea, and we passed Eleusis village without incident. Here our convoy met the Army stream . . . and at a deadly snail's pace the vast cavalcade crept on. Nerves were frayed and any suggestion of a light brought forth a chorus of 'Put that bloody light out' from front and rear. As it was imperative to use lights now and again to negotiate the cliff road, the invective was almost continuous . . . The road was strewn with overturned vehicles . . . one estimate was three hundred overturned on the Corinth–Argos section alone . . . Just before Corinth a convoy of pack mules got mixed up in the general melée . . . we must pay tribute to the magnificent way the soldiers coaxed and handled these animals. On our arrival at Argos, endless units were in groups for miles down the road, but gradually the R.A.F. was sorted out and moved off to the aerodrome. By now (23rd) eleven thousand Army and Air Force had reached Argos, only to learn that two of the ships to take us off had been dive-bombed and were burning—one loaded with high explosive. This blew up with a terrific crash, but passed almost unnoticed in a bombing raid . . . [A description follows of various air attacks, including the one which destroyed the Hurricanes.] At nightfall we again moved through Argos and dispersed on the hillsides three miles beyond, this time minus blankets and kit, and it being too cold to sleep, finished a continuous forty-eight hours without sleep. Dawn (24th) and still no word of a ship, but a little later the first three Me.109's took a look round . . . The usual dive-bombing started shortly afterwards. Later in the day Me.110's flew far and wide at 3,000 feet seeking objectives . . . The squadron had two narrow escapes when sticks of bombs dropped right across our lines . . . A check-up revealed that a party of airmen were missing . . . Towards sunset we were all told to be ready to march to Nauplia. Relief showed on all our faces and no one asked the distance. The six miles were covered in excellent time and we arrived at the water's edge in good order without incident. As the harbour was too shallow for large ships to put alongside, invasion barges were brought in by the Navy and everyone looked on in silent admiration of real efficiency. The last on board arrived about midnight, making seventy sleepless hours in all, and all lay down anywhere, anyhow, to a sleep of sheer exhaustion, oblivious of any dangers the sea might hold and with full confidence, as ever, in the Navy.

Thanks to the naval efficiency which so impressed No. 112 Squadron, and a corresponding lack of enterprise on the part of the *Luftwaffe* and the Italian fleet, the plan of night evacuation worked miraculously well. Doubtless with Dunkirk in mind, Hitler had ordered every precaution against a British escape, yet four-fifths of the troops who had landed in Greece re-embarked in safety. Unable in the dark to find the beaches we were using, the enemy made no attempt to bomb the actual embarkation. Instead he concentrated on attacks by daylight against our troop movements and shipping. But by dawn our returning vessels had normally reached 37°N., at which point they not only came within range of Blenheim fighters from Crete but also passed out of range of the Ju.87's. The advent of our fighters thus coincided with the removal of the deadliest menace to our ships. Long-range bombers persistently attempted to interfere beyond this vital point, but the Blenheims from Crete, despite their slender numbers—there were only fifteen or so in all—succeeded many times in scaring them off. Significantly enough the only major disaster to a loaded vessel occurred when a Dutch ship carrying several hundred men left Nauplia too late to reach 37°N. by the appointed hour. And once our ships approached the anchorage at Suda Bay, they came under additional protection from the single-engined fighters in Crete—the half dozen Fulmars and Gladiators of the Fleet Air Arm, the Gladiators returned from the Epirus, and the six or seven Hurricanes which had survived the bombing at Argos.

In their work of covering our vessels the Blenheim fighters ran many dangers. Not all of these arose from the enemy. On 28th April, for instance, a formation of three Blenheims of No. 203 Squadron made contact with its convoy and was at once fired upon by one of our destroyers. The rest of the story may be told in the words of the Squadron Operations Record Book:

> No damage noticed at time but after eventual recognition L. 9044 caught fire starboard engine and at 0817 aircraft set course for base on port engine. Failed to make Retimo and landed in sea 1½ miles to north. 0850 hrs. Air Gunner got rubber boat out and alongside wing immediately. Navigator was stuck under navigator's table under water, but managed to scramble out, and then turned to help captain of aircraft who was trapped in his seat below water unable to find his release pin, and pulled him out in time. The crew began to paddle for shore and when still one mile away were met by a Greek soldier, Marcos Koumnisakios, who threw them a rope and with the other end tied around his waist proceeded to swim back towing them while they paddled . . . On landing at Retimo, crew were covered by rifles and (perhaps partly owing to colour of captain's hair) thought to be Germans. However, the captain, on hearing an uncertain but familiar accent suggesting British soldiery, gave the inspired cry (after one soundless attempt) of 'We're ——ing British!' and this convinced everyone of the crew's undoubtedly Allied character . . .

The protection of our returning vessels was not the only service rendered by the Royal Air Force during the evacuation. An emergency 'air-lift' for 'V.I.P.s', Headquarters parties, and the like was organized by No. 201 Group at Alexandria. The aircraft employed were the Sunderlands of Nos. 228 and 230 Squadrons, which carried out reconnaissance by day and evacuation by night, the Lodestars and Bombays of No. 267 (Communication) Squadron, and two B.O.A.C. flying-boats. The Lodestars and Bombays made only five trips to Greece before conditions at Menidi and Eleusis made further flights impossible; thereafter, with the two B.O.A.C. aircraft, they concentrated on the Crete–Egypt section of the run.[1] But the Sunderlands made full use of their ability to alight at remote spots along the coast—one of them was attracted to a stranded party by signals from a shaving-mirror—and between them they succeeded in bringing off from Greece nearly nine hundred persons. The King of Greece and most of our senior commanders made their exit in this way; a little earlier on King Peter had been rescued in similar fashion from Yugoslavia. Needless to say, the pilots took on fantastic loads. One Sunderland with an official 'emergency capacity' of thirty bodies staggered off the water with eighty-four.

The merits of intervention in Greece are still a matter of controversy. As far as the Royal Air Force was concerned, the phase before the Germans came on the scene was extremely profitable. Nearly two hundred Italian aircraft were reckoned to have been destroyed, as against forty-seven of our own, and much valuable help was given to the Greeks in other ways. Even after the Germans intervened the strict balance of profit and loss in terms of aircraft was less adverse than might appear from the events of the final days; for though we lost 151 aircraft between 6th and 30th April—of which 87 were damaged machines perforce abandoned at the end—D'Albiac's fighters were doubtless responsible for most of the 164 losses which Operation 'Marita' cost the enemy. These consoling features can scarcely, however, disguise the fact that the committal to Greece of a British expeditionary force and the greater part of the Royal Air

---

[1] The two B.O.A.C. aircraft were used without interrupting the normal running of the Corporation's service. 'As each flying-boat arrived on a normal Horseshoe service at Cairo, its crew was rushed in a fast car along the desert road to Alexandria, to take its turn on the Crete ferry; the same car brought back to Cairo the weary crew from the previous Crete ferry, who at once took over the Horseshoe aircraft and continued its flight to Durban or to Singapore. "Coorong" and "Cambria", with a changing roster of crews in this manner, made thirteen return trips to Crete between 22nd April and 5th May, and brought out a total of 469 British troops. All normal standards were ignored. The method of loading the flying-boats was to allow the troops to file in until the forward door was so low that water began to pour in, then the door was slammed, and the flying-boat took off. On some trips more than fifty passengers were carried in an aircraft built for twenty-one.' (*Merchant Airmen*—the Air Ministry account of British Civil Aviation, 1939–1944.)

Force in the Middle East, while it had extremely strong political arguments in its favour, from the immediate military aspect was quite unsound. The terrain was ideal for defence; but the defenders were far too few to face with any prospect of success the opposition they would meet, while by moving through Yugoslavia the Germans could—and did—make nonsense of the whole Allied deployment. On the air side, the shortage of airfields and anti-aircraft guns was a grave handicap from the start; and when Wilson was compelled to retire south of the Thessalian plain and all the squadrons became crowded on the two or three grounds around Athens, there could be only one end. The Germans, it is true, soon brought many more landing-grounds into use, including those of Salonika—which for a combination of political and military reasons we had never been able to do. But the German attack on Greece coincided with the time when the soil was at last beginning to dry out. A few days in mid-April made all the difference between a sticky morass and a serviceable air-strip; and the transport planes of *Luftflotte 4* provide the rest of the explanation of the enemy's superior mobility.

From the immediate military point of view, then, the decision to face the Germans in Greece was an unsuccessful gamble. The result was not all loss, for by inspiring Yugoslavia to resist we set back the German offensive against Russia by four weeks. The precise effect of that on the fortunes of the war is a matter of speculation. What is beyond dispute is that in so doing we threw away Cyrenaica, and with it our only hope of a swift end to the war in the desert.

*   *   *

The situation in the Middle East now demanded desperate remedies. With a boldness worthy of the occasion, the authorities at home had already decided to run a special convoy through the Mediterranean. The cargo, to the great relief of our harassed commanders, included 306 tanks and 50 Hurricanes. Fortunately the vessels were protected by an unseasonable quantity of cloud as they passed within range of the German bombers in Sicily; Fulmars of the *Ark Royal* beat off the one attack that developed; and on 12th May the entire convoy, less one ship sunk by a mine, docked safely at Alexandria. Meanwhile as part of the same series of operations Benghazi was bombarded and a convoy was passed into Malta from east to west. This, too, benefited from the favourable weather. 'The clouds,' wrote Flight Lieutenant Whittingham at Malta on 8th May 'were right down to the deck. A most unusual occurrence this time of the year in Malta (has not been known for a hundred years), but it was extremely fortunate as a large convoy is coming in.' 'Weather again down to the ground,' he noted on 9th May. 'The cloud remained over the island all day—a miraculous act of Providence.'

By this time the thin trickle of aircraft reinforcement over the Takoradi route was broadening into a steady flow. 'Whereas you have received only 370 from November to now,' announced Churchill to Longmore on 15th April, '528 more are on the way and a further 880 will start before the end of May.' These energetic measures on the part of the authorities in London did much to fill the appalling gaps left by the disasters of Cyrenaica and Greece. Their efforts were fully seconded by those of the commanders at Cairo. Every man and machine that could be spared from East Africa was rushed to Egypt; a new group (No. 204—more or less the old 202), under the well-tried Collishaw, took over the emaciated units in the Western Desert; and into the wasted frames of the squadrons was pumped the life-blood of the new aircraft from home. While Rommel fretfully awaited supplies and the 15th Panzer Division, Egypt was thus replenished and restored, and the danger from the west receded.

In point of fact advanced elements of the 15th Panzer Division had landed at Tripoli on 31st March. By the middle of April these were beginning to appear in the forward area. But the impulsive Rommel was advised by General Paulus, who was then on a mission from German Army Supreme Headquarters, to stay quiet until the rest of the Division arrived; and the view of Paulus (which was also that of the Italians) was echoed in a directive from Keitel on 15th April. This enjoined a pause for the build-up of his own resources, the reinforcement of the *Luftwaffe*, and—above all—'the elimination of British attacks on our rear communications'. Such attacks were to be avoided by 'capturing Tobruk, protecting coastal routes and coastal shipping against sea and air attacks . . . and protecting sea transports from Italy to Libya'. The order was scarcely despatched when its terms were justified in a striking and, to our commanders in Egypt, altogether agreeable fashion. On 16th April our destroyers from Malta, warned by air reconnaissance, intercepted and sank an entire convoy off Sfax. The vessels contained Schutz Regiment 115 and Artillery Regiment 33 of the 15th Panzer Division.

With Egypt for the moment *verboten* Rommel's gaze rested all the more avidly on Tobruk. Eighty miles behind his front-line, it was undoubtedly a powerful thorn in his flesh. To supply and protect the garrison, however, was scarcely less of a worry to our own commanders. Ceaselessly bombed and shot up, and with their airfields under observed artillery fire, the two squadrons within the perimeter faced an impossible task. Within a few days of the investment it was clear that the Lysanders of No. 6 Squadron must be withdrawn, but the Hurricanes for a while kept up the uneven struggle. The fantastic odds reached their peak on 23rd April, when, after an abortive early morning 'scramble', the seven available aircraft of No. 73 Squadron intercepted a force of some sixty German dive-bombers and fighters. In the fierce combats that followed our pilots claimed six of the enemy for only one loss to themselves. But the *Luftwaffe* returned to the charge, and before the day was out another force of forty aircraft appeared on the scene. Once more they were intercepted, and once more our pilots reckoned to have had the better of the exchanges. But when night fell No. 73 Squadron could muster only four serviceable aircraft; and it had lost three Commanding Officers within two weeks. Four months had now passed since the arrival of the squadron pilots in Egypt—four months of continuous action in non-stop advance and retreat across the breadth of Cyrenaica. Human blood and nerves could stand no more, and on 25th April the remnants of No. 73 followed the Lysanders to Egypt. Only the Hurricane flight of No. 6 Squadron then remained in Tobruk; it fought on until 8th May, when it was reduced to four machines. From then on the beleaguered troops had no air cover except fleeting patrols from Sidi Barrani, 120 miles distant.

*   *   *

Elsewhere in the Middle East Command the sombre horizon showed at least two gleams of light. In Malta things were perceptibly improving. In March not a day had passed without visits from *Fliegerkorps X*; and in the early part of the month such havoc had been wrought at the airfields and anchorages that Longmore had perforce withdrawn the Sunderlands and Wellingtons to Egypt. But at the beginning of April the island's defences were strengthened by a dozen Mark II Hurricanes—the Mark I had been out-fought by the Me.109's at heights over 16,000 feet—and thereafter the enemy had matters much less his own way. The Germans still attacked almost ceaselessly, but the damage was not so heavy. By the middle of the month the Wellingtons were back again and bombing Tripoli.

On 27th April another quota of Hurricanes came in safely from the *Ark Royal*. This enabled Maynard to form a second fighter squadron —No. 185—to share the burden of defence. The time was indeed ripe, for No. 261 had been appallingly hard-pressed since the beginning of the year. The strain on this squadron may perhaps be gathered from an extremely feeling remark in the diary of one of its members. A true English 'mem-sahib' at a party on 14th April had asked this pilot how long he had been on the island, had been told '3½ months', and had replied 'Oh, quite a short time'. 'I hope', wrote the outraged airman, 'that when this old cow has a baby she looks forward to the few hours of labour in the same spirit.'

The Hurricanes were not the only new arrivals. During April the advent of a few more Marylands enabled No. 431 Flight to become No. 69 Squadron, and at once made possible a more ambitious programme of reconnaissance. To take advantage of the greater opportunities that would now undoubtedly occur, the Wellingtons were withdrawn at the beginning of May and replaced by a flight of Blenheims from Bomber Command's No. 2 Group. These aircraft had for some time specialized in attacks against German shipping in the English Channel and North Sea, and thenceforward the task of Malta's bombers was less to bomb ports than to sink ships on passage. About the same time a squadron of Beaufighters (No. 252) came out from home to protect the convoy whose safe arrival in Egypt has already been described. Once in the Middle East Command these Beaufighters proved so useful that they were kept there for the rest of the war.

Despite an acute shortage of airfields and maintenance facilities, Maynard's forces were thus steadily growing. Equally encouraging, his principal opponents were about to depart. In May *Fliegerkorps X* began an unobtrusive withdrawal from Sicily to the Balkans, as other German units in turn moved farther east for their *Führer's* next great venture. Soon the island fortress, faced once more only by the Italians, would be free to strike out as it desired; and harassed officers in Rome would debate, not what could be spared for Africa, but how it could get there past the bombers and submarines of Malta.

*   *   *

The successful reinforcement of Egypt and Malta was not the only bright spot in a still gloomy horizon. From East Africa the tidings were not merely good but positively exhilarating. Both wings of the offensive launched in January 1941 had met with complete and uninterrupted success.

From the Sudan General Platt, helped by Slatter's squadrons, had pushed into Eritrea, captured the great natural stronghold of Keren, and swept on to Asmara and Massawa. These successes were not confined to operations on land. As our forces approached Massawa six Italian destroyers put to sea: three were sunk by the Royal Air Force, a fourth by the Fleet Air Arm, and the other two ran aground or scuttled themselves in desperation. By mid-April Platt was moving into Abyssinia from the north, with his task so nearly completed that the 4th Indian Division and most of the air forces involved—four out of six and a half squadrons—were on their way to threatened Egypt.

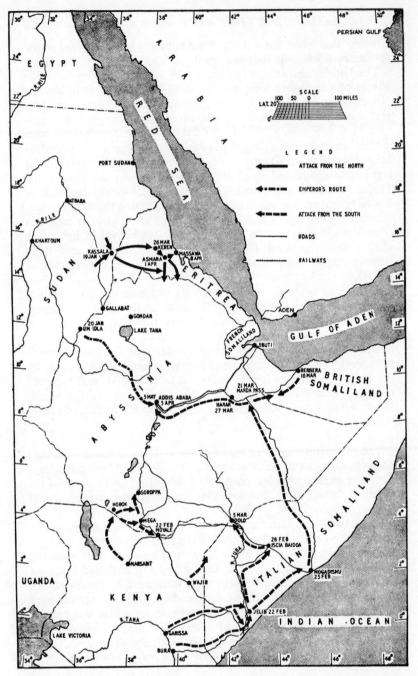

THE CAPTURE OF ITALIAN EAST AFRICA, JANUARY–APRIL 1941

Meantime the other arm of the great pincers—General Cunningham's three divisions from Kenya, with the South African squadrons under Sowrey—had established an equally firm grip on the south. Mogadishu, where the airfield displayed the wrecks of twenty-one Italian aircraft, fell on 25th February; Berbera was recovered by mid-March, after the Aden squadrons had prepared the way for a seaborne expedition; and on 6th April, a few hours after the Germans opened their attack in the Balkans, Cunningham's forces entered Addis Ababa. Before the end of the month three of the Kenya and Aden squadrons were *en route* for Egypt, and the whole campaign, thanks in no small measure to the rapid and complete subjugation of the enemy air force, was on its way to a triumphant conclusion.

Success at one extremity of the Middle East Command, however, usually meant trouble at another. While the sun was slowly breaking through at Malta, and in East Africa the skies were clearing completely, over Iraq the storm-clouds were now gathering in ominous array.

Y

CHAPTER XI

'Middle East': Iraq, Crete and Syria

ON 3rd April an Iraqi politician of chequered career, Rashid Ali, backed by four generals known not without reason as the 'Golden Square', seized power in Baghdad. Scenting danger, the Regent Abdulla Illah had fled the previous day to the protection of the Royal Air Force at Habbaniya—a station some fifty miles west of Baghdad occupied, like those of Basra and Shaibah near the Persian Gulf, under the terms of the Anglo-Iraqi Treaty of 1930. From Habbaniya the Regent was then flown first to Basra, where he took refuge in a British warship, and subsequently to Transjordan.

To this change of régime Britain could hardly be indifferent. The Regent was favourable to our interests, Rashid Ali and his generals were known to be in German pay. The revolt, in fact, was the climax of a steadily growing hostility to us, and friendship with our enemies, on the part of a small but highly dangerous minority in Iraqi political life. Action of the promptest kind was now necessary if we were not to be excluded from the oilfields of Iraq, debarred from ready access to the oilfields of Persia, and faced with an Axis advance on Egypt from an entirely new direction.

On this occasion the British lion allowed no great length of grass to grow beneath his paws. On 16th April Rashid Ali was informed that we intended to avail ourselves of our treaty right to pass military forces along the Iraqi lines of communication. Two days later a contingent of British and Indian troops, intended originally for Malaya, disembarked at Basra. At the same time four hundred men of the King's Own Royal Regiment were flown by No. 31 Squadron from Karachi to Shaibah.

The swiftness of this reaction took Rashid Ali by surprise. But when he learned that two more ships, bearing ancillary troops of the first convoy, were due at Basra on 28th April, he refused permission for them to land until the main contingent had moved out of Iraq. For our part we declined to take this attempt to stand upon legal rights too seriously, and on the morning of 29th April the new arrivals disembarked.

The political temperature in Baghdad now rose to fever heat. By the afternoon Rashid Ali's attitude was so menacing that steps were taken to evacuate some 230 British women and children from the capital. Packed for the most part into Royal Air Force lorries, they were hastily driven to Habbaniya. But they had not long arrived when, under cover of darkness, convoys of a different kind began to set out along the same road. A thousand yards from the British base this second and very much larger group of lorries came to a desert plateau some two hundred feet high. Here the occupants alighted. When the morning of 30th April dawned, Habbaniya and the airfield beyond its gates were dominated by the guns of the Iraqi artillery.

Away in Cairo, that same morning brought Longmore a most unwelcome message from London. In view of changes in the situation in the Middle East the Prime Minister wished him to return home at once for full discussions. Tedder would meantime act in his stead. On 3rd May the Air Commander accordingly took off for London. Though he was not to know it until a fortnight later, his days of command in Cairo—days of brain-racking scarcity, patient achievement, blazing triumph and hapless, abrupt disaster—were at an end. Thenceforth the destinies of Royal Air Force, Middle East, were to rest in other hands—the strong hands, velvet-gloved, of Tedder.

* * *

Of all the stations in the Royal Air Force, Habbaniya is perhaps the most remarkable. Begun in 1934 under the clause of the Anglo-Iraqi Treaty permitting a British base west of the Euphrates, and occupied from 1937, it was designed as the 'permanent Headquarters' of the Royal Air Force in Iraq. Within its seven-miles circumference were not only all the usual buildings of a big station, but also an Aircraft Depot with two large repair shops. The airfield itself, but not the hangars, lay beyond the enclosed perimeter. In 1941 the station contained, besides about 1,200 officers and men of the Royal Air Force, six companies—four Assyrian and two Iraqi— of native Levies. After helping to maintain peace and order in the years 1922–1930, when the Royal Air Force was responsible for the internal security of Iraq, these Levies had been retained mainly to protect our bases. With them were their families, many of whom worked about the station as bearers, laundry hands and the like; and by 1941 other workers, among them many Indians, had swollen the total of non-European inhabitants to about nine thousand. An extensive cantonment, consisting for the most part of small mud-brick dwellings with corrugated iron roofs, housed this considerable body of non-combatants.

So far as anything is agreeably situated in Iraq, Habbaniya may claim that distinction. For its designers had not ignored the fact that under controlled irrigation the soil of the desert will indeed 'blossom like the rose', and the station was carefully sited in an angle of the Euphrates. Along its twenty-eight miles of roads—roads bearing the style of Piccadilly, Cranwell Avenue, Kingsway, and other names redolent of England, Home, and the Royal Air Force—were planted flowering trees, which delighted the passer-by with their enchanting masses of colour and still more enchanting patches of shade. Green lawns everywhere refreshed the eye; to the native growths of palm and cactus had been added clematis, jasmine, lilac, honeysuckle, and many another familiar flower of an English garden. Among the fruits the apple, peach, pear and plum mingled on equal terms with the lime, orange, banana, pomegranate, and *zizyphus jujuba*, or—as it was more commonly known among the airmen—'Tree of Knowledge'. Less enlightening perhaps, but unquestionably more useful, was the food provided by the many vegetable-plots and the large stock farm.

With these products of assisted Nature went all that could be devised in the way of facilities for sport and entertainment. The finest swimming pool in the Royal Air Force, a variety of social clubs, a magnificent gymnasium, an elaborately equipped open-air cinema, a golf course, tennis courts (fifty-six of them), riding stables, a polo-ground-cum-race-course (an airman could buy a third-share in a pony for £2, ride two days a week, and sell his interest in the beast when posted home)—these were but a few of the amenities within the grounds. Outside, beyond the airfield, there was the great Habbaniya Lake—a hundred square miles in area, and used by the B.O.A.C. flying-boats—where long-distance swimmers could test their endurance and the nautically-minded could sail dinghies and other craft. Spiritual needs, too, had not been neglected. Within the station were three magnificent churches devoted respectively to the Anglican, Nonconformist and Roman Catholic creeds.

Nothing, then, had been omitted to make Habbaniya as pleasant a prison as human ingenuity could contrive. For despite all its attractive features, that was how it was generally regarded. At Habbaniya the airmen had everything to alleviate the discomfort of a climate where the summer temperature rises to 120° in the shade, and where it is cooler to stifle with the windows shut than to admit the burning wind from outside. But outside Habbaniya—apart from the lake, and an occasional visit to the dreary arcades and over-priced delights of Baghdad—he had nothing. A stranger in an alien land, his vision was bounded by a steel fence eight feet high, and beyond that the desert. His sentiments, in fact, were summed up perfectly in the local theme-song 'Habbaniya'. The last verse runs:

> Sweet music rising to the sky,
> In tune with song birds fluttering by,
> A garden fair, where all is bliss,
> A place the Air Force would not miss—
>
> *Chorus* To passers by it thus appears,
> To us inside—
> Two bloody years.

The function of the boundary fence—the 'unclimbable' fence, as it was sarcastically termed on the station—was to keep the camp population in, and the Arabs and animals of the desert out. It was not intended as a defence against anything more than local four- or two-footed marauders. This was important; for that tactful but isolated position in the desert, three hundred miles by air from our nearest bases on the Persian Gulf, and five hundred from our bases in Palestine, would obviously mean grave danger for Habbaniya if ever the government in Baghdad turned hostile. On its northern and eastern sides, the camp might indeed derive some protection from the Euphrates; but to the west there was only the open sand, and to the south, beyond the airfield, only the desert plateau. And on this, on the morning of 30th April 1941, nine thousand of Rashid Ali's troops with twenty-eight pieces of artillery were now installed.

The approach of the crisis had not been watched in idleness by the A.O.C. Iraq (Air Vice-Marshal H. G. Smart) and his men at Habbaniya. Though there were no operational units on the station there was No. 4 Flying Training School; and since 5th April the workshops and hangars had echoed to the din of mechanics fitting guns and bomb racks to the trainer-aircraft. By the end of the month some seventy of these, of which nearly sixty were Audaxes and Oxfords, had been made serviceable for operations. The Audaxes, ex-operational machines of about 1930 vintage adapted from the Hart bomber by the addition of a hinged arm for picking up messages—and known from this in the Service as 'an 'art with an 'ook' —had been mostly fitted to carry two 250-pound bombs instead of their 'official' war-load of twenty-pounders; the Oxfords, which had not been designed for armament of any kind, were given an ingenious fitment for carrying eight 20-pound bombs with tails protruding beneath the fuselage. In addition, half-a-dozen Gladiators were sent over from Egypt, to add to the three training fighters which Habbaniya already possessed.

Meanwhile intensive courses in bomb-aiming and air-gunnery had also begun. Few of the instructor pilots (who included some officers of the Royal Hellenic Air Force) had operational experience—if they had, they had either proved unsuitable for combat flying, or had had so much of it that they had been sent to Habbaniya for a rest. In fact most of their recent flying had consisted of 'circuits and bumps'. In their slow machines they could nevertheless soon acquire a fair degree of aiming skill, and they quickly developed into a formidable force. A few other pilots, mostly out of practice, were found among the officers in the Headquarters Unit, the Aircraft Depot and the Military Mission at Baghdad; but all told, the qualified pilots including instructors numbered only some thirty-five. It was therefore decided to promote the more promising pupils, though these had only just finished their initial flying, into the ranks of 'operational' pilots. Those pupils of lesser achievement, and any of the ground staff who felt inclined, volunteered as observers and gunners—for of qualified practitioners in these arts there were only four.

By all these means four bombing 'squadrons' and a flight of Gladiators were formed. The whole, dubbed the Habbaniya Air Striking Force, was placed under the commanding officer of the Training School, Group Captain W. A. B. Savile. At the same time a small landing-ground within the camp, suitable for the Audaxes, was made by combining the golf-course with the polo-ground—a task which involved felling trees, obliterating a road, and levelling the bunkers. Meanwhile eager teams undertook reconnaissance flights, compiled large-scale photo mosaics of Baghdad and the Raschid airfield nearby, and catalogued all possible targets within striking range.

As there were no trained British troops in the camp apart from No. 1 Company of Royal Air Force armoured cars, from 24th April the four hundred men of the K.O.R.R. were flown in from Shaibah. With them came Colonel Roberts, the G.S.O.1 at Basra, who remained to take charge of the ground defences and show himself a most inspiring commander. When Smart and Roberts surveyed the situation on the morning of 30th April they can have had little cause for optimism. Crammed with non-combatants, holding full rations for only twelve days, exposed to attack on two sides, and dominated by the Iraqi guns—a single hit from which might wreck the water tower or power station, and so cripple resistance at a blow—Habbaniya seemed utterly at Rashid Ali's mercy. Of small arms the defenders had far from enough, and of artillery, apart from a few mortars, none.[1] Moreover, Smart had some natural doubts about the Levies, who were all Iraqi subjects—though in point of fact these gallant fighters were soon to give ample proof of their eagerness to join the fray against the rebels.

Soon after dawn Smart sent off an aircraft to report on the strength of the forces which had gathered during the night. An hour later an Iraqi officer appeared at the main gate with a message from the commander on the plateau. It demanded, under threat of heavy shelling, that no person or aircraft should leave the station. Smart's reply was an assurance that any interference by Rashid Ali's forces with our training flights would be considered an act of war. Two further messages from the Iraqis then followed. The first merely repeated the previous demand; the second promised not to begin offensive action while the Royal Air Force refrained from doing so. But meanwhile the forces on the plateau and round about the station were steadily growing, and with them Smart's conviction that the besiegers would attack during the night, when he could make no use of his one source of strength—his aircraft. In the absence of instructions covering the situation, the A.O.C. had some difficulty in deciding what course to pursue; for while he was understandably reluctant to start a private war on his own at a time of great difficulty elsewhere, he could hardly ignore the danger before him. The clearest guidance he had received by the end of the day was a signal from Cairo that he should at once retaliate if the Iraqis opened fire.

The night of 30th April passed without incident. The following morning Smart received from England the directive for which he was waiting; our position at Habbaniya must be restored, and Rashid Ali's troops forced to retire without delay. It was by then too late to issue an ultimatum and carry out a full day's bombing—which Smart considered essential for success—before night fell. He accordingly resolved to wait until the next morning, and then give the briefest notice possible. But as the day of 1st May wore on, the forces on the plateau still grew; twenty-seven additional guns were counted; and by evening Smart decided that it would be fatal to allow the Iraqis to strike the first blow, and therefore that he must act without warning. In this resolve he was supported by the Ambassador at Baghdad, with whom he was in communication by wireless. Meanwhile, against eventualities, Longmore sent ten Wellingtons of No. 70 Squadron

---

[1] There were, however, two ancient field pieces of 1914–1918 which stood ornamentally on a lawn outside the Aircraft Depot. A Royal Artillery artificer was flown in from Basra to recondition these, and after crews and ammunition had also arrived by air the guns were used with success during the later stages of the revolt.

from Egypt to Shaibah. The night wore slowly away, again with every man of the Habbaniya garrison at his post; a signal from the Prime Minister arrived—'if you have to strike, strike hard'; the investing troops still made no move; and at first light on 2nd May No. 4 Flying Training School went into action.

By 0445 the air above the plateau was alive with machines zooming dangerously to and fro in search of the best targets. Bombing began at 0500, when the Shaibah Wellingtons appeared. As soon as they had turned for home, thirty-five Audaxes, Gordons and Oxfords of the Training School continued the attack, diving down to 1,000 feet to make certain of hitting their objectives. Meanwhile the enemy opened fire on our aircraft and shelled the camp and airfield. Casualties to our aircrew quickly mounted. An instructor-pilot and two pupils were killed when an Oxford was shot down in flames; another instructor-pilot, in an Audax, received three bullets in the right shoulder, slumped forward with the machine going out of control, was pulled back into an upright position by his wounded pupil-observer, and brought his aircraft safely down with the use of only one hand before fainting away. One of the Wellingtons from Shaibah, also badly hit, made a forced landing on the Habbaniya airfield, where it stood in the thick of the enemy fire. At once a mechanic drove out from behind the hangars on a tractor, flanked by an armoured car on either side, and attempted to take the crippled machine in tow. He had barely fixed a rope round the tail wheel when the shells smashed into his mount and set the Wellington ablaze. Fortunately he just managed to escape in one of the armoured cars before the bombs exploded and blew both aircraft and tractor sky-high.

By ten o'clock the repeated attacks of the training machines had damped down the fire from the enemy guns. Rashid Ali's aircraft, which were quite as numerous as those of the Training School and were backed by a great deal more operational equipment, had by now appeared on the scene, but had shown themselves to be much less formidable than the shelling. The latter was irritating as well as dangerous, for the shrapnel kept up a disconcerting racket as it clattered on the corrugated iron roofs. Only a pair of nesting storks on the roof of Air Headquarters, and —if legend is true—the Station Warrant Officer, remained completely unperturbed.[1] But fortunately the aim of the gunners was singularly

---

[1] The storks remained on the wireless mast, oblivious of the bombing and shelling, until their two youngsters crashed in premature efforts to become airborne. (The first was seized and devoured by a jackal; the second broke a wing and expired when it found itself about to be X-rayed in the Station Hospital.) The Warrant Officer was reported to have popped his head out of a shelter and yelled at an airman bolting for cover: 'Now then my man—pull your stockings up and don't run around so slovenly.'

poor—or their heart was not in the work—and neither the water tower nor the main power station had been hit. Nor, astonishingly enough, were the enemy shells destroying many of our aircraft on the ground. The Audaxes on the polo ground were screened from observation by trees; and the rest of the aircraft, sheltering behind the hangars just inside the perimeter, were suffering more superficial damage than vital injury. Indeed, the Oxfords and Gordons were actually taking off unharmed in full view of the enemy gunners. To make the exposure as brief as possible, the pilots started up behind the hangars, opened their throttles while still inside the camp, shot out of the gates and on to the runway already well under way, and then made a steep climbing turn away from the plateau. Soon a technique was developed by which the aircraft from the polo-ground bombed the gun-positions while the other aircraft were taking off, and by this means it was possible to get even Douglases and Valentias, bearing loads of women and children, off to Shaibah in safety. The armoured cars also played their part in this by emerging at suitable moments to draw the enemy's fire.

During the afternoon a second flight of Wellingtons (of No. 37 Squadron) arrived at Shaibah from Egypt. It was at once directed against the besiegers of Habbaniya, though by this time fighting had also broken out in southern Iraq. Fortunately the position there was by no means as critical as at Habbaniya, and the local Army Co-operation Squadron (No. 244) at Shaibah, aided a little later by Swordfish from H.M.S. *Hermes*, was able to give our ground forces the support they needed. Reconnaissance, attacking enemy troop concentrations, cutting the Shaibah-Baghdad railway—these were the tasks carried out on the first day by the venerable but invaluable Vincents.

By the end of the day Habbaniya's aircraft had flown 193 sorties for the loss of two machines in the air and three on the ground. A further twenty or so had been rendered unserviceable, but the maintenance staff worked all night, and most of the damaged machines, including another Wellington from Shaibah stranded on the main airfield, were patched up by the following morning. The night passed fairly quietly, but shelling again grew intense at first light. It stopped completely when our aircraft went into action at dawn.

Throughout the rest of 3rd May the Wellingtons and the training machines kept up continuous patrols over the enemy positions, bombing as necessary. In this fashion they induced the Iraqi gunners to remain under cover. Once again the enemy air force accomplished little or nothing, thanks partly to some newly arrived Blenheim fighters of No. 203 Squadron, and partly to raids on Raschid airfield by the Wellingtons. So the second day of the siege gave way to night, and the gunners on the plateau emerged from their trenches to fire their weapons under cover of darkness. Even then, however, they found their aim disturbed. For Colonel Roberts, giving the Levies work after their own hearts, sent out little groups of men to fall silently and murderously upon the rebel gun-crews and sentinels.

With the first light of 4th May, the third day of the siege, the shells again fell thick and fast among the besieged garrison. Once more they died away as soon as our aircraft appeared in the sky. Paralysed by further raids on their bases, the Iraqi aircraft were again unable to play any serious part in the proceedings. But there was another, and far greater, danger from the air—a danger which had been foreseen from the beginning. During the day the Blenheims accordingly headed north for Mosul, in search of the German aircraft now known to be under orders for Iraq.

By this time it was clear that the enemy guns could be effectively silenced, if not disabled, by our aircraft. As the garrison had earned a fair degree of immunity by this means during the day, it was decided to extend the air patrols into the night. Few of the pilots had much experience of night-flying, and no flare-path could be laid out, so the number of aircraft involved was small. The experiment nevertheless proved highly successful. When the moon was up, the Audaxes carried out the task from the polo-ground; when there was no moon the duty fell to the Oxfords, which took off blind from the main airfield and came in with no other aid than their own landing lamp. This was switched on at fifty feet, and switched off again as soon as tyres touched tarmac.

This general pattern of operations was repeated on the following day. The air patrols kept down the shelling; attacks on airfields discouraged the enemy air force; the Douglases and Valentias of No. 31 Squadron arrived from Shaibah with more men of the K.O.R.R. and returned with more evacuees. Continuous air attack of this sort during the day, coupled with the air patrols and ground sorties during the night, soon brought about a complete reversal of the tactical situation. So far from the Iraqis besieging Habbaniya, Habbaniya laid siege to the Iraqis; for with our aircraft operating by night the enemy could no longer bring up his supplies from Baghdad by way of the single bridge across the Euphrates at Felluja. Moreover the incessant bombing and shooting up, coupled with the nightly forays of the Levies, had begun to wear down the morale of the troops on the plateau.

The result was that during the night of 5/6th May the investing enemy folded their tents, like their kinsmen of the song, and as silently stole away. Reconnaissance at first light found the plateau abandoned. At once our armoured cars and infantry set off in pursuit. A sharp encounter followed, in which the Audaxes joined, and the enemy was pushed back beyond the village of Sin el Dhibban. This recovered an important point—the pumping-station on which Habbaniya's sanitary system depended.[1] At the same time over three hundred prisoners and large quantities of equipment were captured. But Rashid Ali had not yet lost hope of restoring the situation, and during the afternoon our aircraft spotted a column of motorized infantry and artillery coming up from Felluja. It was caught near Sin el Dhibban by forty of our pilots, the last of whom, as he turned back to Habbaniya, saw only 'a solid mass of flame 250 yards long', barbed by the flashes of exploding ammunition. A medical officer who afterwards examined the charred and battered remnants has recorded that on its own much smaller scale the destruction was as complete, and as impressive, as that to be observed three years later around Falaise.

Habbaniya could now breathe in comfort, and Tedder was able to send a few more aircraft—Gladiators of No. 94 Squadron and Blenheim bombers of No. 84—across from Egypt. At the same time he withdrew the Wellingtons from Shaibah, for these were badly needed to attack the Libyan ports and the newly acquired German airfields in Greece. The next step was to expel Rashid Ali and restore the lawful Regent. This might have seemed—and indeed did seem—a task for a major expedition from Basra. But the rivers between Basra and Baghdad were in flood, and the rebels astride our communications; and the job was in fact done by Habbaniya itself, in conjunction with a small force which marched across the desert from Transjordan.

On 3rd May a few units had gathered at H.4, a pumping station on the Transjordan branch of the great I.P.C. pipe-line. They consisted only of a half-a-dozen Blenheims from Nos. 84 and 203 Squadrons, a mechanized squadron of the Transjordan Frontier Force, the Desert Patrol of the Arab Legion, and a company of the Essex Regiment. These last were flown from Lydda in the Bombays of No. 216 Squadron, on detachment from Egypt. The little group was under the command of Group Captain L. O. Brown, whose orders were to establish an operational base at the local landing-ground and to prevent the landing-grounds across the frontier at H.3 and Rutbah

[1] Uniquely for the Middle East, Habbaniya had water-borne sewage, which was pumped into the Euphrates at Sin el Dhibban. Our engineers had been withdrawn from the pumping station on the approach of the Iraqi troops, but they had optimistically left the pumps switched on. Though the building was immediately occupied by the Iraqis as an observation and sniping post, the enemy had not the wit (or the malice) to switch off the pumps, and throughout the siege the 12,000 occupants of Habbaniya enjoyed their normal sanitary facilities.

from being used as refuelling points by German aircraft on their way to help the rebels. The successful execution of this task would also help to keep open the approach to Habbaniya and Baghdad from the west.

On 4th May the Transjordan Frontier Force occupied H.3 without opposition, but when ordered to attack an enemy force in the fort at Rutbah refused to proceed farther. Brown, who was well aware of the importance of rooting out the rebel garrison before the Germans appeared, promptly appealed for Royal Air Force armoured cars. They came quickly. On 5th May No. 2 Company was guarding airfields in the Western Desert of Egypt. By the morning of 10th May it was at Rutbah, a thousand miles distant, and in action. The combination of armoured cars and aircraft was too much for the defenders of the fort, and within twenty-four hours the whole area was in our hands.

The way east was now clear. After a little delay further British troops arrived, and the command of the expedition ('Habforce') passed into Army hands. Too late to relieve Habbaniya, since Habbaniya had already freed itself, its task was to link up with the Habbaniya garrison and advance on Baghdad. While the Blenheims remained at H.4 to provide air support and keep a watchful eye on Syria, an advanced detachment of the troops ('Kingcol') accordingly set off across the desert. Surviving the attentions of two or three hostile aircraft in the last stages of the journey, the column completed its arduous march to Habbaniya on 18th May. The identity of the attacking aircraft—Me.110's—underlined the need for a quick move against the capital.

The presence of German aircraft in Iraq had been first established on 13th May, when a Blenheim was attacked by a Me.110 while reconnoitring Mosul. Though it was not known to us then, the previous day the German plans had received an unexpected set-back. An He.111 bearing Major Axel von Blomberg, the newly appointed liaison officer to Rashid Ali and the son of the German field-marshal, had come in to land at Baghdad. As the aircraft flew in low over the north bridge some irresponsible tribesmen fired off a few pot-shots with their rifles. When the reception-party at the airport opened the door of the aircraft they found, not the vigorous adviser and co-ordinator they had expected, but a dead German with a bullet in his head.

The German danger was as yet in its early stages. By way of nipping it in the bud our aircraft intensified their raids on the airfields in northern Iraq, destroyed the hangars at Raschid, and bombed the supply line along the Aleppo–Mosul railway. Despite these efforts three He.111's attacked Habbaniya on 16th May and did more damage to the Aircraft Depot than had been done by the entire rebel air force. From then on, combats with German machines were a daily occurrence. More Blenheim bombers of No. 84 Squadron and fighters of No. 94—Hurricanes as well as Gladiators—arrived from Egypt, but the Germans managed to bring off another effective attack on 20th May. As Habbaniya's 'aircraft warning system' consisted of an accountant or education officer on the roof of Air Headquarters with a pair of field glasses, such incidents were likely to recur until the menace could be eliminated at source. In the absence of more than four aircraft suitable for ground strafing at long range, that was a remedy easier prescribed than applied; and one of the first actions of D'Albiac (who arrived on 18th May to replace Smart, injured in a motor accident) was to ask Tedder for two long-range Hurricanes. These were rare birds at the time, but they duly appeared within a couple of days. Unfortunately one of them was lost over Mosul almost at once, though not before a number of German aircraft had been destroyed on the ground. The pilot, Flight Lieutenant Sir R. A. MacRobert, was the first of three brothers to be killed on operations with the Royal Air Force.

Meanwhile 'Kingcol' and the Habbaniya garrison, strengthened by Gurkhas and other troops flown in from Basra, as well as by the captured Iraqi equipment, had already begun the advance on Baghdad. Between the British forces and their goal lay the Euphrates, and on it the town of Felluja. This was strongly occupied by the enemy, who by now had broken some of the river 'bunds' and flooded the direct approach from the west. However, the resourceful civilian engineers (in uniform) of Habbaniya's Works Services constructed a flying bridge over the river at Sin el Dhibban, and so enabled some of the attacking troops to approach from the north. Another company was flown by No. 216 Squadron's Bombays and the Valentias of Habbaniya's Communication Flight to a position on the north-east, covering the Felluja–Baghdad road, while others still—thanks to the extensive local knowledge of Colonel Cardew, the Chief Engineer— found a way round by the south. These movements were carried out in the early morning of 19th May. To complete the enemy's isolation, telephone communication between the town and Baghdad was then severed. Along one set of lines this was done by the simple expedient of flying an Audax through the wires. Along the other, where the wires were too numerous for this treatment, the pilot landed, climbed on the main plane, and got to work with a pair of shears. The air-gunner meanwhile occupied himself by hacking down the poles with an axe.

With the troops deployed for a converging attack, the Blenheims and the aircraft of the Flying Training School then swooped down in force on the enemy positions, and by late afternoon Felluja had succumbed almost without a fight. The vital bridge over the Euphrates, 'rushed' at a suitable moment, fell into our hands intact. Three days later, on 22nd May, Rashid Ali's forces fought their way back into the town, but were driven out by resolute action on the part of our troops and airmen. During this encounter an enemy lorry bearing gun cotton for the demolition of the bridge was itself demolished in impressive fashion by a well-aimed bomb.

After a halt for further preparations, including repairs to the broken 'bunds', the advance was resumed on 28th May. One column approached the capital from the north, using the newly constructed ferry at Sin el Dhibban; the other—the main force—took the direct route from Felluja. The northern arm was eventually held up; but the main column, which enjoyed nearly all the air support, reached the outskirts of Baghdad on 30th May. The chief obstacles to its progress, the inundations, were checked by local Iraqis anxious to avoid damage to their crops. With this approach of our troops Rashid Ali quickly lost heart, and together with his friends the Italian Minister and the ex-Mufti of Jerusalem decamped on the night of the 28th. On 31st May terms of armistice were agreed with the Mayor of Baghdad. The next day the Regent re-entered the capital amid the plaudits of the multitude, mingled with a few rifle-shots.

The advance of the main column had been marked by a significant incident on 29th May. While our aircraft were bombing Khan Nuqta, the first stronghold along the road, two Italian Cr.42's suddenly appeared. They forced down an Audax; then one fell to a Gladiator, whereupon the other turned tail and fled to base. 'Welcoming parties' for the new arrivals were promptly 'laid on', and the Italian fighters —a complete squadron which had arrived only the previous day— were hotly attacked on the ground. Such further efforts as they made to intervene in the battle for Baghdad were all carried out at a highly respectful distance from our pilots. On 31st May the entire ground staff of the unit, together with some Germans, were rounded up while attempting to escape into Syria.

Thus closed an episode of the highest importance to our fortunes in the Middle East. Encouraged by the disasters to British arms in Cyrenaica and Greece, Rashid Ali had thrown down the gauntlet, then stood irresolute at the edge of the arena. The swiftness with which the challenge was taken up, and the vigour with which Habbaniya struck the first blow, forced him out into the open before he was fully prepared for the fight, and at the same time denied him the initial successes which might have rallied the Iraqi people to his cause. The same factors also robbed him of effective outside help. For the Germans were far too busy with other plans to take proper advantage of the situation; and the death of von Blomberg can only have added to their difficulties. As it was, everything about their movements—even the employment of the aircraft which they sent— betrayed an absence of close liaison with the Iraqis; had the Me.110's been used during the battle of Felluja, for instance, they might have claimed many victims among our ill-armed trainers. Above all, the timing of the episode, though it coincided with a period of great difficulty for us, was very far from perfect for the Germans. Through-out the whole incident their bombers and transports were tied down by their assignment to the invasion of Crete, first by way of prepara-tion, then execution; and by the time the Germans were finished with Crete their airborne forces were shattered and Rashid Ali's brief spell of power was over. What Hitler intended, in fact, is to be seen in his directive of 23rd May. He would support Rashid Ali by means of supplies, a military mission, and air force units in limited numbers; but he would take no decision about a major campaign in the Middle East until after 'Operation Barbarossa'. Fortunately the Russians were not beaten in the eight weeks of the German estimate, and the Iraqi rebels collapsed in four.

That victory in Iraq came swiftly was due, when all credit is given to the work of 'Kingcol' and the other military forces, mainly to the air superiority which we established and maintained. Thanks to this, Habbaniya was first sustained, then relieved, then turned into a base for offensive action. In this connection it is worth remarking that our aircraft could hardly have driven the Iraqis from the plateau had they not also been able to keep Habbaniya in contact with the outside world. Work of enormous value was done by No. 31 Squadron and the local communication flight of Valentias. Troops and supplies were flown in from Basra and Palestine; civilians and wounded were flown out; demolition parties were flown to blow up vital stretches of railway; important Iraqi officials were whisked away to safety and then whisked back again at the right moment. This was a side of the air operations which has often been overlooked, but it deserves a place in history as an early example of how transport aircraft may be used to break a siege.

The half-dozen operational squadrons engaged at one time or another—the Vincents and Wellingtons at Shaibah and the Blen-heims, Gladiators and Hurricanes at Habbaniya—also bore a share in the work which, though vital, has sometimes been forgotten. But no one who has studied the story of the Iraqi Revolt has forgotten, or is ever likely to forget, the achievements of No. 4 Flying Training School; for the rout of an organized army and air force by makeshift crews in training machines, who in less than a month flew some 1,400 sorties against the enemy, was a feat unprecedented in the brief but crowded annals of air warfare. The instructors and pupils, as they climbed with a new and stronger purpose into their familiar cockpits, were doubtless inspired only by the determination to act up to the standards of their comrades in the operational squadrons. But in fact they were doing more than sustain a tradition. They were creating one.

*   *   *

On 20th May, while the struggle in Iraq was still unresolved, German gliders and paratroops descended on Crete. So far from being one of the *Führer*'s long-matured projects, the attack was an improvisation of the most rapid kind. General Student, the originator of the suggestion and the commander of the forces concerned, had proposed the operation to Göring only on 15th April; Hitler had given his approval only on 21st April. The whole affair was thus conceived and executed in little over a month. In these circumstances the attack should, perhaps, have come as a surprise to the defenders. This was not the case. By 26th April our Intelligence was fully informed of the enemy's intention of taking the island by airborne assault, and by 6th May we had most of the detailed orders, together with the probable date of invasion. In no previous operation of the war had we enjoyed any comparable foreknowledge of the German plans. Unfortunately this very considerable advantage could not—or did not—make up for other less favourable factors in the situation.

British troops, it will be remembered, had been acting as a garrison in parts of Crete since November 1940. No Royal Air Force squadrons, however, were permanently based there until April 1941. During the intervening months the island was under military development, in which the Royal Air Force bore its share by preparing airfields, installing radar, and building up dumps of petrol, bombs, and ammunition. Unfortunately much of this work went slowly. Equipment was so scarce on the active fronts that very little could be spared for a rear area which would become of prime importance only if the Greek mainland were lost. In the circumstances it was entirely intelligible that Crete should have ranked low in the scale of priorities. It was less intelligible that those on the spot had no clear idea of development policy, and that inside the seven months of our occupation the British military forces had seven different commanders.

By the beginning of April two airfields and a landing strip were fit for use. All were on the north coast. Maleme (an existing Fleet Air

HABBANIYA AND FELLUJA, 30 APRIL—19 MAY 1941

LEGEND

BUNDS
DEPRESSIONS AND INUNDATIONS
ROADS
TRACKS
TELEG. LINES
IRAQI TROOP POSITIONS
APRIL 30 – MAY 5
LINES OF BRITISH ADVANCE
ON FELLUJA, MAY 19

SCALE

0   1   2   3
MILES

TO BAGHDAD
30 MILES

TRACKS ACROSS PLAIN

AIRBORNE TROOPS

FELLUJA

EUPHRATES

NOTCHFALL REGULATOR

OLD RLY. FORMATION

RUINS OF ANBAR

REGULATOR

CANAL TURN

HAMMOND'S BUND

SIN EL DHIBBAN

H.Q.

R.A.F. CAMP

AIRFIELD

TO RAMADI
13 MILES

LAKE HABBANIYA

Arm airfield) and the landing strip at Retimo were well placed for the protection of Suda Bay, which lay between them; Heraklion (Candia) was a good deal farther east. A fourth ground, at Pediada-Kastelli, south-east of Heraklion, could have been finished in a short time if required. Already by this time Crete was assuming a new importance, for with a British expeditionary force in Greece the Navy needed Suda Bay not merely as a refuelling point but as a main fleet base. Then, quite suddenly, this growing defensive requirement was enormously magnified. As the Allied front in Macedonia crumbled before the German drive, so the role of the garrison in Crete was transformed. From being expected to repel raids on a naval anchorage, it became charged with the total defence of a 180-mile-long island against imminent invasion—and this at a time when its first duty was to give refuge to the defeated forces from the mainland, and when the resources of the Middle East Command were already strained to the utmost.

It was with this double task in mind that on 17th April Longmore appointed Group Captain G. R. Beamish to the position of Senior Air Force Officer, Crete. Before this date the highest-ranking Royal Air Force officer had been a flight lieutenant whose duties, according to an Inter-Services Committee which later enquired into the lessons of the campaign, had been 'ill-defined' and instructions 'inadequate'. Beamish at any rate soon knew what his first job would be. The Blenheims of Nos. 30 and 203 Squadrons from Egypt and the remnants of D'Albiac's fighters must be received and established on the island, so that cover could be provided for the evacuation of Greece. This he accomplished with great success; for the cover, though tenuous, proved surprisingly effective. At all events some twenty-five thousand exhausted British and Dominion troops were brought safely across the sea to Crete. There they were meant to remain only until they could be relieved by fresh units from Egypt.

Unfortunately Wavell's intentions in this matter were thwarted by the swift onrush of events. At the beginning of May the Navy was fully engaged in escorting the vital through-convoy to Alexandria, and after that the German attack was upon the island before anything could be done. In fact even the attempt to replace the troops' lost equipment came to little. Some 27,000 tons of supplies were sent to Crete from Egypt between 1st May and 20th May, but the *Luftwaffe* was so active that most of the ships were forced to turn back, and only 2,700 tons were delivered. As there were only some 3,500 British and trained Greek soldiers in the island apart from the survivors of Greece, the defence of Crete thus rested mainly in the hands

z

of shaken and ill-equipped troops—so ill-equipped that many were without arms and others were reduced to digging trenches with steel helmets. To assist them in the air these troops had only the battered remnants of the three fighter squadrons from Greece (Nos. 33, 80 and 112), together with one equally worn squadron of the Fleet Air Arm—for the Blenheims were needed back in Egypt. By mid-May the combined strength of the four squadrons in Crete was no more than twenty-four machines. And since there was no proper range of tools and spare-parts, those actually serviceable numbered about twelve.

As opposed to our exhausted and ill-provided garrison of 28,500 the Germans had mustered a highly-trained force of some 15,000 airborne and 7,000 seaborne troops. Numerically—and tactically, since the only military movement more vulnerable than a landing by sea is a landing by air—the defenders of Crete were thus stronger on the ground than the attackers. But any such advantage paled into insignificance beside the overwhelming superiority which the Germans could exercise in the air. As against the puny force of a dozen or so Hurricanes, Gladiators and Fulmars, the *Luftwaffe* had available, under *Fliegerkorps VIII* for the supporting operations and *Fliegerkorps XI* for the actual invasion, no less than 650 operational aircraft, 700 transports and 80 gliders. Of the 650 operational machines, 430 were bombers, 180 fighters. For while Crete was now, since the loss of the Greek mainland, virtually outside the periphery of British air power in the Eastern Mediterranean, it was within easy reach from a whole ring of German air bases in the Morea, the Greek islands, and the Dodecanese. Indeed, from the islands of Melos and Skarpanto it was just within that most decisive of distances, the operational radius of a single-engined fighter.

Probably the most disheartening feature of all this, as it appeared to Tedder before the attack, was his inability to reduce the enemy's huge margin of superiority. Crete had two airfields and a landing-strip, and could have had others but for the shortage of defenders. Without doubt the A.O.C.-in-C. could have based on the three available grounds more fighters than the few they now held. But at the most the three airfields could not have taken more than five squadrons of Hurricanes; and at the beginning of May there were not five Hurricane squadrons intact in the whole of the Middle East Command. Even if two or three squadrons could have been spared from their other tasks—which was virtually impossible with Malta under constant assault and Rommel on the borders of Egypt—they would still have been impotent against the overwhelming force of the enemy. To send further squadrons to Crete in the face of such

odds was thus simply, in Tedder's view, to-invite greater losses—
losses which, coming on top of those incurred in Greece, might mean
nothing less than the sacrifice of Egypt. The air commander accordingly resolved to maintain, if possible, a dozen Hurricanes in Crete,
so that the enemy should not have matters all his own way; but he
declined to expose more than this very limited number to the certainty of eventual destruction on the ground. His policy received the
full support of the authorities at home.

Meanwhile Beamish and Major-General Freyberg, the newly
appointed G.O.C., were making the best of a bad job. As it was
known that the German plan hinged on an airborne assault against
our airfields, the incomplete ground at Pediada-Kastelli was obstructed
by trenches and mounds of earth; all spare ground at Heraklion
and Retimo, apart from a narrow flight-path, was blocked by barrels
filled with earth; and at Maleme barrels filled with petrol stood ready
to be ignited by machine-gun fire. Pens were also built to shelter the
fighters. The defensive scheme adopted at the three completed airfields was roughly similar; round each were stationed a few field
guns, the anti-aircraft weapons (machine-guns only at Retimo), two
infantry tanks, and two or three tanks of a lighter calibre. The three
districts and their neighbouring beaches, together with the area
around Canea and Suda Bay as a fourth, were all treated as self-
contained sectors, for with only 28,500 troops Freyberg could
scarcely attempt a wider disposition. Moreover his deployment had
the best of justifications—a knowledge of the enemy's intentions. All
the same, he would have felt more confident of the outcome had
Beamish had more fighters, and had his own anti-aircraft defences,
excluding machine-guns, numbered more than eight 3-inch guns and
twenty Bofors.

Up to the middle of May *Fliegerkorps VIII*, on whom rested the
burden of the preliminary operations, concentrated on Suda Bay and
the sea approaches to the island. The weight of attack was very great,
and though our Gladiators and Hurricanes made many successful
interceptions the Navy suffered severely. Having frustrated our hopes
of re-equipping the garrison, on 14th May the Germans then turned
their attention to our airfields. Their attacks were directed in part
against the ground organisation—though not the landing surfaces,
which they required for their own use—and in part against the surrounding gun positions. Valiantly and repeatedly Beamish's handful
of fighters took the air, but no force of such slender dimensions could
long survive the weight and fury of the German onslaught.

How gallantly the little band of pilots strove to stem the avalanche
may be seen from Squadron Leader E. Howell's description of a

combat on 14th May.[1] Howell, who had succeeded Pattle as commanding officer of No. 33 Squadron, had arrived at Maleme only a day or so previously. Though an experienced Spitfire pilot, he had never before flown a Hurricane:

> I called over one of my newly joined sergeant-pilots and he went over the cockpit with me showing me the position of the various controls. I could not make the radio work .... In the grey dawn. I noticed that the other two pilots were in their places, sitting quietly in the aircraft, waiting ....
>
> Suddenly there was the roar of engines starting up. I saw the other two Hurricanes take off in a cloud of dust. I waved the sergeant away and prepared to start the engine. As soon as it kicked, I noticed the fitter pull the starter battery to one side and run; I thought 'this is efficiency—the boys run about their business!' Then I looked up. Through the subsiding dust, I saw the others twisting and turning among a cloud of Me. 109's. Even as I watched, an enemy aircraft dived into the ground in flames.
>
> I opened the throttle and saw a string of five Messerschmitts coming in over the hill firing at me. It seemed an age before my wheels came off the strip, I went straight into a turn towards the approaching 109's, my wing tip within inches of the ground. The faithful old 'Hurrybus' took it without a murmur, the enemy flashed past and I went over instinctively into a steep turn the other way.
>
> My mind was set on practical things. How to get my undercarriage up, the hood closed, the gunsight switched on, the prop into coarse pitch, the firing button on, the engine temperature down. All the time I kept the nose up, straining to gain height to manœuvre. I found many difficulties. My rear view mirror was not adjusted so that I could see over my tail. This meant that I had to do continuous steep turns with my head back to see what was coming after me. Every time I put my head back, my helmet, which I had borrowed and was much too big for me, slipped over my eyes. Then I could not find the switch to turn on my gunsight. I had to look about inside the cockpit for it. Eventually I found it and saw the familiar red graticule glow ready to aim.
>
> Enemy aircraft kept diving in on me in threes or fives. They were travelling fast and did not stay to fight. They just had a squirt at me and climbed away out of range again. It kept me fully occupied with evasive action. Out of the corner of my eye I saw two aircraft diving earthwards in flames. One was a Hurricane. There was no sign of the other. I was alone in a skyful of Jerries.
>
> All of a sudden, the sky seemed to empty of aircraft . . . Five miles to the south was the airfield. Streams of tracers and red Bofors shells were coming up focused on small black specks which were enemy fighters still strafing it fiercely. Four pillars of black smoke indicated the position of burning wrecks on the ground.
>
> Just level with me and about a mile away two 109's were turning in wide line astern formation. I headed in their direction . . . I drew in closer and closer with an eye on my own tail to make sure that I was

---

[1] In his book *Escape to Live* (Longmans).

not jumped. I restrained myself with difficulty. It is only the novice who opens at long range . . .

[Howell then shoots down the first Me.109 and damages the second. With ammunition exhausted he heads back for Maleme, but finds himself among Bofors fire and turns east for Retimo. He passes a blazing tanker in Suda Bay, lands at Retimo, refuels and rearms, and returns to Maleme.]

A crowd gathered round me as I taxied in . . . . Everyone had assumed that I had been shot down. They had seen my 109 come down and they were delighted that I had opened my score. We had accounted for six Me.109's and had lost the other two Hurricanes, shot down in flames. Sergeant Ripsher had been shot down near the airfield and was credited with two enemy aircraft destroyed. We buried him the next day in a little cemetery by Galatos a few miles down the road. Sergeant Reynish had also accounted for a couple and had baled out of his flaming Hurricane over the sea. We had given him up when he walked in late that evening. He had been two hours in the water and had been picked up by a small Greek fishing-boat. We had also lost one Hurricane on the ground. It had been unserviceable, but could have been flying again within a few hours. Now it was a mass of charred wreckage. We had only one aircraft left. The Fleet Air Arm squadron had lost their Fulmars, burnt out on the ground, as well as a couple of Gladiators. The prelude to invasion had entered upon its last phase.

Only three or four of our fighters were destroyed on the ground in the days that followed; the rest succumbed through sheer wear and tear of combat. Each day two or three Hurricanes were sent over from Egypt to fill the gaps in their ranks, but by the evening of 18th May only four Hurricanes and three Gladiators remained fit for action. With Freyberg's full agreement, Beamish then urged that these should be withdrawn before they were wiped out to the last aircraft. His recommendation was accepted by Tedder and endorsed by the Chief of Air Staff and the Prime Minister. On 19th May the seven survivors took off for Egypt.

During this time Tedder was doing his best to tackle the problem at source by raiding the German air bases in Greece and the Dodecanese. To this end, as already related, he even recalled the two Wellington detachments from Iraq. But night attacks by Wellingtons were a chancy method of destroying aircraft on the ground; and the Air Commander badly felt the lack of some faster aircraft which could have operated by day. Above all, he needed a fast long-range fighter: so much so that he exposed the new Beaufighter squadron at Malta—the only one in the whole Middle East Command—to the risk of refuelling on Crete so that it might come within striking distance of the German bases. But he had also a campaign to fight in Cyrenaica—a campaign which ranked higher than the struggle for Crete—and this, combined with the shortage of suitable aircraft and

CRETE, MAY 1941

the difficulties of range, made the scale of our air attacks too small for effective results.

With the way cleared by the elimination of our fighters, the German airborne assault descended on Crete in the early morning of 20th May. This was three days late on schedule—the enemy had been held up by delay in the arrival of auxiliary petrol tanks for his fighters and shipping for his seaborne expedition. His preparations, however, had been thorough to the last degree, and showed many interesting refinements. Among these may be mentioned the comprehensive medical supplies (including test-tubes of blood for transfusions) dropped by special pink parachutes, and a phrase-sheet in German and phonetic English the first sentence of which ran 'If yu lei yu uill bi schott'. As for the general plan of campaign, this was straightforward. The German troops would descend in the three main areas of Maleme, Canea-Suda-Retimo and Heraklion, occupy the airfields and local beaches, then spread out to form a continuous line sealing off the whole coastal area thus captured. Reinforcements would then land behind this line from both sea and air; an Italian expedition would arrive from the Dodecanese; and in due course the accumulated forces would strike out and overrun the whole island. At Maleme, where the assault was to be launched in the morning, the tactical plan comprised first, an intense air attack lasting over an hour, aimed mainly at the guns and their teams; then, under cover of this, the descent of glider troops and the occupation of positions close to the airfield; next, under covering fire from the glider troops, the descent of the first waves of paratroops; and finally the capture of the airfield and the immediate landing of troop-carrying aircraft. Gliders and paratroops were also to be landed in the morning near Canea. At Heraklion and Retimo, which were to be attacked in the afternoon, the initial assault was entrusted solely to parachutists.

This plan broke down at four out of five points. The paratroops were wiped out or beaten off at Heraklion and Retimo; the glider landings near Canea were effectively dealt with; and the seaborne reinforcements, detected by a Blenheim on reconnaissance from Egypt, were sunk or driven back by the Navy. But the Germans more than made up for these failures by their brilliant, if utterly prodigal, exploitation of the situation at Maleme. Something of what happened there on the first day of the attack may be gathered from a report by Pilot Officer R. K. Crowther, who was in charge of the rear party of No. 30 Squadron:

> At 0430 hours on 20th May, the defence officers inspected all positions and satisfied themselves that everyone was on the alert. A second inspection was carried out at 0600 hours. At 0700 the alarm

was sounded and within a few minutes very severe and prolonged
bombing of the defence positions started. The Bofors crews as the result
of sustained bombing and machine-gunning attacks during the past
seven days were by this time almost completely unnerved, and on this
particular morning soon gave up firing. One Bofors gun was seen to go
into action again but the shooting was rather inaccurate. While the
Camp was being bombed, enemy fighters made prolonged machine-
gun attacks on the Bofors positions and inflicted heavy casualties. At
the same time there was intensive ground strafing of troops over a
wide area in the locality. These attacks lasted for two hours, with the
result that the nerves of our men became ragged, and that intended
reinforcements moving towards the aerodrome were unable to do so. A
fuller effect of the bombing was that the men kept their heads down
and failed to notice the first parachutists dropping. This particularly
applied to those which landed South West of the aerodrome sheltered
by hilly country. Gliders were already seen crashed in the river bed
on the west side of the aerodrome and had apparently been dropped
at the same time. There was no opposition to them except from the
two R.A.F. Lewis guns which kept firing throughout the landing. The
remnants of R.A.F. personnel and New Zealand infantry on the hill-
side were being subjected to persistent ground strafing from a very
low height. The Germans were able to profit by the spare time allowed
them to assemble trench mortars and field guns which later in the
morning were instrumental in driving our men back.

Meanwhile, troop-carrying aircraft were landing along the beach
at intervals of 100 yards. They appeared to land successfully in the
most limited space, and the enemy did not seem to mind whether they
could take off again or not. At least 8 aircraft were seen crashed in
this way. None of these aircraft did take off again to my knowledge.

At the beginning of the attack I reached the pre-arranged position
[on a hill near the airfield] at the rear of the New Zealand troops and
remained there during the morning.

It was here that I gathered a handful of men and obtained a hold;
the men on the deep dug-outs on that side had not been warned of the
approach of parachute troops. After mopping up the parachute troops
here, we discovered that the enemy had obtained a foothold on the
eastern side of the aerodrome, actually above the camp. We gathered
30 New Zealand troops who appeared to be without any leader, and
with my handful of R.A.F. three counter attacks were made, and we
succeeded in re-taking the summit. Throughout this period we were
subjected to severe ground straffing by Me. 109's. The enemy's armament at this stage was very superior to ours, namely, trench mortars,
hand grenades, tommy guns and small field guns. One particularly
objectionable form of aggression was by petrol bombs. These burst
in the undergrowth and encircled us with a ring of flames.

At this time we tried to obtain contact with the remainder of No. 30
Squadron personnel, cut off at the bottom of the valley by the side of
the camp, in order to withdraw them to more secure positions on the
slopes overlooking the aerodrome. The time was now about 1400 hours.
The enemy drove our men who had been taken prisoners in front of
them, using them as a protective screen. Any sign of faltering on their
part was rewarded with a shot in the back. Our men were very

reluctant to open fire and gradually gave ground. A small party of R.A.F. succeeded in outflanking them on one side, and I and a handful of New Zealand troops on the other were able to snipe the Germans in the rear and succeeded thereby in releasing at least 14 prisoners.

Towards the close of the day we discovered that our communications with our forces in rear had been cut, and after an unsuccessful advance made by our two 'I' tanks we decided to withdraw under cover of darkness in order to take up positions with the 23rd Battalion of the New Zealand forces. During the next morning we were unsuccessful in locating them and had to withdraw from our cover under heavy aerial attack for another three miles, where we at last made contact.

In brief, at Maleme the Battle of Crete was lost and won. By landing gliders on the beaches and in the dried-up bed of the river Tavronitis while the air bombardment was still at its height, the Germans caught the defenders with their 'heads down'; the paratroops came in while their opponents in their trenches were still stunned and bewildered from the crash of the bombs; in the ensuing struggle the Germans, denied the airfield, landed transport aircraft on the shore; and by nightfall on 20th May Maleme airfield was virtually in the hands of the enemy. Fresh 'drops' consolidated the position on the following morning, and from noon onwards the Ju.52's began to pour in, landing in a space of 400 or 500 yards and in many cases crashing without hesitation. All our counter-attacks in the next two days failed to restore the situation. By 27th May the Germans had brought in between twenty and thirty thousand troops; the heroic garrisons at Heraklion and Retimo were hopelessly isolated; and ceaseless air attack combined with relentless pressure on the ground had worn down the resistance of the remaining defenders. Once more the fate of a British army depended on the skill and devotion of the Navy.

Throughout the whole of this grim week the Royal Air Force made every effort within its power to sway the fortunes of the battle. From the Canal the Wellingtons, in an unfavourable phase of the moon, continued their raids against the German airfields in Greece and the Dodecanese, or dropped supplies to the defenders of Retimo and Heraklion. From the Western Desert Blenheims, Marylands and Beaufighters, greatly hampered by dust storms over their bases, tried to shake the enemy's hold on Maleme. In reversal of the policy approved just before the attack, it was decided to try to operate fighters again from the island. A hundred airmen were sent from Suda Bay to open up another airstrip in the south, only to be captured before they could complete their task. At Heraklion a landing-space was cleared and a dozen Hurricanes were sent over from Egypt. Two were shot down and three driven back by our own naval barrage as they arrived; four more were damaged in landing on the bombed runway or put out of action by German attack before they could refuel. By way of experiment Hurricanes were fitted with long-range tanks and successfully operated from Egypt with their eight guns still on. All was in vain. Many German aircraft were destroyed, particularly by our attacks on Maleme, but with the size and nature of the forces at his disposal, its commitments in Egypt, and its given distance from Crete and Greece, Tedder was utterly unable to turn the battle in our favour. Numbers, which by no means account for everything in air warfare, in this case tell their story clearly enough. The Germans put up several hundred sorties over Crete every day; our own daily average, including attacks on outside bases, was less than twenty.

Happily the evacuation for the most part went well. The Royal Air Force survivors from Maleme and Suda Bay managed to reach the little port of Sphakia, on the south coast, whence they were rescued by the Navy on the nights of 28/29th and 29/30th May. Once more many of the headquarters staffs, including Beamish and Freyberg, owed their escape to Sunderlands; and once more the ineffectiveness of the *Luftwaffe* at night made the whole evacuation possible. Under cover of the Blenheims and other aircraft from the Western Desert and the Delta, every ship which sailed from Sphakia reached Egypt safely. Other parties, however, were not so fortunate. The troops at Retimo, who numbered among them a dozen members of the Royal Air Force, were cut off completely and killed or captured. Those at Heraklion, including the members of No. 220 A.M.E.S.[1], were picked up successfully from the local harbour, but suffered heavy casualties from air attack while rounding the north-east corner of the island. In this case the convoy, unavoidably late in sailing, failed to reach its scheduled position in time to link up with fighter escort, and was still in Cretan waters when daylight—and the German Air Force—arrived.

The ground staff of the Royal Air Force who fought in the Battle of Crete survived it in roughly the same proportion as their comrades of the Army. Some 14,500 of the 28,000 Imperial troops engaged, and 361 of the 618 members of the Royal Air Force, were brought from the island in safety. The British aircraft losses over the period from 14th May to the end of the campaign amounted to 38 machines; those of the Germans—a gratifying feature—to 220, of which 119 were transports, as well as another 148 damaged. But quite as signifi-cant as the losses of the enemy Air Force were the losses of our own

---

[1] Air Ministry Experimental Station—a cover name for a radar station.

Navy. All told, the struggle for Crete cost the Royal Navy three cruisers and six destroyers sunk, and a battleship, an aircraft carrier, a special service ship, six cruisers and eight destroyers damaged. At this price to its eternal credit and glory the Mediterranean Fleet had defeated a seaborne invasion and rescued a British army; but at this price the Mediterranean Fleet could not continue operating beyond the effective range of the Royal Air Force and within that of the *Luftwaffe*. And as though to point the moral still further, there was the particularly grievous incident of the anti-aircraft vessel *Calcutta*. Ordered off to Cretan waters without any request for cover having been made to the Air Force authorities, she was caught by two Ju.88's and sunk when only a hundred miles out from Alexandria.

The loss of Crete, following on that of Cyrenaica and Greece, led to much bitterness and searching of hearts in Service circles. In London the Prime Minister urged the Secretary of State for Air to make every airfield 'a stronghold of fighting air-groundmen, and not the abode of uniformed civilians in the prime of life protected by detachments of soldiers'. The policy was admirable—and indeed resulted before many months in the formation of the Royal Air Force Regiment—but the phraseology rang somewhat harshly after the supremely gallant fight of the ground crews at Maleme, Heraklion and Retimo. From Alexandria Admiral Cunningham revived an earlier demand for a 'Coastal Command' in Egypt, specifically tied down to work on behalf of the Mediterranean Fleet. In Cairo a whole galaxy of distinguished critics, including the British Ambassador and Captain Lord Louis Mountbatten—the latter more, rather than less, vigorous for having been blown into the sea by a German bomb—taxed Tedder on the deficiencies of our air support. And everywhere the rank and file, as after Dunkirk, made their own distinctive contribution to the debate—from the streets of Cairo, which suddenly became unsafe for solitary airmen, to the prison camps of Germany, where dilapidated figures in blue found themselves regarded with a new disfavour by dilapidated figures in khaki.

The charge that was heard on all sides was roughly the same—that the Air Force had 'let down' the Army. This bred the counter-charge that the Army had not stood up properly to air attack, and that by failing to hold our air bases it had let down both itself and the Air Force. These were the extremes of partisanship; but even among those with little or no partisan feeling the very narrowness of the German victory in Crete gave rise to a hundred questions. Could Crete have been held with more airfields? Or with more fighters? Or if the defenders of Maleme had not been tired troops from Greece? Or if the gun teams had been better protected, and able to stand to their guns during the heaviest bombardment? And, if none of these things could have been done, should we have attempted to hold Crete at all? These were among the queries that sprang to the lips of the coroners in the grand national inquest. It is not the purpose of this narrative to discuss the 'ifs' of history, and the difficulty of giving better air support to the garrison of Crete has already been explained. In a world of speculation, we can at any rate be certain about two things. The Germans captured Crete; and they never again attempted a major airborne operation.

* * *

The fighting in Iraq and Crete, apprehended or actual, had not released the Middle East commanders from their primary duty of hitting back against the Axis forces in Cyrenaica. For it was clearly of vital importance to strike before the enemy could bring up enough supplies and reinforcements to exploit what the chief German military representative at Italian Supreme Headquarters termed 'the unexpected success of the Africa Corps'. A sharp blow, quickly delivered, might well open up the road to Tobruk and recapture the great stretch of landing grounds west of the Egyptian frontier. And this was now essential; for the war in the Middle East was becoming increasingly a struggle for airfields, in which the chief significance of territorial loss or gain lay in whether it brought enemy airmen within easier striking distance of Alexandria, Cairo, and the Canal, or British airmen within more effective range of Benghazi, Tripoli, and the sea routes across the Mediterranean. The sands of the Libyan and Western Deserts, it was only too apparent, had no value in themselves. But whoever held them as bases for his aircraft stood fair to win the prime battle of all—the battle of communications.

On 15th May, though the German invasion of Crete was expected within a matter of days, Wavell's troops in the desert accordingly struck west. The immediate objectives were Capuzzo, Sollum, and a good jumping-off ground for a further advance; the ultimate objective, if the first moves went well, was Tobruk. Collishaw's No. 204 Group was available for support in the forward area, the Wellingtons of No. 257 Wing for operations in the enemy's rear. But the operation fizzled out almost as soon as it had begun. Halfaya, Sollum and Capuzzo fell quickly into our hands, only for the enemy's tanks to strike back and at once recover most of the captured ground. Within three days Halfaya alone remained to us; and this was reoccupied by the enemy in a sharp attack on 27th May.

Fortified by its new accession of tanks, the Army was ready to try again by the middle of June. In the meantime our losses over Crete, coupled with the demands of a fresh task in Syria, had made it no easier for Tedder to provide adequate air support. However, by stripping down the Delta defences and scraping together half-squadrons from units reforming or re-equipping, he managed to build up a total of 200 serviceable aircraft. The air plan for the offensive, arranged to meet the requirements of the G.O.C. Western Desert Force, followed different lines from Collishaw's previous efforts. Preliminary attacks were to be delivered, as usual, against enemy airfields and lines of communication; but as the army moved up to its striking positions most of the fighters were to switch over to continuous patrols above our own troops. With a total of less than a hundred serviceable fighters, such patrols could obviously be carried out by only a few aircraft each time; and Tedder was well aware that this sort of policy, when practised by the Italians, had worn out their fighter force, exposed it to engagements in which it was outnumbered, denied escorts to their bombers, and greatly contributed to our own air superiority. He nevertheless gave the plan his blessing. This was in part because the Army had requested the protective patrols for only three days, in part because he felt it essential to restore the confidence of our troops after their recent experiences in Greece and Crete.

So began Operation 'Battle-axe,' a major attempt to relieve Tobruk. The preliminary air action kept down activity by the enemy air force; and the approach-march of the troops on 14th June, and their operations on the following two days, were duly conducted under the fighter 'umbrella'. This served its purpose well. But by 16th June the leftward of our two armoured columns above the escarpment had again run into a strong concentration of tanks, and within a few hours a second enemy tank force began to threaten the flank of the Indian infantry on the coast. Quickly our armour in the centre, which had worked its way round to the rear of Sollum, was ordered back to interpose itself between the Indians and the enemy; but before it could arrive, the latter had been repulsed by our bombers and the Indians themselves. The Germans, for their part, had no intention of advancing into Egypt; and our air reconnaissance on 18th June thus disclosed the curious spectacle of both armies in retreat. By this time our tank losses were heavy, both from engagements and mechanical breakdowns, and the operation was as extinct as the weapon from which it was named.

* * *

Ever since the French defection of June 1940, the War Cabinet had been exercised by the problem of Syria. So long as this territory continued to acknowledge Vichy, there could be no effective obstacle to enemy plans in the Middle East; for at any time the Germans could persuade or browbeat the French into allowing them the use of Syrian airfields. This permission granted, the *Luftwaffe* would be admirably placed to threaten Palestine, Cyprus, and our oil interests in Iraq and Persia, as well as to bring a far greater weight of attack to bear on the Suez Canal. On 6th May 1941, when the first German aircraft landed in Syria on their way to help Rashid Ali, this danger ceased to be potential and became actual.

Two days later the Foreign Office in London received a circumstantial report of German aircraft landing and refuelling at Damascus —a report which General Dentz, the French High Commissioner in Syria, did not deny. Up to 14th May, however, our reconnaissance failed to detect any signs of the enemy. That morning a Blenheim of No. 203 Squadron, one of the little detachment on the pipe-line at H.4, spotted a Ju.90 taking off from Palmyra. The pilot, Flying Officer A. Watson, asked if he might make a second trip. Shortly after midday he returned with an account of several German aircraft which he had seen refuelling. His appetite whetted, Watson then begged to be allowed to take the only available fighter-Blenheim and indulge in a little ground-strafing. He was referred by Group Captain Brown to Major-General Clarke, the Commander of 'Habforce', who sternly asked the eager warrior if he considered we should declare war on Syria. To the delight of the assembled staff, Watson replied that it would be 'a bloody good idea'. The suggestion was not taken amiss; permission was sought, and obtained, from higher authorities; and at 1615 Watson was told that he might 'commence his act of aggression'. Four other aircraft had by then arrived from Palestine to join in the good work. Before the afternoon was out, the first British bombs and shells had fallen on a Syrian airfield.

In the days that followed, many more raids were made on Syrian airfields, including Rayak and Damascus, and at the beginning of June our aircraft paid attention to a dump of aviation petrol at Beirut. Air operations alone, however, could not dispel the German danger. For that, nothing less than military occupation of the country would suffice. Tedder urged this policy from the start, and on 19th May the Chiefs of Staff ordered the Middle East commanders to prepare to move into Syria at short notice. The force for the purpose was to be as large as they could spare without prejudicing the success of operations in the Western Desert. But with Crete, Iraq, East Africa and Cyrenaica on his hands all at the same time, Wavell found it difficult to muster an expedition of the requisite strength; for it was essential to complete the task cleanly and quickly, and not lock up small but valuable forces in some protracted struggle. True, the six Free French battalions in the Middle East were impatient for action, and at first inclined to think they could manage the job by themselves; but revised estimates of Vichy strength in South Syria quickly induced a more sober frame of mind in General Catroux. And it was scarcely advisable militarily, if we hoped to enforce a rapid submission on the part of the Vichy forces, or politically, if we desired the co-operation of the local Arabs, that the expedition should wear too French a complexion.

On 25th May, against Wavell's inclinations, a force was at length detailed on the basis of the 7th Australian Division, the Free French, an Indian infantry brigade, and part of the 1st Cavalry Division. A cruiser squadron and two Fleet Air Arm squadrons provided the naval component. The Royal Air Force units, under L. O. Brown, now an Air Commodore and A. O. C. Palestine and Transjordan, at the outset consisted of two-and-a-half squadrons of fighters, two of bombers (including a squadron operating from Iraq), and a tactical reconnaissance flight.[1] Their total strength was about sixty aircraft, against which the Vichy Air Force could muster nearly a hundred.

The advance began on 8th June, the Australians moving from Palestine along the coast towards Beirut, the Free French and the Indians from Transjordan towards Damascus. Good initial progress was made, with the Royal Air Force quickly gaining the upper hand over the Vichy airmen. But after the Fleet Air Arm Fulmars, outclassed by the French Moranes and Dewoitines, had lost half their number in one day's work, Brown's fighters were heavily called on to protect our ships. This they did with great success, many times shooting down attacking aircraft; but the diversion naturally reduced the cover available for the troops. Fortunately the bombers and such fighters as could be spared were able to keep the enemy air force fairly well in check by steady pressure against the Vichy airfields.

A few miles south of their objectives both wings of the advance ran into stiff opposition. Encouraged by the weakness of our force, and animated by the desire not only to retain their jobs but also to vindicate before the world the military honour of France, the Vichy troops fought fiercely, and it was only by a great effort that the Free French and the Indians carried Damascus on 21st June. It then became possible, by using the local airfields, to give air support to 'Habforce', which in the interval from 14th May had marched from H.4 to Baghdad and back again across the desert to the outskirts of Palmyra. For a week this column continued to suffer the attentions of Vichy aircraft, but on 28th June six French Glen Martin bombers attacking

---

[1] No. 80 Squadron (Hurricanes), No. 3 Squadron (R.A.A.F.) (Tomahawks), and 'X' Flight (Gladiators); Nos. 11 and 84 Squadrons (Blenheims); and a flight of No. 208 Squadron (Hurricanes).

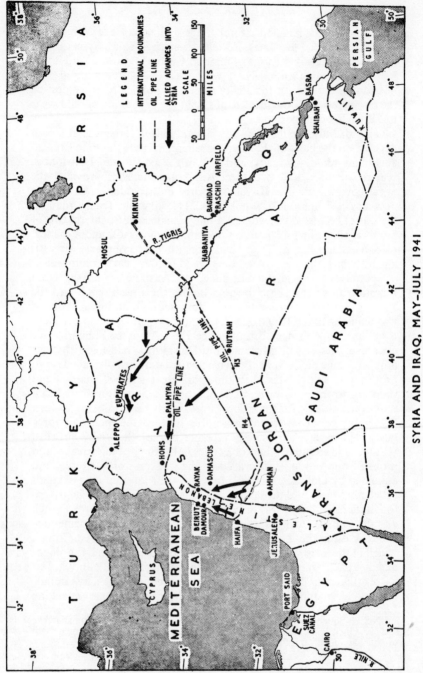

SYRIA AND IRAQ, MAY–JULY 1941

our troops were intercepted and shot down by No. 3 Squadron (R.A.A.F.) flying Tomahawks—American aircraft which after prolonged 'teething troubles' were now at last coming into useful service. After this episode, 'Habforce' was left comparatively unmolested.

The advance was now virtually at a halt. But at this point the abrupt failure of 'Battle-axe' enabled Wavell and Tedder to release further forces from Egypt, and in due course these helped to turn the scale. Meanwhile Brown's aircraft, augmented by Nos. 45 and 260 Squadrons, kept up a continuous attack on airfields, barracks and other military objectives, as well as guarding against the arrival of enemy reinforcements by sea. To this latter end they flew protective and reconnaissance patrols for the naval squadron, bombed the Syrian harbours (especially Beirut) with assistance from the Egypt-based Wellingtons, and attacked Vichy naval and merchant shipping. The troops, however, remained firmly stuck. Exasperated at this slow progress, on 29th June Tedder then ordered an attack on the Residency at Beirut. It was carried out with remarkable accuracy by four Blenheims of No. 11 Squadron, three direct hits being scored and two extremely near misses. The only flaws in an otherwise admirable piece of bombing were the limited damage caused to a substantial structure by the 250-pound bombs, and the unfortunate absence of General Dentz at the time.

During the nights that followed, bombs fell on the residential quarters of Beirut many times when the Royal Air Force was not operating. They were dropped by German aircraft from the Dodecanese—either because the pilots imagined they were over Haifa (which they attacked on several occasions during the campaign), or because they were under orders to stir up local feeling against us.

On 3rd July, 'Habforce' captured Palmyra, then headed swiftly west towards Homs and the coast. Six days later the Australians, supported by air and naval bombardment, at last broke through the main enemy positions at Damour, south of Beirut. At the same time a second force from Iraq, following the Euphrates, was pushing into the extreme north east of the country. Under the combined stress of these movements, the virtual obliteration of his air force, and the failure of his seaborne reinforcements to beat our sea and air blockade, General Dentz then accepted our terms. The 'cease-fire' took effect on 12th July; the formal armistice, after Vichy had bowed to the inevitable, on 14th July.

After the dust of the conflict had settled, General Jeannequin, the Vichy air commander, refought the campaign with his opponent. The Frenchman told Brown that the main factor in his defeat was he activity of our fighters against his airfields. This was certainly

A 2

true; for at a cost of only three fighters damaged on our own side, fifty-five French machines had been destroyed or irreparably damaged on the ground. Many others had sustained damage that was not vital only because our fighters had been woefully short of incendiary ammunition. In air combat ten of our fighters had been lost, some thirty casualties inflicted on the enemy. Moreover our attacks on the Vichy airfields had, said Jeannequin, forced him to base his aircraft far behind the French troops, so that by the end of the campaign what remained of the Vichy Air Force was operating from Aleppo, in the far north of the country. The fact that this airfield was within extreme range of our fighters once they were based at Damascus, in Jeannequin's opinion largely inspired Dentz's decision to capitulate.

*   *   *

On 22nd June, while the Free French were installing themselves in Damascus, the long-prepared German blow fell on Russia. Diplomatic opinion in Moscow, Sir Stafford Cripps had informed the War Cabinet six days earlier, estimated that the Russians might perhaps hold out for three or four weeks. The diplomats were as far from the mark as Hitler's generals; and as the months passed by, and the bloody tide of German victory spent itself against the unconquerable barriers of Russian resistance, it became apparent that a new, and stabilizing, factor had entered the situation in the Middle East. Though the *Luftwaffe* retained some freedom of movement, Hitler's main armies were from now on irrevocably committed to the Russian front. Whatever strength the Germans could bring to bear in Africa —and they had no intention of allowing Libya to pass into our hands by default—they could not, short of crushing Russia or at least breaking through the Caucasus, expose us to the sort of odds we had faced in Greece. And the Italians, whatever their numbers, we now knew would present little trouble.

The crisis which had begun in April 1941 was thus over. Cyrenaica, Greece and Crete had been lost; but Egypt and Iraq had been saved, and Syria and almost the whole of East Africa had passed into our hands. With the Middle East firmly denied to the enemy, the struggle for control of the Mediterranean could begin in earnest, and all available forces could be directed towards that single end. It was thus with the feeling that the way ahead, however hard, should not be impossible, that Tedder settled down to overhaul his repair organization; to digest the manifold lessons of 'Battle-axe'; to perfect his squadrons in the niceties of co-operation with the Army; to wage the long, unremitting battle for air superiority; and to conduct that offensive against the sea communications of the enemy on which all else was to turn.

CHAPTER XII

The Struggle at Sea

The First Battle of the Convoy Routes, the Anti-Shipping Offensive, and the Escape of the 'Scharnhorst' and 'Gneisenau'

'THE main target for the Navy during the Eastern campaign still remains Britain.' Admiral Raeder's 'Barbarossa' directive of 6th March 1941 removed any doubt that might have existed in the minds of his subordinates. Whatever fresh fields of conquest Hitler might discover for his army and air force, the task of the *Deutsche Kriegsmarine* remained obstinately the same.

It was not, then, for want of trying on the part of the enemy that the months following the fateful attack of 22nd June saw a great reduction in our shipping losses. In June, which from our point of view was a big improvement on May and April, the two Axis powers had still managed to sink over 400,000 tons of British, Allied and neutral merchant shipping. But in July they sank only 120,000 tons; and in August, though the total again slightly increased, the U-boats continued to show declining returns. For a few hopeful moments victory in the Battle of the Atlantic seemed almost within our grasp.

This new situation resulted from a combination of factors. Our naval and air action had destroyed, damaged or bottled up most of the German capital ships. Stronger surface forces were accompanying our convoys over longer distances. Evasive routeing was being practised with outstanding success. We had captured or killed the most skilful and experienced of the U-boat crews—including, by May, the last of the 'pre-war' captains. And by no means least, there was the effect of our strengthened and extended air patrols.

Up to March 1941 by far the greater part of our losses had occurred in the Western Approaches. In that month Nos. 107 and 114 Bomber Squadrons were lent to Coastal Command for work over the North Sea, and a strong Coastal force was concentrated in the north-west under No. 15 Group. The effect was almost instantaneous. In April the U-boats began withdrawing to mid-Atlantic. By June they were scoring nine-tenths of their successes beyond the limits of our air patrols. So profound a transformation was, of course, not merely a change of battleground. To reach their new operational areas the U-boats had to spend far longer on patrol, and when they got there they found no such wealth of targets as in the narrower waters nearer home.

This pattern of cause and effect was repeated off the West African coast. Losses suffered towards the end of 1940 led to the decision to form a Sunderland squadron (No. 95) to operate from Bathurst and Freetown. Various difficulties supervened, and it was not until 24th March 1941, that the first two flying-boats started work. By that time the Germans were fully alive to the possibilities of the area, and in May they sank in West African waters no less than thirty ships. Obviously our air patrols, as yet carried out by only five aircraft, were too thin. A reinforcement of six Hudsons—the future No. 200 Squadron—was accordingly sent out from home during June, and during September a further Sunderland Squadron (No. 204) followed. By October, when a West African Command was set up under Air Commodore E. A. B. Rice, the flying effort had increased fourfold in as many months. *Pari passu*, the shipping losses declined. In June the U-boats sank five vessels within six hundred miles of the shore; in July one; in August one; and in September none. Disgusted by this lack of success, to which the diversion of independently routed shipping and the destruction of German supply ships by the Navy also powerfully contributed, Dönitz soon acted as we had hoped. He withdrew his forces from West African waters.

Among the many incidents of this encouraging phase of the struggle, when losses in all waters were lower than at any time since May 1940, one stands supreme. On 27th August 1941, an aircraft captured a U-boat.

In the early morning of that day the crew of a Hudson of No. 269 Squadron, on patrol from Iceland, spotted the swirl which betokens a diving submarine. Visibility was poor, and an hour passed before close search yielded a glimpse of the vessel. The pilot at once seized his chance, but as he came in to attack the depth-charges hung up, and the enemy escaped. His wireless reports, however, had by then brought other aircraft towards the scene, and at 1050 hours—over four hours after the original sighting—a second Hudson of the same squadron, piloted by Squadron Leader J. H. Thompson, came up with the quarry. The U-boat, which was in the act of breaking surface, at once crash-dived, but not before the Hudson launched a salvo of depth-charges. These straddled it squarely as it disappeared beneath the waves. For a few seconds the crew of the aircraft saw only four great plumes of sea and spray; then, as the disturbance subsided, they descried on the surface, its nose slightly down, the *U.570*. Ten or twelve German sailors were on deck. Treated to a burst of the Hudson's guns they scrambled rapidly into the conning-tower, whence they cautiously waved a white article bearing a suspicious resemblance to a dress-shirt. Such, indeed, it proved to be—the captain's. Soon afterwards other members of the crew appeared on deck bearing a large white board. The Hudson reported these curious proceedings to base, then, in foul weather, circled her prize until relieved by a Catalina of No. 209 Squadron. 'Look after our sub., which has shown white flag,' signalled the Hudson. 'O.K.', replied the Catalina; and the watch continued. Shortly before midnight the first trawler came on the scene, but mountainous waves made a boarding-party impossible. Relays of aircraft accordingly kept vigil throughout the night, with the help of flares; and the following afternoon, when the seas had lessened and several more trawlers and a destroyer had arrived, the *U.570* was boarded and taken in tow. Interrogation revealed that she was on her maiden voyage, and that the depth-charges had extinguished her lights and started a small discharge of chlorine. This had demoralized some of the crew, who had insisted on instant surrender. The captain, also on his first operational trip, had lacked the experience or the character to deal with the situation.

The capture of this U-boat had far-reaching effects, for it enabled the Admiralty to study the details of her construction. It also represented not merely a loss to the enemy but a gain to ourselves. Some months later, when the curiosity of our technicians was sufficiently satisfied, the *U.570* was commissioned for service in the Royal Navy as H.M.S. *Graph*—under which name she was soon in action against one of her sister-vessels.

The satisfactory state of affairs of July and August 1941 was not quite maintained in September, when losses increased to 267,000 tons. But only three of the fifty-three ships torpedoed by U-boats were sunk within 350 miles of our air bases, and in the second week of the month convoys brought into British ports the largest volume of goods for any week since August 1939. Another encouraging feature was the success of our ship-borne aircraft. August had already seen the fighter-catapult ship drawing first blood against the Focke-Wulf Condor. Now, in September, came the auxiliary, or escort, carrier—a great improvement on the C.A.M. and F.C. ship in that it carried more aircraft and received them back on deck. Its *début* was triumphant. Five hundred miles south-west of Brest a Condor attacked one of our convoys. From the auxiliary carrier H.M.S. *Audacity*, a captured and converted enemy merchant vessel, a Martlet took off and engaged. The result was quick and decisive—one less Condor to prey upon our shipping.

The most important development of September 1941 was the increasingly generous interpretation of neutrality taken by the United States. Earlier in the year the Americans had decided that there was little point in sending aid across the Atlantic unless it reached its destination. Towards the end of April, American naval and air forces had accordingly begun to search for Axis vessels far out into the western half of the ocean. When they found them, they reported the matter to base in plain language signals, a procedure much appreciated by the Royal and the Royal Canadian Navies. The next step had followed in July, when American forces joined our own in Iceland. Now, at the beginning of September, the Americans announced their intention not merely of reporting but of destroying any Axis raider found approaching the convoy routes between North America and Iceland. Under this arrangement by the middle of the month the United States Navy was escorting convoys two-thirds of the way to Britain. 'In waters we deem necessary to our defence,' thundered President Roosevelt on 11th September, 'American naval forces and American planes will no longer wait until Axis submarines, lurking under the water, or Axis raiders, working on the surface, strike their deadly blow first. . . . Let this warning be clear. From now on, if German or Italian vessels of war enter waters the protection of which is necessary for American defence, they do so at their own peril. . . . ' Four days later Congress modified the Neutrality Act so that American vessels could carry war materials to our possessions in the Near East, the Far East and the Western Hemisphere.

All this was quite enough to make Admiral Dönitz complain to Hitler on 17th September of 'the great difficulties caused by the very strong Anglo-American escorts and the extensive enemy air patrols'. At the same time the German U-boat chief reported that he could achieve results equal to those of the previous year only if he had three or four times as many U-boats in service. In this he was certainly not exaggerating; for at that moment, with an average of some forty operational U-boats at sea, his forces were proving rather less successful than in the autumn of 1940 with an average of nine.[1]

All this was the more remarkable in that our Sunderlands, Whitleys, Hudsons and Catalinas were still only at the beginning of their powers. Formidable enough to inspire the enemy with a determination not to break surface in their presence, they were not formidable enough to destroy him when he did. By the end of September 1941, Coastal Command's 245 attacks on U-boats had resulted in only one sunk, one captured, three destroyed in conjunction with surface craft, and a dozen or so seriously damaged. Dönitz's forces had retired beyond the range of our aircraft, not because these had proved deadly in themselves, but because they were the eyes of the Navy. The use of depth-charges instead of bombs had not yet altered matters. Our aircraft could seek, find, report, strike and wound. They could not yet kill.

It was the firm intention of Sir Philip Joubert to remedy this defect. The new Coastal chief was determined not to rest until the aeroplane was thoroughly lethal to the submarine. In this resolve he was powerfully and ably supported by his staff, among whom special mention must be made of the Senior Naval Officer, Captain D. V. Peyton-Ward—an officer who was at Coastal Command Headquarters throughout the entire war, and who, an ex-submarine officer himself, fully vindicated the principle of 'set a thief to catch a thief'. The months that followed Joubert's accession were accordingly crammed with important tactical and technical developments. Not content with existing weapons, Joubert pressed for heavier types of anti-submarine bomb, bomb-sights for low attack, and depth-charge pistols which would detonate at less than fifty feet below the surface. To make the most of available experience, he ordered all reports of air attacks on U-boats since the beginning of the war to be analysed by the Coastal Command Operational Research Section, so that a standard attack-procedure could be devised. To render the attacker invisible for as long as possible, he encouraged tests with various forms of camouflage (already initiated by Sir Frederick

[1] The growth of the U-boat service may be seen from the following figures:

	Sept. 1939	June 1940	March 1941	Dec. 1941
Number operational .	42	26	30	86
Training force . .	11	18	43	58
New U-boats and working up in the Baltic . . .	4	8	34	92
Total U-boat fleet .	57	52	107	236

Bowhill), with the result that the sides and under-surfaces of all anti-U-boat aircraft were eventually painted white.[1] He also made every effort, in co-operation with the Telecommunications Research Establishment and the Radar Directorate at the Air Ministry, to secure improvements in the two existing marks of A.S.V., besides urging speed in the development of a 10 cm. equipment which promised to be greatly superior. To many other requisites for locating and attacking a submarine in darkness or poor visibility, such as a suitable illuminant and an accurate low-reading altimeter, he and his staff also gave the closest attention. All this activity was to reap its reward later.

Meanwhile the increased shipping losses of September 1941 had once more raised the question of the employment of our bombers. Should they, or should they not, be called upon to play a greater part in the war at sea? In June the Air Staff, with the approval of the War Cabinet, had at last freed Bomber Command from its defensive preoccupations, and had begun a systematic offensive against German transportation and morale. Obviously, a carefully planned strategy so recently undertaken would not be abandoned for any save the most compelling of reasons; and the Air Ministry could point out that even under the existing policy a quarter of our bombing effort was still being directed against German maritime targets. The Admiralty, however, naturally viewed matters from a different standpoint. On 21st October—a date already not without significance in naval history—they accordingly asked for heavier air attack against U-boat bases and construction yards.

This request might have been easier to meet had the naval authorities consented to forgo operations by our bombers against the German warships in Brest. They still expected, however, a harassing scale of attack on these objectives; and before the year was out their demands were to go much higher. Unable to satisfy all requirements, the Air Staff offered a compromise. While agreeing to pay more attention to the construction yards in Germany, since these could be fitted into the general framework of the current offensive, they refused to accept as a priority target the operational bases on the Biscay coast. With this the Admiralty was perforce content. The Air Ministry then issued a new directive to Bomber Command calling for attacks against the yards in Hamburg, Kiel, Bremen and Wilhelmshaven whenever the weather was such that the Commander-in-Chief

---

[1] The aircraft specified in the first order, issued on 19th August 1941, were the Coastal Command Wellingtons, Whitleys and Liberators. Only one Liberator squadron—No. 120—was then in existence; it commenced operations during the following month.

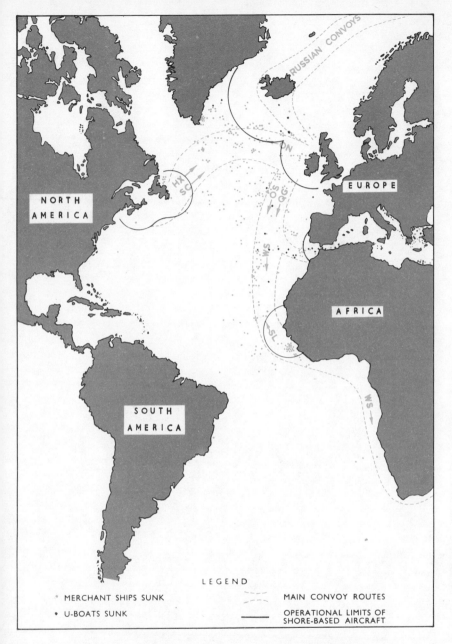

LEGEND

· MERCHANT SHIPS SUNK   - - - MAIN CONVOY ROUTES

• U-BOATS SUNK   —— OPERATIONAL LIMITS OF SHORE-BASED AIRCRAFT

THE BATTLE OF THE ATLANTIC (III), MID-MARCH–DECEMBER 1941

Note (i) In the latter part of April, sweeps and searches replaced close escort. In May 1941 these extended 350 miles from Iceland and N. Ireland.

(ii) Operations from W. African bases began on 24 March 1941.

(iii) Hudsons and Catalinas operated from Gibraltar up to 250 miles.

(iv) Russian convoys commenced August 1941.

[facing page 348]

decided to concentrate on north-west Germany. Only one operational base was mentioned in this document. If the weather was unsuitable over the *Reich*, Bomber Command was recommended to attack Lorient.

On the night of 23/24th November, Lorient was duly attacked by fifty-three Hampdens and Manchesters. No great damage resulted. Apart from an earlier raid on the same town by forty-seven Hampdens and Wellingtons on 4/5th July, this was the only serious attempt to bomb a U-boat base in the second half of 1941. Six or seven times this weight of attack was directed against Brest during December alone, but the targets there were the *Scharnhorst*, *Gneisenau* and *Prinz Eugen*, which lay at the opposite extremity of the port from the U-boats.

In the light of after events, it may well have been a mistake to send in the latter half of 1941 over a thousand sorties against the three German warships and little more than a hundred against the operational bases of the U-boats. Such, however, was the Admiralty's preference. Leaving aside our superiority over the Germans in major vessels, which was seriously impaired by the events of November and December 1941, the most remarkable feature of this choice was that in five of the bases—Lorient, Brest, St. Nazaire, Bordeaux and La Pallice—the Germans were known to be building bomb-proof submarine shelters. And as they had to start by digging down very deep behind caissons, we had an excellent chance of causing flooding and heavy damage by bomb-blast during the early stages of the work. Indeed, the shelters remained susceptible to attack up to the time when their concrete roofs, many feet thick, were in position. But in face of the generally declining losses at sea, the small bomber effort available, the Air Ministry's preoccupation with Germany, and the Admiralty's preoccupation with the *Scharnhorst* and *Gneisenau*, very little was done to hinder their construction. By the beginning of 1942 the chance had passed, for all shelters at Brest and Lorient, and most of those at St. Nazaire and La Pallice, were beyond the stage at which they were likely to be much affected by air attack. The full consequences of the omission were to become plain a year later, when the shipping losses reached a new peak. Our heavy bombers, as described in Volume II (Chapter XIII), were then at last directed in force against Lorient and St. Nazaire. From the cascade of fire and high explosive which descended on the two ports practically nothing emerged intact—except the U-boat pens.

In the closing months of 1941, however, bombardment of the Biscay bases did not appear essential. After the scare of September, the October shipping losses showed a decline to 218,000 tons; and the total for November—100,000 tons, of which only 62,000 tons were sunk by U-boats—was better still. Unfortunately these figures were less a reflection of our counter-measures than of autumn gales in the Atlantic and the development of events elsewhere.

Worried by the mounting success of our naval and air offensive against the Axis convoy routes to Libya, on 26th August Hitler had decided to send six U-boats into the Mediterranean. They reached their destinations in the closing days of September. By the end of the year several more had followed. Five were sunk *en route* and six so damaged that they abandoned the attempt, but eighteen got through. The effect of this move was certainly felt in the new zone of operations, where November saw the loss of the *Ark Royal* and the *Barham*. But it was equally apparent in the Atlantic, where the U-boats found November less profitable than any previous month of the year.

The enemy's increased interest in the Mediterranean made it essential to strengthen our air organization at Gibraltar. Thus far, No. 200 Group had controlled only one Royal Air Force squadron— No. 202, whose London flying-boats had operated from the harbour since the earliest days of the war. These obsolete aircraft had by now given place to Catalinas, but the squadron still retained a few Swordfish float-planes on loan from the Fleet Air Arm. Other Fleet Air Arm Swordfish, of the normal type from carriers, also operated under the Group, using a 'strip' which had been built across the old racecourse on North Front; and during the autumn, long-range A.S.V. had enabled one of these squadrons—No. 812—to perform fine work against U-boats attempting to enter the Straits. The general resources of the Group, however, were clearly inadequate for the new situation, and at the end of November a number of important changes were made. The Group was abolished and a new organization directly responsible to Coastal Command, and known as Royal Air Force Gibraltar, was formed under Air Commodore S. P. Simpson. At the same time, liaison between the Navy and Air Force was greatly improved by the setting-up of an Area Combined Headquarters, working on the lines of those in the United Kingdom. Equally important, ten Hudsons of No. 233 Squadron were sent out from home as a reinforcement.

The prospect before the pilots of this squadron was not enviable. In fast modern aircraft with more than a slight tendency to swing on take-off, they were required to operate from a strip only 950 yards long—a strip beset by winds of unpredictable behaviour and terminating abruptly at the water's edge. The job could certainly be done, for Wellingtons were already using the runway on reinforcement flights to the Middle East. The conditions, however, left no margin for error, and the accident rate for long continued high.

The Hudsons first task was to give a good start to the next homeward bound convoy. Several U-boats were known to be lying in wait, and the departure of the convoy was accordingly delayed until the strongest possible air and surface escort had been assembled. On 14th December, HG76 at length sailed—thirty-two merchant vessels under an escort which included the auxiliary carrier *Audacity*. At once the U-boats gained contact. Gibraltar's Swordfish, however, were also present, and three times during the night of the 14th and the early hours of the 15th they drove off the enemy. At 0815 on the 15th the Hudsons and Catalinas took over, helped by the *Audacity*'s Martlets. The repeated patrols of these aircraft, continued throughout that day and the next, forced the U-boats completely out of touch. Such good fortune could not last; during the 16th the inevitable Focke-Wulf appeared and put the hunters back on the scent. As night came on they drew up with their quarry. The morning of the 17th dawned, the convoy was beyond air range from Gibraltar, the U-boats had their chance. On the next four days no less than nine of them closed in. The escort, however, was fiercely effective and disposed of four of the attackers and two Condors. On our side the losses were two merchant-vessels, a destroyer, and the *Audacity*. So, with superb courage and seamanship, HG76 battled on; and at 1054 on 22nd December it was met, 750 miles out from our Ulster base of Nutts Corner, by a Liberator of No. 120 Squadron. This aircraft at once drove off a shadowing Focke-Wulf, then, two hours later, sighted and attacked a U-boat. At 1620 another Liberator took its place; within three hours it had forced three more U-boats to submerge. Reaching 'prudent limit of endurance', the aircraft then turned for home; but its appearance had been enough, and the enemy decided to break off the action. The next day the convoy came within range of continuous air support from our north-western bases. HG76 had won through, to illustrate what happened when air cover was, and was not, present.

Meantime the war at sea had entered a new climacteric. On 7th December the Japanese struck at Pearl Harbour and Singapore. With the *Prince of Wales*, the *Repulse* and the American Pacific Fleet alike victims of Japanese aircraft, the *Queen Elizabeth* and the *Valiant* damaged by Italian 'human torpedoes', and the merchant shipping losses soaring to 486,000 tons, December 1941 was indeed a black month. In the Atlantic, things still went well; but even there the picture was about to change. Having, for better or worse, declared war on the United States, Germany could now throw the last

restraints on U-boat warfare to the winds. Along the eastern sea-
board of North and Central America there plied an endless variety
of unprotected shipping; and as 1942 opened, six of Dönitz's largest
vessels, sent across to sample the fare, settled in to a rich repast.
The Battle of the Atlantic continued.

*   *   *

Besides playing an increasing part in the defensive struggle against
the U-boats, the Royal Air Force during 1941 developed an offensive
against the enemy's merchant shipping.

At the beginning of the war there was in force, on the British side,
a carefully drawn-up code of regulations governing attacks on
merchant vessels. Its safeguards were so comprehensive that if our
airmen stopped to observe them they were virtually certain to be shot
down. 'Legality' was the order of the day, Bomber and Coastal Commands were in any case heavily engaged against German naval units,
and the enemy's merchant shipping went its way unmolested from the
air.

This state of affairs altered when the Germans attacked Norway
and Denmark in April 1940. Enemy merchant ships were now accom-
plices in treacherous aggression against small and inoffensive
neutrals. Our respect for formalities accordingly declined. In certain
areas the full rigours of search etiquette were relaxed, and our pilots
warmed to the attack.

The process of emancipation from pre-war regulations was completed when the enemy overran France and the Low Countries. The
marine traffic of a nation in control of the whole European coastline
from the North Cape to the Spanish frontier was obviously a matter
of great importance: if allowed to flourish without interference, it
could take a heavy load off overburdened roads and railways. For
the moment, however, we were more concerned with the fact that
German-controlled vessels were about to be used in 'Operation
Sealion'. During the ensuing three months our attacks were accordingly concentrated on the barges and other shipping lying in the
crowded docks and harbours across the Channel. Vessels under way
offered fewer attractions as targets, and were rated lower in our scale
of priority.

By October 1940 conditions were ripening for a change. The
Government had relaxed its scruples to the extent of declaring 'sink
at sight' areas in the North Sea, the English Channel and the Bay of
Biscay; Coastal Command had at last acquired a small but efficient
striking force in the form of the Beauforts of No. 22 Squadron; the
German invasion-flotillas had been dispersed and the days of purely

defensive bombing were drawing to a close. Attacks against ships at sea grew more frequent.

The progress of events at the opening of 1941 added further point to this new offensive. As Hitler was obviously about to strike in the Balkans, the more aircraft we could force him to retain in north-west Europe the better. We were already flying 'Circuses'—offensive sweeps in daylight by escorted bombers against 'fringe' targets, designed to inflict casualties on the German fighter force. If to these we could add systematic attacks on coastal traffic, so forcing the enemy to provide strong and regular fighter escort for his convoys, the effect on developments in Greece might be considerable.

Unfortunately Coastal Command was at this time quite unable to mount a full-scale offensive of this kind in the most obviously profit-able area, the waters to the south and east of our island; for the much more important struggle against the U-boats demanded concentra-tion on the waters to the north and west. The main weight of effort against vessels sailing along the Dutch and Channel coasts was accordingly borne by the 'Circus' forces—the Blenheims of No. 2 Group, Bomber Command. From the middle of March these aircraft bombed 'fringe' targets only when they found no vessels to attack. Between the end of February and the middle of June, Bomber Command carried out twelve, and Coastal Command six, major attacks under fighter escort against previously detected shipping. Both Commands also delivered lesser attacks against ships reported beyond fighter range, and Coastal Command continued to fly a large number of individual search-and-strike missions.

April 24th, 1941, ushered in a fresh development. On that day a flight of Blenheim bombers of No. 101 Squadron was moved to Manston, in Fighter Command's No. 11 Group. Assured of im-mediate escort, the flight began a sustained attempt to close the Straits to all enemy ships during daylight; for the M.T.B.s at Dover could be relied upon to look after matters if the Germans had to make the passage by night. In this modest fashion, with half a dozen bombers, began the 'Channel Stop'—an operation which, with enlarged resources, soon became as good as its name.

By June 1941 the anti-shipping campaign was gathering momen-tum. Single aircraft of Coastal Command, equipped to take full advantage of suitable occasions for attack, were carrying out regular offensive reconnaissance along the enemy coastline from Stadlandet to Lorient. Unarmed Spitfires were periodically securing photographs of all the main ports. Beauforts and Hudsons, in free-lance patrols at irregular intervals, were scouring the Channel and North Sea. And whenever the opportunity arose, the Blenheims of No. 2 Group, escorted within range by Fighter Command, were attacking targets at sea rather than on shore.

The fruits of this activity were soon visible. The enemy convoys began to sail under the protection of stronger surface escorts, special '*flak*-ships' and regular fighter cover. At the same time the Germans began to devote to ship-building resources already earmarked for other purposes. Unfortunately there was also another side to the picture. To score hits our aircraft had to come right down and bomb from mast-height, or little over; and the armament of merchant-ships and escort alike was becoming truly formidable. Between 1st April and 30th June 1941 the Blenheims of No. 2 Group flew over a thousand sorties against merchant-shipping at sea; 297 managed to attack, and 36 were lost. During the same period, 143 aircraft of Coastal Command delivered attacks at a cost of 52 machines. Out of every five aircraft which attacked, one failed to return. As a healthy occupation for aircrew in mid-1941, bombing German ships by day had much less to commend it than bombing German towns by night.

Hitler's invasion of Russia was another landmark in the development of these operations. A few days before the German attack the Chiefs of Bomber, Fighter and Coastal Commands were ordered to report on the best way of forcing the enemy to maintain a strong air force in the West. They recommended that the Blenheims of Bomber Command, in co-operation with Fighter Command, should operate in strength against the Béthune-Lens industrial area and that Coastal Command should attack all enemy shipping reported during daylight in the Channel. When combined with Bomber Command's night raids against communications in the Ruhr such operations would, it was thought, seriously affect the enemy's transport system. The primary object, however, was to make the Germans hold back their fighters from the forthcoming advance into Russia.

These proposals were accepted, and on 27th June Coastal Command's No. 16 Group, employing Nos. 22 (Beaufort) and 59 (Blenheim) Squadrons, began intensive operations against Channel shipping. But the arrangement was scarcely in force when it was succeeded by another. A disagreement between Joubert and Peirse about responsibility for bombing led to a clearer definition of spheres of interest. On 15th July it was agreed that Bomber Command should be primarily responsible for anti-shipping operations over the sea area between Cherbourg and Texel—an eastern limit shortly altered to Wilhelmshaven—and Coastal Command over the rest of the seas round the British Isles. If a target required greater resources than were available in the Command primarily responsible, the other Command would do its best to supply reinforcements. These would be operated by the Command borrowing them. At the same time, to increase the effectiveness of the 'Channel Stop', two squadrons of No. 2 Group were to be stationed permanently near the South-East Coast. These were to be a 'fire brigade', always available for sudden calls—though to create rather than extinguish fires. Fighter Command would help by supplying escort and shooting up the decks before the bombers went in.

This new arrangement came into effect on 18th July. In the months that followed, up to the end of 1941, Coastal Command's No. 18 Group attacked 160 vessels in the northern half of the North Sea. Many of these were undoubtedly carrying Norwegian and Swedish iron ore, a traffic of outstanding importance to the German war economy. Fifteen vessels (34,702 tons) were assessed at the time as sunk, besides many others damaged, and the sinking of sixteen (16,024 tons) has since been verified. The cost was 33 aircraft. During the same period No. 2 Group, Coastal Command's No. 16 Group and Fighter Command, operating between Wilhelmshaven and Cherbourg, found 499 ships to attack. Their sinkings were assessed at forty-two ships (89,429 tons), of which twenty-three (22,993 tons) have since been confirmed. Fifty-five bombers, twenty-three coastal aircraft and four fighters were lost in the course of this work. West of Cherbourg and in the Bay, Coastal Command's No. 19 Group attacked 36 ships at a cost of eight aircraft, and Bomber Command three ships without loss. Between them they sank, according to the contemporary estimate, two vessels. The loss of two vessels in this area has since been confirmed—though one of them did not figure in the claim! All told, 698 merchant ships were thus attacked by the three Commands between 1st July and 31st December 1941. Fifty-nine were thought to have been sunk; at least forty-one are now positively known to have been sunk; and the total cost on our side was 123 aircraft.

This achievement was regarded with different degrees of enthusiasm in different places. The Admiralty throughout expressed a firm belief in the value of the offensive; but the Air Ministry, increasingly disturbed by the cost in aircraft, was less convinced. Its doubts were fully echoed at Bomber Command. Almost from the start Peirse pressed for some of the new Hurricane fighter-bombers, but Portal ruled that these should be operated by Fighter Command. On 9th October, when the first squadron—No. 607—was ready for action, it took over the 'Channel Stop' and to that extent released Peirse from what was by then rapidly becoming a distasteful task. By November the Bomber chief, who a few months earlier had asserted that anti-shipping operations would be 'an economical and profitable

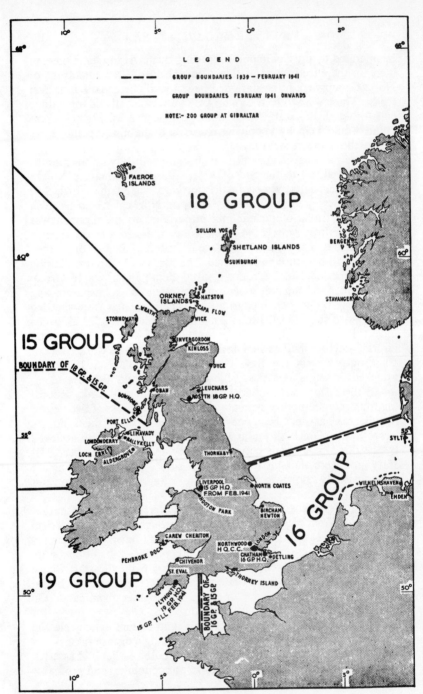

COASTAL COMMAND GROUP BOUNDARIES

role for the light bomber force', had reached the point of asking to be relieved entirely of the work. The Blenheim, he was now convinced, was an unsuitable aircraft for the job—an opinion which reflected, somewhat belatedly, the views of the Blenheim crews. Fortunately his request coincided with an increased requirement for Blenheims in the Middle East, and on 25th November he was freed from responsibility for all except occasional attacks on shipping. Thenceforth primary responsibility over the Wilhelmshaven–Cherbourg area, as over the other sea areas round the British Isles, rested with Coastal Command. Fighter Command, however, continued to operate the 'Channel Stop' in the limited area Manston–Ostend–Dieppe–Beachy Head.

But if the offensive was regarded with growing disillusion in Whitehall and at High Wycombe, it was viewed in another light across the North Sea. On 13th November Raeder made one of his periodic reports to Hitler. 'The decided enemy air superiority in the Western Area', stated the Admiral, 'has made the sea transport situation and the mounting threat to our defence forces more acute. In addition to attacks by aircraft and motor-boats, the enemy is laying mines on a larger scale . . . Utmost demands are made on the *matériel* and personnel of our inadequate escort forces; the physical and nervous strain on the men is very great. By using all available forces it has so far been possible to escort convoys and keep the routes open despite most difficult conditions . . . Losses [in October] include two steamers and one dredger sunk, and sixteen minesweepers, motor minesweepers and patrol boats damaged, some severely. We cannot afford such losses . . . The only way to rectify the position at sea is to reinforce the fighter units, an urgently needed step. According to information from the Air Force, this is not possible for the time being . . . '

Already, then, whatever their cost, our attacks were forcing the Germans into a dilemma—a dilemma in which they must choose between the safety of their ships and the safety of their armies.

* * *

During the late summer of 1941 the *Führer*'s celebrated intuition led him into the belief that the British intended to invade Norway. A venture which would at once deprive Germany of Scandinavian iron-ore and at the same time safeguard the passage of Anglo-American supplies to Russia must inevitably, Hitler thought, appeal to an enemy who knew his business.

On 17th September, when Admiral Raeder was explaining how he proposed to employ his battleships in the Atlantic, the German

B2

dictator therefore suggested a contrary plan. The major units should instead be stationed along the Norwegian coast, where, apart from defending Norway, they would be much safer from air attack than at Brest. The idea made little appeal to Raeder, who was a reasonably sound strategist, and for the moment he was able to maintain his own viewpoint.

Opposition to the *Führer's* opinions was not, however, a characteristic of those who retained high command in the German armed forces. During the next few weeks the long-suffering Admiral accepted Hitler's suggestion that the *Tirpitz*, when ready, should move from Germany to Trondheim; and on 13th November he found himself discussing the possibility of operating the *Scharnhorst*, *Gneisenau* and *Prinz Eugen* from German or Norwegian waters instead of the French Atlantic coast. Again he succeeded in avoiding a decision, but when he admitted that it might be possible to bring the *Prinz Eugen* home through the Channel, Hitler at once asked if the *Scharnhorst* and *Gneisenau* could not be withdrawn by the same route. Raeder replied that such an operation did not appear feasible, but that he would give it further study. Meantime, had he the *Führer's* permission to send the *Scheer* into the Atlantic or the Indian Ocean? He had not. Emphasizing that the 'vital point' was now the Norwegian Sea, Hitler answered that the *Scheer* would be better employed at Trondheim or Narvik.

On 27th December, British forces carried out a 'combined operation' against Vaagsö, an island off the Norwegian coast mid-way between Trondheim and Bergen. At the same time a diversionary raid was made on the Lofotens. Hampdens bombed the Vaagsö defences to cover the approach of the assaulting force, Blenheims attacked the airfield of Herdla some eighty miles to the south, and Blenheims and Beaufighters from Wick and Sumburgh supplied fighter protection. Ten British aircraft were lost and one damaged, as against one destroyed and four damaged of the enemy, but our air action fully achieved its objects, and the operation proved a success. Among other activity, the raiders destroyed industrial plants and defence points, captured German troops and local 'quislings', and embarked Norwegian volunteers for the Allied forces.

This profitable little foray strengthened Hitler's belief in a forthcoming invasion. On 29th December he again held a conference with his naval chiefs. According to the official record, Raeder first gave a preliminary report of the raid, then turned to the question of the *Scharnhorst* and *Gneisenau*. To bring the two battle-cruisers back through the Channel, asserted the German Commander, was 'impossible according to information to date . . . The risk is tremendous . . . It is impossible to safeguard the route sufficiently . . . It is impossible to evade air attacks in the narrow channels swept clear of mines.' But 'impossible' was not a word which the *Führer* cared to hear applied to his own projects. 'If the British go about things properly,' he declared, 'they will attack northern Norway at several points. By means of an all-out attack with their fleet and landing troops, they will try to displace us there, take Narvik if possible, and thus exert pressure on Sweden and Finland. This might be of decisive importance for the outcome of the war. The German fleet must therefore use all its forces for the defence of Norway. It would be expedient to transfer all battleships and pocket-battleships there for this purpose . . . The return of the Brest ships is therefore most desirable.'

Hitler then went on to explain how this could be done. So far from the crews of the three vessels undertaking a programme of practical training, as the Naval Staff maintained was essential, they should put out from Brest without any previous movement, and so take their opponents completely by surprise. In view of the extreme efficiency of the British intelligence services, any preliminary exercise 'would lead to intensified torpedo and bomb attacks, which would sooner or later damage the ships'. The vessels must sail during a spell of bad weather, when the Royal Air Force would be out of action, even if the navigational difficulties of the German crews were thereby increased. And as the main British fleet, including aircraft-carriers, would bar the passage by way of the Iceland Straits, withdrawal could only be made through the Channel. If such a course was impossible, the ships should be decommissioned and the guns and crews sent to Norway. In any case battleships would have no place in future warfare.

These views moved the German Chief of Naval Staff, Vice-Admiral Fricke, to ardent protest. All his arguments, however, were brushed aside. The best that he could do, after hearing Hitler emphasize 'again and again' the importance of defending Norway, was to secure permission to go into the whole question once more.

The fruits of the new investigation were presented to Hitler on 12th January 1942. While confessing that he could not 'take the initiative in advocating such a breakthrough operation,' Raeder stated that he had given orders for the necessary plans to be prepared, and asked the *Führer* for his final decision. Hitler, according to the official records of the conference, at once expressed himself in positive terms—'The naval force at Brest has, above all, the welcome effect of tying up enemy forces and diverting them from making attacks on the German homeland. This advantage will last exactly as long as the enemy considers himself compelled to attack because the ships are undamaged. . . . If he—the *Führer*—could see any chance that the ships might remain undamaged for four or five months and thereafter be employed in operations in the Atlantic . . . he might be more inclined to consider leaving them in Brest. Since, in the opinion of the *Führer*, such a development is not to be expected, he is determined to withdraw the ships from Brest, to avoid exposing them to chance hits day after day.' Moreover, Hitler asserted, northern Norway now appeared likely to be the scene of a large-scale Russian offensive. The entire German Fleet, virtually speaking, was required along the Norwegian coast for purposes of defence.

Having heard the *Führer* deliver himself of what the naval secretary judiciously termed 'these fundamental observations', the Commander of Battleships, Vice-Admiral Ciliax, then outlined the possible plan of operations. There must be a minimum of movement before the break-out. The vessels must leave Brest at night, to achieve surprise, and pass through the Straits of Dover in daylight. This would make the best use of the strong fighter cover that must be provided. The Channel offered the only hope; the northern route was out of the question in view of the imperfect training of the German crews, the lack of air cover, and the disposition of the British Home Fleet.

With all this Hitler found himself in cordial agreement; and after the representatives of the *Luftwaffe* had expressed misgivings, and refused to guarantee immunity for the ships with the available force of 250 fighters, the *Führer* gave his formal decision. The scheme suggested appeared satisfactory. In the light of past experience, the British did not seem capable of making and carrying out lightning decisions, and would probably fail to concentrate their bomber and fighter forces in south-eastern England in the brief time available to them. The Brest group was like 'a patient having cancer, who is doomed unless he submits to an operation. An operation . . . even though it may have to be a drastic one, will offer at least some hope that the patient's life may yet be saved. The passage of our ships through the Channel would be such an operation.' The plan must go forward.

Meanwhile, what of the vessels which were to run the gauntlet of British sea and air power?

Raids by Bomber and Coastal Commands in April 1941, had, it will be remembered, put the *Gneisenau* out of action for several months. The *Scharnhorst* had suffered no direct damage at that time, but the destruction of dockyard facilities had delayed her refit. The third member of the trio, the *Prinz Eugen*, had put into Brest after parting company with the *Bismarck*, and had been spotted there on 4th June by a photographic reconnaissance Spitfire. Various attacks had followed until on the night of 1st/2nd July a bomb found its mark on the cruiser, pierced the fore armoured deck, destroyed the switch room compartment, compass room and transmitting station, and killed fifty-one of the crew. The *Prinz Eugen*, like the *Gneisenau*, was 'out' for some time to come.

Later in the month the *Scharnhorst*, which had thus far escaped all harm, completed her refit. Two hours before midnight on 21st July she sailed south for La Pallice, where her captain hoped to carry out sea trials without undue attention from our aircraft. Her absence from Brest was detected by a Spitfire the following day, and in the early morning of 23rd July another Spitfire picked her up at La Pallice. Bomber and Coastal Commands then attacked at dusk, and again during the night, but without success. It was therefore decided, in spite of the grave hazards attending such a course, to attempt a daylight raid, and on 24th July fifteen of Bomber Command's new Halifaxes took off for La Pallice under fighter escort. At the cost of five bombers they scored five direct hits, forcing the *Scharnhorst* to put back for Brest with 3,000 tons of flood water in her. In foggy weather the vessel was detected and attacked on the way by a Coastal Command Beaufort, but she succeeded in shooting down her assailant. All three ships were now immobilized; and repairs, so the Germans estimated, could not possibly be completed before the end of the year. Unfortunately we were not aware of the full extent of the damage we had inflicted, and in the following months put a good deal of unnecessary work into guarding against an escape.

Apart from two big attacks in September, our raids on the three ships during the late summer and autumn of 1941 were frequent rather than heavy. But in early December, although photographs showed all three vessels still in dry dock, a greater weight of attack was deemed imperative. Japan's entry into the war and our consequent losses in the Pacific, coupled with our previous heavy losses in the Mediterranean, had greatly reduced our superiority over the Germans in capital ships; and at the same time repairs to the three vessels in Brest were reported to be nearly complete. From 11th December our raids on the port, and minelaying outside it, became a nightly routine. On 16th December reconnaissance revealed that the *Prinz Eugen* had left dry dock, and a heavy attack—by 101 aircraft—was promptly delivered the following night. It was followed on 18th December by a daylight raid, forty-one Manchesters, Halifaxes and Stirlings attacking under fighter escort. The second of these operations cost six of our precious 'heavies', but damaged the plating of the *Gneisenau* and so thoroughly wrecked the lock-gates containing the *Scharnhorst* that the vessel was unable to move into the harbour for a month. Frequent and heavy raids continued, including another daylight attack by Halifaxes, and on the evening of 6th January 1942 the *Gneisenau* was again slightly damaged.

All this of course was achieved only by the most sustained gallantry on the part of our crews. To press home an attack on a well-camouflaged warship protected by fighters, balloons and one of the heaviest concentrations of anti-aircraft guns in Europe, and to know that as it was in dry dock not even the best-aimed bombs could sink it, demanded the very highest qualities of morale. But the demand, as in every other task set to the crews of the Royal Air Force, was met to the full. Something of what these young men were called upon to face may be glimpsed from an account by Sergeant J. S. Boucher, a navigator of No. 144 Squadron. The squadron, still armed with Hampdens, was required to find three crews for a daylight raid under cloud cover: 'Three crews', writes Boucher, 'were "drawn out of the hat", and you can imagine our annoyance on being awakened by an orderly at 1.30 a.m. on Christmas Eve to be told that we were to report to the Briefing Room at 2.30 a.m.—especially after a "stand down" evening at such a festive time of the year. Our annoyance was only exceeded by our surprise when the C.O., Group Captain "Gus" Walker, explained the hazardous mission which we were to undertake in a few hours' time. The general opinion amongst the crews was that this was not a job for an obsolescent aircraft like the Hampden with its cruising speed of 140 m.p.h. and its very poor defensive armament. We kept these opinions to ourselves, however . . . '

In this frame of mind the crews climbed into their aircraft. Boucher's machine, piloted by Sergeant P. A. C. McDermott, took off soon after 0600 and made its way to a point west of Ushant:

Cloud was 10/10ths with base at 1,000 feet, and everyone felt relatively safe during this part of the journey. When it was time to turn eastwards for the target the pilot broke cloud at about 900 feet and we could see Ushant right in front of us. Neither of us had had much experience of operating in daylight, and having experienced the fierceness of this target at 12,000 feet at night we both felt a little apprehensive, to say the least—but we did not share our thoughts openly.

The pilot climbed into cloud again and headed south-east. A few minutes later he turned north-east and broke cloud again. The enemy coast was very close and we nipped into cloud again. These zig-zag tactics were continued and accompanied by violent 'jinking' as soon as the coast was crossed. Everyone was strangely silent—apart from my curt navigational directions—until the rear gunner, who was experiencing his first operational flight, asked what the 'tapping noise' was. The wireless-operator told him that it was only 'light flak' bursting as it hit the wings and the fuselage . . . We broke cloud again for a few seconds, just long enough to enable me to give McDermott a course which would bring us over the docks. The *flak* grew more and more intense, and although flying in cloud the aircraft was repeatedly hit. We could see the criss-cross of red tracer shells through the cloud haze a few yards in front of us. It seemed that all the anti-aircraft defences of the docks—as well as those of the battle cruisers—were directed against this one aircraft; and this was most probably the case.

The Hampden broke cloud again at 900 feet above sea-level and I picked out the target about half-a-mile ahead. To make a proper run up under such conditions would have been impossible if one was to survive to complete the task. I leaned over my bomb-sight and pressed the 'tit'. For a few fleeting moments I could see the German gunners frantically firing at us. They seemed so close that I felt myself to be before a firing squad. The pilot opened the throttle and we roared up into cloud again at 180 m.p.h., too soon even to see our bombs burst. The sudden upward movement threw me back into my seat, and a second later there was a yellow flash as a shell exploded, shattering the perspex nose of my cabin and driving me backwards under the floor of the pilot's cockpit. Stunned for a moment, I tried to open my eyes, but the pain was too great. I felt the wet blood on my face. The cold blast of air now passing through the gaping hole in the nose had blown all my maps and my log through the pilot's cockpit window. I crawled back through the fuselage to where the wireless-operator was sitting, and plugged in his 'inter-comm' gear. We were relatively safe now that we were in cloud again and leaving the coast behind us. A rough mental calculation enabled me to give the pilot a course for the Lizard . . .

Damage, wounds and lack of maps did not prevent the crew bringing their aircraft back to England. Of the other two machines, one lost half its tail plane to a balloon cable over Brest, but still struggled home; the other failed to return.

After 6th January our aircraft scored no further successes against the German vessels. On 25th January all three ships were photographed in the harbour. Two of them went back into dry dock during the next few days, but only for short periods. During the closing days of the month our reconnaissance observed the presence of several German torpedo-boats and minesweepers, and in early February these were joined by destroyers. The arrival of so many escorting vessels, the improved condition of the capital ships, and the fact that the *Tirpitz* had now sailed to Trondheim, together convinced the Admiralty that a break-out was imminent.

A British plan known as Operation 'Fuller' had long been in existence to deal with a move by the German vessels. On 2nd February the Admiralty issued an appreciation pointing to an early attempt. It correctly anticipated that the enemy would take the short cut through the Channel, but considered that the ships would sail during daylight (or sail by night and lie up near Cherbourg during the following day), so that they could pass through the Straits of Dover by night. This, of course, was the very reverse of the German plan. The following day the signal 'Executive Fuller' was passed to the home Commands, and the stand-by arrangements and extra patrols arranged under the operational plan were at once brought into force. No large British ships were available to challenge the enemy in the Channel, but our submarine patrols off Brest were strengthened, and the light forces at Dover and in the Thames estuary were brought to a high degree of readiness. On the air side, a whole train of action was initiated. Coastal Command flew extra patrols off the Brittany coast and between Le Havre and Boulogne; our small forces of torpedo-bombers stood ready at St. Eval, Thorney Island and Manston, while another little group at Leuchars awaited the sailing of the *Tirpitz*; and all available aircraft in Bomber Command were bombed up and brought to two hours' notice. Arrangements were also made for fighter cover over the Channel, and for mine-laying in the path of the enemy vessels if they succeeded in passing beyond the range of our light naval forces.

From 4th to 7th February bad weather prevented effective reconnaissance of Brest, but on the 8th the vessels were seen to be still in the port; indeed the *Gneisenau* was back in dry dock. That evening Joubert issued an appreciation from Coastal Command indicating that a break-out was particularly likely between 10th and 15th February. On the 9th, the *Gneisenau* was seen to have returned to the harbour; but on the 10th reconnaissance again proved impossible. Meanwhile, as day succeeded day, the strain on Bomber and Coastal Commands grew ever more intense. With only two squadrons of Hudsons to maintain the night watch off Brest and in the Channel, Joubert found it increasingly difficult to fulfil his task in the face of enemy fighters, bad weather, and repeated failures of A.S.V. equipment; while Peirse could obviously not keep his whole force indefinitely at two hours' notice, able neither to train, nor to strike against other objectives, nor even to secure proper rest. On 10th February the Bomber chief accordingly put a hundred of his aircraft at four hours' readiness, and ordered the rest to stand down.

At 1615 on 11th February a Spitfire of No. 1 Photographic Reconnaissance Unit covered Brest completely for the first time since the 9th. The three major units were all in the main harbour. Six destroyers, together with a large number of minesweepers and torpedo-boats, were also present. The torpedo booms protecting the big ships were still in position, and though the flotilla could obviously depart at short notice there was no definite indication that it

THE U-BOAT WHICH SURRENDERED TO AN AIRCRAFT
This photograph, taken on the following day, shows a naval officer and rating
in a Carley float approaching the U-boat

SHIPPING 'STRIKE'

would do so that night. All the same, sixteen Wellingtons were at once sent off to attack the waiting vessels. They did no damage, but they laid Brest under air-raid warning from 1935 to 2114. The result was that Vice-Admiral Ciliax, who had intended to sail with his whole force that evening at 1930, put to sea some hours late.

The German commander had prepared his plans with supreme care. He had mapped out a course which would take advantage of deep water, yet avoid, as far as possible, detection by our low-scanning radar. He had ordered channels to be swept and marked in our minefields. He had selected a time of departure—four nights before the new moon—which would give him a flood-tide up the Channel and a long initial stretch of darkness. He had arranged for fighter protection throughout the whole of the following day, including a continuous 'umbrella' of sixteen aircraft between 0630 and 1700. He had asked for diversionary raids against our ports and airfields in southern England and 'jamming' against our radar stations in the Straits. He had omitted nothing to give the operation every chance of success. And though he had been prevented from weighing anchor at his appointed hour, he had duly sailed on the night of 11th February without his opponents being aware of the fact.

The German convoy formed up outside Brest and headed out to sea at 2245. At that moment a Coastal Command Hudson of No. 224 Squadron was on patrol 'Stopper'—a routine patrol of over seven months' standing, backed up by others to the south, west and north, and designed to cover the exits from Brest during the hours of darkness. The night was intensely black—so black that the crew of the Hudson could barely see the wing tips of their aircraft—and there was no chance of detecting the enemy by the human eye. But the Hudson was of course fitted with A.S.V.; and at the normal height of the patrol—1,500 to 2,000 feet—this should have been capable of picking up a large ship some thirteen miles away. As it happened, the aircraft was travelling away from the German vessels, towards the south-west extremity of its patrol, when they began to shape towards Ushant; and it was only during the last eight minutes of the next sortie, as the succeeding Hudson approached the northward limit of the patrol, that one of our aircraft came within A.S.V. range of the enemy. This we now know from examination of the recorded tracks of the German ships and the Hudson. It was completely unknown at the time, for the A.S.V. operator in the Hudson saw no 'blip' on his screen which could have been interpreted as anything larger than another aircraft. The apparatus was apparently working well, and it thus remains uncertain why the ships were not picked up during this vital eight minutes.[1]

The German vessels had eluded Coastal Command's main watch. But another patrol—'Line South East', a special measure applied under 'Fuller', now lay across their path. Running from north-west of Ushant towards Jersey, this was intended to detect any vessel turning from Brest into the Channel. At about 0050 on 12th February the German convoy actually crossed the line of this patrol. But at that moment the patrol was not being flown. The A.S.V. having failed, the Hudson had been ordered back to base. And Joubert had sent out no relief—partly because he was short of aircraft, partly because 'Stopper' had reported nothing. For if the ships had sailed before 'Stopper' was established they would by this time be past 'Line South East', and would be picked up by the next patrol farther east.

The second of Coastal Command's night patrols athwart the enemy's route, like the first, had failed. But there remained the third and last—patrol 'Habo', from a point near Cherbourg to a point near Boulogne. This, like 'Stopper', had become a routine measure, and it was flown as usual during the early hours of 12th February. Unfortunately a forecast of dawn fog over our southern airfields caused the aircraft to be recalled at 0630, a little before schedule. At that time the enemy were still well to the westward. Had the aircraft been able to continue the patrol until first light, as normally, it might conceivably have picked up the German vessels. As it was, they sailed past undetected.

So Coastal Command's treble line of defence was pierced, and the enemy had succeeded in his first object of escaping discovery during the night. But he was also likely to avoid being spotted for several hours during the day: for we had arranged no other patrols in the Channel except the routine Fighter Command reconnaissance known as 'Jim Crow', and this went no farther west than the mouth of the Somme. By 1000 the vessels were steaming, still unobserved, past this point. From 0830 onwards, however, our radar stations had begun to

---

[1] The plots indicate that the aircraft was within nine miles of the German ships, i.e. near the limit of A.S.V. range. But the plots might well have been inaccurate, and the actual distances apart somewhat greater. In any case, A.S.V. at the time was not reckoned by crews to be more than fifty per cent reliable.

The 'Stopper' patrol was normally flown by four aircraft consecutively during the night. On this occasion the A.S.V. of the previous (the first) aircraft had broken down, and the patrol was not effectively established until 2238 (instead of 1930). It was naturally assumed during the subsequent British investigations that the vessels had emerged towards the end of this gap in the patrol. In fact, as recorded above, the patrol had been successfully established by the time the ships sailed.

register plots of the German fighter 'umbrella'. These were at first interpreted by No. 11 Group and Fighter Command as air/sea rescue operations; and it was not until 1020, when it became clear that the aircraft were flying in a particular orbit which moved up Channel at a speed of 20–25 knots, that two Spitfires were sent up from Hawkinge to investigate. By then visibility was rapidly declining; and though the two pilots observed a large number of sloops, destroyers and E-boats off Le Touquet, steering north-east, they failed to notice the *Scharnhorst, Gneisenau* or *Prinz Eugen*.[1]

By that time our radar was plotting two ships near Le Touquet. Only vessels of great size could be picked up at such a range. Added to the fact that some of the Kent stations had now been jammed intermittently for the last hour or so, this caused No. 11 Group to send off another reconnaissance. Before the pilot could return, the ships' long immunity from detection had at last ended.

At 1010 Group Captain Victor Beamish, the Station Commander at Kenley, and Wing Commander R. F. Boyd, the 'Wing Leader' of the three Kenley squadrons, had taken off for the French coast. The weather was too bad, in Beamish's opinion, for the younger members of the squadron to operate; and to enliven what appeared to them to be 'one of the quiet days of the war', the two pilots had sought permission to carry out a cross-Channel sweep, 'with the idea of picking up a stray Hun'. Their wish was speedily gratified, for as soon as they came within sight of the enemy coast they encountered a pair of Me.109's. Giving chase, the British airmen within a few moments found themselves over a powerful contingent of the German Fleet— two large warships, as it seemed to them, with an inner screen of destroyers and an outer screen of E-boats. At the same time they were hotly attacked from above by a dozen German fighters. Unable to pull up on to the tails of the enemy, the British pilots dived down through the *flak* from the ships—into which the Me.109's did not attempt to follow—poured their cannon-shells into an E-boat, and made a rapid escape at sea-level. Though neither Beamish nor Boyd knew that a move by the *Scharnhorst* and *Gneisenau* was considered imminent, the import of their discovery did not escape them. They headed back to Kenley at full speed, and at once reported what they had seen. They landed at 1110. By 1125 all naval and air authorities were aware that the enemy battle-cruisers, under strong air and surface escort, were entering the Straits of Dover.

The hunt was now on. But the vessels had already traversed the

---

[1] After the first hasty interrogation, however, the junior pilot stated that one of the vessels seemed to have tripod masts and a high superstructure. This was still being discussed when the positive sighting report was received.

whole length of the Channel; and visibility, poor in the morning, was rapidly becoming worse. Could we bring our strike forces to bear before the lowering clouds and swirling mists of the North Sea, combined with the oncoming gloom of the February afternoon, made our task impossible? During the next two hours our shore-based radar might continue to track the passage of the ships. After that all would depend on the weather, and on the A.S.V., the skill and the good fortune of our shadowing aircrews.

The strike forces scheduled for Operation 'Fuller' included, it will be remembered, a hundred aircraft of Bomber Command. None of these was in the south-east of the country; and all were at four hours' notice. Another 150 aircraft of Bomber Command could also be made available, but with no less delay. With the greatest possible despatch, none of the bomber squadrons could attack before 1500. Nor, though the Air Ministry had at once urged all Commands to exploit to the utmost 'this unique opportunity', could there be any great confidence that the bombers would secure decisive results. Lacking specialized training in work against moving vessels at sea, many of the crews would have difficulty in finding the targets; and with the clouds thick and low, they were unlikely to be able to drop their armour-piercing bombs from the necessary height. The bombers might damage the German battle-cruisers, and divert attention from other forms of attack; but in the given weather conditions Peirse could not, and did not, expect to sink the vessels outright.

As the naval units available consisted of nothing more powerful than destroyers, our main hope was thus pinned on our painfully slender force of torpedo-bombers—the Beauforts of Nos. 42, 86 and 217 Squadrons, and the Fleet Air Arm Swordfish of No. 815 Squadron. At 1130, however, very few of these were within range of the German ships. No. 86, and part of No. 217, were at St. Eval, in Cornwall; the remainder of No. 217 was at Thorney Island, near Portsmouth; and No. 42 was just coming in to land at Coltishall, near Norwich, after flying down from Leuchars—a move ordered by Joubert two days previously, but delayed by snow on airfields. Only the six Swordfish at Manston and the seven Beauforts at Thorney Island were in a position to attack within the next two hours.

The endurance of the Swordfish was very short, and it was essential for them to take off within the hour if they were to get to grips with the enemy. It was also desirable for their attack to coincide with operations by the motor torpedo-boats from Dover and Ramsgate. The naval aircraft were at short notice, and had received very prompt warning; both they and the torpedo-boats could leave without delay. But could a substantial fighter escort be mustered over Manston from Biggin Hill and Hornchurch within the desired time? Approached by the naval authorities, No. 11 Group at once undertook to provide five squadrons—three for cover and two for diversionary attacks—but stated that it would be a 'rush' to get them to Manston by the required hour of 1225.

Between 1200 and 1215 Biggin Hill and Hornchurch both passed word to Manston that their squadrons would be a few minutes late. The controller at Hornchurch spoke personally to Lieutenant Commander Esmonde, the Commanding Officer of the Swordfish squadron, who replied that whatever happened he must leave at 1225. At 1215, Esmonde, sitting in his cockpit, heard that the German vessels were travelling at 27 knots—three or four knots faster than previously estimated. If a quick take-off had been important before, it was now vital. At 1220 he led his flight into the air and circled above Manston.

At 1228, three minutes late on rendezvous, the first of the three escort squadrons—No. 72—reached Manston. This was good enough for Esmonde, who at once turned out to sea, perhaps expecting that the other two squadrons would join up before the attack. If such were his hopes, they were disappointed, for No. 121 Squadron and 401 Squadron, Royal Canadian Air Force, realizing that they would be at least five minutes behind time, avoided Manston and cut straight out across the coast at Deal. Failing to find the Swordfish on their way to the attack, the two squadrons turned back to Manston, drew a blank there, then headed out to sea again. They arrived over the German vessels only a few minutes after the Swordfish had delivered their attack, but were too late to help. They fought a stout engagement, however, with the German fighter force.

Meanwhile the ten Spitfires of No. 72 Squadron were keeping in close touch with their charges. At about 1240 they sighted the enemy ships, and at the same time found themselves attacked by F.W.190's and Me.109's. Fiercely beset by superior forces, the Spitfire pilots lost sight of the Swordfish as they crossed the enemy destroyer screen. Under furious opposition the naval aircraft swept on. First to fall, a victim of the enemy fighters, was the gallant leader, with his crew; but the two remaining aircraft of his section survived the fighter attacks and pressed on into the storm of *flak* now coming up from the vessels. Repeatedly hit, and with their crews wounded, the two Swordfish still headed for one of the two big ships visible through the clouds of mist and smoke. Both crews managed to launch torpedoes before their aircraft, riddled with bullets, struck the sea. Five of the six men were afterwards picked up by our light craft. From the second section of Swordfish, which disappeared from view after crossing the destroyer screen, there were no survivors.

The first attack had thus cost six aircraft and thirteen men. Despite the extreme heroism of the crews—a heroism recognized by the posthumous award to Lieutenant Commander Esmonde of the first Fleet Air Arm Victoria Cross—none of the torpedoes had found its mark. Nor had our other measures met with any greater success. The Dover guns, fired from 1219 until the Swordfish and light naval forces went into action, scored no hits; the torpedoes from the Dover M.T.B.s also missed; the foray by the Ramsgate M.T.B.s miscarried; and four fighter squadrons detailed to attack the escort vessels all failed to find them. Twice more in the next hour Hurricanes equipped with cannon took off from Manston. On both occasions they found and attacked destroyers, but their best efforts could obviously not impede the progress of the main force. By 1321 the two battle-cruisers were passing beyond the effective range of our radar. And they were still completely undamaged.

It was now the turn of the Beauforts at Thorney Island. Seven of these aircraft were available at short notice when the order to attack was received. Two were armed with bombs, which had to be changed to torpedoes, and a third developed a technical fault. Only four of the Beauforts thus took off at 1325, and when they did so they were twenty minutes late on planned rendezvous with their fighter cover at Manston. To make up for this delay both sets of aircraft were ordered while in the air to proceed independently to the targets, of which the position, course and speed were given. The signals were made by the usual means—R/T for the Spitfires and W/T for the Beauforts. Unfortunately No. 16 Group had forgotten that the Beauforts had temporarily changed their W/T for R/T, with the result that the torpedo-bombers did not receive the message. They therefore proceeded to Manston, which they circled for some minutes, unable to understand why the numerous fighters, also circling before departing on other tasks, would have nothing to do with them. Eventually the front section of two Beauforts set off for the French coast, found nothing, and returned to Manston, where they discovered for the first time the nature of their target. Meanwhile the two rear Beauforts, which had lost touch with their leaders, had already landed at Manston, learned their target and the latest position of the ships, and set off towards the Belgian coast. At 1540, about the same time as our destroyers from the Thames estuary were making an extremely brave but ineffective attack, the two pilots sighted a large warship which they took to be the *Prinz Eugen*. Despite intense *flak* they turned in and launched their torpedoes from a thousand yards range. Again the result was failure.

Meanwhile the enemy had suffered his first mishap. At 1431 a mine previously laid by our air forces had exploded under the *Scharnhorst*. The damage was slight, but after some seventy minutes it caused the vessel to drop astern of the *Gneisenau*. The two battle-cruisers were still in company, however, when at 1500 the first of Bomber Command's aircraft came on the scene.

On hearing that the German vessels were entering the Straits of Dover, Peirse had at once warned all his operational groups except the Whitleys to prepare for attack. The force at his disposal, including machines which had operated the previous night and the hundred held at four hours' notice, amounted in all to some 250 aircraft. But the hundred were bombed up with semi-armour-piercing bombs, which had to be dropped from at least 7,000 feet; and cloud was 8/10ths–10/10ths, with base at 700 feet. Unless cloud-gaps occurred at precisely the right place and moment, the bomb-aimers would be faced with an impossible task. But the alternative armament, the general-purpose bomb, which could be dropped effectively from lower heights, would certainly not penetrate decks plated with several inches of steel. In this dilemma, Peirse decided for low attack with G.P. bombs, if the load could be changed without holding up the departure of the aircraft. By this means he hoped to damage the superstructure of the vessels and distract the attention of their crews from the torpedo-bombers.

The first wave of seventy-three bombers began to take off at 1420. Most of them managed to reach the target area, individually or in pairs, between 1455 and 1558, but in the thick low clouds and intermittent rainstorms only ten crews saw the German ships long enough to release their bombs. The next wave, of 134 machines, began to take off at 1437 and arrived in the target area between 1600 and 1706. Twenty of these are known to have delivered attacks. A third, and final, wave of thirty-five aircraft took off at about 1615, and was over the target from 1750 to 1815. Nine managed to attack. All told, 242 aircraft of Bomber Command attempted to find the enemy during the afternoon; and of those that returned, only thirty-nine succeeded in bombing. Our casualties were fifteen aircraft lost, mostly from *flak* and flying into the sea, and twenty damaged. No hits were scored on the vessels.

While these attacks were in progress, the next group of torpedo-bombers was being launched against the enemy. No. 42 Squadron, it will be remembered, was landing at Coltishall on the way down from Leuchars when news of the break-out was received. The Beauforts had originally been ordered down to North Coates, but unfortunately both this and the alternative Coastal airfield at Bircham Newton were snowbound. At Coltishall, which was a fighter station, the squadron arrived to find no facilities for torpedo aircraft. A Mobile Torpedo Servicing Unit had indeed been ordered over from North Coates; but as the unit had not been required to move for several years it belied its name, and reached Coltishall too late to be of service. Nine of the Beauforts had flown down from Leuchars with torpedoes on, and these took off at 1425, despite the fact that their weapons had not been 'topped up'. The remaining five, having no torpedoes, stayed on the ground.

On leaving Coltishall the nine Beauforts headed south. Their instructions were to link up at Manston with fighters and some Hudsons intended for diversionary bombing, and then follow the Hudsons out to sea. When they arrived over the airfield, at 1450, they found the other aircraft already in circuit. The Beauforts promptly tried to form up behind the Hudsons; but on each attempt the Hudsons obstinately endeavoured to get behind the Beauforts. Efforts to attract an answering move from the fighters were equally unavailing: for while the bombers had been told to expect escort all the way to the target, the fighters had been ordered only to supply general cover in the Straits area. The whole formation thus continued to orbit Manston for over half an hour, each element waiting for the other to take the lead. Tiring of this the Beaufort commander finally decided to set a course based on information of the enemy's position given him before he had left Coltishall. As he turned out to sea with his squadron, six of the Hudsons followed him. The remaining five continued to circle till nearly 1600, then, despairing of attracting the company of the fighters, withdrew to Bircham Newton.

In thick cloud and heavy rain the nine Beauforts and six Hudsons now pressed on towards the Dutch coast. The two formations quickly lost touch, but after an A.S.V. contact the Hudsons sighted the enemy and attacked through heavy *flak*. Two of the bombers were shot down, and no damage was done to the ships. A few minutes later six of the nine Beauforts, flying just above sea-level, also came across the main German force—the other three had already released their torpedoes against what were possibly our own destroyers. All six crews attacked with the utmost determination, but though most of the torpedoes were seen to be running well none found its mark.

By this time the two Beauforts of No. 217 Squadron which had failed to find the ships earlier in the afternoon had set off again from Manston. Operating independently, both picked up the *Scharnhorst* off the Dutch coast with the aid of their A.S.V. But their attacks, delivered at 1710 and 1800, were as unsuccessful as all the rest.

One last chance now remained. There were still the Beauforts of Nos. 86 and 217 Squadrons from St. Eval. These had been hastily

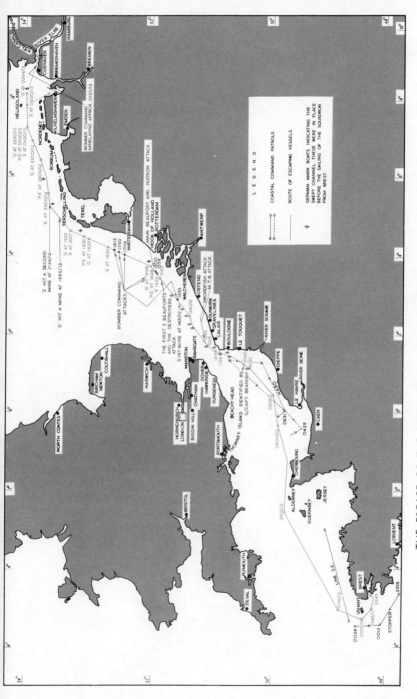

THE ESCAPE OF THE BREST GROUP TO GERMANY, 11–13 FEBRUARY 1942

LEGEND

- - - - COASTAL COMMAND PATROLS

———— ROUTE OF ESCAPING VESSELS

⚓ GERMAN MARK BOATS INDICATING THE
     SWEPT CHANNEL. THESE WERE IN PLACE
     BEFORE THE SAILING OF THE
     SQUADRON FROM BREST.

ordered to Thorney Island, which they reached at 1430. There, after adjusting torpedoes and refuelling, they were ordered to link up with fighters over Coltishall—for by this time the enemy was within easier range of our eastern than our south-eastern bases. The Beauforts reached Coltishall at their appointed time of 1700, but found no sign of the escort they were expecting. Determined to make the most of what remained of the daylight, they at once headed out to a position given them by wireless. At 1805, in the growing dusk, with visibility less than 1,000 yards and cloud base down to 600 feet, they came across four enemy mine-sweepers. One pilot caught sight of what he took to be a big ship, but by then his aircraft was so damaged that he was unable to release his torpedo. Soon darkness was upon them, and at 1830 the Beauforts abandoned their search and set course back for Coltishall. Two of their number, victims of *flak* or the dangerous flying conditions, failed to return.

The ships had now escaped into the night, but all hope of inflicting damage was not yet abandoned. Despite the danger from enemy fighters single aircraft of Coastal Command had been trying to shadow the German formation since about 1600. They obtained two sightings before dark and two or three A.S.V. contacts afterwards—the last of them, against the *Scharnhorst*, as late as 0155 on 13th February. Their reports correctly indicated that the German force had split up, but were too late to be of any value. As a final effort, twenty Hampdens and Manchesters then laid mines in the Elbe estuary during the night. Contrary to the usual version of events, none of these did any damage, but in the course of the evening, mines laid on earlier occasions by our air forces exploded under both the *Scharnhorst* and the *Gneisenau*.[1] The latter, not greatly affected, maintained company with the *Prinz Eugen* and reached the mouth of the Elbe at 0700 on 13th February. The *Scharnhorst*, shaken for the second time, was more seriously damaged. With speed reduced to twelve knots and shipping a thousand tons of water, she nevertheless managed to limp into Wilhelmshaven.

The news of the escape of the German vessels was greeted in England with widespread dismay, not unmixed with indignation. 'Vice-Admiral Ciliax has succeeded where the Duke of Medina Sidonia failed,' wrote *The Times*: 'Nothing more mortifying to the pride of sea-power in Home Waters has happened since the 17th century.' And though opinion in the Services was not as deeply

---

[1] The German records make it clear that the explosions occurred in waters not mined by our aircraft that night. Whether the mines which did the damage had been laid by Bomber Command or by Coastal Command cannot be determined with certainty.

stirred as elsewhere, since in the given conditions of weather and with the naval forces available the Admiralty had entertained no great hopes of success, it was decided to submit the events of 12th February to the examination of a special Board of Inquiry under the Chairmanship of Mr. Justice Bucknill.[1]

After careful examination of a large number of witnesses, ranging in rank from air marshals and admirals to sergeants and leading airmen, the Board established a coherent story of events on our own side. Such criticisms as it offered were expressed in moderate and tentative terms, with full allowance for all the difficulties of the situation. Among other points, the Board considered that after the failure of the first 'Stopper' and 'Line South East' patrols, it would have been 'prudent' to make a daylight reconnaissance by fighter aircraft down the westward half of the Channel. It would also have been 'prudent' to send out a relief when the A.S.V. of the 'Line South East' aircraft failed. Equally, the radar plots of enemy aircraft might have been investigated earlier if No. 11 Group had been 'sufficiently alive to the fact that the German ships might be coming out at about this time'. On the other hand liaison, co-operation and co-ordination between the Services, and between the Commands (which had been criticized in some quarters), in the Board's opinion 'proved on the whole to be satisfactory'. That the earliest attacks were not fully co-ordinated followed inevitably, the Board thought, from the late discovery of the vessels. The state of readiness in Bomber Command— another point of criticism in some quarters—was, the Board concluded, quite reasonable in the circumstances; but the decision to reduce readiness from two to four hours should have been communicated by Bomber Command to the Admiralty. No blame attached to the fighter squadrons that were late for rendezvous; and Lieutenant Commander Esmonde, for his part, was right to leave when only one escorting squadron had appeared.

In sum, the Board considered that apart from the weather and the general weakness of our forces, 'the main reason for our failure to do more damage to the enemy was the fact that his presence was not detected earlier, and this again was due to the breakdown of the night patrols and the omission to send out a morning reconnaissance'. Finally, the Board emphasized how much it had been impressed by 'the countless acts of gallantry' which had come to its notice, and by the 'evident determination of all forces to press home their attacks'.

There is no need to dissent from any of these conclusions—least of all from the last. But, in the light of the information now available,

---

[1] The other members of the Board were Air Chief Marshal Sir Edgar Ludlow-Hewitt and Vice-Admiral Sir Hugh Binney.

no one who studies the sequence of events can fail to be struck by one or two points. Whatever the normal excellence of the liaison arrangements, they did not on this occasion produce effective co-operation between our fighters and our attacking forces. Fortunately the thick weather which protected the German vessels also protected our aircraft. Equally striking, there seems to have been no attempt to inform those concerned all down the line of what was afoot. Too many men in important positions—commanders of stations and squadrons—knew only, as they had known for months, that the German vessels might try to put to sea, but not that there was special reason to believe that they would emerge between 10th and 15th February. Some Beaufort crews took off knowing only that they were looking for enemy ships—possibly even merchant ships; and the two officers who first identified the enemy formation came across it purely by chance. After Joubert's appreciation of 10th February a sort of 'general alert' passed down to comparatively low levels might have avoided at least some of the mistakes and delays.

On the air side, the escape of the *Scharnhorst* and *Gneisenau* was more or less a chapter of accidents. The weather was hopelessly against us; and from the beginning almost everything went wrong that could have done so. Only the skill of the Beauforts in locating the targets under such conditions, together with the unfailing gallantry of the crews, lights up what must otherwise be regarded as an unsatis-factory page in our history. It was not long, however, before British persistence silenced the harsh fanfares of German triumph. On 23rd February the *Prinz Eugen*, despatched to Trondheim by the elated Hitler, was torpedoed by the submarine *Trident*. On the night of 27/28th February the *Gneisenau*, lying in Kiel, suffered two direct hits and the loss of ninety of her crew in a raid by Bomber Command. All three German vessels were out of action for many months. Their position astride our Atlantic communications had been abandoned for nothing. As Raeder himself put it, the German Navy 'in winning a tactical victory suffered a strategic defeat'.

CHAPTER XIII

Towards the Offensive

'You will direct the main effort of the bomber force, until further instructions, towards dislocating the German transportation system, and to destroying the morale of the civil population as a whole, and of the industrial workers in particular.' In these words Air Marshal Sir Richard Peirse, Commander-in-Chief of Bomber Command, was instructed on 9th July 1941 to open a new phase of the air offensive against Germany.

Up to this point Bomber Command had laboured under a host of difficulties. The full extent to which our crews were failing to find, or hit, their correct targets was indeed only just becoming clear; but other obstacles to effective attack on the *Reich*, such as the slow growth of the bomber force and the demands of the Battle of the Atlantic, had for some time been all too painfully apparent. How the diversion of our bombers to maritime objectives continued after July 1941, and from December 1941 to February 1942 occupied the main effort of the Command, has already been described. It remains to trace the progress of the air offensive proper—that assault on industrial targets in Germany, and to a lesser extent in Italy and the occupied territories, which in due course was to rob the enemy of the power to resist the Allied armies, and to reduce so many of his cities to rubble and ruin.

The choice of German transportation as the main objective of our bomber force, and German morale as the secondary, was plainly a confession of failure. We had not succeeded in bombing Germany by day; and we had now found out that attacks by night against small, scattered or well defended targets like oil plants and aircraft factories were inflicting little, if any, vital damage. So much the Air Staff already realized. Considering the question as scientifically as they could from the evidence then available to them, they had come to the conclusion that the crews should at least be able to identify, during the moonlight period, nine great railway centres of Western Germany;

and they were also persuaded, though with less reason, that the available weight of attack, accurately applied to these objectives, would isolate the industrial Ruhr-Rhineland from the rest of the *Reich* and the occupied territories. If this could be achieved the benefit would be felt alike by the Russians, now reeling before the first impact of the German invasion, and by our own army in Africa. Clear moonlight conditions, however, obtain for only one week in four. The bombers must have some target other than railway centres during the remaining three. Only an objective large enough to be found and hit with certainty in the dark would suffice. The conclusion was inescapable that for three weeks out of four we could obtain satisfactory results only, as the directive put it, 'by heavy, concentrated and continuous area attacks of large working-class and industrial areas in carefully selected towns'. Indeed, as the bomber force expanded, and a more impressive weight of bombs could be hurled down on the towns beneath, the Air Staff intended to slacken the attacks on railways and concentrate on an all-out assault against German morale—not, of course, by the deliberate slaughter of civilian populations, but by the destruction of homes, factories, and all the amenities of life in the great industrial cities. They hoped to combine this, however, with daylight raids on precision targets by the new heavy bombers.

To execute this policy, together with subsidiary tasks such as minelaying and attacks on German shipping, Air Marshal Peirse in July 1941 disposed a total of forty-nine squadrons, or nearly 1,000 aircraft. On paper this appeared a formidable force. Eight of the squadrons, however, were Blenheims, now classified as light bombers and suitable only for 'fringe' attacks; and though there were eight squadrons of the new 'heavies', four were not yet operational. Only thirty-seven of the forty-nine squadrons were thus available for the assault against German transportation and morale. Even these thirty-seven squadrons, however, could not play their full part; for less than two-thirds of their crews were fully trained and fit for operations. The drain of experienced crews to the Middle East, coupled with a shortening of the courses in the Operational Training Units in the interests of higher output, had filled the ranks of Bomber Command with 'freshmen'. Indeed, most of the squadrons had to spend one night in three in training. To this grave handicap was to be added a prolonged spell of atrocious weather in the winter of 1941/1942. The result was that for many months the operational effort of the Command remained dishearteningly low. Of the 800 medium and heavy aircraft on strength in the second half of 1941, only some 400 were normally available for operations. As for the nightly total of sorties over Germany, this averaged little more than 60.

These limitations were to become apparent before the new offensive was many weeks old. Meanwhile it was considered desirable to explain our intentions to the Americans. To this end a special review was prepared by the British Chiefs of Staff. 'Our policy at present,' it announced, 'is to concentrate upon targets which affect both the German transportation system and civilian morale, thus exploiting weaknesses already created by the blockade. Since the targets selected lie within highly industrial and thickly populated areas the effect upon German morale is considerable. As our forces increase, we intend to pass to a planned attack on civilian morale with the intensity and continuity which are essential if a final breakdown is to be produced. There is increasing evidence of the effect which even our present limited scale of attack is causing to German life. We have every reason to be confident that if we can expand our forces in accordance with our present programme, and if possible beyond it, that effect will be shattering. We believe that if these methods are applied on a vast scale, the whole structure upon which the German forces are based, the economic system, the machinery for production and destruction, the morale of the nation will be destroyed, and that whatever their present strength the armed forces of Germany would suffer such a radical decline in fighting value and mobility that a direct attack would once more become possible. When that time will come no one can with accuracy predict. It will depend largely on how well we are able with American assistance to keep to our programme of air force expansion and to obtain the necessary shipping. It may be that the methods described above will by themselves be enough to make Germany sue for peace and that the role of the British Army on the continent will be limited to that of an army of occupation. We must, however, be prepared to accelerate victory by landing forces on the Continent to destroy any elements that still resist, and strike into Germany itself . . . '

With this doctrine the Americans were not impressed. Alarmed at the idea of directing a bombing offensive against civilian morale, they urged that we should attack some more specific series of objectives. They also found our conclusions difficult to reconcile with our own 'valorous experience' of German bombardment. These objections, though regarded by the Air Staff as based on misunderstanding, found an echo in a *caveat* put forward at about the same time by the British Prime Minister. Enthusiast as he was for the air offensive, and particularly for the mass bombardment of German towns, Mr. Churchill deprecated some of the larger claims made on its behalf. 'We all hope that the air offensive against Germany will realize the expectations of the Air Staff,' he wrote on 7th October. 'Everything is being done to create the bombing force desired on the largest possible scale, and there is no intention of changing this policy. I deprecate, however, placing unbounded confidence in this means of attack . . . It is the most potent method of impairing the enemy's morale we can use at the present time . . . It may well be that German morale will crack, and that our bombing will play a very important part in bringing the result about. But all things are always on the move simultaneously, and it is quite possible that the Nazi war-making power in 1943 will be so widely spread throughout Europe as to be to a large extent independent of the actual buildings in the homeland. A different picture would be presented if the enemy's air force were so far reduced as to enable heavy accurate daylight bombing of factories to take place. This, however, cannot be done outside the radius of fighter protection, according to what I am at present told. One has to do the best one can, but he is an unwise man who thinks there is any *certain* method of winning this war, or indeed any other war between equals in strength. The only plan is to persevere.'

Throughout the latter half of 1941 Peirse duly persevered. During periods of bright moon he attacked, as his directive ordained, the railway centres; in darkness or during moon when the weather was unfavourable for specific attack on railways, he operated against the 'carefully selected towns', many of which did in fact contain important railway objectives. Against the railway targets results were not impressive; the attacking force was repeatedly foiled by the prevalent haze, and the Ruhr-Rhineland continued to remain in excellent communication with the rest of Germany. The 'area' attacks were more successful. Bielefeld was badly damaged, Münster was treated to an effective four-night 'blitz'—on a return flight from which Sergeant J. A. Ward of No. 75 (New Zealand) Squadron with extraordinary gallantry climbed out on to his starboard wing to extinguish a fire, thereby winning the Victoria Cross—and Aachen and Kassel suffered considerable destruction of both residential and railway property. These last two towns were lightly defended, and had lent much of their civil defence service to other places considered more liable to attack. The result was that our incendiary bombs, though no great load of these was carried, caused fires which quickly spread beyond control.

The general atmosphere of these attacks, when our crews with supreme courage and skill were still navigating their own way to—or near—the target, is admirably captured in a number of first-hand accounts. Of these no one who has read them will forget the remarkable books written by those two outstanding pilots, Group Captain Leonard Cheshire and Wing Commander Guy Gibson. But there are many lesser known volumes which also faithfully depict the ardours and the perils, the 'good shows' and the 'blacks', of the bomber boy's crowded, and customarily brief, existence. Among these is a privately published collection of letters by Flight Sergeant Derek ('Dick') Lord. This young pilot, like many others, carried out a dozen or more operations before his twentieth birthday; and he was not twenty-two when, with thirty or so raids to his credit, and a 'rest' in an instructional job as his reward, he was killed in a flying accident. His account of a raid against Bremerhaven, on the night of 26/27th October 1941, records not only the kind of incident which befell many a crew, but also the appalling difficulty of identifying a target by night in thick weather. The aircraft, a Whitley of No. 77 Squadron, had managed to reach the target area:

> My navigator said: 'Dick, if we are going to prang this place properly, it is about time we started looking for a gap in these bloody fog banks.' I said, 'Right!' and stooged the plane to where the clouds appeared to be less thick.
>
> We found a hole in the black mass of tiny water particles. The Hun found it too, with about thirty of his searchlights.
>
> The light from them seemed to penetrate the very floor of the Whitley. I made no attempt to evade them . . . the navigator wanted a landfall. How he took it, glaring into those millions of candle-power, I cannot attempt to explain, but he did so. He gave me fresh directions and we began our first run.
>
> An orange-coloured searchlight followed our course, shining through the clouds as if such things never existed.
>
> Then the *flak* came, and the tracers and the bomb flashes. Some of the other boys were already on the job. We were flying at 16,000 feet—the remainder of the boys were lower. The shells were exploding at varying heights, mostly, I thought, at about 10,000 feet. I was wrong. We had just finished a tight turn when it happened.
>
> There was a terrific explosion somewhere at the back of my head . . . everything went black and then red, punctured with little green and yellow dots. I heard my radio man say 'My God!' Then everything was silent.
>
> In the silence I could feel myself thinking 'This is it! This is the end of your run . . . you have not done so badly . . . what's this? The seventh raid? You've been lucky—some chaps don't last seven trips . . . '
>
> Something spoke in my ear . . . I say something because it sounded like a very weak loudspeaker . . . 'For Christ's sake, Dick, pull yourself together . . . we're not done yet!'
>
> A light flashed by my eyes . . . it must have been a searchlight. It brought me to my senses with a jerk. I was sprawled over the steering column and the second pilot was pulling at me. I struggled into a sitting position. We were diving madly at the ground, spinning as we did so. The altimeter read 2,500 feet and was fast slipping back to 2,000. Too late to bale out . . . if only I could have died with the explosion! My head was thumping and my right arm felt as heavy as lead. It was still resting on the joystick.

Two thousand feet. The cloud had gone, but the searchlights played on us. Shells burst around us still. In a flash I saw all these things and in the same flash realized that unless we did something very drastic quickly we were going to pile in. The second pilot and myself pulled on the stick. After what seemed an age there was a response from the controls. We stopped spinning and flattened out. The navigator down in the front turret shouted something, but I couldn't make out what it was. The aircraft bucketed, and I thought we had been hit again. Somehow we kept control of the old Whitley and climbed slowly into the shelter of the clouds.

Someone said 'Are you O.K. Dick?' I replied that I was, and was anyone hurt? The second pilot said 'No'. We'd better stooge back and get rid of our eggs,' I suggested.

The navigator laughed . . . 'We dropped them from approximately 1,200 feet, you ass!'

'Oh!' I said, and asked for directions home. Over the North Sea we discussed the dive. 'We were only over Bremerhaven seven minutes', said the wireless-operator, 'but what a seven minutes!'

'What did we hit with the bombs?' I asked.

'God knows,' said the navigator. 'We were diving straight on to a portion of the docks just before you pulled out!'

The Canadian rear gunner called over the inter-com. from his turret, 'The docks ain't where they used to be, Dick! We've gotta small portion in the fuselage right behind me. What the hell d'ya want to dive-bomb the place for? Jeeze, we couldha' made just as good a show from 15,000!'

If thick weather over the target often ruined our operations in 1941, thick weather over base often spelled death to the returning crew. Throughout 1941 very large numbers of aircraft survived the attentions of the enemy over Germany only to crash on landing in England. Such accidents were always most numerous when cloud sat low over our eastern airfields. On 14th July 1941, for instance, No. 7 Squadron at Oakington sent off six aircraft to Hanover. Results were good, but the weather closed down during the return trip. Only one of the six bombers managed to land back at Oakington. Of the others, one ran out of petrol near the coast, another crashed in the centre of Northampton 'much to the disgust of the Chief Constable', and two more sustained damage in landing away from home. Several of the men who baled out were injured and one was killed. No. 7 Squadron, however, were perhaps particularly unfortunate in their experiences of baling out. On one occasion—on the night of 23rd April 1942—an airman who had safely descended was charged twopence by a farmer for a 'phone call to base.

The general effect of our raids at this time may perhaps be gauged by considering the case of Cologne, for which unusually full German records exist. The Rhineland city was within fairly easy reach, and it was not difficult to identify; our raids against it were accordingly much more successful than those against the towns of the Ruhr. Between 1st June 1941 and 28th February 1942, Cologne was attacked as a primary target on thirty-three occasions, including two spells in which it was raided on five successive nights. The aircraft claiming to have reached and bombed the town reported dropping in all about 6,600 high-explosive bombs and 147,000 incendiaries. But the skies above the city were never entirely free from cloud or haze, and the Germans registered the actual fall of only 1,100 high-explosive bombs and 12,000 incendiaries. During the whole nine months bombs damaged 67 industrial plants, 41 transport targets, 10 military installations and 947 residential properties. Twenty-three factories suffered loss of production in varying degrees, but no major works was entirely out of action for more than a month. The number of fires caused was 465, of which 53 were major outbreaks. One hundred and thirty-eight persons were killed, 277 injured, and about 13,000 temporarily lost their homes. All this was not, perhaps, an unprofitable return for 2,000 sorties and the expenditure of 55 aircraft and their crews. But in almost every respect, and particularly in the number of fires and the damage to industrial facilities, these figures were to be exceeded in a single night of 1942—the night in May when the doom of the Third *Reich* first sounded in the thunder of a thousand bombers.

Though it was intended for much more, the attack on transportation and morale during the latter part of 1941 proved in fact to be merely a harassing operation. It had, however, sufficient effectiveness under the best conditions of weather to impress upon the enemy that it must be strenuously opposed. This, rather than any material damage inflicted, was its main achievement. Large numbers of men and women detailed to civil defence, incessant formation of new *flak* batteries, rapid expansion and development of night fighter squadrons, conversion of the searchlight belt behind the Dutch and Belgian coast to G.C.I. radar control—all these were enforced upon the enemy by the activity of our bombers. In turn, of course, this improvement of the enemy's defences caused greater losses in the attacking force. Night raids over Germany in 1940 had cost only 1·6 per cent of sorties. By August 1941 the rate of loss had risen to 3·5 per cent and in November it reached 4·8 per cent. Casualties of this order, added to all the wastage incurred through crashes on return, would have defeated our plans for expanding Bomber Command. By November, therefore, the offensive was virtually in abeyance. The brake was on hard, and but for the renewed calls to attack the *Scharnhorst* and *Gneisenau* our bombers would have conserved their strength in the ensuing weeks for a redoubled effort in the spring of 1942. For by March 1942 a large part of the bomber force was to be equipped with the new aid known as 'Gee'; and this, it was thought, would revolutionize our standards of navigation and bomb-aiming in thick weather.

It was well that there existed this promise of better things to come. For the truth about our night bombing in 1941, though it was little known, was depressing in the extreme. In September 1941 a full assessment was made from photographs taken in a hundred recent raids. It showed that only one in every three aircraft claiming to have attacked had arrived within five miles of its target. Over the Ruhr alone the number of aircraft arriving within five miles of their target was one in ten. Indeed, no greater contrast can be imagined than that between on the one hand the enthusiastic reports of the bomber crews or the travellers' tales from Germany (via Sweden or Switzerland), and on the other the bleak pictures of scarcely damaged towns now being brought back by the photographic Spitfires. The intelligence concerning the campaign was certainly conflicting. But the Air Staff were realists. They accepted in full the distasteful 'evidence in camera' of the photographic reconnaissance machines. And, under the cloak of a complacent publicity which kept everyone happy, they proceeded to build up a force that could do what the optimists imagined was already being done.

* * *

While our night bombers strove to make some impression on the German homeland, our fighters and day bombers struck at the enemy in northern France.

When the *Luftwaffe*'s main daylight assault against this country ended in the autumn of 1940, many squadrons of Fighter Command became free to operate across the Channel. Air Chief Marshal Sholto Douglas's first action on succeeding Sir Hugh Dowding at Stanmore at the end of November 1940 was accordingly to initiate, with the approval of the Air Staff, a policy of 'leaning forward into France'. In this the new Commander-in-Chief was enthusiastically supported by his principal lieutenant, Air Vice-Marshal Trafford Leigh-Mallory, Park's successor at No. 11 Group. And as the Germans showed no sign of resuming intensive operations by day against any British targets other than shipping, the offensive was able to continue without serious distractions.

From December 1940, then, our fighters systematically carried the war into the enemy camp. Either in small numbers by themselves in the operations known as 'Rhubarbs', or in considerable strength accompanied by a few bombers in the operations known as 'Circuses', Douglas's forces gave their opponents no rest. Their objectives were manifold. To destroy enemy machines in the air or on the ground, to shoot up or bomb airfield buildings, ports and communications—all these were within their province. The chief motive underlying the offensive, however, was not so much to cause direct damage as to force the enemy to maintain strong air defences in the West. If, as already mentioned, we could make the Germans strengthen their fighters, anti-aircraft guns and radar posts in France and Belgium at the expense of their forces in south-east Europe, we might perhaps save Greece and Yugoslavia from disappearing into the German maw. At the same time powerful moral advantages would accrue as our pilots grew accustomed to exercising the initiative, and as the enemy became thoroughly imbued with the idea of our superiority in the air.

Up to June 1941 the fighter offensive was waged on no great scale. Nor was there much reaction from the enemy. Between 20th December 1940 and 13th June 1941, 104 'Rhubarbs' resulted in only eighteen engagements with German fighters. In the course of these, we claimed seven enemy aircraft for the loss of eight of our own pilots. During the same period we flew eleven 'Circuses', the largest involving thirty bombers and nearly three hundred fighters. From these twenty-five of our pilots were lost, as against sixteen enemy aircraft claimed. Both 'Rhubarbs' and 'Circuses' achieved, of course, a certain amount of damage on the ground, the 'Circuses' naturally being more profitable in this respect. Including other cross-Channel activity of a similar character, such as the completely ineffective mass sweeps at high level by fighters without bombers, the general exchanges in terms of aircraft were about even. Fifty of our pilots were lost, and fifty-eight enemy aircraft were shot down—fourteen more than we claimed at the time. Whatever its other merits, up till June 1941 the offensive was thus being conducted with economy.

Hitler's attack on the U.S.S.R., as we have already seen, gave still more point to this offensive policy. If it was important to keep German aircraft in the West so that they could not be used against the Greeks, it was still more important to prevent them from being used against the Russians. We accordingly increased the scale of our cross-Channel operations. At once the enemy responded to the threat, challenging our formations wherever they appeared. Between mid-June and the end of July, Fighter Command flew some 8,000 offensive sorties, covering 374 bombers. They resulted, according to our claim, in the destruction of 322 enemy aircraft for the loss of 123 of our own pilots. This seemed a remarkable achievement. The German day fighter force in Northern France was only some 200 aircraft strong, and losses of the order claimed would have meant either its complete

extinction, or its renewal from top to bottom. Unfortunately, however, the more intense fighting had brought the usual overlapping of
claims. We now know that the Germans lost during these six weeks
only 81 fighters, or roughly a quarter of our estimate. All the same,
the strength of the two Fighter *Geschwader* in the West (JG.2 and
JG.26) fell from 200 in June to 140 in August, and serviceability
within these totals from 75 per cent to 60 per cent. Equally, the
Germans found it necessary to recall many experienced pilots from
the East.

An incident typical of the intensive fighting of this period was well
depicted by Flight Lieutenant S. Meares, a fighter pilot of No. 611
Squadron, in a letter to his parents written on 29th June 1941.[1] The
letter first describes how No. 611 Squadron and others had been
'beating up the Heinies', had met 'quite a bit of opposition', and
had enjoyed some 'grand fights'. It then relates the details of one
of the writer's own engagements:

> I had just seen the bombers drop their bombs when I saw a dog-
> fight going on behind me. I turned to join battle and attacked an
> Me.109, who promptly dived vertically towards the ground from
> 20,000 feet. I dived after him and fired a second's burst at him. Then
> I saw another 109 diving after me, firing as hard as he could. I took
> violent evasive action and in a few seconds was at ground level, doing
> almost 500 miles per hour.
> Being well out of the battle and about 50 miles inside France all by
> myself, I felt a little lonely and headed for home, but on the way back
> I passed right over the middle of St. Omer aerodrome, which had two
> Me.109's patrolling it. I thought to myself that this was no place to
> start looking for trouble, and continued on my way. But the Huns did
> not feel like that, and thought that it would please Herr Hitler if they
> shot me down . . . They stalked me, but as I was flying below the level
> of the trees I was able to watch them in the mirror the whole time.
> I waited until the first one was in firing range and then pulled the
> stick back and turned as tightly as I could. 'To me 'orror and amaze-
> ment' I found the Hun was turning inside my turn, which meant he
> could fire and hit me, and I started to perspire a bit. I could not climb
> away because he could outclimb me, and I could not dive as I was
> already flat on the 'deck', and it struck me that I was fighting for my
> life, which is the strangest of sensations. I knew with terrific clearness
> that unless I did something within the next split second I would be one
> of those who did not get home. I was flying about five feet above the
> ground, and pulled the stick back until it would not go any further.
> I blacked out for what seemed to be minutes and when I came to again
> I was flying about 20 feet behind the Hun, and he was obviously
> wondering where I had got to.

---

[1]Meares was very sympathetically portrayed in Ronald Adam's memorable
account of Hornchurch during the Battle of Britain (*Readiness at Dawn*). He was
killed in 1941, leading the first squadron of American volunteers (The 'Eagles').

Realizing how worried he must be, wondering where I had got to, I gave him a little squirt to let him know I was behind him. He then started to do the most amazing display of aerobatics I have ever seen, but I found it quite easy to follow him and every time he made a mistake, I squirted him. He bolted straight back to the aerodrome, and I chased him down his hangars, in between them, over the flying field and back again. He was trying to get his ground defences to shoot me down, then in desperation he turned on his back at about 50 feet and I gave him a long burst and in he went, but it took all the rounds I had got, and I had empty guns.

Realizing I was in a very unhealthy spot, I headed for home, but the second Hun had arrived on the scene. So I had to turn and fight him without any guns. This lasted for about ten minutes and every time I turned for home he came at me again, and I was still about 50 miles from the French coast. This lasted until I was almost exhausted and in a last frantic effort, I got on his tail and when he turned to shake me off, I went the other way, and dived over the top of a hill I had spotted, and turned as quickly as possible and flew under the level of the trees of a wood about a foot off the ground, and he never saw me again. I flew at ground level to Le Touquet and home via Dungeness. I never knew how well I loved England until I saw her shores again. I had learned more about tactics and flying in 20 minutes than in all my flying years . . .

Although our Intelligence was deceived about the number of German aircraft shot down, it was correctly informed about the enemy's movements. The *Luftwaffe's* withdrawals from the eastern front remained confined to pilots, and to the exchange of one unit. This fact, coupled with the rising casualties suffered by our bombers, soon decided the Air Staff to reduce the scale of cross-Channel operations. The decision was taken in August—just when the offensive was in fact beginning to make some inroad into the German fighter force. Beneath the lesser weight of attack the two *Geschwader* soon recovered; and they had no difficulty in keeping up to full strength after November, when our offensive operations were still further curtailed in preparation for the spring of 1942.

Throughout these months, while we were exerting our main cross-Channel effort by day, we were also waging a subsidiary offensive by night. This small but very profitable venture went under the code name 'Intruder'. As early as June 1940 Blenheim night fighters of No. 604 Squadron had patrolled over German-occupied airfields in France in the hope of shooting down returning bombers and generally disrupting the enemy's air operations against this country. From the autumn of 1940 such intrusions had become a regular practice, coastal aircraft and bombers of No. 2 Group taking part as well as fighters. In December 1940, the task became a regular commitment of Fighter Command, and throughout 1941 No. 23 Squadron, equipped first with Blenheims and then with Havocs, bore the main burden of the work. Carrying small bombs as well as guns, and apprised by our wireless interception service of airfields worth visiting, these aircraft were a constant thorn in the enemy flesh; for together with other aircraft of Fighter Command they were responsible during 1941 for nearly 600 'Intruder' sorties. In the course of these, 290 bombing attacks were delivered on airfields, and at least six, and possibly as many as nineteen, German bombers were shot down. Moreover the enemy was often forced to divert his returning pilots to other and less familiar airfields, with the result that many crashed on landing. All this, together with the moral advantage of sapping the enemy's sense of security, we achieved for the loss of ten of our own aircraft.

In proportion to the effort involved, these results were far more impressive than those of the daylight fighter offensive. In the course of the latter we claimed during 1941 the destruction of some 800 enemy fighters, while on our own side we lost 462 fighter pilots. At the time, this rate of roughly two to one in our favour appeared to compensate for the heavy casualties to our pilots—casualties which, in gross, exceeded those incurred during the Battle of Britain. We now know, however, that only 183 German aircraft were in fact shot down. It was the Germans, then, who were scoring at the rate of two to one. We were thus no more successful in shooting down large numbers of enemy fighters than in diverting them from the east. Equally, the 'unrest, possibly developing into revolt' which the Air Staff had hoped to infuse into the French population by our attacks, had not been noticeably in evidence. On the other hand, some useful damage had been done to French industrial objectives, such as power plants; an excuse had been given to French workmen to 'go slow'; and our own forces had gained invaluable experience of offensive operations. It was for such results as these, together with the need to guard against a mass disengagement of German bombers from the east, that a force of seventy-five day-fighter squadrons was retained in this country throughout the latter part of 1941. Whether this was a wise allocation of resources at a time when there were only thirty-four fighter squadrons to sustain our cause in the whole of the Middle and Far East is, perhaps, an open question.

* * *

During an offensive operation on 9th August 1941, Wing Commander Douglas Bader, that remarkable character whose spirit had triumphed so completely over his terrible physical injuries, collided with an Me.109 near Béthune. As he climbed out of his Spitfire, one of his artificial limbs caught in the back of the cockpit. The unfortunate pilot was left dangling from the fuselage while his machine careered rapidly to earth. He had fallen several thousand feet, and was very little distance from the ground when the leather belt which attached the limb to his body gave way, the airman was released, and he was able to complete a successful, if eventful, descent by parachute. Surviving the landing, which broke two of his ribs and for a few moments robbed him of consciousness, Bader revived to find three members of the *Luftwaffe* bending over him. They were removing his parachute harness and his wrist-watch.

As soon as he was taken to hospital, Bader asked his captors to search for his other artificial leg. He suggested that it would still be in, or near, the remains of the aircraft. In case it was not, he also asked if the Germans would signal to England requesting delivery by air of his spare right leg. This, in company with his spare left leg, was in his locker at Tangmere. To his surprise the Germans acceded to both wishes. Within a day or two they retrieved and mended the missing leg; and they also broadcast a message that a Blenheim would be allowed, under certain conditions, to drop the desired object over the airfield at St. Omer. To this message they received no reply, and they were then able to point out to Bader, with much glee, that his comrades had let him down. The Wing Commander, how-ever, had a shrewd idea of how the Royal Air Force would react to such a request. It would deliver him his right leg, but by its own methods, and without obligation to the Germans. He accordingly bided his time and said nothing.

Having recovered his damaged leg, the injured airman at once turned his thoughts to escape. Obviously his only chance was to break out of the hospital before he was transferred to a prison camp. But the hospital was run by the Germans with only a small French kitchen staff; and patients were customarily sent to Germany as soon as they were strong enough to rise from their beds. If anything was to be done it must be done quickly. Seizing a moment when the German orderlies were not watching, Bader soon put his fate in the hands of one of the French maids. The girl agreed to get in touch with English agents on her next day off at the week-end; and the following day she brought the injured pilot a letter from a French peasant couple who promised to shelter him outside St. Omer until he could be passed along the line. When arrangements were perfected their son would wait for him outside the hospital gates every evening after midnight, until the chance came for escape.

The next afternoon—Thursday—Bader was suddenly informed that he was to leave for Germany the following morning. The girl had not yet been able to visit the 'agents' but it was obviously now or never. When she came up with supper Bader told her that he intended to get out that night, and asked that her helper should be waiting outside at 1.45 a.m.

There was now little time to perfect details. The corridors outside the small ward were under constant observation, and Bader had already decided that he would have to climb through the window. The room was on the second floor; and for a man with no legs the difficulties were not inconsiderable. Letting his two comrades of the ward (both badly injured airmen) into his secret, Bader waited until the hospital staff had completed their last round of the evening. He then collected all the sheets in the room, including those of his fellow-patients. This was no easy task; for the two men were lying completely helpless, and Bader, clattering round on his damaged artificial limbs, made an appalling noise. Eventually the job was done; the sheets were knotted together; one end was tied round the leg of the last bedstead; and the bed was pushed up against the wall. Throwing the coil of sheets underneath, Bader returned to his own bed to await the appointed hour.

A few minutes before 1.45 a.m. he rose, strapped on his legs and dressed. He then moved over to the window and threw out the sheets. It was pitch dark outside, and he was quite unable to see if they reached the ground. Trusting to luck, he heaved himself out of the window, bade farewell to his comrades, and lowered himself down his improvised rope. In a few seconds he touched earth, where he found to his amusement several yards of sheet. He then made his way to the appointed spot outside. Across the road he could see the glow of a cigarette. He approached. A man moved forward out of the darkness. A word of recognition, and Bader and his companion were making their way through the town.

The walk was long, and Bader, besides the handicap of his damaged artificial limb, was still dressed in his British uniform. The two men nevertheless proceeded unchallenged, and within an hour or so were safely at the peasants' house. There the elderly couple insisted that Bader stayed until their son-in-law, an Englishman by birth, could come and talk things over.

The following morning the peasant's wife set off for town. She returned with what, to Bader, seemed the very worst kind of news. A cordon had been thrown round the hospital and every house within it was being searched. The peasant and his wife, however, were only amused. Their house was well beyond the enemy ring and they repeatedly assured Bader that the Germans would never look for him so far from the hospital.

The morning turned to afternoon, and all seemed well Suddenly a German staff car drew up outside the house. The escape-plan had been betrayed by another girl worker in the hospital. Guided by the old peasant, Bader at once bolted through the back door and into a garden shed, where he hid beneath some baskets and hay. He heard voices, first inside the house, then nearer at hand. A German soldier opened the door of the shed, rummaged about with the baskets, and went away. Bader breathed a sigh of relief. Then the door opened again, and another German entered. His inspection was more thorough than that of his predecessor. He systematically jabbed his bayonet through the hay until Bader, suddenly realizing what it was when it came within a few inches of his face, could bear it no longer. 'I went yellow, or something,' he explained later; but doubtless his decision was also not unconnected with thought for his hosts. Giving himself up, he denied that he had ever set eyes on the peasant or his wife, and carefully explained that he had entered the garden from the side-gate. His story did not convince the enemy, who in due course hauled off the peasant and his family, together with the helpful girl from the hospital, to forced labour in Germany.[1]

Bader was now placed under close guard, and any further attempt to escape was out of the question. He was taken to German head-quarters in St. Omer. There a surprise awaited him. While he was with his shelterers a number of British aircraft in the course of a normal operation had swept across St. Omer airfield. As the last of them had streaked away, a long yellow box had been seen floating down on a parachute. Surviving the attention of the German gunners on its descent, it had reached the ground, where it was found to be addressed to the Commandant of the airfield for transmission to Wing Commander Douglas Bader, D.S.O., D.F.C. The box was now before him. It contained, of course, his spare right leg from Tangmere.

This incident has been described in some detail because it displays the spirit not only of a British pilot but of the French people. It was the fund of helpfulness and courage among the ordinary men and women of France—stimulated, of course, by Allied successes and the behaviour of the Germans—which eventually translated the shame of Vichy into the glories of the Resistance. What part the Royal Air Force played in the birth and infancy of this great movement must now be briefly related.

In July 1940, almost as soon as the last of the British Expeditionary Force had scrambled back from the ports of Western France, a new organization was set up in London. Its orders were 'to co-ordinate all action by way of subversion and sabotage against the enemy over-

---

[1] Fortunately all survived this. After the war all were able to return to their native land, while the informer, despite Bader's representations, was sentenced by the French to twenty years' imprisonment.

seas'; and it went by the conveniently colourless name of the Special Operations Executive (S.O.E.). Work of this kind was no novelty; indeed, it was old as war itself. A new factor, however, had now entered. With so much of the coast line of Europe under close German supervision, the traditional landing of agents or supplies from small boats presented grave difficulties. Accordingly—it was a precedent first set in 1914–1918, though the trips were shorter then— the gentlemen of the 'cloak-and-dagger brigade' took to travelling by air. To meet their needs a special flight of Royal Air Force Lysanders (No. 419) was set aside in August 1940. It was used alike by S.O.E. and by other secret organizations engaged in clandestine work in Europe.

At that time it was as much as we could do to arm weaponless units of the British Army, let alone groups of 'irregulars' on the Continent. Equally, France, Belgium and Holland were all too near the first shock of defeat to be capable of any great effort on their own behalf. It was also impossible for us to spare many aircraft to stand by, night after night, waiting for the right conditions for a 'special operation'. For a long time the scale of subversive activity accordingly remained small. Despite these facts, however, and despite the great severity of the weather, the winter of 1940–1941 saw a number of organizers, wireless-operators and *coup de main* teams parachuted into western Europe. Besides inspiring or carrying out sabotage, these pioneers helped to prepare the ground for military operations by the Commandos.

During 1941 there was no great increase in the number of aircraft employed on this delivery work. In August 1941 No. 419 Flight became No. 138 (Special Duty) Squadron, but it was not until February 1942 that a second Special Duty Squadron—No. 161— was formed. The nucleus of the new unit was the King's Flight, under Wing Commander E. H. Fielden. By March 1942 the two Squadrons —whose combined strength at this time amounted to a dozen Whitleys, half a dozen Lysanders, two or three Halifaxes and Wellingtons, and a Hudson—were both installed at Tempsford, near Bedford. From this airfield they bore the whole burden of special operations until the autumn of 1943. Only then, as the great day of liberation for the Continent drew nearer, did other squadrons join them in their vital and onerous task.

Broadly speaking, No. 138 and 161 Squadrons carried out two types of operation. One—by far the more frequent—was dropping organizers, agents or supplies by parachute. The other was the 'pick up', in which the aircraft landed to collect some prominent public man, or an agent, or special plans and articles. For the first type of operation the Whitley, and later the Halifax, was the standard aircraft; for the second the nimble Lysander. As time went on No. 161 Squadron became solely responsible for the landings. During 1942 both Squadrons also operated with the bomber force when not required for 'special duties'.

The general procedure in both dropping and landing operations was much the same. Usually the initiative came from an agent in the field or a resistance group, who asked by wireless for a delivery or landing at a certain point. If this point satisfied the requirements of the Royal Air Force, and the operation was approved, the flight was arranged for the earliest possible period of full moonlight. The stores were packed, or agents briefed, and then all depended on the weather. When a favourable forecast was received, a code phrase was broadcast during the day by the B.B.C., usually in the personal messages following the foreign news bulletins. The casual listener might perhaps ponder the significance of some such phrase as '*les lions sont terribles*', but only the initiated knew that this meant attendance at the selected spot that night. Often bad weather prevented the flight after the signal had been given, and the 'reception committee' was then condemned to a long, dangerous and fruitless wait.

Even if the aircraft took off at its appointed time, however, the sortie might prove quite unsuccessful. The weather might close in over the dropping or landing area; the 'reception committee' might be unable to keep its appointment; enemy *flak* or fighters might bring the mission to an abrupt conclusion. Great skill was also required, even under the best conditions, to reach the given pinpoint, and to identify the signal from the ground—usually an arrangement of hand torches and the flash of a letter in morse. The containers or packages, too, had to be dropped from such a height that they would not be damaged, and so accurately that they could be gathered up without delay.[1] As time went on various devices helped the pilot to find his destination. There was, for instance, the radar combination 'Rebecca-Eureka'; 'Rebecca' (carried in the aircraft) transmitted pulses which were received and retransmitted by the ground-beacon 'Eureka' (carried in a suitcase!), so enabling the aircraft to 'home' towards the spot where the beacon was erected. Soon, too, there was the 'S phone', a radio telephone for 'talking' the aircraft down to the

---

[1] On one occasion, following an inaccurate drop, the men at the receiving end had to spend nearly all the night gathering up the containers. Their weariness was increased when several of them were forced by the Germans to spend the next day picking up British leaflets. These had been scattered by another aircraft over a neighbouring area to 'cover' the delivery flight.

right place. Lack of linguistic skill on the part of the crew, or lack of 'flying control' experience on the part of the reception committee made this of limited use for its primary purpose. When a competent linguist was carried in the plane, however, the 'S phone' proved invaluable for exchanging information between ground and air.

Much thought was naturally given to the development of suitable containers for the stores. When the articles were too big for these they were dropped in special coverings of sorbo rubber or hairlok (horse hair impregnated with latex). The loads consisted for the most part of arms, ammunition, food, clothing, wireless equipment, and, in the later days when whole armies were being built up, oil and petrol. A fine variety of other items, however, was delivered on request. At various times during the war our aircraft dropped special socks for the artificial leg of a woman officer in France, sleeping pills, itching powder, and a layette for twins! It is also officially recorded, though perhaps with more doubtful authenticity, that on the first occasion when dried egg was dropped in the Balkans, a message was received back: 'Thanks for the new explosive. Please send instructions for use.'

Most of the difficulties which attended supply-dropping, and many others besides, were present in the case of 'pick up' operations. To make room for passengers the Lysanders were stripped of guns, armour and wireless equipment (except the radio telephone); and the pilot, flying without a navigator, found his way in the moonlight by his maps alone. How fine a margin lay between success and failure may be seen from the first S.O.E. 'pick up' that was attempted. On the night of 4/5th September 1941, a Lysander of No. 138 Squadron, piloted by Flight Lieutenant Nesbitt-Dufort, took off for a point in occupied France. The task was to land one organizer and return with another. The officer to be picked up had engaged rooms for himself and his French assistant in a hotel some ten miles from the agreed landing spot. During the day he heard the warning message over the B.B.C., and prepared to depart that night. The hours went by, darkness at last fell, and the two men were just about to leave the hotel when in came the police. There followed a lengthy examination of papers, from which both emerged triumphant. Free, but very late, they began cycling furiously towards the landing ground. As they approached they heard the Lysander already circling in the darkness, seeking for the lights below. Fearing that the pilot would abandon the attempt before they could reach the appointed spot, they somewhat rashly chose the nearest field which seemed suitable for landing, climbed over the hedge, and laid out their torches. The Lysander put down safely, the passenger leapt out, and after a brief handshake the returning officer climbed in. A quick turn-round, a moment's revving up of the single engine, and the pilot was off again—though not without fouling the telegraph lines. Despite the attachment of several feet of wire to his aircraft, a thick ground mist over base, and the failure of his R/T, he got down safely in England. Meanwhile in France the newly-arrived officer was quietly moving away from the field when he heard a shout. Imagining the enemy to be already on his track, he set off at great speed, hotly pursued by the owner of the voice—the Frenchman who had helped to lay out the flare path.

With greater experience minor mishaps of this kind were usually avoided. Although the dreaded Gestapo remained a constant hazard in North-West Europe, there was only one occasion on which an S.O.E. aircraft was actually ambushed. The pitch of efficiency reached may be judged from the fact that in 112 'pick up' operations, spread over four years, only two Lysanders were lost. Even then one of the pilots was brought out successfully through the 'usual channels'.

Special Operations Executive continued to work on a fairly small scale until the final phases of the war. Only 22 successful sorties were carried out over France in 1941, and only 93 in 1942, as against 615 in 1943 and 2,995 in 1944. By then, as recorded in Volume III (Chapter VIII), massed flights undertaken in daylight were supplying large insurgent areas. Nevertheless there were many great feats of sabotage in the early period, and nearly all depended on air delivery. And soon were to come operations of the very first importance, as when our parachutists blew up the Gorgopotamus Bridge over the Salonika–Athens railway in September 1942 and cut a vital link in Rommel's supply route on the eve of El Alamein, or when a party landed from the air to destroy the Norsk Hydro heavy-water plant and end Germany's one hope of the atom-bomb.

Above all, however, the 'special operations' of these early years enabled us to gain experience, to build up resistance circuits, and to obtain information of priceless value from the occupied countries. The work begun in north-west Europe in 1940 was extended in 1941 to Poland and Czechoslovakia, and in 1942 to Greece and Yugoslavia. From the Middle East No. 148 Squadron, operating over the Balkans, was to emulate the feats of Nos. 138 and 161 Squadrons nearer home. In all this the task of the Royal Air Force was not the most dangerous of all, that of carrying out the action on the ground—though even in this sphere a gallant few like Wing Commander Yeo Thomas were to leave records of imperishable fame. It was in the humbler capacity of 'Carter Paterson' that the Royal Air Force was mainly engaged. But the role was exacting enough; and only the skill and spirit with which it was played enabled Hitler's monstrous edifice to be sapped and mined from within.

* * *

In yet another type of offensive operation at this time the Royal Air Force also bore a share. In the summer of 1940 the 'Commandos' had been born, the Directorate of Combined Operations had been formed, and the principle had been accepted of launching small raids against the coasts of Hitler's Europe. At the same time, with the opening of the Central Landing School at Ringway, the first steps were taken to create a force of paratroops. In this way military raiding parties, like the organizers and saboteurs of the Special Operations Executive or the agents of the Secret Service, could proceed to their assignments by modern methods.[1]

During 1940 only two raids were carried out. Both were minor affairs, and both were seaborne. In 1941 the pace quickened, and two 'combined ops' were mounted within a month. The first of these, the somewhat extravagantly named 'Operation Colossus', was also our first 'airborne' venture. It took place on 10th February, the object being to destroy a large aqueduct at Tragino, in the Italian province of Campagna. This action, it was thought, would cut off the water supplies of Taranto, Brindisi and Bari at a time when these ports were the main supply bases for the Italian forces attacking Greece. The Air Force side of the operation was under the direction of Wing Commander Sir Nigel Norman, the Commandant of the Central Landing Establishment; and the plan was to use six Whitleys, operating from Malta, to drop the parachutists and stores near the objective while two more Whitleys created a diversion elsewhere. In the event, five of the aircraft dropped their men—among them a Royal Air Force flight sergeant interpreter with the encouraging name of Lucky—at or near the right place and time, and by great determination in the face of many unforeseen difficulties the raiders accomplished their mission before they fell into the hands of the enemy. The operation created considerable alarm in southern Italy, but had no noticeable effect on the Italian troops' water supply.

Three weeks later our raiding forces struck at the opposite extremity of Europe, carrying out an entirely successful seaborne

---

[1] The Central Landing School, under the command of Squadron Leader Louis Strange (a famous pilot of the First World War), began training parachutists in July 1940. In September two sections for glider training and technical research were added, and the school was renamed the Central Landing Establishment. The two new sections subsequently split off, becoming respectively No. 1 Glider Training School and the Airborne Forces Experimental Establishment; but the parachute section (No. 1 P.T.S. as it was eventually called) remained at Ringway for the rest of the war.

descent on the Lofotens. Other ventures in 1941 include the operations of 'Layforce' in the Middle East and the raid in December on Vaagsö, already described, while in the opening quarter of 1942 came the great exploit at St. Nazaire. To all these the Royal Air Force contributed by reconnaissance, direct support, fighter cover, or diversionary operations. So far as the Service itself was concerned, however, the most important combined operation before the great assault at Dieppe, to be described in a later volume, was the airborne raid on the German radar station at Bruneval.

Behind the Bruneval raid there was a long story. As our bomber and fighter offensive over the Continent had progressed, so its success had come to depend more and more on our knowledge of the German radar system. At the outbreak of war we had not known that the Germans possessed radar at all, but during 1940 and 1941 we had steadily built up an accurate picture of their air defences. Partly through photographic reconnaissance, partly through more secret sources of intelligence, we had located nearly all their early warning radar installations, those *Freyas*, as the Germans termed them, which corresponded to our own long-range stations on the coast. During 1941 we had also found out, however, that the Germans possessed another type of apparatus used for detection and tracking at short range, an apparatus performing the functions of our own Gun-Laying and Ground Controlled Interception Sets. This was known as a *Würzburg*; already capable in 1940 of controlling *flak* and searchlights, it had since been adapted to control night fighters. Obviously, we must take its full measure very quickly if our aircraft were not to suffer greatly increased losses.[1]

As soon as the existence of the set came to our notice, we accordingly re-examined our photographs of enemy-held territory with the utmost care. Of these there were many thousands; and as the *Würzburg* was known to be extremely small, the task bore an uncomfortable resemblance to the proverbial hunt for needles in haystacks. It was suspected, however, that a *Würzburg* might be found near an ordinary *Freya*. Attention was therefore concentrated on the vicinity of these; and eventually a member of the Scientific Intelligence Staff in the Air Ministry discovered a small and unexplained dot in a photograph of a *Freya* at Bruneval, near Le Havre. Several other photographs of the same site were examined before it became certain that this was not a speck of dust. After that the next step was obviously to secure a low-level photograph of the

---

[1] In the early days of the war, German fighters had not operated under ground control. This was because they had concentrated on offensive tactics to the neglect of defence.

suspected point. Dr. R. V. Jones has described how this was done. 'Before we had time to put in an official request, our suspicions came to the notice of a photographic pilot—Squadron Leader Tony Hill, who promptly took off unofficially to have a look at it. He came back with the exciting news that it looked like what we expected, a large electric bowl-fire; but he was disappointed that his camera had failed to work. He was about to take-off again next day, again unofficially, when he was stopped because three aircraft from a rival squadron were officially scheduled to be taking photographs in the same area at the same time. He thereupon taxied his aircraft over to the others and told them if he found any of them within twenty miles of the target he would shoot them down. He went out and got his photographs unmolested. They were among the classics of the war, and led directly to the Bruneval raid.'

The existence of the *Würzburg* being thus confirmed, our radio experts began to plan counter-measures. To assist the progress of these it was decided to examine the apparatus at close quarters. Details of local geography and defences having been obtained from members of the French Resistance, a combined operation was prepared, under the code name 'Biting', to seize certain vital parts of the equipment. The plan was for the Whitleys of No. 51 Squadron, led by Wing Commander P. C. Pickard—already well known as the pilot in the documentary film 'Target for To-Night' and later to achieve undying fame as the leader of the raid on Amiens prison—to drop a company of paratroops in the area, and for these to be withdrawn afterwards by sea. Diversionary bombing was to take place before and during the operation, and fighter cover was to be given to the naval forces on their way home. Among those to be dropped by parachute was Flight Sergeant C. W. H. Cox, a Royal Air Force radar mechanic, who had volunteered to help in the task of dismantling. The fact that he had never before left the shores of his native country or travelled in an aeroplane apparently only whetted his appetite for the venture.

After a period of intensive training and preparation, during which the troops and aircrews learnt every feature of the ground by means of models prepared from air photographs, the operation was carried out on the night of 27/28th February 1942. All but two of the twelve Whitleys put down their loads at the right time and place. The parachutists made their drop without opposition, and quickly gathered up demolition material, arms and signalling equipment from the containers. While one contingent moved against the defences on the cliff and the beach below, the main assault party split into three. One section stormed an isolated house near the radar post, a second took up covering positions, and the third, including Flight Sergeant Cox, made for the apparatus itself. Here a sharp struggle ensued. It resulted in the death or capture of all the six Germans present. By that time enemy troops in a farm some 450 yards distant had two machine guns trained on the *Würzburg*; but despite accurate fire from these the raiders took photographs of the complete equipment. Then Cox and his helpers, working in the dark with the utmost coolness and skill, began to extract the desired parts. Two machine-gun bullets struck the apparatus under the Flight Sergeant's hand, but the work still went on. When they had what they wanted the raiders blew up the rest, then retired towards the beach. A further sharp struggle and the troops were able to call in the unfailing Navy, already waiting off shore.

At the small cost of fifteen casualties—and the Germans suffered many more—we were thus able to improve our acquaintance with a vital element in the German air defences. The result was that we could apply our counter-measures, such as jamming, or low flying, or 'saturation' by large numbers of aircraft, with all the greater effect. Another victory had been recorded in the 'radio war', that ceaseless battle of wits which was to determine the future of our bombing offensive, and with it the course of the whole titanic conflict.

*   *   *

While the Royal Air Force was thus pressing the enemy hard in Europe, a new opponent, strong, resolute and treacherous, had appeared 'from out the fiery portal of the East'. On 7th December 1941 the Japanese blow fell with stunning effect, and for a while all that we had so painfully achieved since 1940 seemed in hazard. Yet, through the dark days ahead, when defeat in Cyrenaica pressed hard upon disaster in Malaya and Burma, the British Commonwealth could take comfort from the fact that in 1940 it had faced far greater perils, and still survived. That it had been able to do so, that it had contrived to defy the heavy odds against it and to battle on alone until time and the folly of the enemy brought the help of two great Allies, was due to several factors, of which not the least was the work of the Royal Air Force. And that the Royal Air Force had been able to save Britain in 1940, and then to carry war with progressive force into the German homeland, was due in turn to many things, of which two stand foremost. One was the sound judgment and receptiveness to new ideas of those, from Trenchard onwards, who, in the brief span of twenty years and despite strictly limited resources and a climate of public opinion for long unfavourable, had made the Royal Air Force what it was in 1939. The other, transcending even this, was the sustained excellence of technique and morale among its crews.

For in war in the air, even more than on the land or the sea, the power of the weapon depends in the end upon the individual quality of the fighting man; and in this the Royal Air Force of 1939–1941 may have been equalled, but has certainly never been surpassed. Manifestly, it was still true to say of the Royal Air Force in the Second World War, as the official historian wrote of it in the First, that 'when the builders have been praised for their faith and for their skill, the last word of wonder and reverence must be kept for the splendid grain of the stuff that was given them to use in the architecture of their success.'

APPENDIX I

Members of the Air Council, 1934–1941

SECRETARY OF STATE FOR AIR

	Date of Appointment
The Most Hon. The Marquess of Londonderry, K.G., P.C., M.V.O.	9th November 1931
The Rt. Hon. Viscount Swinton, P.C., G.B.E., M.C.	7th June 1935
The Rt. Hon. Sir Kingsley Wood, M.P.	16th May 1938
The Rt. Hon. Sir Samuel J. G. Hoare, Bart., G.C.S.I., G.B.E., C.M.G., M.P.	5th April 1940
The Rt. Hon. Sir Archibald Sinclair, Bart., K.T., C.M.G., M.P.	11th May 1940

PARLIAMENTARY UNDER-SECRETARY OF STATE FOR AIR

The Rt. Hon. Sir Philip A. G. D. Sassoon, Bart., G.B.E., C.M.G., M.P.	3rd September 1931
Lieutenant Colonel A. J. Muirhead, M.C., M.P.	28th May 1937
Captain The Rt. Hon. H. H. Balfour, M.C., M.P.	16th May 1938
Lord Sherwood (Under-Secretary of State, House of Lords)	22nd July 1941

CHIEF OF THE AIR STAFF

Marshal of the Royal Air Force Sir Edward L. Ellington, G.C.B., C.M.G., C.B.E.	22nd May 1933
Marshal of the Royal Air Force Sir Cyril L. N. Newall, G.C.B., C.M.G., C.B.E., A.M.	1st September 1937
Air Chief Marshal Sir Charles F. A. Portal, K.C.B., D.S.O., M.C.	25th October 1940

AIR MEMBER FOR PERSONNEL

Air Marshal Sir Frederick W. Bowhill, K.C.B., C.M.G., D.S.O.	31st July 1933
Air Marshal Sir William G. S. Mitchell, K.C.B., C.B.E., D.S.O., M.C., A.F.C.	1st July 1937
Air Marshal C. F. A. Portal, C.B., D.S.O., M.C.	1st February 1939
Air Marshal E. L. Gossage, C.B., C.V.O., D.S.O., M.C.	3rd April 1940
Air Marshal P. Babington, C.B., M.C., A.F.C.	1st December 1940

AIR MEMBER FOR SUPPLY AND ORGANIZATION

Air Chief Marshal Sir Cyril L. N. Newall, K.C.B., C.M.G., C.B.E., A.M.	14th January 1935
Air Marshal W. L. Welsh, C.B., D.S.C., A.F.C.	1st September 1937
Air Chief Marshal Sir Christopher L. Courtney, K.C.B., C.B.E., D.S.O.	15th January 1940

Date of Appointment

AIR MEMBER FOR TRAINING

Air Marshal A. G. R. Garrod, C.B., O.B.E., M.C.,   8th July 1940
D.F.C.

AIR MEMBER FOR SUPPLY AND RESEARCH[1]

Air Marshal Sir Hugh C. T. Dowding, K.C.B.,   1st September 1930
C.M.G.

AIR MEMBER FOR RESEARCH AND DEVELOPMENT

Air Marshal Sir Hugh C. T. Dowding, K.C.B.,   14th January 1935
C.M.G.
Air Marshal Sir Wilfrid R. Freeman, K.C.B.,   1st April 1936
D.S.O., M.C.

AIR MEMBER FOR DEVELOPMENT AND PRODUCTION

Air Chief Marshal Sir Wilfrid R. Freeman, K.C.B.,   1st August 1938
D.S.O., M.C.

SECRETARY OF THE AIR MINISTRY[2]

Sir Christopher Ll. Bullock, K.C.B., C.B.E.   20th January 1931
Colonel Sir Donald Banks, K.C.B., D.S.O., M.C.   9th August 1936

PERMANENT UNDER-SECRETARY OF STATE FOR AIR

Colonel Sir Donald Banks, K.C.B., D.S.O., M.C.   March 1938
Sir Arthur W. Street, K.C.B., K.B.E., C.M.G., C.I.E.,   1st June 1939
M.C

ADDITIONAL MEMBERS

The Rt. Hon. Earl Winterton, M.P. (Deputy to   14th March 1938–
Secretary of State for Air)   15th May 1938
E. J. H. Lemon, Esq., O.B.E., M.I.MECH.E.,   Aug.1938–April 1940
(Director-General of Production)
Sir Arthur W. Street, K.B.E., C.B., C.M.G., C.I.E.,   19th January–31st
M.C. (Acting Permanent Under-Secretary of   May 1939
State)
Sir Harold G. Howitt, D.S.O., M.C., F.C.A.   18th September 1939
onwards
Sir Charles Craven, O.B.E. (Civil Member for   1st May–Nov. 1940
Development and Production)
Air Marshal Sir Richard E. C. Peirse, K.C.B.,
D.S.O., A.F.C.
(a) Deputy Chief of the Air Staff   30th October 1939–
21st April 1940
(b) Vice-Chief of the Air Staff   22nd April–
4th October 1940

---

[1] This appointment became Air Member for Research and Development (14th January 1935) which in turn became Air Member for Development and Production (1st August 1938). The appointment ceased after the formation of the Ministry of Aircraft Production.

[2] Designated Permanent Under-Secretary of State for Air, March 1938.

	Date of Appointment
Sir Henry Tizard, K.C.B., A.F.C., F.R.S.	June 1941 onwards
Air Chief Marshal Sir Wilfrid R. Freeman, K.C.B., D.S.O., M.C.	
(a) Representing Ministry of Aircraft Production	August–Nov. 1940
(b) Vice-Chief of the Air Staff	Nov. 1940–Oct. 1942
Air Marshal F. J. Linnell, C.B., O.B.E. (Controller of Research and Development, Ministry of Aircraft Production representative)	5th June 1941 onwards

APPENDIX II

Air Officers Commanding-in-Chief, 1936–1941

HOME

BOMBER COMMAND

Air Chief Marshal Sir John M. Steel, G.C.B., K.B.E., C.M.G.	14th July 1936
Air Chief Marshal Sir Edgar R. Ludlow-Hewitt, K.C.B., C.M.G., D.S.O., M.C.	12th September 1937
Air Marshal Sir Charles F. A. Portal, K.C.B., D.S.O., M.C.	3rd April 1940
Air Marshal Sir Richard E. C. Peirse, K.C.B., D.S.O., A.F.C.	5th October 1940

FIGHTER COMMAND

Air Chief Marshal Sir Hugh C. T. Dowding, G.C.B., G.C.V.O., C.M.G., A.D.C.	14th July 1936
Air Marshal Sir W. Sholto Douglas, K.C.B., M.C., D.F.C.	25th November 1940

COASTAL COMMAND

Air Marshal Sir Arthur M. Longmore, K.C.B., D.S.O.	14th July 1936
Air Marshal P. B. Joubert de la Ferté, C.B., C.M.G., D.S.O.	1st September 1936
Air Chief Marshal Sir Frederick W. Bowhill, K.C.B., C.M.G., D.S.O.	18th August 1937
Air Chief Marshal Sir Philip B. Joubert de la Ferté, K.C.B., C.M.G., D.S.O.	14th June 1941

BRITISH AIR FORCES IN FRANCE[1]

Air Marshal A. S. Barratt, C.B., C.M.G., M.C.	15th January 1940

ARMY CO-OPERATION COMMAND

Air Marshal Sir Arthur S. Barratt, K.C.B., C.M.G., M.C.	20th November 1940

TRAINING COMMAND[2]

Air Marshal Sir Charles S. Burnett, K.C.B., C.B.E., D.S.O.	1st May 1936

---

[1] The Advanced Air Striking Force and the Air Component, which were brought under Air Vice-Marshal Barratt's Command on this date, were commanded by Air Vice-Marshal P. H. L. Playfair, C.B., C.V.O., M.C. and Air Vice-Marshal C. H. B. Blount, O.B.E., M.C., respectively.

[2] Disbanded on formation of Flying Training and Technical Training Commands—27th May 1940.

Date of Appointment

Air Chief Marshal Sir Arthur M. Longmore,   1st July 1939
K.C.B., D.S.O.

FLYING TRAINING COMMAND

Air Marshal L. A. Pattinson, C.B., D.S.O., M.C.,   27th May 1940
D.F.C.
Air Marshal Sir William L. Welsh, K.C.B., D.S.C.,   7th July 1941
A.F.C.

MAINTENANCE COMMAND

Air Marshal J. S. T. Bradley, C.B.E.   31st March 1938

TECHNICAL TRAINING COMMAND

Air Marshal Sir William L. Welsh, K.C.B., D.S.C.,   27th May 1940
A.F.C.
Air Marshal J. T. Babington, C.B., C.B.E., D.S.O.   7th July 1941

OVERSEAS

COMMANDER-IN-CHIEF, FAR EAST[1]

Air Chief Marshal Sir H. Robert M. Brooke-Popham,   18th November 1940
G.C.V.O., K.C.B., C.M.G., D.S.O., A.F.C.

ROYAL AIR FORCE, MIDDLE EAST

Air Chief Marshal Sir William G. S. Mitchell,   1st April 1939
K.C.B., C.B.E., D.S.O., M.C., A.F.C.
Air Chief Marshal Sir Arthur M. Longmore,   13th May 1940
G.C.B., D.S.O.
Air Marshal A. W. Tedder, C.B.   1st June 1941

AIR FORCES IN INDIA

Air Marshal Sir John F. A. Higgins, K.C.B., K.B.E.,   6th October 1939
D.S.O., A.F.C.
Air Marshal Sir Patrick H. L. Playfair, K.B.E.,   26th September 1940
C.B., C.V.O., M.C.

R.A.F. FERRY COMMAND

Air Chief Marshal Sir Frederick W. Bowhill,   18th July 1941
G.B.E., K.C.B., C.M.G., D.S.O.

---

[1] Royal Air Force Far East was not at this date under the command of an Air Officer Commanding-in-Chief. R.A.F. units in the Force were, however, under the command of Air Vice-Marshal J. T. Babington, C.B., C.B.E., D.S.O., from September 1938 to April 1941, and Air Vice-Marshal C. W. H. Pulford, C.B., O.B.E., A.F.C., from April, 1941 to February 1942. From 18th November 1940 to 27th December 1941, however, Air Chief Marshal Sir Robert Brooke-Popham was Commander-in-Chief, Far East, with supreme control over land and air, but not naval, forces.

APPENDIX III

Royal Air Force Command Organization, September 1939

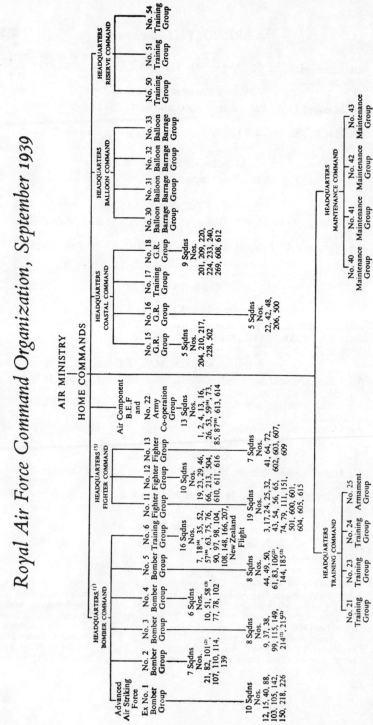

AIR MINISTRY

HOME COMMANDS

HEADQUARTERS[1] BOMBER COMMAND

Advanced Air Striking Force
Ex No. 1 Bomber Group
10 Sqdns Nos. 12, 15, 40, 88, 103, 105, 142, 150, 218, 226

No. 2 Bomber Group
7 Sqdns Nos. 21, 82, 101[2], 107, 110, 114, 139

No. 3 Bomber Group
8 Sqdns Nos. 9, 37, 38, 99, 115, 149, 214[2], 215[2]

No. 4 Bomber Group
6 Sqdns Nos. 10, 51, 58[1], 77, 78, 102

No. 5 Bomber Group
8 Sqdns Nos. 44, 49, 50, 61, 83, 106[2], 144, 185[2]

No. 6 Bomber Training Group
16 Sqdns Nos. 7, 18[a], 35, 52, 57[a], 63, 75, 76, 90, 97, 98, 104, 108, 148, 166, 207, New Zealand Flight

HEADQUARTERS[5] FIGHTER COMMAND

No. 11 Fighter Group
19 Sqdns Nos. 3, 17, 24, 25, 32, 43, 54, 56, 65, 74, 79, 111, 151, 501, 600, 601, 604, 605, 615

No. 12 Fighter Group
10 Sqdns Nos. 19, 23, 29, 46, 66, 213, 504, 610, 611, 616

No. 13 Fighter Group
7 Sqdns Nos. 41, 64, 72, 602, 603, 607, 609

Air Component B.E.F and No. 22 Army Co-operation Group
13 Sqdns Nos. 1, 2, 4, 13, 16, 26, 53, 59[a], 73, 85, 87[a], 613, 614

HEADQUARTERS COASTAL COMMAND

No. 15 G.R. Group
5 Sqdns Nos. 204, 210, 217, 228, 502

No. 16 G.R. Group
5 Sqdns Nos. 22, 42, 48, 206, 500

No. 17 Training Group

No. 18 G.R. Group
9 Sqdns Nos. 201, 209, 220, 224, 233, 240, 269, 608, 612

HEADQUARTERS BALLOON COMMAND

No. 30 Balloon Barrage Group

No. 31 Balloon Barrage Group

No. 32 Balloon Barrage Group

No. 33 Balloon Barrage Group

HEADQUARTERS RESERVE COMMAND

No. 50 Training Group

No. 51 Training Group

No. 54 Training Group

HEADQUARTERS TRAINING COMMAND

No. 21 Training Group

No. 23 Training Group

No. 24 Training Group

No. 25 Armament Group

HEADQUARTERS MAINTENANCE COMMAND

No. 40 Maintenance Group

No. 41 Maintenance Group

No. 42 Maintenance Group

No. 43 Maintenance Group

OVERSEAS COMMANDS

ROYAL AIR FORCE MIDDLE EAST

- Egypt Group
  10 Sqdns
  Nos.
  14, 30, 33, 70,
  45, 55, 208, 211,
  113, 216

- No. 252 Fighter Wing
  2 Sqdns
  Nos.
  80, 112

- Sudan Wing
  2 Sqdns
  Nos.
  47, 223

ROYAL AIR FORCE IN PALESTINE AND TRANSJORDAN
No. 6 Sqdn

BRITISH FORCES IN IRAQ
No. 84 Sqdn

BRITISH FORCES IN ADEN
3 Sqdns
Nos.
8, 94, 203

ROYAL AIR FORCE MEDITERRANEAN
No. 202 Sqdn

AIR FORCES IN INDIA

- No. 1 (Indian) Group
  4 Sqdns
  Nos.
  5, 20, 27, 60

- 2 Sqdns
  Nos.
  28, 31

- INDIAN AIR FORCE
  No. 1 Sqdn

ROYAL AIR FORCE FAR EAST
9 Sqdns
Nos.
11, 34, 36,
39, 62, 100,
205, 230, 273

NOTES
(1) Bomber Command Order of Battle as at 27th September
(2) Reserve Squadrons
(3) Loaned to Coastal Command 30th September 1939/February 1940
(4) Proceeded to France for Air Component of Field Force
(5) Fighter Command Order of Battle as at 9th September
G.R.—General Reconnaissance

APPENDIX IV

Royal Air Force Command Organization, January 1941

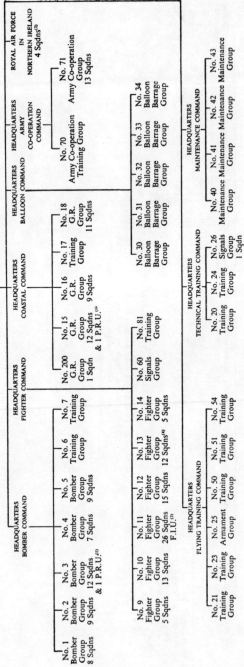

OVERSEAS COMMANDS

HEADQUARTERS*
ROYAL AIR FORCE——1 (Bomber Transport) Sqdn
MIDDLE EAST

ROYAL AIR FORCE IN PALESTINE AND TRANS-JORDAN
1 Sqdn

BRITISH FORCES IN IRAQ
1 Sqdn

BRITISH FORCES IN ADEN
3 Sqdns

ROYAL AIR FORCE MEDITERRANEAN
4 Sqdns

- No. 201 G.R. Group
  1 Sqdn and 1 G.R. Unit
- No. 202 Composite Group
  10 Sqdns
- No. 203 Fighter/Bomber Group
  5 Sqdns
- No. 252 Fighter Wing
  1 Sqdn
- No. 257 Bomber Wing
  3 Sqdns

HEADQUARTERS BRITISH AIR FORCES, GREECE
4 Sqdns

AIR HEADQUARTERS EAST AFRICA
8 Sqdns

AIR FORCES IN INDIA

- INDIAN AIR FORCE
  1 Sqdn
- No. 1 (Indian) Group
- 7 Sqdns[5]

ROYAL AIR FORCE FAR EAST
9 Sqdns

NOTES
(1) Photographic Reconnaissance Unit
(2) Including one squadron of No. 13 Group, Fighter Command
(3) Fighter Interception Unit
(4) Including one squadron in Northern Ireland
(5) Some of these squadrons were controlled by No. 1 (Indian) Group for operations on the North-West Frontier
G.R. General Reconnaissance

* From 11th June 1940, the Air Officer Commanding-in-Chief, Middle East, commanded all Royal Air Force units stationed or operating in Egypt, Sudan, Palestine and Trans-Jordan, East Africa, Aden and Somaliland, Iraq and adjacent territories, Cyprus, Turkey, Balkans, Mediterranean Sea and Persian Gulf. The Air Officers Commanding Iraq, Mediterranean, and Aden continued to exercise local administrative control.

APPENDIX V

First-line Aircraft—British, German and Italian Air Forces

DATE	R.A.F.[1]	GERMAN[4]	ITALIAN
30th September 1938	1,982	3,307	
3rd September 1939	1,911[2]	4,161	
1st August 1940	2,913[3]	4,549	1,529[5] (June)

[1] These figures are based on the official 'establishment' for the initial equipment (I.E.) of squadrons, home and overseas. In addition, there was an immediate reserve (I.R.) varying from 4 to 5 aircraft per squadron. After June 1944 this initial equipment and immediate reserve were grouped together in what became known as unit equipment (U.E.).

[2] The decline in first-line aircraft in September 1939 as compared with September 1938 was due (a) to the withdrawal of obsolescent aircraft, and (b) to the relegation of certain 'non-mobilizable' bomber squadrons to form a reserve and operational training organization at the outbreak of war.

[3] Includes aircraft of Dominion and Allied air forces under R.A.F. control.

[4] The German figures, which are extracted from Luftwaffe records, are for actual strength. They include in each case a powerful force of transport aircraft— 308 in September 1938, 552 in September 1939, 375 in August 1940.

[5] This figure is an official Italian total to the nearest available date.

APPENDIX VI

Principal Operational Aircraft of the Royal Air Force, 1939–1941

BOMBER

AIRCRAFT NAME AND MARK	MAXIMUM SPEED	SERVICE CEILING	RANGE AND ASSOCIATED BOMB LOAD	ARMAMENT
	m.p.h. feet	feet	miles lb.	
Battle I	241 at 13,000	23,500	1,050 – 1,000	2 × ·303″
Blenheim IV	266 at 11,800	22,000	1,460 – 1,000	5 × ·303″
Halifax I	273 at 17,750	18,200	1,840 – 6,750 or 850 – 13,000	8 × ·303″
Hampden I	254 at 13,800	19,000	1,885 – 2,000 or 1,200 – 4,000	8 × ·303″
Manchester I	265 at 17,000	19,200	1,630 – 8,100 or 1,200 – 10,350	12 × ·303″
Maryland I	278 at 11,800	26,000	1,210 – 1,500 or 1,080 – 2,000	8 × ·303″
Stirling I	260 at 10,500	17,200	2,050 – 3,500 or 740 – 14,000	8 × ·303″
Wellington IC	235 at 15,500	18,000	2,550 – 1,000 or 1,200 – 4,500	6 × ·303″
Wellington II	247 at 17,000	20,000	2,450 – 1,250 or 1,400 – 4,500	6 × ·303″
Wellington IV	229 at 13,000	20,000	2,180 – 500 or 980 – 4,000	6 × ·303″
Whitley V	222 at 17,000	17,600	1,650 – 3,000 or 470 – 7,000	5 × ·303″

FIGHTER

AIRCRAFT NAME AND MARK	MAXIMUM SPEED	SERVICE CEILING	CLIMB-TIME TO HEIGHT	ARMAMENT
	m.p.h. feet	feet	minutes feet	
Beaufighter I F	324 at 11,750	27,000	9·4 to 15,000	6 × ·303″ 4 × 20 mm.
Blenheim IV F	266 at 11,800	26,500	10 to 15,000	7 × ·303″
Gladiator	245 at 15,000	32,500	7 to 15,000	4 × ·303″
Hurricane I	316 at 17,500	33,200	6·3 to 15,000	8 × ·303″
Hurricane II A	342 at 22,000	37,000	8·2 to 20,000	8 × ·303″
Hurricane II B	342 at 22,000	36,500	8·4 to 20,000	12 × ·303″
Hurricane II C	339 at 22,000	35,600	9·1 to 20,000	4 × 20 mm.
Spitfire I	355 at 19,000	34,000	6·2 to 15,000	8 × ·303″
Spitfire V	375 at 20,250	38,000	7 to 20,000	2 × 20 mm. 4 × ·303″
Tomahawk I	338 at 16,000	30,500	7·8 to 15,000	2 × ·5″ 4 × ·303″

COASTAL

AIRCRAFT NAME AND MARK	CRUISING SPEED AND ENDURANCE	ASSOCIATED BOMB (OR DEPTH CHARGE) LOAD	ARMAMENT
	knots hours		
Anson I	103 – 5½	200 lb.	4 × ·303″
Beaufighter I C	180 – 5	—	4 × 20 mm. 6 × ·303″
Beaufort I (T.B.)	150 – 6	1,500 lb. or 1 × 18″ torpedo	4 × ·303″
Blenheim IV F	150 – 6	—	6 × ·303″
Hudson I	125 – 6	750 lb.	7 × ·303″
London II (F.B.)	86 – 5·2	2,000 lb.	3 × ·303″
Stranraer (F.B.)	92 – 7·2	1,000 lb.	3 × ·303″
Sunderland I (F.B.)	115 – 12	2,000 lb.	7 × ·303″
Vildebeest IV (T.B.)	82 – 4·3	1,000 lb. or 1 × 18″ torpedo	2 × ·303″
Wellington I C	125 – 10·6	1,500 lb.	6 × ·303″
Whitley V	110 – 9	1,500 lb.	5 × ·303″

NOTES

(i) MAXIMUM SPEED was only possible for an extremely limited period. Apart from tactical manœuvring, bomber and fighter aircraft in the main flew at speeds between 'most economical cruising' and 'maximum continuous cruising'. Varying with the different aircraft, these speeds were respectively between 55–80% and 80–90% of the maximum speed.

(ii) SERVICE CEILING. The height at which the rate of climb has a certain defined low value (in British practice 100 feet per minute). Ceilings quoted are for aircraft with full load.

(iii) RANGE AND ASSOCIATED BOMB LOAD. The main purpose of this table is to give some idea of the relative performances of the various aircraft. The figures quoted relate to aircraft flying at 'most economical cruising' speed at the specified height (i.e. the speed and height at which the greatest range could be obtained). Allowance is made for take off but not for landing, the range quoted being the maximum distance the aircraft could cover in still air 'flying to dry tanks'. Furthermore in the planning of operations a reduction of range of about 25% had to be made for navigational errors, tactical manœuvring, weather conditions and other factors.

(iv) ENDURANCE. The time an aircraft can continue flying under given conditions without refuelling. This being a vital factor of Coastal Command operations an economical cruising speed, consistent with maximum safe endurance as determined under normal operational conditions, is quoted.

(v) (F.B.) Flying Boat. (T.B.) Torpedo Bomber.

APPENDIX VII

Principal Operational Aircraft of the German Air Force, 1939–1941

BOMBER AND RECONNAISSANCE

AIRCRAFT	MAXIMUM SPEED	SERVICE CEILING	RANGE AND ASSOCIATED BOMB LOAD	ARMAMENT
	m.p.h. feet	feet	miles lb.	
Junkers (Ju.) 87B[1]	245 at 15,000	23,500	360 – 1,100	3 × 7·9 mm.
Henschel (Hs.) 126	230 at 13,000	25,000	530 – 620	5 × 7·9 mm.
Dornier (Do.) 17	255 at 15,000	21,000	1,440 – 1,100 or 890 – 2,200	7 × 7·9 mm. 1 × 20 mm.
Heinkel (He.) 111	240 at 14,000	26,000	1,510 – 2,200	7 × 7·9 mm. 2 × 20 mm.
Junkers (Ju.) 88 A4	287 at 14,000	22,700	1,280 – 4,400	7 × 7·9 mm. 1 × 20 mm.
Dornier (Do.) 215	275 at 15,000	28,000	1,450 – 1,100 or 900 – 2,200	7 × 7·9 mm. 1 × 20 mm.
Focke-Wulf (F.W.) 200[2]	240 at 13,600	20,500	2,150 – 3,600 or 2,700 (Recce. only)	3 × 13 mm. 3 × 15/20 mm.

[1] The *Stuka* dive-bomber.
[2] Known as the Condor.

FIGHTER

AIRCRAFT	MAXIMUM SPEED	SERVICE CEILING	CLIMB-TIME TO HEIGHT	ARMAMENT
	m.p.h. feet	feet	minutes feet	
Messerschmitt (Me.) 109E	355 at 18,000	35,000	6·2 to 16,500	2 × 7·9 mm. 2 × 20 mm.
Messerschmitt (Me.) 109F	395 at 22,000	36,500	5·75 to 17,000	2 × 7·9 mm. 3 × 20 mm.
Messerschmitt (Me.) 109G	400 at 22,000	38,500	6 to 19,000	2 × 7·9/13 mm. 3 × 20 mm.
Messerschmitt (Me.) 110D[1]	360 at 20,000	34,000	8·5 to 18,000	6 × 7·9 mm. 2 × 20 mm.
Focke-Wulf (F.W.) 190	385 at 19,000	36,000	6·5 to 18,000	2 × 7·9 mm. 4 × 20 mm.
Junkers (Ju.) 88 C6	295 at 14,000	24,200	13·8 to 16,500	7 × 7·9 mm. 3 × 20 mm.

[1] Marks E and F were of similar performance.

Notes (i), (ii) and (iii) on page 412 apply in general to the above tables.

APPENDIX VIII

Principal Operational Aircraft of the Italian Air Force, 1940–1941

BOMBER AND RECONNAISSANCE

AIRCRAFT	MAXIMUM SPEED	SERVICE CEILING	RANGE AND ASSOCIATED BOMB LOAD	ARMAMENT
	m.p.h. feet	*feet*	*miles lb.*	
Savoia Marchetti (S.)79	255 at 13,000	21,500	1,570 – 1,100 or	3 × 12·7 mm.
			1,190 – 2,750	2 × 7·7 mm.
Savoia Marchetti (S.)81	210 at 15,000	24,500	1,030 – 2,200 or	6 × 7·7 mm.
			895 – 4,400	
Savoia Marchetti (S.)82	205 at 7,000	17,000	2,200 – 3,200	1 × 12·7 mm.
				4 × 7·7 mm.
Cantieri Riuniti (Cant) Z.506[1]	230 at 13,000	19,000	1,685 – 1,750	1 × 12·7 mm.
			1,465 – 2,640	3 × 7·7 mm.
Cantieri Riuniti (Cant) Z.1007b	280 at 13,000	27,500	1,650 – 1,100	2 × 7·7 mm.
				2 × 12·7 mm.
Fiat B.R.20	255 at 13,500	25,000	1,350 – 2,200	2 × 7·7 mm.
				1 × 12·7 mm.

[1] Seaplane bomber.

FIGHTER

AIRCRAFT	MAXIMUM SPEED	SERVICE CEILING	CLIMB-TIME TO HEIGHT	ARMAMENT
	m.p.h. feet	*feet*	*minutes feet*	
Fiat C.R.32	233 at 10,000	28,000	5·3 to 10,000	2 × 12·7 mm.
Fiat C.R.42	270 at 13,100	32,000	5·5 to 13,000	2 × 12·7 mm.
Fiat G.50	300 at 14,500	32,000	6·4 to 15,000	2 × 12·7 mm..
Fiat G.55	380 at 20,000	38,000	5·8 to 20,000	2 × 12·7 mm.
				3 × 20 mm.
Aer Macchi C.200	310 at 15,000	32,000	6·25 to 15,000	2 × 12·7 mm.
Aer Macchi C.202	345 at 18,000	32.000	8·2 to 18,000	2 × 12·7 mm.

Notes (i), (ii) and (iii) on page 412 apply in general to the above tables.

APPENDIX IX

Royal Air Force Middle East Subordinate Commands, 1940–1941[1]

Date of Appointment

ROYAL AIR FORCE IN PALESTINE AND TRANS-JORDAN[2]
Air Commodore J. H. D'Albiac, D.S.O.   16th August 1939
Air Commodore J. W. B. Grigson, D.S.O., D.F.C.   1st December 1940

BRITISH FORCES IN IRAQ[3]
Air Vice-Marshal H. G. Smart, O.B.E., D.F.C.,   23rd November 1939
A.F.C.
Air Vice-Marshal J. H. D'Albiac, C.B., D.S.O.   17th May 1941

ROYAL AIR FORCE, MEDITERRANEAN
Air Commodore R. Leckie, D.S.O., D.S.C., D.F.C.   17th December 1938
Air Vice-Marshal F. H. M. Maynard, C.B., A.F.C.   26th January 1940
Air Vice-Marshal H. P. Lloyd, C.B.E., M.C., D.F.C.   1st June 1941

BRITISH FORCES IN ADEN
Air Vice-Marshal G. R. M. Reid, C.B., D.S.O.,   2nd September 1938
M.C.
Air Vice-Marshal F. G. D. Hards, C.B.E., D.S.C.,   10th September 1941
D.F.C.

HEADQUARTERS, BRITISH FORCES IN GREECE
Air Vice-Marshal J. H. D'Albiac, D.S.O.   15th November 1940

AIR HEADQUARTERS, WESTERN DESERT
Air Vice-Marshal A. Coningham, C.B., D.S.O.,   9th October 1941
M.C., D.F.C., A.F.C.

AIR HEADQUARTERS, SUDAN[4]
Group Captain C. E. V. Porter   1st May 1940
Air Commodore L. H. Slatter, C.B., O.B.E., D.S.C.,   17th August 1940
D.F.C.
Air Commodore C. B. S. Spackman, D.F.C.   13th July 1941

AIR HEADQUARTERS, EAST AFRICA
Air Commodore W. Sowrey, C.B.E., D.F.C., A.F.C.   19th October 1940

AIR HEADQUARTERS, EGYPT
Air Commodore T. W. Elmhirst, A.F.C.   1st December 1941

[1] The Air Officer Commanding-in-Chief, Middle East, commanded all Royal Air Force Units stationed or operating in Egypt, Sudan, Palestine and Trans-Jordan, East Africa, Aden and Somaliland, Iraq and adjacent territories, Cyprus, Turkey, Balkans, Mediterranean Sea and Persian Gulf.
[2] Air Headquarters, Royal Air Force, Levant, 1st December 1941.
[3] Air Headquarters, Royal Air Force in Iraq, 1st May 1941.
[4] Headquarters No. 203 Group, 17th August 1940.

APPENDIX X

Order of Battle, Fighter Command, 8th August 1940

HEADQUARTERS NO. 10 GROUP
(Box, Wilts)

Squadrons Nos.

92 (Spitfires), Pembrey
87 (Hurricanes), Exeter
213 (Hurricanes), Exeter
234 (Spitfires), St. Eval
247 (Gladiator), Roborough
(1 Flight only)
238 (Hurricanes), Middle Wallop
609 (Spitfires), Middle Wallop
604 (Blenheims), Middle Wallop
152 (Spitfires), Warmwell

HEADQUARTERS NO. 11 GROUP
(Uxbridge)

Squadrons Nos.

17 (Hurricanes), Debden
85 (Hurricanes), Martlesham
56 (Hurricanes), Rochford
151 (Hurricanes), North Weald
25 (Blenheims), Martlesham
54 (Spitfires), Hornchurch
65 (Spitfires), Hornchurch
74 (Spitfires), Hornchurch
41 (Spitfires), Hornchurch
43 (Hurricanes), Tangmere
145 (Hurricanes), Westhampnett
601 (Hurricanes), Tangmere
1 (Hurricanes), Northolt
257 (Hurricanes), Northolt
615 (Hurricanes), Kenley
64 (Spitfires), Kenley
111 (Hurricanes), Croydon
32 (Hurricanes), Biggin Hill
610 (Spitfires), Biggin Hill
501 (Hurricanes), Gravesend
600 (Blenheims), Manston

HEADQUARTERS NO. 12 GROUP
(Watnall, Notts)

Squadrons Nos.

73 (Hurricanes), Church Fenton
249 (Hurricanes), Church Fenton
616 (Spitfires), Leconfield
222 (Spitfires), Kirton-in-Lindsey
264 (Defiants), Kirton-in-Lindsey
('A' Flight at Ringway)
46 (Hurricanes), Digby
611 (Spitfires), Digby
29 (Blenheims), Digby
242 (Hurricanes), Coltishall
66 (Spitfires), Coltishall
229 (Hurricanes), Wittering
266 (Spitfires), Wittering
23 (Blenheims), Colly Weston
19 (Spitfires), Duxford

HEADQUARTERS NO. 13 GROUP
(Newcastle-on-Tyne)

Squadrons Nos.

79 (Spitfires), Acklington
607 (Hurricanes), Usworth
72 (Spitfires), Acklington
605 (Hurricanes), Drem
232 (Hurricanes), Turnhouse
253 (Hurricanes), Turnhouse
141 (Defiants), Prestwick
219 (Blenheims), Catterick
245 (Hurricanes), Aldergrove
3 (Hurricanes), Wick
504 (Hurricanes), Castletown
232 (Hurricanes), Sumburgh
(1 Flight only)
603 (Spitfires), 'A' Flight at Dyce
'B' Flight at
Montrose

APPENDIX XI

Glossary of Code Names and Abbreviations

A.A.S.F.	Advanced Air Striking Force.
'ABIGAIL'	Bomber operation in December 1940 designed to produce the 'maximum possible destruction in a selected German town'.
A.D.G.B.	Air Defence of Great Britain.
A.I.	Air interception—radar set carried by fighters.
A.M.E.S.	Air Ministry Experimental Station (i.e. radar station).
A/S.	Anti-submarine.
A.S.V.	Air-to-surface vessel—Airborne search and homing radar used for anti-U-boat and anti-shipping operations.
'BARBAROSSA'	(German) Code-name for invasion of Russia.
'BATTLE-AXE'	Operation to relieve Tobruk—Western Desert, June 1941.
'BITING'	Raid on enemy radar installation at Bruneval, 27/28th February 1942.
'CIRCUS'	Offensive operation by fighters and bombers on the Continent to prevent the withdrawal of the G.A.F. to the eastern front.
'COLOSSUS'	Airborne combined operation against an aqueduct at Tragino on 10/11th February 1941.
D.W.I.	Directional Wireless Installation (mine-exploding device on aircraft).
'DYNAMO'	Evacuation from Dunkirk, 26th May–4th June 1940.
E.A.	Enemy aircraft.
E.T.A.	Estimated time of arrival.
'EUREKA'	Portable ground radio-beacon.
F.C.	Fighter Catapult (ship).
FREYA	German radar installation for long-range detection.
'FULLER'	Counter-measures against the escape of the *Scharnhorst* and *Gneisenau* from Brest.
'GEE'	Medium range radio aid to navigation employing ground transmitters and airborne receiver.
G.L.	Gun-laying (radar).
G.P.	General Purpose (bomb).
'HABFORCE'	Force sent from Trans-Jordan across desert to relieve Habbaniya in May 1941.

'HADDOCK' Organization for operating British bombers from South of France against Italian targets—June 1940.

H.E. High-explosive.

'HEADACHE' Counter-measures against German navigational beams.

I.F.F. Identification friend or foe—device on aircraft for identifying 'friendlies' to radar stations.

'INTRUDER' Night operations designed to impede the enemy in his use of airfields.

J.G. *Jagdgeschwader*, i.e. German Fighter Group.

K.G. *Kampfgeschwader*, i.e. German Bomber Group.

K.Gr. *Kampfgruppe*, i.e. German Bomber Wing.

'KNICKEBEIN' (German) Navigational beam.

'LAYFORCE' Commando force operating in Middle East.

'MARITA' (German) Invasion of Greece and Yugoslavia.

'MOONLIGHT SONATA' (German) Operation against Coventry—November 1940.

M.T. Mechanical transport.

'MUTTON' The Long Aerial Mine.

'NICKELS' Leaflets.

O.K.L. *Oberkommando der Luftwaffe*, i.e. High Command of the G.A.F.

O.K.W *Oberkommando der Wehrmacht*, i.e. High Command of the German Armed Forces.

O.T.U. Operational Training Unit.

P.A.C. Parachute and Cable defence.

P.R.U. Photographic Reconnaissance Unit.

R.D.F. Radio direction-finding—early name for radar.

'RHUBARB' Offensive operations by fighters designed to make enemy retain strong air forces in western Europe.

R/T. Radio-telephony.

S.A.P. Semi-armour piercing (bombs).

'SEALION' (German) Plan for invasion of England—1940.

S.L.C. Searchlight Control (radar).

'STOPPER' Coastal Command patrol outside Brest.

'STRAFGERICHT' (German) Bombing of Belgrade—April 1941.

STUKA *Sturzkampfflugzeug*, i.e. dive-bomber.

T.R.E. Telecommunications Research Establishment.

'UMBRELLA' (German) Projected attack on Birmingham—November 1940.

U.P.	Unrotating projectile (rocket).
V.H.F.	Very high frequency (R/T).
'WESERÜBUNG'	(German) Plan for invasion of Norway and Denmark—1940.
W/T.	Wireless telegraphy.
WÜRZBURG	(German) Ground radar system used for controlling searchlights, anti-aircraft guns and night-fighter aircraft.
X-GERÄT ⎱ Y-GERÄT ⎰	(German) Navigational radio devices.

INDEX

Aachen, 379
Aalborg, 88, 94
Aandalsnes, 85-6, 88-94, 104-5
Abbeville, 127-8
Abyssinia, operations in, 249, 307-9
Addis Ababa, 250, 309
Addison, Air Vice-Marshal E. B., 209
Adem, El, 241, 270, 292
Aden, British Forces in, 26, 407, 409, 415
Admiral von Scheer, German pocket-battleship, 39-40, 47, 223, 358
Advanced Air Striking Force, 32, 34, 37, 41, 109, 113-21, 125-7, 129, 133, 145, 147-50
Organization of, 406
Agheila, El, 280, 288
A.I., 202-3, 214-15
Air Component, Field Force, see British Expeditionary Force
Air Council, Members of, 401-3
Air Defence of Great Britain, 21
Airborne Forces Experimental Establishment, 395n.
Airborne operations:
British, 395-8
German, 82, 107, 114-15, 324, 326, 331-4
Aircraft, see under Royal Air Force, German Air Force and Italian Air Force, and under respective types
Aircraft Production (British), 17, 152, 154, 217-18
Aircraft Production, Ministry of, 152, 221
Air/Sea Rescue, 159-60
Albania, operations in, 285-6
Albert Canal, bombing of bridges, 116-18
Alexandria, 246
Aliakmon, River, 283-5
Altmark, German fleet auxiliary, 57, 77
A.M.E.S., *No. 220*, 334
Andover, 166
Anson, aircraft, 56, 412
Antelat, 289-90
Anti-aircraft defences, U.K., 1940, 157, 202, 213
Antwerp, 186
'Area Bombing', 234
Arendal, 81
Argus, British aircraft carrier, 249, 263
Ark Royal, British aircraft carrier, 59, 89, 93-4, 103-4, 226, 304, 350
Armoured Car Companies: *No. 1*, 314; *No. 2*, 269, 320

Army, British:
Divisions:
1st Cavalry, 339; 2nd Armoured, 289-90; 4th Indian, 271-2, 307; 6th Australian, 293; 7th Armoured, 271-2, 279; 7th Australian, 291, 339; 51st, 145; New Zealand, 293n.
Brigades, armoured:
1st, 293n., 295; 3rd, 290-1
Regiment:
Royal Tank, 271
Army Co-operation Command, 26, 404, 408
Army, German:
Corps: XIX, 129, 135; Africa, 287
Divisions: 5th Light, 287; 15th Panzer, 305; Adolf Hitler S.S. Motorized, 299
Army, Italian, 60th Infantry Division, 277
Asmara, 307
Assab, 252
A.S.V., 220, 227, 348, 350, 364-6, 366n.
Atcherley, Wg. Cdr. R. L. R., 96-7
Athenia, British S.S., 59
Auchinleck, Lt.-General Sir Claude J. E., 98, 103, 105
Audacity, British auxiliary aircraft carrier, 346, 351
Audax, aircraft, 313
Auxiliary Air Force, 16
Avonmouth, 212, 214

Babington, Air Marshal J. T., 405, 405n.
Babington, Air Marshal P., 401
Back Component, 127, 131
Bader, Wg. Cdr., D. R. S., 193, 197, 387-90
Baldwin, Air Vice-Marshal J. E. A., 46
Baldwin, The Rt. Hon. S., 1, 2, 11-13
Balfour, Captain the Rt. Hon. H. H., 401
Ball, A/C, 229
Balloon Command, 26, 157, 406, 408
Balloon defence, 16, 68, 160
Balloon Development Establishment, 49
Balloon Unit, 'M', 49
Banak, 96-7
Bandon, Wg. Cdr. the Earl of, 129
Banks, Col. Sir Donald, 402
Bardia, 245, 272-3, 292
Bardufoss, 96-9, 102
Barham, British battleship, 350
Bari, 264

ROYAL AIR FORCE 1939–45

Volume 1

The Fight at Odds 1939–41

DENIS RICHARDS

Rearmament and pre-war planning. Early war
operations. Norway and France. The Battle of Britain
and the Blitz. The bombing of Germany. Air
operations in the war at sea. The Mediterranean and
the Middle East.

Volume 2

The Fight Avails 1941–43

DENIS RICHARDS AND HILARY ST G. SAUNDERS

The Far East. The U-boat war and anti-shipping
operations. The Western Desert, Malta and Tunisia.
The strategic bombing offensive. Sicily. The invasion
of Italy (with subsequent operations up to the fall of
Rome, May 1944).

Volume 3

The Fight is Won 1943–45

HILARY ST G. SAUNDERS

*With concluding chapter by Hilary St G. Saunders and
Denis Richards*

The combined bombing offensive. The Atlantic and
the Bay of Biscay. The liberation of North-West
Europe – plans and preparations. Normandy and the
battle for France. Flying bombs and rockets. Italy and
the Balkans. The advance into Germany and the final
surrender. Victory in Burma and the Far East. The war
in the air – the balance sheet.